DATE DUE

DISRAELI

STANLEY WEINTRAUB

DISRAELI

A Biography

T·T

TRUMAN TALLEY BOOKS/DUTTON/NEW YORK

TRUMAN TALLEY BOOKS/DUTTON

Published by the Penguin Group
Penguin Books USA Inc., 375 Hudson Street, New York, New York 10014, U.S.A.
Penguin Books Ltd, 27 Wrights Lane, London W8 5TZ, England
Penguin Books Australia Ltd, Ringwood, Victoria, Australia
Penguin Books Canada Ltd, 10 Alcorn Avenue, Toronto, Ontario, Canada M4V 3B2
Penguin Books (N.Z.) Ltd, 182–190 Wairau Road, Auckland 10, New Zealand

Penguin Books Ltd, Registered Offices:
Harmondsworth, Middlesex, England

First published by Truman Talley Books/Dutton, an imprint of Dutton Signet,
a division of Penguin Books USA Inc.
Distributed in Canada by McClelland & Stewart Inc.

First Printing, October, 1993
1   3   5   7   9   10   8   6   4   2

LIBRARY OF CONGRESS CATALOGING-IN-PUBLICATION DATA:
Weintraub, Stanley, 1929–
Disraeli : a biography / Stanley Weintraub.
p.   cm.
Includes index.
ISBN 0-525-93668-8
1. Disraeli, Benjamin, Earl of Beaconsfield, 1804–1881. 2. Great Britain—Politics and
government—1837–1901. 3. Prime ministers—Great Britain—Biography. I. Title
DA564.B3W45   1993
941.08—dc20   93-16498
                                                                        CIP

Printed in the United States of America
Set in Goudy

Designed by Steven N. Stathakis

In memory of my father,
Benjamin Weintraub,
and my father-in-law,
Benjamin Horwitz,
who each shared a name
with Disraeli

Contents

Preface "FORTI NIHIL DIFFICILE"   xi

SON OF MY RIGHT HAND, *1804–1837*   1

    I. *1837* "I HAVE THE TWO GREATEST STIMULANTS
        IN THE WORLD TO ACTION, YOUTH AND DEBT."   3

    II. *1804–1817* "I WAS BORN IN A LIBRARY."   17

    III. *1817–1824* "ON A SUDDEN I SEEMED ENDOWED
        WITH NEW POWERS."   33

    IV. *1824–1826* "BITTERER . . . THAN ALL, IS WAKING
        FROM OUR FIRST DELUSION!"   48

    V. *1826–1830* "I WAS DEVOURED BY AMBITION
        I DID NOT SEE ANY MEANS OF GRATIFYING."   65

    VI. *1830–1831* "WHY THEN THE WORLD'S MINE OYSTER."   89

    VII. *1831–1833* "THERE IS NO EDUCATION LIKE ADVERSITY." 115

VIII. *1833–1834* "... A FAIR LADY OF MY ACQUAINTANCE." 137

IX. *1834–1837* "... THE DAZZLING FARCE OF LIFE." 156

REBEL IN THE HOUSE, *1837–1862* 173

X. *1837–1841* "THE TIME WILL COME WHEN
YOU WILL HEAR ME." 175

XI. *1841–1844* "I ALREADY FIND MYSELF WITHOUT
EFFORT THE LEADER OF A PARTY,
CHIEFLY OF THE YOUTH." 198

XII. *1844–1846* "THE TWO NATIONS" 220

XIII. *1846–1847* "... INTO THE ENEMY'S PORT." 249

XIV. *1848–1850* "OPPORTUNITY IS MORE POWERFUL
EVEN THAN CONQUERORS OR PROPHETS." 275

XV. *1851–1853* "... WE CANNOT COMPLAIN OF
FORTUNE." 300

XVI. *1853–1856* "... THE BITTER CUP OF ILL SUCCESS." 327

XVII. *1856–1858* "... SO FOND OF MR DIZZY." 348

XVIII. *1858–1862* "... THE FIELD OF BATTLE." 370

THE HIGH GAME, *1862–1874* 389

XIX. *1862–1866* "... MIRAGES THAT RISE UP BEFORE
THE POLITICAL EYE." 391

XX. *Ralph and Kate* "... A REVIVING TOUCH
OF NATURE IN ONE OF HER MOST POPULAR
AND AGREEABLE FORMS." 419

XXI. *1866–1868* "... THE MINISTRY BY HIMSELF" 437

XXII. *1868* "... THE GREASY POLE." 459

XXIII. *1869–1872* "BUT NOW THEY HAVE TURNED ME
OUT OF PLACE." 476

XXIV. *1872–1874* "THE AGE OF RUINS IS PAST." 500

THE ELYSIAN FIELDS, 1874–1881   523

XXV. *1874–1875* "I LIVE FOR POWER AND THE
AFFECTIONS."   525

XXVI. *1875–1876* "WHAT'S THE USE OF POWER IF YOU
DON'T MAKE PEOPLE DO WHAT THEY DON'T LIKE?"   548

XXVII. *1876–1878* "I AM DEAD, DEAD BUT IN THE
ELYSIAN FIELDS."   563

XXVIII. *1878–1880* "EVERYTHING, THEY SAY, COMES
TOO LATE. IT IS SOMETHING IF IT COMES."   599

XXIX. *1880–1881* "I HAVE HAD A GOOD INNINGS AND
CANNOT AGREE WITH THE GREAT KING THAT
ALL IS VANITY."   628

XXX. *1881* "EVERY PROCESSION MUST END."   659

Sources   666

Acknowledgments   692

Index   695

Sixteen pages of illustrations follow page 274

"FORTI NIHIL DIFFICILE"

Preface

WHEN BENJAMIN DISRAELI DETERMINED THAT HIS RISING STATUS RE-
quired a personal motto, he chose *forti nihil difficile,* or "Nothing
is difficult to the strong." Strength of will, one assumes. From the
bourgeois home of a bibliophile father of "alien" origins, Disraeli
persevered, through will and guile, into the aristocratic world that
did not want him. He attracted a litany of labels that boded ill for
his aspirations—*poseur, debtor, womanizer, adventurer, hack, charlatan, dandy, liar, hypocrite, radical, opportunist.* . . . The tag intended to be most damaging was *Jew.*

Whether or not Disraeli identified himself as a Jew he
was always perceived as one—not only by his friends and colleagues, but especially by his enemies, of whom there were
many. His archrival, W. E. Gladstone, saw Disraeli as motivated
by "Jew feelings," while Gladstone's tame historian, Edward Freeman, used the label "loathsome Jew" and Bishop Wilberforce
"Eastern Jew." Although recognizing reality—that his name
remained a career liability—Disraeli never gave any thought

to changing it, other than to drop his father's apostrophe for simplicity.

While Disraeli was *"der alte Jude"* to the admiring Bismarck, he was "the Hebrew conjuror" to the curmudgeonly Carlyle, "under all his trappings, the absurd Jew-boy" to the bitchy Lytton Strachey, and "the tawdry old Jew" to the snobbish Henry James. There was an element of exasperated admiration even in the calumnies and the contradictions, and Disraeli made use of them. Prejudice propelled him, energizing his colorful career and molding him into one of the unforgettable personalities of his century. "Success is the child of audacity," he announced while still in his twenties. No one in his time better applied the maxim.

A public figure who invented his legend in the glare of publicity, Disraeli was sometimes scoffed at by Jewish contemporaries who saw his loyalties as little more than exaggerated historical nostalgia. Yet to most Englishmen he was "the Asian mystery," who once claimed that he was "the blank page between the Old Testament and the New." *Disraeli: A Biography* attempts to fill in that blank page in order to better fill out the man.

Benjamin is Hebrew for "son of my right hand," the name given by the biblical patriarch Jacob to his favorite child. *D'Israeli*, or "of Israel," was a common Levantine tag for "Jew," despite Disraeli's claim that it was rare, and even unique. He liked to think of himself as unique, and in the England of his time he was. The names he neither rejected nor replaced suggest the Judaic dimension in his life that determined his personality yet collided at every turn with the unswerving ambitions made possible by his father's impulsive decision to allow Benjamin's Anglican conversion when a boy of twelve.

His rise to be at the right hand of Queen Victoria—"the top of the greasy pole," he put it—was a fifty-year struggle not only against the Liberal opposition but against the grandees in his own party, the Conservatives. It was a good thing, a contemporary observed, that Tories read no books, especially Disraeli's, as his would have made them uncomfortable. While he seemed to celebrate the patrician class he had forced to accept him—at the end he was even an Earl—he saw through its poverty of values and excoriated it for its purposelessness. Even as Prime Minister he was perceived as an outsider because he had no choice in his origins, an opportunist because he had to make the most of his chances, an adventurer because a life in politics left no alternatives.

Biographers have often charged Disraeli with reckless mendacity in fabricating his past and dishonest expediency in fashioning political policy. Yet he was a writer of fiction who recognized the need to capture his audience's imagination and a politician who exploited the hypocrisies of partisan electioneering. As he had a character in one of his novels confide, "The necessities of things are sterner stuff than the hopes of men." For him the overwhelming necessity was for power, and his relentless quest for it was not a prescription for a life of easy satisfactions. Complimented on being able to live "a pleasant life," one of his characters retorts, "Yes, but life should be more than pleasant; an ox in a pasture has a pleasant life." Disraeli chose power over pasture. If, in the process, he was guilty of any number of outrageous things of which role-model heroes are innocent, it is fortunate for his biographer—and the reader. That he succeeded, although at first a loser at everything, was also opportune for England.

In the House of Commons in 1859 Disraeli remarked, "Finality is not the language of politics." It is also not the language of biography. The first life of Disraeli had already been written by 1859; this one will not be the last. Compelling figures who have made a difference in the world will be put under the biographer's lens again and again. *Disraeli: A Biography* examines major documents and data hitherto unknown or unused and employs the perspectives of medicine, sexuality, and other biographical lenses which help get to the roots of behavior. Among my other lenses are the recorded impressions of Americans who encountered Disraeli, revealing angles of vision seldom if ever employed before. And there is the perhaps controversial prism of possible paternity.

No life is lived in a vacuum. Disraeli's crowded career includes a supporting cast of men and women—especially women—who abetted his climb or made it less than easy. Physicians nearly killed him with cures for his depression; bailiffs tried to seize him with arrest warrants for unpaid debts. He bedded several ladies for their connections, married another for her money. To get anywhere in his own party he had to destroy the leaders he could not co-opt, and to win as a gentleman over the opposition he had to deny himself his most powerful weapon—publicizing its pious leader's penchant for "rescuing" prostitutes. To get anywhere with the Establishment, Disraeli had to overcome, by what one adversary on his own side described as "splendid perseverance," what was lightly dismissed as "social difficulties." Despite being Benjamin Disraeli he presided at 10 Downing Street when it was the seat of the greatest empire the world had ever known, and—even before his publisher knew any more than the title—he accepted the fattest contract any English author had ever been offered for a novel.

For Disraeli *forti nihil difficile* was more than a platitude; it was a challenge. However remarkable we find individuals with a relentless appetite for achievement, they make us uneasy. However much we are amused by them, we also deplore people who have a flair for self-advertisement and a disconcerting wit that turns conventional wisdom upside down. Disraeli is difficult to love. A life of Disraeli cannot be a saint's life, although all the more fascinating for that. "Adventures are for the adventurous," he claimed. This is an adventure.

SON OF MY RIGHT HAND

1804–1837

I

"I HAVE THE TWO GREATEST STIMULANTS IN THE WORLD TO ACTION, YOUTH AND DEBT."

1837

THE CANDIDATE SEEMED TO EVERYONE BUT HIMSELF AS OUT OF PLACE as a peacock in a chicken coop. East of Sevenoaks in Kent, only two weeks into the reign of eighteen-year-old Queen Victoria, a crowd had gathered at the Corn Exchange in the borough of Maidstone to gawk at, more than to listen to, the curious young man on the platform. The stodgy structure, pride of the town, had been built two years earlier to furnish a roof over the local grain merchants' stalls. It had quickly become the local meeting point, even for aspiring politicians.

A canary waistcoat topped the strident green trousers of the outsider from London. His gold chains glittered. As he gesticulated, his beringed fingers sometimes reached toward his pomaded black curls. On that summery Monday evening—July 3, 1837—he hardly appeared to be the sort of tribune in whom the people's trust might be vested, but that impediment seemed of no concern as he exhorted constituents to elect him to the new Parliament. For five years he had been trying to gain a seat in the

Commons and had little to show from three previous attempts but mounting debts and a carefully marshaled patience.

Pride and ambition sent Benjamin Disraeli back to the hustings, but now prison seemed likely if Parliament failed him. Short of death there were few ways to avoid paying overdue bills. One could flee the country or become immune, as an M.P., from arrest for debt. In Disraeli's first novel, written at twenty when he was already deep in debt—both achievements evidenced a young man in a hurry—one character remarks of another in what seems prophetic of the author's own story, "The only way to keep him out of the House of Corrections was to get him into the House of Commons."

Disraeli was pleased to find the Sheriff's Officer, he claimed audaciously to his sister Sarah, "among my staunchest supporters. I suppose gratitude." Officers of the Sheriff received a commission for each writ served.

"Shylock!" someone shouted. Others took up the cry. It was a singularly inappropriate epithet to use against Disraeli. For years he had been so much in servitude to the Shylocks of the City—who knew no religious exclusion—that each time he emerged to campaign he risked writs, "sponging houses," and prison. It might no longer be possible, he worried to Sarah, "to prevent a disgraceful catastrophe."

He had put a scene in a sponging house into his heavily autobiographical novel of the previous year. In addition to an idealized version of himself, the major figures included Count Alfred D'Orsay and Lady Sykes, a former mistress. Playing with fire, Disraeli had used her Christian name in the title, *Henrietta Temple*. D'Orsay, a dandy like Disraeli, was also an artist. The Count's principal occupations, however, were to be himself and to be lover of Marguerite, Lady Blessington, who wrote society novels frenziedly to finance their lifestyle. Disraeli's novel suggested that the author's acquaintance with sponging houses—from which the victim went free when squeezed dry, or went to debtor's prison—was real, and that when he found himself in one, he had been extricated by D'Orsay.

"Old clo's!" someone in the crowd at Maidstone jeered, and others picked up the even less appropriate catcall. Selling secondhand clothes was the cliché occupation of the Jewish underclass; yet Disraeli's flamboyant dress was foppish to the last degree. Further, his family, including many of the Basevis and the Lindos, had little to do with that embarrassing majority of their brethren in England to whom the malediction applied, eschewing the community as well as the theology.

Gansevoort Melville, brother of the future author of *Moby-Dick*, would write a few years later, "We rode on the top of an omnibus to Whitefriars to visit the Jew quarter and the old clothes exchanges. We visited three of these—crowded with Jews young & old & replete with old garments, cast-off finery, old shoes, & every possible variety of second-hand integuments. We must have seen in the lanes & at the Rag fairs some 26 or 28,000 Jews—a dirty, ill-favored, undersized set."

This seemed an inferior caste, not the historic race with which Benjamin Disraeli chose to identify, complete to keeping the surname which he could have jettisoned for a less foreign one. Francis Cohen, the son of Isaac D'Israeli's stockbroker friend Meyer, had married, converted to the Anglicanism of his wife, and taken the maiden name of her mother. Litterateur and lawyer in the Middle Temple, he had already been knighted in 1832 as Sir Francis Palgrave.

Invective, Disraeli had learned in his first campaign, in that very year of 1832, was part of politics. He could not and would not hide from his origins. Whatever the risks, it seemed better to make political capital of them. Since he had already canvassed the town for two days, he knew that many in his audience were nonvoters who had come to be entertained. The real voters were to be purchased with the Tory incumbent's golden sovereigns. Running for the second local seat, Disraeli was performing for the local press, for whose reporters it was important to overawe the burghers. Maidstone was his stage, and Disraeli's listeners discovered that he merely talked through their epithets and their laughter, elaborating methodically on his broadsheet address distributed the previous Saturday.

He was, he had declared, "an uncompromising adherent to that ancient Constitution which was once the boast of our Fathers, and is still the Blessing of their Children." The Reform Bill

The High Street, High Wycombe, looking West. *Engraved from a painting by E. J. Niemann.*

of 1832, which had opened more seats to be contested, remained, to Disraeli, a threat to national equilibrium. "I wish to see the Crown enjoy its Prerogative, both Houses of Parliament their equal Privileges"—the Reform Bill had weakened the Lords—"and . . . that universal and hereditary Freedom which has been the noble consequence of our finely balanced scheme of legislative power."

Ignoring further taunts about his ancestry, Disraeli went on (it was also a period of emotional anti-Catholicism in much of England) to emphasize his stand, paradoxical as was his logic, that Protestantism was "the best guarantee for religious Toleration and orthodox Purity." The "national Church"—the Crown being peculiarly defender of several faiths—was, he claimed, an institution devoted to civil as well as "spiritual liberties." And, recognizing that the country was gradually losing its political power to the city, he identified himself (as his father lived in a Buckinghamshire suburb of London) as "Resident in an agricultural County, and deeply interested in the Land," the fortunes of which he would watch over "with vigilant solicitude."

"I think I made the best speech I ever made yet . . . and

more than an hour in length," he wrote to Sarah. And on returning to London he announced to her confidently that he had
"completed a most TRIUMPHANT CANVASS. . . . I doubt whe[the]r
there will be a contest."

Until June 30, only a few days earlier, Disraeli had no idea
that he would be vying for a seat at Maidstone. Promised for his
party services an opportunity with real prospects, he had to wait
for a by-election to fill a vacancy, or for the death of the old King
and the dissolution of Parliament automatic upon the accession of
the new sovereign. William IV had been seriously ill over the
winter, and Disraeli wondered whether he could remain out of
debtor's prison long enough to be nominated for the Commons.
And for which seat?

By May 3, he reported to Sarah, he had finished page 109 of
the second volume of *Venetia*. It was being set in type as he finished each chapter. Two weeks earlier he explained to William
Pyne, who was pressing him for money, that he had 150 pages to
go, and in his distractions and anxiety "indeed I know not how
I can repay you. . . . I find it difficult to command the Muse amid
all these vexations." Assisting his muse, Disraeli borrowed an
aside from Macaulay, some dialogue for his Shelleyan figure from
the poet's *Discourse on the Manners of the Ancients*, and for pad-
ding he paraphrased a long extract from *Don Quixote*.

While the urgent question was whether he could finish the
novel and collect some money for it before the bailiffs came for
him, he had to worry, too, about whether the King could survive
beyond Princess Victoria's eighteenth birthday on May 24. A new
regime meant new elections and new possibilities for a seat. If the
Princess succeeded before then, a regency under her mother, the
despised Duchess of Kent, would occur, altering all political expectations, including whether Victoria might succeed at all.
Disraeli's survey of constituencies and by-election possibilities
ranged all of England, and to create more claims for himself he
assisted strenuously in other by-elections. On May 18 William appeared at a levee, listless and seated. The King was failing, but he
would outlast the Duchess's ambition.

At smart balls and banquets in London, the talk was of William's likely death and of its social and political repercussions.

Disraeli dined among the marquesses and earls and their ladies, grandees of whom he had no experience when he had written his novel *The Young Duke* (1831)—and his father had scoffed, "What does Ben know of dukes?" The bulletins from Windsor Castle were pessimistic, then the reverse. One dinner party at posh Bridgewater House—the residence of Lord Francis Egerton, the literary-minded second son of the Duke of Sutherland and the M.P. for South Lancashire—for (Disraeli wrote to his sister) "about one thousand persons," was to show off the picture galleries, specially lit for the occasion, but the conversation was of the impending dissolution of Parliament. The King had been given "four and twenty hours." The next day, June 15, Disraeli walked to St. James's Palace to see the latest medical bulletin posted. The curious onlookers, he told Sarah, were "an inspiring sight."

A day later, with William still hanging on, Disraeli saw the Earl of Munster, the King's illegitimate son George Augustus Frederick Fitz-Clarence, who reported that William was no longer "in peril." It was empty optimism, but the King insisted that he would see Waterloo Day, June 18, through. Between attending dinner parties at night and writing evasive letters to creditors by day, Disraeli was unable to follow the throngs to Vauxhall Gardens that Friday—Waterloo Day was a holiday—to watch "the monster balloon rise." His political and literary prospects, he assured claimants for money, were excellent, and payment certain. While new writs were left for him at his father's house at Bradenham, Disraeli pursued the good life as a favorite of fashionable ladies. At the Comtesse de Montalembert's (the former Eliza Forbes, a minor writer, had married a titled émigré) his hostess lionized him "so dreadfully," he boasted to Sarah, "that I was actually forced to run for my life. She even produced *Venetia* and was going to read a passage out loud, when I seized my hat and rushed downstairs, leaving the graceful society of Lady Egerton, much to my vexation." Disraeli flourished in the company of attractive and often older married women, and had met the "charming" Anna Elizabeth Grey-Egerton only the week before at Lady Londonderry's—a "demon" hostess in his opinion, but a useful one.

The King was dying, Disraeli reported, "like an old lion."

According to Fitz-Clarence, who brought to William's bedside a Union Jack that had been sent by the Duke of Wellington, his royal father had said, "Unfurl it and let me feel it. Glorious day." In the early morning hours of the 29th, the King died, and Privy Councillors were summoned to Kensington Palace, the residence of the new sovereign. Disraeli's patron, Lord Lyndhurst, took Disraeli with him to wait in an anteroom while the former Lord Chancellor, Ben reported to Sarah, "kissed the Queen's hand which all agreed was remarkably sweet and soft." Doll-like in size and in a black mourning dress, Victoria "read her address well and was perfectly composed tho' alone in the council chamber and attended by no women."

At the small, pseudo-Grecian bastion of Toryism that was the Carlton Club, along club-lined Pall Mall, hundreds crowded in, once the Privy Council had adjourned, to ponder strategies for winning the next Parliament. First offered the borough of Ashburton in Devonshire to contest, reputedly a safe seat, Disraeli turned it down, perhaps because of its remoteness from London. Other offers, he was certain, would follow—and his impulse proved a good one, as Ashburton would not return a Conservative until 1852. While High Wycombe, his father's district, was again a possibility because Charles Grey was stepping down to become an equerry to the Queen, the party outlook there seemed unpromising. Disraeli had been defeated there before. Yet there would be a seat for him somewhere, he confided to Sarah from the smoky hubbub of the Carlton, for in "the extraordinary hustle and bustle of the eventful moment," which had already lasted beyond midnight, "deputations from the country . . . , places that want candidates and candidates that want places," still milled about and bargained. The suspense was "harassing and engrossing."

For Whigs as well as Tories, the sorting-out process required continuing intelligence from the constituencies. Incumbents were canvassing their reelection prospects and prospective candidates testing their chances and staying in or withdrawing. "O politics, thou splendid juggle!" Disraeli had exulted in *Vivian Grey*, before the fiction had become fact.

For him, the decisive juggle came on the 30th. Most districts

were two-member constituencies, and he was friendly with
Charles Fancourt, one of the sitting members for Barnstaple, a
harbor town in far western Devon, even more remote than
Ashburton but a safer bet. He could campaign in tandem with a
popular incumbent. Still, neither man was honest to the other
about the situation. Disraeli was looking for a seat near
London—it was the infancy of railways and many districts seldom
saw their members after a campaign unless they actually had authentic homes nearby. And Fancourt was negotiating to become
an aide-de-camp to the new King Ernest of Hanover, uncle to the
Queen and, in England, the Duke of Cumberland. (Had Victoria
not survived to reign, the kingdom would have gone to the unpopular Ernest as the next living brother in line of succession after George IV and William IV.)

Maidstone in Kent—much closer to the capital—also
elected two members, but since there was a sitting Whig, local
Tories had intended to present only one, Wyndham Lewis, their
incumbent. When reports that seemed genuine suggested that the
Whig M.P. was not planning to run again, Lewis—who had
known Disraeli for four years, and whose wife, Mary Anne, doted
on him—proposed him for the other seat. Lewis felt sure that he
could command 750 "plumpers"—voters who chose to cast only
one vote—to cast a second for Disraeli. With only 1,400 voters
eligible, many of whom would not bother to cast a ballot, the seat
seemed a certainty. "My darling," Ben wrote to Sarah at
Bradenham on June 30, "The clouds have at length dispelled, and
my prospects seem as bright as the day. At 6 o'clock this evening
I start for Maidstone with Wyndham Lewis." And on July 3,
Disraeli made his first appearance at a public meeting in the borough at the Corn Exchange.

Unperturbed by hostile epithets and optimistic about the results after canvassing the borough, Disraeli traveled with
Wyndham Lewis back to London late in the week. No opposition
had emerged to either of them, the only Whig candidate, Abraham Wildey Robarts, M.P. from Maidstone since 1818, having
confirmed that he would not campaign again. But candidates and
alliances were still being negotiated, with grumbles coming from
Barnstaple as late as the 8th that neither Fancourt nor Disraeli

had announced for the local seats. The news had not yet come to the outer reaches of Devon that both aspirants were making other arrangements. When it did, on the 10th, Fancourt warned his friend that there would be "the deuce to pay" for Ben's "non-appearance."

Excited and unaware of his son's continued toying with two constituencies, Isaac D'Israeli paid a midweek visit to London to hear his son's account of likely triumphs at Maidstone and retired, "full of confidence and satisfaction," to Dunn's lodging house, where Ben had procured a room for him overnight. "Nothing could be better," Ben crowed to Sarah in a note. He would have been less pleased if he had known what the Dowager Marchioness of Salisbury had penned in her diary the night before after having dined with him at the Londonderrys' mansion at Rosebank. "I never met him before. He bears the mark of the Jew strikingly about him, and at times his way of speaking reminded me so much of Lord Lyndhurst. . . . He is evidently very clever, but superlatively vulgar." Clearly Disraeli had acquired more from the Lord Chancellor than ambition and had been aping his style. The politician, the peacock, and the patronymic had clashed.

On Monday the 17th the Queen visited the House of Lords to officially prorogue—dissolve—Parliament; then, at a Privy Council session, she asked for a proclamation calling for new elections. Disraeli was a spectator at the Lords ("everything gay and splendid" he told Sarah) and events seemed to be going so well that he wrote to her again at the end of the week that he was apparently to be the only new candidate on the Conservative side "who has not an opposition." He could take time off to cobble up for Lady Blessington "a Syrian sketch of 4 or 5 pages" for her annual hack volume, *Heath's Book of Beauty.*

Balloting was traditionally spread over several days, and polling for various constituencies held over a space of days, which meant that Disraeli would vote in his own home district after the ballots were completely counted at Maidstone. To sail in unopposed "was thought impossible in these times," he boasted to Sarah, quoting his last turn-down for financing. "So much for the 'maddest of all mad acts,' my Uncle G's prescience, and B.E.L.'s unrivalled powers of Encouragement."

Even campaign funds seemed no further problem. No votes had to be bought beyond those already guaranteed to Wyndham Lewis. Still, Ben's own debts remained serious enough. He had been campaigning for a variety of seats for so long that he had exhausted his borrowing capacity, even from his father, his last resort after costly undertakings in politics and in love. His mother's family had been no use. They saw no hope for him, as a Jew, in politics, although they were hardly more Jewish than Ben, most of them marrying out of the faith. His uncle, George Basevi, a prosperous lawyer, whom Ben privately called "George Base," had been applied to unsuccessfully before. This time he discussed the matter with his son Nathaniel, Ben's cousin and already an eminent barrister, and the Basevis agreed that there was no future in Parliament for their persistent and ambitious relative. Even George's arty son, George, Jr., was already a successful architect while Ben, they explained to him, seemed little more than an adventurer and an outsider to the very people in politics whom he needed as colleagues. When Ben told his uncle and cousin what he thought of their unfamilial lack of support they repeated that they were acting for his own good. It was time he settled down to something at which he could succeed.

Ben went then to "B.E.L."—his cousin Benjamin Ephraim Lindo—son of his mother's elder sister Sarah (another Basevi). Ten years older than Disraeli, he was businesslike and in a position to help. Again there was no encouragement, and the concerns of the family seemed justified when, on the 23rd, a Sunday, an opponent materialized. Nomination Day in Maidstone was July 24. "That notorious bore, Colonel Thompson," Ben reported to Sarah, had arrived in town "avowing his readiness to serve the Electors." Thomas Perronet Thompson, co-proprietor of the *Westminster Review* and author of such pamphlets as *The True Theory of Rent* and *A Catechism on the Corn Laws*, was in his middle fifties and had been Radical M.P. for Hull since 1835. Suddenly it seemed as if Disraeli should have spent less time at the Carlton Club talking politics and more in Maidstone.

Years after Disraeli's death the weekly *World* ran "a very circumstantial story . . . told by the Conservative agent at Maidstone" that when a rival appeared on the scene and things looked bad, "Mr Disraeli came into the garden behind the Star Hotel, the Conservative headquarters, and, throwing himself on the grass, declared that he should be beaten, and that if so, his career was over, and he was ruined. Mrs Wyndham Lewis, who was sitting there, tried to cheer him up and raise his hopes, but finding that course unsuccessful, took the Conservative agent aside, and, giving him a large sum of money, said, 'Spend that, and more if you want it—all that is necessary; but Mr Disraeli must be returned.' " When she later estimated her expenses at Maidstone at far more than the figure reported by Wyndham Lewis, it may have meant that the Tory agent had indeed come back. Maidstone electors expected to be bribed handsomely.

Before an appreciative Nomination Day audience, Perronet Thompson's proposer, alluding sarcastically to his rival's origins, dismissed "Mr Disraeli—I hope I pronounce his name right." It was exactly what the Basevis had feared, and indeed there was some question about whether the second syllable should be pronounced "rail" or "reel," or whether the name should be elongated into Disra-ee-li, which further emphasized its alien nature.

John Hollams, then a young man, remembered Disraeli the next day "addressing the mob from the window of his committeeroom at the Bell Hotel," confessing that although it was his fourth contested election, he was confident this time of success. "He was not popular with the mob. They offered him bacon, ham, etc. and repeatedly suggested that he was a Jew; but he was very ready in replying to them. Taking up the slur directly, Disraeli did not dally long in his remarks before he referred to 'Colonel Perronet Thompson—I hope I pronounce his name aright.' It did not help, Hollams remembered, that Disraeli's appearance "was very remarkable—long black hair in curls—and he was dressed in an extraordinary way, the extreme, it may be supposed, of fashion."

Some of his political aims were no less remarkable. Although Disraeli claimed to be a "Radical Conservative"—an evolution toward political orthodoxy from his beginnings as nonparty Radical—he saw no contradiction in terms. He would lay out a career in adapting popular causes (the Radical thrust) to the Conservative agenda, and found one for the citizenry of Maidstone in the anomalies of the Whig-inspired and widely unpopular New Poor Law of 1834. The chief tax burden of maintaining it fell upon "rates"—property taxes. In rural areas until only a few years before the act, there had been riots and destruction of farm machinery by the unemployed and the underpaid, often led by militant craftsmen, one of them the Radical cobbler John Adams of Maidstone. Kent had experienced more agitation about joblessness and low wages than most counties, and many attributed the relative calm to the callous austerity of the Poor Law.

The law encouraged people to work by making relief for the indigent as unattractive as possible. No longer were the legally poor to maintain themselves, if possible, in their own dwellings; they were to be forced into workhouses maintained by public funds, segregated by sex and meanly fed. To plead poverty meant deprivation of freedom, separation from spouse (and deprivation of sex), conditions of labor and diet akin to prison life. Dickens and his like would dramatize the discontent and the debased existence created by the Poor Law, which, by institutionalizing relief, made it more costly and less humane.

On the hustings Disraeli called the law cruel and urged its repeal, as it was based "upon the principle that relief to the poor is a charity. I maintain," he declared to the Maidstone electorate, "that it is a right!" Anticipating Bernard Shaw's *Major Barbara* by seventy years, he insisted that social regeneration could not be so coldly bureaucratized. "To sum up my feelings in a sentence—I consider that this Act has disgraced the country more than any other upon record. Both a moral crime and a political blunder, it announces to the world that in England poverty is a crime."*

While a popular cause among the poor, repeal frightened rate-payers upon whom the act depended and who actually had

---

*Poverty, says Andrew Undershaft, the millionaire factory owner in Shaw's 1905 play, is "the worst of crimes. All the other crimes are virtues beside it. . . . Poverty blights whole cities; spreads horrible pestilences; strikes dead the very souls of all who come within sight, sound, or smell of it." Oswald Millbank, the enlightened millionaire manufacturer in Disraeli's novel *Coningsby* (1844), and his utopian— even smokeless—factory community "in a green valley of Lancaster," anticipate Shaw's Undershaft and the planned factory town of Perivale St Andrews.

Mrs Wyndham Lewis. *From a miniature at Hughenden, painted in 1829 by Rochard.*

the right to vote. After all, its supporters in both parties claimed, it was philosophically sound to make the dole painful, and other forms of poor relief might cost more. The problem as always was that human dignity required meaningful jobs—work, rather than the workhouse. Political parties never were effective at that.

The tally at the close of the first day's balloting showed Lewis with 707 votes, Disraeli with 616, and Thompson with 412. "The constituency nearly exhausted," Ben—signing his name hastily as "Dizzy"—wrote to Sarah. There were not enough likely voters left to reverse the count. Pleased with his prospects, he returned to his lodgings at 8 Down Street, Piccadilly, en route to

Bradenham to cast his own vote at Aylesbury. Eventually the Tories would gain thirty-four seats, to a total of 309 against 349 for
the Whigs and Radicals. He had affixed Wyndham Lewis's purple
campaign colors to his own candidacy, and won—not because of
his own appeal, he understood, but because his partner's money
and the local political machine that it purchased had brought
him in. He had no doubts that once in the Commons, he could
build his own reputation.

Mrs Wyndham Lewis was satisfied on both counts. To her
brother, Major Viney Evans, Mary Anne exulted that her husband had not only topped the poll but "succeeded in bringing in
another Conservative with him—his friend Mr Disraeli—one of
the greatest writers and finest orators of the day—age about
30. . . . Mr Disraeli's being so fine a speaker joined to *my humble
worth* carried everything before us." She had been there for the final days, the chief enthusiast. "Can you not fancy me driving
about the town—encouraging our friends and playing the Amiable to a pitch of distraction[?]" And with victory some of the local women "clasp'd Wyndham in their arms and kissed him again
and again in spite of his struggles—which set Mr Disraeli and
your Whizzy in screams of laughter."

She was ready with a prophecy for her brother. "Mark what
I say. . . . Mr Disraeli will, in a very few years be one of the greatest men of his day—his great talents back'd by his friends. . . .
Wyndham's power to keep him in Parliament will ensure him success. They call him my Parliamentary Protégé." Happily, she
signed her letter "Whiz."

From Bradenham his other chief supporter, Sarah, wrote to
Ben, "A few days back the *Morning Herald* said something of two
men being returned to Parliament of whom great things were expected. Who is the second?"

II

"I WAS BORN IN A LIBRARY."

1804–1817

ON DECEMBER 28, 1804—THE 26TH DAY OF TEBET, 5565 IN THE JEW-
ish calendar—a large family group gathered at 6 King's Road,
Bedford Row,* overlooking Gray's Inn Garden, to observe and
celebrate a *brit milah*—a circumcision. Religious law required that
the observance take place on the eighth day of the male child's
life, which had begun at 5:30 A.M. on December 21. More than
the required ten adult men, accoutered in black hats and morning
coats, were present to make up the *minyan*. As it was still a
lying-in time for the mother, Miriam D'Israeli (she called herself
Maria), one of the men fetched her firstborn son and brought him
to the room where the rite was to be performed.

The *kiseh Eliyahu* (Elijah's chair) had been brought from
Bevis Marks Synagogue, as well as a second chair for the *mohel*
(circumciser). It had a pull-out drawer below the seat for the necessary surgical implements. According to 1 Kings 19:10–14, the

---

*Now renamed and renumbered 22 Theobald's Road.

Prophet Elijah had complained to God that Israel was again neglecting the divine covenant, one of its many lapses in biblical history. According to tradition, God had then enjoined Elijah (and by extension his representatives) to be present at each circumcision to witness Israel's symbolic loyalty to the higher law as instructed in Leviticus 12:3. In Elijah's spacious chair sat the child's designated godfather, in actuality his grandfather. Benjamin D'Israeli had waited into his seventy-fourth year for a grandson. The grumpy godmother (and grandmother), Sarah, waited in an adjoining room with the women.

The *sandik,* or proxy, who had gathered up the child from his mother—his title, curiously, came from the Greek *syndikos,* or counsel—held the infant firmly on the *kiseh Eliyahu.* Turning toward the "throne of Elijah," the *mohel,* David Abarbanel Lindo, the boy's uncle, dexterously applied the tiny protective shield and then swiftly made the single, circular, cut.

Two cups of wine were at hand. The *mohel* used one for rinsing his mouth before draining whatever drops of blood oozed from the wound—a primitive form of antisepsis—and to dip in a finger and, as needed, offer it to the child to suck, to quiet its crying. The other cup was for a ceremonial blessing. After prayers for the boy's long life, David Lindo asked the father, Isaac D'Israeli, by what name his son was to be called. "Benjamin," Isaac said—in honor of his father. Perhaps, too, since the child was a firstborn son, the name had an additional and more literal resonance— "son of my right hand."

Further prayers followed; then the godfather returned young Benjamin to the room of women, which included the infant's sister Sarah, whose second birthday would be the next day. Everyone tucked into wine, coffee and tea, chocolates, and sweet cakes. The *minyan* then proceeded to Maria's room to look in and to offer a prayer for the preservation of mother and child. Young Benjamin D'Israeli had participated in the only Judaic rite in which he would be a central figure.

As the next day was a Saturday, the Sabbath, the two ceremonial chairs remained at 6 King's Road an extra day, after which a carriage came to return them to the synagogue. Named for the narrow street intersecting with Heneage Lane, Bevis Marks was a corruption of Buries Marks, the mark or site of the mansion of the abbots of Bury St. Edmunds in Suffolk, which had stood there in the twelfth century. At the synagogue in Aldgate, officially Sha'ar Hashamayim ("Gate of Heaven") but always colloquially Bevis Marks, the record of the *brit milah* was entered in the register in the customary Portuguese (which gave the mother's name as *Mariam*). Sha'ar Hashamayim had been founded in 1656, on the upper floor of a house in Creechurch Lane, as the Spanish and Portuguese Jews' Congregation. Their first house of worship after the legal return of the Jews to England—the few thousand who had not been slaughtered in the thirteenth century were banished in 1290—it was at first a curiosity to outsiders. Samuel Pepys of the Admiralty Office visited it on October 14, 1663, recording in his diary a celebration of *Simchat Torah*.

The congregation had quickly outgrown its temporary site, and built a structure of its own in Bevis Marks in 1701, moving the oak benches on which the male worshippers had sat to become the back rows of the new hall. Women were restricted to the balcony. Otherwise, the building—discreetly unidentifiable unless one entered its courtyard—owed its interior in part to the manner of Christopher Wren, and something, too, in its severe simplicity, to the example of the Dissenters' Chapel. In Jewish tradition the raised reading platform was in the center, and above the Ark were not only the symbolic Tablets of the Law, with the Ten Commandments, but the inscription in Hebrew, "Know thou before Whom thou standest."

So the elder Benjamin D'Israeli found it when he came to London from Italy in 1748 as a young man of eighteen. A Jew, unless he were fleeing his religious identity, would join a local congregation, and young D'Israeli was drawn to the Spanish and Portuguese synagogue with which Italians had affinities. Many Italian Jews, as Benjamin's grandson and namesake suggested as a reflection of his own claimed ancestry, descended "from one of those Hebrew families whom the Inquisition forced to emigrate from the Spanish Peninsula at the end of the fifteenth century, and . . . found a refuge in the more tolerant territories of the Venetian Republic." On their resettlement, the younger Benjamin would write imaginatively in 1848 in his memoir of his father, a

century after the D'Israeli for whom he was named arrived in
England, his ancestors "dropped their Gothic surname." Now,
"grateful to the God of Jacob who had sustained them through
unprecedented trials and guarded them through unheard-of perils,
they assumed the name of D'Israeli, a name never borne before,
or since, by any other family, in order that their race might be for
ever recognised." (The family name was Israeli until the first Benjamin added the *D'* in England.)

Under "the protection of the lion of St Mark," he added,
which was appropriate, "since the patron saint of the [Venetian]
Republic was himself a child of Israel," the Israelis flourished as
merchants until the younger son of one of them, "son of his right
hand," was sent to England to pursue the family's business.

An inveterate romantic, the younger Benjamin invented
material for the blank spaces in his history and embellished the
rest so happily that he soon believed it himself. It was a characteristic best seen in that of a feisty Victorian contemporary, an expatriate from America who had lived in Russia as a boy while his
father built railroads for the Czar. A judge in a celebrated libel
trial had asked this American (the plaintiff) where he was born,
and James A. McNeill Whistler had responded, "St. Petersburg"—it had been a place replete with romantic and exotic associations for him.

According to court records, so the judge observed, Whistler
had been born in Lowell, Massachusetts.

"I do not choose to be born in Lowell, Massachusetts," Whistler insisted—and Disraeli did not choose to have his antecedents
emerge from sleepy provincial Cento in Ferrara, the papal state
where they had settled after, very likely, generations in Turkey or
North Africa. The Cento community had been augmented by
Spanish and Portuguese émigrés, into which the family of Israeli
may have married. The association which the later Benjamin often
claimed with the Sephardic "aristocracy" (*Sefarad* was Spain) and
the post–1492 *converso* "secret Jews" were little more than wishful
fantasies—guesses, at best—turned into facts by a facile pen.

Writing his fanciful autobiography, *Contarini Fleming* (1832),
he imagined the Venice with which he identified with a reverent
nostalgia. "The marble palaces of my ancestors rose on each side,

like a series of vast and solemn temples. How sublime were their broad fronts bathed in the mystic light whose softening tints concealed the ravages of time, and made us dream only of their eternity! . . . I viewed them with a devotion which I cannot believe could have been surpassed in the most patriotic period of the republic. How willingly I would have given my life to have once more filled their mighty halls."

Disraeli's surname itself, rather than an exclusive adoption of his grandfather's family, was only a Levantine tag for a Jew—there was even at the time another Benjamin D'Israeli in Dublin—but the younger Benjamin, who dropped the exotic apostrophe (very likely in the Middle East the accepted version had been al Israeli), found a reason to suffuse the name with a romantic past.

The earliest Italians of his surname of whom there are surviving records are Isaac and Abraham Israel, who in 1613 were members of the Sephardic community of Venice, and David and Jacob Israel of Tunis, who resided in the Jewish community of Livorno (Leghorn) in 1644. The earliest of his own family whom Benjamin Disraeli could trace was the Isaac Israeli of Cento nearly a century later, father of his grandfather Benjamin. What Ben did not know was that the bride of his great-grandfather Isaac was a Rossi, or De'Rossi, and that Enrichetta De'Rossi according to local tradition came, thus, from one of the four noble families of Jerusalem who had been brought from Israel to Rome as captives of the Emperor Titus, becoming the ancestors of the first eminent Italian-Jewish families. It was a heritage that Ben might have seized upon.

Benjamin Israeli had arrived in England at eighteen, sent by his family to exploit his knowledge of the Italian straw bonnet trade. He found work in the establishment founded in 1740 by Joseph and Pellegrin Treves of Venice in Fenchurch Street, between Leadenhall Street and Eastcheap. Eight years later, D'Israeli, as he had become, had risen sufficiently in his compatriots' business to marry Rebecca Mendes Furtado, whose family had indeed fled Portugal and the Inquisition. It was an Iberian connection of which the younger Benjamin would have been proud, but Rebecca died in 1764, leaving her husband with a daughter, Rachel, who was to eventually settle and raise a family in Livorno. The younger Benjamin's grandmother would be D'Israeli's second wife, marrying her husband a year after his bereavement.

The new marriage rehabilitated D'Israeli's fortunes. Going into business on his own in 1759 as an importer of goods and also speculating in stocks and shares, he quickly found himself in financial distress. One record dated April 22, 1760, is a suit in Chancery demanding payment of £63/11s./4d. long overdue, for twenty-three blocks of Italian marble shipped to Benjamin D'Israeli and associates by Ephraim De Aguilar, described as a merchant of Leghorn. D'Israeli had been chronically unable to pay his bills, yet on marrying Sarah he thrived as a wholesale merchant and jobber through the good offices of his new father-in-law, who had the added distinction, the younger Benjamin thought, of being related to the aristocratic Sephardic family of Villa Real* and also to the Chief Rabbi of Venice, Simon Calimani. Benjamin the younger would build edifices of ancestry upon both associations.

The beautiful and proud Sarah Shiprut de Gabay, who married Benjamin D'Israeli in 1765 and conceived their only child, Isaac, born the next year, chafed at the religious snobbery that limited her life. As her grandson would put it, "The lady was ambitious of social distinction, and she resented upon her unfortunate race the slights and disappointments to which it exposed her." Old Broad Street, a fashionable area of the city in the seventeenth century near busy Threadneedle Street, was still dwelt in by bankers and merchants, but Sarah scorned Jews and the others snubbed her. In response she pressed Benjamin in 1780 to relocate to the country, and he moved to Enfield, just to the north of what was then urban London, where he created an Italian garden in which he entertained his friends. He kept his importing firm in London and retained his membership at Bevis Marks, serving an honorific term of office as inspector of the synagogue's charity schools.

In 1794 he resettled at Woodford, even farther from the chimney pots of London, where he toyed for three years at being

---

*Actually not the famous Portuguese family of Villa Real, but a Livorno clan of the same name.

a gentleman farmer. One can imagine the upwardly mobile Jewish merchant in the print "A Cockney and his Wife going to Wycombe" (1805), by H. Humphrey of 27 St. James's Street, in which a well-dressed businessman for whom "Cockney" is clearly a euphemism, his grossly fat, overdressed wife at his side, drives a two-wheeler westward. While whipping his abused and underfed horse he recalls, "Vednesday vas a veek, my Vife & I vent to Vest Vycombe, & vether it vas the Vind, or vether it vas the Veather—or vat it vas!—Ve vip'd, & vip'd, & vip'd!—I could not get off a Valk!" It would be old Benjamin's son, Isaac, who would later move his family to Wycombe.

Nothing D'Israeli did satisfied Sarah, "who never pardoned him for his name." Nursing her frustrations, she became, so her grandson remembered her, "a demon" only comparable with viragos like Catherine the Great, "so mortified by her social position that she lived until eighty without indulging in a tender expression." Possibly using the springboard of Ben's memoir of his father, George Eliot in her novel *Daniel Deronda* (written in 1874–75) wrote of an English-educated and baptized young man whose once beautiful but now ravaged mother, from a Portuguese-Jewish family resettled in Genoa, had rejected the yoke of her husband, Ephraim Charisi, and lived as a Gentile. Daniel is physically "a young copy" of the grandfather he never knew, who had insisted upon "fettering" Leonora to a faith she found repellent. "I was to feel everything I did not feel," she explains unrepentantly to Daniel, "and believe everything I did not believe. I was to feel awe for the bit of parchment in [the] mezuzah* over the door; to dread lest a bit of butter should touch a bit of meat; to think it beautiful that men should bind the *tephillin*† on them,

---

*The *mezuzah* is a small tubular case containing a piece of parchment on which are inscribed in Hebrew the biblical passages from Deuteronomy which form part of the *Shema* prayer ("Hear, O' Israel, the Lord our God, the Lord is One!"), the core of monotheistic faith. Following the biblical injunction "And thou shalt write them upon the doorposts of thy house and within thy gates," the mezuzah is so fixed at the entrance of the dwelling of an observant Jew.

†Hebrew for phylacteries, or "frontlets," small boxes or cubes containing prayers from Exodus and Deuteronomy, bound briefly during morning prayers to the forehead and the upper left arm of a male Orthodox Jew to signify worship of God with the head and the heart.

and women not,—to adore the wisdom of such laws, however silly they might seem to me. I was to love the long prayers in the ugly synagogue, and the howling, and the gabbling, and the dreadful fasts, and the tiresome feasts, and my father's endless discoursing about Our People. . . . I was to care for ever about what Israel had been; and I did not care at all. I cared for the wide world, and all that I could represent in it."

Returning to London and retiring from business, Benjamin D'Israeli joined the committee which built the new Stock Exchange, and lived placidly at Church Street, Stoke Newington, just above Hackney, a "kind, good-natured man," the younger Benjamin recalled, "who was in the habit of giving me presents when his wife was away." For Isaac, who grew up in the acrid atmosphere of his mother's discontent, it was inevitable that her only offspring developed to be as unlike his parents as was possible. He was "lost in reverie, fond of solitude, . . . seeking no better company than a book," and with "a mind utterly unfitted for every species of business."

Isaac seems to have had only a sketchy Jewish education, probably furnished by a tutor who visited occasionally at his school in Enfield. Disliking schooling altogether, especially the regimen and the discipline, he ran away once, his son wrote, and "was brought back, having been found lying on a tombstone in a Hackney churchyard." Relieved, his father "embraced him and gave him a pony," but the reconciliation was short-lived, for after uneasy months of "unusual abstraction and irritability," Isaac "produced a poem." His father was "seriously alarmed." It seemed clear that Isaac would not be useful in the importing business, and "decisive measures were required to eradicate this evil."

"It was resolved," the younger Benjamin explained, "that my father should be sent abroad, where a new scene and a new language might divert his mind from the ignominious pursuit which so fatally attracted him." The elder D'Israeli had little experience of literature, and associated poets with a satiric William Hogarth print he had in his house of "an unfortunate wight in a garret . . . inditing an ode to riches, while dunned for his milk-score." Isaac was "consigned like a bale of goods to my grandfather's correspondent at Amsterdam, who had instructions to place him at some collegium of repute in that city." Holland, the epitome of entre-preneurial acumen, a nation without natural resources that ex-isted entirely by its commercial skills, was exactly the place for Isaac's reformation.

When Isaac returned home from Amsterdam in November 1784, gaunt, long-haired, and curious in "intolerable garments," Benjamin, once the initial shock had abated, "dwelt on the united solicitude of his parents" for their son's future good, "and broke to him their intention, if it were agreeable to him, to place him in the establishment of a great merchant of Bordeaux." It was the wrong kind of place, Isaac explained. He had just written "a poem of considerable length which he wished to publish, against Commerce, which was the corrupter of man." And he took his manuscript to the eminent Dr. Samuel Johnson at his house at 8 Bolt Court, just above Fleet Street. There, Isaac was met at the door by Francis Barber, Johnson's black Jamaican servant, who told the young poet to return again in a week, and to be sure to be punctual. "But the packet was returned to him unopened, with a message that the illustrious doctor was too ill to read anything. The unhappy and obscure aspirant, who received this disheart-ening message, accepted it, in his utter despondency, as a me-chanical excuse. But alas! the cause was too true; and a few weeks later, [on December 13, 1784] . . . the great soul of Johnson quitted earth."

If the younger Benjamin learned anything from his father be-yond a love for books, it was to cultivate and utilize his connec-tions. When the death of Samuel Johnson sent him elsewhere with his packet of verse, Isaac turned to Henry James Pye, a pe-destrian poet whose sister-in-law, Mrs. Jael Pye, also a scribbler, was the daughter of a wealthy and literary-minded businessman known to the D'Israelis, Solomon Mendes. Nearly fifty, Pye was an M.P., an Oxonian, and a country gentleman who dabbled in Pindaric odes and could recognize in Isaac another poet as defi-cient as he was in traces of the Muse. But Pye had the necessary background to impress Isaac's father. Visiting the house at Enfield, he persuaded the amiable but disappointed D'Israeli to permit his son to follow his own bent.

Always ambivalent about Judaism, Isaac, who would write to

Francis Douce in 1794 that religion had drained Jews of their genius—"Ten centuries have not produced Ten great men"—wrote about one of them, "A sublime Metaphysician" of European stature, Moses Mendelssohn, in his novel, *Vaurien*, three years later. Vaurien, the hero, is a Frenchman who tries to transplant revolution to England and visits a Jewish philosopher, based upon the revered Mendelssohn, to suggest "[re]assembling the dispersed Hebrews," scattered, he believes, for having rejected Christ. The Diaspora had begun long before that, the philosopher tells Vaurien, for Jews retained their identity through the Mosaic Law and did not need to coalesce about a place; but he also felt that the ways by which Jews now flourished—Isaac was thinking of the inhibitions upon himself—limited their cultural impact. "Literary Jews must always be rare. . . . Their most malignant and powerful enemies will be found among their domestic associates." Foremost among them, Isaac thought sourly, was his own father, who changed his mind yet again and sent Isaac back to the Continent for further business training. Still, the opportunity of Paris meant bookshops and literary talk and immersion in Voltaire.

When Isaac returned from his apprenticeship and a family financed—and then very fashionable—"grand tour" of France, the Rhineland, and Italy in 1788–89 and went back to writing, Benjamin D'Israeli had to reconcile himself to his earlier bargain. The advice, after all, came from the new Poet Laureate: Pye had succeeded Thomas Warton in 1790. His exalted status would subject the new Laureate, no worse than some others before and since, to ridicule from London literati, but the elder Benjamin was remote from such sophisticates. When, in 1791, Isaac published, through John Murray, an anecdotal, antiquarian book, *Curiosities of Literature*—an immediate success—the family decision, however reluctant, seemed vindicated.

Since Isaac had kept his Voltairean heresies under his hat, he found himself rewarded in the year he established the beginnings of a literary reputation. His grandmother, Esther Shiprut, grieved at her daughter's hostility to the faith of her family, had cut Sarah out of her will, leaving a substantial sum directly to Isaac, her only grandson. At twenty-five, he possessed independent means and could spend his days in the British Museum and his nights among his own books. It seemed a pattern likely to endure for a lifetime. But much as he wanted to become an imaginative writer, creative genius failed to visit, and in the middle 1790s he suffered a nervous breakdown. "There came over my father," Benjamin would write after he had been afflicted by, and survived, much the same kind of malady, "that mysterious illness to which the youth of men of sensibility, and especially literary men, is frequently subject—a failing of nervous energy." Among its causes was "restless and indefinite purpose," and among its symptoms was "lassitude and despondency." Medical men, he added, from his own experience, "misled by the superficial symptoms, and not seeking to acquaint themselves with the psychology of their patients, arrive at erroneous, often fatal, conclusions."

In Isaac's case, Dr. Turton imagined the onset of consumption, and recommended a warmer climate. Since the Continent was then "disturbed" in the aftermath of the French Revolution, Devonshire was substituted, a remedy concurred in by Dr. Wolcot, a Devon man himself, who gave Isaac letters of recommendation to literary persons in Exeter.

Late in 1796, Isaac's bookish cronies discovered him back in the British Museum, taking notes for new projects and writing a novel. It appeared that the pattern of his life would be as before. But on February 10, 1802, he married Maria Basevi, daughter of Naphtali Basevi, a prosperous Italian-Jewish merchant once of Verona, now of Billiter Square, Bloomsbury, who like Isaac's father had emigrated to England as a young man. Maria's father, a merchant in London since 1762, had become President of the Jewish Board of Deputies in 1801. (Banker William Manning at No. 8 Billiter Square was one of Naphtali Basevi's friends and neighbors. The future Cardinal Manning proved more successful at his trade than did his grandfather. However respected, the firm of Manning & Vaughan failed, thereby disproving to some City merchants the suspicion that its senior partner had some Jewish blood in his veins.)

The uncle of Maria's mother, Solomon Rieti, had developed the amusement gardens by the Thames at Ranelagh in Chelsea in 1741. Under its enormous rotunda and in its broad gardens, pleasure seekers, for a twelvepence entrance fee, ate, drank, milled about, or merely gawked at the others who did. (Ranelagh would be swallowed up by new construction in 1803.) Other Basevis were barristers and businessmen, few of them as concerned as was Naphtali about maintaining a Jewish identity.

Literary life was no struggle in a garret for Isaac and Maria. Isaac's *Curiosities of Literature* opened doors for *An Essay on the Manners and Genius of the Literary Character* (1795), *Miscellanies, or Literary Recreations* (1796), and succeeding popular compilations which diverted him, perhaps contentedly, from more challenging literary efforts. Their funds were ample, and Maria proved a compliant helpmate, bearing his eccentricities and his children with equanimity. As Isaac would write, a year after his marriage, to Francis Douce, with Maria's individuality already submerged, "I have never yet found her desires to interfere with my wishes; my pleasures are her pleasures, & my friends are her friends."

"He was a complete literary character," his son Ben explained, "a man who really passed his life in a library. Even marriage produced no change in these habits. He rose early to enter the chamber where he lived alone with his books, and at night his lamp was ever lit in the same walls. . . . He disliked business, and he never required relaxation; he was absorbed in his pursuits." When Isaac took a walk, it was to visit booksellers. When he joined a club, it was to use its library. When others went to the country to ramble, he would find a nook in which to sit and work over something he had written. The external world concerned him little. References to contemporary events so seldom appeared in his books and letters as to suggest that he read everything but newspapers. "He had," Ben concluded, "not a single passion or prejudice." Much of that personality would emerge in the character of Horace Grey, father of the autobiographical protagonist of Benjamin's first novel, *Vivian Grey* (1826).

The birth of a daughter, Sarah, on December 29, 1802, loyally named for Isaac's unpleasant mother, changed little in his life. Nor did the birth of Ben two years later—"born in a library," he would say. But a boy required some parental decisions. He would have to go to school when he was old enough, and at six young Ben entered Miss Roper's, "a very high class establishment" in Islington, not far off. When he was nine or ten, Ben was shipped off to a boarding school at Elliott Place, Blackheath, run by a Nonconformist minister, the Rev. John Potticary, where, during prayers, Ben and another Jewish pupil, Moses Saqui, "stood back"—a conspicuous exercise in self-alienation. The two boys also had weekly lessons in Hebrew, on Saturday, when school met only half a day, from a visiting teacher, probably to prepare them for bar mitzvah at thirteen.

Facts about Ben's early schooling are sparse. He confided few reliable recollections in letters, and committed fewer to print except in fictional guise. "I was always a bad learner," he recalled in the person of Contarini Fleming, "and although I loved knowledge from my cradle I liked to acquire it my own way. I think I was born with a detestation of grammars." He sensed "the folly of learning words instead of ideas" and "read every book that I could get hold of." At Potticary's the choices were narrow. Students were "victims of the grammar and the lexicon. . . . Our limited intelligence," he wrote as Contarini, "was confined to the literature of two dead languages, and it was necessary to acquire those languages in order to obtain the knowledge they embalmed." The key word was *embalmed*. "To study man from the past," he added, looking back, "is to suppose that man is ever the same animal, which I do not."

He was apparently good at telling stories and fancied himself as an actor. At least once he took part in a school play, acting Gratiano to Saqui's Shylock. Contarini Fleming, too, is "mad for the playhouse," and having shown, otherwise, "so little relish for what is called amusement," he receives permission from his father to go to performances of plays. "I now had a pursuit, for when I was not a spectator at the theatre, at home I was an actor. I required no audience; I was happier alone."

At school Ben edited what passed for the Academy paper, compiling its contents and selling copies for one-third of a penny (computed from the price of a sheet of gingerbread sold by a visiting hawker on Saturdays), and he subscribed—sharing the penny-per-issue cost with several boys—to *Bell's Weekly Messenger*. But whether it was this school, where he was an outsider, or the next, where he was less so, Ben, like his father before him, hated it. A fictionalized echo resonates in Contarini Fleming's ex-

perience, his irreconcilable names as well as his Italianate appearance contributing to his unhappiness. He did not look back on
his schoolboy days "with fondness," Contarini remembers. He
could not share the sentimental attitudes that turned that difficult time into a "sweet prime, free from anxiety, and fragrant with
innocence. . . . I was a most miserable child; and school I detested
more than ever I abhorred the world in the darkest moments of
my . . . manhood."

While Ben was at Potticary's, Isaac's family was increasing. A
son, Naphtali, had been born in 1807 but did not survive the
year. Raphael was born in 1809 and Jacobus in 1813. Their
names, Naphtali's recognizing Maria D'Israeli's father, suggest a
continuing if not ardent tie with Bevis Marks. In the year of Jacobus's birth, however, when Isaac was selected to be a warden of
the congregation, he rejected the honor, explaining that his
bookworm character ill fitted any kind of external office. According to the *ascamot,* or laws of the synagogue, he was informed,
any congregant who declined offices which rotated among the
membership was subject to a fine of forty pounds. Isaac refused
any assessment and remained at odds with the Bevis Marks authorities.

During the summer of 1816, when Ben was eleven, he became very ill. His D'Israeli grandfather was "in great anxiety for
poor little Ben." "Alarmed" and "afeared" for his grandson, he
wrote to a relative, "God preserve him and grant that he may get
the better and recover!" Ben recovered, but was never a sturdy
child—or adult. If, as seems likely, Disraeli in *Venetia* gave his
Lord Byron figure as a boy the suggestion of his younger self, he
had been "pale and slender, with long curling black hair and large
black eyes, which occasionally, by their transient flashes, agreeably relieved a face . . . somewhat shy and sullen."

In November, "Old Mr. Israel," as he was known to his
neighbors in Stoke Newington, died at eighty-six. The new legacy
left Isaac a wealthy man. A year later the family would move to
a large house in fashionable Bloomsbury Square, a short walk to
Isaac's beloved British Museum. No longer inhibited by what old
Benjamin might do with his will, Isaac—long in arrears anyway
and unobservant even longer—resigned as a member of the syn-

agogue in March 1817,* an action which his widowed mother, who had long rejected Judaism as a misfortune, could not have deplored. (In fact when she died in 1825 she was buried at her request at Willesden Church rather than beside her husband.)

Young Ben was left, as he approached his crucial thirteenth birthday, in religious limbo. The book of Jewish ritual in use in London since 1780 then prescribed, "All *Jewish* Parents are reckoned to be accountable for the Sins of their Sons, till they are thirteen Years old, but no longer; and therefore when Boys arrive to their thirteenth Year, they are for the first Time called up to the Law that is read on the Altar in their Synagogue on the Sabbath-Day, and read a Chapter or more in the Law themselves, . . . entering into Man's State, in Regard of becoming accountable for himself, from that Day."

If Ben returned to Potticary's for the next academic year, his religious tutor would visit again for weekly lessons, in part to prepare Ben for bar mitzvah although his family no longer had a synagogue in which to celebrate the rite. Isaac's literary friend Sharon Turner offered a drastic solution. Fussy and given to homiletics, he was a transplanted Yorkshireman of forty-nine who lived nearby in Red Lion Square and practiced law in chambers in the Temple. One of his clients was John Murray, Isaac's publisher.

A bookworm like Isaac but also a devout Anglican, Turner had taught himself Norse and Icelandic in the British Museum, where he and Isaac often met, and had written a multivolume history of England, beginning with the Romans and continuing into the sixteenth century. Why, he proposed, leave the children in an equivocal position when baptism into the Church of England, however perfunctory, could give them better chances in life, opening doors closed to them by law and by prejudice?

Taking the two younger boys, who were too young to have any objections, with him when Isaac (in Ben's recollection) "half-consented," Turner hurried to St. Andrew's, Holborn, where

---

*Among the fanciful stories about Isaac and Ben is that the event occurred when Ben was nine, and that Isaac had "promptly turned Christian on account of a quarrel about his pew."

on July 11, 1817, Ralph and James, as they became, were baptized by the Rev. William Hart Coleridge, nephew of the poet. The older children remained reluctant. It took until July 31 before Ben accompanied Sharon Turner to St. Andrew's, where the baptismal register listed him as number 633 that year, his abode as King's Road (the D'Israeli family had not yet moved to Bloomsbury Square), and his father's "Quality, Trade or Profession" as "Gentleman." The ceremony was performed by the Rev. John Thimbleby. (Sarah held back until August 28; her parents were never baptized.)

The few drops of holy water would, in time, work their miracles.

III

"ON A SUDDEN I SEEMED ENDOWED
WITH NEW POWERS."

1817–1824

FOR BEN THE NEW TERM AT POTTICARY'S WAS OUT OF THE QUESTION. To leave for the summer as a Jew and return in the autumn as a Christian guaranteed an avalanche of derision. Better that he go to a school where his background, despite his proudly unchanged name, was blurred. Although no religious test was now an obstacle to Oxford or Cambridge, Isaac bypassed the traditional vestibules to "Oxbridge." Ben had been deflected from bar mitzvah to baptismal font and was bookish and precocious, but was he ready for an esteemed Church of England public school—an Eton or a Harrow? That was too much, too soon for the son of Isaac's right hand. Rather, Ben was enrolled at a Unitarian school, Higham Hall.

In December 1817, instead of being escorted to a synagogue reading desk and, before the open scroll of the Torah, being introduced to the congregation as "Benyamin di Yitzhak Israeli," to chant from the Pentateuch, he was attending prayers at the Rev. Mr. Eli Cogan's academy just above Walthamstow. "I never believed in Merrie Xmas," he would later confide, but just after his thirteenth birthday he celebrated his first Christmas.

Isaac knew Dr. Cogan as a frequenter of antiquarian booksellers in London, which—along with his liberal religion—recommended the headmaster as an appropriate mentor for a D'Israeli. His father had, however (Ben recalled in a fragmentary autobiography), first thought of Winchester. While Isaac made the ultimate decisions at the house on Bloomsbury Square, it is possible that the choice of school was at least in part that of the unassertive Maria. Her intervention is suggested in *Vivian Grey*, where Vivian's father "was for Eton but his lady was one of those women whom nothing in the world can persuade that a public school is anything but a place where boys are roasted alive, and so with tears, taunts, and supplications, the point . . . was conceded."

Isaac may have been particularly pleased by Dr. Cogan's boast, in a letter, that he was "almost entirely, and in Greek altogether, self-taught." Still, his curriculum paralleled the greater public schools. "The first class," Ben recalled late in life, "dealt with Aeschylus, Aristophanes, Aristotle, Plato, and the Greek Orators. I could never reach this stage, though I listened to many of the interpretations and expositions of the master with interest and admiration." After tedious construing, Ben once went to Cogan to have Terence explicated, and he "would himself interpret the scene. It was acting—full of humour."

While Ben never reached the first class and "was not eminent even in the second," he was exposed to the Greek and Roman monuments. "In Greek, all Herodotus; much of Thucydides; the greater part of the *Iliad*; something of the *Odyssey*; the *Ajax, Oedipus Rex* and *Antigone* of Sophocles; the *Idylls* . . . ; and Xenophon. . . . In Latin he bathed us in Cicero . . . ; Caesar; much of Livy; something of Tacitus; all Virgil and Horace; some of the best things in Catullus and the elegiac poets; the first book of Lucretius; and all Terence."

A schoolboy notebook confirms his reading. "Virgil—2nd book of the Georgics," he observed, ". . . begins with a splendid invocation to Bacchus; it, however, all vanishes in a sleepy lecture on grafting boughs and lopping trees." He "wonder[ed] extremely why Lucretius is not a greater favorite," and found the editors of his edition of the *Iliad* "equally contemptible. They mistake incapacity for originality, . . . advocating every ridiculous [interpretative] system." At first he preferred "the elegant and musical Orations of Cicero" to the catchwords of Demosthenes, for "though his speeches are replete with Virtue, Patriotism and Courage, history tells me he was a Villain, a Partisan, and a Poltroon." Later, despite Ben's dependence upon a "hateful lexicon," his imagination was "fired" by the "irresistible" eloquence of Demosthenes: "I must own that Cicero is his inferior."

During Ben's first year in his new school, where he was unsettled and at odds with his environment, his father was busy writing his *History of Men of Genius*, which Murray would publish in 1818. Some of its observations seem not only out of Isaac's own experience, but out of what he saw happening to his son, much more of a potential genius to Isaac than he ever perceived himself to be. "The education of the youth," he observed, "may not be the education of his genius." Ironically, given Isaac's uncharitable disposition toward the faith of his fathers, culminating in the wholesale baptism of his children, one of the heroes of his book was Moses Mendelssohn, the "Jewish Socrates" of eighteenth-century Germany. What he represented for Isaac was in character. Although Mendelssohn did not spurn his Judaism, he did reject an education limited to "the Talmudical dreamers" who were the schooling of his boyhood. He could not exploit "the philosophy of his age" through a "barren idiom" incapable of original speculations and solved his dilemmas through self-education—to Isaac the best pedagogy of all.

"There is no place in the world," Disraeli would claim in *Vivian Grey*, "where greater homage is paid to talent than at an English school." Young Ben's fictional alter ego was talented, although "more deficient than most of his own age in accurate classical attainments, and he found himself, in talents and various acquirements, immeasurably their superior. . . . Vivian Grey's English verses and Vivian Grey's English themes were the subject of universal commendation. Some young lads made copies of these productions, to enrich, at the Christmas holidays, their sisters' albums; while . . . fellows who were writing Latin Dissertations and Greek Odes, which might have made the fortune of the

Classical Journal, were looked on by the multitude as . . . great dunderheads."

Ben was also a natural storyteller, and Beatrix Potter recalled decades later being regaled by a Mrs. Gibson, Cogan's then elderly daughter, about how Disraeli "used to keep the boys awake half the night romancing."

The multitude was rather small—fifty or sixty boys from the "middling class" of prosperous businessmen and professionals. The boys at Higham Hall who were permitted the Rev. Cogan's liberal instruction in religion discovered advantages over the others, and suddenly Ben was again among the outsiders. Those who espoused the Church of England had to walk to a distant church on Sunday mornings. The big midday dinner would be underway when they returned, and the Anglicans found the portions picked over. Lacking the religious fervor that made the sacrifice seem worthwhile, Ben suggested that while they were at Higham Hall they become Unitarians.

From Contarini's experience—Disraeli subtitled the novel "a psychological autobiography"—we learn that Ben

> was placed in the heart of a little and busy world. For the first time in my life I was surrounded by struggling and excited beings. Joy, hope, sorrow, ambition, craft, courage, wit, dulness, cowardice, beneficence, awkwardness, grace, avarice, generosity, wealth, poverty, beauty, hideousness, tyranny, suffering, hypocrisy, truth, love, hatred, energy, inertness, they were all there, and all sounded and moved and acted about me. Light laughs and bitter cries and deep imprecations, and the deeds of the friendly, the prodigal, and the tyrant, and the exploits of the brave, the graceful, and the gay, and the flying words of native wit and the pompous sentences of acquired knowledge—how new, how exciting, how wonderful!

The reality was less wonderful. He was taunted about his origins, which his profile and his ebony curls could not conceal. Despite his school dress he was often greeted with cries of "old clo's!" Contarini and Vivian both fight, and thrash, schoolboy bullies, the reason clear between the lines of *Contarini Fleming*, where the protagonist, as is obvious from his name, is of mixed, part-Italian, nationality. "Did I tremble? Did I sink into my innermost self? Did I fly? Never. As I gazed upon them, a new principle rose up in my breast, and I perceived only beings whom I was determined to control. They came up to me with a curious glance of half-suppressed glee, breathless and mocking. They asked me questions of gay nonsense with a serious voice and a solemn look. I answered in their kind. On a sudden I seemed endowed with new powers."

In *Vivian Grey* the opponent "was a burly big-limbed animal," and Vivian "delicate in frame and more youthful," but "his match in spirit, and . . . ten times his match in [boxing] science." His adversary is floored, but the master arrives to stop the fight and close off any response from Vivian with "I understand that you always have an answer ready. I do not quote Scripture lightly, . . . but 'Take heed that you offend not, even with your tongue.' Now, sir, to your room."

In *Contarini Fleming*, "There never was a more unequal match," but the hero, aroused, was like "a demon that had usurped his shape." Contarini flies at the bully "as the hail upon the tall corn. . . . I felt not his best blow, I beat down his fine guard, and I sent him to the ground, stunned and giddy. . . . Again I flew upon him. . . . I believe he was terrified by my frantic air." In "a voice of madness" Contarini cries for the bully to "come on," and when he could no longer rise, "I placed my knee upon his chest. . . . 'Apologise,' I exclaimed; 'apologise.'

" 'Never,' he replied.

"Some advanced to interfere. 'Off,' I shouted; 'Off, off.' I seized the fallen chief, rushed through the gate, and dragged him like Achilles through the mead. At the bottom there was a dunghill."

Resentment made Disraeli a fighter, but won few friends at school. From his earliest years, his novels suggest, he was attracted to older women, upon whom he had boyhood crushes. At Higham Hall, they also suggest, he had a typical public school infatuation for a "shy, timid" schoolmate, fictionalized as "Musaeus" in *Contarini Fleming:* "It seemed to me that I never beheld so lovely and so pensive a countenance. . . . Oh! days of rare and pure felicity, when Musaeus and myself with our arms around each other's neck wandered together amid the meads and shady woods that formed our limits! I lavished upon him all the fanciful love that I had long stored up; and the mighty passions that lay yet dormant in my obscure soul now first began to stir."

When they part for the holidays, the separation seems almost an "execution," but in the new term the returning object of desire seems a bore. A new goal has altered priorities—"ambition, which now each day became more quickening." Higham Hall no longer seemed relevant to Disraeli's restless adolescence. He has Contarini run away from his school. And in the summer of 1820 Disraeli at fifteen returned to Bloomsbury Square determined to stay. The authorities were in rare agreement with their charge, writing to Isaac D'Israeli that Ben appeared to be "of foreign and seditious mind, incapable of acquiring the spirit of the school."

Always untraditional, Isaac may have felt that Ben's best strategy lay in reading literature and philosophy in the well-stocked D'Israeli library and eventually in family connections— reading law while apprenticed to a Basevi.* But until his sixteenth birthday he was too young for a solicitor's office. To begin to "know everything," Ben began with his father's books. The scene is colorfully fictionalized in *Vivian Grey* where, "the system of private education having so decidedly failed," the hero begins an indisciplined program of reading at home. "Nothing could be a greater failure than the first weeks of his 'course of study.' He was perpetually violating the sanctity of the drawing-room . . . and outraging the propriety of morning visitors by bursting into his mother's boudoir† with lexicons and slippers."

---

*Isaac had written to solicitor William Tooke (a founder of the University of London) on February 25, 1819, introducing "my nephew Mr. N. Basevi, who was called to the Bar recently—and has now settled himself in Lincoln's Inn. . . . As I believe there are opportunities, in the pressure of business, which are favourable to try young practitioners, I consider it as a duty incumbent on us all, to obtrude the name of a young friend on these occasions."
†*Boudoir* was used in the sense of a small elegantly furnished room in which a lady received her intimate friends.

His father set some rules, and one can hear Isaac in Horace Grey: "This will never do; you must adopt some system for your studies, and some locality for your reading. Have a room to your-self; set apart certain hours in the day for your books, and allow no consideration on earth to influence you to violate their sacred-ness; and above all, my dear boy, keep your papers in order. I find a dissertation on 'The Commerce of Carthage' stuck in my large paper copy of 'Dibdin's Decameron,' and an 'Essay on the Meta-physics of Music' (pray, my dear fellow, beware of magazine scrib-bling) cracking the back of Montfaucon's 'Monarchie.'"

The boy "apologised, promised, protested, and finally sat down 'TO READ.' He had laid the foundations of accurate clas-sical knowledge . . . and twelve hours a day and self-banishment from society overcame, in twelve months, the ill effects of his im-perfect education." When his attempt at self-study seemed too limited, "he flew to his father, and confessed . . . that his favourites were not all-sufficient."

While Ben began with the idea that the external world had to be spurned if he were to make any headway in his father's vast library, the world came knocking anyway. His parents had many friends, and Isaac enjoyed the company of his literary cronies, who in turn were fond of Maria's cooking. Isaac's publisher, the second John Murray, was a frequent visitor. His father, who had died in 1793, had been the publisher of *Curiosities of Literature*. The younger Murray had moved the business from Fleet Street to Albemarle Street, off Piccadilly, founded the Tory-leaning *Quar-terly Review*, and published, among others, Ben's hero, Lord Byron, whose *Childe Harold* (1817) had seized young men's imag-inations. And Byron, who admired "Israeli's" work, was now, as a self-exile, doubly to be honored from afar at Bloomsbury Square.

Since a seat for Ben at the D'Israeli dinner table when liter-ary guests were present could have been an occasion for a bright boy full of himself to make a fool of himself, Isaac apparently set some rules for that, too, remembered in Contarini Fleming's ad-vice from his father:

"Do not talk too much at present; do not *try* to talk. But whenever you speak, speak with self-possession.

Speak in a subdued tone, and always looks at the person whom you are addressing. Before one can engage in general conversation with any effect, there is a certain acquaintance with trifling but amusing subjects which must first be attained. You will soon pick up sufficient [background] by listening and observing. Never argue. . . . If a person differ from you, bow and turn the conversation. . . . Talk to women, talk to women as much as you can. This is the best school. This is the way to gain fluency, because you need not care what they say, and had better not be sensible. They, too, will rally you on many points, and as they are women you will not be offended. Nothing is of so much importance and of so much use to a young man entering life as to be well criticised by women."

Despite a satirical edge in the instructions, the counsel is very likely well-meant, and Ben was an apt pupil, even accompanying his father to dinners at such homes as Murray's. Impressed, across the table, by Ben's astuteness on theatrical matters, Murray offered the young man—only fifteen—a consulting assignment. William Charles Macready, a brilliant young tragedian who at twenty-one was already a rival to Edmund Kean, was going to play the title role in Charles Edward Walker's *Wallace* at Covent Garden. Murray had been offered publication rights. Would Ben read the manuscript and suggest a course of action?

Ben did. "I ran my eye over 3 acts of Wallace," he reported confidently, "and as far as I can form an opinion I could not conceive these acts to be as effective on the stage as you seemed to expect," and he went on to assess the drama's defects. His letter concluded with a double-edged pun, as the issue of the play had come up at a dinner at which another guest had been an Italian Egyptologist large in girth, Giovanni Battista Belzoni, "I hope you got your dinner in comfort when you got rid of me and that gentle Pyramid."

As Ben predicted, the play was not a success. Forearmed, Murray passed on the rights, and *Wallace* was published by actor and editor William Oxberry.

Isaac D'Israeli, 1834. *From a drawing by S. P. Denning*

At one gathering at Murray's, Isaac and Ben (now nearly eighteen) were joined by poet Tom Moore and Murray's business associates Walter Hamilton and Stuart Newton. "Moore very entertaining," Ben noted in a diary scrap, appreciative of Moore's way with a pun. The poet had just returned across the Channel from a long residence abroad, and Isaac had observed over Murray's characteristic English wine, which Moore had, at least diplomatically, praised as excellent, "You'll miss the French wines."

"Yes, the return to port is awful."

He'd get used to the English liquid, Isaac predicted, but Moore saw difficulties.

"French wines spoil one for a while. The transition is too sudden from the wines of France to the port of Dover."

Moore had visited Lord Byron, and talk shifted to Murray's star poet. Was he "much altered?" Isaac asked.

"Yes, his face has swelled out and he is getting fat; his hair is gray and his countenance has lost that 'spiritual expression.' His teeth are getting bad."

They talked of a dentist in England that Byron hoped to consult if he returned, and Ben observed that the man had died, ensuring that Byron "certainly won't come."

Moore noted that Byron's manner of dress had become "very extraordinary," which Isaac took to mean slovenly.

"Oh, no! No! He's very dandified, and yet not an English dandy. When I saw him he was dressed in a curious foreign cap, a frogged great coat, and had a gold chain round his neck and pushed into his waistcoat. I asked him if he wore a glass and [he] took it out, when I found fixed to it a set of trinkets. He also had another gold chain tight round his neck, something like a collar."

Byron, Moore added, was talking of buying land and living in South America, and when he told their mutual friend Scrope Davies about it, and that Byron was growing fat, Davies said, "Then he'll never come to England."

They talked of other writers, Moore noting that Samuel Rogers, a brilliant conversationalist yet a mediocre poet, would be "matchless" if he could write as well as he spoke, "but his faculties desert him as soon as he touches a pen."

Isaac agreed that "many men of talent have been so circumstanced," and Moore recalled a friend who had confessed, "It seems that directly I take a [quill] pen into my hand it remembers and acknowledges its allegiance to its mother goose."

They moved to Thomas De Quincey and his striking *Confessions of an English Opium Eater,* which Isaac called "an extraordinary piece of writing."

"I thought it an ambitious style," said Moore, "and full of bad taste."

"You should allow for the opium," said Isaac. "You know it is a genuine work."

Moore was surprised. He had assumed that it was fiction.

Ben scribbled it all down as quickly as he could, to capture the style of each of the speakers while keeping his recorded input to a modest minimum. Later he would exploit some of it in his own fiction, putting the exchange about Byron into book IV of *Vivian Grey*, and giving his dialogue by such means an authenticity that belied his years. Few fathers would have taken teenage sons to gentlemen's dinners, and few such sons would have been accepted as near equals. Yet Ben's future, as far as his father was concerned, lay outside literature. Once sixteen, Ben was to read law and to become somebody. But from papers left at Hughenden it is clear that Isaac's love of books was too profound for there to have been any real pressure on Ben.

Mr. Grey's advice to Vivian suggests what was going on at Bloomsbury Square. He should not "consider himself a peculiar boy"—a young genius. "Take the advice of one who had committed as many—aye, more—follies than yourself. Try to ascertain what may be the chief objects of your existence in this world. I want you to take no theological dogmas for granted, nor to satisfy your doubts by ceasing to think; but whether we are in this world in a state of probation for another, or at death we cease altogether, human feelings tell me that we have some duties to perform to our fellow-creatures, to our friends, and to ourselves."

A different fictional father—Contarini Fleming's—suggests that his son might find it interesting "to turn over Voltaire" (Isaac's favorite author). "I drew out *Zadig*. Never shall I forget the effect this work produced on me. What I had long been seeking offered itself. This strange mixture of brilliant fantasy and poignant truth, this unrivalled blending of ideal creation and worldly wisdom, it all seemed to speak to my two natures. . . . I delivered myself up to the full abandonment of its wild and brilliant grace. I devoured them all, volume after volume."

Not the Voltairean that his father was, Ben was already finding a middle path toward a Tory scepticism. Traditions meant nothing to Isaac, but their values were already apparent to his teenage son. On reading Voltaire's critique of the *Oedipus* of Sophocles he characterized it in his notebook as "a furious denunciation against Oracles and Superstition, brazen pipes and flagitious priests." And he reflected, foreshadowing his later self,

"This is a speech worthy of a French *Illumin*; but in the heroic age [of Greece] *Philosophers* did not exist, and the good men were contented to obey and consult those institutions which from their youth upward they were taught to respect and reverence."

The notebook diaries record Ben's guided self-education. Greek grammar was "miserable work indeed." *Mitford's History of Greece* was "wretched, scarcely English, a striking contrast to the cadenced periods of the Decline and Fall." Written across an end paper of the *Historical Almanac* for 1821 is an ambitious quotation from Petrarch, whom he was obviously reading: "I desire to be known to posterity; if I cannot succeed, may I be known to my own age, or at least to my friends."

Six weeks short of seventeen, on November 10, 1821, Ben was articled to the law firm of Messrs. Swain, Stevens, Maples, Pearce and Hunt of 6 Frederick's Place, Old Jewry, just below the venerable Guildhall. The indenture was signed by William Stevens, one of the partners, Isaac D'Israeli, and Ben, and is the last known occasion when he used the apostrophe in his name. The opportunity for Ben to learn the Law in one of the leading firms in London cost Isaac four hundred guineas.* Informally, the investment had another aspect not put into writing. Maples had a daughter, "by no means," Ben recalled, "without charm, either personally or intellectually." But he was gauche and inexperienced, and his visits to the Maples household, with Ben dressed in his finest black velvet suit, from Byronic ruffles to black silk stockings decorated by red clocks, came to nothing. Eventually the young lady would tell Ben, "You have too much genius for Frederick's Place; it will never do."

Bored, Ben remained a solicitor's clerk in title, but, he claimed many years later, more useful to Maples and to himself

---

*Gentlemen computed in guineas, tradesmen in pounds. As a guinea represented twenty-one shillings rather than the pound's plebeian twenty, it cost the equivalent of £420 to permit Ben to apprentice at Swain, Stevens, where he received no salary. At the time, a London family with several servants could have lived comfortably on £150 a year; servants' wages ranged from £10 a year (a head butler) to £1 (a scullery maid). A case of a dozen bottles of excellent sherry or port cost about £2; one could dine well at a tavern, including beer, for a shilling (now a five pence coin).

than that. "My business was to be private secretary of the busiest partner. . . . He dictated to me every day his correspondence which was as extensive as a Minister's, and when the clients arrived I did not leave the room but remained not only to learn my business but to become acquainted with my future clients." The assumption was that he would remain, and move up, at Frederick's Place, but "the rest of my life was not in harmony with this practice and business. . . . I became pensive and restless." Still, the years from seventeen to nearly twenty were not mere imprisonment in a stultifying solicitor's chambers. The apprenticeship, he thought decades later, "gave me great facility with my pen and no inconsiderable knowledge of human nature."

Some of his work, the extant evidence confirms, was not in stuffy chambers. At least once he was sent to Eton, where but for his peculiar circumstances, he might have been wandering about in scholar's garb. For a law case, Thomas Frederick Maples needed to know the exact historic name of the school. From nearby Windsor, making the day's last post, Ben wrote that both the Provost of the college and his clerk were out, but from a lease on record the school's ancient name seemed to be "the Coll. Royal of the Blessed Mary of Eton near unto Windsor in the Co. of Bucks."

When Ben parted from the firm a year later, Isaac tried to interest him in Oxford, to which he might have gone had he followed the Eton path. Oxford had a religious test on matriculation, but that was no longer a problem. Cambridge barred non-Anglicans through compulsory church attendance, but again that hardly mattered. But Ben was already dreaming of a career combining literature and politics. John Murray had given him ideas about writing, and he thought of trying his hand at both political journalism and political satire. Not sufficiently well connected, he guessed, to make a political career on his own— besides, he was still perceived as a Jew—he might be the power propelling someone else's. The law office experience suggested to Disraeli—although he had now dropped the un-English apostrophe he had clung to the un-English name—that he might manipulate men.

His first surviving literary effort showed little promise that he was making a prudent career choice. With his friend, and Sarah's future suitor, William Meredith (twenty-one to Disraeli's nineteen) he put together a verse play, *Rumpel Stiltskin*, in two hand-produced copies, with illustrations apparently by Sarah. A political parable purportedly written in 1596, it was mediocre in the extreme. Dated from Oxford, as Meredith was still a student at Brasenose, it was very likely written in London, where the Meredith family—with a country seat in Worcestershire—had a house at Nottingham Place, to the northeast of Bloomsbury. The families were close—one of Meredith's two sisters, Georgiana, was even thought of as a future wife for Ben.

More ambitiously, Ben had written a political satire, "The Adventures of a certain Mr Aylmer Papillon in a terra incognita." On May 24, 1824, he sent what he claimed was all but two chapters of it to John Murray, confessing that he had mislaid the rest—hardly a communication of enthusiasm in the production. The novel was, he explained, about "the present fashion of getting on in the world," about which Ben, in May 1824, at nineteen, knew little. Its organization can be guessed at from Ben's explanation that the missing chapters—the second and the last—"have no particular connection with the story."

He was still at Frederick's Place a month later, when he assumed that Murray's reluctance to comment upon the "indiscretion" was implicit rejection. Since the "crude production" was "certainly too late for this season, and . . . obsolete in the next," Disraeli suggested that, as Murray had "some small experience in burning MSS, you will be perhaps so kind as to consign it to the flames." Seemingly a reckless remark, putting "Aylmer Papillon"—as he instructed—"behind the fire" may indicate how comfortable Disraeli felt with the publisher. It was John Murray who, in May, had burned Byron's manuscript memoirs rather than risk their incendiary publication.

The two lost chapters survived by having been mislaid. They later turned up among Disraeli's papers, and foreshadow his 1828 political satire *The Voyage of Captain Popanilla*, which also borrows from Swift and Voltaire and the once popular literature of imaginary voyages.

By July, Disraeli and Meredith, who had just come down from Brasenose, were taken on a shortened version of a grand tour by Isaac. An excursion of the sort was expected after completion of a university degree, but Ben took his tour without the preliminary benefit of Oxbridge. His "pensive and restless" state at Swain, Stevens, Maples, Pearce and Hunt appears to be code for the beginnings of depression, and Isaac was applying the cure of a change of scenery. As they left, it was with the declared intention of Ben's returning to Frederick's Place after the holiday restored his health, but when they embarked on the Channel crossing from Dover to Ostend, Ben did not tell his father that Swain, Stevens had seen the last of their clerk.

IV

"BITTERER ... THAN ALL, IS WAKING FROM
OUR FIRST DELUSION! FOR THEN
WE FEEL THE NOTHINGNESS OF SELF,
THAT HELL OF SANGUINE SPIRITS."

1824–1826

FLANDERS IN 1824 WAS STILL PART OF THE KINGDOM OF THE NETHER-
lands, under the sway of a disliked Dutch king. Little of that rest-
lessness among the Belgians, who in 1830 would invite the future
Queen Victoria's uncle, Leopold, to become their first sovereign,
was apparent to Isaac and Benjamin D'Israeli as they toured with
William Meredith through Ostend, Ghent, Antwerp, Brussels,
and Spa, and on into the Rhineland. Ben's seven journal-like letters to Sarah, and a fragmentary diary from late July into the last
days of August, stored up impressions that he reused in a dozen
years of fiction writing. He reveled in the paintings of Rubens,
Rembrandt, and Van Dyck; in church and public and "grand mai-
son" architecture; in food and wine and the ambience of inns and
conveyances; in aristocrats, literati, and serving maids; in trying
out his awkward French and his halting German. "Meredith and
myself," he wrote to Sarah, "talk French with a mixture of sublimity and sangfroid perfectly inimitable."

To rein in his young men, Isaac—"the Governor" to William

and Ben—was at his most hortatory, prompting a letter to Sarah from Brussels, "The sermones gubernatoriae are [by] this time rather diminished." In nearly every sizeable city they visited the opera houses, experiencing among other productions Cherubini's *Medea* and Mozart's *Magic Flute*. With Isaac leading the way, stout black stock in hand, they explored the inevitable bookshops, Ben finding the Flemish proprietors, eager to promote their wares, "horrid Dons." They sampled the famed waters of Spa—"a kind of Champaigne au naturel"—and in Heidelberg they went to a casino (akin to a London "club" where for the price of coffee one could read the local newspapers) and "billiardized" as well as caught up on *The Times* and *Galignani's Messenger*, the continental English-language paper for many decades.

Ben saved his negative impressions for his journal, which kept some of his stronger wit from Sarah. Approaching Cologne, he wondered whether German beggars would be even more of a burden than Belgian ones, "but the traveller is well trained in Flanders for even the very Nursery of Mendicity. Your carriage never leaves an inn yard without a crowd of supplicating attendants and three old women, a dozen young ones, half a dozen men, and all the children of the village attend[ing] you on your whole journey. The old women seem to have the best breath." The road from Spa into Germany via "mean" Aix (now Aachen) was "actually studded with crucifixes" and populated with more beggars "than [in] Callot's [etchings]. If you stop at an inn, one side the lame, on the other the blind—a swarm of alert naked children surround your carriage."

Benjamin confronted a world utterly unlike England, yet little more than a night's sailing away. On the road to Aix he noted a man "standing with his right arm extended like an eastern faquir . . . the palm of his right hand . . . conveniently bent for the reception of *Groschen*." Even the system of conveying passengers was different, the budding proponent of marketplace competition observing that accommodations were "wretched because the posting [of passengers] in Germany was a state monopoly." However "squalid" the villages were, each had churches adorned with paintings by Renaissance masters, and many had ancient town halls at least partially still Roman.

Sublimity of another sort magnetized Ben. His conversion left him with no theology yet with an increased susceptibility to ritual. He would be drawn often to the rites of Roman Catholicism, which on political grounds he had to reject, because of its aesthetic appeal and its roots in his own ancestry. At Ghent on August 6 he left the "nasal" singing at St. Michael's (which had been recommended to him for its music) for the Cathedral of St. Nicholas, arriving in time for high mass. "A dozen priests in splendid unity, clouds of incense, and Mozart's sublimest masses by an orchestra before which San Carlo might grow pale," he noted in his journal, knowing the orchestra of the San Carlo Opera only by reputation. "The effect inconceivably grand. The host raised, and I flung myself on the ground."

His letters to Sarah were more conventional travelogues, with praise of the scenery, the food, the company. But nowhere did he record his later claim, "I determined when descending these magical waters [of the Rhine] that I would not be a lawyer." In *Vivian Grey* he rejected the profession with, "Pooh! law and bad jokes till we are forty; and then with the most brilliant success the prospect of gout and a coronet." Yet, while he spurned any return to Frederick's Place, he mollified his father by consenting to read for the bar. Admitted as a student at Lincoln's Inn on November 18, 1824, Benjamin failed to take his status seriously from the first day. A fever of financial speculation was on one of its irregular cycles through the City, and Ben had, by then, already succumbed.

Impatient to be someone in the world, yet certain that birth had closed politics to him, he fixed upon wealth as strategy, and with little money but what he could borrow had joined Thomas Mullett Evans, a solicitor's clerk he knew from Frederick's Place, in buying mining stock on credit. Since Ben was not even twenty, a minor ineligible to secure a lawful loan, he (and Evans) used Robert Messer, son of a stockbroker, to acquire stock for them in companies doing business in Latin America. Mexico and the other former Spanish colonies to its south were gradually gaining their independence, and the mineral wealth that had tempted Cortés and Pizarro still beckoned to the investor who bet upon the soundness and stability of the new republics.

Even the cautious John Murray was drawn in by the young Disraeli, who was still reading manuscripts for him, and Ben now proposed not only to have Murray publish—on a commission basis—a pamphlet Ben would write to lure the moneyed and counteract prophecies of ruin, but to purchase some of the stock himself. By late December (Ben had returned from the Continent in September) he and two partners owed £400, but a paper profit was still predicted, and he was being encouraged by a promoter of mining shares, John Diston Powles, the backer of the pamphlets, whom Ben had known as a client at Swain, Stevens.

The Anglo-Mexican Mining Association's shares, £33 on December 10, rose to £158 by January 11; the Colombian Mining Association, its shares at £19, bulged to £82. Quick wealth seemed certain. Powles urged Ben and his friends to buy more shares, and as prices began to decline, Ben, high and dry on the margin, rushed into print his first publication under John Murray's masthead: nearly a hundred pages of shameless propaganda equating mining stock purchases with inevitable prosperity. *An Enquiry into the Plans, Progress and Policy of the American Mining Companies,* published anonymously in March 1825 and Disraeli's first "book," took a high-minded tone but was meant to reverse looming financial embarrassments. Within a month he rushed out another publication, *Lawyers and Legislators: or Notes on the American Mining Companies,* a polemic against further government restrictions upon "the laws regulating the investment of capital." Because he had gambled on slim margins yet wanted to keep his father from embarrassment, Ben, it appears from a desperate letter to Robert Messer, had gone for assistance to his uncle, the elder George Basevi. Temporarily bailed out, Ben based his confidence about repayment upon a rise in stock prices, which, he confessed to Messer, had fallen to their lowest point to date. Ben's enormous paper worth of £6,000 was mostly irretrievable debt.

Lawyers and Legislators suggested that of the two ways in which South American mining shares were viewed—as "a desirable investment" or as "rash and ruinous" speculation—history had shown that when the countries were free of "wars and revolution," the mines were productive. He vowed no repetition of the "South Sea Bubble" disaster, the speculative mania of 1721 when the market was manipulated for the unscrupulous profits of a few. The new situation was different, Disraeli explained, and investors needed no special legal protection. "The South Sea scheme was not visionary, for nothing was to be seen. . . . It was not wonderful, therefore, that the loose livers in society [in the reign of George I] did not neglect the opportunity which human folly offered them." The parallel alleged was a "perfect fallacy."

In his first projection—he was still only twenty—of an imperialist vision for England, he suggested that since the nation had "no new resources" in the home islands to develop, "we intend the whole world [as] the theatre of our action," as otherwise the wealth of Englishmen sat useless. "A rich nation that keeps its capital to itself is like a magnifico in solitude." That would not have been the way of "the Merchant Adventurers of England . . . whose enterprise was the foundation of our present glory." Although Powles had pressed Disraeli to write the two pamphlets— and there would be yet another—the service to Powles as well as to himself did little to restore confidence in what the Duke of Wellington dismissed as "bubble securities." As they slipped further, Disraeli rushed out *The Present State of Mexico*, largely a translation of a report to the Mexican Congress by Minister for Home and Foreign Affairs Don Lucas Alamán. Disraeli's introduction described him as a "perfect and practical patriot" although he was being paid by external mining interests to protect their investments.

While the three pamphlets promoted shares the unsoundness of which the young author could not have hidden from himself, he had been apprenticed to the Law, in which one made the best case possible for one's client. His training at Swain, Maples and his literary education under Isaac had both been effective enough that, at the least, his *Lawyers and Legislators* pamphlet was a readable and persuasive brief with the flair of a real writer and with touches of invention that foreshadowed the future novelist.

In a draft of a letter to Robert Messer which he thought better of and did not send, sometime in the summer of 1825, Ben exuded a spurious air of confidence about his mining shares, estimating them "at the lowest price they have yet sunk" as worth

£6,000. He predicted that they would double in value by the end of 1825, bringing him an income more than adequate to repay his debts. He talked vaguely of other investments, including a new newspaper, and of seven months "of unwearied exertion" and "harrowing care" that were producing results "which when I contemplate [them] I feel actually dizzy." He considered his fortune "as made," or at the least he wanted to convey that impression. Yet the key phrase was his dizziness with contemplation of the hazards of new fortune. He hoped soon, he planned to tell Messer, to be "upon a rock," but he was on a roller coaster, and the dizziness was real.

As Ben hinted in the unsent letter to Messer, he was dreaming of alternative avenues to success if the shares gamble failed. Isaac had his dreams, too, of becoming, where his father had failed, a country squire, and living out his declining years in the soft hills of suburban London—close enough to run in to see a publisher, explore a bookshop, check out a literary anecdote in his beloved British Museum. Experimenting, he rented a house for the season through the good offices of a lawyer friend, Benjamin Austen, whose energetic wife, Sara, had assisted the owner in getting his first book published. Hyde Heath House, near Amersham, just to the northeast of High Wycombe, belonged to Robert Plumer Ward, who had just achieved popular success with an anonymously released society novel. *Tremaine* was a satire in the "silver fork" school in which the aristocratic characters might be identified with real-life figures by using one of a variety of "keys" supplied by eager journalists. Ward, a client of Austen's, was a sixty-year-old retired civil servant whose sudden literary notoriety had sent him scurrying into retreat from London.

In the venue in which *Tremaine* was written, Benjamin began his own equivalent.* Although his experience of fashionable

---

*A curious link between Ward and Disraeli beyond "Tremaine's" (Ben's word for him) support for *Vivian Grey* and the D'Israeli family's rental of Ward's house in the country was that Ward was half Jewish. His father, John Ward, had married Rebecca Raphael of Gibraltar, daughter of a merchant from Genoa. Ben would praise Ward's second novel, *De Vere*, fulsomely and even dedicate his *Popanilla* to one of the more unlikely of Sephardim.

"Author of Vivian Grey." *Pen-and-ink sketch of Disraeli by Daniel Maclise*, Fraser's Magazine, May 1833.

life was almost nonexistent, he opened with what he knew. Vivian Grey, his hero—and Ben's own age—is a young man brought up by a retiring, bookish father and educated in his father's vast library after he leaves a school much like Dr. Cogan's. Having used up his little experience but for the law office and the Rhineland holiday, Benjamin might have turned in those unprofitable directions if another opportunity to link his fortunes to Murray's had not arisen. While the novel brightly evoked Ben's background, raised several notches socially, it had nowhere to go; but Murray was beginning to talk in circles to which Ben had access about the possibilities of a London daily of Tory persuasion that might rival *The Times*. Since 1818 Murray had been toying with the idea of a newspaper; in 1820 he became a partner of John Wilson Croker with the *Guardian*, published from Windsor and quickly a failure. Flush with profits from his other publishing ventures, he was eager to try again, this time with a morning paper printed in London.

With his infectious gift for persuasion, Ben put the novel aside and linked himself to the venture, offering his energy and his freedom to be Murray's legs while the publisher managed his other enterprises. Rather than merely watch the mining shares in which they both had interests slowly implode—yet hoping all the while that they would make a comeback as business revived in the autumn—Ben proposed himself as the go-between among all the professionals necessary to launch and run a newspaper. Murray's *Quarterly Review* had long been a successful mix of political and cultural points of view. He had dreamed of a widely circulated organ of opinion that would bear the imprint of Canningite politics.

A bold and popular Tory liberal,* Sir George Canning was even admired by Byron, who wrote that he was "bred a statesman" but "born a wit." Disraeli's very model of a future prime minister, Canning had responded to the charge that he was a political adventurer by contending that he found public confidence more important than aristocratic lineage or rigid politics, and "if that be to be an adventurer, I plead guilty." He would not exchange that situation, he declared, "for all the advantages which might be derived from an ancestry of a hundred generations."

Disraeli would eulogize him later as "someone never to be mentioned . . . in the House of Commons without emotion . . . and we all sympathize with him in his fierce struggle with supreme prejudice and sublime mediocrity." Foreign Minister in 1825, he had been quick to recognize the independence from Spain of the breakaway republics of South America, and he fought to end slavery and the slave trade. To bring into being a new morning newspaper in the Canning interest, one that sup-

*Liberal then suggested an opponent of absolutism, from the Spanish *liberales*, opponents of the despotic Ferdinand VII.

ported new nations whose mines Disraeli's threatened shares sought to exploit, and besides, to be part of the power structure, was to realize grand dreams. "I may obtain not only considerable profit," he predicted to Robert Messer, to whom he owed money, "but [it] will materially assist me in gaining the object of my highest ambition. The daily journal must if properly managed soon become the leading newspaper, and I shall possess a considerable share of it."

At twenty young Disraeli saw himself as a power broker, and one can read Isaac's cautionary words in Mr. Grey's admonition, "Vivian, beware of endeavouring to become a great man in a hurry. One such attempt in ten thousand may succeed: these are fearful odds. Admirer as you are of Lord Bacon, you may perhaps remember a certain parable of his, called 'Memnon, or a youth too forward.' I hope you are not going to be one of those sons of Aurora 'who, puffed up with the glittering show of vanity and ostentation, attempt actions above their strength. . . .' Is neglecting to mature your mind, my boy, exactly the way to win the races?"

Later, a sadder and wiser Murray blamed Disraeli's "unrelenting excitement and importunity" for the venture, but a canny and businesslike Scot of forty-six would not have fallen for a youth's enthusiasm as easily as Murray went into the exploration of the possibilities; and Disraeli was abetted by a sophisticated speculator, John Diston Powles. Yet Murray demonstrated his confidence in Disraeli further by giving him an assignment to edit and slightly rewrite a life of the Scottish-born American sailor adventurer, John Paul Jones, whose daredevil exploits had an ironic symmetry to Ben's visionary exploits on dry land. Murray's edition, which would emerge before the year was out, never identified the American author, Theophilus Smart, and was neither improved by Disraeli's intervention nor by his listless and uninformative preface. Ben was too busy with his own adventures.

Late in September, when Murray acquainted his friend Isaac with the book, D'Israeli responded, "Had the editor of 'Paul Jones' consulted me a little, I could probably have furnished him with an account of the miserable end of his hero; and I am astonished it is not found, as you tell me, in your American biography." John Paul Jones, bored with inaction in the new nation, had joined the Russian navy as a rear admiral, became disappointed with his situation and moved, embittered and in poor health, to Paris in 1790. Dying there in 1792, at forty-five, he had been buried in an unmarked grave. Yet Isaac's rueful point was not the book's failure to exploit the drama of its subject's life, but Ben's failure to consult his father about his earliest publication projects.

Although Murray wanted to rush his newspaper out on November 1, it was only on August 3 that he signed an agreement with his two partners to underwrite it. Murray was to put up half the funds needed, Powles and Disraeli a quarter each. In May, Ben had written to the uneasy Murray, "Be easy about your mines." After prophesying a doubling of the faltering stock's value by December, he was proposing his nearly worthless mining shares, only fractionally his in any case, as his start-up portion. Each party, the agreement specified, would be responsible for the expenses and risk in proportion to their contributions, while Murray would be the manager of the enterprise. Since Disraeli was the least occupied of the triumvirate, he was assigned the task of negotiating with the proposed editor, John Gibson Lockhart, the ambitious thirty-year-old son-in-law of Sir Walter Scott, and later his biographer. A literary journalist with ties to *Blackwood's Magazine*, Lockhart had, in Murray's eyes, the virtues of being a gentleman and a Scot, ties to the best-selling author of the day, and increasing visibility in print. That he was too young and inexperienced, and innocent of London, could not have registered upon a flourishing publisher, heady with money, who used a twenty-year-old school dropout as executive assistant, financial adviser, and partner.

At Murray's expense, Disraeli began the long journey to Edinburgh overland by post chaise on September 12, stopping evenings to sleep at Stamford, York, and Newcastle, and arriving, finally, at eleven on the 16th in the Scottish capital, where—being as far north as Halsingborg in Sweden—the sky still showed some remnants of summer twilight. For Murray's emissary, who knew nothing of England above the Home Counties, the journey was a revelation of the great expanse of Britain in the last prerailway days. York seemed especially splendid, with its cathedral soaring above any Ben had seen in Belgium, Holland, and

Germany, and a music festival in progress that made it seem, he wrote to Murray, "a perfect Carnival." Since the establishment of the new paper was still being kept in confidence in London, Benjamin proposed to Murray "some cloak" for the great personages he expected to see, in case the mails were tampered with, but the codes were largely a game for a young man negotiating business that was over his head. Lockhart was "Melrose," and Scott was "the Chevalier." Canning was "X." Disraeli—"the political Puck" as he described himself—was "O." Spacious, stately, uncrowded Edinburgh left him in raptures, and a Scottish breakfast of cold grouse and marmalade seemed the perfect beginning for the business day.

Business began badly when Lockhart affected to be surprised that his visitor was not the famous writer Isaac D'Israeli, but only his callow son. Murray had written that he was sending "Mr. B. D'Israeli, son of my oldest friend," yet Lockhart, in Benjamin's report, showed "an evident disappointment at seeing me. Everything looked as black as possible." The reception seems a calculated ploy to put the young man in as weak a negotiating position as possible. Lockhart did not want to drudge at a chancy newspaper; nor did his father-in-law, who doted on his daughter Sophia and frail young grandson John Hugh, want Lockhart to leave Scotland. But Scott sought whatever he could extract from Murray for his son-in-law if nothing onerous were involved. Despite the vast commercial success of the *Waverley* novels, Scott was worried about his investments in the ambitious publishing ventures of James Ballantyne, and Ballantyne's bankruptcy early the next year would plunge Scott himself into debt. It was better that Lockhart seize the opportunity for his own independence.

A lawyer friend in London, William Wright, who was close to Murray, had prepared Scott and Lockhart by reporting that Benjamin was a "sensible clever young fellow; his judgment however wants sobering down; he has never had to struggle . . . in difficult situations. At present his chief exertions as to matters of decision have been with regard to the selection of his food . . . and his clothing and, though he is honest and, I take it, wiser than his father, he is inexperienced and untried in this world." But Scott and his son-in-law listened courteously, as Wright also reported what young Disraeli did not know—that Murray was willing to oust the editor he had chosen for his *Quarterly Review* the year before, John Taylor Coleridge, a nephew of the poet, to get Lockhart, who had been an aspirant for the position, for the newspaper. Like Lockhart a barrister, Coleridge was becoming too busy in his practice to indulge his hobby further, however remunerative. (In time he would become an eminent judge.)

After seeing young Disraeli, Lockhart wrote to Murray that he was not a candidate. Murray could take that as the hesitancy of negotiation. Benjamin remained enthusiastic, urging Murray to use his connections to secure a parliamentary seat for Lockhart, to increase his clout as editor. And after a fortnight as Lockhart's guest at Chiefswood, and a long audience with Sir Walter at Abbotsford, Disraeli and Lockhart set out together on an exploratory journey to London. For Ben it was a dream about power and influence in the middle of which he had awakened and found it real.

To his friend William Stewart Rose, Scott sneered about the young man he had treated with warmly false friendliness, "Here has been a visitor of Lockhart's, a sprig of the rod of Aaron, young D'Israeli. In point of talents he reminded us of his father." Benjamin was, he added, a young coxcomb, and indeed he had come calling in velvet and ruffles, an aspiring dandy. It was not Sir Walter's style. The Rebecca of his *Ivanhoe* had been a fantasy Jewess; Disraeli validated all of Scott's negative stereotypes.

Pleased with Ben's progress in Scotland, Murray shared his letters from his emissary with Isaac, still ensconced at Amersham, who wrote back with both pride and concern on September 29, "How deeply I feel obliged and gratified by your confidential communication! I read repeatedly the third letter of our young plenipotentiary. I know nothing against him but his youth—a fault which a few seasons of experience will infallibly correct." Isaac thought that the experience of the law office "would greatly serve [Ben] in matters of business. His views are vast, but they are based on good sense, and his is most determinedly serious when he sets to work." On October 9, following further shared news from Scotland "about him on whom we now both alike rest our hopes and our confidence," Isaac added with fatherly pride, "The more I think of this whole affair, from its obscure beginnings, the more I am quite overcome by what he has already achieved." But Murray, he concluded diplomatically, deserved much of the credit for "the grand view you take of this new intellectual steam engine."

By now it was clear to Murray that to secure Lockhart for the newspaper in some capacity he had to offer him the *Quarterly*. On arrival in London, Lockhart found a letter proposing that for £1,000 a year, plus additional sums for articles, he become the editor. Also, for some affiliation with the newspaper for an experimental three years, including articles for it, Lockhart could double his income. It was a handsome proposal, kept at first from Disraeli. Lockhart accepted and went back to Scotland to prepare his family to relocate in a climate more propitious for John Hugh. Disraeli worked through October and November to lease a large house in Great George Street, employed his cousin George Basevi as architect to redesign the interior, and contracted with correspondents in Britain and abroad to be the paper's representatives. "The most celebrated men in Europe," he boasted to an uncelebrated German he was engaging as contributor. Murray, he promised, would make their paper "the focus of the information of the whole world." Murray himself wrote to prospective correspondents at Hamburg, Maastricht, Genoa, Trieste, and Gibraltar in much the same vein, adopting the phrase "the focus of the information of the whole world."

One writer signed by Disraeli to the pleasure of both Lockhart and Murray was William Maginn, a witty Irishman who would be sent to Paris for the paper, then returned to write humorous material in London. Although Maginn assured Disraeli (so he told Lockhart) "that as to the success of the paper doubt could not exist," it took two months to sign him, and afterward he drank more at the paper's expense than he wrote.

Disraeli's lengthy and detailed correspondence with Lockhart over the launching of the newspaper, soon postponed to January 1826, suggests a greater managerial role for Lockhart than evidenced from his gentlemanly protestations of September. Lockhart even received a list of correspondents arranged for as far off as Smyrna, Constantinople, and the Levant, and (on November 23, 1825) confidential reports on the "official scamps" who were trying to undermine his relationship with Murray. Associated with the *Quarterly Review* were a group of Londoners in influential positions, chief among them John Wilson Croker at the Admiralty. All were unhappy that Murray—in their correspondence to Lockhart, "the Emperor"—had failed to consult them about the arrangements, which meant dumping their man as *Quarterly* editor. "Trash," Disraeli wrote, ". . . has too long been bandied about, as to your character."

Urging Lockhart to lose no time in returning to London, Disraeli added, "It is *absolutely necessary*, that you and I should have a conversation before you see Murray." Benjamin was eager to be the "very attached friend" in reporting the conspiracies afoot, to keep lines open to someone who might help him realize his ambitions. Included in his letter on the 28th—Ben had just returned on the 21st from a second, hurried, trip to Scotland which hardly suggested a small role for Lockhart—was a copy of the scurrilous weekly *The Age*, which had a reference to Lockhart's famous father-in-law.

Lockhart was still in Scotland in the last days of November when word leaked out about the new venture, and Disraeli reported gleefully to him on December 1 that London papers were suddenly concerned about losing their best professionals to a well-financed new Tory rival. But Murray's distractions in the waning months of 1825 were too great to be able to manage a sound launching. The market in South American mining shares was slumping badly, and all three investors in the paper had counted on a rise in the shares and quick profits from them to finance the paper. With other publishing ventures to run, Murray had no manager or editor overseeing the new paper, although far too many prying advisers. Still, he boasted to the absent Lockhart that *The Times* had offended so many supporters that there was also talk elsewhere of "setting up a paper." Even the Rothschilds were allegedly interested.

Expected then to begin publication in December, the paper had neither printing presses nor a management, and until Benjamin came up with a title for Murray—*The Representative*, Lockhart noted with satisfaction on December 21—it had no name. But four days earlier (and unmentioned by Lockhart) the expected crash had come. Bankruptcies and abruptly closed banks paralyzed financial London. Even the Bank of England was threatened. Powles and Disraeli had nothing but unpayable debts, and in the panic Powles reneged even on the printing bills for the pamphlets Disraeli had arranged for him with Murray. *The Representative* would fill the paper's masthead, Lockhart had affirmed, "if Mr. Powles does not produce some thundering objection." Powles, however, had already disappeared ahead of the bills, in debt for over £120,000. Disraeli, too, was no more heard from in the gloomy new offices of the paper, and *Vivian Grey* suggests one last unhappy meeting, in which the Marquess (an equivalent here for Murray) "raved! he stamped! he blasphemed! but the whole of his abuse was leveled against his former 'monstrous clever' young friend, of whose character he had so often boasted that his own was the prototype, but who was now an adventurer—a swindler—a scoundrel—a liar—a base, deluding, flattering, fawning villain."

When *The Representative* emerged on January 26, 1826, Disraeli was represented on it only by the writers he had hired, most of them less than useless without an aggressive managing editor. Only one reference to him survives from the faltering early days of the paper, a letter from Lockhart to Murray suggesting that Ben wanted to apply to J. W. Croker, Secretary to the Admiralty, for some unknown reason, perhaps prospective employment. "I think Mr B. Disraeli," Lockhart wrote coldly, "ought to tell you what it is that he wishes to say to Mr Croker on a business *of yours* ere he asks of you a letter to the Secretary. If there really be something worth saying, I certainly know nobody that would say it better, but I confess I think, all things considered, you have no need of anybody to come between you and Mr Croker. What can it be?" There would be no letter of introduction, and Ben disappeared from the history of *The Representative*. Murray took to his bed and, to his wife's distress, to his whisky bottle, and rumors of both enlivened London gossip.

When the paper ceased publication six months later, unread and unlamented (except by Disraeli), Murray was out £26,000 in addition to his mining shares losses. He had to give up his ostentatious house in Whitehall Place and his summer villa at Wimbledon and move the family back above his offices in Albemarle Street. It would take Ben thirty years, and some luck, to pay his debts. He had no experience from which anyone should have entrusted him, barely now twenty-one, to run a London newspaper, but as he boasted through Contarini Fleming, "If a person have imagination, experience seems to me of little use."

Ben did not go into hiding to lick his wounds; he had nowhere to go but home. Vivian Grey, facing the collapse of his own hopes, "wept as men can but once weep in this world. . . . All his boasted philosophy vanished; his artificial feelings fled him. Insulted nature reasserted her long spurned authority." And the "once proud" Vivian "felt too humble even to curse himself."

Ben brooded over the twin calamities, but not for long, although the agony would surface in at least two early novels, emerging after *Vivian Grey* in *The Young Duke* (1831), where his private tears were "blood." In "the desolation of the beautiful ruin," he assessed, if we accept the musings of his second novel, the bitterness of recognizing self-deception:

> Bitter are hope deferred, and self-reproach, and power unrecognised. Bitter is poverty; bitterer still is debt. It is bitter to be neglected; it is more bitter to be misunderstood. . . . Bitter are a broken friendship and a dying love. Bitter a woman scorned, a man betrayed! Bitter is the secret woe which none can share. . . . Bitter are old age without respect, manhood without wealth, youth without fame. . . .
>
> But bitterer far than this, than these, than all, is waking from our first delusion! For then we first feel the nothingness of self; that hell of sanguine spirits. All is dreary, blank, and cold. The sun of hope sets without a ray, and the dim night of dark despair shadows only phantoms. The spirits that guard round us in our pride have gone. Fancy, weeping, flies. Imagination droops her glittering pinions and sinks into the earth. Courage has no heart, and love seems a traitor.

In a letter of May 21, 1826, he tried to explain his side of the matter to Anne Murray, the publisher's wife, as the affair had shattered relations between their families. Murray had "over-stepped the bounds" in calumniating him, he wrote; at the same time, without his knowledge, Maria D'Israeli followed her son's plea with a very different kind of letter to John Murray. No one would accept stories that the paper was ruined "through the mis-management and bad conduct of my Son," she told him force-fully. ". . . It would not be believed that the experienced publisher of Albemarle Street could be deceived by the plans of a boy of twenty whom you had known from his cradle and whose resources you must have as well known as his Father and had you conde-scended to consult that Father the folly might not have been committed."

"From his cradle" had been no mere metaphor. On Decem-ber 22, 1804, the day after Ben's birth, Isaac had written on be-half of Maria and himself to thank Murray for "the interesting note you have sent us on the birth of our boy." Murray had not yet married, nor had a son—the third John Murray—himself.

The failure of *The Representative*, Maria charged, lay with the proprietor rather than with her son, and his allegations were only "hurting the character and future prospects of a young Man to whose Father you subscribe yourself his faithful friend." And she would no longer hold her tongue among their mutual acquain-tances if it meant keeping Ben "under an odium which can be explained away by the truth being told." It was only in Murray's "versatile imagination" that Ben had been a "prodigy" and a "perfect being" rather than "*a mere mortal* and a very young man."

In old age, Disraeli denied in a letter to an inquirer that the breach* between his father and Murray had anything to do with the demise of the paper, but he knew otherwise. When Horace Grey berates his son, "Vivian, you are a juggler," the voice of the injured Isaac D'Israeli can be heard. The son's eagerness for in-stant success had destroyed the most intimate and productive friendship in his father's life.

---

*The relationship would resume, but on nothing like its former terms.

V

"I WAS DEVOURED BY AMBITION I DID NOT SEE ANY MEANS OF GRATIFYING."

1826–1830

"I ALWAYS DISCOUNTENANCE READING *VIVIAN GREY*," DISRAELI TOLD Lady Bradford in 1874. "I have no opinion of books written by boys." It would be easy to look at *Vivian Grey* as a young writer's revenge upon John Murray, but the newspaper imbroglio was only an episode, disguised, and the novel had been begun months earlier and put aside. In old age he allegedly told a friend, when asked what passion gave the most lasting pleasure, "Revenge. A man will enjoy that when even Avarice has ceased to please." If he abandoned avarice in the wake of catastrophe, he needed both money and occupation; and Murray's accusations, which his wife Sophia blamed on his taking to his bottle at night as *The Representative* rolled up new debts daily, made Benjamin unemployable.

His barely begun novel seemed the only route back. Given his tarnished name, what better way to place *Vivian Grey* before the public than the method used by Ward in *Tremaine* and with such continuing success by the author of *Waverley*? Scott had first appeared as novelist promoted as "The Great Unknown." Ben had visited him twice at Abbotsford and understood that the open secret of Scott's anonymity had enhanced his baronial lifestyle by selling more of his books. With the impudence of ambition he began with a title-page epigraph lifted from *The Merry Wives of Windsor:* "Why then the world's mine oyster / Which with my sword I'll open." Writing with fresh enthusiasm and the material of new experience, Ben completed the ten chapters of the first book and was well into the second when he thought of Sara Austen. After her success with *Tremaine*, she might well be his literary adviser too, and she was close at hand. The Austens, friends of his parents, lived at 33 Guildford Street, off Russell Square. He could not go to Murray with his book, yet Mrs. Austen had placed *Tremaine* with an enterprising publisher of fiction, Henry Colburn. Ben sent Mrs. Austen a letter and the first book of *Vivian Grey*, about a clever young man insinuating himself into Society.

Eight years older than Ben, but in sophistication much older than that, Sara Austen was attractive, well-to-do, and well connected. Childless, and with a dull lawyer husband, she was eager to occupy herself with something that promised to be as thrilling as *Tremaine*—even more so, as Ward's daughters had rewritten his manuscript to efface his hand, and she might do the same for young Ben. On February 26 she responded. "I am *quite delighted* with it, & *enter into the spirit of* the book entirely." She offered herself as "an Ally upon trust," and sought permission to write, without betraying his secret, to Colburn. Then she added, with a certainty that Benjamin would comprehend the indiscretion, "I am in a state of complete excitation on the subject—Remember that you have the entrée whenever you like to come—at all hours—In the morn[ing] I am generally alone."

To deflect suspicion, she intended to be seen in public with him only when Sarah D'Israeli could accompany them, and her letter was sent with a servant as if from her husband—"I trust this very *unladylike* paper will veil my correspondence." And while she insisted that "*ceremony* must be completely banished on this subject," between the lines it was clear that she had in mind an intrigue with a clever and good-looking young man she had seen socially only a few times. That it was an impulsive new design is manifest from her not even recalling his name: "I forget M[r.] DI's Christ[ian] Initial, so must direct Jun[ior]."

Beautiful and bored, Sara Austen conducted her flirtation using the safest of all stratagems—the full knowledge of her husband and of the D'Israeli family. It may be that the entrance in the seventeenth chapter of a pretty woman of thirty with a bent for intrigue, Mrs. Felix Lorraine,* marks the place in the manuscript where Mrs. Austen entered Ben's life. How much extracurricular intrigue ripened cannot be known. Although Sara's later letters suggest an emotional code, she apparently destroyed Ben's letters of the *Vivian Grey* period.

From the first fresh page of the novel he had every intention of extracting from the experience of *The Representative* what he needed to give it satirical bite. To that he added all the little he and Sara Austen knew of high society. Even Ben's journey to Scotland to enlist Lockhart is appropriated for the plot, relocated to Wales. Murray is inflated into a Marquess, and a drunken one at that. Vivian is the dandified, impudent young rascal of an intermediary who persuades the Marquess of Carabas and others into forming a new political party which, racked by internal dissension, eventually fails. With it go the ambitions of Vivian Grey, whose brash maxim had been: "A smile for a friend, and a sneer for the world, is the way to govern mankind."

Relying on his own experience, Benjamin intended to create for his young Englishman a sentimental education into manhood—as Goethe had done in *Wilhelm Meister*. He also confided later to his diary, "In *Vivian Grey* I have portrayed my active and real ambition." As Vivian admits, "I am no cold-blooded philosopher that would despise that for which . . . men, real men, should alone exist. Power! Oh! what sleepless nights, what days of hot anxiety! what exertions of mind and body! what travail! what hatred! what fierce encounters! what dangers of all possible kinds, would I not endure with a joyous spirit to gain it!" As he described the experience in *Contarini Fleming*, "My thoughts, my

*"Keys" to the novel identified her with Lady Caroline Lamb, estranged wife of the future Viscount Melbourne. Her affair with Lord Byron had been one of the notorious scandals of the previous decade.

passion, the rush of my invention, were too quick for my pen. Page followed page; as a sheet was finished I threw it on the floor; I was amazed at the rapid and prolific production, yet I could not stop to wonder." Neither could Mrs. Austen as she recopied Ben's manuscript, making only a few suggestions to excise what contemporaries might have called "puppyness" (a youthful innocence of his milieu). Through Contarini in 1832 Disraeli confessed, "In depicting the scenes of society in which my hero was forced to move, I suddenly dashed, not only into the most slashing satire, but even into malignant personality. All the bitterness of my heart, occasioned by my wretched existence among their false circles, found its full vent. Never was anything so imprudent. Everybody figured, and all parties and opinions alike suffered."

Toward the end of March the two volumes of *Vivian Grey*, in Sara Austen's hand, were with Colburn's typesetters, and Ben had £200 for the copyright—all he would see from its sales. Purchasing the copyright in lieu of royalties was then a traditional way of doing business in commercial publishing, and Colburn, who had paid Ward £500, was taking no chances with what appeared to him to be a risky and often absurd work. But Ben and Sara were exhilarated, although aware that once they had seen the proofs through the press there would be no further excuse for their conspiratorial mornings together in Guildford Street.

Adept at puffing a book, Colburn published two literary journals in which he could slyly refer to the imminent release of a bold new novel by "a talented young man of high life." Alluding to Byron's rakish narrative in verse, he called *Vivian Grey* "a sort of *Don Juan* in prose." Taking the hints, *John Bull* on April 17 declared, "This individual, whose adventures among the great are now in the press, we hear will be found to be anything but *insipid*. He is reported to be truly '*an original*': insidious, daring, decisive." Books went from manuscript to the printed page, and from thence to the shops, quickly in the pre-electronic age, and on April 22, barely a month after the last pages were delivered to Colburn by Sara Austen, readers were buying the book. Journals attributed authorship to a dozen men of note, Colburn doing his best to mislead—and to sell more books.

Vivian Grey's raciness appealed to book buyers, and only

Robert Plumer Ward got close at first to its secret, suggesting teasingly to Sara Austen that she had very likely written it herself. Then William Jerdan in the *Literary Gazette* (which Colburn owned jointly with William Longman) shrewdly guessed that the anonymous author knew too little about society to have come from its ranks, yet too much about literary matters, about which "the mere man of fashion knows nothing and cares less." Meanwhile "keys" to the identity of the characters were published, including one on May 24 in *The Star Chamber*, a minor periodical issued by friends of Disraeli's, which seemed intended to put readers off the scent. Possibly, as self-protection, the author himself was doing the misleading. "Everybody," he wrote later in *Contarini Fleming*, "took a delight in detecting the originals of my portraits. Various keys were handed about, all different, and not content with recognizing the very few sketches from life there really were, and which were sufficiently obvious and not very malignant, they mischievously insisted, that not a human shadow glided over my pages which might not be traced to its substance."

Most of the caricatures of real people were too remote to be recognizable by an ordinary reader—Carabas as Murray, or other grotesques. A few minor characters were almost without disguise. Comic playwright and practical joker Theodore Hook, notorious for his "Berners Street Hoax" of 1809—where people ranging from the Duke of Gloucester and the Lord Mayor to firemen and chimney sweeps were summoned to the house of an outraged Mrs. Tottenham, to whom he had conceived a dislike—was obviously "Stanislaus Hoax." And the ostentatious socialite "Mrs. Million" needed no key to be recognized as the imperious Harriot Mellon, a stage comedienne who had married one of the richest men in England, the banker Thomas Coutts, when he was eighty, becoming his millionairess widow in 1822 when he died at eighty-seven.

By early summer a reversal was in progress. Critics did not want to be caught as fools. *Vivian Grey*, *Blackwood's* decided, had been written by an outsider—by "an obscure person for whom nobody cares a straw." Sara Austen, who had been copying out the reviews and commentaries, became more and more concerned, writing to Ben (as "My d[ear] Sir") of "the astounding intelligence of y[ou]r *name* being confidently mentioned"—a report she traced through Ward to Jerdan. "Don't be *nervous* ab[out] V.G.—We'll blind them yet—I have never committed you *by even a look*—it's only a guess which may be averted."

Rather than own up to a popular success, Disraeli worried that exposure might lead Colburn's commercial enemies to settle old scores at the novelist's expense. Also, people of note identified in the keys might feel aggrieved, further blocking the author's ambitions and possibly frustrating his chances of further publication. *John Bull* cut off all avenues of retreat in reporting on June 15, punning in the process on how the author pronounced his name, that when old Samuel Rogers had guessed that the author was D'Israeli, his friend exclaimed in disbelief, "Indeed! Are you sure?"

" 'Tis *really*," came the answer—but *John Bull* observed, it was the son rather than the father.

Only the youth of twenty would have written so impudently. It was not only that the novel flippantly ridiculed real people; much of it was hastily and badly written, exposing Ben's social and political naiveté. The more second thoughts that critics who had been taken in earlier allowed themselves, the more they fastened upon how little the author really knew of manners and fashions. Disraeli soon protested that the affectations of Vivian Grey were meant to expose his shallow character to ridicule, yet that remained no defense for his own solecisms, and it would not be until 1853 that the author, still ashamed of what he had perpetrated, permitted a new edition, which he heavily cut and patched. Contarini Fleming, his own first book battered by critics, suffers a "sickness of heart. . . . I was ridiculous. It was time to die." Held up to "public scorn" for his "mingled pretension and weakness," he could not defend what his publisher had touted as a major satire except by deploring it as a youthful indiscretion.

Thwarted, Disraeli drifted into depression. Blaming his condition on "overtaxing his brain," family doctors recommended confinement in a darkened room, rest, and change. In his sequel to *Vivian Grey*, the despondent Vivian, when he "remembered his existence . . . found himself in bed. The curtains of his couch were closed; but as he stared around him . . . a face that recalled everything . . . gazed upon him with a look of affectionate anxiety." It was his father, looking in, then quietly drawing the curtains.

Vivian is semiconscious for six weeks, after which the past seemed "like a hot and feverish dream. Here he was once more in his own quiet room, watched over by his beloved parents," and he wonders if there had "ever existed such beings as the Marquess, and Mrs Lorraine . . . or were they only the actors in a vision?"

After another relapse, from which he rallies, Vivian tells his father gloomily, "I fear that I shall live!"

"Hope, rather, my beloved," says Horace Grey. ". . . At your age, life cannot be the lost game you think it. . . . I shall yet see my boy the honour to society which he deserves to be."

"Alas! my father," Vivian explains, "you know not what I feel. The springiness of my brain is gone."

An undated note from Sara Austen invited Ben to recover under her care, "to lie on the sofa & eat boiled lamb & be quiet as you please," a suggestion that seems to combine flirtation and concern. Another, more anxious, begins with safe commonplaces, then turns into a passionate code which the pair must have shared on earlier occasions. "I cannot continue my note thus coldly," she added. "My shaking hand will tell you that I am nervous with the shock of your illness. *What is the matter?* For God's sake take care of yourself. I dare not say for my sake do so. . . . So indeed I must pray. Do everything that you are desired. If without risk you can come out tomorrow, let me see you at twelve or any hour which will suit you better. I shall not leave the house till I have seen you. I shall be miserably anxious till I do . . . ; my spirits are gone till you bring a renewal of them."

Although Mrs. Austen realized that abetting Ben had created the conditions for his collapse, her appeal raised other emotions to the surface. Whatever the extent of her devotion, and however circumspectly it would be played out thereafter, there was nothing of the maternal in it.

To assist in Ben's recovery, and also because Mrs. D'Israeli, in appropriate nineteenth-century fashion, was often vaguely unwell, Isaac made plans to summer quietly in the sea air at Dover. Sara Austen had other ideas as far as Ben was concerned. He needed the distractions of the Continent, and she needed him. To make both discreetly possible, she prevailed upon her husband to take her on a holiday to Switzerland and to have young Ben accompany them to recuperate. It would all be very proper. Ben had no funds, but Austen would lend whatever was necessary and keep a careful accounting for later repayment. At Sara's dictation, he was to write the letter inviting Ben. Austen would do almost anything for his lovely, imperious wife, apparently including shamming a degree of myopia.

Ben was instructed to "peruse the note with attention, and consider the offer with care"—almost certainly Sara's hint to read between the lines of the message. His response was affectedly gay, pointing out that he would be a "sober and honest" companion, "except when I am entrusted the key to the wine cellar, when I must candidly confess I have an ugly habit of stealing the Claret, getting drunk, and kissing the maids." The entire letter, manic, perhaps, to Austen, might have been decrypted by Sara as elaborately flirtatious. And so Ralph, "Jem," Sarah, and the elder D'Israelis summered in somnolent, proper Dover without Ben, who embarked in early August with the Austens on a steam packet to Boulogne.

How much of a *ménage à trois* the holidayers were can only be guessed at. To Isaac, Ben wrote from Paris that he was in the best health he had experienced in three years. Austen spent the first days of travel being ill. Sara Austen wrote to Sarah D'Israeli that her brother "seems to enjoy everything, *pour ou contre,* and has just said high mass for a third bottle of burgundy." Traveling south from Paris to Lyons, they stopped at Moulins, Henry Layard, then a boy and later to play an important role in Disraeli's life, remembered. "My uncle and aunt . . . were accompanied by Benjamin Disraeli. . . . I still retain a vivid recollection of his appearance, his black curly hair, his affected manner, and his somewhat fantastic dress."

At Geneva, Ben reported to Isaac, he would "take a row on the lake every night with Maurice, Lord Byron's celebrated boatman." Byron had been dead for two years, his fame burgeoning posthumously, and the "handsome and very vain" boatman regaled Ben with stories of his employer, including the dramatic storm described in the third canto of *Childe Harold*. Whether either or both Austens were also aboard was usually left unsaid, although once Ben reported being out on the lake until dawn, with Austen, after too much wine at dinner, asleep on Ben's cloak while lightning flashed across the water. Disraeli was re-enacting Byron's myth.

After Geneva their stagecoach crossed to the Italian lakes through the Simplon Pass, paused at Lago Maggiore, then continued southward into Lombardy. From Milan they posted across the waist of Italy to Venice, encountering Cento, the town from which the first Benjamin D'Israeli had emigrated to England; but the younger Benjamin's notes offer no indication that he knew of his family's origins there. "I have not had a moment[']s illness," he assured Isaac, adding, "My fellow travellers are very kind and very accommodating." Yet the few references to "Austen" are seldom paralleled by allusions to Sara, who was writing, meanwhile, in affectedly maternal fashion, about her charge that "your Brother" ("Mr. Ben" to them as they traveled) was in "perfect health" and was enjoying exotic Italian cuisine that *"half killed"* her husband. "He feels, & really is, better than he has been since his *very young days."*

At Venice, where the D'Israelis had relatives, Ben made no attempt to locate them, absorbing his history through art and architecture and vistas of the Lago de Guarda. Returning through Bologna, Florence, Spezia, Genoa, and Turin, the pilgrims took in more scenery and more ruins, Ben storing up memories for as yet unthought-of books. Turning toward home, he summed up for his father the experience of "Five capitals and twelve great cities, innumerable remains of antiquity and the choicest specimens of modern art have told me what man has done and is doing. I feel now that it is not prejudice, when I declare that England with all her imperfections is worth all the world together, and I hope it is not misanthropy when I feel that I love lakes and mountains better than courts and cities, and trees better than men."

Ben was on his way over the Appenines from Genoa to Turin on October 6 when Sharon Turner wrote to Isaac to dissuade him from publishing anything angry about Murray and *The Rep-*

resentative. Ben was still being blamed for the debacle, and Isaac was seething about it. Why make yourself notorious, Turner asked, and become "the football of all the dinner-tables, tea-tables, and gossiping . . . ? Therefore, as I have said to Murray, I say to you: Let Oblivion absorb the whole question as soon as possible." Murray replied to Turner unpersuasively that Isaac was "totally wrong in supposing that my indignation against his son arises in the smallest degree from the sum I have lost by yielding to that son's unrelenting excitement and importunity. . . . From me his son had received nothing but the most unbounded confi-

Sara Austen (1828). *Pencil sketches by Daniel Maclise.*

dence and parental attachment; my fault was in having loved, not wisely, but too well."

Almost certainly the letter, stubbornly placing the blame for the fiasco upon a youth hardly twenty when it happened, was meant for Isaac's eyes. Relations between D'Israeli and Murray would resume on a chilly and formal basis only as they needed each other.

That Sara was often at least over Ben's shoulder is apparent from his laconic reference from Lyons to "all my papers." He had not only kept a journal but begun a continuation of *Vivian Grey*,

Benjamin Austen (1828).

for which Mrs. Austen played her established role of adviser, inspirer, and copyist. The sequel was occupational therapy, and with
Austen busily computing Ben's share of the travel expenses
daily—the eventual total would be £151—Ben needed Colburn's
money. Writing (October 13, 1826) to his sister, Ben could hardly
elaborate upon all of Mrs. Austen's possible services to him, but
one wonders about such lines as "Nothing can have been more
prosperous than our whole journey. Not a single contretemp and
my compagnons de voyage uniformly agreeable. Everything that I
wished has been realized, and more than I wished granted." Perhaps having hinted at too much, Ben turned quickly to a travelogue, then noted that the letter "completes my travels." He and
the Austens would now cross the Channel no later than his
letter.

In London, Henry Colburn pressed Disraeli to assist a journalist, William Jerdan, to compile a key to the characters in *Vivian Grey* as publicity for the new novel, a continuation of Vivian's
adventures, for which Mrs. Austen arranged payment (for the
copyright) of £500. While confessing that incidents and people
were "founded" on experience, Disraeli begged off linking people
with characters. The novel was not "a gallery of portraits" but,
rather, "a faithful picture of human nature in general." (Perhaps
to deflect any linkage to Sara Austen, he turned "Mrs. Lorraine"
in the continuation into a scheming monster.) And he pressed on
to finish the sequel, exploiting his Rhineland journey of two years
earlier. This time, to appease further the moralistic readers of the
earlier novel, the hero's ambitions are thwarted, and he is even
given, at the close, a tongue-lashing by his father. "Vivian," Horace Grey declares, "you are a juggler," and he decries "the deception of your sleight of hand tricks. . . ." Vivian would be doomed,
Mr. Grey warns, to "self-contempt. . . . Let me warn you not to
fall into the usual error of youth in fancying that the circle you
move in is precisely the world itself. Do not imagine that there
are not other beings . . . governed by finer sympathies, by more
generous passions."

Little in the continuation of *Vivian Grey* resembled the real
world. Vivian's adventures among Englishmen are undramatic although they include a fatal duel. His involvement in the petty

politics of minor German principalities fails to amuse. The interest lies in the subtext—an ambitious young Benjamin Disraeli in search of himself. More than a mere amanuensis this time, Sara Austen had offered literary advice, suggesting better management of exits and entrances, and improvements in style. But the heart of her "Dis" was not in the work, which he wrote only to pay his debts, and as he finished the final pages in the last days of 1826, it was largely with disappointment that the notoriety of the earlier portion had not been enough to secure a thousand pounds for the sequel. "He says," Sara wrote to him after seeing Colburn, "Scott had only 300*l* for his first work."

Only Colburn's puffs were enthusiastic when the continuation, in three small volumes, was released on February 23, 1827. A contrite Vivian Grey was less glamorous than a scheming, sardonic one. Possibly at Sara's urging, Robert Plumer Ward wrote warmly to Disraeli on March 10 that the second part was "far, far superior to the first." Ward claimed to be "lost in astonishment, not only at the natural powers, but the *acquisitions* of one so young." In turn Disraeli praised Ward's new novel, *De Vere*, and more significantly for his honor, he wrote to John Murray, enclosing £140 as payment for the mining pamphlets commissioned by the bankrupt Powles. If the amount proved insufficient, he added, aware that Murray was not likely to respond himself, "I will be obliged your clerk instantly informing me of it." But by then, the excitement and the pressure of completing the sequel, and the scorn with which it was greeted, had sunk the author into gloom.

Quick fame and rapid descent into debt had left Ben with a craving for instant resolution of his difficulties. Given his living at the extremes of accomplishment, he could not afford a gradual cultivation of the world's good opinion. His sister would report to him happily, once his next novel was out, that according to visiting Americans, "*The Young Duke* is the text-book of the United States, from which they preach and read, and learn the important requisite manners." One American on the other side of the Atlantic was already beginning to borrow from Disraeli—the very index of literary success, even if not translated into desperately needed pounds and pence. Although Disraeli never learned of it, a prolific and inventive writer for the magazines, Edgar Allan

Poe, would through the 1830s publish stories lifted from *Vivian Grey*, *The Young Duke*, and even the next novel, *Alroy*. In one story, "Loss of Breath," flashing through the mind of the dying hero on the gallows are "falsities in the Pelham novels, beauties in Vivian Grey—more beauties in Vivian Grey—profundity in Vivian Grey—genius in Vivian Grey—everything in Vivian Grey." Another story, "King Pest the First," burlesques Disraeli's novel, while "The Duke de l'Omlette" borrows flippantly from Disraeli's Duke of St. James and his exotic milieu. Other stories would lift Oriental extravagances of setting, complete to particulars, from *Alroy*, and if mimicry by a future American master were implicit praise, Benjamin was being paid the ultimate compliment, but one he would never know. Rather, he remained a failure.

Isaac's response was to cajole Ben back into the law. Since he had already renounced the boredom of a solicitor's occupation with its law-office focus, Isaac suggested that Ben should at least qualify as a barrister, and represent clients before the bar. In April, he was entered on the rolls of Lincoln's Inn, which required some nominal attendance. He ate some dinners and paid his dues but soon was ill and with his family at Fyfield in Oxfordshire, where the D'Israelis were joined by the Austens. Despite their having taken the premises for an extended stay, both families shortly quitted Fyfield and Ben cultivated a new lapse into depression in London.

After a setback, his hero in the sequel to *Vivian Grey* had confessed that the "springiness" of his mind was gone. Such was Disraeli's condition in July 1827 when he wrote to Benjamin Austen, then taking the sea air in Ramsgate: "I continue just 'as ill' as ever. Little else I have to tell you, being in the situation of those youthful jackanapes at school—who write home to their parents every week to tell them that they have nothing to say." It was a clever ploy, suggesting that the schemer of twenty-two was hardly more than a boy, for looking in on him was Sara, having not accompanied Austen to the seaside, while Ben's family was conveniently away visiting friends near Fulmer in Buckinghamshire. "Your good lady, I am aware," he added breezily, "sends you daily bulletins and I am quite sure that nothing certain or contingent in this odd world can possibly escape the comprehensive circuit of her lively pen."

The complaisant Austen may have needed such self-consciously lighthearted reassurance. Sara and Ben were traversing a thin line between a clandestine affair and a quasi-maternal relationship that appeared open and innocent. However far it went—and perhaps it was more anguished than physical—they were playing a dangerous game, and frustration that was not related to his career may have been contributing to Ben's cycles of despondency.

The outside world intruded but little into Ben's often darkened rooms as 1827 slipped into 1828, and he was moved from London to country cottage to London and back once more into country solitude. "Physician followed physician, and surgeon, surgeon, without benefit," he wrote of Contarini Fleming, who was obviously here Ben himself. "They all held different opinions. . . . One told me to be quiet; another, to exert myself: one declared that I must be stimulated; another, that I must be soothed. I was, in turn, to be ever on horseback, and ever on a sofa. I was bled, blistered, boiled, starved, poisoned, electrified, galvanised; and at the end of a year found myself with exactly the same oppression on my brain."

In "moody silence" he read a little, even enjoying the *Memoirs* of Benvenuto Cellini (translated into English in 1822). He tried writing fragments of fiction and a few letters seeking news of the burgeoning interest on his mining shares debts—not a likely means of speeding his recovery—from Thomas Mullet Evans. Isaac referred to Benjamin's wretched state as "a blank in his existence. His complaint is one of those perplexing cases . . . in an ardent and excitable mind." The medical profession labeled it as "chronic inflammation of the brain," which meant only an inability to understand it, and to Sharon Turner from Bloomsbury Square in March 1828 Benjamin described himself as "slowly recovering from one of those tremendous disorganisations which happen to all men at some period of their lives."

Understanding its origins in the frustrations of energy and intellect he added, frankly, "Whether I shall ever do anything which may mark me out from the crowd I know not. I am one of those to whom moderate reputation can give no pleasure, and in all probability, am incapable of achieving a great one." He claimed that he was learning to accept his destiny "with composure," which was less than true although he needed to think it was so. By the end of the year he was indeed getting about more, pressed into activity by Isaac's practice of leasing country places for the summer and autumn, and Ben's own desire to return to active life in London. "He who desires but acts not," William Blake had written in one of his proverbs, "breeds pestilence."

London drew Ben for yet another reason. When Sara Austen was away from the city she would direct letters to Ben to her own Guildford Street address, and he could only collect them on his own. In the interstices of his lassitude, abetted once more by Sara, he had turned his early "Papillon" novella, much of which he had permitted John Murray to burn, into *The Voyage of Captain Popanilla*, a satirical look at Benthamite utilitarianism in the narrative vein of Swift and Voltaire. Again Mrs. Austen was intermediary with Colburn, who published it on June 3, 1828, with a second edition the next year.

Despite the new edition, both printings were small, and the success smaller. It may have been Sara Austen's idea to have the book dedicated to Plumer Ward, who then touted it as in the spirit of Voltaire and Swift, but despite some witty and imaginative pages it would have taken a Nostradamus to see in its attacks on mainstream Toryism a future Conservative leader. Ben's own physicians were another target, as Popanilla is told that he "had overworked his brain; that he must take more exercise; that he must breathe more air; that he must have relaxation; that he must have change of scene."

Change came in the summer of 1829 when Isaac took a long-term lease of Bradenham House in Buckinghamshire, a few miles from High Wycombe. Since the venerable manor house, remodeled in Queen Anne style in the early eighteenth century and set among 1,351 largely wooded acres, was being battled over in Chancery, it could be occupied until the case was settled, and the D'Israelis remained there for nineteen years. Curiously, Isaac as squire of the manor acquired the living at Bradenham Church, just down the slope from the house, which meant that he, a Jew, albeit a nonobservant one, had the right to present candidates as rector.

In a letter to poet and critic Robert Southey, Poet Laureate since 1813 (as Scott wasn't interested), Isaac blamed leaving "London with all its hourly seductions" upon "the precarious health of several members of my family." Only Ben fit that description, and Isaac could have sent Ben off to the country himself had "the salubrity of the soil and air" not been personally appealing. Past sixty now, he was ready to eschew the smoke and fog and filth of London, and he could live among his books in the Chiltern Hills as readily as in Bloomsbury. A Thames coach departing daily from the Green Man in London for High Wycombe would drop off parcels of books or printer's proofs directly at the gates of Bradenham House.

In *Endymion* (1880), Disraeli recalled the setting lovingly:

> . . . an old hall with gable ends and lattice windows, standing in grounds which once were stately, and where there are yet glade-like terraces of yew trees, which give an air of dignity to a neglected scene. In the front of the hall huge gates of iron . . . opened on a village green, round which were clustered the cottages of the parish with only one exception, and that was the vicarage house, a modern building . . . surrounded by a small but brilliant garden. The church was contiguous to the hall, and had been raised by the lord on a portion of his domain. Behind the hall and its enclosure the country was common land but picturesque. It had once been a beech forest, and though the timber had been greatly cleared, the green land was still occasionally dotted, sometimes with groups and sometimes with single trees, while the juniper which here abounded, and rose to a great height, gave a rich wildness to the scene and sustained its forest character.

Like his Popanilla, Disraeli convalesced in a country setting, which for all its salubriousness failed to relieve his despondency. His writing was leading nowhere and his hopes for a political career, dependent upon a parliamentary seat, had no place to go. He was put under further sedation, coming out of it intermittently to transact the faltering business in his life. To Lady Derby, wife of his foreign minister, as they walked near Hughenden half a century later, Disraeli exaggerated, "It was here that I passed my miserable youth."

"Why miserable?" she asked.

"I was," he said, "devoured by ambition I did not see any means of gratifying."

More than ambition had gone awry. Benjamin Austen had been enlisted to search for an affordable country location, presumably at Isaac's expense, for Ben, so that he could establish himself for a run for Parliament. Now Ben wrote that Stockton, a Warwickshire parish southwest of Rugby, was "no go." Isaac had decided that the current state of "agricultural distress" was too great to chance the investment, although, Ben confided, it "would have exactly suited me." Living without illusion—one apprehended the worst of oneself in depression—he had defiantly begun, in the absence of other opportunities, a pilgrimage of the spirit, researching in his father's vast library the history, more myth than fact, of the doomed twelfth-century Jewish hero David Alroy, who rose up with his followers against Islamic oppression. "The fact is," he explained to Austen, "I am

'spell-bound within the clustering Cyclades'

and go I must, tho' I fear I must hack for it." Quoting Byron's *Corsair* about the fabled, but real, islands that bridged Turkey to Greece, he was alluding cryptically to the spell of the East. Even Greece was largely Turkish, only partly freed from Ottoman rule by the uprising to which Byron had given his final months.

Although Ben wanted to capture the feel of the East for his book, Isaac declared that lengthy travel was out of the question for a chronic invalid. His "too indulgent sire," Disraeli explained to Austen, had "at once knocked on the head" such ideas. Unlike the Rhineland therapy, which Isaac had financed, voyaging to the disease-ridden eastern Mediterranean was dangerous. To earn his way, Ben would have to put David Alroy aside for a money-spinner, and for the support of Austen's pocketbook.

Confiding in Austen left the stolid solicitor more puzzled as

he read, for Ben's language, brash as ever, seemed to need de-
crypting, especially as he went on about his writing activities. As
Austen knew, Ben's literary accomplice remained the fond Mrs.
Austen, and Disraeli referred to his writing in terms of seemingly
jocular sexual innuendo which might have pricked a sense of concern even in the phlegmatic and uxorious Austen. Ben seemed to
be alluding to his urgent need to compose a different book, in a
popular vein, to offer to the sleazy salesmanship of Colburn. He
was not, Disraeli assured Sara's husband, "a literary prostitute . . .
tho' I have more than once been subject to temptations which
might have been the *ruination* of a less virtuous woman. My muse
however is still a virgin, but the mystical flower, I fear, must soon
be plucked. Colburn I suppose will be the bawd."

Was he suggesting, and the letter went on in much the same
fashion—women were "delightful creatures, particularly if they
are pretty, which they all are, but then they chatter"—that despite the proximity, and perhaps more, of a particular pretty
woman he had *not* succumbed to that temptation? In the other
direction, Sara wrote to Ben in her own cryptic fashion of an accident with a lighted candle that resulted in "a prettily singed
head," and remembered to add, since Sarah D'Israeli had been ill,
"I *grieve & rejoice* in the same moment—to hear that you have
both been ill, but are better again—that you have been idle, but
are trying to work—I take part so much in all that concerns *you
all* now, that a great deal of my happiness depends upon 'the family.' "

Ben had begun a new novel that would become *The Young
Duke*—"What does Ben know of dukes?" Isaac said—but the
medical treatment of his case, now in the hands of the fashionable George Buckley Bolton of 3 King Street, London, soon relaxed him into a vegetative state. Whenever Ben's despondency
worsened, he was cupped, to remove what was thought to be excessive blood from the brain. Further, he wrote to Austen, he was
"nearly in a *trance* from the digitalis. I sleep literally sixteen out
of the twenty-four hours, and am quite dozy now." Digitalis, a
rather new discovery by the profession although used in English
folk medicine for centuries, was extracted from the dried leaves of
plants in the foxglove family. It slowed the heart muscle. Used to

regulate a rapid heartbeat, digitalis was prescribed by Bolton to prevent Disraeli from becoming excitable. In that respect it was completely effective. But what Bolton had done was to prescribe a depressant for depression.

"With regard to myself, in a word," Ben wrote on March 7, 1830, to "My dear Madame"—an unusually distant description for Sara Austen—"I cannot be worse." He had not seen her, he confided from Bradenham, because London was of all places, in his present condition, "least suited to me." In a letter to Austen a few months earlier he had explained that it might be impossible for him to call upon "Madam[e]" because he was "necessarily betrayed by her, and in consequence 'the heathen rage most furiously.' " It was one of his usual circumlocutions. He could be pounced upon by sheriff's officers, ready with their writs in behalf of his creditors, if he visited Guildford Street, an address he was known to frequent. The allusion to the *Book of Common Prayer* did not identify the heathen, but he could also have meant his own father, who was impatient with Ben's irresponsibility.

He hoped to be "quitting England" soon, in hopes of recovery, Ben added in his March 7 letter to Austen. "When I was in town last," he explained wryly, "I consulted secretly many eminent [medical] men. I received from them no consolation. Without any exception, they approved of Mr Bolton's treatment, tho' they were *not* surprised that it produced no benefit." Vain about his ebony curls, which so well complemented his dandy dress, he had a new concern worse than the grave. "I grieve to say my hair grows badly, and I think more grey, which I can unfeignedly declare—occasions me more anguish than even the prospect of death."

What he failed to tell Sara Austen, who did not realize yet that she was falling out of his life, was that he had taken to dyeing his hair, which would make the contrast between the artificial blackness and his natural pallor startling. He told Sara little now and even avoided her because the most effective ministrations had come from Dr. Bolton's wife Clarissa, who often accompanied him to Bradenham. "Clara" had become devoted to Ben when the couple prolonged their stay to continue his treatment, a "house call" well within Isaac's ability to pay, but with consequences unexpected by the family if not by Bolton, who abetted his wife's amatory hobbies.

Mrs. Bolton's interest in her husband's patient could hardly be concealed in the confines of Bradenham. Isaac had already maintained that a drastic change of scene might be too much for Ben. Could the family dismiss the fashionable Bolton, who seemed to be doing all the proper things, on suspicion that his wife may have been doing some improper ones? Ben was even writing again, often with speed and energy if not with literary genius. In the hours when he was not prostrated by Bolton's digitalis, he was prostituting himself in the penning of a romantic novel to make money, and part of its sunny mood came not from the warm spring of 1830 and the attractions of Buckinghamshire in flower, but from the occasional presence of Clara Bolton, a love interest hardly ascertainable from the demure and chaste heroine of *The Young Duke*.

William Meredith, Sarah D'Israeli's perennial fiancé, was to accompany Ben on his travels. The engagement had dragged on because the uncle whose heir Meredith was had been reluctant to countenance his marriage to a Jewess—baptized or not. The understanding was that if his affection survived the long separation, a wedding could follow. Meredith had some money of his own, but Ben had to sell his new novel in order to supplement his line of travel credit of £500, arranged through Austen with Hanson Brothers, London, and addressed to bankers in Malta, Constantinople, and Smyrna. Although Disraeli had already told Colburn about *The Young Duke* on February 14, announcing that he had written "*a volume and* ½" of a fashionable novel, with "positive Exile, probable Death, and possible Damnation" hanging over him, he needed an assurance of interest in it, even if he could only finish it in time for "next Season." Then hoping to restore his, and his family's, relations with John Murray, he also offered *The Young Duke* to Albemarle Street on the condition that Murray meet with him. "I cannot crudely deliver my MS to anyone," he explained in a letter on May 9, 1830. "I must have the honor of seeing you, or your critic." As substitute he suggested Lockhart, who was, Ben believed, rightly, "influenced by no undue partiality towards me."

Murray replied the next day, declining to meet Ben in person, but assuring him of "the strictest honour and impartiality" if the manuscript were left at his office. Ben refused. He would try the "bawd," Colburn, once more—this time (since he was keeping his distance from Sara Austen) himself. Visiting London in general had become extremely hazardous. Creditors were closing in, one of them, Robert Messer, claiming debts of £1,500 for Ben's share of mining stocks now worthless, yet on which the interest was mounting. To another partner in his failed speculations, Thomas Mullett Evans, Ben wrote, on the same Sunday that he offered Murray his novel, that nothing had gone right. "Life has not afforded me a moment[']s ease; and after having lived in perfect solitude for nearly eighteen months, I am about to be shipped off," he lied, "for the last resource of a warmer climate." He would have to leave without settling his "distracted affairs," which was "bitter." But there were "so many harrowing interests [that] solicit the attention of my weakened mind."

Now he saw his speculative fever of 1825 as the phenomenon of a disordered brain, and apologized to Evans for having "suffered from my madness." Although, Ben closed, he was "only the inmate of an unsocial hotel," he found something within himself "that whispers to me I shall yet weather this fearful storm."

For most patients sunk in depression, even a doleful hope seemed an improvement, yet his manic periods could have been as much Disraelian pose as the swinging pendulum of his emotional cycle. However legitimately ill he remained, he understood the license his perceived condition afforded him. When he had left home in late March to go down to London, he had told Isaac that one of his needs was to be cupped by his physician, which suggested that the malady dragged on. He may very well have needed more the services of the physician's fond wife, and a vignette remains in William Meredith's diary for March 29—Ben was to discuss travel plans to the East with Meredith—of a very different Disraeli than the moody invalid who had left Bradenham:

B.D. to dine with me. He came up Regent Street, when it was crowded, in his blue surtout, a pair of military light blue trousers, black stockings with red stripes, and shoes! "The people," he said, "quite made way for me as I passed. It was like the opening of the Red Sea, which I now perfectly believe from experience. Even well-dressed people stopped to look at me." I should think so! He was in excellent spirits, full of schemes for the projected journey to Stamboul and Jerusalem; full, as usual, also of capital stories, but he could make a story out of nothing.

Pleased with the way *The Young Duke* was going, but under no illusions that he was contributing to literature, Ben boasted to Meredith, "It is a series of scenes, every one of which would make the fortune of a fashionable novel: I am confident of its success, and that it will complete the corruption of public taste."

During that London spring, operating when in London out of the Union Hotel in Cockspur Street, which intersected the Strand at Whitehall, he had also met and made a friend of the well-connected young novelist and aspiring politician who still called himself Lytton Bulwer, and whose *Pelham* had been as much in the silver-fork spirit of *Vivian Grey* as Disraeli's novel was in the vein of Plumer Ward's *Tremaine*. At the novelist's house on Hertford Street, Disraeli had dinner with Bulwer, his brother Henry, and two other ambitious young men, an occasion recalled wittily decades later in the dinner party in *Endymion* (1880) given by Mr. Bertie Tremaine and his brother, Mr. Tremaine Bertie.

Henry Bulwer remembered Disraeli as accoutered in "green velvet trousers, a canary coloured waistcoat, low shoes, silver buckles, lace at his wrists, his hair in ringlets." Disraeli in sober old age denied the green trousers and claimed that he only wore buckles in his shoes at audiences with the Queen. He preferred instead to recall what had become, more than thirty years later, of the five seemingly pleasure-loving young men. "I have been twice the leader of the House of Commons, Edward Bulwer has been Secretary of State, Henry Bulwer is at this moment H. M. Ambassador at Constantinople, Charles Villiers is at this moment a Cabinet Minister, and Alexander Cockburn is Lord Chief Justice of England."

Disraeli was to embark from London, for the first leg of his voyage to the East, on May 29, a Saturday. To bid his family good-bye he returned briefly to Bradenham House, writing from there on May 27 a final appeal to the dour John Murray, offering to make "great sacrifices" to be published someday from Albemarle Street. The next day, from London, he signed a statement to Thomas Jones, a fashionable physician and once a Bloomsbury Square neighbor. Since 1825 and the implosion of the mining shares bubble, Ben had been borrowing from Jones. The document confirmed an indebtedness of £3,000, unpaid interest of £175 more, "and in case the property which I may leave behind me will not meet this engagement, I request my dear father to make good the same." In effect it was his last will and testament, symbolic in every way. He had little in the world but his ambitions and his debts, and both, despite his long bout with giant despair, were rising.

VI

"WHY THEN THE WORLD'S MINE OYSTER."

1830–1831

A VOYAGE TO THE MIDDLE EAST REQUIRED, AS FIRST STAGE, SAILING to Falmouth, the Cornish port near Penzance from which monthly steam packets departed for Malta. Disraeli and Meredith left London early on May 29, on the steamer *Shannon*, Disraeli posting before they embarked a letter to Benjamin Austen—on whose credit he was traveling—extending diplomatic hope that he would meet the Austens in Naples. "Remember me most kindly to my kind friend Madame," he added discreetly. ". . . I can't say much for my confounded head, which has retrograded with the weather, but continued [Mediterranean] heat may yet cure me. . . . I will be sanguine, for if I despair, all is over."

A rough passage against contrary winds brought them to Falmouth hours late, near dawn on June 1. From the Royal Hotel, Ben reported his arrival to Sarah, apologizing that he had little to write as yet, and since the addressee then paid to receive mail, "I fear you will grumble at postage for such empty letters, but in time you will have fuller ones." But he had met a resident who had nearly every book Isaac had published, and Ben transmitted his acquaintance's admiration. "He literally knows my father's works *by heart*, and thinks our revered sire the greatest man that ever lived. He says that Byron got all his literature from padre, and adduces instances which have even escaped us."

While the packet to Gibraltar and Malta lay by awaiting government dispatches to the two colonies, Disraeli shopped and went sightseeing, drawing on the stay in *Henrietta Temple*. In the novel, Ferdinand Armine, who would also follow his creator to the Mediterranean, waits for the mail to be put aboard, spending leisure hours visiting Pendennis Castle and other sights and, his appetite stimulated, enjoying in the "cheerful hotel the mutton of Dartmoor and the cream of Devon."

Steaming across the usually stormy (Sarah called it "frightful") Bay of Biscay and around the Portuguese coast, the HMS *Messenger* arrived in Gibraltar in mid-June, the travelers missing the drama at home of the dying of the obese and enfeebled old King. Assuming that Ben would have to get his first mail from home at his next port of call, Sarah forwarded to Malta the news about George IV, and about the accession of his unpredictable brother, William IV. "We are most outrageously loyal," she wrote about the new King, the former Duke of Clarence, who was mending fences with the public after George IV's arrogant ways.

That Gibraltar was "agreeable" was a premature assessment which Disraeli quickly upscaled in a letter to his father: "This rock is a wonderful place." The colony was not only picturesque but full of friendly people, from "moors with costume as radiant as a rainbow" and "Jews with gaberdines and scull caps" to Genoese and Spaniards and Highlander garrison troops. In the large Merchants' Library, he reported to his father, "are all your works," and both it and the Garrison Library had copies of "another book s[ai]d to be written by a member of our family, and which is looked upon at Gibraltar as one of the masterpieces of the 19th Cent[ur]y. You may feel their intellectual pulse from this."

The Royal Lieutenant Governor, the courtly General Sir George Don, then seventy-six, had come as second-in-command under the chronically absent Duke of Kent, who died in 1820 when his infant daughter, Princess Victoria, was eight months old. Still the real authority under another absentee, Sir George had been shrugging off retirement for years, and until it came the following April he was a generous host. A wealthy man eager to spend his considerable fortune, he had "ornamented Gibraltar," Ben wrote to Bradenham, "as a lover does his mistress."* Wining and dining Disraeli and Meredith, he also recommended excursions into favorite spots in southern Spain, a beautiful, harsh, and legendary region of highwaymen, smugglers, and dusky senoritas about which Ben knew from the romances of Lesage and Cervantes. The bandits, he was told, "commit no personal violence, but lay you on the ground and clean out your pockets. If you have less than sixteen dollars, they shoot you; that is the tariff." He took care to have "little more," but to his disappointment he was unchallenged. Yet he picked up color for later writings, including a forgettable tragedy, *Count Alarcos*.

In Gibraltar itself, colonial society gave Disraeli opportunities to display his most dandified wardrobe, sometimes even in the mornings, and he tried out the new waistcoat studs given to him by his mother. "I have also," he reported to Isaac on July 1, "the fame of being the first who ever passed the Straits with two canes, a morning and an evening cane. I change my cane as the gun fires, and hope to carry them both on to Cairo. It is wonderful the effect these magical wands produce." Oscar Wilde would pick up, and make notorious, such self-advertising mannerisms as he learned from the example of Disraeli, and in the title of his only novel he even echoed Disraeli's *Vivian Grey*—and a German episode in Disraeli's book may have furnished the idea at the heart of *The Picture of Dorian Gray*. The mysteriously handsome nobleman Max Rodenstein in Disraeli's sequel will not permit his mother, the Baroness, to have his portrait painted, fearing that any likeness would mean his death. While he is away as a serving officer his parents receive a case with his portrait, and the Baroness, certain that she sees the eyes move, grows pale. "Again the eyes trembled, there was a melancholy smile, and then they closed. The clock of Rodenstein Castle struck." Three days later

*Sir George Don died in 1832. A monument to him would be erected in his beloved Gibraltar, designed by Disraeli's cousin George Basevi.

the news of the Battle of Leipzig* arrived, confirming that "at the very moment that the eyes of the portrait closed Rodenstein had been pierced by a Polish Lancer!" (Wilde's Dorian would kill himself by stabbing his own portrait.)

Another possible foreshadowing of *Dorian Gray* is in Disraeli's *Venetia*, where the heroine of the title, mesmerized by the portrait of her father in his young manhood (Marmion Herbert is a fictionalized Shelley), determines to exorcise that enchantment once and for all. "She seized the ancient dagger . . . and plunged it into the canvas; then tearing with unflinching resolution the severed parts, she scattered the fragments over the chamber."

While feminine society in Gibraltar was plentiful, and Ben basked in admiration of his plumage, he took a blow to his vanity—at least so he wrote home. "I am sorry to say all my hair is coming off," he reported, "just at the moment it had attained the highest perfection and was universally mistaken for a wig." He was "obliged to let the women pull it, merely to satisfy their ——— curiosity." Maria would offer to send a wig to a future port of call, but despite the theatricalized fears, Ben never lost his ebony locks. In any case, his chief triumph with the women, so he reported, was with Lady Don, who, although seventy, was not only "excessively acute and *piquante*" but a charmer in conversation who attracted him as much as "a blooming beauty in Mayfair." Disraeli was at his best with older women.

In Spain on horseback, he and Meredith visited, in formerly Moorish country near Cadiz, the castle of Medina Sidonia. Among Spanish Christians of Jewish origin had been the eminent Duke of Medina Sidonia. Disraeli would adopt the name for two of his characters, a subordinate figure in *Count Alarcos* and a mysterious and ubiquitous Jew, the philosophical banker Sidonia of *Coningsby* and *Tancred*. The Spanish scenes themselves would be recalled in novels like *Henrietta Temple* and *Contarini Fleming*, and

---

*The Battle of Leipzig, October 16–19, 1813, a decisive defeat for Napoleon, pitted Austrian, Prussian, Swedish, Russian, and other forces against a French army little more than half the allied strength. It marked the end of the Napoleonic empire east of the Rhine.

the heroine of *Coningsby* would claim Spanish descent via her mother (as would Disraeli himself). Even in *Alroy*, one of the spurs for the journey, features of the Alhambra at Seville—the greatest of all Moorish palaces in Spain—would be written into the palace of the Caliph of Baghdad. "I thought that enthusiasm was dead within me, and nothing could be new," Ben wrote to Sarah on August 9 as he was preparing to leave for Malta. But Moorish ruins and Murillo paintings had "upset my theory." Yet, he hastened to add, "there is no place like Bradenham, and each moment I feel better, I want to come back."

He was not fully recovered. "The moment I attempt to meditate . . . or in any way call the greater powers of intellect into operation, that moment I feel I am a lost man. The palpitations in my heart and head increase in violence, an indescribable feeling of idiocy comes over me, and for hours I am plunged into a state of the darkest despair. When the curse has subsided to its usual grade of horror, my sanguine temper calls me again to life and hope." His general health, he insisted nevertheless, was "never better." He did not give way "except under a paroxysm," and he was "determined to prove to all that I am not suffering under hypochondria." He was going to give himself a personal deadline. "I pursue this life only for a year; if at the end of that period I find no relief, I resign myself to my fate. . . . I am serious. Prepare yourself for this, but hope [for] better things."

On August 19, 1830, despite a "devil of a Levanter" often "full in our teeth," Disraeli and Meredith debarked in Malta from the *Columbian* and were lodged for a week in mandatory quarantine in the isolation of the vast Lazaretto.* As the place into which travelers from the Middle East and North Africa poured, Malta protected itself from infection via the Lazaretto, after a week of which the "capital hotel," Beverly's, seemed even more luxurious than it was. But from the tedium of quarantine Ben wrote a long letter to "Sa" about Spain. When Colburn finally published *The Young Duke*, Ben instructed her to tell Ralph, a copy was to be sent to Gibraltar inscribed, "Lady Don, by desire of the author."

---

*Originally a hospital for contagious diseases, especially leprosy, the label was adopted for places of detention for travelers under quarantine.

She was, he explained, "the cleverest and most charming woman I ever met."

Since even Royal Navy captains shared "the bore of our quarantine," he and Meredith acquired instant acquaintances of some standing in Malta, and left the Lazaretto with invitations to shipboard dinners, later fictionalized in *Lothair* (1870), in Valetta harbor. In Valetta itself Disraeli met an old acquaintance, James Clay, a year younger but an Oxford contemporary of Meredith. Clay drew an income from his father and grandfather, London merchants and shipowners, and considered life an opportunity for indulgence in gambling, sport, sailing, and sex. To assist him was his own Leporello, "Tita," Byron's former gondolier and manservant. Giovanni Battista Falcieri had been in Greece with the poet—even at his deathbed in Missolonghi six years earlier. "His moustachios touch the earth," Disraeli wrote home in some awe at encountering the shade of Byron in the haunts of *Childe Harold*.

Clay, who had chartered a fifty-five-ton yacht for travels eastward, brought his reputation with him. Incautiously, Ben told his father that Clay was "immensely improved and quite a hero. He has been here a month and has already beat the whole Garrison at Rackets and billiards and other wicked games." No sportsman, Ben reported watching others at the racket court and being struck by an erratic ball. "I picked it up, and observing a young rifleman . . . , I humbly requested him to forward its passage . . . , as I really had never thrown a ball in my life." But he would learn a few other pastimes under Clay's tutelage. "Conceive me," he wrote to Benjamin Austen, "with a Turkish pipe seven feet long puffing on a sofa." Similarly he wrote to Ralph that smoking "relieve [s] my head." It was also a convivial activity in Clay's company.

Inevitably, the straitlaced D'Israeli family disapproved of the genial but debauched Clay, and when Ben wanted to accept an offer to share expenses on the yacht in which he had already spent "very agreeable hours," Meredith, so Ben understated to Ralph, "was averse to the plan." Sarah would write sharply to her brother, "How you come to be in a boat sailing with him on the Aegean Sea I cannot understand." Nevertheless, Ben persuaded

Meredith to become Clay's passenger at a "fair" rate, and to be dropped off at whatever port they decided to leave Clay. And while Meredith shrank from such contamination en route to Corfu and the Greek mainland, Ben gloried in his new role. "You sho[ul]d see me," he bragged to Ralph in mid-September, "in the costume [of a] Greek pirate. A blood red shirt with [sil]ver studs as big as shillings, an immense [sca]rf full of pistols and daggers, [a] red cap, red slippers, blue broad striped . . . jacket and trousers. Excessively wicked!"*

Hoping, probably, that the wickedness would be accepted at home as playacting, Ben described his new companions, Clay and Tita, in lighthearted terms. The family was not amused; nor was the reluctant Meredith. Still, they set sail on the *Susan* for Corfu, "a stormy, but not disagreeable, passage," Ben wrote to Isaac on October 10. Corfu (now Kerkira) was more authentically Greek than Greece—"a poor village," Benjamin observed, "but a most lovely island, offering all you can expect from Grecian scenery." The largest of the Ionian group, it was once owned by the Venetian republic. Briefly French, after Napoleon it was ceded to England. Corfu had never been, like continental Greece, part of Ottoman Turkey. Across a narrow strait was Turkish Albania and Greece. Albania, he wrote, was "in a state of insurrection. I am glad to say the Porte [is] every where triumphant."

In a letter from Malta, Disraeli had warned Benjamin Austen not to be surprised "if you hear something very strange indeed" from the next stopping place. What he was hinting at was his quixotic plan, he confessed later, "to join the Turkish army as a volunteer in the Albanian War." The idea was not new: He had suggested it as an option for his hero in the *Vivian Grey* sequel, where he deplored "the cunning, intriguing Greek, who served well his imperial master, the Russian." Although Tory merchants in Malta favored the Turks, in part because Greek pirates preyed upon British commerce in the Mediterranean, Disraeli, especially now that he was in the company of the legendary Tita, might have been expected to be sympathetic to the cause that had fired Byron and his generation—Greek freedom.

*Damaged by fire, the letter requires emendation where charred and cropped.

Disraeli would write a novel based upon Byron and Shelley, *Venetia*. Yet the cause of Greece remained an exception. In part as a Tory and in part as a Jew, Disraeli seemed as pro-Turk as he was anti-Russian all his life. The ramshackle, polyglot Ottoman Empire seemed the only real barrier to Russian expansionism into the Middle East and the Mediterranean. To him the Greeks, like the other rebellious Balkan peoples, were unwitting Czarist surrogates, agents of Russian barbarism. Further, despite notorious lapses, Jews in Ottoman lands lived more freely than under czarism, and would continue to do so under Islam until the struggle for the Holy Land began in earnest after 1918 with the awakening of a Jewish nationalism which Disraeli had espoused decades earlier.

Looking for an excuse to meet the Ottoman ruler, Disraeli prevailed upon the Lord High Commissioner of the Ionian Islands, General Sir Frederick Adams, to direct a message to Grand Vizier Reschid Mehmet Pasha, in some vague British interest. Accompanied by Meredith and Clay, Disraeli would deliver it to the Grand Vizier at his headquarters in Yannina (Ioánnina), now south of the Albanian border in Greece. Disraeli reveled in the adventure, which he put into *Contarini Fleming* without much change. It was the first time he had heard the call of the muezzin from a minaret, the first time he had enjoyed exotic Turkish hospitality. Disraeli delayed until 1845, in a note to *Alroy*, recording that "His Highness sent to myself and my traveling companions a course from his table, singers, and dancing girls." They also dined with Mehmet Pasha. Ben understood, he told his father, that as a guest it was discourteous to not eat and drink with abandon, and they ate "a most capital supper" with their fingers, and in great quantities. "We must drink," he wrote, as "a compliment," and they quaffed the Bey's brandy "in rivers." In the middle of the night he found himself "sleeping on the [Bey's] Divan, rolled up in its sacred carpet."

Although purple crags in the "dying glory" of Greek sunsets were thrilling, what was more so, he wrote with deliberate outrageousness, was experiencing "the delight of being made much of by a man who was daily decapitating half the Province." The Turkish depredations were not atrocities only because Disraeli was

young and because he was being made much of—as representative
of the King of England—and because he did not actually see any
horrors. It was "a wondrous week. To lionize and be a lion at the
same time is a hard fate. When I walked out I was followed by a
crowd; when I stopped to buy anything, I was encompassed by a
circle."

Fame dazzled him, even such fleeting and spurious popular
enthusiasm. Still, he concluded to his "dearest father"—and there
was no question that his father remained the most important being in Ben's life—that he now remembered "the barbaric splendor, and turbulent existence, which I have just quitted, with
disgust" when recalling "the feelings, in the indulgence of which
I can alone find happiness, and from which an inexorable destiny
seems resolved to shut me out." The contrast was only geographical. An audience with "His Highness" as someone of political
importance symbolized what he wanted for himself, only not *that*
Highness.

Using the letter to his father as the basis, Disraeli drafted another account of the audience with the Grand Vizier to send to
Henry Colburn for publication in his *Court Journal*, complaining
at the same time about the delay in release of *The Young Duke*, "I
very much fear that you are injuriously procrastinating its appearance." "A Visit to the Grand Vizier" would appear on January 29,
1831 (he wrote Colburn on November 18, 1830); the novel was
not published until April.

The Yannina episode reappeared at length in part V of
Contarini Fleming, where the hero is given the opportunity denied
to Disraeli and to *The Court Journal* because the insurrection in
Albania was waning. Contarini goes off to battle in a colorful
"general charge" that excites feelings "of energy and peril," despite the often "horrible spectacles," a "wonderful and glorious
moment in existence." Returning to his tent, he drinks "a flask of
Zitza wine" at one gulp with "the highest sensual pleasure." By
moonlight he canters back over the field of battle to revisit the
Vizier seated on a carpet in a cypress grove. The great man gives
Disraeli's hero "the pipe of honor from his own lips." What Ben
had actually written to his father was, "I gave him my pipe as a
memorial of having got tipsey together."

The boundaries of the new Greece were undefined in November 1830, and the nation lacked a head of state. Prince
Leopold of Saxe-Coburg, widower of George IV's only legitimate
offspring, Princess Charlotte of Wales,* had refused the questionable kingdom, and European powers were still looking for a candidate. (Leopold would be offered Belgium, a less hazardous
throne, in June 1831.) "I really believe," Disraeli joked in a letter
to Benjamin Austen, "that if I had 25,000£ to throw away I
might increase my headache by wearing a crown."

Much of the Balkans was still Turkish after centuries of Ottoman occupation—alien, Islamic, "Eastern," even in Disraeli's
imagination "Arabian." Camel caravans transported one back in
time to David Alroy's half-legendary day, and even to the Bible.
In Athens, still occupied by the Turks, Disraeli, Meredith, and
Clay inspected the reopened Parthenon and the Temple of The-
seus before embarking once more (Meredith with increasing reluctance) on the *Susan*, this time for Turkey itself. Each new
setting encountered was the "most truly beautiful" Disraeli had
seen. When Constantinople came romantically into view near
sunset early in December as they sailed up the Dardanelles, "it
baffles all description," Ben wrote breathlessly to his father; "tho'
so often described; an immense mass of buildings, cupolas, cypress
groves and minarets. I feel an excitement I thought was dead."
He had said much the same about the Alhambra and Seville.

Postponing his urge to sample the pleasures of the city at the
edge of Asia, he searched out, he wrote to Isaac, "a pile of
Galignanis." *Galignani's Messenger* was full of news of political turmoil in England. The Duke of Wellington's administration, paralyzed by Tory squabbling, had ended with the resignation of the
hero of Waterloo; the new King, fearing riots, had canceled the
traditional Lord Mayor's Day (November 10) visit to the City.
"What a confusion!" Ben remarked to his father. "What a capital
Pantomime . . .!" He dashed off similar epithets to Benjamin
Austen and to Edward Lytton Bulwer. His "Turkish prejudices,"
he added to Bulwer, were "very much confirmed" by what he had

*Charlotte had died in childbirth in 1817, opening the succession to the still un-
born Victoria.

experienced in Turkish lands. Although he itched to be back in London to exploit politically the opportunities inherent in what *Galignani* had reported, he was in the Middle East for a purpose and might never return.

While Meredith chafed, Disraeli and Clay explored the pleasures of Constantinople. "The life of this people greatly accords with my taste, which is naturally somewhat indolent and melancholy," he asserted to Bulwer, half-believing what he wrote. "To repose in voluptuous ottomans, and smoke superb pipes, daily to indulge in the luxuries of a bath which requires half a dozen attendants for its perfection, to court the air in a carved caique by shores which are a continual scene and to find no exertion greater than a canter on a barb,* is I think a far more sensible life than all the bustle of clubs, and all the boring [tedium] of [ladies'] saloons!"

With the letter went Turkish slippers for Bulwer's fractious wife, Rosina, and a tobacco pouch for Bulwer himself. Another pair of slippers went to Sara Austen, with a letter about his travels telling her what he thought she would want to hear—that Athens was "the most beautiful assemblage of all that is interesting in art and nature." She would not have appreciated his encomiums to Turkish life—nor did Meredith, who did not join his companions on their dissipations, which included the carnal delights of Constantinople's brothels and would cause Disraeli later to confide to Clay, "Mercury has succeeded to Venus." Ben was lucky: The doses of mercury, in his case at least, cured the complaints of love.

Constantinople was full of delights, with its bazaars where even "a common pair of slippers," he wrote to Isaac, could be as colorful as "the warmest beam of a southern sunset." The markets were like the Burlington Arcade expanded to a square mile of intersecting passages and "full of every product of the Empire from diamonds to dates." And the broad Bosporus combined the attractions of an ocean with the riverside of the Thames and the Rhine. The polyglot population—mostly Turks, Greeks, Jews, and Armenians, he explained—lived in harmony, and in "characteristic" costumes that suggested an "Eastern fairy tale." He had not been presented to Mahmoud II, a Turk of forty-five who had been

---

*A breed of lithe horses from Barbary, known for speed and endurance.

ruler of the Ottoman Empire for twenty-two years, but had "seen
the Sultan several times." Much like a "European Prince," he appeared more affable than his Western counterparts, "mixes with
his subjects, interferes in all their pursuits and taxes them most
unmercifully." He dressed in European style and embodied to
Disraeli a positive future for a nation already written off as "the
sick man of Europe." The Sultan, he explained, had to struggle
against "unprecedented conspiracy." A conglomerate of nationalities, Turkey seemed full of intrigues foreshadowing its breakup.

    Disraeli wanted to believe in the comparative blessings of
Ottoman sovereignty in the Middle East. He preferred tradition,
stability, and enlightened (when possible) aristocracy to seething
nationalisms and mobocracy, and the unchanging Turkish empire
he saw at the end of a six-foot hookah would shape his foreign
policy perceptions all his life.

    On January 11 he wrote home that he and Clay expected to
be in Egypt in about ten days. Then he would return to England
via Malta. Yet two factors altered Disraeli's itinerary. First, he
wanted to explore Jerusalem, the very object of his travels from
the start, and Clay was willing if Meredith balked. Weary of
Disraeli's and Clay's debaucheries, some of which may have been
brag, Meredith determined to go overland along the Turkish coast
to Smyrna, at that time the great Greek city compared to which
Athens was a village with ruins. He would then find a vessel to
Egypt, to link up again with Disraeli for the voyage home.
Meredith's decision, Ben wrote to Sarah two months later on arriving in Alexandria, was "very mad," as the country he stubbornly elected to see from the saddle was "unsatisfactory." Unlike
the friend he could no longer understand, Ben was traveling for
material for books as well as to clear his head. On both counts he
was doing well, and the sensual delights were a bonus. But leaving
Constantinople was more of a problem than he and Clay had anticipated. The ambassador, Sir Robert Gordon, a younger brother
of Lord Aberdeen, a former foreign secretary and a future prime
minister, had taken a fancy to the young gentlemen, and offered
them rooms in the ambassadorial palace to induce them to stay.
When, with difficulty, they extricated themselves, Gordon parted
from them "in a pet."

Becalmed once they exited the Dardanelles, they lay at nightfall off the coast of ancient Troy, where Meredith was to wander, and Disraeli remembered, in a note appended to *Alroy*, hearing from the yacht "the most singular screams at intervals through the night," the sounds of "jackals on their evening prowl." Clay was behind schedule when they reached Smyrna, intending to debark only to reprovision the *Susan*, but it remained at anchor for ten days, lashed by "unceasing rains and terrible gales of wind." Yet there, Ben reported to Sarah, "we found Meredith in a very decent bivoack." When Disraeli and Clay left, it was again without Meredith. He would meet them in Egypt, he promised, using as excuse his desire, Ben wrote in exasperation, to explore "the unseen relics of some unheard of cock and bull city." Alone of the three, William Meredith was anticipating marriage on his return, and unlike his companions, he was keeping chaste in body and soul.

Although gales kept Clay and Disraeli from landing at Rhodes, they managed a day in Cyprus, which, he explained to Sarah cautiously, was "more delightful to me as the residence of Fortunatus"—the legendary possessor of a magical flying hat— "than as the rosy realm of Venus." At the Cyprian port of Famagusta, Clay hired a pilot to steer them to Jaffa, a difficult harbor but the shortest land route from the coast to Jerusalem.

The first sight of "Syria"—Disraeli meant the mountains of lower Lebanon—was of a snow-covered range dominated by distant Mount Hermon. All of the Holy Land, extending into contemporary Jordan, was a Syrian province of the Ottomans, and when they made landfall at Jaffa they were still in provincial Syria. Even there, Disraeli found Venetians—not spurious Venetians like himself, but an expatriate named Damiani who had become more Oriental than the local aristocracy. Damiani dressed in "flowing robes of crimson silk" and offered them a dinner in his gardens (which included orchards of oranges, citrons, and pomegranates) of "rice, spices, pistachio nuts, perfumed rotis, and dazzling confectionery." Starved of Europeans, he urged them to stay for a month.

Eager to see Jerusalem, they set out on horseback the next day, "a party of six, well mounted and armed," across the plain

and into what Disraeli described without exaggeration as "the severe and savage mountains of Judea." Overnight, they sought hospitality in a "Latin convent, an immense establishment, well kept
up, but with only one monk." It was the Hospice of St.
Nicodemus and St. Joseph of Arimathea, a hotel for travelers and
pilgrims, and a money-making enterprise rather than a purely religious one. No trail was safe, as local brigands often waylaid and
robbed travelers, or merely extracted protection money, but toward the close of the second day they saw Jerusalem from the
Mount of Olives. Disraeli's awe as expressed to his sister was paralleled by lines he would give to Contarini Fleming.

From the Mount of Olives, he told Sarah, he could look
across to the city that had been his object:

> Jerusalem is entirely surrounded by an old feudal wall
> with towers and gates of the time of the crusaders and
> in perfect preservation; as the town is built upon a hill,
> you can from the opposite height discern the roof of al-
> most every house. In the front is the magnificent
> mosque built upon the site of the Temple, with its beau-
> tiful gardens and fantastic gates—a variety of domes and
> towers rise in all directions, the houses are of a bright
> stone. I was thunderstruck. I saw before me apparently
> a gorgeous city. Nothing can be conceived more wild
> and terrible and barren than the surrounding scenery,
> dark, stony and severe, but the ground is thrown about
> in such picturesque undulations, that the mind is full of
> the sublime, not the beautiful, and rich and waving
> woods and sparkling cultivation would be misplaced.
> The city on the other side is in the plain, the ravine
> not being all around. It is, as it were, in a bowl of
> mountains. I have jotted down materials for description;
> I have not space to describe. I leave it to your lively
> imagination to fill up the rest. Except Athens, I never
> saw anything more essentially striking. . . . I will not
> place it below the city of Minerva. Athens and Jerusa-
> lem in their glory must have been the finest representa-
> tions of the beautiful and sublime.

Jerusalem, with the Dome of the Rock in the background, at the time of Disraeli's visit in 1831. *From a contemporary engraving.*

Never one to waste his impressions, Disraeli would put another lengthy description of Jerusalem from the Mount of Olives, this time by moonlight, in *Tancred,* a novel that owes even more to his experience of the Holy Land than either *Alroy* or *Contarini Fleming.* Yet those works, too, are suffused with his ardor for the stark land that stirred his imagination, and for the astonishing city that seemed, even within the old walls, more history than reality. Jerusalem in 1830, in Robert Blake's words, "bore little resemblance to the rhapsodic vision of the Psalmists. It was a poverty-stricken Turkish city which, however, happened to contain some of the most sacrosanct places hallowed by the three great monotheistic religions of the world." Its gritty reality disappears in Disraeli's enthusiasm. Jerusalem was, he told Sarah, "the most delightful [place] of all our travels," certainly more for what it fed his fancy than for its mean streets and barren hills.

Again Clay and Disraeli resorted to the only hotels available—the monasteries. St. Salvador belonged to the Franciscan Order, official overseers of such holy sites as the Church of the Holy Sepulchre. The Franciscans also owned guest houses, one of which—after a night in the monastery—was alloted to

them, along with servants. Clay could afford it. Provisions were
sent in daily. There were no public eating places. "We dined,"
Disraeli told Sarah, ". . . on the roof of our house by moonlight—
visited the Holy Sepulchre of course, tho' avoided the other
Coglionerias [frauds]; . . . but the Eastern will believe anything.
Surprised at the number of remains at Jerusalem—tho' some more
ancient than Herod. The tombs of the Kings very fine. Weather
delicious—mild summer heat—made an immense sensation—
received visits from the Vicar General of the Pope, the Spanish
Prior, etc."

Ben took many more notes than turned up in his letters.
Vivid passages in the novels appear to be firsthand observation
rather than later gleanings from histories and guidebooks. In sixteen months of travels he wrote only thirty letters which have
survived, seventeen to the family—these for the most part colorful narratives he intended to exploit for books. *Contarini Fleming*
and *Alroy* and *Tancred* include details not in the letters that almost certainly are not merely from memory. Disraeli never mentioned, for example, his attempt to slip into the Mosque of Omar,
closed to infidels, until he wrote author's notes* to an 1843 edition of *Alroy:*

> I endeavoured to enter it at the hazard of my life. I was
> detected and surrounded by a horde of turbaned fanat-
> ics, and escaped with difficulty; but I saw enough to feel
> that minute inspection would not belie the general
> character I formed of it from the Mount of Olives. I
> caught a glorious glimpse of splendid courts and light
> airy gates of Saracenic triumph, flights of noble steps,
> long arcades, and interior gardens, where silver foun-
> tains spouted their tall streams amid the taller cypresses.

Another note suggests that he really worked at examining the
tombs of the Hasmonean "kings"—the Maccabeean princes.

*Disraeli's notes to *Alroy* also show that he had read such works, probably in his father's library, as the Hebraist John Lightfoot's commentaries on the Talmud
(1822–25) and Leon of Modena's *Rites and Ceremonies of the Jews.*

"There is no grand portal; you crawl into the tombs by a small opening in one of the sides. There are a few small chambers with niches, recesses, and sarcophagi, some sculptured in the same flowing style as the frieze."

In *Contarini Fleming*, he would hint at an attempt to enter the mosque as if he belonged: A European ("Frank"), he wrote, does so

> at the risk of his life. The Turks of Syria have not been contaminated by the heresies of their enlightened Sultan. In Damascus it is impossible to appear in the Frank dress without being pelted: and although they would condescend perhaps, at Jerusalem to permit an infidel dog to walk about in his national dress, he would not escape many a curse and many a scornful exclamation of "Giaour!" There is only one way to travel in the East with ease, and that is with an appearance of pomp. The Turks are much influenced by the exterior, and although they are not mercenary, a well-dressed and well-attended infidel will command respect.

While the Islamic sites were aesthetically appealing, the Christian ones failed to stir any religious emotion and in some cases, he wrote (in *Contarini Fleming*), were cynically fraudulent. Within the walls of the Church of the Holy Sepulchre, Contarini charges, the ecclesiastical authorities "have contrived to assemble the scenes of a vast number of incidents in the life of the Saviour, with a highly romantic violation of the unity of place. . . . The truth is, the whole is an ingenious imposture of a comparatively recent date, and we are indebted to that favoured individual, the Empress Helen, for this exceedingly clever creation, as well as for the discovery of the true cross." The Church, he added, was as much a marketplace as a point of pious pilgrimage. "The court is crowded with the vendors of relics and rosaries . . . and in its bustle and lounging character rather reminded me of an exchange than a temple."

Of Jewish places of worship he saw nothing. Jews had lived in Jerusalem continuously despite the Diaspora. They represented the largest religious community in the sparsely populated region, but by Ottoman edict were only permitted to occupy the worst possible quarter of the city. Most Turks knew only poor and cowed Jews, except for the rare courtiers and entrepreneurs needed to conduct their affairs. Disraeli's Jews of the Holy Land are not city dwellers in miserable back streets, but landowners who live spacious lives, at least in *Contarini Fleming* and *Tancred*. In the first is the banker Adam Besso, "a rich Hebrew merchant . . . , one of the finest-hearted fellows in the world, and generous as he is rich." At Besso's, "near the Gate of Sion," one encountered "some intelligent society," and—one almost sees Isaac here—Besso, "although sincere in his creed, was the least bigoted of his tribe."

In *Tancred*, Besso reappears. And in gardenlike grounds on the southern side of the Mount of Olives, "such as Gethsemane might have been in those days of political justice when Jerusalem belonged to the Jews"—very likely appropriated from Damiani's estate near Jaffa—Tancred, Lord Montacute, finds the lovely Jewess Eva, without question like no one he could have met on either side of the Jordan.

From Jerusalem, Clay and Disraeli returned the way they had come and embarked on the waiting *Susan*. They arrived in Alexandria on March 12, 1831, and a week later, as Ben was writing a long letter to Sarah to fill the family in on where he had been and what he had seen, Meredith turned up on a Turkish ship from Smyrna. In a desperate appeal to Ben from the harbor, he described a "horrid passage" and the threat, giving his vessel and port of departure, of a month's quarantine. "He w[ill] go mad," Ben guessed to Sarah before going to the Governor General's office to plead Meredith's case. Although under the suzerainty of the Turkish Sultan, Egypt was ruled by a Pasha, Mehemet Ali, whose powers extended into Arabia and as far to the south as the Sudan. Because of the presence of the partner of Samuel Briggs of Briggs and Thurburn, cotton brokers, Disraeli and companions would have the run of Egypt despite the Sultan's sweeping police powers. Disraeli had a letter from Briggs in London, describing Ben as a son of a famous author. The firm was Mehemet Ali's agent in London. Meredith was released.

Before the reunion with Meredith, Disraeli and Clay had arranged to go up the Nile to Luxor and Thebes—and beyond "to the very confines of Nubia." Meredith insisted on traveling separately, prompting Ben to write to Sarah, who had learned of Meredith's going on his own through Turkey, "I am glad that you are not as astonished . . . at Meredith and myself parting [in Constantinople]." Ben was not surprised that Meredith was off again alone. Meredith wanted no connection with Clay, and Ben no longer cared. Meredith was dull and proper, Clay lively and improper. Ben professed to Sarah to be "very sorry" at her unease over this companion who had eliminated her fiancé from his life "as he has been to me a highly agreeable one. I owe much to his constant attentions. It is a great thing to travel with a man for months and that he sh[oul]d never occasion you an uneasy moment. . . . Indeed I am greatly indebted to him for much comfort." Clay also saved him, he said, from boredom, which was an understatement.

Much of April and almost all of May were needed for the Nile journey, "in a capital boat, which the Consul had provided for us with cabins and every convenience." The *dahabeeyah* first took them from Alexandria through the Delta and on to Cairo. The "villages of mud," clustered in palm groves, were beautiful at a distance, and the river "perfectly magical" by moonlight. After the great Sphinx and the Pyramids—they climbed the largest of the three—the upper Nile with its hundreds of miles of monumental ruins left Disraeli grasping for words. "Conceive," he explained to Sarah, "a feverish and tumultuous dream full of triumphal gates, processions of paintings, interminable walls of heroic sculpture, granite colossi of Gods and Kings, prodigious obelisks, avenues of Sphynx[e]s and halls of a thousand columns, thirty feet in girth and of a proportionate height. My eyes and mind yet ache with grandeur so little in union with our own littleness." Italy and Greece were "mere toys."

Although Ben was "very well indeed," Clay had joked earlier to Meredith that Disraeli, who had embarked on the long voyage in part to convalesce, "ought never to travel without a nurse." But now both Clay and Tita were ill. Clay's "intermittent fever" was probably malaria; Tita was down with dysentery, the other almost unavoidable souvenir of the Nile. "Never ill before in his life," Disraeli wrote about his friend, "he is exceedingly frightened."

"Thus you see," Ben remarked from Cairo in his May 28 letter to Sarah, "the strong men have fallen while I who am a habitual invalid am firm on my legs—but the reason is this, that I—being somewhat indolent and feeble, live *a la Turque* while Clay and Giovanni are always in action and have done nothing but shoot and swim from morning to night."

The latest packet brought "wonderful news . . . in a pile of Galignani's" that made Disraeli eager to get home. The Reform Bill introduced by Lord John Russell in the House of Commons had survived, by one vote, a second reading on March 23, then failed through the tactic of an amendment a month later. King William had dissolved Parliament and new elections had brought in a Whig majority determined upon Reform. If it happened, there would be more seats to contest and fewer seats that were family fiefdoms.

Disraeli thrived on the sybaritic life—his long hookah, his coffee boiled with spices, his pomegranate sherbet, the oranges, citrons, limes, and—best of all—bananas. But he also longed to be back, he declared, with his father, "dearest of men, fleshing our quills together . . . , now that I have got use of my brain for the first time in my life."

While he waited for Meredith to return and for Clay and Tita to recover, Disraeli kept busy writing, perhaps the reason why *Contarini Fleming* bears so many marks of the travelogue and includes long passages nearly parallel to letters to Sarah. The novel, he recalled in a preface to the 1845 edition, had been "written with great care, after deep meditation, and in a beautiful and distant land favourable to composition, with nothing in it to attract the passions of the hour." Exploiting his connections in Egypt he arranged for himself an audience with the Pasha in his palace at Shubra Khit, on a branch of the Nile east of Alexandria, at which they discussed the comparative merits of popular and absolute rule. Probably romanticized in the telling,* the ac-

---

*"You spit pearls," Mehemet Ali compliments Disraeli on his political sagacity.

count was published in December 1835 in the form of a political pamphlet as *Vindication of the English Constitution in a letter to a Noble and Learned Lord*. (The dedicatee, whom in 1831 he had yet to meet, would be the former Lord Chancellor, Lord Lyndhurst.)

Toward the end of June, Meredith returned to Cairo somewhat unwell, just as Clay left for Alexandria to arrange crew and provisions for the return voyage. Ben had been amusing himself in conversations with Paul Emile Botta, an Italian physician who lived in the Egyptian style and dabbled in archeology. In *Contarini Fleming*, he became (his talk transmuted almost directly onto the pages of the novel as Disraeli wrote) Count Marigny, "a sceptic and absolute materialist, yet influenced by noble views." Not all his views were sufficiently elevated for the novel—his enthusiasms included opium and exotic sex—but he was fortunately at hand when, ten days before departure for home, Meredith's ailment proved to be smallpox.

A doctor had earlier assured Disraeli that Meredith did not have a virulent form of the disease and might even recover unmarked. But on the afternoon of July 19, as Disraeli was talking with Botta in a nearby room, a servant came crying that Meredith had fainted. Rushing to the bedside, Botta opened a vein and realized that Meredith's heart function had ceased.

Disraeli was prostrated, and Botta had a new patient, staying with his friend through "a night of horror" and into the morning. Then, his drafts of letters degenerating into anguished scrawls, Ben tried to frame the dread news for Bradenham. He began one to his father headed "READ THIS ALONE."

"If you were not a great philosopher, as well as a good man," he began, "I do not think that I could summon courage to communicate to you the terrible intelligence which is now to be imparted by this trembling pen; but I have such confidence in your wisdom, as well as in your virtue, that it is your assistance to which I look in the saddest office that has ever yet devolved upon me."

With that letter, crowded with graphic medical details, was the most heartfelt page that Disraeli ever penned: the separate letter to Sarah. More than almost anything else he wrote, it also reveals his instinctive recourse to the Bible, as it became almost a Song of Songs to a sister. "Ere you open this page," he began to "My Own Sa!" their father "will have imparted to you with all the tenderness of parental love the terrible intelligence which I have scarcely found courage enough to communicate to him." And he told her what he knew would mean—as she was nearly twenty-nine—a life thereafter of lonely near-widowhood.

"Oh! my sister," he went on, "in this hour of overwhelming affliction my thoughts are only for you. Alas! my beloved! if you are lost to me, where, where, am I to fly for refuge! I have no wife, I have no betrothed, nor since I have been better acquainted with my own mind and temper, and situation, have I sought them. Live then my heart's treasure for one who has ever loved you with a surpassing love, and who would cheerfully have yielded his own existence to have saved you the bitterness of reading this. Yes! my beloved! be my genius, my solace, my companion, my joy! We will never part, and if I cannot be to you all of our lost friend, at least we feel that Life can never be a blank while illumined by the pure and perfect love of a Sister and a Brother!"

Unable to gather the courage to write to Meredith's parents, Disraeli wrote instead to his dead friend's sister, Georgiana, wishing that he could "mingle the tears I am fast shedding with your own." Yet mourning for William Meredith had little to do with Meredith, who had vanished as friend when Clay appeared. The loss was his own family's—their hopes focused upon Ben's future—and Sarah's. His letter suggesting that Sarah live for him, however egomaniacal it appears out of the context of their lives, exactly mirrored her needs and her likely future. Having for years put all her prospects into marriage with Meredith, she had no alternatives for a meaningful existence other than as helpmate to her father or to her brother. It explains his comment, decades later, when his friend Philip Rose expressed pity that Sarah had not lived to see his becoming Prime Minister, "Ah, poor Sa, poor Sa! We've lost our audience; we've lost our audience."

Soon in double quarantine because cholera had broken out in Egypt, Disraeli spent much of August and September either sailing to Malta or mired there. He had time to write more of

Sarah Disraeli, 1828. *From a drawing by Daniel Maclise.*

Contarini Fleming and much of *Alroy.* Unknown to him, Sarah had written on the first day of August, "We should be more sat-isfied could we hear that you & William are well for in these days of universal plague we know not what we fear, and fancy all sorts of evils."

In *Alroy,* he would claim, he had portrayed his "ideal ambition"—puzzling words given its extravagances of plot and its stilted poetic diction. What did the novelized story of the rise and fall of the Jewish adventurer Menahem ben Solomon al-Ruhi on the frontiers of Persia have to do with its author's confiding, as he wrote to his father from the HMS *Hermes,* off Cape St. Vincent, on October 17, 1831: "If the Reform Bill pass, I intend to offer

myself for the seat at Wycomb[e]"? Humiliated by Jewish captivity to Baghdad, David Alroy raises up a Jewish insurrection
against the Caliph and in victory assumes the Caliphate himself;
but he marries the passionate Schirene, daughter of the
Caliph—a gentile—and a denouement much like the Samson
and Delilah story becomes inevitable. Using her considerable sexual wiles, she entraps him, then arranges his overthrow. Although
he is offered escape from death by impalement on condition that
he bow before the Prophet of Islam, he refuses, and he escapes
torture only by tricking the victorious "King of Karasme" into be-
heading him with one sword stroke. As his head falls "a smile of
triumphant derision seemed to play upon [Alroy's] dying features."

The cunning evasion of torture—"David el-David" could
not avoid death—came from Disraeli's reading of Maimonides in
a Latin translation by David Gans. Asked by his captor what evidence Alroy had that he was the Messiah, "he replied that they
might cut off his head and that he would return to life." Alroy,
of course, dies, but "the boldness and arrogance of his heart" in
seeking a future beyond dispersion for his people survives, as do
questions about why Disraeli chose a subject so unpromising for
his political aspirations at just the moment when Parliament
seemed to beckon.

Was Disraeli aiming at restoring Jerusalem to the Jews? Obviously not yet, although he was already thinking of the justice of
it. "If I speak in heat, I speak in zeal," Alroy tells the seer,
Jabaster. "You ask me what I wish: my answer is, a national existence, which we have not. You ask me what I wish: my answer is,
the Land of Promise. You ask me what I wish: my answer is, Jerusalem. You ask me what I wish: my answer is, the Temple, all
we forfeited, all we have yearned after, all for which we have
fought, our beauteous country, our holy creed, our simple manners, and our ancient customs."

Did it make sense for a prospective adventurer in politics to
publish a novel glorying in his Jewish origins at a time when observant Jews were barred from Parliament? "Alas! alas!" Alroy
confesses to Jabaster, "there was a glorious prime when Israel
stood aloof from other nations, a fair and holy thing that God

had hallowed. We were then a chosen family. . . . We shunned the stranger as an unclean thing that must defile our solitary sanctity, and keeping to ourselves and to our God, our lives flowed on in one great solemn tide of deep religion, making the meanest of our multitude feel greater than the kings of other lands." But now, Alroy believes, they must become part of the larger world. "It was a glorious time: I thought it had returned; but I awake from this, as [from] other dreams."

Apparently the author saw no way that the issue of origins would not come up if a candidate were named Benjamin Disraeli. He would anticipate that aggressively. In a political poem—and he was no poet, as it proved—of 1834, *The Revolutionary Epick*, he referred to *Alroy* in the preface as that "celebration of a gorgeous incident in that sacred and romantic people from whom I derive my blood and name." Like David Alroy he would not deny who he was, and he would strive against the odds.

In his letter to Isaac from the *Hermes*, Ben also wrote of meeting Henry Stanley aboard ship, renewing an acquaintance made in Spain. He was the younger brother of Lord Stanley, the future fourteenth Earl of Derby and a Prime Minister to figure large in Disraeli's life. The encounter would be the second catastrophe of the travels. Edward Stanley was one of the most promising younger Tory politicians. Henry Stanley was a charming ne'er-do-well from a moneyed and landed family who on returning to London disappeared into the "Hell" (gaming house) in St. James's Street run by the notorious Effie Bond. At first Lord Stanley blamed Disraeli for luring Henry there, but Disraeli—his hands clean (although he was embarrassed by the allegation)—delayed for days his return to Bradenham to help locate the erring playboy. According to Sir Philip Rose—commenting years later—the longstanding hostility of Stanley toward Disraeli that followed (tinged by anti-Semitism), emanated from "the resentment of a proud man at a stranger having become mixed up in the family secrets, and [his] cognizance of a brother's misconduct."

Ben was less than eager to return to a house still in mourning. He was in Bradenham for a few days in early November, claiming a feverish cold had kept him at the Union Hotel in London. From then until he took regular lodging for himself in London in mid-February he ran in and out of the city, seeing doctors, including Bolton. To his family he blamed his indispositions on severe colds and a chest inflammation. But, he confided to Benjamin Austen, putting off "Madame" in the process, "I am pretty well, having just left off a six weeks course of Mercury—which has pulled me down, but head all right, and working like a Tiger." While mercury was prescribed for other afflictions than venereal ones, Clay had written to his friend from Venice, having taken a leisurely way back to England, "Between us we have contrived to stumble on all the thorns with which . . . Venus guards her roses; for while you were cursing the greater evils, I contrived to secure the minor, viz. a glut from over-exertion and crabs."

Having longed for Bradenham and eager to try for the seat at nearby Wycombe if the Reform Bill passed, Disraeli needed London more. He was nowhere without social and political connections, and each meant the other. Yet he was beginning under more handicaps than he surmised. He knew about the encumbrances of inauspicious birth, untraditional schooling and lack of lands and "old money," but Edward Bulwer identified still another. People who counted were afraid that Disraeli might "clap them into a Book."

VII

"THERE IS NO EDUCATION LIKE ADVERSITY."

1831–1833

"IF THE REFORM BILL PASS," BEN HAD DECLARED TO HIS FAMILY WHILE voyaging home, "I intend to offer myself for Wycomb[e]." Unwilling to risk everything on what would be perceived as an arrogant gamble, and in desperate need to pay his debts, he was writing furiously. *Contarini Fleming*, he hoped, would be his *Childe Harold*, while *Alroy* would further startle literary London by taking the offensive in the matter of his origins.

Oversimplifying his electoral hazards, he expected to slip the property qualification which gentlemen seeking seats in Commons had to meet by the usual device of a nominal transfer of property. Unreformed in the pending legislation was the requirement, on the books since 1710, to own property worth £600 a year for a county seat and £300 a year for a borough seat. Had that been his only hurdle, a stroke of a friendly pen would circumvent it. But his lack of party and family connections, his impolitic behavior and impossible debts, and the burden of his birth, suggested to those who knew him that the effort to win a Parliamentary seat would be an exercise in futility.

To Disraeli his antecedents were the least of his concerns. No professing Jew could take the House of Commons oath "on the true faith of a Christian," but others baptized out of Judaism had been M.P.s. "Pitt's Jew," the future Lord Eardley, was elected in 1770 as Samson Gideon. In 1802 Sir Manasseh Lopes had been elected for Romney, and in 1812 for Barnstable; but he was no role model as he became involved in scandal and was imprisoned for bribery and corruption. There was also Ralph Bernal, elected for Lincoln in 1818 and still a power in the House, whose father had, like Disraeli's, left Bevis Marks Synagogue; and there was the eminent economist David Ricardo, elected for Portarlington in 1819, and serving until his death four years later. Since altering the name that had brought him notoriety was out of the question, Disraeli expected racial slurs, and with no plans, either, to change his ways, he anticipated personal attacks. With confidence in his destiny he could weather both, but given such handicaps, his backers required something more akin to faith.

Seeking London connections, Ben took lodgings in the fashionable St. James's district and used the people he knew to help launch him into society. (He rejected Bloomsbury, where the Austens still lived, as too intellectual for his needs.) Bulwer promised to push Ben's cause with the clubs and even took him to London brothels (a Bulwer letter refers to meeting "at the Naughty House"). While an applicant could buy his way into a brothel, to a club's admissions committee one was only a supplicant. The Travelers' and the very literary Athenaeum—where Isaac was a member—turned Ben down. He tried to sell his exotic Turkish pipes to raise funds to keep going, and he tried as well to open Benjamin Austen's pocketbook. He pressed John Murray to publish "The Psychological Romance"—his working title for *Contarini Fleming*—and began a political satire that he hoped would bring him credibility, *England and France: or a Cure for the Ministerial Gallomania*.

To Sarah, explaining that he had acquired Cabinet papers from the French émigré opposition about relations with England, Ben confided that his intention was to "not only ensure my election but [to] produce me a political reputation." He had seen almost no one who mattered socially, he added, deliberately keeping dark for the moment his renewed intimacy with the Boltons, who lived in King Street, St. James's, very close to Ben's own rooms at 35 Duke Street, where he had moved from temporary quarters at 15 Pall Mall East.

It was easy to reopen relations with the Boltons, as Dr. George Buckley Bolton had been his physician, and Ben still needed one. It was even easier to reopen Clara Bolton's arms, and Mrs. Bolton fancied herself a society hostess with an invitation list appropriate to sponsor Ben's political ambitions. She also speeded Ben into her bed, which was something he anticipated, and which Sarah soon discovered. Clara was eager to find a wife with means and status for her lover, and regularly invited potential brides to be looked over along with a variety of supposedly influential politicians. Some of the foreigners of alleged power and connections at her table were as shady as the Boltons themselves, and one of them, Baron Moritz von Haber, became what Disraeli interpreted as confidant and ally. Six years older than Disraeli, von Haber was the son of a Karlsruhe banker, Salomon Haber, who was successful enough, although a Jew, to be ennobled by the Grand Duchy of Baden in 1829. The younger Haber, who operated out of the Hague, adopted an unearned *von* and openly supported the deposed Charles X of France over the bourgeois King Louis Philippe.

Disraeli, who loved intrigue and assumed that it was the lever that moved governments, considered von Haber (so he told Sarah) "a noble spy . . . who moves in the first circles, and is altog[ethe]r one of the most remarkable men I have ever met." Some of the allegations in *Gallomania*, far less sensational than Disraeli imagined them to be, would come from Haber, who was out to discredit the French regime. Through Haber, Ben also met Count Alexis Orlov, who was in London to represent the Czar in the London conference to create Belgium from the restless lower provinces of the Netherlands. Since the French had a stake in what happened to Dutch Flanders, and the Russians wanted to keep the English and French apart, Disraeli offered Orlov a preview of *Gallomania*. Not remotely near the sources of real power,

Disraeli nevertheless felt smug about his ability to influence events.

In November 1831, Ben's cocky manner belied his desperate situation. "I have not *literally*," he confided to Robert Messer, who was pressing him to pay at least something on his mining share debts, "a shilling in the world; my renovated health maintains my Courage and I am vigorously working." He hoped to have his affairs "arranged" within the year, but harassment would upset his equilibrium. "Decide," he challenged, "whether it shall be disturbed. I have no friend in the world that I can ask to lend me five pounds. . . . I have not a tradesman who is paid. . . . Repose & Quiet & all will receive justice; anxiety & suspense, & I shall be as little advanced this time [next] year, the only year in which from my health, I have had anything like a chance." He hadn't, Ben added from Bradenham, even enough money "to pay my voyage to the Metropolis."

By November 11, he was, nevertheless, in London and had seen Bolton, who, he told his sister, was "richer than ever"—a clue, perhaps, to Ben's means of getting on in the metropolis. The Boltons were not close to politicians of real importance, or to the more influential members of the aristocracy, who considered Clara a vulgar upstart, yet "Madame" knew people who knew people, and Ben used one connection to acquire another. "Mrs. B.," he wrote, telling Sarah on March 1, 1832, about a dinner party, "was a blaze of jewels, and looked like Juno, only instead of a peacock, she had a dog in her lap called Fairy." Given his intimacy with Clara Bolton—which was hardly a secret, as she displayed him along with the ormolu pillars and gold plate in her drawing room—Ben found it awkward to visit the Austens, but tied to Benjamin Austen by burgeoning debts, he had himself "ticketed" for Sara's table on March 3.

Even in the intellectual environs of the British Museum the talk that March revolved about the Reform Bill, which would pass its second reading in the Commons on March 22 by the paper-thin margin of 302 to 301. "The jaw of Peel fell," the young Whig Thomas Babington Macaulay wrote to a friend, but the Tory leader of the opposition had one more chance to defeat the bill, and a majority of the Lords remained hostile, sparking riots in the unenfranchised cities and towns violent enough for King William to fear for his head.

Ben's chances required either a vacancy and by-election or a new seat to arise out of Reform. The bill, he explained to Sarah early in March, "is in a most crazy state," with the King having offered Earl Grey "a carte blanche" to ask for as many new peers to be named as were necessary to outvote the recalcitrant Lords. "It is not the Reform Bill that has shaken the aristocracy," Disraeli's Sidonia would observe in *Coningsby*, ". . . but the means by which that Bill was carried." If Grey failed his opportunity, Ben predicted to his sister—and Grey did not, as the peerage took fright at the prospect of its own dilution—the Prime Minister would forfeit his career. And he added, confidently, "I care very little, what ever may be the result, as, under all circumstances, I hope to float uppermost."

While he awaited his chance, Ben tried to improve his political and financial prospects. From home he was urged to marry one of Meredith's sisters; at the Boltons he was warned not to fall in love: "You must have a brilliant star like yourself." Meanwhile, of course, Clara would manage him. On the literary side, Murray dithered over the "Psychological Romance," for which Ben asked (on March 4) for an advance of £200, as the reader's report was late. And the political gamble of *Gallomania* went on, in hopes of newspaper serialization.

Sarah's salutation from Ben improved to "My dearest Angel" when Murray forwarded his reader's response. Suffering from an eye infection, Henry Milman had been nearly blind and had to have the novel read to him by his wife; yet he understood that he had encountered a work in the school of Johann Wolfgang von Goethe's *Wilhelm Meister,* which Thomas Carlyle had translated in 1824. "It is a very remarkable production," Milman wrote, "—very wild, very extravagant, very German, very powerful, very poetical. It will, I think, be much read—as far as one dare predict the capricious taste of the day—much admired, and much abused. . . . Some passages will scandalize the rigidly orthodox."

Milman advised Murray to publish it, but with a more marketable title. It read, he thought, less like a "Romance" than a "real history," and if readers disputed whether or not it were actual autobiography, "This will add to its notoriety." What must have pleased Disraeli most, however, was Milman's labeling it "a 'Childe Harold' in prose." Ben had aspired to the Byronic, and his first reader had perceived it, finding the novel up to the parallel.

Ben racked his brain—and Sarah's—for a new title, while insisting that "Psychological" had to be part of it. Titles often have defeated the works advertised beneath them, and Murray would have no success with *Contarini Fleming: A Psychological Autobiography*. Later Disraeli would note in his diary that *Vivian Grey*, *Alroy* (then still unfinished), and *Contarini Fleming* presented the secret history of his own feelings: *Vivian Grey* his active and real ambitions, *Alroy* his ideal ambitions, and *Contarini Fleming* the development of his poetic temperament. In actuality *Contarini* represents all three and demonstrates its author's certainty about his powers and uncertainty about how to exploit them. Until politics prevailed he would continue to try to have it both ways. Yet *Contarini* was a watershed work, a very serious undertaking suffused in places by the spirit of its models, *Childe Harold* and *Wilhelm Meister*. Goethe himself, and Heine, wrote approvingly of it, Disraeli would recall with pride. A major work of its decade, it deserved better from the English press, where it would be received condescendingly, or worse, ignored.

Had the novel succeeded resoundingly, Ben might have never run for office. His real goal was neither political nor literary. It was sheer fame, as he confessed publicly through his alter ego Contarini Fleming, whose father places his arm affectionately upon Contarini's after the success of a bold political stroke. "My son," says the gentle Baron, whose right hand he has now literally become, "you will be Prime Minister of ———" and Disraeli leaves out the name of their small state, the Baron adding, provocatively, "perhaps something greater." The reader is not left in much doubt about the identity of the greater kingdom. "I should have killed myself if I had not been supported by my ambition," Contarini confides, "which now each day became more quickening, so that the desire of distinction and of astounding action raged in my soul, and when I realised that so many years must elapse before I could realise my ideal, I gnashed my teeth in silent rage and cursed my existence."

As with Disraeli, the frustration of Contarini's early ambitions precipitates a lapse into depression. Disabled by "brain fever," Contarini finds "existence, on the terms I now possess it, an intolerable burden." For fifteen months, he explains as the cure ("a country course") is tapering off, "an idea has not crossed my brain." But, sighs Contarini, "Alas! what is life! At this age I hoped to be famous."

While at the close of the novel Contarini rejects glory, at least temporarily, for reflection, Disraeli at twenty-seven had already used up in his own cure—the Mediterranean voyage—all the time for reflection he was willing to spare. His own options were the repellent one of returning to a law office, and the gamble of attempting to live by his wits. Contarini's illness, a venerable family friend advises the young man's father, "was nothing to be alarmed about," and "just as much a part of your necessary education," he tells Contarini himself, "as travel or study." Yet the gap to the goal still yawned. He had not only to live through the interim but to do so in the proper style. A success was someone perceived as such.

With *Contarini* in production and little money to show for it, Ben put off Austen, who was pressing for repayment of his loans, by claiming that he had "another [novel] finished and in my portfolio." This was presumably *Alroy*—as *Gallomania* (nearly completed with the help of a chapter by Haber) was fuzzy political invective which, when published reluctantly by Murray, left readers uncertain about Disraeli's real views and did him little good politically or financially. Stubbornly, Disraeli made it *seem* important.

Essential to him were the almost nightly dinner parties which offered elegant food and drink at no cost but the refurbishing of his costume; information he could use, from Parliamentary and Cabinet talk to high gossip; a stage upon which to perform; and the company of beautiful women and their well-placed escorts. Ben's invitations came on the strength of his hostesses' knowledge of his capacity to entertain. He was an exotic presence in a velvet suit lined with satin in a contrasting color, embroidered waistcoats, gold rings and chains, and a variety of tasseled canes for extra effect. And he could tell a story, dazzle

Benjamin Disraeli, 1828. *From a drawing by Daniel Maclise.*

with repartee, or coin an aphorism that inverted absurdity into witty sense. His letters to "Dearest Sa" are often chronicles of dizzying orbits about London Society, each furnishing slightly less than the whole truth and slightly more of an estimate of Ben's political and literary standing than the often dismaying reality. Still, Sarah, desperately lonely at Bradenham, could sense in his progress through crowded drawing rooms and gilded dining rooms incremental successes on Ben's part, and more about the ladies than the men.

Ben's instincts told him that male-dominated politics was indirectly but materially influenced by the wives and mistresses of the movers and shakers. For him one of the most valuable ac-

quaintances would be Frances Anne, Marchioness of Londonderry, four years his elder and second wife of the immensely
wealthy 3rd Marquess. As Mistress of Holdernesse House on Park
Lane she was so haughty that Londoners would joke about her invitations: "Are you going to see Lady Londonderry insult her
guests tonight?" At one of her costume balls she presided in a
dress Ben described to Sarah as "literally embroidered with emeralds and diamonds from top to toe. It looked like armor, and she
like a Rhinoceros." He was more—if not altogether—tactful later
in Sybil (1845), a copy of which he presented to her. There she
is the "Marchioness of Deloraine," who "had great knowledge of
society, and some acquaintance with human nature, which she
fancied she had fathomed to its centre; . . . very worldly, she was
nevertheless not devoid of impulse; she was animated, and would
have been extremely agreeable, if she had not restlessly aspired to
wit; and would certainly have exercised much more influence in
society, if she had not been so anxious to show it."

At a soiree on April 1, Ben was introduced at her "particular
desire," to Mrs. Mary Anne Wyndham Lewis, he told Sarah. "A
pretty little woman," she was also "a flirt and a rattle; indeed
gifted with a volubility I sh[oul]d think unequaled, and of which
I can convey no idea. She told me that she liked silent, melancholy, men. I answered that I had no doubt of it." Twelve years
older than Ben, she was married to the Tory M.P. for Maidstone,
a well-to-do Welsh colliery proprietor and a part-owner of an iron
foundry, with a home overlooking Hyde Park at fashionable
Grosvenor Gate. Before long Mrs. Wyndham Lewis fancied Ben
as her protégé.

Many women of a certain age looked upon the strikingly
garbed and handsome Disraeli not as a potential young lover but
as potential husband for some wealthy young woman they could
sponsor. While Ben was cautiously responsive, none seemed to
suit, and even Sarah warned him that a young lady with £25,000
was very likely used to spending "the greatest part of it on herself." He was aware of that, he confided, but "love" would never
be a consideration. All his friends who had married "for love and
beauty"—he was thinking in particular of Rosina Bulwer—"either
beat their wives or live apart from them. . . . I may commit many

follies in life, but I never intend to marry for 'love,' which I am sure is a guarantee of infelicity."

The dislike was mutual. Rosina saw Ben as a bad influence upon her husband, with whom she quarreled over his absences and his intermittent affection. Years later when she took up novel-writing herself she portrayed Ben spitefully, in *Very Successful* (1856), as Mr. Jericho Jabber, a *"Jew-d'esprit"* who affected dandy attire and whose mannerisms included posturing with a handkerchief, hooking his thumbs in the armholes of his elaborate waistcoat and "ostentatiously admiring the ceiling."

Another hostile witness was Sydney Owenson, Lady Morgan, the sharp-tongued Dublin novelist whose romantic *The Wild Irish Girl,* published in 1806 when she was twenty-three, gave her literary éclat on both islands. At her home on Kildare Street she had her "Lady Morgan's School" of young well-born Irishmen to whom she spoke seditiously of the wickedness of absentee Tory landlords; visiting London on book business and to enjoy the hospitality of the absentee landlords and their social lioness wives, she would run into such "flumflamaree novel writers" as "that outrageous coxcomb Disraeli, outraging the privilege a young man has of being absurd." She had met him through the "unamiable" but Irish-born Rosina Bulwer (who was once discovered adding fresh flowers to her dining room as "fumigation"—in order "to get rid of the brogue" after entertaining Daniel O'Connell and several other Irish M.P.s invited by her husband). All that Lady Morgan claimed in common with Disraeli was a publisher, Henry Colburn. She thought that the young novelist slipped out of rooms in which he saw her because she had his measure, but he was more interested in people who could promote his prospects. Sydney Morgan's fading influence was limited to the backwater of Dublin.

After the dinner party at which he had met "Mrs Wyndham," Disraeli remained with some of the men until four in the morning, smoking. Making conversation, an Army officer, Lt. Col. Henry Webster, said, "Take care, my good fellow, I lost the most beautiful woman in the world by smoking. It has prevented more liaisons than the dread of a duel, or"—and he referred to the divorce court—"Doctors Commons." "You have proved, then," Disraeli quipped, pleased with himself, "that it is a very moral habit." (Years later, having cut back his own smoking to gatherings of men when it seemed a social necessity, he would call tobacco "The Grave of Love.")

Pinning his hopes to be considered a new Byron on *Contarini Fleming*, and to be a prospective Canning on *Gallomania*, he was seeing both through the proof stages, assuring a sceptical but co-operative John Murray the younger, that the political exposé would make "a sensation." Ben was certain that "a great noise in *The Times*" would ensure an audience for him thereafter. And on April 20 *The Times* reviewed *Gallomania*, validating half of his prophecy. It would be a "hit" with anti-reform Tories, *The Times* predicted, as in both domestic and foreign affairs it was "coloured with absolutism." Counting upon the anonymous authorship to provoke speculation, and upon the celebrity of eventual identifi-cation when the work had established a credibility his own repu-tation could not give it, Disraeli was unrewarded on both counts. *Gallomania* overturned no ministries and was at best a minor em-barrassment. He acknowledged his role in it three years later, when it made less difference, still unwilling to concede that a po-litical career was not made from the top, but rather by careful planning and hard work at the bottom.

Another of Disraeli's influential older women was Marguerite, Countess of Blessington, a widowed onetime beauty of forty-three who had known Byron, kept a literary salon, and edited an ex-pensive annual, *Heath's Book of Beauty*. Possibly more glamorous than anything in her book was her longtime companion, Count D'Orsay, whose place in the household ensured the absence of the ultrarespectable from her mansion in Seamore Place. Alfred D'Orsay had lived with Lady Blessington in a ménage à trois with her husband since 1821, when the young count, at twenty, had moved in. Seven years later, the complaisant Blessington bro-kered the espousal of a daughter from an earlier marriage to D'Orsay, a very likely unconsummated arrangement that scandal-ized London and further ostracized Lady Blessington, who filled her salon with wits and dandies rather than the wealthy and well connected. Sometimes she managed both at Gore House. "I re-member one Sunday," journalist and cartoonist George Augustus

Sala wrote, "seeing Mr Disraeli, Madame Doche, the author of *Vanity Fair*, a privy councillor, a Sardinian attaché, the Marquess of Normanby, Flexmore the clown, and the Wizard of the North, all pressing to enter the whilom boudoir of the Blessington."

When Disraeli first encountered D'Orsay in Bond Street (so he wrote to Sarah) he confronted the ultimate in dandyism. It was "a splendour I cannot describe, so dishevelled were his curls, so brilliant his bijouteries and the shifting tints of his party-coloured costume. He knows who I am, and has I suppose been crammed by Lady Blessington." At a time when he needed them, Ben would have few more loyal friends than Alfred D'Orsay and Marguerite.

With *Gallomania* faltering almost upon publication, Disraeli shifted his hopes to *Contarini Fleming*, which he had assured John Murray would have an immediate success. He also felt that it would have permanent literary value, but Murray's firm was not interested in the future of literature. Murray had told Disraeli of a conversation with Washington Irving, who had asked a large price for "heavy tomes" which Murray saw as risky. Irving countered with talk of posterity and the "badness of public taste." Murray, Ben told Sarah, "said that authors who wrote for Posterity must publish on their own account."

Contarini Fleming, on which author and publisher were to share the profits equally, was to be another victim of the badness of public taste—Murray and Disraeli would each earn £18. On May 12, as Ben wrote about the latest political events to Sarah, publication was a week away, and his only news of the book was that socialite novelist Letitia E. Landon, whose works and person he made fun of privately, had reviewed it from proofs and called it a work of genius. Bulwer seemed to know the literary gossip from every quarter and again he was right, although "L.E.L." would set off no rush to the bookshops.

The major event of mid-May was the refusal of the Duke of Wellington to attempt a Tory ministry to replace the Whig Earl Grey. There was no support in the Commons for an antireform government. Ben had written excitedly to Sarah on the day he had news of L.E.L.'s review that the Duke was in. Three days later he wrote dejectedly that the Whigs were "again in, and on their own terms." That meant that William IV could no longer renege upon Grey's proposal to name as many peers as necessary to overwhelm the hostility to the bill in the Lords. And the Lords felt further pressure from the streets, with the *Morning Chronicle* on the 18th announcing "the eve of the barricades." There were riots in some cities and mobs marching in others, with England as near to revolution as it would get in the nineteenth century.

The pressure on the Lords grew through the waning days of May and into June. On June 4 the bill was read for the third and final time in the Lords, with most of the beaten opposition abstaining. Reform passed 106 to 22. Crowds paraded in London with placards urging the King to give his royal assent personally. When he peevishly refused, Reform became law automatically on June 7, the Clerk of Parliament declaring, according to the procedure in such unusual circumstances, *"Le Roi le veult."* Street violence ebbed slowly, with the Duke of Wellington nearly mobbed—and not this time by well-wishers—on June 18, Waterloo Day.

In that atmosphere, when no literate person in England cared about anything else, *Contarini Fleming* was released and, here and there (where there was newspaper space amid the political columns), reviewed. It could not console Disraeli, although he pretended great pleasure that William Beckford, the reclusive and eccentric author of the ornate Arabian tale *Vathek* (1787), its style modeled on Voltaire, praised *Contarini* in a letter with "how wildly original! How full of intense thought! How awakening! How delightful!" The wealthy Beckford's pleasure palace at Fonthill had been commemorated in Byron's *Childe Harold,* Disraeli's own prototype for *Contarini,* which brought history full circle—but the novel, emerging in the wrong time and place, went unpurchased and unread.

His name suggesting his Venetian mother and Nordic father, Contarini Fleming is the son of the Baron's first marriage, olive-complexioned and "different" in the mythical Germanic kingdom where Baron Fleming is Foreign Minister. Although young Fleming studies at a university, the pedantry in which he finds "disgusting," Contarini's real education takes place in his father's library and as aide in his father's office. He is possessed by polit-

ical ambition, thrilled by the burgeoning of the poetic temperament in himself, and buoyed by the admiration of beautiful (and
older) women who embody his ardor for recognition and accomplishment.

A shrewd political intervention for his father brings Contarini
to an awareness of his potential. "I felt all my energies. I walked up
and down the hall in a frenzy of ambition, and I thirsted for action.
There seemed to me no achievement of which I was not capable. . . . In imagination I shook thrones and founded empires."

Contarini writes a novel based upon his experience, *Man-
stein*—an echo of Byron's *Manfred*—which is praised until the
identity of the young author is discovered (an echo of *Vivian
Grey*), after which the work is excoriated. Crushed, he wants to
die, but settles for self-exile in Venice, where he seeks his roots.
Meeting his last Contarini cousin, the beautiful Alcesté, who is
betrothed to another, he elopes with her but after some months
of bliss she dies in childbirth, their son stillborn.

To find new purpose in life, the desolate Contarini turns
again to the pursuit of fame, despite what he has learned of its
frustrations. "There is no education," Disraeli would write in his
last novel, *Endymion*, "like adversity." Surviving, like Disraeli, a
nervous breakdown, Contarini banishes his sorrows by energetic
travel, also like Disraeli, across the Mediterranean to the Holy
Land and back as far as Italy. There, a philosophical friend, the
painter Peter Winter, advises him to put his intelligence, rather
than only his physical self, "in motion. Act, act, act, act without
ceasing, and you will no longer talk of the vanity of life." Now
heir to his late father's fortune, Baron Contarini Fleming settles
near Naples to write and to plan a return to politics.

If in exposing his ambitions and his contradictions in fiction
Disraeli hoped to work them out, he was no more successful than
was the novel. He remained an outsider, which made a career in
politics more difficult than one in letters, and writing was failing
him. Nothing symbolized his problems better than a malicious
tale told by Rosina Bulwer about Disraeli's rising from a cane-
seated drawing room chair, unaware that its imprint was upon his
velvet trousers. "Who is that?" asked old Samuel Rogers, a better
gossip than poet.

"Oh!" said Rosina, "young Disraeli, the Jew."

"Rather," quipped Rogers, "the wandering Jew, with the brand of *Cane* on him."

Since Rogers knew Isaac as well as Ben, the truth of the tale is in its intent rather than its reality. "Rogers hates me," Ben would write in his diary in 1834. "I can hardly believe, as he gives out, that V[ivian] G[rey] is ye cause. Considering his age, I endeavoured to conciliate him, but it is impossible. I think I will give him cause to hate me." Disraeli hardly had to try.

In the first days of June, Ben rushed a message to Benjamin Austen with the usual apologies for nonpayment of debts and the dramatic announcement that he had heard from Wycombe "that the crisis has commenced." He needed a horse quickly, "and if you let me, I will purchase yours." Disraeli was a believer in the shameless adage that debts made the borrower and lender partners. Austen knew that Ben was waiting for the expected resignation of Sir Thomas Baring to campaign for his seat in the Commons. With the Reform Act likely to empty further seats, abolish others, and create new ones, few candidates were likely to arise for a seat with such a short tenure, and in fact the High Wycombe campaign would be the last by-election under the old franchise.

Ben's stance as a candidate posed immediate problems. Although by disposition a Conservative, he could hardly campaign on the party's hostility to Reform, now a discredited issue. "Toryism is worn out," he explained to Austen, "& I cannot condescend to be a Whig." When his hero in *The Young Duke* surveys his alternatives, we see, with some satirical exaggeration, Disraeli's dilemma:

I must be consistent, and not compromise my principles, which will never do in England—more than once a year. Let me see: what are they? Am I a Whig or a Tory? I forget. As for the Tories, I admire antiquity, particularly a ruin. . . . I think I am a Tory. But then the Whigs give such good dinners, and are the most amusing. I think I am a Whig; but then they are so moral and morality is my forte: I must be a Tory. But the

Whigs dress so much better; and an ill-dressed party, like an ill-dressed man, must be wrong. Yes! I am a decided Whig. And yet—I feel like Garrick between Tragedy and Comedy. I think I will be a Whig and a Tory alternate nights. . . . I have no objection, according to the fashion of the day, to take a place under a Tory ministry, provided I may vote against them.

Since no other candidate emerged for so ephemeral a seat, Disraeli hoped that he had only to lay his credentials before the minuscule electorate and distribute a handbill about the hustings to win without challenge. Even a party designation seemed unnecessary, and he declared himself *"decidedly liberal"* in principles and a believer in Reform. He had letters of support to publicize, procured by Bulwer, from the liberal M.P. Joseph Hume and the Irish radical Daniel O'Connell, neither of whom he knew. But the Whigs wanted a real Whig, not an avowed independent, and to Ben's dismay entered Lt. Col. Charles Grey, second son of the Prime Minister.

The same age as Disraeli, Grey—whose considerable rank at twenty-seven was purchasable by influential families—was on half-pay from the army while he acted as a private secretary for his father. While he had no political experience and was a halting speaker, Grey had the prime asset of name recognition—and a name that was not, as was being said, "oriental." Placards appeared in Wycombe announcing his arrival on Saturday afternoon, June 9, to campaign. The quiet canvass Disraeli had hoped for was out, but the afternoon went, nevertheless, to his satisfaction. First, Grey was an hour late. He came, Ben wrote smugly to Sara Austen, "with a hired mob and a band. Never was such a failure. After parading the town with his paid voices, he made a stammering speech of ten minutes from his phaeton."

The crowd outside the Red Lion was ready to be entertained, having been refreshing itself at the bar of the Red Lion since the expected 4:30 arrival. From his carriage, Charles Grey stammered out what he confessed was his first public address—a declaration that he would stand by his father's principles, and that his father had engineered the passage of the great Reform Bill. It was clear to Disraeli that the crowd—unfortunately hardly an eligible voter in it—understood that Grey was a novice with a parent's famous surname.

"I jumped up on the Portico of the Red Lion and gave it [to] them for an hour and ¼," Ben crowed. He discovered that he could raise an audience and keep it listening. Ben was a performer, and not only his costume was theatrical. At one crescendo he pointed dramatically to the life-sized figure of a lion on the portico and prophesied, "When the poll is declared, I shall be there"—he reached out an arm in the direction of the lion's head—"and my opponent," he concluded dramatically, pointing to the lion's tail, "will be there." The crowd roared its appreciation of the candidate's wit.

"I can give you no idea of the effect," he told Sara Austen. "I made them all mad [with delight]. A great many absolutely *cried.* I never made so many friends in my life or converted so many enemies. All the women are on my side—and wear my colors, pink and white. Do the same. The Colonel returned to town in the evening absolutely astounded." Well might Grey have been amazed. Disraeli was at his sarcastic best. The following Wednesday he made his own formal entrance into Wycombe, accompanied by his two brothers and a few friends, standing in an open carriage drawn by four horses. The cost was borne by the complaisant Dr. Bolton, who also put up a bond of £2,500 to prevent the candidate's arrest for debt. Mrs. Bolton had made artificial flowers and tassels in Ben's pink-and-white to be displayed by his supporters, and even a pink and white collar for Sarah's dog—a rival, Clara teased, for her affections.

The carriage had paused en route at the Bird-in-Hand, a public house outside Wycombe, to assemble supporters from nearby villages, and it was a colorful assemblage that entered the borough, although Disraeli himself had determined to eschew color for a look of simple dignity. He wore a coat of black velvet, lined with white satin, beneath which could be seen an embroidered waistcoat across which were displayed several heavy gold chains. His hands, garbed in white kid gloves, clutched an ivory cane with a black tassel.

A band led the way past the Adam-designed marketplace

and the venerable Guild Hall to the Red Lion, where Ben made his formal address. It was, the *Bucks Gazette* reported, an able and amusing speech, and the crowd gaping at Disraeli's splendid costume found itself laughing and cheering. He was sure that he had made a good impression, but few if any lawful voters were present. Still, he had carefully sought out the other M.P. in the two-candidate borough, Robert Smith (later the 2nd Lord Carrington), to ensure his neutrality. Smith had given no assurances, but Disraeli thought that he detected no enthusiasm for Grey.

In the days leading up to the balloting on June 26, it became clear that Smith was using his considerable local influence in the Colonel's behalf. Yet such efforts were hardly necessary as Disraeli had exposed his Tory loyalties by appointing as his manager a party hack, John Nash, while enlisting the public support of the unpopular Tory mayor, John Carter.

The election procedures, three weeks after the Reform Bill had become law, were a mixture of new and old. A hustings was erected before the town hall for the "open" election, yet the candidates were formally nominated inside the hall with only the mayor and his burgesses present. At thirty minutes after noon, the candidates were introduced and Mayor Carter made a speech announcing that future elections would give more citizens the right to vote. Then a second and open nomination ceremony placed Disraeli and Grey before the electorate, and each was given a final opportunity to speak.

When the cheers and catcalls died down, Disraeli promised to promote Reform and the happiness of the many over the benefits of the few. Offering brevity to his opponent's brilliance, Grey promised to support the abolition of unnecessary government jobs that were a burden upon the taxpayer. Then most of the few eligible voters appeared to cast ballots, with the tally for Grey 20 votes to Disraeli's 12.

The announcement made, Grey rose to thank his electors. Disraeli charged up and lashed at Baring and Smith and others who promised not to interfere, and attacked the *Bucks Gazette* for favoritism. As Baring tried to respond, a Disraeli claque drowned him out, but the boos faded when the traditional ceremony of chairing the winner began and Grey was cheered by the departing throng.

For Disraeli the campaign had hardly begun. Since Parliament would be dissolved by the end of the year, the very next month he began to canvass the future "ten pound householders." The Reform Act continued the franchise for adult males who owned freehold property valued at an income of no less than forty shillings a year. It conferred the franchise on adult males with a leasehold worth at least £10 a year, or who rented land for cultivation worth £50 a year. In borough constituencies, adult males who owned or occupied rental property worth £10 a year qualified for the vote if they had paid all property taxes, had proved a one-year residency, and had not been on poor relief in any of the previous twelve months.

Also, anyone eligible under any system now voided retained eligibility, and the rules might be evaded by any male of means or influence via a receipt for a year's lease or other qualifying paper. And while the £10 qualification was the key to vastly greater urban representation, the basic ascendancy of the governing class remained what it had been before 1832. In 1831, 366,000 adult males in England and Wales had been eligible to vote. Following the Reform Bill, 653,000 voters were franchised—still only eighteen percent of adult males. Elsewhere the extension of the franchise was more dramatic only because so few had been eligible before. In Scotland, where a handful of voters had elected members to Parliament, the numbers rose from 4,000 to 64,000; in Ireland from 39,000 to 93,000. At the least, the door to the popular vote had been pushed ajar.

Addressed to "the Free and Independent Electors of Wycombe," Disraeli's announcement of new candidacy cloaked as a concession statement recognized the broader base of the franchise, and promised that the last election was only "the first struggle" for the emancipation of the borough from "foreign" hands—the Grey family. "Gentlemen," he declared from Bradenham on June 27, 1832, "there are instances in which defeat is no disgrace, and victory no triumph."

For the General Election under the Reform rules in December, three candidates emerged for the two Wycombe seats. With the reelection of Robert Smith a foregone conclusion, the contest was again between Grey and Disraeli, who, despite his Bradenham House address, was as much an outsider as Grey. His life was in London, and—what was even more apparent to his Buckinghamshire electorate—so was his life-style. While accepting his advertising, the *Bucks Gazette* chided him in an editorial as politically a Tory in Whig clothing, and personally only a dandy from a constituency of Mayfair fops. "Good Mr. Disraeli," it lectured him, "this will never do. This is more ridiculous than the fopperies of the ebony cane, or the ruffled shirt, or the capers you cut upon the hustings."

While Disraeli's Byronic garb was being castigated as inappropriate for the representative of a staid chair-manufacturing town, Byron's Tita turned up in Buckinghamshire, and at Ben's request, Giovanni Falcieri was hired by Isaac to be a factotum at Bradenham. Tita was, Ben wrote to John Murray, Byron's publisher, "one of the most deserving creatures in the world" and "so intimately connected with the lost bard." And in that same first week in July, Isaac went off to Byron's alma mater, Oxford, to receive an honorary doctorate in Civil Law. An honorary degree was the only kind open to a Jew.* Modestly, he had written to Benjamin Austen, "I have myself a public engagement which must take me to . . . the University of Oxford—on the 1st or 2nd of July to receive the honorary degree there." And he added, almost certainly a comment upon his son's quixotic aspirations for office: "As for politics I really wish not to interchange an opinion with any one. Both parties as usual are equally unreasonable."

Although the London "season" was ebbing, Ben remained. "Madame"—Clara Bolton—was still in town, and for Disraeli her services were more than personal. In his diary he noted cynically, "Bolton and his wife, a decoy duck." Her political salon, he explained to Sarah, who remained appalled but largely uncomplaining, was "better than a club." Until the next Wycombe campaign

---

*Until 1854 non-Anglicans could not matriculate and graduate B.A. at Oxford; until 1871 only Anglicans could receive an M.A. The exclusions did not apply to honorary degrees, as such recipients did not belong to the university, often being foreign dignitaries of diverse faiths.

geared up in the autumn, he was pressing to finish *Alroy*, "who flourishes," he wrote to Sarah on August 4, "like a young cedar of Lebanon."

When Clara departed London, Ben decamped for Bradenham with Bulwer, but returned when Mrs. Bolton came back, "quite recovered, altho' with a slight scar," he reported to Sarah, suggesting that Clara had undergone minor surgery. For Sarah it was all a relief, as it postponed indefinitely the visit to Bradenham that Mrs. Bolton was proposing to make and which the embarrassed D'Israelis could not have refused.

Just as the campaigning season resumed in October, Ben received the bad news that Murray had refused to consider *Alroy*— even to read it. Despite private praise from such literati as Madame D'Arblay (the novelist Fanny Burney) and William Beckford, *Contarini Fleming* had been a public failure. Colburn, who had quarreled with his partner Richard Bentley, was temporarily without financing to continue in business. Desperate for money to stall his creditors, Disraeli turned to Saunders and Otley, now in the fashionable novel trade. *Alroy* was clearly unfashionable in content, but the new publishers may have banked on Disraeli's return thereafter to fiction of the "silver fork" variety. Quickly, Disraeli turned over the £300 to his chief banker, Benjamin Austen, clearing up all but the interest on the loan which had made *Alroy* possible, and he began trying, through Austen and "Tremaine" Ward, to secure a spurious property qualification in another county, in order to run a third time for the Commons if, as he expected, his second Wycombe bid failed. In August he had visited the House and chatted with his rival, Charles Grey, even conceiving a liking for him. (In later years they would conduct the Queen's business together in amity.)

Again Ben ran as Radical independent, denying to the electorate of Wycombe in his manifesto of October 1 that he was employing "that much abused epithet" to "escape an explicit avowal of my opinions." Explicitly, he vowed "to ameliorate the condition of the lower orders, to rouse the dormant energies of the country, to liberate our shackled industry, and re-animate our expiring credit." As for the notorious Corn Laws, which protected domestic grain producers by levying heavy duties on imported grain, almost putting bread out of reach of city dwellers, Disraeli ambiguously offered to support "any change the basis of which is to relieve the consumer without injuring the farmer." In general he offered fence-sitting positions which might enable him, if elected, to join either major party. Queried about Ben's political beliefs, Clara Bolton averred that her protégé was "v[ery] wise not to quibble at such minor things as . . . scraps of paper."

With *Alroy* now in press and other novels behind him, Disraeli knew that he could not escape from innuendo about his Jewishness and from dismissal as a hack writer. Neither allegation would come, he knew, from Charles Grey, but on November 10 *The Times* reported remarks by a Whig candidate for the county, John Cam Hobhouse (later Lord Broughton), who had been a friend of Byron, that Disraeli was known to his countrymen only as "the author of a few miserable novels in which he had described either the society in which he had lived himself, or a state of society which had no existence." *The Times* noted "cheers and laughter," after which Dr. George Mitford, also on the platform, observed that in his county of Berkshire "they were not troubled with any Jews." Despite the wider franchise and his legal residence in Bradenham, Disraeli remained an outsider, and the loans he received, backed by Bulwer and Clay this time, were only additions to a burgeoning debt. As a politician, Disraeli remained a poor investment.

On December 12 he was at the bottom of the poll. To Smith's 179 and Grey's 140, Disraeli managed only 119 votes. It was his last run as an independent. To a friend, Mrs. Bolton explained that Ben was "a new man without any party." He would not repeat the mistake.

Early in 1833 Disraeli made two abortive attempts to run elsewhere, but withdrew when official candidates were proposed by the Tories. He was moving in the direction of the Conservatives, and considered himself a "Radical Tory." In his own way he would always be that, proposing his candidacy abortively at Marylebone with the themes of government by "great spirits"— men of character and charisma—who could "maintain the glory of the Empire and . . . secure the happiness of the People." Men, in other words, like the future Disraeli.

VIII

"... A FAIR LADY OF MY ACQUAINTANCE."

1833–1834

DISRAELI WOULD CONTEST WYCOMBE WITH COLONEL GREY ONCE more, in 1834, but as 1833 began he was busy with other ventures, political, literary, pecuniary—and amatory. From his fantasy world in which he could not separate ambition from reality he claimed to publishers Saunders and Otley, who were preparing *Alroy* for release in March, that he would "give up Literature" unless he could assure himself of £3,000 a year by it—a baronial sum. Then he went off with Bulwer for a holiday in Bath, living on borrowed funds as if he had the dreamed-of income.

In its architecture and its amusements Bath seemed suspended in the century of the first Georges, but Bulwer and Disraeli avoided the fashionable parts of town, taking furnished rooms at a pound a week each in a quiet area where they could spend the daylight hours remote from distractions, smoking Latakia tobacco and plying their pens. Bulwer was finishing *England and the English*, which he would dedicate to Isaac D'Israeli. Ben was under greater pressure. Saunders and Otley had found *Alroy* too short to be stretched into the conventional three volumes, and wanted a short fiction to pad out the last volume. What Ben produced was the Eastern tale "The Rise of Iskander," which took a week and read as if it had. He told Sarah that it was "a pretty thing," but it was largely an imaginative recasting of his Albanian adventure.

For friends who wanted shorter works from him, he had already completed, and in part published, a classical pastiche, "Ixion in Heaven," which appeared in Colburn's *New Monthly Magazine* in December 1832 and February 1833. A reviewer in *The Age* acknowledged its cleverness but labeled it not "very Christian-like," a failing attributed not to its being in the spirit of Lucian but to the author's "Jewish persuasion." The charge, based entirely on his name, better fit *The Wondrous Tale of Alroy*, published that March, of which critic William Maginn—once rumored as the author of *Vivian Grey*—wrote in *Fraser's Magazine* in May, "O' reader dear! do pray a look here, and you will spy the curly hair and forehead fair, and nose so high and gleaming eye of Benjamin Dis-ra-e-li, the wondrous boy who wrote *Alroy*, in rhyme and prose, only to show, how long ago victorious Judah's banner rose. . . ." With it appeared a pen and ink portrait by Daniel Maclise of a younger-than-life, Byronic, Disraeli.

Maclise's portrait was more of a success than the novel, which, while it went into a second printing, only served politically to confirm Disraeli's unacceptable Jewishness. He had described it as "the secret history of my feelings," the last work in a trilogy that left his ambitions no secret whatever. Brazenly, *Alroy* declared in effect that if English society turned upon aristocratic ancestry, its author could win at the game of lineage. David Alroy, of the blood of King David, boasts his "deep conviction of superior race" and dreams of leading his scattered people to Jerusalem. He fails, done in by a latter-day Delilah, the novel's Schirene, daughter of the Caliph of Baghdad, but Disraeli had no intention of letting his ambitions succumb to fleshly delights. In fact, the most interesting females in his social world, an increasingly elegant one ranging from Upper Bohemia to Upper Crust, remained older women with powers beyond the bedroom. Lady Stepney, he told Sarah, was "a very young old woman indeed"—

she was about fifty—and authoress Mrs. Sheridan, who had three dazzling daughters, was "very young and pretty" at fifty-four. Despite the passionate Schirene, another woman loomed significantly between the lines of *Alroy*, the hero's sister, Miriam, for whom he has a "pure and perfect love," much as Benjamin had for the dedicatee of the novel, Sarah. The Sheridan sisters were drawn to Schirene, and one of them, Helen Blackwood, wife of a naval officer and later Marchioness of Dufferin, even signed her letters to Benjamin "Schirene." But Disraeli needed the influential society hostesses more, even the octogenarian Countess of Cork and Orrery, once an intimate of Dr. Samuel Johnson, who would become the racy Lady Bellair in *Henrietta Temple*.

Helen Blackwood, however, was a favorite of Disraeli's, not a vehicle for his ambitions, and when she announced that she was enchanted by the quirky *Curiosities of Literature* and wanted to meet the author, Disraeli worked at persuading his difficult father. Isaac was reclusive at best, and unhappy about what he knew of his son's debts, the extent of which Benjamin could hardly confess. One day, however (as the Blackwoods' son, Frederick, then a child, later recalled), Disraeli appeared in Helen's drawing room with Isaac in tow. Looking at his father "as if he were a piece of ornamental china," he began, "Madam, I have brought you my father. I have been reconciled to my father on two conditions. The first was that he should come to see you; the second that he should pay my debts."

However modest their commercial success, Disraeli's novels enhanced his social successes, which he attempted to parlay into political ones—something the Sheridan sisters predicted would be impossible. His audacity, which Helen felt was awesome, was exceeded only by his dress. When she first met him at a dinner party, so she told American diplomat and historian John Lothrop Motley in 1858, it included "a black velvet coat lined with satin, purple trousers with a gold band running down the outside seam, a scarlet waistcoat, long lace ruffles falling down to the tips of his fingers, white gloves with several brilliant rings outside them, and long black ringlets rippling down his shoulders." Since she liked him, Mrs. Blackwood warned that he was making a fool of himself by a costume more fantastic than anyone with serious aspirations ought to display, and he began to modify his plumage, although not his audacity, which was his weapon against ridicule.

Caroline Norton, her sister, was not yet separated from her boorish barrister husband, a failed Tory politician who had lost his seat in the Commons in 1830 and was appointed a police magistrate by Lord Melbourne, with whom she had found more congenial consolation. Melbourne, a handsome widower whose late wife, Lady Caroline Lamb, had been notorious for her tragicomic relationship with Lord Byron, could hardly keep the liaison discreet, as Caroline Norton, one of the writing Sheridans, wrote popular, if trashy, society novels, and was nearly as much of an exhibitionist as Disraeli. Yet at a dinner given by her husband before their separation she had been flabbergasted by Disraeli's reckless wit. George Chapple Norton, "my insufferable brother-in-law" in Lady Dufferin's description to Motley, had offered Disraeli a glass of wine with the claim that his guest had never tasted a vintage that fine. Sipping it, Disraeli agreed that it was indeed very good. "Well," Norton boasted, "I have got wine twenty times as good in my cellar."

"No doubt, no doubt," said Disraeli as he looked at the others round the table, "but, my dear fellow, this is quite good enough for such *canaille* as you have got today."

Memorable, too, was Disraeli's quip at a dinner where waiters had served cuisine turned tepid after being trundled long distances from the kitchens below. When his glass was filled he sighed dramatically, setting his wine down after a sip, "Thank God for something warm at last!"

Such episodes were consistent with his love of the theatrical gesture, which some critics claimed had gone too far in his newest novel. Still, in the *Court Journal*, Catherine Gore saw the "wild excess" in *Alroy* as a new style which might be imitated by other writers of historical fiction. It carried over unhelpfully, however, into his oratorical manner and his political writings, which he hoped might lead political power brokers to find him a safe parliamentary seat. His problem, unfortunately, was that his manner suggested that he was not a sufficiently safe candidate, and an opening in the London constituency of Marylebone was not offered to him.

He looked for other opportunities, and also for a marriage of political advantage, particularly among the heiresses whose prospective fortunes might relieve him of his debts. One candidate was Lady Charlotte Bertie, who was clever and literary but very likely had nothing like the £25,000 a year Ben thought she possessed. Even at that, Sarah warned jealously that "improvident blood more than half fills her veins."

Having met Ben in one of his Byronic moments at the premiere of Rossini's *Tancredi* at the King's Theatre, Charlotte described him in a diary entry for May 18 as "wild, enthusiastic, and poetical. . . . The brilliancy of my companion infected me and we ran on about poetry, about Venice, and Baghdad, and Damascus, and my eye lit up and my cheek burned, and in the pause of the beautiful music . . . my words flowed almost as rapidly as his. He tells me that . . . nothing could compensate him for an obscure youth—not even glorious old age. I cannot understand his trying to get into Parliament. . . . With all his enthusiasm and contradictions he pleased me and we were very good friends, I think."

Charlotte Bertie was obviously ripe for wooing, but Ben's parents and sister wanted him to settle down with a Meredith sister. Only one remained. He was too late for Georgina, who married in May, and soon was considered insufficiently serious by Ellen, who received what she realized was a perfunctory offer. Mrs. Meredith, Sarah reported, was "annihilated" by Ben's loveless proposal, and relations between the families became strained.

It did not help that Ben's father was having the firm of Moxon publish at the same time—in order to capitalize upon the publicity of *Alroy*—his crotchety book *The Genius of Judaism*. Although Isaac's thrust was that Judaism was a religious fossil, with dietary and other ritual practices that were obsolete—he raised pigs at Bradenham as if to prove his point—he also confirmed by the book another Judaic link with his ostensibly Anglican son. And almost despite his convictions, or his claimed lack of them, Isaac found "many admirable things" in Jewish religious literature, in the *Gemara* and in the Talmud—"beautiful inventions," he insisted as a confirmed Voltairean. But he was also devoted to the works of the German-Jewish philosopher of the European Enlightenment, Moses Mendelssohn (grandfather of the composer), who perceived danger in all dogmatic religions. Isaac saw the ideal outcome as the assimilation of Jewish genius into the majority religion—not for theological reasons but for humanistic ones. It would not happen, he predicted, through Christian missionary efforts, to which Jews would be forever hostile, but only through their perceived natural affinities.

Although Ben would later find much of that view politic, there was none of it in the deeply felt *Alroy*. His father, however, crankily aloof from his brethren, required reinforcement of his prejudices, which Ben, eager for Isaac's support, sometimes supplied. In a particularly nasty example, several years later (December 15, 1835), he told his father of meeting Isaac Lyon Goldsmid, financier, philanthropist, a founder of the University of London and University College Hospital, and leader in the Ashkenazic community—Jews whose post-exile origins were north of the Mediterranean. Friendly with the Whig leaders who sought Jewish emancipation and in 1841 the first Jewish baronet, Goldsmid was on the opposite political side. "I had great fun with Isaac [and his son] about the holy people," Ben crowed, "and quizzed them very much." (*Quizzed* was used in the now obsolete sense of *ridiculed.*) "I asked the son, if he were Jew, why he called himself Francis Henry; and I quizzed and mystified them in every possible manner, and opened their minds. They gaped and received the oracles with staring eyes."

It was not one of Benjamin's finer moments. The younger Goldsmid, whom Benjamin also labeled "a solemn fool," would be, as Sir Francis, the first Jewish Q.C. in 1858 and Liberal M.P. from Reading in 1859. He might well have responded by asking D'Israeli the Younger, as he was often referred to, why as a Christian he retained his Hebraic names. Given the possibility of such a rejoinder, the substance of the encounter may have been largely an invention to amuse his father. Whether or not it happened, the letter reflected Ben's own discomfort about his equivocal identity.

In his dedication of *Alroy, or The Prince of the Captivity* to Sarah, Benjamin linked her to a gazelle he had seen in the mountains of Zion, and his sister had responded with gratitude for "all the beautiful expressions of love you have poured out to me." But Benjamin needed a physical passion more than a paper one, with none of the cynicism of a Clara Bolton type of relationship or the sentiment of a marriage that would damage his hopes.

Alroy hurt his ambitions far less than its absurdities and its linkages with Judaism might have, given the times. In *Fraser's Magazine* in May he appeared in the "Gallery of Literary Characters" as a "clever fellow" with some "striking books" but "preposterous" politics and "fustian" language. In truth his political ideas were still so unfocused that he could repeat to Sarah a joke about himself that had been going the rounds. Having allegedly offered himself for the seat at Marylebone, he was asked on what he intended to stand and he gibed, "On my head!"

Despite rebuffs he was in excellent humor. "A fair lady of my acquaintance"—as he described her deceptively casually to a friend—offered to stage a "political dejeuner" for him, and she was soon seeing him at other times of the day—and night. Henrietta Sykes, the Henrietta Temple of the later novel, was the dark-haired, bosomy wife of Sir Francis Sykes. A baronet whose family had become wealthy in the East India trade, he possessed a country house, Basildon Park; a yacht on which he spent much time, allegedly for his health; and a town house in Upper Grosvenor Street, a short walk from Disraeli's bachelor quarters at 35 Duke Street. The daughter of Henry Villebois of Marham Hall, Suffolk, the sultry Henrietta had married Sir Francis in 1821, when Ben was not yet seventeen, and had borne him four children, the oldest then eleven, and all of them usually kept out of sight in the country.

Since the Sykeses had done their marital duty, Sir Francis now felt free to indulge his health obsessions, which required fishing and shooting and the ministrations of the ubiquitous Dr. George Buckley Bolton. Sykes also found the intimacies of Mrs. Bolton therapeutic, as once had Ben, and Clara and Sykes were content to go out in public together if Lady Sykes were appropriately chaperoned, which to Sir Francis meant encouraging Henrietta's interest in Disraeli. With Dr. Bolton off elsewhere counting his money, a very agreeable quartet might have arranged itself, the more comfortable for Sykes's preference for distant venues more conducive to health than London. But Clara Bolton balked at including Disraeli. He had been disloyal to her—the very reason why she had sought new consolation—and was to be excluded from the arrangements. She insisted that Henrietta find a substitute lover.

Disraeli's bliss had been immediate, passionate, and public. And it was reciprocated. He and Henrietta were seen at the opera (once with Lady Charlotte Bertie, to confuse prying eyes), at dinner parties (one at the Wyndham Lewises' that first April), at ro-

Henrietta, Lady Sykes. *Painted by A. E. Chalon (from* Heath's Book of Beauty, *1837).*

mantic walks in Hyde Park, at Lady Sykes's weekly ball at her town house. No bluestocking beauty like the Sheridan sisters, Henrietta was interested in *bon société*, in entertainments, in "that white couch" (as she told Ben), and in pillow talk.

To Henrietta he was quickly "Amin"—and she was already too possessive about her Amin to buy "Madame's" bargain. She "wrote and destroyed a dozen notes" to Clara, "some too hot, others too cold," Henrietta explained in a letter to Disraeli about her determination to have it out with Mrs. Bolton in person:

At last, thinks I, I will walk [to Park Lane] and tell her my opinion upon the fracas between myself and my Lord. I did so, found *his* cab[riole]t at the door, which was open, walked in sans knocking, and up to the drawing room sans being announced. Fancy their consternation! I really thought Francis would have fainted.

Lady S (stiff as a poker and perfectly cool): "Mrs Bolton I have called upon you in consequence of a scene which I am perfectly aware I owe entirely to you and I am here to have an understanding, as from what has passed there can be no reserve betwixt us three. Sir F is aware of my role, this intimacy with Disraeli. It has suited all parties to be a great deal together, not certainly from the intimacy of the Ladies, for I have never expressed a friendship for you. I have never been even commonly Ladylike in my conduct to you, and when together Disraeli and I, Francis and you, formed two distinct parties, and . . . should he leave London tomorrow your doors *I would never enter.* . . . I will give Francis the sanction of my acquiescence on the strict condition of his not again violating by unjust and ungenerous threats ties which he himself has sanctioned and which both himself and yourself *know* have been necessary to carry on your own game. . . . So chuse. Before I leave this House the solemn promise must be given *never* to mention Disraeli's name as a bug bear."

Mrs Bolton: "It was from Disappointment I complained and not from malice. Disraeli is a heartless

wretch. I have stuck up for him for years. Our acquaintance has been of nine years standing. *Here are his letters*, vowing undying friendship, unspeakable obligation,
but I repay them now with scorn. As for you and I, I
have too much dignity to wish our acquaintance on any
other footing than you have placed it. Disraeli has influenced his *dear* family to desert me, witness his father
never having called upon me, and through him your
character has gone—I heard from good authority. No
one would visit you next year on his account and he
will leave you, he has left you, I know him well and he
is everywhere despised."

I was enraged and contradicted the falsehood but
dearest even if memory would serve of what avail would
be the repetition of our eloquence? Suffice for you and
I that we are victorious. Madame cried and wrung her
hands. F[rancis] cried and begged me to be merciful. I
did *not cry* and had apologies from both.

With new license to love Henrietta, and such evidence of
her tigerish devotion, Disraeli wore her like a jewel. At Bradenham House his family worried about what they were hearing from
London, although little information came from Ben. "Your silence," Sarah wrote on May 12, ". . . gives us much pain and anxiety," and Isaac added, "You cannot imagine how greatly I am
distressed by your unaccountable silence. I never ask you for idle
letters—but nearly a fortnight has elapsed and we do not know
how or where you are!" Sarah had already been furnished half
truths in lighthearted letters from her brother, and might have
guessed from the number of references to "Lady Sykes"—usually
tucked into laundry lists of fashionable people—that she was no
ordinary socialite and certainly no dowager hostess. It should
have been no surprise when, early in June, Ben pried an invitation to Bradenham for her, "as Sir Fra[nci]s is going down in the
yacht for a week. . . . My mother need not be alarmed as it is impossible for anyone to be more perfectly unaffected, and give less
trouble."

Curiously it was at the same time that Ben had received,

through Sarah, a definitive no from the Meredith family about betrothal to Ellen, on grounds that no affection existed between them. Ben had hardly seen Ellen, and the "cutting indifference" with which he had been charged was genuine. He had never offered that fraud called "Love," he explained to Sarah, who thought she had been in love with the dead Meredith and would wear her bereavement all her life. In the circles in which Ben moved, marriage often made love possible—but with someone else. A young man, he later thought, should ripen under the ministrations of a married woman before he settled into marriage himself. "For my part," he wrote a political associate years after, "I think that even Princes sh[oul]d sow their wild oats, & not step out as paterfamilias from the nursery, or middy's berth."

With Henrietta there was no possibility of marriage, much opportunity for intimacies, and a certainty of scandal. Upper Bohemia accepted complaisant husbands, gentlemen escorts, and aristocratic ladies of light virtue not actually caught *en flagrante;* the country preferred quieter dalliances where looking the other way was possible. To ward off the worst gossip, Lady Sykes arrived with her maid, her page, and Eva, her three-year-old daughter, for a weekend which stretched into midweek and stretched the resources of the house. If Disraeli attempted to deflect tattling tongues by taking Lady Sykes on a visit to Velvet Lawn as a Sunday outing, it served more to expose her to the local squirearchy. Velvet Lawn, the grounds of Chequers Court (now the official residence of each prime minister), was known for its deep green, mossy turf, and the occasion—fashionable country folk visiting the exotic setting—suggested to Disraeli a *fête champêtre* masque he would set down when Sarah asked him to compose something to be printed and sold for benefit of the Buckinghamshire Infirmary.

A month later he confessed to Sarah that "not a word" had yet been written. Then he hastily penned a sketch, signed "by the author of *Vivian Grey,*" for performance by a narrator, dancers, and singers. A pastoral paean to the Vale of Aylesbury, "so fair and soothing after all the rustle & turmoil of what is called 'the World,'" it included a Disraeliesque young man—"The Green Cavalier"—in green velvet who thrills to a young lady playing a guitar, a Black page in crimson, a "Ritornella" by a "Baron" who sings, "Now is the hour / to leave thy bower," and further lyrics of equivalent quality.

Despite his new passion for Henrietta, one ballad—he would put it in his novel *Henrietta Temple*—evoked the defeated Disraeli of past history:

My heart is like a silent lute
Some careless hand has thrown aside;
Those chords are dumb, these lines are mute,
That once sent forth a voice of praise.

But after a drinking song in which another knight "pledges that . . . this earth / That has seen our mirth / Shall now count as holy ground," the Lady orders everyone to the Castle, "but not before we have seen the silver moon rise upon *Velvet Lawn*."

Printed in seventy-five copies at Sarah's order for sale at the hospital's benefit bazaar, it survives in only one copy at Windsor Castle. But it represented Disraeli as sensitive to his county's philanthropies while leaving him free to cultivate his larger ambitions in what he had described in *Velvet Lawn* as "the rustle and turmoil" of "the World," which to him remained London. There, a leading article on Saturday, June 15, would paraphrase from one of his political pamphlets on the "aristocratic principle" in government. A validation of how he might best employ his pen, it was more than a massage to his ego. Political writing might earn for him that next chance at a Parliamentary seat.

Ben owed Sarah something and intervened with Rivingtons about the firm's publishing a Sunday school catechism she had written which exemplified the family's manner of handling what remained of their Jewishness. The "fair author," Ben explained, realizing that the New Testament is put into the hands of children unversed in the Old, has "repaired their ignorance of the preceding Scriptures" and its "history of the peculiar people of God, and the connection of the prophecies from the time of Abraham to their completion in the coming of our Saviour." That was about as pious as he would get regarding the faith adopted for him, toward which his adherence remained broadly political and an inch deep.

While evading Austen and the payments of overdue debts, Disraeli continued to cut a playboy swath across Upper Bohemia. Often with Lady Sykes, he sampled "the cream of blueism"— intellectual ladies—at Madame la Marquise de Montalembert's, met "all the Bonapartes . . . at Lady Cork's," and at Letetia Mitford's on Upper Berkeley Street, at a private concert by diva Maria Malibran, he fancied the contralto (a favorite of young Princess Victoria) as heroine of an opera based upon his *Alroy*. With Ben entangled with a married lady and nuptials for him an unlikely prospect, Mary Anne Wyndham Lewis, who was often in his orbit and among the many older women seeking to arrange his future, married off her husband's Dowlais iron foundry partner, Josiah John Guest, to Charlotte Bertie. His "flame," Ben told Sarah, was going to marry "a Croesus of the forge, . . . older than Wyndham, much uglier. . . . So much for a romantic lady." For Ben, romance and marriage remained things apart. For the moment, one had crowded out the other. As Lady Charlotte Guest, and then as a wealthy, remarriageable widow, she would indulge her collecting interests—and also translate the Welsh epic *The Mabionogion*.

Sarah pressed him for "the truth" about his London life, but Ben responded to Sarah's curiosity only by sending a box of venison from Lady Sykes with her overdue bread and butter letter. When he went to Southend in Essex in November to work on his intended claim to Byronic political fame, *The Revolutionary Epick*, it was no surprise to Sarah that although he had two rooms of his own and claimed to eat breakfast alone, Porter's Grange, his address, was actually a property rented by Sir Francis Sykes. The sea air, he reported, agreed with him, but more agreeable was the company, especially since Sir Francis preferred shooting birds in the North to remaining at home. Disraeli found rapture in indoor sport.

Through February (1834), when not with Henrietta, Disraeli put his hours into his political poem, its third book, he boasted to Sarah, surpassing his "most sanguine expectations." By the last day of November he had contracted with Saunders and Otley to publish the epic as well as a future novel but still needed infusions of money and tried the device of writing to Sara Austen for advice on the poem while pleading separately to her husband for a further loan. He had reduced his personal expenses to almost nothing, he told Benjamin Austen honestly, not explaining how he had managed the feat. The new work would be his *Childe Harold*. "The conception," he told Mrs. Austen, "seems to me sublime. All depends on the execution."

Austen responded that he "looked . . . with fear and trembling" upon Ben's activities, and had been "tried too often." Writing under a Bradenham address, Ben lied in return that all his debts were "electioneering expenses," and that he did not want to appeal to his father because in seeking a political career "I have opposed his most earnest wishes." Meanwhile, seeking funds by other means, he offered (from Southend) publisher Richard Bentley a short novel he had written with his sister, based upon his failed electioneering career, *A Year at Hartlebury*. It was equal, he assured Bentley, to *Vivian Grey* and possessed "the elements of great popularity."

Work on the novel (on Ben's part, largely in the late summer of 1833 before he returned to Henrietta's bosom) was his effort to find occupation for his sister other than in handling Ben's or their father's affairs. He had already intervened with Rivingtons for her, and she was attempting to find a niche with essays, poems, and stories that evidenced only a frail talent. Having given great anxiety to his family, which watched, they thought, Ben's genius frenetically wasting itself on vain ambitions, he cooperated in Sarah's efforts to find herself in fiction, leaving her the nonpolitical elements of the plot, and writing his portions in her labored style before escaping to Southend and Henrietta.

Hartlebury Manor was Bradenham House; Sarah was the novel's heroine, Miss Helen Molesworth; the young radical politician, Aubrey Bohun, was Ben. The authors signed themselves "Cherry and Fair Star," curiously the title of an Easter melodrama, *Cherry and Fair Star or, The Children of Cyprus*, of anonymous authorship, which opened at the Theatre Royal, Covent Garden, on April 8, 1822. Had Ben, at seventeen, seen it? More likely, Sarah had remembered it (it had been revived in 1832), seizing the names for her novel and writing a curious preface identifying the joint authors as husband and wife. With the likelihood of marrying gone, she had hoped to remain surrogate wife to Ben, a role now fast vanishing. If the novel succeeded, perhaps she could keep him at least as collaborator, sharing a life in the lines of their manuscripts. "Our honeymoon being over," she wrote in the preface as "Fair Star," "we have amused ourselves during the autumn by writing a novel. All we hope is that the Public will deem our literary union as felicitous as we find our personal one."

When Bentley returned it, Sarah asked Ben to offer the novel to the publishers of *Alroy*. Saunders and Otley estimated its marginal worth by offering £20 for it, possibly on the strength of Ben's nine chapters on Bohun's election in the second volume. Sarah wrote most of the rest, including, at the close, the blackmailed Bohun's unexplained murder, as he is going to a rendezvous with a tavernkeeper's wife. A review in *The Examiner* (April 27, 1834) would see "no trace of a female hand in the book," a strange observation after such unmuscular lines as "The sun was rising in the light blue sky, and spangled the dewy grass and glittering hawthorn with drops of lustre." It was not a work for the ages, and Ben did not offer to collaborate further, effectively ending Sarah's career in fiction. Yet a little of Disraeli lives in Bohun's "If I live, I must be a great man."

At Christmas, while Henrietta returned to London and her children, Ben evaded Bradenham and worked on the *Epick* at Southend. It was as perverse an effort, in its way, as *Alroy* had been, but Disraeli had not yet learned to exploit his authentic strengths. Decades later he explained to Lady Bradford about *Alroy* that since his generation had become "satiated" by verse of great poets he had been determined "to give them poetry without numbers. . . . Society decided against the experiment and it was a disappointment to me." Neither was he a satirical poet in the fashion of Pope or Byron, and the writing did not come easily. As he confessed to Sarah about his additions and corrections, estimating that he still had "something like 1,500 lines" to write, "If blotting will make a perfect poem, mine ought to be eternal." By

February he was more optimistic. "The book," he assured her, still from Southend, "surpasses all my hopes."

Among his hopes was that the Duke of Wellington, a Tory icon, would accept the dedication, and in early March, still secluded in Southend, he appealed to the "immortal name." Cautiously, writing at right angles across the lines of Disraeli's letter, the Duke, on March 7, although "much flattered," declined the dubious honor. The verses went to press without a dedication and the first of what would be three small volumes appeared on Tuesday, March 25. (The second and third were ready in June.)

Isaac offered fatherly praise that concealed a warning. "I am struck by the sublimity of the theme," he wrote on March 14, "by the many vigorous passages exquisitely argued—highly original. . . . You have put to the test the public attention for a mode of writing . . . which had become obsolete." If he achieved his object, Isaac concluded, it would be "a durable triumph," but Ben should not despair if it were read only by the "few."

By then the author had concluded, as he confessed to Benjamin Austen, whom he was still attempting to solicit, "I am not sanguine of its pleasing the million." And indeed he was correct. Back in London in April after a brief visit to Bradenham, he confided to Sarah that he had checked on sales at Edward Moxon's. "Of the Epick: three copies this week, which Moxon thinks 3 more than he expected."

Reviewing it in the *Monthly Depository*, William Johnson Fox had some frank words for an author in whom he perceived signs of genius yet who was "in danger of being a failure." His advice: "Let him go into Parliament; let him fall in love; let him be converted, and go out into the heathen lands as a missionary; . . . let him do, be, or suffer anything that will give him singleness of aim, concentration, intensity, to his great and varied faculties, and he will be redeemed to the high destiny to which he was born."

Such reaction was far better than Ben had expected. He knew in his heart when committing the work to print that poetry was not his metier, yet also that any activity leading him more effectively into the closed world of politics was worth chancing. For that, Lady Sykes was still useful as an entrée into the right drawing rooms, and after some months apart they were renewing their amours in London, where Disraeli had taken nominal lodgings at 31A Park Street. His actual domicile was 34 Upper Grosvenor Street, with Henrietta. Not only was the arrangement satisfactory to Sir Francis but when he had left for a long holiday on the Continent—this time free from Mrs. Bolton, whom he now regarded, he told Ben, with "disgust"—Disraeli had accompanied him to the Channel boat at Harwich.

Through the spring and summer of 1834 Sarah received at Bradenham letters that detailed the dinners and dances at which Ben preened himself, and in which he would note, lightly, "Lady Sykes was there." She was openly everywhere with Ben, from balls at the great houses to Henrietta's bedroom at Upper Grosvenor Street. In at least one of the luxurious new settings where Disraeli was welcomed with Henrietta, such recklessness was the norm: "Lady Blessington's house," he explained to Sarah early in June, "is a great focus of the [Earl of] Durham party." Durham led the radical wing of the Whigs, and Ben was hoping that splits among the Whigs might lead to another dissolution of Parliament and another electoral opportunity. Yet the real attraction of Gore House, overlooking Hyde Park, was the Countess of Blessington and the exquisite Count D'Orsay, son of a Bonapartist general. That the Count looked on Disraeli as an equal was success of a sort. Thomas Carlyle described the six-foot-three-inch D'Orsay as the Phoebus Apollo of dandyism, "built like a tower, with floods of dark auburn hair, with a beauty, and adornment unsurpassed on this planet."

Connoisseurs of fine cuisine, pictures, books, brilliant company, and spirited conversation still came to Gore House despite its shadow of scandal, their hostess's mode of life supported by her frantic production of romantic novels and her opulent annual. Disraeli would contribute a story, "The Consul's Daughter," for the 1836 number, and Henrietta's sensuous full-length portrait by Alfred Edward Chalon, which Benjamin told Sarah on its completion in July was "marvellous," the painter's "chef d'ouevre," would appear in 1837.

The litany of elegant ladies and peers he would meet at bohemian and fashionable houses and identify to Sarah, who lived vicariously in Ben's letters, would include many whose personalities, and even whose names, he pillaged later for his novels. At the home of Lady Dudley Crichton-Stuart, daughter of Lucien Bonaparte, he encountered the notorious Marquess of Hertford, the future model for Lord Monmouth in Disraeli's *Coningsby* (1844) as well as Thackeray's Lord Steyne in *Vanity Fair* (1847). In the same month of June 1834 he met a Coningsby at Lady Cork's—George Coningsby, 5th Earl of Essex—and a week later, Lady Tankerville (D'Orsay's sister-in-law), whose name, Corisande, he would give to the heroine of *Lothair* (1870).*

A visiting young American writer, Nathaniel Parker Willis, who met Disraeli at Lady Blessington's that hectic June, recorded in the *New York Mirror* "that fiery vein of eloquence which, hearing many times after, and always with new delight, has stamped Disraeli in my mind as the most wonderful talker I have ever had the fortune to meet." Yet Ben could make fun of his own eloquence when he recognized the posturing. "If he catches himself in a rhetorical sentence, he mocks at it in the next breath. He is satirical, contemptuous, pathetic, humorous, everything in a moment." (Disraeli described Willis to Sarah as "highly polished and even elegant"—unusual in a Yankee.) Lady Cork had told Lord Carrington of Ben's social success, he boasted, that he was the finest writer in London and the one who gave *ton* to a party. "He does not care for people," Ben quoted her (June 19), "because they are lords; he must have fashion, or beauty, or wit, or something." She was even having her maid bind his *Epick* in crimson velvet, for which she had laid out seventeen shillings.

Through Lady Tankerville he was able to join Almack's, the most exclusive social club in London, and at a dinner at Caroline Norton's he met Viscount Melbourne, Home Secretary but about to become Prime Minister, and announced that he, Benjamin Disraeli, twice defeated for a seat in the Commons, intended some day to be prime minister himself. Melbourne was politely blunt. "No chance of that in our time. It is all arranged and settled." After Earl Grey, or soon after his immediate successor, Melbourne prophesied, the prime minister would be a peer "who has

---

*The name *Lothair* itself would be anticipated in Disraeli's short story of 1835, "The Carrier-Pigeon."

every requisite for the position, in the prime of life and fame, of old blood, high rank, great fortune, and greater ability. . . . Nobody can compete with Stanley. I heard him the other night in the Commons . . . : he rose like a young eagle above them all. . . . There is nothing like him."

Melbourne meant Edward Stanley. Five years Disraeli's elder, Lord Stanley had already mastered the House with his rhetoric, and he represented the same political generation. "If you are going to enter politics and mean to stick to it, I dare say you will do very well, for you have ability and enterprise; and if you are careful how you steer, no doubt you will get into some port at last. But you must put all these foolish notions out of your head: they won't do at all."

For Disraeli, who was busy scratching out a satirical short story for Henry Colburn to secure a hundred pounds to live on, it was advice to take very seriously. For a political career of even modest goals, one needed money and status, and the Stanleys were considered the uncrowned kings of Lancashire. Sir John Stanley of the manor of Stanlegh, founder of the family's fortunes, had emerged in the reign of Edward II. The Stanleys had acquired castles and estates and influence through a succession of sovereigns. Sir John's grandson, the 1st Earl of Derby, had placed the crown of Richard III upon the head of Henry VII at Bosworth Field in 1485. What business had a young upstart, whose Jewish grandfather had come from Cento in Italy to sell straw hats, to aspire to become prime minister?

IX

"... THE DAZZLING FARCE OF LIFE."

1834–1837

IN HENRY COLBURN'S *NEW MONTHLY MAGAZINE* FOR JULY AND AU-
gust 1834, Disraeli published "The Infernal Marriage," clever di-
alogues in the manner of Lucian, about the carrying off of the
beautiful Proserpine by Pluto. The satire suggested something of
the author's wry realism about himself. "I have no [good] opinion
of a literary son-in-law," says Jupiter to Proserpine's mother, Ce-
res, about Apollo as alternative husband for their daughter.
"These scribblers are at present the fashion, and are very well to
ask to dinner but I confess a more intimate connection with them
is not at all to my taste." And, says Tantalus about the values of
religious propriety, "I am convinced . . . that, provided a man frequent the temples, and observe with strictness the sacred festivals,
such is the force of public opinion, that there is no crime which
he may not commit without hazard."

"Long live hypocrisy!" exclaims Ixion. ". . . If I began life
anew, I would be more observant in my sacrifices."

In such hastily written pieces, completed too quickly for

second thoughts, is the private Ben beneath the public Disraeli.

On July 16, 1834, Melbourne succeeded the second Earl Grey as Prime Minister, heading a government that kept in office a powerful peer whose influence upon Disraeli would be profound. The American-born John Singleton Copley, whose portrait painter father had taken him to England at the age of three, was, as Baron Lyndhurst, former Attorney General, Master of the Rolls, and three times Lord Chancellor. His Whig opponents had made him Chief Baron of the Exchequer. Sixty-two but still virile and handsome, he was a raffish widower with the most acute legal mind in England and one of the sharpest eyes for a shapely figure. He resembled, Disraeli would write later, "a high-bred falcon." To Sarah he confided on meeting Lyndhurst that he liked him "very much." So did the ladies. Once asked by Lady Tankerville whether he believed in platonic friendship with women, Lyndhurst quipped, "After, not before."

Following the London social season, Disraeli returned to Bradenham and Henrietta to her husband—and, on occasion, to Lyndhurst. Having assessed her charms and Disraeli's abilities, the opportunistic peer had decided to sample both. Loyal to her "Amin" yet casual about sexual favors, she wrote to Ben unsentimentally about the Baron, whom both now thought of as potential political patron: "I can make him do as I like, so whatever arrangement you think best, tell *me* & I will perform it. . . . My Beloved, every thought, every feeling of my heart is yours. . . . I shall never be happy until I am clasped to your bosom & be not sorrowful. . . . L[or]d Lyndhurst is anxious you should be in the House. Seriously, he is a most excellent being & I am sure I can make him [do] what I please. . . . Love me Ever. Never doubt how fondly I worship you. You are entwined with the feeling of my Soul. I shake so I can't write. . . . Kiss me a million times." Henrietta would often sign throbbingly passionate letters "Your Mother." Not a matter of disparity in age, it recognized the elemental nurturing dimension that would always sustain, beyond sex, her Amin's relationships with women.

Writing to Lady Blessington early in August from the bosom of his parents' establishment, Disraeli, apart from Henrietta and worried now about his prospects with her as well as his future in general, confided that he felt "as desolate as a ghost." Two months later he was writing Benjamin Austen that his life at Bradenham had been "literally a blank." He had experienced, he explained to Austen two weeks later (October 24, 1834), "a strange illness that kept me to my sofa . . . , great pains in the legs and extraord[inar]y languor. . . . I struggled against it for some time, but mounting my horse one day, I had a slight determin[a-ti]on of blood to my head, and was obliged to throw myself on the floor of the hall. This frightened me remembering old sufferings." It seemed a revisit of his old enemy, from which sudden recovery came by way of a therapeutic summons from London to return to Henrietta, who had been promised supplementary support by Lyndhurst.

In early November 1834 Disraeli's restoration of fortune began. He had dinner with Lyndhurst and his two teenage daughters (Lady Sykes went unmentioned in his report to Sarah), went to Covent Garden (Henrietta, very likely in the adjacent seat, went unidentified) to see Henry Denvil play in Byron's *Manfred,* and had his portrait in profile drawn by D'Orsay. Soon Lady Blessington had given him a splendid new waistcoat in payment for his brief *Book of Beauty* fiction, "The Carrier-Pigeon," and Disraeli, playing both sides, was exploring electioneering prospects with both the Earl of Durham and Lord Lyndhurst.

Parliament was dissolved on December 29 after William IV refused to accept Lord John Russell, whom he considered too liberal, as replacement for the dilatory Melbourne as Prime Minister. In the interim, the King sent for the ultra-Tory Duke of Wellington, who refused office and recommended Sir Robert Peel. But with Peel in Italy on holiday and communications primitive, Wellington agreed to a caretaker government pending Peel's return, with Lyndhurst again as Lord Chancellor. Disraeli had been apprised of the impending election by Lyndhurst and had begun, a month earlier, to recall his adherents for a third try at High Wycombe, meeting with them at the Lion on December 1. But Lyndhurst mobilized no concrete support until Disraeli wrote that Durham had assured a seat "for the mere legal expences," so long as the campaign was run as an unaffiliated Radical—"anything in short but joining the Tories." All that Lyndhurst had managed was the unsuccessful lobbying of the local Tory leader in Disraeli's district, Lord Carrington, although Ben had assured Sarah of Lyndhurst's confidence that Carrington would "swallow the leek." When he resisted, Lyndhurst turned to Charles Fulke Greville, Clerk of the Privy Council, to use his influence with Lord George Bentinck, his cousin, to secure Disraeli's candidacy for the seat at King's Lynn. Bentinck "won't hear of" Disraeli, Greville responded. Later, under very different circumstances, Bentinck would become Benjamin's closest political ally, but at that time a dandy writer of uncertifiable loyalty named Disraeli seemed unsuitable for a Norfolk constituency.

Lyndhurst was left with promises to make good for Lady Sykes, if not for their mutual friend, and managed to extract £500 from central Tory funds to assist Disraeli as—for the third time—a Radical, on grounds that no Conservative candidate had been nominated. Once again he faced Charles Grey.

Disraeli's campaign address at High Wycombe on December 16 attacked the government for claiming the Reform Bill. The Whig establishment, he charged, contained "scarcely an original member of that celebrated Cabinet." It reminded him, Disraeli joked in one of his earliest uses of the homely anecdote in a political address, of Andrew Ducrow, the celebrated circus performer who could ride upon six lithe horses at once. But one by one as the horses were "seized with the staggers," they were replaced by jackasses. "What a change! Behold the hero in the amphitheatre, the spangled jacket thrown on one side, the cork slippers on the other. Puffing, panting, and perspiring, he pokes one sullen brute, thwacks another, cuffs a third, and curses a fourth, while one brays to the audience, and another rolls in the sawdust." The spectacle was akin to the Reform Prime Minister and his Cabinet: "The spirited and snow-white steeds have gradually changed into an equal number of sullen and obstinate donkeys."

Wellington offered Tory funds to print a pamphlet version of the address, then titled "The Crisis Examined," and asked for fifty copies. With embarrassment, Disraeli sent one to Lord Durham. Although the speech described the Earl as a man of "character" among Whigs, it nevertheless placed him in a "united" Cabinet

with the politicians whom Disraeli excoriated. "I sh[oul]d grieve,"
he explained, if Durham felt thought of "in any other terms but
those of high and deserved consideration."

While not yet an acknowledged Tory, Disraeli had destroyed
any chances of accommodation with the Whigs. Had he the finances for a real fight, he wrote cockily to Benjamin Austen in
yet another equine metaphor, "I might canter over the C[ount]y,
for my popularity is irresistible." But on January 7, 1835, the poll
closed with the reelection of the incumbents, and Disraeli—by
nineteen votes—again last. He took the defeat well. At a Conservative dinner at Wycombe chaired by Lyndhurst's friend Lord
Chandos a fortnight later, Disraeli's presence belatedly acknowledging his Tory credentials, he claimed, "I am not at all disheart-
ened. I do not in any way feel like a beaten man. Perhaps it is
because I am used to it. I will say of myself like the famous Italian
general, who being asked in his old age why he was always victorious, replied, it was because he had always been beaten in his
youth."

To Wellington he wrote less jauntily, hoping for further political support. "I am now a cipher," he confessed, "but if the devotion of my energies to your cause . . . can ever avail you, your
Grace may count upon me, who seeks no greater satisfaction than
that of serving a really great man."

Throwing his father into the fray, Ben brought Isaac together
with Lyndhurst at dinner late in January, then brought him to
Lady Blessington's. Other political dinners followed, at one of
which, where the main course was swan stuffed with truffles
("very white and tender," Ben reported to Sarah), he met "young
Gladstone." Just turned twenty-five, William Ewart Gladstone,
M.P. since 1832, was already a junior lord of the Treasury. When
a by-election came up at Taunton, Lyndhurst arranged to have
Disraeli slated the Tory nominee. His opponent, who had been in
office since 1830, was Henry Labouchere, who had also been
named Master of the Mint by the Whig ministry.

Had Labouchere's adversary not been Disraeli, the campaign
might have gone almost unnoticed. But under the sartorial influence of D'Orsay, who had become his great friend, the black-
ringleted candidate campaigned in dandy garb more appropriate

for St. James's Park than Somersetshire. More notorious than his curls and chains and pantaloons, however, was his attack on the Whigs for having "seized the bloody hand" of the Irish leader in the Commons, Daniel O'Connell.

Disraeli's culminating speech to the electors of Taunton on April 29, 1835, was largely lighthearted. After alluding once more to the "bloody hand" charge, he asserted that "dismemberment" of the United Kingdom could not take place "without a civil war." More significantly, he said, was the accusation that he could not be a serious legislator because he had written a novel.

"A good one!" someone cried, and Disraeli responded, "I am glad there is a critic in the crowd who joins me in opinion. I trust there is no disgrace, gentlemen, in being an author." It was not shameful, he exaggerated, to have published a book read by thousands of fellow countrymen, and "translated into every language in civilised Europe." He trusted "that one who is an author by gift of nature is as good as one who is Master of the Mint by the gift of Lord Melbourne." Disraeli had second thoughts, too. "This I do know, gentlemen, that twelve months hence I shall still be the author of *Vivian Grey*, though I shall be much surprised if at the [end of the] same period my honourable opponent be still Master of the Mint."

Refusing to see anyone but the occupiers of Ireland as bloody, O'Connell fired his choicest invective at the "unprincipled" Disraeli. "He was the worst possible type of Jew," O'Connell charged from Dublin. "He has just the qualities of the impenitent thief on the cross, and I verily believe, if Mr. Disraeli's family herald[ry] were to be examined and his genealogy traced, the same personage would be discovered to be the heir ... of the exalted individual to whom I allude."

O'Connell's diatribe was only the strongest of the racist attacks. "The Jew," the Rev. Sydney Smith wrote to his daughter on June 3, 1835, was called "Old clothes!" by the children as he arrived for a speech, and to suggest the itinerant peddler, they "offered to sell him sealing-wax and slippers."

The election results left Disraeli with his fourth loss in as many attempts, with 282 votes to Labouchere's 452, even before news of O'Connell's slur reached London. After consulting

D'Orsay—duels were still popular in France—Disraeli issued a challenge to Morgan O'Connell, as his father, having killed a man in a duel, had vowed never again to engage in one. No offer could have been more public, Disraeli making his intentions known in letters to *The Morning Post* and *The Times*, vowing "inextinguishable hatred with which I shall pursue his existence."

The affair kept Disraeli from brooding over his loss at Taunton, even after a magistrate, on appeal from the O'Connells, bound Disraeli over to keep the peace. He would get into the Commons sooner or later, he vowed, and pursue the bigoted M.P. there; and by letters in the press he kept the controversy going. It did put Disraeli into drawing room and dinner table conversation although by early July he was writing insincerely to Edwards Beadon, a Taunton solicitor, that he was "no friend" of "paper warfare," as it was "fruitless."

With Melbourne's government back in office after the brief moment of Peel, another general election finally loomed, and Lyndhurst, preparing for it, employed Disraeli as informal private secretary and Tory publicist. It was then, at Ben's request, early in July, that Sarah again invited Lady Sykes to visit Bradenham, this time with Lord Lyndhurst. "I have half a mind to keep away," Ben claimed on July 3, but he came as part of the threesome. Nearly half a century later, Sir Philip Rose, later Disraeli's personal attorney, wrote, "I can well remember the scandal in the country at this connection and especially at the visit of Lady Sykes to Bradenham accompanied by Lord L and the indignation aroused in the neighbourhood at D having introduced his reputed mistress and her Paramour to his *Home* and made them the associates of his Sister as well as of his father and mother."

Although Disraeli was risking local opprobrium, two months later Lyndhurst and Lady Sykes would pay a second visit. And there was a further risk. Henrietta's willingness to share her bed could lead to losing her to Lyndhurst. But the Lord Chancellor, as Disraeli usually called him, accepted his part of the bargain.

One result was Disraeli's series of fourteen leading articles in *The Morning Post* beginning late in August which supported Lyndhurst's political positions and reminded readers of Whig alliances with Radicals and Irish members in order to stay in power.

Anonymity permitted him to give full rein to his gift for invective, describing various representatives of the people as *toadeaters, plunderers, parasites*, and *Popish dupes*. One M.P. had the qualities of a butterman, another of a chandler, a third "would make an admirable cad, or a first-rate conductor of an omnibus." Nevertheless, Disraeli also enunciated what would be the most consistent of his political themes, that the Tories were truly the national party in representing the authentic diversity of national interests. That he was recognized as the anonymous author enhanced his reputation, as did his December manifesto, *A Vindication of the English Constitution in a letter to a noble and learned Lord*, addressed to Lyndhurst and again stressing that the Conservatives were the party pledged to represent the national institutions of Monarch, Church, and People, while the Whigs were allegedly little more than "that Venetian oligarchy."

Having sent her *The Morning Post* every day to make sure that the family did not miss his columns, Ben boasted to Sarah (August 20, 1835) that it was "the only paper now read." In its pages "some great unknown has suddenly risen, whose exploits form almost the sole staple of political conversation, and all conversation is now political. The back numbers for last week cannot be obtained for love or money, and the sale has increased nearly one-third. All attempts at discovering the writer have been baffled, and the mystery adds to the keen interest which the articles excite."

Introduced by Lyndhurst to Thomas Barnes, editor of *The Times*, Disraeli found a new market for his political circulation-raising, but Barnes, alarmed at the clever scurrility, cautioned him about his "most surprising disdain for the law of libel." Continuing his polemical journalism for Lyndhurst, early in 1836 Disraeli would begin his series signed "Runnymede"—nineteen articles promoting Tory principles as he and Lyndhurst saw them. Publication further promoted Disraeli's status as a future Conservative voice although his authorship was known only to the elect. (In "The Spirit of Whiggism," published in a collection of his Runnymede letters, Disraeli coined his paradox that "European revolution is a struggle against privilege; an English revolution is a struggle for it.")

As Disraeli's political sponsor, Lord Lyndhurst was useful in keeping his protégé's ambitions afloat, yet he secured no office or even any realistic candidacy for Disraeli; in Disraeli's amorous life, Lyndhurst represented an interruption in the idyll. From Lady Sykes's standpoint, Lyndhurst paid his way, as she otherwise would have to maintain an extravagant style far beyond Disraeli's almost nonexistent financial capacities on the £1,500 a year she received from Sir Francis in his absence. "The truth is that Sir Francis is rather a queer person," Lyndhurst acknowledged coldly, but also odd was the ménage that Henrietta maintained. While Disraeli's romantic opportunities diminished, his political reputation progressed and his frenetic social life continued. He even managed election to the essential Tory bastion, the Carlton Club. Everything, nevertheless, had its price. Speculation about Lyndhurst's role in his and Henrietta's life enlivened Mayfair gossip and appeared to validate views of Disraeli as shameless opportunist.

Yet it was Lady Sykes who had taken possession of Disraeli. When apart, she shamelessly teased him at a distance. Escape from desire became almost impossible. Her voluptuousness leaped from her letters, which he kept all his life. One message, dated one o'clock in the morning, and "In bed," asked whether he had "thought of his Henrietta this morning and wished her to be snugly placed by him in that comfortable couch sipping coffee and kisses at the same time." She loved him "even to madness," and denied that her aim was only to show her power over him. "I swear," she confided, "I suffer the torments of the damned when you are away and although there is nothing I would not sacrifice to give you a moment's enjoyment I cannot bear that your amusement should spring from any other source than myself." And she hoped that her selfishness did not make him angry, for she wished that they were "never separated for a moment."

"I feel I am not the vain frivolous being I am set down to be and with you for my guiding star," she declared, "what would I not do to retain and cherish the love I've gained." Nothing Henrietta did or wrote, but for her seduction of Lyndhurst in Disraeli's behalf, suggests that her aims were to inspire her Amin to greatness.

The Runnymede letters had ended with *The Times* of May 15, 1836, but not Disraeli's industrious political journalism, which included a leading article in *The Times* on a Lyndhurst speech, a new series on a "Popanilla" scheme called "A New Voyage of Sinbad the Sailor, Recently Discovered" (eleven articles beginning on December 15), further articles signed "Runnymede," several signed "Skelton Jun[ior]," verses and sketches for the *Book of Beauty*, even book reviews. With his debts still plaguing him, as well as the disasters of new speculations with Haber, he enlisted William Pyne of the Pyne and Richards law firm, who handled Sir Francis Sykes's business in his absence, to stave off the sheriff, promising infusions of new funds from imaginary positions offered and future writing projects, and finally sending Pyne a cheese from the Bradenham House dairy. Pyne's instructions were also to furnish Henrietta's household expenses, which Sykes discovered only in 1838 had been overpaid during 1836 by £2,000, with no receipts to account for the funds. Appealing to Sykes's sense of "honour" regarding Henrietta, Pyne kept the matter quiet,* but the unrecorded transactions may have been part of what Disraeli had described to Pyne as "our system"—an elaborate juggling of paper to keep him just short of bankruptcy.

Hoping for money from Henry Colburn, Disraeli returned to a novel of which he had long before written the first "book" (ten brief chapters). The early pages had exploited his memories of Gibraltar and Malta in the person of young Captain Ferdinand Armine, a handsome Englishman of a minority religion (he is from an old Catholic family) and reckless habits who is a man of fashion but not of means. As Disraeli began the second part of the novel, *Henrietta Temple* became a nostalgic backward look at his unraveling amour with Henrietta Sykes.

In "Calantha," a poem written at the time for the *Book of Beauty*, Disraeli had closed with the line, "Love is a dream without repose." It was almost a gloss on the state of his affair with Lady Sykes, for whom he still cared much, but whose attentions were increasingly elsewhere. In the novel his fanciful Henrietta is

---

*Pyne was also the intermediary in the publication of *Whigs and Whiggism* by "Runnymede"—to capitalize upon the promotional value in Disraeli's anonymity.

a virginal beauty of eighteen, sheltered in the country by a devoted father. Captain Armine—his surname suggests the real Henrietta's tag for Benjamin, "Amin"—is urged by his love to "get into Parliament," but he responds (the time of the novel is prior to Catholic political relief) that he is of the wrong faith. His family urges him to solve the dilemma of his debts—bailiffs lie in wait—by marrying the wealthy Katherine Grandison, but he rejects her for Henrietta, in whose love vulgar ambitions fade and fame seems no more than a "juggle," political aspirations mere "childish games."

Close friends of Disraeli and of Lady Sykes like Count D'Orsay, to whom the novel is dedicated and who is the engaging Count Alcibiades de Mirabel of the tale, very likely found the characters readily identifiable and *Henrietta Temple* a source of delicious table talk. Something of the passion in the early relationship with Lady Sykes survives in the novel, in tender lines close to Henrietta's letters, as when Miss Temple, writing Ferdinand Armine that she had kissed his pillow, explains, "I could not help it, dearest; when I thought that his darling head had rested there so often and so lately, I could not refrain from pressing my lips to that favoured resting-place, and I am afraid shed a tear besides." Disraeli mined the real Henrietta's fervent letters for those of the fictional Henrietta, giving them their sentimental authenticity.* A reviewer of a later Disraeli novel, in 1844, would recall "the depth of affectionateness which we remember in the love-letters of Henrietta Temple (the best we have met with in modern fiction)," not realizing the documentary advantages possessed by the novelist.

Disraeli's real-life arrangements with Henrietta, under pressure from her possessiveness, were bound to fall apart, and did. Sir Francis had returned; Lord Lyndhurst still hovered nearby in expectations of accommodation; and Lady Sykes's bosom, and pillow, became less and less available. In his letters to Sarah, Henrietta's name still appeared, but usually in tandem with her

---

*"The Consul's Daughter," in the *Book of Beauty* for 1836, also had a heroine named Henrietta, a young woman "of singular beauty." Obviously its author was not bent on concealing his idyll with a flesh-and-blood Henrietta.

husband, with whom Disraeli now shared an opera box as well as Lady Sykes. Her portrait was being drawn by Daniel Maclise, he boasted to Sarah in April. The Irishman's portraits—he had already done Isaac and Ben—appeared in *Fraser's Magazine* and were an index of social fame, but in the case of Henrietta a different sort of fame would ensue. As Disraeli was bringing *Henrietta Temple* to a conclusion redolent with sentimental innocence, Lady Sykes was beginning an affair with Maclise.

For Disraeli the end was signaled at Basildon Park, Reading. He returned to London with Lyndhurst. Henrietta had pleaded illness and sent them both off. On the evidence of her disappearance from his correspondence it was the last of Lady Sykes for Disraeli. In his scrappy diary he noted under "Autumn of 1836"—obviously recorded well after the fact—"Parted forever from Henrietta." In December—the month of the novel's release—London gossip finally reached him about the absent Henrietta's new amour, and letters of consolation began arriving. To one from D'Orsay he responded, "As a man of the world, you will perhaps laugh at me and think me very silly for being the slave of such feelings, when perhaps I ought to congratulate myself that an intimacy which must have, I suppose, sooner or later concluded, has terminated in a manner which may cost my heart a pang but certainly not my conscience. But it is in vain to reason with those who feel. In calmer moments I may be of your opinion; at present I am wretched." He felt no bitterness toward Henrietta, he confessed. "I am indebted [to her] for the happiest years of my life."

Henrietta even wrote what was probably a last letter to Ben just after publication of the novel, a presentation copy of which she had received. "You know I am not very eloquent in expressing my feelings," she wrote—although Disraeli had paid her the compliment of exploiting her love letters in the novel—but she was happy about the "brilliant success" he had achieved. Sir Francis had been "*tolerably* kind" to her, she added, suggesting that he had discovered nothing yet about Maclise, who was still painting a Sykes family group. In fact Sykes thought that the only reason for Disraeli's absences had been "your application to your

books," and "he frightened me," Henrietta confessed, "by projecting a trip to Bradenham." Finding excuses, she staved off a little
longer his discovery that Disraeli had been replaced in her affections by someone else.

Sir Francis may have been the last person in London to
know, returning home unexpectedly on July 4, 1837, to find
Maclise in bed with his wife. Sykes instructed his lawyers to institute proceedings against the artist for "criminal conversation,"
charges eventually dropped. Henrietta, publicly disgraced, vanished from London society.*

That Sir Francis was eager to visit Bradenham made it clear
to Disraeli that, although the journey would never happen, he remained persona grata to Henrietta's husband. There were no visitors during the quiet Christmas of 1836. Disraeli remained at
Bradenham well into the new year, avoiding creditors and consol-
ing himself that sales of *Henrietta Temple* had been reported
"brisk." The snow was deep and the isolation restorative. "I assure you," he wrote to William Pyne on December 26, "when I
reached the old hall and found the beech blocks crackling and
blazing, I felt no common sentiments of gratitude. . . ." Temporarily he was free from "the plague [of] women, the wear and tear of
politics and the dunning of creditors."

With Lyndhurst promising a safe seat to contest the next
time, Disraeli's attentions refocused upon the new session of Parliament and the health of the King. The death of the failing William IV would bring down the government and necessitate new
elections. But before such events could occur, Disraeli, who had
returned to London to stay temporarily with Count D'Orsay—for
appearance's sake he lived next door to Lady Blessington's Gore
House—had to rush back overnight to his home county. A sudden by-election had come up, and with Lord Chandos he jolted
by carriage, without sleep, to be at Aylesbury in time to campaign

---

*Maclise was untouched by the scandal. His artistic stock continued to rise.
Queen Victoria, who heard about the episode from Lord Melbourne, would purchase two of the Irishman's pictures in 1839, and after her marriage would buy additional Maclises as gifts for Prince Albert, including an *Undine* embellished by
callipygian nudes.

for the Tory candidate the next morning. On the evening of February 16 he collapsed outside the George Inn and was taken to Bradenham, put to bed, and leeched. He was still shaky a fortnight later in London. His homeopathic physician, Dr. Frederick Quin, diagnosed a "bilious swoon" and railed against the use of leeches. Never sturdy physically, Disraeli would renew late in life his loyalty to homeopathic medicine, which favored minute doses of drugs in the treatment of ailments.

With Bradenham more safe from messengers with writs than London, he returned to the country as quickly as he could, awaiting his own political chance and continuing, from the country, his "Sinbad" letters for *The Times*. Exploiting Byron and Shelley in a new novel, *Venetia, or the Poet's Daughter*, begun over the new year at Bradenham, he continued at it between letters to impatient lawyers and creditors. There was something elegiac about the last novel before Disraeli's Parliamentary years. Cadurcis, his Byron figure, pens a poem which foreshadows the shift in the author's own fortunes that would turn his energies fully toward politics:

My tale is done; and if some deem it strange
My fancy thus should droop, deign then to learn
My tale is truth: imagination's range
Its bounds exact may touch not: to discern
Far stranger things than poets ever feign,
In life's perplexing annals, is the fate
Of those who act, and musing penetrate
The mystery of Fortune: to whose reign
The haughtiest brow must bend.

Henrietta Temple had sold 1,250 copies in two months, and he was optimistic that the new novel would pay off further obligations, but his father was increasingly irritable over the burden of debt—he would have been horrified had he learned what Ben actually owed—and the apparent dissipation of talent. At one awkward moment he would write to D'Orsay that Isaac was "very gouty and grumpy. I have just left him, as he is too unwell to get

Bradenham. *From a watercolour by Mrs. Partridge, circa. 1850.*

out at night, and sits at home reading the Pickwick papers* and
bullying his sons." Ben had already written to Benjamin Austen,
the most exasperated if not the most impatient of a queue of creditors, that he had reassured his father without revealing "anything
disagreeable."

As much as Disraeli could manage on his forays to London,
he pretended unconcern at society dinners, theater parties, and
his political haven, the Carlton Club. Parliamentary elections
were almost certain by summer; he had to buy only a little more
time. "My arrest at this moment," he explained to a creditor,
would frustrate his hopes and do no good for those pressing him
for payment. Somehow the sun shone, and despite all his cultivation of grand Establishment bigwigs, his deliverance would come
through the good offices of an iron foundry proprietor of little political consequence and his "flirt and rattle" of a wife.

D'Orsay's reaction after the ballots were counted at
Maidstone was to send his friend advice on how to handle his
post-Henrietta status: "You will not make love! You will not in-

*Dickens's novel was appearing, to an increasingly enthusiastic readership, in
twelve monthly parts.

trigue! You have your seat; do not risk anything! If you meet with a widow, then marry!" "It is odd," Disraeli would write early in September to Rosina Bulwer, who had congratulated him on his finally winning a seat in the Commons, "that my electioneering struggle sh[oul]d terminate in being M.P. for Maidstone. As I am already a believer in destiny, it required not this strange occurrence, and doubly strange from the manner in which it took place, to confirm me in my Oriental creed. . . . But we are the children of the gods, and are never more the slaves of circumstances than when we deem ourselves their masters. What may next happen in the dazzling farce of life the Fates only know." The concept was curiously close to a line of dialogue from "The Infernal Marriage": "All is ordained, but man is nevertheless master of his own actions." It was a question lifted from Rabbi Akiba's *Ethics of the Fathers*, incorporated in the traditional Hebrew prayer book.

REBEL
IN THE
HOUSE
1837–1862

X

"THE TIME WILL COME WHEN
YOU WILL HEAR ME."

1837–1841

DISRAELI'S MAIDEN SPEECH IN THE COMMONS LATE ON THE NIGHT OF December 7, 1837, was a public embarrassment; his first significant vote, two days earlier, was a private one. Since Members of Parliament were unpaid and those without incomes usually spent their mornings and afternoons earning their daily bread, the House conducted its business in the waning hours of the day, often into the early hours of the next. Having vowed, after his failed attempt in 1835 to lure Daniel O'Connell into a duel, to meet him instead "at Philippi"—the House—Disraeli now had his opportunity to answer one of the dominant personalities in the chamber. The ruddy Irishman's invective was justly feared, but Disraeli, neglecting the first rule of debate—that one should never speak on a subject upon which one is unprepared—caught the Speaker's eye and rose.

The scene could have been a painting by Rembrandt, and little but the substitution of hissing new gaslight for candlelight would have been different. Members wore frock coats of dark colors, usually black, and most perched on their benches with their tall silk hats on their heads. Removing their hats only when addressing the Chair, they clapped them on again as they sat down. A tilt of one's headgear forward over the eyes suggested boredom with the address and sometimes evidenced real slumber. The usual response to a statement that awakened attention was a "Hear! Hear!"—and the tone indicated pleasure or disapproval. An effective hit might touch several chords, while a swelling chorus might be reported parenthetically in Hansard's *Debates* as "Cheers."

When Disraeli removed his hat to address the subject of Irish election returns, he knew it would awaken the M.P. from County Kerry whom he had compared, in the *Letters of Runnymede,* to a crocodile. O'Connell and his claque were ready. Once Disraeli began, in an affected delivery which he believed represented sarcasm, he was drowned out in hisses, hoots, catcalls, drumming of feet, and general uproar. The tumult reminded him, he explained to Lady Caroline Maxse, of what he had read about "the earlier legislative scenes of the French revolution." So maniacal was the hubbub that his courage in going on gained him sympathy even from the Opposition. "I have begun several things many times," he shouted above the screaming, "and I have often succeeded at the last—though many predicted I would fail." After all, he was there in the House even though it had taken five tries. "I will sit down now," he concluded, raising his voice even higher, "but the time will come when you will hear me."

Isaac would write on December 10, "I wish your debut had been more auspicious ... but I am always fearful that 'theatrical games' will not do for the English Commons." The Attorney General, Sir John Campbell, was kinder. Meeting Disraeli—to whom he had never spoken before—in the Lobby, he asked, cordially, "Now, Mr Disraeli, could you tell me how you finished one sentence in your speech—we are anxious to know: 'In one hand the keys of St Peter and in the other ———'?" The shouts had drowned out the rest, and it was never completed in the published text of the debate in *Hansard.* "—in the other, the cap of Liberty," said Disraeli, pleased.

"A good picture," said Sir John, and he disowned the noisy

"party at the Bar, over whom we had no control." Encouragingly he added, "You have nothing to be afraid of."

Doing Lyndhurst's dirty work in *The Morning Chronicle* two years earlier, Disraeli had anonymously characterized Campbell as "this shrewd, coarse, manoeuvering Pict," and a "bowing, fawning, jobbing progeny of haggis and cockaleekie."

The next evening, Disraeli's friend Edward Bulwer arranged dinner with O'Connell's colleague in the Commons, Richard Lalor Sheil, a playwright as well as a politician. "Now get rid of your genius for a session," Sheil advised. "Speak often, for you must not show yourself cowed, but speak shortly. Be quiet; try to be dull." Eventually, Sheil predicted, after listening to monotonous facts and figures, Members "will sigh for the wit and eloquence which they know are in you."

Two evenings before Disraeli's debut came a decision which left him ashamed of his cowardice, however lightly he tried to rationalize it to Sarah. Sir George Carroll and Sir Moses Montefiore, the Sheriffs of the City of London, appeared at the bar of the House, as was their privilege on behalf of the Corporation of the City, to present a petition and take their places in the gallery to hear the plea examined. Sir Moses was the first Jewish Sheriff, only recently knighted by the young Queen, and Disraeli did not realize until the debate began that the petition "was the Jew Question by a sidewind."

Catholic Emancipation had come in 1829, and Lord John Russell on behalf of the Whigs had been attempting to extend relief from religious oaths of office to Quakers and Moravians, but the "sidewind" was George Grote's motion to extend the bill's coverage to all denominations, which raised the matter of relief to Jews. The debate quickly focused on that, and Disraeli recognized that not a Tory vote was likely to be cast in favor—unless it were his. "Nobody looked at me," he explained about his obvious unease, "and I was not at all uncomfortable, but voted in the majority (only of 12) with the utmost sangfroid." In the debates of 1841 and 1845 he remained silent but voted for emancipation, first speaking in its favor in 1847. In his first month in Parliament his timidity had totally overwhelmed his loyalties.

"The Church of England," a wry saying went—and Disraeli knew—"is the Tory party at prayer."

Fiction was now less important than faction. Novels had brought him little income but some recognition in society. What Disraeli needed was acknowledgment of his political value by his party. Still struggling to stave off creditors, he claimed to William Pyne from Bradenham that under pressure from "the highest quarter," *The Times* had commissioned him to write articles anticipating the sittings of Parliament after the new year. Since the management of *The Times* knew that Disraeli's polemics sold papers, he may have arranged the "Old England" series (ten columns signed "Coeur de Lion" which appeared between January 3 and January 15) himself. "Bye the bye," the often grumpy Thomas Carlyle wrote to his brother Alexander on the 10th, "a man in the *Times* Newspaper, for the last ten days, is writing diligently a series of papers called 'Old England' extravagantly in my manner; so that several friends actually thought it was I! I did not see them till last night; and had a good laugh over them then. It is that dog Thackeray . . . , I am persuaded, and no other."

One debt which Disraeli now had to pay, and for which his political journalism earned far too little, was his share of election expenses, including bribes, at Maidstone. He had promised Wyndham Lewis £500 by January 1, and owed him at least £4,559/7s./0d. To settle his debts, he almost needed a Rothschild, but an arranged marriage into a wealthy Jewish family was an impossibility. Although the choice of a spouse out of the faith was still a rare event for an observant family, the choice of a convert out of the faith was unheard of. As for Disraeli's political future, a marriage to a Jewess would have been devastating. Still he was drawn to the Rothschilds.

In mid-February, at a concert for London elite at the Grafton Street town house of Robert Parnther he met not only his new patroness, Mary Anne Wyndham Lewis, "very proud . . . of being there," he told Sarah, but many of the London Rothschilds, "the most picturesque group" present. Hannah de Rothschild was still in mourning dress; her late husband, Nathan Mayer de Rothschild, patriarch of the family, had died on July 28, 1836, and nineteenth-century widows often wore some aspect of mourning the rest of their lives. "Above all," Disraeli wrote, was "the young bride, or rather wife, from Frankfort, universally admired, tall, graceful, dark, and . . . picturesquely dressed." Striking in yellow silk and "magnificent pearls," she was "quite a Murillo." Charlotte, Nathan Mayer's daughter, had married her cousin Anselm de Rothschild of Frankfurt. The three sons of Nathan Mayer were Lionel, who had succeeded to his father's position in the London branch of the banking firm, and his brothers, Anthony and Mayer. Disraeli would see much of them in later years but only after he felt comfortable in their company. In the first months of 1838 he had marginally enough social standing beyond High Bohemia to be invited to mingle not only with dukes but with Rothschilds.

Soon after Parliament resumed, Disraeli listened for the first time to one of his party's reputed comers, son of a wealthy Liverpool merchant. "Gladstone spoke very well," Ben reported to Sarah, "tho' with the unavoidable want of interest which accompanies elaborate speeches which you know are to lead to no result. . . ." He began choosing his own occasions with care, not venturing to speak in the Commons again until March 16, this time defending the Corn Laws, which protected the agricultural interest from cheap grain imports and kept the price of bread high. ("Stable," claimed its adherents.) This time he was heard, and even congratulated by Tory leaders. He had arisen with anxiety, still in shock over the events of two days before, when Wyndham Lewis had fallen from his chair at 2 Grosvenor Gate, dead of a heart attack. "To complete my vexations," Disraeli wrote hastily to Pyne, "my colleague has just fallen down in a fit and died!" As cold as the note seemed, Disraeli's immediate realization was that Lewis's estate would have to be settled, and he would be pressed to pay nearly five thousand pounds in campaign debts. That seemed a greater catastrophe than the death of his amiable partner in Maidstone, to whom he had never really been close. He was "overwhelmed," Ben wrote to Sarah, "incapable of any exertion."

One exertion was immediately necessary. He went to Grosvenor Gate to console Wyndham Lewis's widow, and learned that her husband's property would go, according to his will, to his brother, subject to her life interest. There were no children. She was forty-five and had been married since 1815 but seemed to

have acquired little polish from a match that, given her background as daughter of an obscure naval lieutenant from Glou-
stershire who had died in 1793, when she was only one, had
promised to be brilliant. Pretty and small in figure, she did not
look her age and claimed to be four years younger than she was.
What she could not hide was her lack of education and a disin-
terest in compensating for it that caused her absurdities to become notorious. She could never remember, Disraeli once joked,
who came first, the Greeks or the Romans.

Once she began consulting with him about her confused affairs, he began to weigh marrying her for her money. Her physical
attractions were fading, and she had little property of her own,
but she had use of Wyndham Lewis's in her lifetime. At thirty-
three Disraeli knew he could not afford to marry for love, yet he
had to begin to convince himself, as well as Mary Anne, that he
was at least half in love with her. Unsure how to begin, within a
month of her widowhood he ceased addressing his many sympathetic notes to her as "My dearest Mrs. Wyndham" and omitted
salutations altogether. Finally, on April 19, from Bradenham, he
dropped a strong hint. "My father's health," he wrote to her,
"gives me *the greatest possible uneasiness*. Altho' an eldest son, it
seems to me that I should scarcely survive his loss. The first wish
of my life has ever been, that after all his kindness to me, and all
the anxiety which I have cost him, he sh[oul]d live to see me settled and steady, and successful to his heart[']s content."

From Clifton, a Bristol suburb where her elderly mother,
Mrs. Eleanor Yate, lived, Mary Anne responded after several
weeks that she had been writing to no one, that her heart was
still "too full & anxious *at times* to bear up against the misery
which almost destroys me." She was glad to hear that Ben was
spending so much of his time with the Lyndhursts—in his mid-
sixties Lord Lyndhurst had happily remarried and would soon
have a daughter by his young wife—"because the more you go
there, or to any other married lady,* the less likely you are to

*Sarah Bradford, in her book *Disraeli* (London, 1982), misidentifies "Lady L" as
Lady Londonderry. But Disraeli had been spending many evenings "en
famille"—as he told Sarah—with Lyndhurst and his new wife, Georgiana.

think of marrying yourself some odious woman. I hate married men. I would as soon you were dead. *Rather selfish!* Yes I am, but most sincere (& kind)."

They had exchanged the strongest of hints. Augustus Fitzhardinge Berkeley, who had been interested in her even before she had married Wyndham Lewis, feeling now that he would be again thwarted, reported to Mary Anne society prognostications that were still premature—"the babbling world already gives you to the Tory novelist."

"Unfurl your wings," Disraeli responded to her intimations, "and fly away home." She returned, sending ahead Wyndham Lewis's gold watch chains for her "dear kind friend Dizz" to wear; and he responded that, "in public, I wore *your chains*. I hope you are not ashamed of your slave." The passionate metaphor was intended to be unsubtle, and soon Mary Anne signed herself "your poor little whitebait" and "your little Dove." She visited at Bradenham and called herself, in advance, as "the *comfort & joy* of your life." By then he was writing to "my sweetest love." It was not until October that she sent him symbolic kisses by letter, but the "happy evenings together" about which she wrote when they were apart seem still to have been tender yet unphysical. Ruffled feelings often broke through, with Mary Anne worried that she was being wooed only for her money, while Ben argued that it was "in vain to struggle with Destiny."

Disraeli's first public embarrassment as M.P. came early in June, after John Minet Fector, former M.P. for Dover but defeated in 1837, had been elected to Wyndham Lewis's vacant seat. Maidstone's grasping electors, reputedly the most corrupt in England, had validated their reputation by suing Fector and Disraeli for promised bribes unpaid. The sleazy practice was common, but Disraeli rebutted the "disgusting" charge in letters to London papers, claiming no responsibility for "expenses of the contest . . . defrayed by my lamented colleague" in the general election nor for Fector's alleged guilt. Instead he blamed "the vile license of a loose-tongued lawyer" hired by certain electors of Maidstone. Eventually Disraeli had to apologize in court, however defiantly, for having accused the barrister, Charles Austin, of libeling him. The affair dragged out, draining dignity from his parliamentary seat. Mary Anne quietly offered the money to pay his court costs, and on November 22 the embarrassment was over, Disraeli returning most of the way—as far as Paddingdon Station—on the new rail line, powered by a new engine "of unprecedented power," he wrote to her on reaching Bradenham. The North Star—pride of Isambard Kingdom Brunel's Great Western Railway—had reached thirty-six miles an hour, and would exceed that the next month.

While the Maidstone case had simmered in June, Disraeli used his perquisites as M.P. to attend the coronation of Victoria at Westminster Abbey. Taking his place required court dress— breeches and silk stockings—which Ben donned at 2:30 A.M. in order to be seated in time for the morning pageant. "It turned out that I had a very fine leg, which I never knew before!" he reported to Mary Anne. Lightly as he made the point, he was nevertheless reminding the widow of forty-five that he was an attractive younger man, and her own, if she wanted him.

How intimate they became through the year can hardly be judged by their letters, even though symbolic kisses must have represented real ones. When they were apart in December, Ben wrote to her, "I pass my nights and days in scenes of fascinating rapture. Till I embrace you, I shall not know what calmness is. I write this to beg you to have your hand *ungloved*, when you arrive, so that you may stand by me, and I may hold and clasp and feel your soft delicious hand . . . , or I shall be insane with disappointment." The lines sounded circumspect enough to suggest that fleshly passion had gone no farther. Yet three weeks earlier, when down with influenza at Bradenham, he had written to Mary Anne, "I have been obliged to betake myself to bed again, and wish you were with me there." Almost certainly they had lost little time in reaching a physical stage in what was still courtship. Mary Anne had not yet been willing to set a date for marriage, feeling that an appropriate mourning period had not yet passed.

At Bradenham, with Parliament not sitting and his love unavailable, Disraeli had been tended through his influenza by his mother, and having indulged in amorous verse to Mary Anne, he produced lines on December 1, to "My Mother, nursing me on her birth-day." It was a rare acknowledgment in a father-dominated household to Maria D'Israeli.

> O mayst thou be,
> For many years, the link that sweetly binds
> My memory to the past! Pursue thy way,
> Calm and content,

he wrote. And so her life had been as wife and mother.

In his hiatus from politics he also tried writing a play, *Count Alarcos*. "I am convinced," he explained to Mary Anne, "that to write a great tragedy is the chef-d'oeuvre of literary skill." But however many draft pages of blank verse he confessed to burning, which he thought "a good sign," the result was as mediocre as were most poetic plays aspiring toward Shakespearean grandeur. The story of Count Alarcos had intrigued him since hearing a ballad in Spain, but Disraeli could not capture its Websterish horrors. When he offered it to the great tragedian of the decade, William Charles Macready, even a supporting exhortation from Count D'Orsay—penned because Lady Blessington liked the play—failed to move the impresario of Covent Garden. All he had known of Disraeli was his maiden speech. Macready had been in the gallery to hear the debate. In his diary he had noted Disraeli's "farcical failure." The *Count Alarcos* script, he predicted in a new entry, on February 21, 1839, "will never come to any good." Disraeli had to resort to publishing it, earning the faint praise of a few friends. Thomas Wakley, M.P. for Finsbury, a surgeon and the first editor of *The Lancet*, called *Count Alarcos* "the finest play since Shakespeare," Ben boasted to Sarah. Wakley, however, was the wrong kind of editor from whom to value literary judgments.

Count Alarcos is memorable for the anatomical solecism, when Alarcos rejects his countess, "Another breast should bear my children." More positively there is the mocking inversion, "Absence cures love." And there is Oran the Moor's skeptical taunt:

> "Show me Christian acts,
> And they may prompt to Christian thought."

Count D'Orsay had learned of the drama's completion from Disraeli early in the new year, responding jocularly, "When I read in the beginning of your letter, The Tragedy is finished, I thought that you were married. . . . How is it that you leave her in London by herself?" Disraeli had to explain that as he was awaiting the new sitting of Parliament on February 5, his prospects, marital and financial, had begun unraveling. Talk in their circles in London about Disraeli as adventurer and Mrs. Wyndham Lewis as purchaser of a younger man's between-sheets favors had become painful to both. While insisting that she was only waiting to wed until a mourning year passed in mid-March, Mary Anne hesitated to set a date, and began pressing him to repay, at the least, his legal debts, or prove by his failure that he was trifling with her for her money. When apart, their letters were replete with kisses; together they quarreled as to how long Disraeli would have to endure society gossip which described him, he claimed, as a wealthy widow's "hired lover." She branded his haste "selfish." On February 7, in the second of what would be four letters to her that day, Disraeli addressed her unsparingly as "My dear Mrs Wyndham" and spoke of leaving her house not in anger "but in deep sorrow and mortification." It was a brief farewell: He promised to "soon be to you a dream." Then he determined upon emptying his bitter cup, and wrote a third letter, one of the longest in his life.

She was a woman of the world, he began, and she understood their relative positions and what each had to lose. "The continuance of the present state of affairs," he wrote bluntly, "could only render you *disreputable*, me it wo[ul]d render *infamous*. There is only one construction which Society . . . puts upon a connection between a woman, who is supposed to be rich, and a man whom she avowedly loves, and does not marry. In England especially there is no stigma more damning."

He had to choose, Disraeli charged, between being ridiculous or being contemptible. Honor required his being recognized as having been jilted by her, the lesser scandal. Then he gambled by confessing what was almost the entire truth:

> I avow [that] when I first made my advances to you, I
> was influenced by no romantic feelings. My father had

long wished me to marry; my settling in life was the implied, tho' not stipulated, condition of a disposition of his property, which would have been convenient to me. I myself, about to commence a practical career, wished for the solace of a home, and shrunk from all the torturing passions of intrigue. I was not blind to worldly advantages in such an alliance, but I had already proved that my heart was not to be purchased. I found you in sorrow, and my heart was touched. I found you, as I thought, amiable, tender, and yet acute and gifted with no ordinary mind; one whom I co[ul]d look upon with pride as the partner of my life, who could sympathize with all my projects and feelings, console me in the moments of depression, share my hour of triumph, and work with me for our honor and our happiness.

Her personal fortune, he confessed, was far less than he had hoped, and if the adventurer he was alleged to be, he would have already reneged upon their engagement. The alliance would not benefit him socially or politically, he claimed. "I can live, as I live, with[ou]t disgrace, until the inevitable progress of events gives me that independence which is all I require. . . . No, I wo[ul]d not condescend to be the minion of a princess;* and not all the gold of Ophir sho[ul]d lead me to the altar." What his nature required was that his life should be "perpetual love."

The problem "must quickly be solved," he insisted, and closed with the prophecy that in the "penal hour of retribution," some time hence, she would recall "the passionate heart that you have forfeited, and the genius that you have betrayed." Then, having sent the long letter off, he had further thoughts about his strong language, and wrote a brief fourth note. Neither party, he explained, had done the other justice, and his affection for her survived. If she wished to see him on the morrow to convey her feelings in person, he would come. "I am certain I never meant

*The penniless Prince Albert of Saxe-Coburg-Gotha, a tiny German dukedom, had just been announced as future husband for Queen Victoria, giving rise to rude jokes about his being purchased to sire the succession.

to write a *cruel* letter, but is it a true one? That is the question; and if you think that I have expressed the truth, shun that Disraeli whom you perhaps still love."

"For Gods sake come to me," she responded, confessing her concern over "the *apparent* impropriety of my present position." And she closed, "I am devoted to you."

Disraeli had salvaged his destiny, but the marriage would not take place until the close of the parliamentary session. Since it was assured, he could pay more attention to politics, then enlivened by the Court scandal of Victoria's having accused one of her mother's favorite Ladies of the Bedchamber, Flora Hastings, of being pregnant by the Duchess of Kent's comptroller and likely lover, Sir John Conroy. When Lady Flora would prove the slander erroneous by dying of a cancer that had bloated her belly, political concerns turned to the more foreboding matter of a possible insurrection of the Chartists, whose convention, running concurrently with Parliament, was preparing a petition of grievances to be delivered to the Government.

"I am full of Chartism," he wrote to Sarah in July 1839, and in another letter, "We are all talking of the making of pikes here and the arming of the Chartists." Rumors—some accurate—of clandestine pike-forging and other militant preparations for revolution had alarmed Parliament while not spurring any measures for political or social amelioration. On January 15, 1840, as the two Houses were about to resume sessions after the Christmas and New Year holidays, Benjamin would alarm Sarah unduly, "Last night all the town was terrified with the expected risings of the Chartists—the troops ordered to be ready, the police [dispatched] in all dir[ecti]ons, and the fire engines all full as incendiarism was to break out in several quarters." Perhaps, he backtracked, it was all a hoax. Ministers were informed, he had heard, that the Chartists were planning "to set the Thames on fire."

The Charter, later called by Winston Churchill "the last despairing cry of poverty against the Machine Age," demanded universal male suffrage, equal election districts, annual Parliaments, removal of the property qualification for Parliament, the secret ballot, and salaries for Members. Whatever the merits of the Chartist case, they hoped to win support because they represented the feared, seething mass of the underprivileged and unrepresented. Middle-class support was rejected, as it might dilute the message, yet only through the empowered middle class could they make any parliamentary headway. It was an adversarial perspective that would lead Disraeli, in *Sybil* (1845), to see Britain already divided into the rich and the poor, almost as separate nations.

Chartism as a force would fade, but most elements of the petition would find their way into law. Disraeli's condemnation of centralized relief in the new Poor Law of 1839, which took the Chartist view unpopular in his own party, was based on the humane elements associated with local administration, and lost otherwise in the bureaucracy. But centralization was cheaper, the only matter that counted with the majority. It proved, once more, to Disraeli that the Reform Act of 1832 had given power without responsibility to legislators outside the British tradition of governance. The new ruling class which seemed bound to consolidate its sway further seemed to him interested largely in keeping both trouble and expense as little as possible.

In *Sybil*, Disraeli would recall the monster petition of the People's Parliament "carried down to Parliament on a triumphal car, accompanied by all the delegates in solemn procession. It was necessary to construct a machine in order to introduce the large bulk of parchment, signed by a million and a half of persons, into the House of Commons, and . . . its vast form remained on the floor of the House during the discussion." The debate had been delayed by the "Bedchamber Crisis" precipitated by Victoria's impolitic refusal to dismiss her chief Court ladies, who were Whigs, in favor of ladies from Sir Robert Peel's party. The Queen—behaving unconstitutionally according to interpreters of that unwritten document—kept her ladies. As a result she kept her prime minister as well, Peel after two days of dithering refusing to accept office without what was little more than a symbolic perquisite. Melbourne remained.

That debate over the Charter could be more important than trivial patronage was lost on Parliament, and by the time consideration began, the Chartist convention had moved to seething Birmingham, a sink of industrial unemployment and agitation. A bloody riot followed, and Lord John Russell, the Home Secretary, asked the Commons to fund a local Birmingham constabulary to suppress further violence. One of the three to vote against the resolution, Disraeli rose to ask that an investigation into the causes ("the pedigree of sedition") precede any use of force. By then the House had decided, 235–46, to ignore the Charter, and Disraeli, having it both ways, declared the instrument an inappropriate device for change and remained with his party. Yet he was one of five to vote against harsh punishment for Chartist leaders, prophesying that the Radical agitators of the present might be the ruling class of the future. "Although Jack Straw was hanged," he warned, "a Lord John Straw may become a Secretary of State."

In the debate on the Petition, he invited a rebuke from the Chancellor of the Exchequer for reminding the Commons, "Nobody can deny that the Chartists labour under great grievances. Look at the House; it has been sitting now for five months. What has it done for the people? Nothing. The Government sees everything in the brightest colours; everything is the best in the best of worlds. The Government is busy making peers, creating baronets, at the very moment when a social insurrection is at the threshold." The Tory Radical side of Disraeli would emerge often enough to cause the leadership to question his party loyalty, but his ambitions as a Tory were sometimes checked by his sense of history. The electoral forces of the future were stirring, and he would not turn a blind eye to them. As his oracular figure in *Coningsby* would say a few years later, "I have been of opinion that revolutions are not to be evaded."

As the Chartist agitation wound its way in and out of the Commons, Disraeli and Mrs. Wyndham Lewis married and settled down to live happily ever after. But the happiness was uncertain, given the extent of his debts as well as his efforts to keep the worst from his wife. Her jealousy of his ties to his family made it necessary for Sarah to write to the Carlton Club, with occasional letters—like placebos—mailed to Grosvenor Gate. The wedding itself had to be postponed because of the death of John Viney Evans, Mary Anne's brother, early in July, but when they were apart, Disraeli wrote to her as "my dear wife" to reinforce expectations.

Evans's death had given Mary Anne new reasons of propriety to delay the marriage even further.

In August, with the date of the very private ceremony finally fixed, Isaac proposed a financial settlement which would help ease Ben's burden of debt. Nearly a year later the negotiations with lenders were still dragging on, with Ben apparently attempting to reduce some of the claims against him, astronomically magnified by interest over the years, on grounds that he was under age when the commitments had been made and thus legally incompetent to have become a debtor. The Carlton Club received his sensitive correspondence. (William Pyne was informed that good financial news could be sent to Grosvenor Gate.)

The ring was purchased and the license obtained on August 24, and in the next week Ben visited and wrote to his Basevi and Lindo relatives to formally announce the impending wedding to which none of them would be invited. Nor would the D'Israeli family be present at fashionable St. George's, Hanover Square, on the morning of Wednesday, August 28. Ben arrived by way of the home of his best man, Lord Lyndhurst, and Mary Anne, in "a travelling dress of exotic brilliancy" (as Ben wrote to Sarah), was given away by her mother's distinguished cousin, William Scrope, a landscape painter and well-known Wiltshire sportsman. Although one of Lyndhurst's horses was "seized with the staggers" en route to the church, the married couple had other equipage for their trip to Tunbridge Wells. Isaac's present to Mrs. Disraeli had been a new carriage, in which the newlyweds were attended by their own servants in livery of silver, brown, and gold.

At Bradenham the family celebrated afterward without the bride and groom, hosting a dinner and dance for the household servants. Carefully buttering up her new father-in-law, Mary Anne wrote to "dear Papa" the next day, "I wish you could see your happy children." Tunbridge Wells, however, was less than a happy honeymoon venue. Since the rain never stopped, they escaped to Dover, from which they took a packet to Calais and went on to Baden-Baden and Munich, returning via Paris in the last week of November.

It was mid-December before the Disraelis returned to Bradenham, bringing with them Mary Anne's aged mother. They found Isaac failing in sight, with the devoted Sarah working on his books with him. Out of Ben's life, unable to find a life of her own, she had new employment.

For Mary Anne, life with Ben was not at first markedly different. She had been the wife of an M.P. before, and she was living in her own house off Park Lane. But Ben's life had a dimension to it which was new to her experience. As he wrote to Sarah early in December, before the visit to Bradenham, on the previous Saturday evening he and Mary Anne had "dined en famille with Mrs. Montefiore to meet Anthony Rothschild who is to marry one of the Montefiores. . . . There were Rothschilds[,] Montefiores, Alberts, and Disraelis—not a Xtian name, but Mary Anne bearing it like a philosopher." He had dined with the Montefiores at their home in Great Stanhope Street, Mayfair, for the first time that March, "very different to what I expected," he confessed to Sarah. The family was "extremely well bred; great repose yet . . . *savoir vivre.*" Through Isaac he had never experienced such exemplars of the rejected culture, and Maria's Basevis and Lindos were only nominal Jews, most of them in the process of assimilation. When canvassing for votes, Disraeli regularly suffered gibes of "old clo's"—which represented Jewry in the public perception, and even his own, far more than did a remote Montefiore or a mythic Rothschild. Some months later he boasted to Sarah that at a dinner he had sat next to Lionel de Rothschild, whom he would admire above most men. An outsider in both worlds, Disraeli would not be cultivated by London's Jewish community, or even by its elite. Yet he would become close to a very few, and Mary Anne would not be excluded.

Mary Anne would herself be an effective hostess although, lacking a large staff, she would often have the food sent in and hire extra servants to wear her livery. "I have asked nearly sixty MPs to dine with me," he told Sarah on February 12, 1840, "and 40 have come. I shall rest upon my oars. There is scarcely any one of station in the House of Commons or society that I have not paid this attention to, which was most politic." Reporting on such political dinners, the scurrilous weekly, *The Satirist,* added its usual anti-Semitic twist. "Was ever such an impudent, indolent, Hebrew varlet as this fellow, D'Israeli? 'Ma shon Pen' as the old man was wont to call him, is somebody now, at all events!" That the sophisticated master of the language, Isaac D'Israeli, referred to his "pretty Ben" in a spurious Cockney was only the first of the inventions in Barnard Gregory's weekly "Censor of the Times." Disraeli the Younger, he went on, was now

> able to give dinners to "leading members of the Conservative party," and he has a "mansion". . . . Laugh not, gentle reader, a "mansion." But how came him by that mansion? Why, there lived a simple old fellow of the name of Lewis, whose ancestors are said by some people to have been Jews, and to have rejoiced in the patronymic of Levi; be this as it may, the old buck married the grand-daughter of a Welsh dairymaid—a smart, pretty, good-tempered milliner girl. The old boy took it into his head to die one day, and leave his buxom widow some three or four thousand pounds a year. "Younk Pen" happened to thrust his beard in the way— she liked its shape—a "bargain" was struck—"Pen" hopped into the shoes of the old fellow, and now he "poasts" of having a "mansion". . . . We trust the police will keep an eye on him.

It was no coincidence that in the same rag, published from 334 Strand, the editor published in his "Chit-Chat" column a couplet attacking both Disraeli and his bride:

> *"They call me Jew," D'Israeli cried—"I'm none,"*
> *"Though," quoth my lady, "he's got the cut of one!"*

A few weeks earlier *The Satirist* had prepared for the pun on circumcision with the vicious invention, purportedly from a pamphlet published in 1805 by a converted Moldavian rabbi, that when a Jewish child was circumcised, "the haham (or doctor) takes a goblet of wine, in which they put a drop of blood of the circumcision and a *drop of blood of a murdered Christian*. After having mixed it, the haham puts his finger into the goblet, and then puts it into the mouth of the child twice, saying, 'I have given thee thy blood and thy life.' "

To employ the libel and slander laws would only have given Gregory's publication publicity and Disraeli notoriety, of which he had enough. Gregory would even refer imaginatively to Disraeli's "Hebrew accent and dialect," which would have surprised those who heard him speak on the hustings or in the Commons. Uncowed—even energized—by the bigotry and unafraid to speak his mind despite his lack of seniority, Disraeli made his presence in Parliament increasingly visible. And the sense that he was a future force expanded his circle of influential acquaintances beyond the High Bohemia of Count D'Orsay, Lady Cork, and Edward Bulwer. Still, that somewhat raffish collection continued to be useful in ways which the future had not yet intimated to him. At Bulwer's rented house on the Thames, for example, he encountered the exiled Prince Louis Napoleon, who offered to take him, and Mary Anne, to meet a boat downstream that was bringing more guests to the breakfast party. They hailed a passing boatman from the terrace; Louis Napoleon confidently took the oars himself, and, Disraeli recalled many years later, "for a time we went on very well. At last, to escape the swell of a steamer that was approaching, the Prince contrived to row into a mud-bank in the middle of the river, and there we were stuck. Nothing could get us off." Mary Anne, usually alarmed by less, scolded Louis Napoleon, "You should not undertake things which you cannot accomplish. You are always, sir, too adventurous." Watching from the bank, the boatman found another craft and rowed off to the rescue, returning them to Craven Cottage.

Dining with Emperor Napoleon III at the Tuileries in 1856, Mary Anne recalled the incident, and the former Louis Napoleon confessed to it. "Just like him," said Empress Eugénie. The old connection would prove useful as both men made their claims upon destiny, but Louis Napoleon almost lost his chance by failing to heed Mrs. Disraeli's advice. On August 6, 1840, having set off for France to try to overthrow King Louis-Philippe's government, he and some of his cohorts were landed from a steamer at Boulogne. Failing to win over the local garrison, they signaled for a launch from the steamer, but too many men scrambled to get into it and it overturned. Swimming for safety, Napoleon Bona-parte's ambitious nephew was captured, tried in Paris, and impris-oned, escaping in 1846 to try again.

Nothing would give Disraeli more continuing grief than his finances, which seemed always well beyond his capacity to repair. While William Pyne tried, his manipulations could not take the place of money, and he was usually at odds with Disraeli as to strategy. On January 1, 1840, Disraeli had written with bravado to Pyne, whose health was then too poor to enable him to attend to much business, "I have only my own exertions to trust to, and I must therefore consult my own judgment as to my own conduct. *I wish everything to be left to me at this moment*, and I feel confident under these circumstances, that before the spring passes away, ev-ery claim on me will be arranged to the complete satisfaction of all parties concerned." Spring came and went without any of the predicted miracles occurring. What was worse, Isaac having, he thought, settled sufficient funds upon his son to enable him to marry in confidence, found in his mail in that first year of the Penny Post a demand from Thomas Jones, one of Ben's creditors from the South American mining share days.

Despairingly, Isaac responded through Sarah, who had read the letter to him, that he had no idea such debts still existed. De-spite his "heavy infirmity" he had recently taken some pecuniary steps for his son that he had expected "would conduce to his per-manent comfort," and did not have the resources to do more. "It is a long time," he added, "since from the disordered state of my sight I have been able to write with my own hand. . . . Your letter has been read to me, & I have listened to it with astonish-ment. . . . I learn for the first time with surprise and sorrow that any one should have entered into pecuniary matters with any son of mine at a period of life when he was not only legally, but I should think morally incompetent to regulate himself."

"Let it suffice," Ben advised Sarah, who had sent a draft of Isaac's letter to him (probably on May 30, 1840), "that the affair is not of the slightest importance—that Jones has not a leg to stand on from a legal point of view." He professed certainty re-garding his finances that he would "effect a complete, thoro' and permanent arrangem[en]t."

The arrangements would be so lacking in completeness that on July 13, 1840, he had to write to Pyne that an R. Manning, who conducted an office for service of writs, had arrived at Grosvenor Gate to demand payment of overdue annual fees on at least £5,000 of further debt. There would still be £4,000 owed as late as 1876, which Disraeli settled with the deceased creditor's estate. But he wrote Pyne that he had the servants turn Manning out. One surviving writ served on Disraeli, in the name of a Sir Benjamin Smith, at Grosvenor Gate, on July 21, 1840, in the amount of £500 plus £2/4s. in costs, also notes interest of five percent per month until satisfied. (Interest rates from such lenders often ranged upward from an annual forty percent to whatever the desperate debtor was willing to accept to pay off previous loans.)

Disraeli's fiscal chaos, ever worsening with huge interest aggregates, was bound to reach Mary Anne, and on November 1 he wrote to the long-suffering Pyne that a writ delivered in his absence had "produced a terrible domestic crisis." It did not help that Lady Blessington's 1841 *Book of Beauty* had just appeared with Chalon's bare-shouldered portrait of Mary Anne and Disraeli's accompanying verses on her perfection. (*The Satirist*, always at Disraeli, criticized him for pretending that his matronly spouse of "forty-nine or fifty" was "of angelic form and grace.")* No flattery could now conceal from Mary Anne the financial disgrace that loomed, yet much of her husband's debts were beyond her capacity to repay, and some still remained concealed from her. At a time when a family could live comfortably on £100 a year, the money owed by Disraeli was enormous.

The culprit who opened the Pandora's Box of his improvidence was George Samuel Ford, a solicitor with offices in Henrietta Street, Covent Garden. Ford was also a moneylender. Disraeli had little choice but to put his financial affairs in the hands of Ford by March 1841, as that month a sheriff's offi-

*Nathaniel Montefiore, who liked "Mr Disi," confessed skepticism in a letter to his sister Louisa de Rothschild that readers would see in Mrs. Disraeli anything more than "one of the numberless worshippers who . . . kneel in vain at the altar of Beauty."

cer, J. L. Nathan, had arrived, Disraeli wrote to Pyne, with a judgment "signed ag[ain]st me, and an executive virtually put in my house. . . ." (Apparently a sheriff's official was armed with a writ which authorized access to 2 Grosvenor Gate to oversee its execution.) And there was another action pending, related to a bill for £800 which he had backed for the delinquent D'Orsay. Disraeli had to borrow at forty percent interest from Ford to avoid another judgment. He was, he confessed to Pyne a few weeks later, "badly distressed" for "pocket money"—he needed £500, which demand he reduced two days later to £300 in hopes of securing something. The urgency was the expensive dinner party he and Mary Anne had just given (May 6, 1841) for the Duke of Buckingham and Chandos, the Marquess of Salisbury, Henry Goulburn (soon to be Peel's Chancellor of the Exchequer), and other influential peers and politicians. In the face of his financial catastrophe, Disraeli was entertaining as if he had no worldly cares, and rising to speak in the House with assurance and effect—"many fine hits," he would boast to Sarah on May 15, 1841.

In theory, Disraeli remained safe as long as he remained an M.P. A verse published in 1840 quoted an M.P. as boasting:

I may become immerged in debt,
And leave my creditors to fret,
Without a chance to ever get
My person in a legal net;
My fingers I can gaily snap,
When at my knocker they may rap;
My shoulder, too, defies the tap
Of every caption-loving chap . . .

In truth, the embarrassments of public indebtedness—and creditors knew the value of bad publicity—might cost a Member his next election, and then his liberty.

Although while an M.P. he could not be imprisoned for debt, all his goods could be seized, and sheriffs would inventory everything movable at Grosvenor Gate, from an ormolu clock in the drawing room to a featherbed bolster in the attic. And with

Parliament to be dissolved on June 23, 1841, there was a chance that he would be subject to arrest.* He had to regain a seat. The mercenary electors at Maidstone, many of them first empowered by the reforms of 1832, would have to be foregone. The selling of votes had burgeoned, one of the unsavory side effects of enfranchising segments of society new to the ballot. Disraeli could not afford new bribes even had he wanted to buy votes, and the suit against him by Maidstone's finest citizens still rankled. Early in June, when he knew that dissolution was impending, he arranged to run from Shrewsbury. It was the best he could do. An apparently safe Tory constituency in Shropshire, it was nearly a twelve hours' journey from London—six hours by train to Wolverhampton and six more (since there was as yet no rail link) by road. Again Disraeli had a partner for a second seat, this time George Tomline, a local landowner nine years Disraeli's junior who had represented Sudbury in 1840–41.

The prospects looked good, and Disraeli prepared for release on June 18 an electioneering appeal for the pair that stressed his favorite theme of "old Constitutional Principles" threatened by "the new self-interested doctrines of Government." Six days later a broadsheet appeared, boldly and blackly headed: "JUDGMENTS AGAINST B DISRAELI, Esq." Three separate listings appeared—in the Queen's Bench, in the Common Pleas, and in the Exchequer. They totaled over £22,000, and all were genuine and incontrovertible. In the list of unsatisfied debts, the broadsheet declared, were included "the names of unhappy Tailors, Hosiers, Upholsterers, Jew Money Lenders (for this Child of Israel was not satisfied with merely spoiling the Egyptians), Spunging Housekeepers and, in short, persons of every denomination who were foolish enough to trust him."

The "Honest Electors of Shrewsbury" were asked whether

---

*Arrest, subsequent embarrassment, and release, but not jailing. In 1838, imprisonment on mesne process—under a court order prior to final judgment—had been abolished. Its excuse had been to prevent a debtor's fleeing the jurisdiction, but was widely employed for intimidation and extortion. One could still be jailed on final process—on determination by a court and judge. Debtors' prisons themselves faded away in the 1860s and 1870s, when regular penal institutions began to be utilized.

they wished to be represented by such an unprincipled delinquent. "Take warning by your brethren at Maidstone, whom Benjamin cannot face again. He seeks a place in Parliament merely for the purpose of avoiding the necessity of a Prison."

Pretending not to be mortified, Disraeli issued his own broadsheet the next day, declaring the charges "UTTERLY FALSE" and blaming several judgments upon his standing security for "a noble friend"—the unidentified D'Orsay. The attack, he claimed, was "unprecedented for its malignity and its meanness," and he did not believe, in any case, "that the merit of a man mainly depends upon his Property." But the battle had also been joined at a different level, and he faced taunts of "Bring a bit of pork for the Jew," with morsels of roast pig displayed on sticks and held as close to him as the malefactors could approach. In the midst of a speech he observed a man advancing toward the platform leading a small cart drawn by a donkey—often called a "Jerusalem pony" after the arrival of Jesus in Jerusalem on a donkey described in the Gospel of St. Luke. When the man halted in front of him, Disraeli paused in his address and asked, "What is the meaning of your equipage, my friend?"

"Well," he said, having hoped to be asked, "I be come here to take you back to Jerusalem!"

There was no appropriate response that Disraeli could think of. He offered a wan smile and went on with his address.

Unhelpful to his electioneering, given local sensitivities, he employed at one point a familiar metaphor at odds with conventional religion. "What are we after all?" he asked the Shrewsbury crowd, to the distress of George Tomline. "What are even the best of us? Mites crawling about a cheese!"

Polling began on Tuesday morning June 29, 1841, with results announced by the Mayor at noon the next day. Tomline and Disraeli led, with Tomline's 793 votes just ahead of the outsider Disraeli's 785. "In half an hour I shall be chaired," Ben wrote to his mother while awaiting the beginning of the traditional victory procession. With relief he also wrote to Sarah that he had been "only five days out of Parl[iamen]t!" Once more, he had evaded debtor's prison.

XI

"I ALREADY FIND MYSELF WITHOUT EFFORT
THE LEADER OF A PARTY,
CHIEFLY OF THE YOUTH."

1841–1844

LATE IN 1840 THE SHORT-LIVED *LONDON MAGAZINE, CHARIVARI AND Courier des Dames* disinterred Disraeli's vow in his maiden speech in the Commons that he would be heard, and it went on to taunt, "That time has never arrived." He had "renewed his efforts repeatedly," the anonymous scold charged, even "moderating his tone into a semblance of humility, but Disraeli was only sometimes listened to. He had not made the slightest impression in the House, *and we may fairly predict he never will.*" Accompanying was a sardonic caricature of the aspiring statesman, with a bird following Disraeli's footsteps and mimicking his already characteristic stooping walk. The forecast appeared well founded.

If Disraeli had made the slightest impression upon his party leader, Sir Robert Peel (again Prime Minister), the evidence was not in any feelers about a possible appointment. Dour and aloof, Peel displayed little warmth even to his closest associates, and Disraeli had looked in vain for encouragement of his hopes in a thin smile or a word of compliment through a third party. Son of

a wealthy cotton manufacturer and a product of Harrow and Oxford, Peel had inherited a recent baronetcy, had never had to run
for a contested seat, and was seen as suspect in his sympathy for
the landed class. He had no rivals for primacy once Wellington
had relinquished further ambitions, and he expected loyal support
in Parliament as builder of national consensus.

Most younger politicians with Peel's background sought more
congenial seats on the Whig side of the aisle, where Members
were beginning to call themselves Liberals while the Tories were
identifying themselves as Conservatives. An anomaly on either
side, Disraeli came neither from old money nor new, neither from
country nor factory town. Older than such of his competitors as
William Ewart Gladstone who had the benefits of birth or
wealth—or both—in acquiring safe seats as soon as they came of
age, and who had already acquired experience and seniority in
the legislative club, the M.P. from Shrewsbury counted, to catch
up, upon his loyalty in fighting hopeless battles and in propagan-
dizing for Tory causes.

With a Conservative majority of ninety-one, Peel named a
Cabinet that included five prime ministers, past, present, and future. Again in a sub-Cabinet post was Gladstone, then thirty-two.
Feeling humiliated, Disraeli pressed his case with Peel on September 5, 1841. Since 1834 he had fought four elections for the party,
"expended great sums," and "exerted my utmost for the propagation of your policy." And he had a special claim, he added, about
which he could not remain silent. "I have had to struggle against
a storm of political hate and malice, which few men have ever
experienced, . . . sustained under these trials by the conviction
that the day would come when the foremost man of this country
would publickly testify that he had some respect for my ability
and my character." To remain unrecognized seemed an "overwhelming" injustice.

A "long convers[ati]on" with Peel at a social gathering the
previous March was Disraeli's only reason for expecting office.
Postelection talk between husband and wife may have recalled
the occasion. Probably without Disraeli's knowledge—the idea
that she would have groveled to the Prime Minister in his behalf
would have embarrassed him and reduced his credit—Mary Anne

had solicited Peel the night before, "overwhelmed with anxiety" that rejection would crush her husband's career. "Literature," she reminded Peel, "he has abandoned for politics."

Some of her phrases echoed Disraeli's, but very likely only because he had confided his hopes so often. Her own claim was that at Maidstone alone she had raised or spent from her own resources "more than £40,000." (Since Disraeli's share of the joint expenses of campaigning for the two seats had been calculated at just over £4,500, either the Wyndham Lewises had been estimating his costs modestly then, given his inability to pay, or Mary Anne had now inflated their investment on the basis of what had since been made public about electoral corruption in Maidstone.)

To keep her husband from discovering her intervention she urged Peel not to reply to her "humble petition." Yet she must have known that Disraeli was writing on his own that Sunday morning in a last-ditch appeal for a minor place.

On Monday morning, September 6, 1841, London newspapers published a list of appointments. "All is over," Disraeli mourned to Sarah. He was consoled in the devotion of Mary Anne, for whom, he lied, he had "aspired to this baffled dignity." From Peel he received a response expressing surprise that Disraeli had thought he had been promised office. Disraeli claimed that Peel had "misconceived my meaning." What Peel had misconceived was Disraeli's ability to make himself too crucial a personage to exclude. But that lay in strategies which Disraeli had not yet formulated.

Although he wanted to flee from his disappointments and debts and did take a packet with Mary Anne to Caen, his burdens followed. A petition to invalidate his election and that of Tomline on grounds of bribery was filed with the Commons by several hostile citizens of Shrewsbury, and Disraeli's paper-thin property qualification was further challenged. There would be some awkward months until the charge was withdrawn. Although his seat was immunizing him from years behind bars, if he returned to England, he told Pyne from France, it would be "to a nest of hornets."

The hornets were swarming when Disraeli reappeared in London. While Mary Anne attended to her failing mother, Mrs.

Yate, he slipped off to Bradenham until the new Parliament opened. Early in February, Mary Anne took Mrs. Yate to Bradenham, where there were more servants to help care for her. The Disraelis were employing a minimum of household staff and paring expenses further by claiming Isaac's hospitality at Bradenham, an obligation Isaac accepted happily. He doted upon Mary Anne, who had quickly established an affectionate relationship with the sedentary and now nearly sightless old man.

Whatever political triumphs Ben achieved in her absence were magnified in his letters. Between gushy endearments that he knew would please her were accounts of his austere domestic life. He kissed her "vacant pillow" each night, "dined at home" daily, confined his alcoholic intake to "port and water," and sympathized with every imaginary rudeness she touchily sensed from the family in her awareness of her parasitism. Realizing that Mrs. Yate could not last much longer, the Disraelis arranged to settle some of their debts by borrowing £5,000 from Ford, at five percent interest, on the expectations of an inheritance of approximately that amount. As Ben put it on February 24, 1842, in that manner they had coped with "two of the principal usurers."

At the end of the month he brought the loan papers for her signature, then returned by rail to London "at the rate of nearly fifty miles an hour." He had new instructions in her absence. As she could not dress his hair, she had advised him to send for Prince Albert's coiffeur, Herr Breidenbach, who had a salon nearby at 88 Park Street, Grosvenor Square. Ben was to "tell him the way I dress it, . . . *to cut it,* but do not let him *cut* it, only; DRESS IT and if he dresses it too formal, you can always pull it about a little." When he described "Breidenbach[']s first experiment," she responded with the urgent ardor of absence, "I am now & ever your devoted Wife your own little slave your darling yr friend sweetheart companion & bedfellow—your own property."

From Grosvenor Gate he reported on the impact of one of his speeches—even "Peel, giving me a cheer," and Sir Richard Vyvyan taking him aside to congratulate him for not consulting "a single note—a great demonstration." Peel had warned that he would not support the proposal to be advanced (the merging of the consular and diplomatic services) and Disraeli knew that he had to be prepared for a vigorous response from Viscount Palmerston, Foreign Secretary in the departed Whig administration, whom he planned to accuse of appointing political hacks to the denigrated consular posts.

Palmerston could cut his opponents up in a courtly manner and had twenty years of practice at it. Turning back Disraeli's charge, he reminded the Commons that the "hon. Gentleman himself" would have seized a political appointment in the Tory government had one been offered. Unembarrassed, Disraeli reminded the Commons that Palmerston had even jumped parties to retain office himself, and was "a consummate master" of the art. The silence at his incautiousness in challenging "the noble Viscount" turned to cheers from his side of the aisle.

At supper at Crockford's afterward—he had made an exception to his practice in order to bask in his triumph among clubmen cronies—the Tory wit and former M.P. Horace Twiss, then writing political leaders for *The Times*, compared him ("between mighty mouthfuls") to Palmerston, Disraeli wrote to Mary Anne, calling his seemingly extemporaneous speech delivery "the completest case of having a man on the hip that I can remember in Parliam[en]t." The mastery of facts in a conversational style, in apparently effortless recall, would become the hallmark of a Disraeli performance, filling the benches far in advance when it was known he would rise. Like a Macready he would painstakingly prepare his lines, perfecting his technique in the solitude of nearly empty Grosvenor Gate.

On March 11 he wrote to Mary Anne, still at Bradenham, "I already find myself with[ou]t effort the leader of a party—chiefly of the youth, & new members." In numbers he had no new party, but a few junior Members had begun clustering about him in search of a spokesman for such Tory principles as they perceived were being abandoned by Peel. One was George Smythe, son of Lord Strangford, M.P. for Canterbury, known for his sideburned profile and his way with the ladies. Ben had already described him to Mary Anne as "very radical indeed & [as] unprincipled as his little agreeable self." Less lightweight, Disraeli thought, was the M.P. from Newark, Lord John Manners, second son of the 5th

Duke of Rutland. At twenty-four, he was only eight months younger than Smythe and also in his first Parliamentary seat, from a
family constituency. At twenty he had written a poem, "England's
Trust," which evinced a nostalgic medievalism, redolent of Walter
Scott, in which

> Each knew his place—king, peasant, peer or priest,
> The greatest owned connexion with the least;
> From rank to rank the generous feeling ran,
> And linked society as man to man.

It was a world, Manners concluded, "free from modern restless-
ness," in which tradition-minded citizens possessed "nobility of
character." Disraeli was quickly attracted to him.

A third, Alexander Baillie-Cochrane, M.P. for Bridport as a
"Liberal-Conservative," was two years older than Manners, son of
an Admiral of the Fleet, inheritor from his mother of a Lanarkshire estate, and a product of Eton and Cambridge. When he
spoke against the New Poor Law of 1834 as legislation without
compassion, he earned Disraeli's attention.

At Bradenham, Mary Anne relished Disraeli's Parliamentary
gossip. The bibulous 3rd Marquess of Hertford, as dissolute as he
was rich, had died on March 1—"of putrefaction," Ben wrote.
Complicated by dozens of codicils which countermanded each
other, the Marquess's will was as convoluted as his life, which included scheming stewards, resident prostitutes, and illegitimate
progeny. One of his largest and least scandalous bequests, it
quickly emerged, would go to the Galway-born Tory propagandist
John Wilson Croker, who had coined the word *Conservative* for
his party in an article in January 1840. Disraeli would make fictional use of both men, as he would of his young M.P. friends.
Not yet realizing that the characters and situations would become
his to exploit, he wrote to Mary Anne on March 11 about Hertford's death, "[Alexander] Pope c[oul]d do it justice."

While others of Disraeli's acquaintance who were grandly in
debt lived abroad to escape their creditors, he survived in London
month by month, shielded by his Parliamentary seat and the
patchwork of new loans for old. Even had the Commons not been

in session, he could not leave because of Mrs. Yate, who was finally moved in April by special invalid carriage from Bradenham
so that she could die at Grosvenor Gate. The end came on the
morning of May 29. With the Disraelis having borrowed against
her estate, there was little left to inherit, and in part to live more
frugally (Ben claimed that Mary Anne was broken by her bereavement and needed "country air") they planned a lengthy stay
in France once the House ended its sittings on August 12. Although Disraeli did rise on several further occasions after his encounter with Palmerston in March—once to belabor Peel—he
was more subdued than usual. Minor office would have furnished
a salary and increased dignity, but he closed the session with no
prospects of either.

On September 19, 1842, the Disraelis left by the Tower
Dock for France, Ben putting his confidential affairs in Sarah's
hands. His letters to her from the Hotel de l'Europe in Paris were
a catalogue of visits and visitors, *dejeuners* and dinners. He discussed English affairs almost as often as if he were in London,
talking politics with Henry Hope, M.P. for Gloucester and millionaire squire of a vast country estate, The Deepdene, and with
Alexander Baillie-Cochrane and George Smythe. Earlier, Smythe
had met with John Manners in Geneva, where they mulled over
an alliance of like-minded Members. "If we keep together," Manners noted in his journal late in June, "we might be formidable;
considerable attention is being paid even now to our movement."
What he meant was the minuscule "new party" which Disraeli
had described in March. Manners had followed up the Geneva
idea with an approach to Disraeli, then still in London.

Realistically, given party discipline and the possible temptations of place, Disraeli anticipated few adherents. His response
was clear from another note by Manners: "D'Israeli wishes us to
form a party with certain general principles, not to interfere with
acceptance of office. He says even six men acting so together
would have great weight. . . . I think . . . there never was a House
of Commons in which there was so much young talent frittered
away." One of the alleged talents, George Smythe, wrote to Manners after seeing Disraeli in Paris in October, "Dizzy has much
more parliamentary power than I had any notion of," and he

went on to list possible allies, including John Walter, proprietor of *The Times*. Nevertheless, Smythe worried that any alliance with the mercurial Disraeli would quickly become, as he joked to Manners, a "Diz-Union." Since each had more to gain than to lose, the result, gathering momentum in Paris in the closing months of 1842, would be "Young England," a much publicized movement that in size, and more, was briefly the David to Peel's Goliath. In a speech at Bingley in October 1844 Disraeli would credit its name to a taunt "given us in derision." (First to use the tag was Joseph Hume, a Radical M.P. who used it early in 1843.)

Paris was enlivened for the Disraelis by more than politics. Through one of Count D'Orsay's sisters, the Duchesse de Gramont, they were introduced to the French aristocracy, and through Lyndhurst's elderly father-in-law, Lewis Goldsmith, once an agent for Napoleon, they had entrée into yet another segment of French society. Henry Bulwer of the Paris embassy was a valuable contact, and the Rothschilds and Montefiores of London arranged for access to Anthony de Rothschild's uncle, the head of the Paris branch of the family enterprises, Baron Jacob James Mayer de Rothschild. "I believe you know my nephew," said the Baron on introducing himself. "A happy mixture," Ben described him to Sarah, "of the French dandy & the orange boy."

Early in January the Disraelis went to a ball at the palatial residence of Baron Solomon Mayer de Rothschild, nearly seventy, who had established the Vienna offices of the financial empire and was second son of the already legendary Mayer Amschel Rothschild, the founding father. It was "an unrivalled palace," Ben told Sarah, "more gorgeous than the Tuileries," and with exotic dishes in such profusion that there were "pineapples plentiful as blackberries." Mary Anne was even lent a Rothschild box at the Opéra, "lined in crimson velvet" and adjoining the royal boxes.

Inevitably the august Disraelian connections, which included Lord Cowley, the ambassador, led to invitations from King Louis-Philippe. "Mr Disraeli had never been to St Cloud in the evening," the King explained to his aide, General Marie de Baudrand. "I wish to present him to the Queen." The Court was in mourning for the Duc de Orléans, killed in a carriage accident, and Her Majesty seemed "tall, & sad, with white hair, a dignified

& graceful phantom." The King, however, sought a pipeline into British politics, and Disraeli, ecstatic over his opportunities "in the domesticity of a Court," in several visits spent hours with Louis-Philippe, moving quickly from the conspiracy-minded journalist of *Gallomania* to proponent of closer Anglo-French ties. If the Rothschilds could maintain amicably interlocking banking baronies that crossed national frontiers, why not nations with shared interests?

The link with Louis-Philippe dramatically enhanced Disraeli's reputation in Paris, and inflated his own sense of importance, Baillie-Cochrane writing on December 2, and invoking Byron's heroic poem, to John Manners, "Disraeli's salons rival Law[es]'s* under the Regent. Guizot, Thiers, Molé, Decazes and God wots how many *dei minores* are found in his antechamber, while the great man himself is closeted with Louis-Philippe at St Cloud, and already pictures himself as the founder of some new dynasty with his Manfred love-locks stamped on the current coin of the realm."

The sardonic and even spiteful remark raised, for the first time, the paradox presented by Disraeli to aspiring Tory politicians. Like him or not, they needed him. He could make his way, and they theirs with him. He would promote their ideas better than they could, and while the arrogance of his ambition seemed written on his sleeve, he might just bring it off.

A vision of Queen Anne's political strategist, Lord Bolingbroke, might be forgiven Disraeli as he found himself in political demand not in his own country but in France as 1842 slipped into 1843. In Tory opposition a century earlier, Bolingbroke was reputed to have received secret financial assistance from the King of France. Possibly Disraeli was hinting at his potential usefulness to France as a policy maker in England if he could gain some power over a group of "swing" votes and secure covert financial support to help his friends fight elections. There was no treason in it, but Young England and King Louis-Philippe would both vanish from the stage before the "vast combinations" about which Disraeli dreamed could materialize.

*Composer Henry Lawes's house in the London of Oliver Cromwell was a haven for the aristocracy of the Interregnum as well as for ex-Royalists.

Late in January Disraeli returned to London to prepare for the new session of Parliament and closeted himself first with his usurers. In the Commons he quickly found his opportunity to link France with English interests by speaking in behalf of commercial treaties with neighboring nations that might open markets for domestic industry and agriculture. But not even his small cadre of Young Englanders were of one mind about the cure for what was being called "the Condition of England." Traditionally protectionist regarding agricultural products, Conservatives claimed to represent the landed interests whose power was being eroded by industry and the commerce in its merchandise, both in the Whiggish hands of the burgeoning middle classes who stood to gain the most from further electoral reform.

In the Prime Minister's shifting away from the Corn Laws, and Protection as Tory ideology, lay the opportunity for opposition to Peel within the party. William Cobden, Disraeli's own age and far more famous, Radical M.P. from Stockport and a founder of the Anti–Corn Law League, had fanned Free Trade agitation in and out of Parliament, and was turning Peel into a convert, the Prime Minister citing the national interest. Provincial Tory newspapers began accusing Peel of abandoning traditional principles, which in Disraeli's reading meant a modernized feudalism.

Young England would proselytize for a nostalgic Old England that never was as "Merrie" as its proponents described it, and revolved about attachment to the land through the institutions of Monarchy, Aristocracy, and Church, and their noblesse oblige toward a peasantry that now included the industrial labor force. It was a myth that gained power from the revival of a romanticized medievalism in art and architecture as well as in literature—and, through the Oxford Movement, an Anglicanism ritualized almost into Romanism. The Church of England—so Manners, Smythe, Cochrane, and their circle believed—had to lead the spiritual revival against materialism, which had degraded society. Evangelicalism could not be depended upon, as it had been embraced by factory owners and factory workers alike and was allied to Capitalism, which created value from manufactures rather than from land. Disraeli claimed to share his friends' sentimental Toryism, causing Smythe to explain to Manners: "Dizzy's attachment to moderate Oxfordism is something like Bonaparte's to moderate Mahomedanism." Manners confided to his journal: "Could I only satisfy myself that D'Israeli believed all that he said, I should be more happy; his historical views are quite mine, but does he believe them?" While conceding some truth to the Young England view, Karl Marx was another skeptic, seeing it as "half lamentation, half lampoon; half echo of the past, half menace of the future; at times by its witty and incisive criticism, striking the bourgeoisie in the very heart's core." To Marx it was a dreamy sentimentalism, with a "total incapacity to comprehend the march of history."

While Marx never cared about working within existing systems, Disraeli linked his ambitions to the Tories, and reform to traditional values espoused by Tories. In line with that pragmatism, Disraeli went with Mary Anne to Shrewsbury early in May 1843 to take part in local ceremonials, watch the races, and explain his votes in Parliament to his constituents. He spoke for an hour and twenty minutes and received loud cheers when he finished (perhaps because he had finished). Even London papers, not merely the friendly *Times* and *Chronicle*, reported him. Carefully, he backed Peel by interpreting the Prime Minister's moves as little more than periodic revisions of the tariffs, but Disraeli insisted that England could not countenance "hostile tariffs" and "free imports." One could not have free trade, he said, "unless the person you deal with is as liberal as yourself."

Trade policies, he declared, had to support "the landed interest, . . . the foundation of our national greatness." He applied the term broadly, to include "that great building up of our laws and manners which is . . . the ancient polity of the realm, and the ancient constitution of the realm." The "manners and duties" of Englishmen were supported by ownership of land, for their "great sympathy" with traditional values "proceeds from the fact that they have some stake in the realm."

The summer months were a heady period for Young England. Disraeli gained in visibility as its obvious leader. With the backing of John Walter, interested backbenchers met in London in a room at *The Times*, which referred to them as the "New Party," and at Walter's country home, Bearwood. Disraeli brought Mary

Anne to Bearwood, prompting Walter's daughter Catherine to describe her as "the greatest curiosity I ever met," while "D'Issy" was "the oddest being I ever saw." Having not been so odd to the French branch of the Rothschilds, the Disraelis found their English cousins increasingly welcoming. They were invited to dinner on June 22 by the Anthony de Rothschilds, whom they had seen in Paris, and the widowed Hannah Rothschild included them on July 29 in the party at Gunnersbury Park, near Acton, to greet King Ernest of Hanover, Victoria's uncle, and other royals. The late Nathan Mayer de Rothschild's "beautiful park and villa," Ben wrote to Sarah, who was still visiting the great vicariously through her brother's letters, were "worthy of an Italian Prince, though decorated with a taste and splendor which a French financier in the olden times could alone have rivalled."

In the Commons, Disraeli still attempted to appear sufficiently a party loyalist to support all measures but the few he had chosen over which to duel with Peel. And he turned that flexibility into a principle: Since Peel himself was abandoning policies that had returned the Tories at the ballot box, Conservatives who had campaigned upon those policies were not obligated to follow their leader away from established party positions. The Irish Arms Bill was one, and Smythe, Manners and Cochrane voted with Disraeli. Disraeli even indicted the Government as "do-nothing," and Peel turned on "the member for Shrewsbury." Excoriating him for ambition without practical ideas, the Prime Minister predicted that Disraeli would never "realise this vision of a great statesman." Uncowed, he returned a few days later to attack the Government's Irish and Turkish policies and to point to "dissatisfaction and distress at home."

It was August 9, as the session was winding down, that Disraeli joined the debate initiated when William Smith O'Brien asked for an inquiry on Irish grievances. Disraeli had done his homework and knew his history, describing the problem as not rooted in politics or religion but in tenure of land and overpopulation in a nonindustrial country where there was little work to be had. If one changed churches or cabinets, he contended, the degrading social conditions would not be improved. Nor was an Irish Arms Bill up for its third reading the solution either to agitation or

to despair, as Ireland was being governed "in a manner which con-
duces only to the injury of both countries." The "state of things"
was "the bane of England and the opprobrium of Europe."

He spoke from behind the benches of the Prime Minister
and Home Secretary, who reacted, a reporter from the Whiggish
Morning Chronicle wryly observed, uncomfortably. Peel "palli-
ate[d] the effects of the castigation by industriously rubbing his
nose," while Graham, "edging occasionally round, would look up
into the face of the orator with that sort of uneasy smile by which
one sometimes tries to convey the idea of being not only perfectly
at ease, but exceedingly amused."

A few days later, after Palmerston opened a debate on Middle Eastern policy, Disraeli rose again, this time to ask whether
England would defend its own interests in the region by maintaining the independence and integrity of the crumbling Ottoman Empire, and particularly its hold upon the Dardanelles, upon
which Russia had designs. In both cases he would keep to his positions throughout his parliamentary career.

Charles Greville characterized Disraeli and his little group in
a diary entry on August 11 as "abusive and impertinent." Writing
to John Wilson Croker a week later, Graham sneered, "With respect to Young England, the puppets are moved by Disraeli, who
is the ablest among them; I consider him unprincipled and disappointed. . . . I think with you that they will return to the crib after prancing, capering, and snorting; but a crack or two of the
whip well applied may hasten and insure their return. Disraeli
alone is mischievous. . . . It would be better for the party if he
were driven into the ranks of our open enemies." John Gibson
Lockhart, still running the *Quarterly Review*, told Croker that
Smythe was "the cleverest of the set" and that Disraeli and Peter
Borthwick, a newcomer, were unruly because they were "very ne-
cessitous, and wanted places, of course." Pleased with his precarious new eminence, Disraeli was peeved early in 1844 when Peel
failed to send him the usual party circular inviting M.P.s to attend
a meeting prior to the opening of Parliament. He had already
been surprised the month before when his effrontery at asking
Tory leaders for a post for his brother James was coldly rejected,
since he had secured a job for Ralph through Lyndhurst in 1841.

Graham wrote to Peel about the "impudent" request, given Disraeli's "conduct and language" in the previous session, and the Prime Minister confided to being pleased that "such a man puts his shabbiness upon record. . . . However it is a bridle in his mouth." Disraeli was slow to learn that he could not have it both ways. Independence had its price.

Invited by Henry Hope to The Deepdene, Dorking, the Disraelis arrived on September 5, 1843, and remained until September 28. Attacks on Young England from the loyalist Tory press, and on Disraeli in particular, had become so numerous that he was planning to write rejoinders while at The Deepdene. One diatribe he quoted to Sarah on August 29 scorned the Young Englander who "thinks himself equal both to Wm. Pitt & Wm. Shakespeare." Whether that was the trigger for Disraeli's new novel can only be guessed at.

The young squire of Wotton Hall, Surrey, the twenty-one-year-old William John Evelyn (a future Conservative M.P.), was at The Deepdene, "a young Oxonian and full of Young England,"* Ben wrote to Sarah from the Carlton Club on the day he returned. "We are going to Manchester and Liverpool—a rapid visit which I must make—and after a respite of forty-eight hours for business we should like to come to Bradenham for as long as you will have us. I am writing and want a workroom; therefore, if it does not inconvenience anybody, let me have my old writing-room next to your room. The journals daily descant on the 'new party' that has arisen to give new colour to modern politics."

All of the letter's contents emerged in some form in *Coningsby, or The New Generation*, the novel he began at The Deepdene and would dedicate to his host, Henry Hope. The handsome young Harry Coningsby possessed the innocence and idealism of young Evelyn and the physical characteristics of the sophisticated sinner George Smythe; even Disraeli's visit to Manchester still in the future would figure significantly in the book.

*Evelyn would never be that close to Disraeli again. When he was returned to Parliament for West Surrey in 1849, Disraeli, remembering him, sent him a congratulatory note. Although he was a loyal Tory and attended Mary Anne's crushes for Members at Grosvenor Gate, there was never another private meeting with Disraeli.

John Manners appeared as Lord Henry Sidney and Baillie-Cochrane as Lord Buckhurst. The Marquess of Hertford and his entourage, complete to the ignoble lord's melodramatic death, furnished the denouement, Hertford fictionalized into Coningsby's cranky and monstrous grandfather, Lord Monmouth, who describes Harry's windy Young England formulas about reverence for duty, authority and property as "fantastical puerilities." Disraeli took from life Hertford's own confidant, Tory publicist J. W. Croker—who would be astounded at the unkind accuracy of the image—as Monmouth's craven factotum, Rigby.

For his political setting, Disraeli chose the shaping event of his time, the Reform Bill of 1832, after which he would sweep through the decade. The plot, which is unimportant except as the vehicle for Disraeli's ideas, concerns the political and emotional education of a priggish young man of good family—a daydream Disraeli in Smythe's clothes—who eventually inherits a great deal of money, finds public service in politics, and secures a wife equal to his fortune. Disraeli had intended some political writing while at The Deepdene, and discussed his ideas with Henry Hope. It was Hope, he later claimed, who first urged him to package his message in literary form. Fiction, Disraeli duly concluded, was the form which, "in the temper of the times, offered the best chance of influencing opinion." Enlarging his audience might even earn some desperately needed money.

As he began his novel-with-a-purpose—it would have too much purpose to reach the highest levels as imaginative literature—Disraeli may have had little idea how subversive to contemporary Toryism it would become, or how little emphasis he would give to Young England's nostalgic medievalism. One theme, dramatized by the propagandist Rigby and the wirepullers Tadpole and Taper, was that politics was becoming dominated by party newspapers and political operatives. All three technicians busy themselves devising deceptive political slogans, and Taper comes up with a new party cry:

"Ancient institutions and modern improvements, I suppose, Mr. Tadpole?"

"Ameliorations is the better word; ameliorations. Nobody knows exactly what it means."
". . . The time has gone by for Tory governments.
What the country requires is a sound Conservative government."
"A sound Conservative government," said Taper,
musingly. "I understand: Tory men and Whig measures."

Traditional Conservatives were skewered in the reactionary
and rotten Lord Monmouth, who was interested exclusively in
conserving his wealth and his perquisites, while the new Tory,
whose message was embodied in Taper's maxim, was the unnamed
Peel. He was identified cautiously only as the Prime Minister—
author (as indeed he was) of what had become the party guide,
his "Tamworth Manifesto" of 1834, "an attempt," according to
the author of Coningsby, "to construct a party without principles."
It would ensure that "forms and phrases are religiously cherished
in order to make the semblance of a creed," while "bend[ing] to
the passion or combination of the hour."
    Despite the pauses in the plot for thoughtful paragraphs that
might otherwise have been articles in The Times, Disraeli leav-
ened his narrative with wit and with graphic scenes of political
and social life in the great houses of London and the parks and
manors of the country aristocracy, scenes written as if for an audience of Sarah D'Israelis. Monmouth's baronial seat, Beaumanoir, gave readers a look into Belvoir Castle, home of the Dukes of
Rutland. Lady Everingham's early afternoon "breakfasts" at her
magnificent "cottage" on the Thames combined the Rosebank of
the Marchioness of Londonderry with sumptuous Rothschild
houses: "The weather was as bright as the romances of Boccaccio;
there were pyramids of strawberries, in bowls colossal enough to
hold orange-trees; and the choicest band filled the air with en-
chanting strains, while a brilliant multitude sauntered on turf like
velvet, or roamed in desultory existence amid the quivering
shades of winding walks."
    Coningsby began as an examination of the nature of political
parties—who should be included in the electorate and who should
not—and how parties must change to conserve the old England as

it adapted to the new; the novel became an examination into "the Condition of England" as well as another self-examination of Disraeli as Jew. He faced his identity in the mirror every day, as well as in the relentless public perception of him as an outsider. He could fight his way in life only by turning his identity to his advantage, and his creation of the enigmatic Sidonia, who has no other name, embodied Disraeli's racial Judaism rather than the religion that would still have kept him from office. (In his only reference to religion, Sidonia tells Coningsby, "I am of that faith that the Apostles professed before they followed their Master.") However godlike in his potential power, Sidonia eschews its exercise because as a Jew he is barred from politics, a paradox possibly explainable on grounds that whatever else he might be able to effect, he could not expunge bigotry from history. To W. F. Monypenny, Disraeli's first major biographer (with G. E. Buckle), Sidonia was "the deity of Disraeli's religion," an emanation of pure, if passionless, intelligence. "Brains," Sidonia argues in Disraeli's behalf, "every day become more precious than blood. You must give men new ideas, you must teach them new words, you must modify their manners, you must change their laws, you must root out prejudices, subvert [obsolete] convictions, if you wish to be great."

Disraeli's Sidonia—the most striking character in all his fiction—was more myth than reality although often described as carved from "Baron Rothschild." By 1844 Disraeli knew the younger generation of Rothschilds but was not yet close to any of the three sons of Nathan Mayer, who never exploited his Austrian barony and had died in 1835, leaving the management of the London branch he founded to his eldest son, Lionel. But the Rothschilds were already nearly mythic, and Disraeli's mysterious, solitary Sidonia, most influential banker in Europe and beyond political frontiers, is also a Spinoza born into the Rothschild inheritance— and Spinoza was one of Isaac D'Israeli's heroes as well as Ben's.

Sidonia's Judaism "walled him out from the pursuits of a citizen" and left him without desire for progeny, or at least without what other men called love. Woman was to him "a toy," and man merely "a machine." "What we call the heart," he dismisses, "is a nervous sensation. . . . The affections are the children of ignorance; when the horizon of our experience expands, and models multiply, love and admiration imperceptibly vanish." The only charm in life, he concludes, is "the sense of existence." He becomes, by happy accident for Harry Coningsby, his informal mentor. Coningsby, of course, is not up to the mental strain of absorbing all that Sidonia has to offer, but by providing Sidonia with a listener he furnishes Disraeli with a way of talking about Jewishness that his readership would accept as also beyond Disraeli. "The only human quality that interested Sidonia was Intellect," Disraeli writes, and from Sidonia's rarefied perspective he views European politics and culture as a man without a country, for Jews, as a dispersed people, had none.

To save themselves, the Sidonias of Aragon had turned Christian during the Inquisition. When they established themselves elsewhere in Europe they returned to the synagogue and to the profession of banking. "Shut out from universities and schools," young Sidonia studied mathematics and philosophy in England with a Sephardic tutor, significantly named Rebello, who had always been a Jew, then learned his profession through residence with uncles—suggesting the Rothschilds—in Naples and Frankfurt. When he came of age, he "made arrangements with the heads of the houses that bore his name" about the management of his fortune and traveled the world, including Asia, Africa, and the Americas, to "exhaust the sources of human knowledge." He saw himself as "a lone being, alike without cares and without duties," and although "without affections," he was "susceptible of deep emotions, but not for individuals. . . . Public approbation was [also] worthless to him." It was "a temperament . . . peculiar to the East."

One of Sidonia's preoccupations was "in his descent and in the fortunes of his race." He was "proud of his origin, and confident in the future of his kind," for in his travels "Sidonia had visited and examined the Hebrew communities of the world. He had found, in general, the lower orders debased; the superior immersed in sordid pursuits; but he perceived that the[ir] intellectual development was not impaired. This gave him hope. He was persuaded that organisation would outlive persecution. When he reflected on what they had endured, it was only marvellous that the race had not disappeared. They had defied exile, massacre, spoliation, the degrading influence of the constant pursuit of gain; they had defied Time."

Sidonia's residence largely in England is explained by his temperament. "The somewhat hard and literal character of English life suited one who shrank from sensibility." But all over Europe the imaginative Sidonia—or Disraeli—sees crypto-Jews managing affairs: professors, ambassadors, generals, councillors, and cabinet members. Even in the recesses of history, Sidonia claims, this had happened: In the Spain from which his own family had come, many of the first Jesuits were Jews. Someone would write to the *Morning Post* questioning the Jesuit connection, observing that his research showed that the constitution of the Jesuit order expressly forbade admission of persons of Jewish extraction. Disraeli responded learnedly that the earliest texts had no such clause, apparently prompted by later Italian Jesuits who were jealous of their "Nuevo-Christiano colleagues." Sarah would write that Isaac thought that the long, scholarly letter was one of Ben's "most skilful answers," but wondered how he had found his information. Disraeli did not explain that he was a politician and a novelist.

While Sidonia's world to the conspiracy-minded Disraeli is "governed by very different personages from what is imagined by those who are not behind the scenes," young Coningsby is "startled" by the confidence and wonders, if it is so, "Why has not your race* produced great poets, great orators, great writers?"

Because of persecution and pariah status, Sidonia responds, in a paean to Judaic pride one must assume is shared by Disraeli:

Favoured by Nature and by Nature's God, we produced the lyre of David; we gave you Isaiah and Ezekiel. . . . Favoured by Nature we still remain: but in exact pro-

---

Race was not used by Disraeli in any scientific sense, but rather to refer to persons of common descent, a people or a nation, much as Thomas Hooker, the Nonconformist preacher, declared in 1594 that his flock had to acknowledge "our own forefathers, or else disdain the race of Christ." Disraeli applies it to separate Jewish origins from religious practice. That *race* would be misused in the literature and politics of anti-Semitism in the nineteenth and twentieth centuries seems unconnected with Sidonia's practice in *Coningsby* and *Tancred*, although Sidonia's claims would be used to validate an alleged international financial conspiracy.

portion as we have been favoured by Nature we have been persecuted by Man. After a thousand struggles; after acts of heroic courage that Rome has never equalled; deeds of divine patriotism that Athens, and Sparta, and Carthage have never excelled; we have endured fifteen hundred years of supernatural slavery, during which, every device that can degrade or destroy man has been the destiny that we have sustained and baffled. The Hebrew child has entered adolescence only to learn that he was the pariah of that ungrateful Europe that owes to him the best part of its laws, a fine portion of its literature, all its religion. Great poets require a public; we have been content with the immortal melodies that we sung more than two thousand years ago by the waters of Babylon and wept. They record our triumphs; they solace our affliction. Great orators are the creatures of popular assemblies; we were permitted only by stealth to meet even in our temples. And as for great writers, the catalogue is not blank. What are all the schoolmen, Aquinas himself, to Maimonides? And as for modern philosophy, all springs from Spinoza.

New impetus came to the writing of *Coningsby* from the "Grand Soirée" organized by the Manchester Athenaeum in the Great Free Trade Hall on October 5. Three thousand Mancunians crowded the hall to see the popular novelist Charles Dickens, who was in the chair, and their political hero Richard Cobden, a founder of the Athenaeum in 1835. Disraeli was a late addition, to help encompass, as advertised, "men of all parties." Learning that he was in Manchester on other political business and staying at the Mosley Arms, Cobden sent E. W. Watkin, a Manchester alderman, to invite him. At first Disraeli declined: He would have to be ready to speak the same day. But, Mary Anne recalled, "They sent a deputation of ladies, which, you know, he could not refuse; so he went."

Given the occasion, Dickens alluded to education and improvement, and Disraeli, after referring to his "honorable friend Mr Cobden," who preceded him, and to the "Lancashire witches" whose occult powers had drawn him there, went on to challenge the wealthy manufacturers of Manchester "to sympathize with the fair inventions of art" and "the poetic creations of the human intellect" by offering them the examples of the great merchants of Venice, the bankers of Florence, the manufacturers of Flanders, all patrons to genius. Closing, Dickens announced a later lecture by John Roby, a popular local banker who had become an author himself with a book, *The Traditions of Lancashire*. Afterwards, he promised, he would be "most happy, in conjunction with Mr Disraeli," whom he privately detested but whose talk he praised as "very brilliant and eloquent," to collaborate with his fellow novelist in writing a description of Mr. Roby on the platform, "the best . . . that our joint abilities can produce."

Applause and laughter followed, giving Disraeli a triumph in the enemy's lair. More significant in the long term was the experience of a city prospering on new manufacturing technology, even in the new amenities of urban life. Disraeli gave the opportunity to Coningsby, who confesses that he longs to travel, especially to see Athens.

"The Age of Ruins is past," says Sidonia. "Have you seen Manchester?" Coningsby will go to Manchester, but not before he and Sidonia meet again at Beaumanoir, where there is banter about the relative values of the New Poor Law and the new feudalism, which was only "dancing around a May-pole," and fed no one. Other obsolete customs survive honorably, contends Lord Henry Sidney, pointing to the Order of the Garter. But, counters Lord Everingham, the Spirit of the Age is "Utility," and Coningsby finds Utility in the "illumined factories, with more windows than Italian palaces, and smoking chimneys taller than Egyptian obelisks." When he also finds an enlightened industrial prince, Oswald Milbank,* and his beautiful daughter, Edith, Utility acquires a romantic penumbra.

Parliament did not meet again until February, and the

---

*Milbank gives Disraeli yet another opportunity to devalue what England considered aristocratic ancestry. "Ancient lineage!" Milbank scoffs, "I never heard of a peer with an ancient lineage. The real old families of this country are to be found among the peasantry; the gentry, too, may lay some claim to old blood."

Disraelis remained at Bradenham through much of the winter while *Coningsby* reached completion. London remained only as far away as the newspapers and magazines, one of which was *Punch*, which had already recognized a rich target in Disraeli, and had established early in its existence a penchant for anti-Semitic humor. Since writing *Coningsby* kept its author particularly attuned to such derision, he was quick to respond to the issue of February 17, 1844, which reproached the *Morning Post* for referring to a Jew as a gentleman. On March 2 *Punch* responded to a letter charging malice, and signed "a Jew," by claiming ironic intent. Disraeli wrote to Richard Wright, a solicitor to the proprietors, asking to see him personally, having already made "many ineffectual efforts. . . . Cannot you keep yr friend, Punch, in order? He gets malevolent with[ou]t being playful."

Disraeli's agreement with his publisher was to share profits on the traditional three small volumes in which novels were packaged. Henry Colburn delivered the first proofs late in March. *Coningsby* went on sale in London on May 11, and the first thousand copies were gone in a fortnight. Three thousand copies of the guinea-and-a-half first edition would bring Disraeli £1,000. The first significant political novel in England, it was bought for its politics as well as for its interest as contemporary fiction. Praising its political characters as "perfect portraits," Lord Palmerston sent his brother a copy of *Coningsby* with a list of identifications. Henry Hope was "enchanted" with it, Ben told Sarah, and John Manners was "full of mild rapture." Even more so was Smythe, who wrote to Disraeli, "I am so dazzled, bewildered, tipsy with admiration, the most passionate and wild!" As reviews began to appear, Hannah de Rothschild wrote to her daughter-in-law Charlotte that she thought that the author was "rather adept in dwelling upon the good qualities of Sidonia's race. In raising many arguments for their emancipation he cleverly introduced many circumstances one might recognise." She had written to him, Hannah added, "expressing our admiration of his spiritual production."

At the request of her husband, Lionel, Hannah's eldest child, Baroness de Rothschild invited the Disraelis for dinner on Sunday, May 19. Within days of publication, Disraeli would be dining with a Sidonia.

XII

"THE TWO NATIONS"

1844–1846

DISRAELI WAS GETTING NOTICED; *CONINGSBY* WAS SELLING. WHAT matter if the hostile responses, public and private, were as numerous as were the positive reviews? If he were identified as Mr. *Disraeli* there was no certainty that the critic was favorably disposed; if, however, the author's name was spelled *D'Israeli* the likelihood of anti-Semitic bias was strong. Even writer friends welcome in his home, and in whose homes he had dined, were quick with such carping as, in *Hood's Magazine*, June 1844, that there was "much that is Jewish in Mr. D'Israeli's general view of society, and in the very notion of Young England." The author, who signed himself "Old England," was Richard Monckton Milnes, traveler, wit, and Tory M.P. for Pontefract, who elsewhere made fun of Disraeli's neomedievalism with

> Oh! flog me at the old cart's tail
> I surely should enjoy
> That fine old English punishment,

I witnessed when a boy!
I should not heed the mocking crowd,
I should not feel the pain,
If one old English custom
Could be brought back again!

What the facetious lines did not reveal was Milnes's jealousy at not being among Disraeli's friends who were characters in *Coningsby*. Several of the youngish originals were at Grosvenor Gate when Mary Anne offered, "Would you like to go and see the room where Dizzy was brought to bed of *Coningsby?*" George Smythe took the lead in scampering upstairs to the bedroom floor where he pushed in the wrong door in the semidarkness and stumbled into Disraeli's bathtub.

"I know nothing of the place of his birth," the sodden Smythe reported to Mrs. Disraeli about Coningsby, "but I have been in the room where he was recently baptized."

W. M. Thackeray's caustic review in the *Morning Chronicle* (May 13, 1844) found the critic enjoying Disraeli's "superb coxcombry" even as he attacked it. *Coningsby* was "the fashionable novel, pushed . . . to its extremist verge," a "dandy-social, dandy-political, dandy-religious" fiction. It was also Carlylean, he suggested, thinking of *Heroes and Hero-Worship*. Carlyle, however, had written to Milnes two months before that Young England would serve its ideals better by "honestly recognising what was dead, and leaving the dead to bury that, [and] address itself frankly to the magnificent but as yet chaotic and appalling Future." While Thackeray found the novel naive, he acknowledged the "rare faculties of power and mind" that went into it, and in the *Pictorial Times*, applying himself to the popular newspaper sport of identifying personalities fictionalized (including Lord Hertford, whom he would exploit himself), Thackeray wrote about Rigby, the caricature of Croker, "a better portrait of a parasite has never been written since Juvenal's days."

Thomas Milner Gibson's wife, Susanne, suggested to Mary Anne that Disraeli and Thackeray should meet, and on August

"Rafael Mendoza" (Disraeli) in Thackeray's *Codlingsby* (1847): "D'you want to look at a nishe coat?"

11 Thackeray wrote in his diary of "a pleasant dinner at Disraelis." When *Vanity Fair* began to appear in monthly numbers in 1847, however, he may have worried that readers would question his borrowing Hertford from Disraeli. To downgrade his source he produced a lampoon for *Punch. Codlingsby*, "by B. de Shrewsbury Esq." would have a long fuse. Not until 1880, in *Endymion*, did Disraeli even the score by creating his pathologically envious critic, "St. Barbe."

Punch, meanwhile, published a vicious cartoon (June 22, 1844) showing a Cheapside old clothes dealer fitting out a child-like Young England in dandy dress. Beneath it were the lines,

The novel of Coningsby clearly discloses
The pride of the world are the children of Moses.
Mosaic, the bankers—the soldiers, the sailors,
The statesmen—and so by-the-by, are the tailors.

Thackeray would also illustrate his satire with an "Old Clo' " vendor fitting out a very callow Young England gentleman, but his comic figure in *Codlingsby* was "Rafael Mendoza," an absurd combination of entrepreneur, sportsman, and philosopher with a Sephardic name suggesting prizefighter Daniel Mendoza of Byron's day as well as Disraeli's Sidonia. Preceding Thackeray in the very year of *Coningsby*, and possibly his inspiration, was William North's pseudonymous two-volume *Anti-Coningsby; or, The New Generation Grown Old*, published as "by An Embryo, M.P." It imagined the resignation of Peel and Coningsby being sent for by the Queen. The new Prime Minister is a protégé of "Mr Ben Sidonia," a solemn man with black corkscrew curls who employs bribery and other devices to keep hostile M.P.s under control.

Ben Sidonia erects an obelisk to Coningsby in Trafalgar Square, but the obelisk is pulled down in a futuristic 1850 by an angry mob which sees "Israel" as "one chain of wars, conspiracies, seditions, and rascalities. . . . They may acquire wealth, they may obtain rank, title, and nobility, but whilst they think and act like Jews they will remain in their present humiliating and degraded position for ever!" Parodying Sidonia's attribution of much of the world's culture to Jews and crypto-Jews, *Anti-Coningsby* reveals that every villain since the patriarch Jacob was "of Hebrew race"—Robespierre, Captain Kidd, Jack Sheppard, and a litany of other "Mosaic Arabs."

In contrast to such diatribes was a lengthy, three-part review of *Coningsby* in *The League*, lauding the author's "intelligent Judaism." When Disraeli discovered that the critic, William Cooke Taylor, had written an anonymous article, "Jewish Emancipation," in 1833, which in passing had praised the "creative genius" in *Alroy*, he wrote (May 27, 1844) to Taylor, "much touched" by his "sustained sympathy." He asked to "become personally acquainted," and they soon met. When the Disraelis celebrated Isaac's seventy-ninth birthday at Grosvenor Gate on May 11,

1845, Maria, Sarah, and Ralph were there, and the only nonfam-
ily guest was Dr. Cooke Taylor.

Charles Dickens in his serial *The Chimes* began satirizing
Coningsby more overtly than his colleague John Forster cared for,
and retreated, conceding (November 1, 1844), "As you dislike
the Young England gentleman I shall knock him out, and replace
him by a man . . . who recognizes no virtue in anything but the
good old times, and talks of them, parrot-like, whatever the matter is."* Dickens's friend Macready, who had dismissed *Count
Alarcos* as unplayable, found that he had to read *Coningsby*—
everyone else seemed to be conversant with it—and he found it
difficult to disparage. "I have been much interested and pleased,"
he noted in his diary on August 20. "There is occasionally a
gaudiness of style and sometimes the affectations of a coxcombi-
cal mind, but there are character, pathos, humour, and graphic
power assisting . . . a well-arranged story."

Others of Disraeli's detractors were quick to read the book,
often to their disappointment. John Gibson Lockhart had borrowed it from John Murray II and read it through early in May.
"I return Disraeli's very impudent and amazingly vainglorious
piece of malignity," he wrote to Murray. "It is cleverer far than
anything of his I have seen before, however, and I don't doubt it
will have a great run." To his son Walter two days later, Lockhart
wrote, "Ben Disraeli, the Jew scamp, has published a very blackguard novel. . . . Awful vanity of the Hebrew!" Even W. E. Gladstone, who usually read improving works, spent much of five days
in June reading *Coningsby*, perhaps to become better acquainted
with Peel's opposition, while historical painter Benjamin Robert
Haydon discovered inspiration in the novel, copying quotations
from it into his diary in August, and finding so much "very high
talent" in *Coningsby* that he wrote to tell the author so. When
they saw each other on August 24 Haydon recorded finding

---

*Forster's disapproval apparently affected Dickens's *Dombey and Son*, for the Parliamentary reporter now a success as a novelist intended to put his experience of
the House into the 1847 serial, and did out-Rigby Disraeli in his creation of
"Carker." Warned to keep Dombey out of politics or risk his run of popularity, he
put Dombey instead into a house of business in which he behaves as if in Parliament.

Disraeli "much improved since I met him at Caroline Norton's, [in] 1832, in velvet trowsers & ruffles, and where he did the Dandy." And Disraeli *had* changed, even sartorially, now affecting a statesmanlike black. But in September he ordered a yellow-striped waistcoat for Thomas Farmer, his under-butler.

With *Coningsby* bringing him fame beyond its sales figures, Disraeli was a lion of the London season, and he and Mary Anne contributed to it themselves. A dinner on June 24—with a guest list that included Mrs. Montefiore and Baron and Baroness Lionel de Rothschild, as well as Sir Josiah and Lady Charlotte Guest—was followed by a reception for two hundred. Mary Anne hired four extra waiters, two additional serving women, and a butler's assistant to help, anticipating royalty money from Colburn to cover expenses. The next day the publisher came through with a check for £645/11s/8d. representing most of the first two printings of a thousand copies each. A third was in preparation.

A fourth printing would further validate Disraeli's success, but a fifth would not emerge until 1849, the occasion for the distinguished critic G. H. Lewes to excoriate "the weight of trash" and "tawdry falsehood" in the book while spelling the author's name with the telltale apostrophe not on the title page. "D'Israeli's" prose exposed "that love of ornament, which is characteristic of his race: they are the mosaic chains and rings with which the young gentlemen of Hebrew persuasion adorn their persons." He was not "moralizing," he claimed to readers of the *British Quarterly Review*, but "is it the disgrace of our literature, or the disgrace of our Parliament, that the only man who has risen into political eminence through literary ability is that clever, sarcastic, extravagant, reckless, disrespectable and disrespected person who formerly styled himself 'D'Israeli the Younger'?"

The novel brought Disraeli closer to Lionel de Rothschild. The week before the dinner at Grosvenor Gate, the Baron had invited the Disraelis to what Sir John Cam Hobhouse described as "a grand entertainment in a fine house, Piccadilly Terrace." The guests on June 16, 1844, were largely Whig politicians on the order of Lord Landsdowne and Lord John Russell, Rothschild's strategy being a meeting of minds between the formal Opposition (Hobhouse in pre-Victoria days had coined the

term "His Majesty's Opposition") and anti-Peel Tories. Emboldened by external inflation of Young England's minuscule numbers,
Disraeli confided overconfidently that he thought they could
bring Peel down "by five o'clock the next day."

If they did, Hobhouse asked skeptically, who would govern?
Disraeli proposed Russell, but the Whig positions on the Poor
Law, the Corn Laws, and Ireland would have to be turned around.

"I shook my head at this," Hobhouse recalled about the impossible scheme, but Disraeli "declared that Peel had completely
failed to keep his party together and must *go*, if not now at least
very speedily." Hobhouse had read *Coningsby*, and his praise had
encouraged Disraeli, who spoke, Sir John thought, "with that sort
of confidence which sometimes belongs to men of genius, and
sometimes to very impudent pretenders." *Coningsby*, Disraeli said,
was "a hit," and people "from all parts of the country" had written to him informing him that he had done "the one thing need-
ful." He had "told the truth." But he was deaf to the truth from
others, that the Whigs would not trim their traditional principles,
and that Peel's control over his own party remained overwhelming.

The test came on a vote on sugar duties, Disraeli rising to
chide the Prime Minister for backtracking on his opposition to
slavery by supporting cheap, slave-grown sugar and for enforcing
party discipline on the issue. Peel's "horror of slavery," Disraeli
mocked, did not extend to his own backbenchers. "There the
gang is still assembled, and there the thong of the whip still
sounds." Whether the cheers came for his message or his effrontery, the uproar was loud and sustained, and the leadership, including Peel, Stanley, and Graham, Hobhouse remembered, "sat
in most painful silence and submission to the rebuke. . . . I never
saw them look so wretched."

While Peel was being excoriated for his abandonment of
party interests, no one doubted that Disraeli was also making the
Prime Minister pay a price for rejecting him. As Monckton Milnes
put it in a letter to C. J. MacCarthy on October 14, 1844, "I am
so angry with Peel for passing over out-and-out the best speaker
among us younger men for a pack of illiterate lordlings, that I am
not sorry to see the consequences. Disraeli has no Christian senti-

mentalities about him; none of your forgiveness of injuries; he is a son of the old jealous implacable Jehovah."

Even so, Disraeli remained no more than a gadfly, and Peel commanded his cohorts unyieldingly. Since he opposed most industrial reforms, few Tories other than Disraeli's small faction supported a Ten Hours' amendment to a factory regulatory bill, a proposal by Lord Ashley,* the Evangelical reformer and a Whig, to reduce the employment of women and children from a brutal twelve hours a day. Introducing education clauses into the bill, an attempt to turn schoolmasters into propagandists, Sir James Graham told the Commons, "The police and the soldiers have done their duty; the time is arrived when moral and religious instructors must go forth to reclaim the people from the errors of their ways." Ashley's friend Gladstone proposed a meek compromise limiting working hours to eleven, but at first the original amendment passed with ninety Conservative defections, apparently defeating the Government. Not so easily cowed, Peel whipped his followers into reversing their votes. For Disraeli it was a demonstration of how raw political power worked, and how little of it he had.

If the incident had an impact beyond reminding Disraeli of his impotence in the House, it was to propel the only other source of persuasion available to him, his pen. When Smythe wrote to him, probably early in August, asking, "How are the two nations?" Disraeli, Smythe knew, was at work on a sequel to *Coningsby* about Chartism, labor, and the downtrodden. In *Sybil, or The Two Nations*, set in 1837 and continuing the earlier novel in time (although *Coningsby* actually went on into 1849), Charles Egremont, an idealistic aristocrat on the order of Harry Coningsby, meets several strangers in the countryside. One of them, the socialist editor Stephen Morley, responds to Egremont's proud boast that the young Queen "reigns over the greatest nation that ever existed" with, "Which nation?"

Egremont is baffled and silent. "Yes," the stranger continues. "Two nations; between whom there is no intercourse and no sympathy; who are as ignorant of each other's habits, thought, and

*Afterwards the 7th Earl of Shaftesbury.

feelings, as if they were dwellers in different zones, or inhabitants of different planets; who are formed by a different breeding, are fed by a different food, are ordered by different manners, and are not governed by the same laws."

"You speak of—" said Egremont, hesitantly.

"THE RICH AND THE POOR."

Factory legislation had drawn Disraeli back to the graphic Blue Books, the reports of Parliamentary commissions, especially the painful *Second Report of the Children's Employment Commission,* which had been released in February 1843. Nothing at the time better exposed the sordid state of England, as it included in two volumes of appendices the results of hundreds of interviews. It had already inspired Elizabeth Barrett [Browning]'s poem "The Cry of the Children," published in *Blackwood's* in August 1843.

The striking evidence gave Disraeli the opportunity to be specific, and to the Blue Book testimony he could add his recent memories of Chartist agitation. He had been to factory communities himself, and would be in Manchester, at the invitation of the Athenaeum, twice more in 1844. Writing to a Shrewsbury supporter on August 29, 1844, he summed up what seems to have been his intentions as he worked on *Sybil.* "The 'Condition of England' question of wh[ich] they now heard so much"—he was referring to a speech he had just given in his constituency—"was shortly this: one half of the population of the country was overworked and the other half underpaid. Hence the fearful diminution of the term of human life in Lancashire; hence the fires of Suffolk,* the two causes producing the same result, the degradation of the species."

How much of *Sybil* its author had already shared with Young England was evidenced not only by Smythe's query but by a report in *The Times* of a speech which Lord John Manners had given at the Manchester Athenaeum on August 26, about which Disraeli was "charmed." Manners had excoriated the "modern system" which had divided society into two classes, "and two only—rich and poor." Accompanied by Manners and Baillie-Cochrane, Disraeli saw more of the other nation while in the north of Eng-

*The "Captain Swing" and similar protests which included rick burnings.

land for his chairing of the annual Manchester Athenaeum Soirée, the fund-raiser over which Charles Dickens had presided the year before. Smythe had returned to England from a summer pursuing Angela Burdett-Coutts, whose banking fortune, Disraeli hoped, might further Young England causes. The wayward Smythe, however, had been distracted by a prettier face and the opportunity, if it ever existed, had faded by the time he joined the others in Manchester. Still, his father, Lord Strangford, awaiting impatiently an opportune marriage for his son, was assured by Manners' father, the Duke of Rutland, that at the Manchester soiree, which might have embarrassed both of them, "not a syllable of party feeling or politics was uttered even by the arch-president," a "designing person" of no "integrity of purpose."

Sarah thought that her brother's nonpolitical address was "sublime," especially his claims for the beneficial results of better educating the working population. "Knowledge," he challenged the Mancunians, using a metaphor from the story of Jacob, "is like the mystic ladder in the patriarch's dream"—it maintained "the communication between man and heaven." Intellect had arrived in the market place, and only when it was exploited could the young become "the Masters of Posterity."

Referring to a quotation from the *Odyssey* that his Whig adversary Richard Cobden, the Member from Stockport, had used about travels in the Eastern Mediterranean, Disraeli returned, in effect, to the dreams of Sidonia, his own experience of Jerusalem, and his pride in the "intellectual refinement" of the people from whom he had sprung. "I can still remember that olive-crowned plain, that sunset crag, that citadel famed of ineffable beauty! That was a brilliant civilization developed by a gifted race more than 2,000 years ago: at a time when the ancestors of the manufacturers of Manchester, who now clothe the world, were themselves covered with skins and tattoos like the red men of the wilderness." It was curious flattery of his audience.

In the months following the publication of *Coningsby*, some of the letters Disraeli received came from old Etonians who corrected him on minor points about Harry Coningsby's schooldays, and a few questioned Sidonia's sweeping identification of makers and shapers of contemporary Europe as secret or former Jews. One skeptic, writing from Berlin, was Monckton Milnes, who had been traveling between Parliamentary sittings. The Disraelis had visited the Milneses at their Yorkshire estate, Fryston, in October, after the Manchester events, and were regaled there by turtle soup, truffles, and champagne, and by amateur theatricals, including a scene based on Dickens's new novel, *Martin Chuzzlewit*. Milnes played the disreputable, umbrella-toting Mrs. Sarah Gamp. Outside the skit, Mary Anne played her usual role, now familiar in society—the aging former beauty who wore girlish clothes at fifty-two and told stories, all of them very likely true, about her devotion to her "Dizzy."

The long weekend at Fryston displayed Disraeli ready at forty to make the leap forward into a leadership role. Once an ebony-ringleted dandy so draped with gold chains that behind his back remarks flew that he resembled an escapee from a slave ship, he now made no attempt to dominate a dinner table with smart repartee. Although Lady Elizabeth Spencer-Stanhope, writing to her husband, saw Disraeli's "manner" as "half-foreign," he dressed soberly and he was subdued in speech—unlike Mrs. Disraeli, who was "very amusing and off-hand, saying everything that comes uppermost and unfeignedly devoted to her D'Izzy." Lady Elizabeth's "simple and *sincere* tribute" to Mary Anne about her husband as they parted "brought tears to her eyes." Lady Elizabeth's son, Walter, writing separately to his father, perceived Disraeli as someone more than a mere seven years' occupant of a seat in the Commons. "The *great man* seems a very unaffected good sort of fellow, and of more importance in his appearance and features than one would suppose from the [newspaper] caricatures." The statesmanlike Disraeli may have been as much of a role as the former Byronic adventurer, but it was more comfortable to play.

Milnes had toyed with casting his lot with Young England, but was bored as an M.P., loved travel, and longed for Henry Bulwer's post, then vacant, at the embassy in Paris. Bulwer had gone to Madrid. Milnes had already written to Gladstone to intercede for him with Peel, but would remain as coldly neglected by the Prime Minister as if he had joined the enemy. To Disraeli, who found the toadyish "Dicky" Milnes "irresistibly comic," with "a countenance cut out of an orange," Milnes, "with great earnestness—tears in his eyes," appealed that he had sometimes voted with Young England and by rights should have figured in *Conings-by*. Three years later he would appear in *Tancred* as the eccentric Mr. Vavasour, "a social favourite; a poet, and a real poet, quite a troubadour; as well as a member of Parliament; travelled, sweet-tempered and good-hearted; very amusing and very clever."

That Mr. Vavasour, whose "merry wit" is attributed ominously to the bottle, first appears at a dinner party given by Sidonia may be due to Disraeli's long memory about Milnes's disputing Sidonia's German attributions. Disraeli used *Syrian* almost interchangeably with *Hebrew* (the Holy Land was politically part of Turkish Syria), and on December 29, 1844, responded to Milnes lightly, as if Sidonia's suspicions had been confirmed: "I suppose you find yourself in the midst of these Syrian celebrities where you are."

After Fryston the Disraelis had combined politics and pleasure at other country seats in the North and in Young England spirit attended the festivities on October 11 marking the opening of the Cottingley Allotment Gardens in Yorkshire. The fifteen acres set aside as gardens to be tilled by laborers for their own use were provided by the aunt of the Radical Tory M.P. William Busfield Ferrand of Bingley, who had a reputation for excoriating mill owners who exploited their employees. When his Bill for the Allotment of Waste Lands, which he called "an act of justice to the poor," failed of passage, he pursued his campaign by private example, and Disraeli spoke at the celebration, denouncing class barriers and calling for landowners to share uncultivated parcels.

There had been a parade, a dinner, and even a series of cricket matches in which the classes mixed, Ferrand having founded a Bingley Cricket Club. Lord John Manners reportedly captained one of the teams, and Disraeli went in to bat with a local shoemaker—an episode unique in his political life. Afterward, at a grand dinner, with Disraeli and Manners on either side of him, Ferrand rose to respond to a toast in his honor, declaring to the two hundred guests from every station that "if there be one position more than another in which an English country gentleman may stand proud and happy in his own parish, it is when he is surrounded by every grade of society within it, cheering him when his health is proposed at a vast meeting like the present." It was the hopeful outcome of Disraeli's novel of the "two nations" lifted from its pages into brief reality.

Early in the new year, just before the Parliamentary session, the Disraelis were guests at Stowe, the seat of his longtime friend the Duke of Buckingham and Chandos, for the visit of Victoria and Albert. "We were for the first half hour in the vestibule," Mary Anne wrote to Sarah, "half lit up and no seats or fire; only a little hot air and a great deal of cold wind. . . . Fancy dear shivering Dizzy, and cross Mary Anne." Always too warm, the Queen did not notice. For her the event had more significance than honoring a powerful aristocrat by her presence. Since Victoria was meeting resistance in getting her subjects to accept her German prince, who had been only a younger son in a tiny principality, the event was more political than social. The Duke, "who is immensely proud," she wrote in her journal, brought the after-dinner coffee to Albert himself. It was as close an encounter with Victoria as Disraeli had experienced, but his reputation had reached her before he did. When he came into view, she remarked to her hostess, the Duchess, "There's Mr. Disraeli."

Although at Stowe Sir Robert Peel shook hands cordially with Disraeli, it was almost like two pugilists on entering the ring, for 1845 was not only the year of publication of *Sybil*, but of open warfare with the Prime Minister. Sparring over a Post Office matter—the Home Office's opening of letters—Disraeli turned the issue into Peel's heavy hand on dissent in the party and his shift toward the Opposition's views. "I do not believe he is looking toward any coalition," Disraeli scoffed, "although many of my constituents do. The right honourable gentleman has only to remain where he is. The right honourable gentleman caught the Whigs bathing, and walked away with their clothes. He . . . is himself a strict conservative—of their garments."

Delighted with the debate, Lady Palmerston wrote to Mrs. William Huskisson, the widow of the Whig worthy, "I hope you read d'Israeli's excellent speech last Friday; it kept the House in a roar of laughter and I am sure you will not have been sorry to see the severe truths that he inflicted on Peel."

By then a sixpenny weekly paper had appeared, *Young Eng-*

land or, the Social Condition of the Empire, first published on January 4, 1845. The prospectus from publisher Richard Bentley
advertised, in Disraelian terms, that Young England, "while it sup-
ports our venerable institutions, . . . will urge the generally acknowledged demands of the present times; while it proposes or
advocates changes tending to promote the prosperity and happiness of all classes, it will be with the sincere desire to impart renewed vigour and strength to ancient institutions." An engraving
of Windsor Castle illustrated the handbill, under which were lines
from the Queen's Speech on ameliorating social conditions "for
the happiness and contentment of her people." Peel carefully
placed a copy of the advertisement among his papers.

Disraeli was more outraged than Peel. He had not promoted
the venture and felt that it would confuse supporters at such influential papers as The Times. But he could not control the name
any more than he could control Lord Ranelagh, who dabbled in
political writing and kept the paper up until he ran into debt.
Unfortunately for Disraeli, it expired only after it had endorsed
Peel's bill to increase support for the Roman Catholic Seminary at
Maynooth, inland from Dublin, from an annual £9,000 to £30,000.
Although the school was in desperate straits, Peel's intention was
less to assist the education of priests than to evidence sympathy of
a symbolic sort for the plight of Ireland, which seemed always to be
experiencing hard times, and was already suffering from a potato
blight that would worsen into authentic famine.

Disraeli, whose responses to Roman Catholicism in his fiction and in his public statements seemed akin to paddling a
canoe—first one side, then the other—examined the underside of
the Maynooth proposal to look for further evidences of hypocrisy
among Peel's closest supporters. It was easy to observe that Tories
long represented anti-Rome sentiment in Parliament, and that
government subsidy of the preparation of priests represented support of a religion other than the Established Church.

What Disraeli found most delicious was that Peel's devoted
lieutenant, a master of casuistry, had published a book in 1838,
The State in its Relations to the Church, in which he had declared
that the State had "a true and a moral personality," and should,
therefore, profess and support a religion. Now that very author,

W. E. Gladstone, had spoken in favor of public funds being voted to sustain a communion other than the Established Church. In an act of research rather than piety, the Member from Shrewsbury, perhaps alone among those arrayed against the Maynooth grant, had actually read the book.

Maynooth fit the Peelite pattern, Disraeli charged, of "giving up principles." Gladstone, he mocked in Young England metaphors, was "the last paladin of principle, the very chivalry of abstraction."

With little assistance from party regulars—"only four or five young gentlemen," Croker disparaged—Disraeli sparred with Peel on every bill that would offer him an opening. In March, debating a measure to relieve agricultural distress, the gadfly from Shrewsbury contended that if the nation were to adopt Free Trade, it should have it from William Cobden rather than from the leader of a party pledged to Protection. "Dissolve, if you please," Disraeli challenged, "the Parliament you have betrayed, and appeal to the people who, I believe, mistrust you."

While Disraeli tried, at considerable risk to himself, to force Peel into a political corner, the Prime Minister affected an air of nonrecognition of his troublesome colleague's existence. *Punch* (March 15, 1845) pictured a disconsolate Disraeli pondering why, with his "confess'd ability" and even his attempted "servility," Peel had ignored him with "Belial's own tranquility" and relegated him to "the ranks." Lacking "birth," he had nevertheless acquired the *"manners of nobility,"* but all else having failed,

> *Well, I've been pretty mild as yet,*
> *But now I'll try scurrility;*
> *It's very hard if that don't get*
> *Me more than mere civility.*

Orthodox Tories elected unashamedly on a "no Popery!" pledge, although no admirers of Disraeli, announced against Peel on religious grounds. Disraeli, on the other hand, objected to the Maynooth bill on grounds of political theory. The party system, he contended, was preserved by the conflict of opposing ideas. When one party adopts the policies of the other, except in times of national crisis, the system breaks down. As for advancing "the cure of souls" as a reason for the bill, he didn't think that mattered. Priests would be produced anyway. Peel, so Disraeli charged, had become a "middleman" among factions rather than the spokesman for his party.

The charges were cruel to Maynooth, but Disraeli was out to destroy Peel on the principle that Parliamentary checks and balances required "a constitutional Opposition" which should not have to arise from within the party in power. That they thoroughly disliked each other left little room for compromise. As Croker would say later of Disraeli, "Nothing is so dangerous as those *sharp blades* in adventurous hands."

"Peel hung his head down," Sir John Hobhouse observed, "changing colour and drawing his hat over his eyes, and [Sir James] Graham grinned a sort of compelled smile, and looked a great deal at me . . . to see how we took the attack. Our front row was well behaved, but Russell, and Palmerston, and George Grey, whispered to me, 'It is all true,' and . . . Macaulay looked happy."

Young Gulliver and the Brobdingnag Minister. *Punch*, April 5, 1845. Although outmatched, Disraeli attacks the formidable Sir Robert Peel anyway.

According to Greville's diary, Disraeli's charges were "well bepraised . . . by Whig and Tory papers and all the haters of Peel, who now comprise a large majority of the world." But they cost Disraeli both Manners and Smythe, who were praised by Peel for their votes, and with Whig support and a minority of his own party, the Prime Minister got his bill through. There were prices to pay on all sides. With Manners and Smythe went Young England, while Disraeli put Gladstone's own seat in the Commons in jeopardy. "The Irish Church question is on me like a nightmare," Gladstone confessed. It was "a Trojan horse, full of armed men." But this was a Trojan horse with a rider. "They hunt him like a fox," Greville wrote of Peel's predicament, "and they are eager to run him down and kill him in the open."

The outcome of Maynooth was that Peel continued to dominate Parliament, but with fewer of his own cohorts. Paradoxically, Disraeli was simultaneously vindicating party loyalty from the benches—the issue upon which he grappled with Peel—while eschewing party orthodoxy in *Sybil* and in his continuing and open sympathy with the Chartists, whose causes were central to his novel. Recognizing Disraeli's interest, a self-educated shoemaker, preacher, and musician came to Grosvenor Gate for help in securing a publisher for his ponderous long poem *The Purgatory of Suicides*. His identity on the title page was "Thomas Cooper, Chartist."

In Spenserian stanzas written when Cooper was in prison following the Manchester riots, he told the stories of men and women in history who had taken their lives and awaited in a cavernlike purgatory their return to an earthly paradise. Bitter and despairing, it questioned whether life was worth living when people were doomed to oppression and cruelty.

At noon on a Sunday early in May, Cooper knocked on Disraeli's door and was admitted by "a tall Hebrew" (he thought) "in livery," and escorted up a stairway to a small room at the top of the house, the study. There he told his tale, and Disraeli's face—"one of great intellectual beauty" in Cooper's recollection twenty-six years later—lit up. "I wish I had seen you before I finished my last novel," he said. "My heroine, Sybil, is a Chartist." Cooper put his manuscript into Disraeli's hands, and asked that Edward Moxon be asked to consider it. "But Moxon is not my publisher," Disraeli said. "I offered him a poem of my own some years ago, but he declined to take it." Cooper explained that he wanted to deal with someone with poetry on his list. "You think he must sympathise with you," Disraeli said. ". . . You forget he is a tradesman, too, and poetry doesn't sell well nowadays." But he agreed to read Cooper's work, and told him to come back; when Cooper did, he gave him a note for Moxon.

"Disraeli knows that poetry is a drug on the market," Moxon said. "He does not offer me one of his own novels." Still, he took the lugubrious poem to read, returning it with regrets when Cooper came for it. Disappointed, Cooper appealed again to Disraeli, this time for an introduction to the publisher of the great man's novels, Henry Colburn, and a letter was dispatched, asking for "a kind and impartial hearing."

When Cooper was again turned down, he walked back to Grosvenor Gate and asked for a note to Chapman & Hall. Disraeli thought about it, then said, "No, I know nothing of them personally. But I will give you a note to [William Harrison] Ainsworth, and desire him to recommend you to Chapman & Hall."

Ainsworth, a novelist and magazine editor, reminded Cooper that poetry was selling badly, but sent him to John Forster, editor of the *Examiner* and Chapman & Hall's consultant. "A stout, severe man," Forster, who had been left Cooper's parcel, complete to the dedication of the book to one of his heroes, Thomas Carlyle, examined the poet "with the spirit of a bitter Whig examining a poor Chartist at the bar." Opening to the cover page he asked, "I suppose you have no objection to alter[ing] the title you gave yourself? I certainly advise you to strike the 'Chartist' out."

"Nay, sir," said Cooper, "I shall not strike it out. Mr Disraeli advised me not to let anyone persuade me to strike it out, and I mean to abide by his advice."

Stubbornly, the poet went on to yet another firm, and *The Purgatory of Suicides: A Prison-Rhyme in Ten Books* was published in August by Jeremiah How.

Cooper had been released from Stafford Gaol on May 4, in

the week of publication of Disraeli's Chartist novel. On the 9th, two days before Cooper saw Disraeli, Dickens had written to Lady Blessington, curious about the new novel, "Has the Sybil spoken yet?" He knew his audience, for the Countess was one of the first recipients of the book, which, once she read it through, she acknowledged generously to Mary Anne on May 12. "This book *must* do great good," she predicted. "It is not more full of sensibility, than of wisdom, and is calculated to excite a warm sympathy for the classes whose hardships, as well as the dangerous results they produce, are so powerfully illustrated. How well the selfish policy and shallow as well as selfish, which marks some of the Statesmen of our time, is exposed! And what an exquisitely drawn figure is Sybil! Dis has achieved a great work."

Sybil evokes what has been called the "hungry forties" in England, where the industrial North is drawn on the evidence of the Blue Books, on Chartist writings, and on Disraeli's experience. The major plot line is simple. Charles Egremont is a younger son of the late Earl Marney, whose estates include the ruins of Marney Abbey. It is a time of Chartist agitation and rick-burning. Going out into the countryside to explore the problem, Egremont meets a Roman Catholic priest, a philosophical artisan of Chartist leanings, and the lovely daughter of the artisan. While Egremont is attracted to Sybil Gerard, he is expected to marry the wealthy and intellectual Lady Joan Fitz-Warene, who can finance his career. As Chartist violence and Establishment rejection play themselves out, the romantic *mésalliance* goes through cycles of despair and hope, ending in a melodramatic series of disasters in which Walter Gerard (who proves in fairy-tale fashion to have been the dispossessed heir to vast lands) is killed, and Egremont's brother, the present earl, dies, cut down by a Chartist band seeking revenge. The lovers, one a daughter of the people but both well-born after all, are reunited, with Egremont the new earl.

Disraeli's opportunities to explore the failings of the Reform Act and of the New Poor Law are many. Although there are vicious employers like Shuffle and Screw, there is also Trafford's mill, where employees are human beings living in a model, if sterile, industrial town, unlike other laborers who must use a vividly realized "tommy shop" (company store), where the pathetic wages are paid in the form of overpriced provisions. The Chartist convention is contrasted to Parliament's triviality, and a scene of what is clearly high life at glittering Crockford's to the miserable squatters' slum of Wodgate (based upon the Blue Books and a harrowing example of the underside of factory life). In his stark clash of vivid settings, Disraeli also drew degraded women and children working in the mine pits and fashionable ladies in luxurious clothes with little to do amid lush country house settings. The mining scene, drawn from Blue Book testimony, could have been written by Friedrich Engels. It was intended to shock, and it did:

They come forth; the mine delivers its gang and the pit its bondsmen; the forge is silent and the engine is still. The plain is covered with the swarming multitude— bands of stalwart men, broad-chested and muscular, wet with toil, and black as the children of the tropics; troops of youth—alas! of both sexes—though neither their raiment nor their language indicates the difference. All are clad in male attire, and oaths that men might shudder at issue from lips born to breathe words of sweetness. Yet these are to be, some are, the mothers of England! But can we wonder at the hideous coarseness of their language when we remember the savage rudeness of their lives? Naked to the waist, an iron chain fastened to a belt of leather runs between their legs clad in canvas trousers; while, on hands and feet, an English girl for twelve, sometimes for sixteen, hours a day hauls and hurries tubs of coals up subterranean roads, dark, precipitous, and plashy—circumstances that seem to have escaped the notice of the Society for the Abolition of Negro Slavery. Those worthy gentlemen, too, appear to have been singularly unconscious of the sufferings of the little trappers, which was remarkable, as many of them were in their own employ.

Hostile critics made the most of the melodramatic coincidences and the sentimentality, and claimed distortion in the depiction of privation and in the idealism of the oppressed, but the few working class readers of *Sybil* who wrote to Disraeli knew otherwise. A Mrs. M. Baylis, who signed herself "A Mechanics Wife," thanked him "for the gift you have conferred on our class, by the works which have lately issued from your pen." She urged him not to "pause" with *Sybil* but to "*go on*" with his "stirring words" and "*truthful* description" of conditions, which she blamed "more than half" on "the ignorance of the Aristocracy," which Disraeli was redeeming. "It is you who must open their eyes to the truth, 'tis the pages of *Coningsby* and *Sybil* and such works that will remove the chain of prejudice, and heartlessness, which their want of knowledge has bound around them." Movingly she urged, "Ere this day twelvemonth present us with another gift, place in the hands of the children of England another work which shall teach *both nations* the great lessons which must be learnt. You are one of our political leaders you are a member of that House which holds such vast power in its hands, you are listened to within its wall use then your voice and pen for that suffering body who stand so much in need."

Her address was 12 Sussex Terrace, Camden Town, then a respectable London district of artisans, bakers, shoemakers, dressmakers, carpenters. She was not one of the desperately poor, but had she been, her access to the book and to writing skills would have been very limited.

One of the first Victorians to use the novel to lodge an indictment, Disraeli raised issues to which the Establishment remained indifferent almost to the last years of the century, and often many decades into the next. Two were joined in a single paragraph, "baby farming" and the hypocrisy of philanthropies to spread the Gospel abroad while poverty spread degradation at home:

> About a fortnight after his mother had introduced him into the world, she returned to her factory, and put her infant out to nurse—that is to say, paid threepence a week to an old woman, who takes charge of these newborn babes for the day, and gives them back at night to their mothers, as they hurriedly return from the scene of their labour to the dungeon or the den, which is still by

courtesy called "home." The expense is not great: laudanum and treacle, administered in the shape of some
popular elixir, affords these innocents a brief taste of the
sweets of existence, and, keeping them quiet, prepares
them for the silence of their impending grave. Infan-
ticide is practised as extensively and as legally in
England, as it is on the banks of the Ganges; a circumstance which apparently has not yet engaged the attention of the Society for the Propagation of the Gospel in
Foreign Parts.

Sybil herself rues the decline of the English people, brutal-
ized by poverty and overwork, yet once "the truest, the freest, and
the bravest, the best-natured and the best-looking, the happiest
and most religious race upon the surface of the globe; and think
of them now, with all their crimes and all their slavish sufferings,
their soured spirits and their stunted forms; their lives without enjoyment, and their deaths without hope." And her father adds
that the great men of Britain "have never made any use of us but
as tools; and that the people can never have their rights until
they produce competent champions from their own order." Poverty, he observes, had become a crime rather than a symptom of
decay—the evidence, so the idealistic Egremont believes, in
Young England fashion, that the aristocracy had neglected its duties within the social fabric.

Advocacy of no specific legislative agenda was *Sybil*'s
strength. Disraeli's goal was to afflict the consciences of the ruling
classes and bestir them into curing the ills of England while conserving the usable past that a real social upheaval would erase. To
that end he wrote, as in the London slum scene which Sybil
views from a cab, with a Hogarthian intensity that only Dickens
was beginning to reach:

Now dark streets of frippery and old stores, now market-
places of entrails and carrion, with gutters running gore;
sometimes the way was enveloped in yeasty fumes of a
colossal brewery, and sometimes they plunged into a
labyrinth of lanes teeming with life, and where the dog-

stealer and the pickpocket, the burglar and the assassin found a sympathetic multitude of all ages; comrades for every enterprise; and a market for every booty.

The long summer twilight was just expiring; the pale shadows of the moon were just stealing on; the gas was beginning to glare in shops of tripe and bacon, and the paper lanterns to adorn the stall and the stand. They crossed a broad street which seemed to be the metropolis of the district; it flamed with gin-palaces; a multitude were sauntering in the mild though tainted air; bargaining, blaspheming, drinking, wrangling; and varying their business with their potations, their fierce strife and their impious irreverence, with flashes of rich humour, gleams of native wit, and racy phrases of idiomatic slang.

Disraeli's Peelite colleague Gladstone read *Sybil* with enough interest and concern that he made two pages of notes, eager to set down its faults in fact and logic. On social matters he saw the characters as "chattering on subjects of which it is impossible that they can know anything." Yet he noted one political passage as "capital," and marked another for its revelation of "the two faced effects of the Peel legislation." On religious matters he thought that *Sybil* was "full of Erastian complacency," an obvious objection for someone who saw the Church as above the State, and he noted some "Hebreo-Christian" elements, which were many more than he marked, as Disraeli's intention was to blur the border between Judaism and Christianity. Thus Mary is "the blessed Hebrew maiden," the early apostles are "Hebrew," and, says Aubrey St. Lys, a young Roman Catholic priest, Jesus "announced Himself as the last of the prophets," one of the "heirs of the patriarchs." In this apostolic succession, "the second Testament is avowedly a supplement," and Christianity is "completed Judaism," St. Lys insists, "or it is nothing." Rome has nothing to do with it: "The law was not thundered forth from the Capitolian mount."

Moved by *Sybil* and *Coningsby*, the fervently Evangelical Charles Kingsley, despite his denials, paid Disraeli the compliment of imitation in his first novel, *Yeast*, published in *Fraser's Magazine* in 1848–49 and in book form in 1851. Chartism, the condition of rural England, the Roman Catholic subplot, the mysteriously omniscient stranger much like Sidonia, all emerge in Kingsley's fiction. *Fraser's* itself had the dubious distinction in June 1845 of publishing an anonymous review of *Sybil* which poked unsavory fun at Disraeli's dedication of the novel to "a perfect wife!" by suggesting—and however true, it was tasteless—that the author had married for money.

Mary Anne had acquired Judaeo-Christian ideas in her inimitable fashion from her Dizzy. After Charlotte de Rothschild was delivered of her youngest son later in the year of *Sybil*, Mrs Disraeli gushed, on her first visit to see the child, "My dear, that beautiful baby may be the future Messiah whom we are led to expect—who knows? And you will be the most favoured of women!" Louisa's daughter Constance recalled that Leopold afterwards, while still a young child, was referred to in the family as "Little Messiah."

Disraeli himself was moving closer to Lionel de Rothschild's family. One surviving letter of his to Charlotte, in June 1845, well before the birth of Leopold, urged her to "bring the beauteous children"—then Leonora, Evelina, Nathaniel, and Alfred—to Grosvenor Gate for a view of the Queen's parade in Hyde Park in honor of the visit of her uncle, King Leopold I of the Belgians. And Disraeli would tell the Baroness that when she wanted to observe a debate in the House, "You have only to ask for Mrs Disraeli's place." Sharing his sympathies as well as his Parliamentary privileges, Mary Anne wrote to Charlotte in July, when the Jews' Oaths of Abjuration Bill passed its second reading in the Commons, to express happiness at "the glorious result of the debate."

Unaware of her own good-hearted absurdities, Mary Anne once rushed to Charlotte—it was just before the Disraelis departed on September 9, 1845, for France—and pulled hard on the bell at Piccadilly Terrace. She fell "into my reluctant arms," the Baroness wrote to Louisa about their "excellent and eccentric friend." It was six in the evening, and Charlotte had just returned from the sickbed of her mother-in-law, Hannah:

"I am quite out of breath, my dear, I have been running so fast, we have no horses, no carriage, no servants, we are going abroad, I have been so busy correcting proof-sheets, the publishers are so tiresome, we ought to have been gone a month ago; I should have called upon you long ere now, I have been so nervous, so excited, so agitated, poor Dis' has been sitting up the whole night writing; I want to speak to you on business, pray send the darling children away" &c., &c., for it would, without any exaggeration, take more than ten pages to put down conscientiously all the lady's words, not noting exclamations and gestures and tears. You know, dear Louisa, that I am easily terrified and almost speechless. I had never seen her in such a state of excitement before, and all I could do was to gasp out—"Has anything happened?"

Mrs Disraeli heaved a deep sigh and said: "This is a farewell visit, I may never see you again—life is so uncertain. . . . Disi and I may be blown up on the railroad or in the steamer, there is not a human body that loves me in this world, and besides my adored husband I care for no one on earth, but *I* love your glorious race, I am rich, I am prosperous, I think it right to entertain serious thought, to look calmly upon one's end" &c., &c.

Mrs Disraeli's conversation is not exactly remarkable for clearness of thought, precision of language, or for a proper concatenation of images, ideas and phrases, nevertheless, I had always been able to comprehend and to reply, but on that memorable Friday, I was quite at a loss to understand her meaning. *Je vous fais grâce de mes réponses*, as they are not particularly interesting. I tried to calm and quiet my visitor who, after having enumerated her goods and chattels to me, took a paper out of her pocket saying: "This is my Will and you must read it, show it to the dear Baron, and take care of it for me." I answered that she must be aware of my feelings, that I should ever be truly grateful for such a proof of confidence, but could not accept such a great responsibility. "But you must listen," replied the inexorable lady: she opened the paper and read aloud:

> "In the event of my beloved Husband preceding me to the grave, I leave and bequeath to Evelina de Rothschild [Charlotte's daughter, age six] all my personal property."

I leave you to picture to yourself my amazement and embarrassment. Mrs Disraeli rose and would hear no answer, no objection.

"I love the Jews—I have attached myself to your children and she is my favourite, she shall, she must wear the butterfly." Away rushed the testatrix, leaving the testament in my unworthy hands. I passed a miserable night, witnessing all the horrors of boilers bursting on the railroad and steamboats being blown up, and seeing myself as chief mourner at our poor friend's funeral. Then there was a Ball at the French Embassy; I was an old Mamma and Evy looked overpowered by the weight of the emerald tiara, and the diamond butterfly was fluttering round her shoulders. The next morning I breakfasted in a hurry, walked in a hurry to the abode of genius and his wife, to whom I returned the Will. There was a scene, a very disagreeable one, and then all was over—*the dream and the reality* . . .

The proofs which Mary Anne had been reading were new prefaces to *Alroy* and *Contarini Fleming*, which Henry Colburn, on the heels of the Young England novels, was reissuing. With the *Alroy* preface establishing the historical background Disraeli had added some striking lines of verse lamenting that, with the bards of Israel gone, his pen had to be their replacement:

> *And where are thou,*
> *My Country! On thy voiceless shore,*
> *The heroic lay is silent now;*
> *The heroic bosom beats no more.*
> *And must thy lyre, so long divine,*
> *Degenerate into hands like mine!*

When the Channel steamer docked at Boulogne, Disraeli reported to Sarah, placards in bookshops were advertising *Sybil*.
Mary Anne had been ailing, as her visit to Baroness de
Rothschild had evidenced, and the two months in the Flanders
town of Cassel, east of St.-Omer and closer to the Belgian border,
were restorative. Left to themselves, they arose with the villagers
at 5:30, eating simple local fare and enjoying at dinner the excellent French wines—unlike Alfred Mountchesney in *Sybil*, who responds to complaints about the "cursed bad wine" in England
with a riposte anticipating Oscar Wilde: "I rather like bad wine;
one gets so bored with good wine."

The nearest house was a nunnery, and life was quiet, exactly
right to get on with the sequel to *Coningsby* and *Sybil*, to complete what Disraeli now intended to be a trilogy in which he
would return Sidonia, who had no role in *Sybil*. He and Mary
Anne had brought boxes of books with them, some as reference
for what would become *Tancred, or the New Crusade*, and Disraeli
began writing almost as soon as he settled down in Cassel. But he
was still thinking it out more than writing it out, and walking was
good for contemplation. The weather was mild, and they wandered through most of the nearby villages, returning to keep up
with the news through *Galignani's Messenger* and papers forwarded
from London. Left behind at home were a pair of Blue Books,
Correspondence Relative to the Affairs of Syria, many pages of which
dealt with religious matters in the Turkish Middle East. Sarah was
asked to send it. By November 10 Mary Anne estimated that they
had logged three hundred miles on foot through Flanders, more
miles than pages written. Like the locals, they went to bed each
evening no later than nine-thirty.

From Paris early in December—they had left Flanders on
November 26—Disraeli wrote to Lionel de Rothschild, congratu-
lating him on the birth of Leopold, his third son, "I hope he will
prove worthy of his pure and sacred race." Having seen King
Louis-Philippe, the visiting M.P. reported on his conversations—
another information source for the always *au courant* Baron. And
Disraeli used his opening to seek investment advice, although he
owed a staggering amount of money. With Rothschild acumen behind his book income, he thought he could make a profit out of

railroads. James de Rothschild had opened his Paris–St.-Germain line in 1837 and his Paris–Versailles line in 1839, and had put large sums into his *Chemin de Fer du Nord*, connecting Paris with the industrial northeast, floating a stock issue of 150 million francs, five percent of which quietly went as gifts to French politicians and journalists. When the line had opened to great acclaim on June 13, 1846, everyone with a small amount to invest wanted to put it into French railroads, even though three weeks after the opening a train wreck killed thirty-seven people—the fault of an engine driver going too fast round a curve, not of a Rothschild. Nevertheless, a spate of anti-Semitic attacks followed, including a pamphlet, *The History of Rothschild I, King of the Jews*, which was responded to by another, *Reply by Rothschild the First, King of the Jews, to Satan the Last, King of the Slanderers*. James de Rothschild was asked by the author for a reward, which was refused. It had not been commissioned.

Disraeli already had Rothschild manage his very modest 150 shares of Paris & Strasbourg stock; now he asked Baron Lionel, "I feel half inclined to purchase Foreign Railway shares in spite of the surrounding gloom and terror. Do you think we have seen the worst? And what do you recommend?"

No response survives, but the Rothschild branches would remain cautious about financial relations with Disraeli despite the sums being small, as English politics was different from the easy French variety, and they were wary of being seen as monetarily involved with any London politician.

Although Peel had resigned on December 5, and was recognized for political resilience, Disraeli told Louis-Philippe confidently that he did not expect him back. After meeting with François Guizot, the King's chief adviser, who had long worked to checkmate Palmerston in Europe, Disraeli sent a long letter to Palmerston on December 14, giving the details of his conversations with both Guizot and Louis-Philippe. Clearly, Disraeli expected the equally resilient Palmerston to be back in the Foreign Office, and was making points as someone with an influential network that included not only Rothschilds but kings and *éminences grises*. By December 20, Peel, to Disraeli's disappointment, was back at Downing Street. Lord John Russell had been

unable to form a Liberal ministry, and Gladstone was in the revived cabinet, succeeding Stanley at the Colonial Office. And
the breakup of Young England would be formalized in a letter to
Disraeli from George Smythe. He had been rewarded for his support of Peel with the Undersecretaryship of Foreign Affairs under
the Earl of Aberdeen. Smythe had been involved in numerous
foreign affairs but none of a nature that would fit him for office.
"Everything conspires to make you think me a blackguard,"
Smythe began accurately.

While still in Paris, Disraeli learned from Sarah that a Frenchman, Henri Avigdor—the Sephardic origin of the name was obvious—who was then a guest of Sir Isaac Lyon Goldsmid in London,
had left a monograph at Grosvenor Gate. Dedicated to Disraeli, it
was a response to an anti-Semitic book by Théophile Hallez, *Des
Juifs en France*. Disraeli went to Avigdor's publisher in the rue de la
Paix and picked up another copy, writing to the author on December 28, "You have greatly honored me by the dedication to my
name of your reply to the attack of M. Hallez upon our ancient race.
I have not seen his book, but I dare say, that the children of Israel,
who baffled the Pharaohs, the Assyrian Kings & the Roman Cae-
sars, to say nothing of the Crusades & the Inquisition, will not be
overwhelmed by M. Hallez, of whom I never heard."

Remaining into the new year, the Disraelis made full use of
their French social and political connections, which were inter-
twined to a greater extent in Paris than in London. They went to
a sumptuous ball for eight hundred at Solomon de Rothschild's
mansion, and Disraeli had further conversations with the King
when he returned to the Tuileries from St.-Cloud. With his
mornings still free from political correspondence, Disraeli pressed
on with *Tancred*, which was to be set in England and in the Holy
Land.

Back in England late on January 16, 1846, he found the mixture as before: debts and politics. "Everyone wants money," he
said, putting off a creditor. But Disraeli could not get on with
Tancred, which might earn some, as public business pressed—
Parliament was to resume on January 22. Peel had almost been
forced to exit in Disraeli's absence. Now he was determined to
bring Peel down.

XIII

"... INTO THE ENEMY'S PORT."

1846–1847

DISRAELI WAS STILL ON A BACK BENCH WHEN THE QUEEN OPENED Parliament on January 22, 1846. The Government had put no direct reference to the Corn Laws into Victoria's speech, but Peel's remarks following the traditional acceptance of the address included the admission that his views on Protection had "undergone a change." The ship of state needed, from a foreign trade standpoint, to be navigated differently, and he could not "undertake to direct the course of the vessel by observations taken in the year 1842." He expected his party to follow his lead, and he would not remain in office on any "servile tenure."

Warned that they would be permitted no contrary opinions, the Tories sat in silence. Lord John Russell responded for the other side, whose policies Peel had apparently adopted, in a rambling response which indicated that he had nothing more to add. Disraeli rose with a cannonade of clever metaphors, including one describing Peel as the nurse who murdered the infant under her care. Then a nautical salvo broke through the laughter.

Disraeli recalled a Turkish admiral "in the late war in the Levant" who was entrusted with an immense fleet intended to preserve the empire, and who departed with the embraces of the Sultan and the blessings of the muftis. "Away went the fleet," Disraeli continued, "but what was the Sultan's consternation when the Lord High-Admiral steered at once into the enemy's port!"

Called a traitor for his surrender, Disraeli went on, the Admiral confessed as much, but explained that it was useless to prolong a struggle in which he did not believe. And so he was, "at this moment, the First Lord of the Admiralty at Constantinople under the new reign."

"Let men stand by the principle by which they rise, right or wrong," concluded Disraeli, passionately, but with his hands in his pockets to inhibit excessive flamboyance. Only if there remained "a demarcation between parties" could the party survive, and with it "the power and influence of Parliament itself." Furious about what he saw as a spurious claim to principle, Robert Browning fumed to Elizabeth Barrett, "So the Young England imbeciles hold that 'belief' is the admirable point—in what, they judge comparatively immaterial!" In the Commons, where Young England was already nearly forgotten, the chamber erupted with cheers, and anti-Peel Protectionists realized that they had a leader if they wanted him. Five evenings later, when Peel unveiled his scheme, the agricultural interests learned that the Corn Laws would be repealed in stages, but the bad news was doled out in a deliberately plodding speech filled with promises of compensatory taxation relief. Peel thought that tediousness in delivery—his ally, Gladstone, labeled it "righteous dullness"—would defuse discontent. Another tactic, especially useful when dealing with Disraeli, was to refuse to condescend to a question. "Sir," he would say gravely, turning to the Speaker, "I will not waste the time of the House in making any reply to the venomous attacks of the Honourable Member from Shrewsbury." Never warm in speech, Peel could be icy with contempt.

There was little question that the Prime Minister would win on repeal. His only opposition was within his own party. Tory loyalists and Liberals would carry Free Trade. Yet repeal at the cost of a Tory insurrection might mean the splintering of the party,

A Political Application of an Old Fable. *Punch*, May 30, 1846. An unsympathetic view of Disraeli's attacks upon Sir Robert Peel.

with Protectionist vindictiveness registered in every division until the Government came down. On February 11 Peel told the Queen that he could undo the Corn Laws, but only at the cost of his job. "Nobody now doubts," Greville observed in his diary the next day, "that the question will be carried and that Peel will go out soon after."

What had happened was that Disraeli had secured a hero about whom the disillusioned squirearchy could rally. Lord George Bentinck had volunteered himself. The second son of the eccentric 4th Duke of Portland, who communicated with his family only in writing, Bentinck had been in Parliament from King's

Lynn for eighteen years but was known only outside politics. So well-to-do, Disraeli wrote of him, but not for print, "Bentinck had no wardrobe. He always had a complete new suit of clothes on a chair in his bedroom." In his first eight years as an M.P. he had not risen to address the Commons once, but his racing stable, one of the best in England, spoke for him in the country. One of his horses had won the Oaks; he expected to win the Derby; and he had immense prestige among racing men for his integrity and his zeal to raise the ethics of competition. Listening to Peel, he thought he recognized the political equivalent of the tricksters and defaulters he encountered on the turf. Yet when debate on the Corn Laws began on February 9, he felt that he lacked the parliamentary skills to contribute.

Disraeli did not speak again on repeal until February 29, by which time he realized that however few were his friends and confidants in the House, he now had committed allies. Leaguing themselves against Peel on any grounds, they also opposed a new Coercion Bill for Ireland, introduced on February 23 when the Prime Minister felt that it would be obscured by the wrangling over Free Trade.

When, three weeks after the debate had begun, Bentinck rose for the first time, it was, in Disraeli's words, "long past the noon of night." Bentinck was still seething over what he took to be a flouting of protocol by Prince Albert, who had appeared in the gallery of the House on the first night of debate to offer implicit support to Peel, whom he admired. In a long and convoluted sentence Bentinck charged that the Prince had "allowed himself to be seduced by the first minister of the Crown . . . to give semblance of the personal sanction of Her Majesty to a measure which . . . a great majority of the landed aristocracy of England, of Scotland, and of Ireland imagine fraught with great injury if not ruin to them." The sentence was nearly two hundred words long. Bentinck knew he needed help with the art of debate, and finally, on March 31, he wrote a stiff and formal letter to Disraeli suggesting that they act in concert.

For the perennial outsider the partnership with Lord George Bentinck was a recipe for success. His position and reputation commanded respect, and the picture of Bentinck leading and

Disraeli seconding was exactly right in the circumstances. Lord George proved more than facade, rising to his role while Disraeli managed offstage. Toward the end of March, when Disraeli was ill and at home, Bentinck wrote to him, "For God's sake get quite right before you venture out, as we shall want you after Easter in earnest."

Out of action through April, Disraeli was back in May for the third reading of the Corn Importation Bill, now politically entangled with Irish Coercion, which many Liberals, especially Irish M.P.s, could not support. Peel had pressed on with both measures, and late at night on May 15 Disraeli was recognized.

The most frustrated listener in the House through much of the Corn Laws debate had been Gladstone, who had lost his seat, but at that moment his exasperation was compounded. Peel, at least, would have opportunities to respond, but until Gladstone was again returned in August 1847, he could only be a spectator in the Strangers' Gallery. After Disraeli's memorable philippic on January 22, Gladstone had written, gloomily, "Read last night's debate. The skies are dark enough. It was vexing not to be at Peel's side when he most needed help." The most practical consolation was that it was now easier to fit in his three daily hours for devotions.

From the outside, Gladstone did what he could for Peel, hosting a reception at 13 Carlton House Terrace on February 11 "attended by all Young England," one of the dwindling occasions other than within the nearby Carlton Club, or in the nonpolitical salons of society matrons, when Tories of the warring factions could be brought together. Toward the end of March, as Peel was being increasingly buffeted, Gladstone reached for divine rationalization of his ouster by his constituency. "A most gracious purpose of God," he wrote, "has spared me the most wearing part of my labours that my resumption of office"—he had been Colonial Minister—"should have brought, the bitter feuds of Parliament: but my heart does not answer in lively thankfulness."

When Disraeli rose in May to pillory Peel, Gladstone to his further chagrin was absent even from the Gallery, ill with influenza. (In his diary he attributed his afflictions to his Cabinet dinner, the previous year, when there were thirteen at table.) He would later read what Disraeli said in *Hansard*, and could imagine exactly how the cruel, if brilliant, lines would come to life in Disraeli's languid, half-drawling manner. In debate he appeared to his adversaries to be "lying in wait for points," and he lay in wait, too, to puncture affectation, as when Gladstone once paused dramatically, seemingly losing the thread of his thinking, and Disraeli leaned forward from his bench helpfully with "Your last word was *revolution.*"

Disraeli spoke for nearly three hours, his invective carrying easily over the hissing of the gaslights. Like an actor he would draw a handkerchief from his pocket to prepare his audience for a telling remark—a "hit"—and aimed at his target. Peel's ideas were neither his party's, nor his own, Disraeli charged. The Prime Minister "has traded on the ideas and intelligence of others. His life has been one great Appropriation Clause. He is a burglar of others' intellect. . . . There is no statesman who has committed political petty larceny on so great a scale."

He had already had his say on "cheap bread" and was winding up his remarks, each hit followed by loud protectionist cheers. "I know that the public mind is polluted with economic fancies," Disraeli concluded. There was a depraved idea that one could become rich, or richer, "without the interference of industry and toil. . . . Confidence in public men" was disappearing, and he expected "an awakening of bitterness." But he ended on an idealistic note about rejecting easy solutions and returning "to those principles which made England great," and sat down to a noisy ovation.

Peel arose to jeers, but was not going to let an opportunist wound him mortally. He fired back with his most powerful weapon, recollecting Disraeli's letter of 1841 appealing to him for an undersecretaryship. If the right honorable gentleman had always held so low an opinion of the Prime Minister's character, "It is . . . surprising that he should have been ready, as I think he was, to unite his fortunes with mine in office, thus implying the strongest proof which any public man can give of confidence in the honor and integrity of a Minister of the Crown."

Disraeli responded with a flat lie. He had "never directly or indirectly solicited office," although had he been offered "a very slight office" at the time, he would have accepted it. Stories would float about for decades that Peel had the letter in his pocket but was too gentlemanly to exploit it. Had he had access to it in that moment of his humiliation and Disraeli's reckless-ness, he almost certainly would have used it. What is surprising is that he did not release it to the newspapers the next day. It might have finished Disraeli in politics. Possibly Peel had difficulty lo-cating it among the papers of three decades, and by the time it was located it was too late to matter.

At four in the morning of Saturday, May 16, the third read-ing of Corn Law repeal was carried, 327 to 229. Of the 328 Con-servatives who voted, only 106 supported Peel. Few readers would have noticed in the papers that carried long accounts of the proceedings—possibly not even Disraeli—the news that the day before, at Little Missenden in Buckinghamshire, Henrietta, widow of the late Sir Francis Sykes, had died.

Debate on the Irish Coercion Bill was joined on June 8, with Bentinck emotionally accusing Peel of having no Tories on his side but "forty paid janissaries and some seventy other renegades," numbers that closely matched the Corn Laws figures. Recrimina-tions between Peelites and anti-Peel Tories were bitter, yet Disraeli had no inhibitions about dining with the enemy when the opponent was someone he liked, like Richard Cobden, one of the most eloquent Radical supporters of Peel's bill. Cobden, D'Orsay, Kinglake,* "Suleiman Pasha" (actually D. J. A. Sève, a French officer recruited to modernize the Egyptian army), and Prince Louis Napoleon also breakfasted at Monckton Milnes's rooms at No. 26 Pall Mall on June 12 to celebrate Louis Napo-leon's return to England. He had escaped from a French prison on May 25, making his way across the Channel. Disraeli almost for-got the Coercion Bill when Napoleon took him aside to an al-cove with a bow window to confide that he had secured support in France to restore his family—meaning himself—to the imperial throne. "I thought," Disraeli would recall, "I was talking to a madman."

*A. W. Kinglake had published Eöthen, a book of travels in the Middle East, in 1844.

Asked what would happen if Christ reappeared, Carlyle quipped, "Monckton Milnes would ask Him to breakfast." Possibly the progress of *Tancred*, suspended in the heat of politics, can be dated from Milnes's eclectic *déjeuner*, for in chapter XX Disraeli would write, "Mr Vavasour's breakfasts were renowned. Whatever your creed, class, or country, one might almost add your character, you were a welcome guest at his matutinal meal, provided you were celebrated. . . . Individuals met at his hospitable house who had never met before, but who for years had been cherishing in solitude mutual detestation, . . . and paid each other in his presence the compliments which veiled their ineffable disgust."

By midafternoon Disraeli was at the Carlton Club, preparing to return to the Commons. He sent a note to Mary Anne by messenger, "As I cannot bear to be away from you the whole day, & as it is now nearly four o'c[loc]k, I send this . . . to beg that you will call for me at the Carlton, where I shall remain until ½ past five, so that we may be together a little."

The usual flood of social invitations suggested that the Irish debate was not supposed to interfere with the Season, but little else was on anyone's mind in London. Famine in Ireland, industrial distress in England, concerns that a widespread sense of injustice might lead to revolutionary violence on both British isles were as nothing once Peel's adversaries saw his vulnerability and their chances. The Whigs (soon to be Liberals) saw an opportunity to return to office; the Protectionists sought control of what would inevitably be a wounded and weakened party, but one, at least, representing traditional Tory values. As Bentinck had put it, in a speech that sounded much like Disraeli, "I trust the House will recollect I am fighting the battle of a party whose leaders have deserted them."

Reporting to the Queen, Peel on June 22 described his plight as "the result of a foul conspiracy concocted by Mr Disraeli and Lord George Bentinck," whose motives were entirely "malignant." The inevitable was approaching, and both she and Prince Albert realized that Peel was only hanging on to an office that had lost its savor. His party split into loyal and disloyal factions, he would not have been able to stand it much longer, Peel confided.

On Thursday, June 26, the day after a crowded *fête champêtre* at Gunnersbury, the Lionel de Rothschild estate, came the division in Commons that would turn the government over to the Whigs. "With the legions of the Protectionists watching their prey in grim silence, while the Liberal sections were united in hostile manoeuvres against the government," Disraeli wrote in his life of Lord George Bentinck, "it was recognised at once that the great minister had a staff without an army; not a reconnoitring could take place without the whole cabinet being under orders, and scarcely a sharpshooter sailed from the opposite ranks without the prime minister returning his fire in person." Voting against Peel, and the Irish Bill, were sixty-nine Protectionists. Seventy-four Tories abstained. The Opposition, whom Peel had hoped to conciliate, voted its own interest.

"My darling," Disraeli wrote to Mary Anne in a note to be rushed to Grosvenor Gate by messenger, "I shall be home for dinner before or by ½ past seven. The Ministry have resigned. All 'Coningsby' and 'Young England' the general exclamation here." In reality his little group had faded away and a Protectionist party had arisen in its place, but Disraeli's campaign in print and from the back benches of the House, abetted by the prestige of Bentinck, who had found his voice and followers, had done Peel in.

Bentinck had come out, Disraeli would say, "like a lion forced out of his lair." In the tradition of the turf, he competed to win, vigorous in "the ardour of his friendships, even the fierceness of his hates and prejudices." To underline his determination, Bentinck sold his race horses. And in the House he was a curious contrast to Disraeli, whose speeches were dramatic in content while understated in delivery. Bentinck spoke as fiercely as he hunted and rode, Peelite whip John Young observing with hostility that when Lord George made "a furious onslaught on the Government . . . his voice was raised to screaming pitch—his eye gleamed like a wild animal at feeding time, and his whole deportment was so excited that no man out of Bedlam ever came near it." It would be a paradoxical partnership, the ultimate outsider and the patrician sportsman, but it was based upon mutual regard and lasted until Bentinck's untimely death.

"I little thought . . . that I should ever live to praise Peel," Charles Dickens wrote to his publisher Thomas Chapman on July 3. "But d'Israeli and that Dunghill Lord"—Bentinck was often so pilloried in *Punch*—"have so disgusted me, that I felt disposed to champion him."

For the Whigs, technically outnumbered in the Commons, Lord John Russell's government was a caretaker affair until he could dissolve Parliament and go to the people for a mandate. Bentinck and Disraeli had no intention of letting Peel back in, and Russell could count on that in the interim. But the Tories, if they were ever to repossess Downing Street, could not remain divided. The Protectionist partnership spent much of the summer traveling to political gatherings to rally their forces, making it clear that Edward Stanley, in the Lords since September 1844, was effectively head of the authentic party.

After visiting Bentinck's constituency at King's Lynn, Disraeli went to Belvoir Castle, the seat of the Duke of Rutland, Manner's father, and the "Beaumanoir" of *Coningsby*. There was more political talk. Bentinck had evidenced no stomach for prolonged struggles in the Commons and was not in as good health as his noble presence suggested. The wing of the Tories he represented, in actuality the Country party, needed Disraeli as leader in the House of Commons, but he was unrepresentative of the squirearchy in a property and family sense and in his seat for Shrewsbury, an uncomfortable urban constituency, as he had already learned. Without land of his own, could he be potential leader of the landowning interests? He needed to represent a county, and what better one than the Buckinghamshire of Bradenham House? But that property was tied up in litigation, the reason that Isaac could rent it.

Pending any further inheritance on Isaac's death, and any substantial earnings from Disraeli's writings, the Bentincks—Lord George and his elder brother, the Marquess of Titchfield—proposed quietly advancing the wherewithal for a country property. Disraeli was still overwhelmingly in debt, even with the burgeoning bills from his minority ignored, and Mary Anne's income, largely from a life interest in the Wyndham Lewis estate, supported their tenure at Grosvenor Gate and interest on acknowledged debts of close to £20,000. Hughenden Manor, a mile north of High Wycombe, had been on the market since John Norris had died in 1845. It was a white-stuccoed three-story building of unpretentious appearance set in 750 acres of farmland and woods, and like Bradenham House had a small church on the property nearby. The price asked, which included the estimated value of its timber, was about £35,000. Disraeli had no anticipated resources to repay a sum that large. Most of what he expected to receive from his father had already been advanced. Much of what would be left would go to Sarah. The matter remained in abeyance when Ben and Mary Anne went off to Bradenham early in September so that work on *Tancred* could be completed before Parliament met again.

When Bentinck visited Bradenham early in December to plan strategy for the new session, there was further talk with Isaac about what Bentinck spelled as "Huendon." Disraeli immediately alerted his two deputies in London, Richard Wright, a lawyer with a wide spectrum of influential clients who had been handling financial matters for him, and Philip Rose, another lawyer who had become his confidential agent for every kind of business, with their correspondence directed away from Mary Anne to the Carlton Club. The Hughenden opportunity was a way out of Shrewsbury, and dissolution loomed in 1847. Yet Disraeli was so busy with *Tancred*, he claimed in a letter to Lady Londonderry on December 26, that if Bentinck had not visited, "I sh[oul]d not even know who, at the present moment, was Prime Minister."

Tancred, Lord Montacute, the young protagonist of the closing novel in Disraeli's trilogy, was a new species for him—a religious enthusiast. The first part of the narrative, set in England, exploited a long experience of castles and country estates. Tancred, an innocent, knows little more than Eton and Oxford. Even there he was insulated from experience, as his father, the Duke of Bellamont, had taken a house nearby to keep watch on his only child. Tancred was expected to take his place in his social milieu, in Parliament, and on his extensive lands. The Duchess, his mother, has already selected a bride for him, but Tancred insists that he must first find himself. For that, the impractical young man insists upon emulating the Crusader De Montacutes of six centuries earlier and strengthening his faith and sense of duty in the Holy Land. Even the worldly Bishop of London, urgently sent for by the Duke, fails to sway Tancred, who seeks "heavenly messengers." Bellamont gives in. A son in doubt is better than a son in debt. Going to Jerusalem, shrugs the Duke, "is at least better than going to the Jews, which most men do at his time of life." His Duchess disagrees, confessing, "I would rather that he should be ruined than die."

"Men do not die as they used [to]," his lordship says. "Ask the annuity offices; they have all raised their rates."

Preparations and farewells take Tancred into the society of *Coningsby* and *Sybil*, even to encore performances by some of the characters, including the ubiquitous and even more mysterious Sidonia. One book which Tancred is given to further his religious education is *Revelations of Chaos*, described by Lady Constance as a book that "explains everything." In 1845 the Disraelis had encountered *Vestiges of the Natural History of Creation*, published anonymously by Robert Chambers the year before. "Dizzy is enchanted with it," Mary Anne had reported. A precursor to Darwin's *Origins of the Species*, it was much discussed—in religious circles only with outrage—and Disraeli satirized its reception as Lady Constance explains its gist. "Everything is explained by geology and astronomy, and in this way. It shows you exactly how a star is formed; nothing can be so pretty! A cluster of vapour, the cream of the Milky Way, a sort of celestial cheese, churned into light, you must read it, 'tis charming."

"Nobody ever saw a star formed," Tancred retorts.

But, Lady Constance goes on, what is most interesting of all is the explanation of man's development. "The principle is perpetually going on. . . . First there was nothing; then there was something; then, I forget the next. I think there were shells, then fishes; then we came, let me see, did we come next? Never mind that, we came at last. And the next change will be something very superior to us, something with wings. Ah! That's it: we were fishes and I believe we shall be crows."

"I do not believe I ever was a fish," insists Tancred.

It is all proved, Lady Constance continues. It is scientific and beyond contradiction. "You see exactly how everything is made; how many worlds there have been; how long they lasted; what went before, what comes next. We are a link in the chain, as inferior animals were that preceded us: we in turn shall be inferior; all that will remain of us will be some relics in . . . red sandstone. This is development. We had fins; we may have wings."

Such revelations are too distasteful for Tancred, who must flee irreligious modern horrors. He had much actual company in his time, leading Disraeli to comment on evolutionary speculations tongue-in-cheek. Ambiguity, however wryly put, cost few votes, but shrewd old Lord Lyndhurst, who did not have to campaign for anything, could growl to Disraeli, "nothing will induce me to believe that the human species could have sprung from one pair." It became a political, rather than a scientific, statement when, in Oxford, in 1864, Disraeli quipped about the contradictions between evolution and faith, "The question is this; is man an ape or an angel? My Lords, I am on the side of the angels." He recognized the desire of human beings for belief in something beyond themselves ("Duty," contends Tancred, "cannot exist without faith"), but Disraeli, like his father, was a confirmed skeptic.*

"A man cannot go to Jerusalem as he would to Birmingham, by the next train," says the Duke of Bellamont, but he arranges things through Sidonia, and Tancred goes off to plumb "the Asian mystery," arriving with unlimited credit and unlimited naiveté. Quickly he is enchanted by the land of the Bible, and also by the beautiful Eva Besso, daughter of a Jewish agent of Sidonia's, whom Tancred urges to read the life of Jesus in the Gospels:

> "I have read it. The English bishop here has given me the book. It is a good one, written, I observe, entirely by Jews. I find in it many things with which I agree; and if there be some from which I dissent, it may be that I do not comprehend them."

*In an 1842 commonplace book Disraeli had written, "Many nations have lived very comfortably without kings, but no nation has lived without a priest."

"You are already half a Christian!" said Tancred, with animation.

"But the Christianity which I draw from your book does not agree with the Christianity which you practise," said the lady, "and I fear, therefore, it may be heretical."

"The Christian Church would be your guide."

"Which?" inquired the lady; "there are so many in Jerusalem. There is the good bishop who presented me with this volume, and who is himself a Hebrew: he is a Church; there is the Latin Church, which was founded by a Hebrew; there is the Armenian Church, which belongs to an Eastern nation who, like the Hebrews, have lost their country and are scattered in every clime; there is the Abyssinian Church, who hold us in great honour, and practise many of our rites and ceremonies; and there are the Greek, the Maronite, and the Coptic Churches, who do not favour us, but who do not treat us as grossly as they treat each other. In this perplexity it may be wise to remain within the pale of a church older than all of them, the church in which Jesus was born and which he never quitted, for he was born a Jew, lived a Jew, and died a Jew; as became a Prince of the House of David, which you do and must acknowledge him to have been. Your sacred genealogies prove the fact; and if you could not establish it, the whole fabric of your faith falls to the ground."

"If I had no confidence in any Church," said Tancred, with agitation, "I would fall down before God and beseech him to enlighten me; and, in this land," he added, in a tone of excitement, "I cannot believe that the appeal to the Mercy-seat would be made in vain."

"But human wit ought to be exhausted before we presume to invoke divine interposition," said the lady.

Tancred's adventures echo Disraeli's memories of Jerusalem and environs, while the characters seem nineteenth-century reincarnations of figures from *Alroy*. Eva has a foster brother, the raffish and engaging Emir Fakredeen, raised by Adam Besso largely so that Disraeli can contrast Arab and Jewish Semitic types. ("Arabs," says a wry observer, "are only Jews on horseback.") Fakredeen is intensely greedy for lands and power. "You will never succeed," Eva warns. "Intrigue will be your ruin."

"Intrigue!" says Fakredeen. "It is life! It is the only thing! . . . If you wish to produce a result, you must make combinations."

Through Fakredeen's machinations, Tancred, while exploring a mountain pass, is captured for ransom and, after some complications of plot, is rescued and brought back to Jerusalem. (When alone in the stony wilderness he has had an apparent mystical experience which satisfies his longing for affirmation of faith, Disraeli having implied throughout that belief not palpably fraudulent is essential to most humans.) Finding Eva once more, Tancred professes his love for her, but she softly refuses him, for more reasons than her prior betrothal to her cousin Hillel, of Aleppo, whose admiration of Voltaire is no bar. As for Tancred, he is, she explains to him, "a son of Europe and of Christ," an outsider in her world. "There are those to whom I belong; and to whom you belong." But she permits her pretty head to fall on his shoulder, and none too soon, for shouts are heard in the near distance. A party of guides and servants are approaching, escorting the Duke and Duchess of Bellamont, who have just arrived in Jerusalem.

Here—abruptly—the novel ends. Will Tancred resist his rescue? Had Disraeli intended to carry the plot further? *Tancred* seems to close with the opening of Parliament in 1847, but also because there were no alternatives that would not alienate his readers. Ambiguity was the safest strategy. And Disraeli was pleased with the result, although his deep feeling about his ancestry resonates so powerfully through the novel as to have seemed to a less committed writer politically hazardous. It was *Alroy*, written as he first aspired to Parliament, all over again, only this time he was looking ahead to its front bench and beyond.

Very little of Disraeli's pride in what he called *race* was covert in *Tancred*, but at least one element was. Sidonia's confidential courier who assists Tancred is an Italian named Francis Baroni, which he explains to the young man's surprise identifies him as a Sephardi. He is a Jew from Cento, the town from which the author's grandfather, an earlier Benjamin D'Israeli, emigrated to England. "Good Arabic, my lord. Baroni; that is, the son of Aaron; the name of old clothesmen in London, and of caliphs in Baghdad." Disraeli was throwing the jeers and the caricatures back at their makers.*

The story of the Baroni family offered Disraeli the opportunity to suggest a little of the early history of Sidonia, who appears in flashback at twenty (he is about forty in *Tancred*) in an obscure Flemish village much like those in which Disraeli wandered with Mary Anne in the autumn he began the novel. There the young Sidonia, already many times a millionaire with managers handling his banking affairs across Europe, encounters a family of talented Italian-Jewish traveling players eking out a living, and befriends them. Their fifteen-year-old son is a younger Francis Baroni. Asked about his ambitions, he tells Sidonia, "I have no wish to be idle; but there are two things which I have always desired: first, that I should travel; and, secondly, that nobody should ever know me." Like the others, he is granted his wishes.

Almost an autonomous short story—titled boldly, like no other segment of a Disraeli novel, "The History of the Baroni Family"—the story within a story reveals a gentle Sidonia that is a facet of his mystery-man personality unseen in *Coningsby* or elsewhere in *Tancred*. The "History" remains one of Disraeli's happiest creations in fiction.

Other family undercurrents seem inserted in the novel for Disraeli's private satisfaction. An influential Spanish priest in Jerusalem is named Alonzo Lara, suggesting the aristocratic Sephardic family of his grandfather's first wife; and the Mesdemoiselles de Laurella, the haughty Thérèse and Sophonisbe, suggest Disraeli's own grandmother. Educated in Smyrna and then Marseilles, they return "ashamed of their race, and not fanatically devoted to their religion, which might be true, but was not fashionable."

Disraeli had followed the political changes in Syrian Israel

---

*Ironically, in a cruel gesture more than ten years earlier, Disraeli had ridiculed (Sir) Francis Goldsmid for using the name *Francis* although a professing Jew.

carefully since his visit in 1831. In his imagination he had never left, and as an M.P. he was aware of the interventions of the Great Powers into Ottoman affairs, the "Eastern Question", which after 1840 was never out of the newspapers. Further, the persecutions of Jews in the area, especially over trumped-up accusations of ritual murders, had even brought Sir Moses Montefiore, on behalf of the European Jewish communities and with the approval of Queen Victoria, to visit the Sultan and request a *firman* from him declaring the innocence of the accused. He would undertake similar missions, with less success in alleviating persecution, to Russia in 1845, to Italy in 1859, to Morocco in 1863, and to Romania in 1867, when he was nearly eighty-four. In 1848, when republican uprisings had forced Pope Pius IX from Rome and he appealed to Charles de Rothschild of the Naples house for help, he and James de Rothschild of the Paris branch extended financial help on condition that the ghettos in the Papal States come down. Pius took the money but reneged on emancipation.

As they occurred, such developments were well known to Disraeli from political sources and from the press. He also had access to Montefiore and Rothschild homes in London. His Eastern settings in *Tancred* were up to date through 1846, even to Eva's remark about the "good bishop" of the Anglican See of Jerusalem being "a Hebrew." In 1841 the British and Prussian crowns had agreed to alternate appointments to the post. The first appointee was an ex-rabbi from Posen who had become a missionary of the London Society for Promoting Christianity among the Jews. Despite the delicacy of his own convert status, Disraeli sardonically tells, through Baroni, of the Bishop's sparse congregation, "consisting of his own family, the English and Prussian consuls, and five Jews, whom they have converted at twenty piastres a-week; but I know they are going to strike for wages."

Even so, Disraeli conceded while having no real interest in theology, Christianity was useful to Jews. "It secures their history & their literature being known to all Xdom," he noted in a memorandum. "Every day the Church publickly reads its history, & keeps alive the memory of its public characters; & has diffused its poetry throughout the world." It was impolitic of Jews, he thought, to "oppose" a "Jewish Institution" that was insuring the survival of Judaic culture. Yet, despite his own situation as nominal Anglican, Disraeli espoused continuity over conversion, as he made clear in the novel in the case of the "good bishop," in the exchanges between Eva and Tancred, and in the poignant description of the celebration of *Sukkot*, the Feast of Tabernacles. "The vineyards of Israel," Disraeli wrote, fifty years before the term *Zionism* first appeared in print, "have ceased to exist, but the eternal law enjoins the children of Israel still to celebrate the vintage. A race that persist in celebrating their vintage, although they have no fruits to gather, will regain their vineyards." It was easier to mark the festival in warm Mediterranean regions, he notes, "But picture to yourself the child of Israel in the dingy suburb of the squalid corner of some bleak northern town. . . . The law has told him, though a denizen in an icy clime, that he must dwell for seven days in a bower." The symbolic dwelling followed God's injunction in Leviticus 23:43 to construct for *Sukkot* bowerlike shelters to recall those erected in the Sinai wilderness "when I brought them out of the land of Egypt," as well as the encampments of pilgrims in Jerusalem for the harvest festival at the time of *Sukkot*, which marks the reception by Moses, as described in Exodus, of the tablets of the Law.

Disraeli in *Tancred* relates the observance sensitively to the devout London Jew of his own day who "goes early to some Whitechapel market, [and] purchases some willow boughs . . . brought, probably, from one of the neighbouring rivers of Essex, hastens home, cleans out the yard of his miserable tenement, builds his bower, decks it, even profusely, with the finest flowers and fruits that he can procure, the myrtle and the citron never forgotten. . . . After the service of his synagogue, he sups late with his wife and his children in the open air, as if he were in the pleasant villages of Galilee, beneath its sweet and starry sky." He raises his glass of wine and repeats the *kiddush* prayer, and breaks and distributes the bread, "much," Disraeli writes, "as Jesus must have done as a young man." And as his wife and children join in the chant "in honour of the vintage," a group of "Anglo-Saxons," perhaps so respectable as to pay £10 a year in rent and thus become eligible for the franchise, pass by, and one, overhearing, sneers, "I say, Buggins, what's that row?"

"Oh! it's those cursed Jews! We've a lot of 'em here. It's one of their horrible feasts. The Lord Mayor ought to interfere."

In 1855, David Salomons, a City alderman, would become the first Jewish Lord Mayor of London. It was possible because in 1845 the Jewish Disabilities Removal Act, opening municipal office to Jews, passed successfully through the Commons and was then guided by Lyndhurst through the Lords. It had been introduced in the House by Sir Robert Peel.

English religion is entirely a creation of Parliament, Fakredeen claims. "The English are really neither Jews nor Christians, but follow a sort of religion of their own, which is made every year by their bishops . . . in what they call a parliament, a college of muftis." And Eva wonders why "these Saxon and Celtic societies" persecute the people from whom they acquired their religion. "We agree," she taunts Tancred about Catholicism and Protestantism, "that half Christendom worships a Jewess, and the other half a Jew. . . . Which is the superior race, the worshipped or the worshippers?"

While "the greatest of legislators, the greatest of administrators, and the greatest of reformers"—Moses, Solomon, and Jesus—represent what no other race, "extinct or living," can boast, and a litany of other illustrious Jews from David to the composer Mendelssohn (even less a Jew than Disraeli) are cited, Tancred, heir to a dukedom, confesses, "Alas! I am sprung from a horde of Baltic pirates, who were never heard of during the greater annals of the world, a descent which I have been educated to believe was the greatest of honours." But the creed from the East, an ethical monotheism Disraeli described as "completed Judaism" with Jesus as culminating prophet, had civilized Tancred's forebears into "kings and princes."

Parliament reassembled on January 19, 1847, just as Mary Anne was writing Charlotte de Rothschild, "The first proofs of 'Tancred' are now on the table. How much I hope you may be here when he is presented to the public, for I am sure you will sympathise with me in my child's fate." Whether it was the novel or its author she was claiming as her spiritual child is unclear, but she understood that while its content might please the Baroness, it would have hard going among the critics. Thomas Carlyle, who

The Rising Generation—in Parliament. *Punch*, January 30, 1847.
PEEL. *"Well, my little Man, what are you going to do this Session, Eh?"*
D————LI. (the Juvenile) *"Why—aw—aw—I've made arrangements—
aw—to smash—aw—Everybody."*

had referred to Tancred de Hauteville in his *Past and Present* as a knight in the First Crusade, growled in a letter to Robert Browning that "d'Israeli's *Tancred* (readable to the end of the first volume), a kind of transcendent spiritual Houndsditch, marks an epoch in the history of this poor country." The upper class English settings so unflatteringly depicted pleased the curmudgeon of No. 24 Cheyne Row, but to him the Eastern scenes were akin to the stretch of London's East End occupied since the seventeenth century by Jewish secondhand clothes sellers, their merchandise still identified in the name of Petticoat Lane.

Across from Lord John Russell, the Prime Minister, Bentinck and Disraeli moved to the front bench in the Commons to rep-resent the Opposition. The Opposition leader in the House of Lords, Stanley, although no friend of Disraeli's, had been a defec-tor from Peel's Cabinet. Peelites were almost a party apart. While politics drifted in expectation of new elections, Disraeli moved to establish himself as a candidate for Buckinghamshire, signing an agreement for purchase of Hughenden Manor on March 2. As yet he had promises, but no money, and was able to forestall a settle-ment on grounds that a proper evaluation had to be made of the woodlands "down to 1/ per stick," as specified to the estate agent the next day.

Positioning himself for the county seat, he went to Aylesbury early in March for the Lent assizes to meet the circuit judges and to be a guest of Baron Mayer de Rothschild, brother of Lionel and Anthony, who had become High Sheriff of the county, and was hosting a series of Buckinghamshire notables. As befit a county eminence, Rothschild had purchased an estate, Mentmore, and would begin construction of an awesome manor on the site in 1851. For the series of dinners at John Kersey Fowler's White Hart Hotel, Disraeli wrote to Sarah from Grosvenor Gate, Rothschild had imported "a legion of French cooks and wines" to the astonishment of the proprietor. For Disraeli, it enabled him to meet people who mattered in his quest for a new seat, while the dinners made certain that it would become public knowledge that he was acquiring Hughenden.

Tancred appeared in the bookshops the next week, on March 17. "There is an accession to my family," he wrote to the loyal Lady Londonderry two days earlier in sending her a copy; "& as you have always been gracious to my offspring, I hope you will re-ceive 'Tancred' kindly." Several of the Rothschilds received cop-ies, as did Lord John Manners, who reappeared as Henry Sidney (rather than Sydney as in *Coningsby*), and Isaac responded through Sarah, who had read it to him by March 19, "Wonderful book—in which every succeeding adventure is more original than the preceding. . . . Did the East ever produce anything so thoroughly completely Eastern?" It was, he added, "magical" and "profound," and he approved of the conclusion—"the untying of so many knots by one felicitous stroke."

Thirty years later, Disraeli told Benjamin Jowett, the Regius Professor of Greek at Oxford, that he still liked *Tancred* the best of all his novels. And he told another friend that whenever he wanted to refresh his knowledge of the East, he turned back to *Tancred*. The author was not alone. Many readers of fiction found their first contemporary view of the East in *Tancred*. Young Isabel Arundell at sixteen was "inspired . . . with all the ideas and yearnings for a wild Oriental life." It was "my second Bible." She carried it everywhere and claimed to know it by heart. Years later, when she went to Syria as Richard Burton's wife, she recalled, memories of *Tancred* made her feel "as if I had lived that life for years." Yet the work bewildered readers as much as it entertained, and despite its later reprintings in cheap editions, the first two printings of 2,250 copies in all brought the author only £775 the first year, a disappointment after *Coningsby* and *Sybil*.

Among the reviewers, predictably, Monckton Milnes—Mr. Vavasour—was dissatisfied with the metamorphosis of living people into fictional characters. "The immediate interest which these personalities confer on the works," he contended in the *Edinburgh Review*, "is dearly purchased; for the moment a character is known to represent Lord——— or Mr———, it loses all power as a work of art." *The Court Journal*, while predicting that the novel would extend Disraeli's fame, observed, "To the Hebrew fraternity it will be particularly acceptable, for the author goes much farther than he has done in his previous works toward exalting the character, talents, and religion of the Jews." It was "clever," *Punch* conceded, adding, in "old clo's" metaphor, "We shall soon begin to suspect that MR DISRAELI is the poet of MOSES AND SON'S Establishment." In his commonplace book, Milnes quoted Carlyle as expostulating, "I cannot stand Disraeli trying to force his Jewish jackasseries on the world." And *The Times*, usually friendly toward Disraeli, questioned whether his purpose was "to convert the whole world, converted Jews and all, back to Judaism!" It prompted a response from Jacob Franklin's paper, *The Voice of Judaism*, that there should be room in the world for both Gentiles and Jews:

> If Sidonia buys a noble estate in Bucks, he not only does not act against the precepts of Judaism, but he lit-erally follows the counsel of the prophet, who thus ad-vised Israel, saying, "This captivity is long: build ye houses and dwell in them; and plant gardens and eat the fruit of them: (Jerem. XXIX, 28); and if Sidonia's first cousin is high-sheriff of a county, he only follows the noble example set to him by Daniel, Hananiah, Meshael, and Azarish. . . . The truth is, the Jews never secluded themselves from the Christians—it was the Christians who excluded the Jews.

In Boston, patrician young poet James Russell Lowell, who would be Minister to Great Britain 1880–85, wrote in the *North American Review* for July that he was unable to find any "cohe-sion" or "art" in *Tancred*. There were "one or two excellent land-scapes, and some detached thought worth remembering," and he reminded his readers that "the earnestness of a charlatan is only a profounder kind of charlatanism." The Gospels were "read backward, after the Hebrew fashion," while the "girds at Sir Rob-ert Peel" were upon a man "who . . . has shown himself capable of one thing beyond Mr D'Israeli's reach—success, which always gives a man some hold or other, however questionable, upon pos-terity."

Parliament was not formally dissolved until mid-July, but Disraeli had declared for one of the three Buckinghamshire seats on May 22 and began campaigning in hopes of an uncontested election. He could not afford a repetition of Maidstone or Shrewsbury.

When the possibility of more candidates than seats loomed, and that Charles Cavendish might be a rival rather than a col-league, he exhorted the electors of Aylesbury (June 26, 1847), in true Sidonia fashion, that his own "pedigree" was "as good and even superior to the Cavendishes; but as my opponent and his representative have chosen to narrow the question to that issue,

I accept. . ." Like *Tancred*, it was a bold embrace of his origins, the claim to an elitism beyond property confiscated from monasteries or seized in civil wars. He was not going to let his adversaries define his ancestry for him. Further, as Sidonia had boasted, he derived from a continuing aristocracy of intellect. "Let him"— the scion of the Cavendishes—"pride himself on his blood; I have confidence in my brains." Although he had his own racial chauvinism, he preferred to point his audience closer to home. "I have a father, more than eighty years of age," he reminded his listeners, "who is a freeholder of the county of Buckingham, and who intends to record his vote for his son when the day of election arrives. I would not change that father, who for half a century has laboured to form the tastes and instruct the minds of his fellow countrymen, for any Duke alive or dead."

Disraeli's campaign had been marred by the death of his mother on April 21 after a long illness, very likely cancer. She was seventy-one. Isaac, too, was ailing, and on Sarah's appeal, Ben rushed to Bradenham to help break the dread news to him. The agents for Hughenden, in fact, assumed that their prospective purchaser was using delaying tactics—technicalities about the timber estimates—to await Isaac's own death, in order to secure the funds for settlement of the property. A contract had been signed on June 5, 1847, in order to validate Disraeli's claim to hold Buckinghamshire land, but it was not until April 3, 1848, that he actually took title to Hughenden. A serious economic slump, largely because of overambitious railway expansion, had followed elections, and many banks closed their doors. It had become difficult for the Bentincks to borrow money on their lands to advance to Disraeli, but the slump also had a positive impact. Railways reduced their orders for ties, and Disraeli saved about £800 on the timber valuation. Yet he had to borrow £13,000 beyond what the Bentincks had furnished to raise an amount in excess of £35,000 to complete the purchase.

Disraeli had already been acting in some ways as if he possessed Hughenden. In the summer of 1847 he had sent, at Sarah's request, trout from what would be his own streams for Isaac's increasingly limited diet as he failed further. But in the Aylesbury address Disraeli cautiously had distanced himself from legal ownership. "Return me to Parliament," he urged, "not because I am a relative of the Duke of Devonshire"—as was Cavendish—"not because my broad lands stretch from Buckingham to Aylesbury, but because my public character has shown you that I may be trusted, and what is more, that I am capable." Implicitly he was responding to attacks such as in *Punch* on June 26, where he was "The Political Cheapjack," the peddler with his wagon, an anti-Semitic caricature on the order of an "old clo's" seller. "Now then my Bucks," Disraeli is quoted as offering constituents, "let me have the pleasure of making you a few Presents—an assortment of valuable Pledges, warranted never to break."

On the morning of August 4, the traditional nomination of candidates was held in Aylesbury at the County Hall, before the High Sheriff, Baron Mayer de Rothschild. Only in the last minutes did Disraeli become assured that no sudden new candidacy would complicate the balloting. On the withdrawal of John Gibbs, who spoke first and offered some humorous remarks about not going forward, Rothschild declared as duly elected Caledon George Du Pre, Charles Compton Cavendish, and Disraeli. What followed was less auspicious. Perceived by some as an interloper, Disraeli was met with hisses and heckling, but he was used to that at elections and talked through the racket. A larger problem was that there were election expenses after all, amounting to £1,345/16s./4d. Even that relatively small amount was beyond Disraeli's capacity to pay: he was struggling, still, to acquire Hughenden. Philip Rose had to arrange a loan on a mortgage upon Disraeli's life insurance policies.

The election results produced 325 Whigs, Liberals (the two designations had not fully meshed), Radicals, and Irish pledged to the Government and 330 Conservatives, about a third of them Peelites likely to vote Russell's way, giving him a thin but secure margin. Looking dignified and earnest in their black suits, Bentinck and Disraeli again took their seats on the front bench, three places from Sir Robert Peel.

One Liberal elected from the City of London would not appear in the House to be sworn in "on the true faith of a Christian"—Lionel de Rothschild. He was awaiting the outcome of Lord John Russell's promised resolution to remove "the civil

and political disabilities affecting Her Majesty's Jewish subjects."
On principle he would stand for election again and again until he
could take an oath that would open Parliament to professing
Jews, and on principle his constituents would reelect him. In the
year that Disraeli had first run for office, a Jew could not vote if
he refused to take a Christian elector's oath, administered at
whim; he could not practice law, or be a magistrate or judge; he
could not be employed at any school but a private Jewish one.
Catholics, however, had been relieved from all civil disabilities,
and the only conspicuous one still a humiliation to Jews denied
them the right to sit in Parliament. To Disraeli this suggested a
way out that might spare the Commons—and himself—a painful
debate, and spare him the need to stand up. To Lord John Manners he proposed that Lionel de Rothschild could ask to take the
Roman Catholic oath, which included no restrictive language.
Manners explained that one had to be a Roman Catholic to be
offered it, which Disraeli hadn't realized. The matter would be
stalled in the Lords anyway, he guessed: "The peril is not so
imminent."

While fighting for party leadership, it was an awkward moment to be counted on a matter that was anathema to most Tories, and he preferred to see it arise, rather, in the other House,
where it was certain to lose, making it moot in the Commons.
After all he had written in *Tancred*, would he have to eat his own
words?

Disraeli as Prime Minister. Painting by J. E. Millais.
National Portrait Gallery.

Bevis Marks Synagogue.

TOP: *Maria D'Israeli, Disraeli's mother. From a picture by J. Downman. Hughenden.* BOTTOM: *Benjamin D'Israeli, Disraeli's grandfather and namesake. Hughenden.*

Disraeli at forty-seven, as flatteringly painted by Sir Francis Grant in 1852. Hughenden.

Mary Anne Disraeli, 1840. From a picture by A.E. Chalon. Hughenden.

TOP: *Count D'Orsay, 1841.* BOTTOM: *Lord George Bentinck.*

TOP: Edward Henry, Lord Stanley, later 15th Earl of Derby, by Sir Francis Grant. Hughenden. BOTTOM: Edward George Geoffrey, 14th Earl of Derby, by Sir Francis Grant. Hughenden.

Hughenden Manor, 1848.

Hughenden Manor, as added to in the 1860s.

ABOVE: The dining room at Hughenden, with the Queen's gift portrait of herself. BELOW: Peace with Honour (1886), by Theodore Blake Wirgman. The Earl of Beaconsfield reporting to Queen Victoria on his return home after concluding the Berlin Treaty in 1878. Reproduced by permission of the Prince of Wales Hotel, Niagara-on-the-Lake, Ontario, Canada.

TOP: Lady Dorothy Walpole [Nevill] at twenty, *painted by Richard* Buckner. BOTTOM: Henrietta, Lady Sykes, *painted by A.E.* Chalon (*from Heath's* Book of Beauty, *1837*)

TOP: *Disraeli, looking youthful at thirty-five in 1840, by A.E. Chalon. Hughenden.* BOTTOM, LEFT: *Kate at about thirty, looking strikingly like Disraeli at that age. Falk Studios, Sydney, Australia.* BOTTOM, RIGHT: *The porcelain figurine given to Kate. It is still in the possession of her family in New Zealand.*

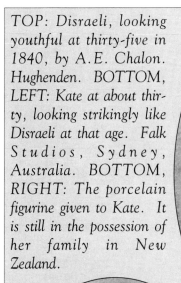

TOP: *Baron Lionel de Rothschild. From a portrait in the offices of his firm.* BOTTOM: *Selina, Countess of Bradford. From a portrait by Edward Clifford.*

TOP: *Sir Philip Rose, Disraeli's confidential agent and attorney, in a painting by Van Havermant. Hughenden.* BOTTOM: *Robert, 3rd Marquis of Salisbury. Hughenden.*

ABOVE, LEFT: *Palmerston Selling Off.* Punch, March 13, 1858, *on Palmerston's relinquishing office to the Conservatives. Disraeli, the Conservative Party's strategist, is seen as the cliché Jewish old clothes peddler.* ABOVE, RIGHT: *The Political Egg-Dance.* Punch, June 29, 1867, *on Disraeli's cautious management of the Reform Bill in committee, enabling him to defeat crippling amendments moved by the Opposition.* BELOW: *The True Specific.* Funny Folks, November 22, 1879, *on Disraeli campaigning: the medicine man offering magical elixirs.*

The Right Hon. Benjamin Disraeli, Earl of Beaconsfield, K.G.
Engraved by W. Roffe, from a photograph by Jabez Hughes, taken by
command of H.M. the Queen.

TOP: Viscountess Beaconsfield, in an idealized portrait by G.F. Middleton, painted when she was eighty. BOTTOM: Disraeli as Prime Minister, 1875. A publicity photograph produced by the Woodbury Process. Collection of B. and H. Henisch.

XIV

"OPPORTUNITY IS MORE POWERFUL EVEN
THAN CONQUERORS OR PROPHETS."

1848–1850

THE DEBATE OVER THE "JEW BILL" WAS DISRAELI'S FIRST TEST AS party leader. In fiction, where his characters could speak for him, he had already made his position clear, and he had been counted in favor of similar resolutions that had failed. But the front bench was different. On the floor, few Tories other than Peelites supported amending the Members' oath, Gladstone rising to ask why Jews were excluded when Unitarians, "who refuse the whole of the most vital doctrines of the Gospel," were admitted.

His colleague holding the other Oxford University seat, Sir Robert Inglis, was quick with an answer: "The Jews are voluntary strangers here, and have no claim to become citizens but by conforming to our moral law, which is the Gospel."

Realizing months before that the matter would come up as soon as the City's ballots were counted, Lord George Bentinck expected to be pressed into opposing it by the Country faction, and Croker had urged him as early as September to be a loyal Tory. He had always voted "in favour of the Jews," he responded.

His family in fact had traditionally been Whig, and he had brought his Whiggish views on civil and religious liberties with him, but as leader of the Tory faction, could he be his own man? It was not "a great national concern" like the Roman Catholic question had been, he explained to Croker. "The Jew Question I look upon as a personal matter, as I would a great private estate or Divorce Bill. . . . Disraeli, of course, will warmly support the Jews, first from hereditary prepossession in their favour, and next because he and the Rothschilds are great allies." Besides, Bentinck suggested, realizing that Croker was a conduit to the most reactionary Tories, "The Rothschilds all stand high in private character," and the City's confidence in the Baron was "such a pronunciation of public opinion" that it was "like [County] Clare electing O'Connell, Yorkshire Wilberforce."

To Lord John Manners, Bentinck called the Jewish question "a terrible annoyance. I never saw anything like the prejudice which exists against them." He planned to vote for the resolution, as he had done before, but also, this time, because "I don't like letting Disraeli vote by himself apart from the party." And to Disraeli he confided, "L[or]d Stanley & all the party are pressing me hard to surrender my opinions about the Jews."

Nominally second in precedence to Bentinck, Disraeli was disconcerted to find, as the debate began, that Lord George was absent, "enfeebled by illness." Taking the floor himself, he encouraged support of the resolution not on grounds of ethics and fairness—religious bigots could not be so persuaded—but on dogma: "The best reason for admitting the Jews is because they can show so near an affinity to you. Where is your Christianity if you do not believe in their Judaism?" It was the discussion between Tancred and Eva rendered pragmatically. Cries of disapproval arose as he went on to accuse his fellow M.P.s of being "influenced by the darkest superstitions of the darkest ages that ever existed in this country." Gladstone recalled, "I remember once sitting next to John Russell when D. was making a speech on Jewish emancipation. 'Look at him,' said J.R., 'how manfully he sticks to it, tho' he knows that every word he is saying is gall and wormwood to every man who sits around and behind him.' "

For his peroration Disraeli turned to reckless sanctimony

rather than the implicit shame and pretense expected from an assimilated Jew:

> I cannot sit in this House with any misconception of my opinion on this subject. Whatever may be the consequences on the seat I hold . . . I cannot, for one, give a vote which is not in deference to what I believe to be the true principles of religion. Yes, it is as a Christian that I will not take upon me the awful responsibility of excluding from the legislature those who are from the religion in the bosom of which my Lord and Saviour was born.

He sat down to stony silence from the Country Tories, and even to some dismay from supporters of the amendment. Yet to Disraeli it was his least precarious strategy.

Bentinck "was entreated not to vote at all; to stay away, which the severe indisposition under which he was then labouring warranted," Disraeli recalled. ". . . After long and deep and painful pondering, when the hour arrived, he rose from his bed of sickness, walked into the House of Commons, and not only voted, but spoke in favour of his convictions." There was "great dissatisfaction" among the squires, an overwhelming majority of whom voted against him; Bentinck, exhausted and exasperated, resigned from the party leadership two days before Christmas, 1847.

A sardonic letter to the editor in the *Morning Post* would suggest that since Jews stank, once a change of House rules admitted them, "old clothesmen, lead-pencil sellers, and all the fragrant tribe of Hebrews from the Stock Exchange will swarm into the Commons . . . so as grievously to deteriorate the atmosphere." Before "the savoury Israelites invade the Christian Senate," it recommended, "some effective plan of ventilation" had to be installed. It was signed *Nāsus*—Latin for "nose."

At Bradenham, Isaac D'Israeli learned how the debates had gone from Sarah, who read to him from the newspaper accounts. "Papa," she wrote, "thinks Dis' speech the most important ever delivered in the House of Commons: stamped with all the characteristic novelty and boldness of the orator." The motion had even been carried—by sixty-seven votes. Offered afterwards in the Lords, dominated by the squirearchy, it was overwhelmingly defeated.

While Isaac, who was without theology, thought that the son of his right hand had made a speech for the ages, he had no idea how poorly it would go down with the people it was intended to support. Observant Jews would scoff at Disraeli's calling them half-Christians (he called himself privately the blank page between the Old Testament and the New) and would deplore his failure to appreciate the religious laws, even dietary ones, that still bound many of them. Isaac had railed at their obsolescence; Ben merely forgot their existence, except when friends like the Rothschilds regretted their inability to dine at Grosvenor Gate. When the Duke of Richmond sent Disraeli a haunch of venison just as he was about to leave London, he sent it on unthinkingly, with the kindest of greetings, to Charlotte de Rothschild, "it never striking me for an instant," he explained to Sarah, "that it was unclean meat, wh[ich]: I fear it is. How[eve]r, as I mentioned the donor, as they love Lords, notwithst[andin]g they throw out their [oaths] Bill, I think they will swallow it." The jocularity, even the concluding pun, may have masked his embarrassment, for he did not parade the militant modernism of his father. It was poor politics.

On January 19, 1848, cradled in the faithful Tita's arms, Isaac died. He was eighty-one. He had never replaced the faith of his fathers with any other, but the churchyard at Bradenham was conveniently down the slope from the house in which he had lived for twenty years, and he was buried there. It was said at the time that at seventy-six, several years earlier, although disabled by blindness and gout, he had made a journey to London to attend the consecration of the first Reform Synagogue. Whether or not it happened, it would have been in character. The Reform movement had its origins in Germany, and D'Israeli had been sympathetic to the views of Moses Mendelssohn, who believed in cultural emancipation from outworn ritual.

Since Ben had written many of his novels at Bradenham,

even the trilogy of Coningsby, Sybil, and Tancred, his dream to his
father, written long before from the Mediterranean, of "fleshing
our quills together," had been fulfilled. To the end, he would
write in a memoir of Isaac he prepared as preface to a posthumous
edition of Curiosities of Literature, "Everything interested him;
and blind, and [nearly] eighty-two, he was still susceptible as a
child. One of his last acts was to compose some verses of gay gratitude to his daughter-in-law, who was his London correspondent,
and to whose lively pen his last years were indebted for constant
amusement." And Disraeli noted his father's contributions to the
knowledge and the literary taste of Englishmen. "It will be conceded," the writer once known as D'Israeli the Younger summed
up, "that in his life and labours, he repaid England for the protection and the hospitality which this country accorded to his father
a century ago."

More literary man than politician, with popular novels and
plays behind him, Edward Bulwer-Lytton—he had added the surname on inheriting Knebworth in 1843—wrote to his old friend
about Isaac, whom he had revered, "I regarded and admired him
much. . . . He had at least the happiness to enjoy the fame of his
son." Another friend, Count D'Orsay, contributed a pen-and-ink
portrait of "Isaack Disraeli," as The Illustrated London News mis-
spelled both his names, to an obituary notice that concluded:
"Many a mind has been excited to literary effort and success by
his graceful and entertaining lucubrations."

Isaac's will left Ben as executor and principal heir, the estate
being valued for probate at £10,803, but that only identified
Isaac's stock in public companies, actually £10,803/16s./1d., of
which Sarah and Ben were each to receive one-third, James and
Ralph sharing equally the final third. Isaac also possessed
£11,666/13s./4d invested in 3 percent Consols (Consolidated
Bank Annuities), which had its origins in Maria's marriage settlement. Having received so much from his father earlier, Ben was
to draw only 5 percent, after which Sarah would retain two-thirds
of the remainder, James and Ralph each a sixth. Ben, as seemed
appropriate, inherited Isaac's books, while his collection of
prints—including some by the then still underrated William
Blake—was left to "my beloved daughter-in-law, Mary Anne

Disraeli." When the furniture, except what she wanted to take with her, was sold, Sarah let a house in Hastings despite her brother's concerns that "watering-places" were "melancholy." Any location was likely to be melancholy for Sarah, who at forty-six was alone. With a clerkship in Chancery at £400 a year, Ralph already lived in London, and "Jem" farmed unsatisfactorily in Buckinghamshire, annoying his successful brother about a sinecure until Benjamin found him a post in the Treasury in 1852, where he was no more unfit than many others in patronage jobs.

Desperate for cash, Benjamin sold most of his father's library of twenty-five thousand volumes at Sotheby's on March 16, 1849. Isaac had explained, "The Octavos are my Infantry, my Cavalry are the Quartos, and the Folios are my Artillery." Some of the volumes, carefully picked over, were transferred to Hughenden. Significantly, many of these were books of Judaica, very likely already utilized more than once by Benjamin in his own writings from *Alroy* to *Tancred*. They included histories of the Jews in Spain, France, Italy, and England; books on the Inquisition; editions of *The Song of Songs* and the *Book of Joel; Transactions of the Parisian Sanhedrin* (1771) and *Apologie de Spinosa et du Spinosisme; Protection of the Jews of Palestine* and the *Travels of Rabbi Benjamin; A Defence of the Old Testament* (1797) and *Bibliotheca Judaica;* Menasseh Ben Israel's *The Term of Life* (1699), in Hebrew, and the *Memoirs of Moses Mendelssohn; The Traditions of the Jews* (1742) and *A Succinct Account of the Rules and Covenants of the Jews.* These, and more like them, Disraeli kept all his life.*

Parliament reassembled on February 3, 1848. When Bentinck entered the House, Disraeli wrote, he "walked up to the head of the second bench below the gangway, on the opposition

---

*Disraeli's knowledge of Jewish ritual has been dismissed by many as niggling to nonexistent, but his library evidences his continuing access to such information, and such examples as the *Sukkot* passage in *Tancred* demonstrated his ability to use what he knew. His claim that Christianity was only "completed Judaism" was more a political than a theological stance. He was, after all, a very visible convert, thanks to his father, and an ambitious politician seeking public acceptance in a churchy age.

side." Moving back a row was Bentinck's announcement that the Protectionist faction had to look for another leader, and having dissuaded Disraeli from resigning with him, he expected to see his friend on the front bench once more, possibly in tandem with another squire. Anticipating the Tory dilemma, Greville wrote on January 7, "Nobody can think of a successor to Bentinck. . . . It seems they detest Disraeli, their only man of talent, and in fact they have nobody [else]."

Few of the future luminaries among the Tories saw Protection as anything more than an anachronism, and like Gladstone had followed Peel. The most competent on the Country side were relatively old men like John Charles Herries, who had served as Chancellor of the Exchequer and President of the Board of Trade, but he had entered Parliament in 1823 and was sixty-seven. There was Thomas Baring, financial expert and a master on his feet of what Disraeli called the "parliamentary point." But he preferred running the family banking firm. Others with experience were elderly, uninterested, or unavailable—but for Disraeli, who seemed to kingmakers among the squirearchy completely wrong for the role yet all they had.

The grating irony to the Tory old guard was that both Baring and Herries, men of acknowledged probity, seemed disqualified by their support of the "Jew Bill." As a debater, Baring was second only to Disraeli, but he had proven insufficiently antediluvian; Herries was similarly suspect. Of his Jewish sympathies Beresford wrote to Stanley, "He says they are better than Roman Catholics! Now bigoted Protestant as I am, I prefer a Christian to a Jew or an infidel." Not yet finished blocking the door, Beresford, in his capacity as Tory Whip, insisted to Stanley that ability was not the only criterion for leadership in the Commons. "I consider . . . that any man is entitled to *bid* for it, in the only mode in which it can be obtained, by the display of superior ability and power in debate; but these will not do alone, and personal influence must be added to them to enable anyone to hold the post; and in this respect Disraeli labours under disadvantages which I do not think he can overcome."

Arguing Disraeli's merits, Bentinck told Lord Stanley frankly that the "reward" Disraeli had so far received from his party

"would leave a blot upon the fair name of the Country Gentlemen of England." And he added, "I tell you none of all this could
have happened, had you played a generous part." His words were
even stronger to Croker, to whom he predicted that "before two
sessions are out," Disraeli would be "the chosen leader of the
party; but I think it will not be under Lord Stanley's banner."

Observing the fractiousness was no better for Bentinck than
being in it, and seeing him looking drawn and careworn at the
first race meeting of the spring where he was suddenly an outsider, Isabella Forester Anson, wife of the Whig M.P. George
Anson, exclaimed, "For Heaven's sake, George, let me persuade
you to cut politics and come back to the turf, or you will be dead
in six months!"

Since the Country faction had to have someone represent its
interests, Lord John Manners's elder brother, his title a household
word because inn signs around England memorialized a soldier
predecessor, was chosen without opposition, but also without his
enthusiasm for the role. A few weeks later, when the Marquis of
Granby resigned the office he hadn't wanted, the Protectionists
remained in confusion. Herries next declined the honor, after
which Bentinck and Disraeli formed a shadow leadership, formally unrecognized. "There was . . . no organised debate and no
party discipline," Disraeli wrote. "No one was requested to take a
part, and no attendance was ever summoned. . . . The situation,
however, it cannot be denied, was a dangerous one for a great
party to persevere in, but no permanent damage accrued, because
almost everyone hoped that . . . the difficulty would find a natural
solution in the virtual chief reassuming his formal and responsible
post."

As most in Parliament agreed on urgent measures to prop up
the faltering economy and to cope with the famine in Ireland,
there were no serious confrontations. For continued hits at Peel,
Macready called Disraeli a "Jack-Pudding," but Peel could yet fill
the continuing vacuum of leadership. From Gladstone's perspective, Disraeli merely "played with the subject" of Protection for
his own ends. Even so, Stanley had no one else to sum up for the
fractured party in the Commons at the end of the session.

Aside from the question of the leadership gap, Disraeli had

his hands full with the settlement of his father's estate and the completion of the Hughenden sale. While his share of Isaac D'Israeli's estate was no fortune, added to the loan of £25,000 from the Bentincks, the Hughenden property was almost within reach. Immensely wealthy, the Duke of Portland could have made up the difference with his own pen, but he was uninterested and let his sons arrange matters. Disraeli was content. The Duke was old; his elder son was sickly and childless; Lord George Bentinck seemed certain to become Duke, and Benjamin Disraeli had no better friend in England.

There had been other great friends, but somehow they had been drawn apart by circumstances. Bulwer-Lytton remained (until 1852) on the opposite political side, had made large sums by his novels and plays, and still lived the raffish life which anyone with ambitions for office had to forgo. D'Orsay had embarrassed Disraeli by gambling debts for which he had stood guarantor, and the Count's liaison with the ageing Lady Blessington persisted as a public scandal. They were running out of resources to continue the social splash they craved—even to keep up a pretense of their style in London. In a note Disraeli made on March 13, as he was hanging on to the informal leadership in the Commons, he confessed to himself, "Agreed to dine at Gore House today, Lady Blessington having asked me every day. But I dislike going there, D'Orsay being in such high spirits, quite unchanged, but Lady Blessington very altered—silent, subdued, and broken. She told me another year would kill her, and complained bitterly that after having fought against so much prejudice, and made a sort of position . . . , and not owing a shilling in the world, she is perhaps to see it all shattered and scattered to the winds. I think it is horrid." Disraeli was embarrassed for them.

There was some awkwardness, too, in his post–"Jew Bill" relationship with the Rothschilds, as his argument for altering the oath, while politically cautious for him, had rested on religious grounds which they found spurious. At a dinner party just before the debate in December 1847, at the town house of Louise and Anthony de Rothschild, "Disi," Louise—a Montefiore—noted in her diary, "spoke of the Jews' life in his strange Tancredian strain, saying we must ask for our rights and privileges, not for concessions and liberty of conscience. I wonder whether he will have the courage to speak to the House in the same manner."

What he had argued was a special relationship with Christianity that evaded the uncompromising ethics of both Lord John Russell and Lord George Bentinck about freedom of conscience. Contesting for leadership in a party committed to the idea of a Christian society was awkward for an M.P. perceived of as a Jew, and the Rothschilds were undeceived by his sophisms. And there was another cause for discomfort, especially with Lionel de Rothschild. Disraeli was desperate for funds to bridge the gap in resources that prevented him from assuming the Hughenden property, a sum hardly noticeable to a Rothschild, but the most he could do in talking over money matters with Baron Lionel had been to discuss small railway investments. He could not admit his plight, however much the Rothschilds were aware of it, and they could not be seen as buying him off in any way. As a result he dealt primarily with Drummond's, a rival banking and brokerage house, and some delicacies that were neither political nor social existed between Disraeli and the Baron. How did someone who had to borrow money to support his debts talk finance with a Rothschild?

The Parliamentary session dragged on to no Disraelian advantage. At Lady Palmerston's late in July he confessed to Sir John Hobhouse that the Liberal ministry "might last as long as it liked. It was a weak Government, and therefore durable. Strong Governments always fell to pieces." In August, Disraeli attacked Palmerston's foreign policy in what Hobhouse called "an amusing and striking speech," answered cogently by the Foreign Minister; and on August 30, in his summing-up, Disraeli, accepted by but without portfolio as spokesman for the Tories, entertained the Commons with clever comparisons between Don Quixote's illusions and Russell's ministry, and again argued, "I say you can have no Parliamentary government if you have no party government."

A week later, on September 6, 1848, Disraeli finally became a country gentleman, writing to Mary Anne, "It is all done, and you are the Lady of Hughenden." Although the Marquis of Titchfield had become squeamish about lending some of the money, a third brother, Lord Henry Bentinck, had joined in, and

the sale had gone through. For Lord George Bentinck it had been
a frustrating session and an exasperating season, as while he labored in the House library gathering agricultural statistics for a
speech, a former horse of his, *Surplice*, had won the Derby. The
next day, May 25, when Disraeli encountered him over his led-
gers, Bentinck groaned, "All my life I have been trying for this,
and for what have I sacrificed it?"

Disraeli attempted some solace, and Bentinck said, "You do
not know what the Derby is!"

"Yes, I do; it is the Blue Riband of the Turf."

"It is the Blue Riband of the Turf," he agreed, and sat down
again to a folio of statistics.

As soon as the session ended, Bentinck returned to his country home, Welbeck Abbey, hoping not to have to return in any
leadership role. After breakfast on September 21, he went to his
study to write letters, completing one of seven sheets to Disraeli.
At four in the afternoon he took his walking stick and started
down a footpath to Thoresby, the seat of Lord Manvers, where he
planned an overnight visit, his valet going separately by carriage
with Bentinck's belongings. When it grew dark and his master
had not yet arrived, he returned to Welbeck and with the groom
began a lantern-lit search. About a mile from the Abbey they
found Bentinck lying face down, dead of a heart attack. He was
forty-six.

In a letter to Lord Henry Bentinck, Disraeli called Lord
George's death "the greatest sorrow I have ever experienced." In
the next session he rose to mourn: "In the midst of the Parliamentary strife his plume can soar no more for us to rally round."
And in his memory Disraeli began preparing *Lord George Bentinck, a Political Biography*.

"No one but Disraeli can fill his place," Malmesbury wrote
in his diary. Disraeli was beyond comparison and without a rival
in the party, he thought. Few denied it, but powers like Stanley
wanted someone else—anyone else. Meanwhile, with Bentinck's
death raising new complications about Hughenden, Disraeli had
other distractions. On October 18 he spent four hours with Lord
Henry at the request of the Duke of Portland, who claimed that
his deceased son's estate could only be settled if Disraeli repaid

what he had just borrowed. He could only do that, Disraeli said, by selling the property and resigning his seat. Lord Henry, M.P. for Nottinghamshire, responded that neither he nor his father wanted that.

"It would be no object to them & no pleasure to me," Disraeli told Mary Anne he had said, "unless I played the high game in public life, & I c[oul]d not do that with[ou]t being on a rock." (He meant being solidly settled.) He explained to Lord Henry that Mary Anne's assets from the Wyndham Lewis estate were only for her lifetime use, but that she had become, through deaths, the sole executor of that will. Somehow that was accepted as a guarantee. Lord Henry, Disraeli reported with relief, "was resolved I sh[oul]d play the great game; & I sh[oul]d trust to him."

While the Tory leadership remained unsettled, the Disraelis visited the Hobhouse estate, Erle Stoke, meeting for the first time the novelist of *Crotchet Castle* and *Headlong Hall*, Thomas Love Peacock, whose satiric conversation novels were more praised than read. Disraeli lamented that he had so little time for reading classical literature, adding (Hobhouse noted on December 22), "that the summit of human bliss was to be possessed of £300 a year & live a retired life amongst books." He confessed delight in reading Peacock and called him his "master," but Peacock confided to Hobhouse, "I did not know he was my pupil!"

A week later Disraeli was possessed of twice the blissful sum he had suggested to Peacock, Edward Moxon having paid £600 for a memoir of Isaac to preface the fourteenth edition of *Curiosities of Literature*, which would lead off a collected edition of his father's works the son thought fit to reprint. Given his debts and his standard of living, the pounds passed quickly through Disraeli's hands.

While he was still at Erle Stoke he learned that Louis Napoleon, who earlier in the year had been living in London on small sums borrowed from his friends, no longer had to worry about his next meal. Back in France since February as beneficiary of the coup that had ousted Louis-Philippe, the adventurer had been elected President of the new republic.

As 1848 waned, with Parliament about to sit, Edward Stanley offered Disraeli the effective leadership in the Commons as long as someone else—he proposed Herries—bore the title. "I am doing you bare justice," he appealed, "when I say that as a debater there is no one of our party who can pretend to compete with you; and the powers of your mind, your large [fund of] general information, and the ability you possess to make yourself both heard and felt, must at all times give you a commanding position in the House of Commons, and a preponderating influence." But he felt that formalizing that role would not meet with "cheerful approval" from the party faithful.

Refusing the duties without the office, Disraeli announced his willingness to act "alone and unshackled." A Disraeli independent of the Tories could be a catastrophe for them, Stanley understood. Retreating, he wrote again on January 6, urging a triumvirate with Granby and Herries, who were intended as facades to make Disraeli's leadership palatable to the party. Henry Bentinck added his own perverse plea. Tories would accept Disraeli if he did not use his position to push the "Jew Question, . . . a measure obnoxious to them," although Disraeli could "claim for yourself the right of individually following the same course you had followed before, . . . to take the line that you would deem fair to your own Church." Lord Henry assumed that Disraeli was still a practicing Jew, whatever oath he had taken as an M.P.

Disraeli was then in Brighton, having taken the train south for political instruction from Prince Metternich, in exile at seventy-five, after the uprisings of 1848 had reached Austria. They had first met on May 17, 1848, introduced by Lord Londonderry, whose conservatism was sufficiently profound to earn Metternich's trust. The old fox had been at the center of European affairs since the Congress of Vienna in 1815 and confidently expected the revolutions to subside. Progress, he explained, is discredited "by the misery which spreads about it."

Consulting "Professor Metternich," Disraeli wrote to Mary Anne on January 7, "I never heard such divine talk; he gave me the most masterly exposition of European affairs. . . . He was indeed quite brilliant, and his eyes sometimes laughed with sunny sympathy with his shining thoughts." On January 25 Metternich followed up his advice with a long letter in French urging Disraeli to lead not a Protectionist party but a Conservative one—that his faction would inevitably fail if identified with a single divisive issue. For some months while in England, Metternich was a sounding board for Disraeli, not only for ideas but for expedients. To C. Rivers Wilson, who became his assistant at the Treasury, he recalled that he utilized Metternich to assess "how far my speeches in Parliament were effective. . . . He would say, for instance, 'your peroration was too long this time, your tropes and metaphors too redundant that time.' " Since Disraeli spoke from notes, or extemporaneously, he apparently furnished the Prince with texts from *Hansard* and from newspapers. One, he told Wilson, did not excite much attention in the House, but was "decidedly in advance of anything I had done before."

"Well," said Metternich, "your speech reminded me of one of the great orators of former times."

"But which?" Disraeli asked, trying on the Prince such names as Cicero and Demosthenes.

"Not Demosthenes," Metternich objected, before deflating Disraeli altogether. "I am thinking of St Augustine."

"There is a peculiar irony," Monypenny and Buckle observed in their biography, "in contemplating the mind of the most determined enemy of Parliamentary government applying itself to solving a difficulty in the working of Parliamentary institutions." Yet Metternich read the leading London dailies, and when Disraeli condemned the Liberal tendency to treat foreign affairs as a matter of sentiment rather than pragmatic politics, and in another speech criticized Palmerston's obsession with "new-fangled" and divisive doctrines of nationality, the old Viennese was impressed. He wrote to Baron Wessenberg, the Austrian foreign minister, to call his attention to the remarks.

Some influential Tories complained to Stanley as the opening of Parliament approached that intrigues were afoot to force a disreputable character upon them. It is too easy to claim *disreputable* as code for *Jew*. More than that troubled the Tory whips in the Commons, Charles Newdegate, a county member for Warwickshire, and William Beresford, M.P. for Harwich. Newdegate admitted finding nothing in Disraeli's conduct to suggest the "want of confidence so many seem to feel." What left Tories uneasy, he explained to Lord Stanley, was "attributable to some circumstances of his earlier life with which I am not familiar, but have little doubt you are." Gossip about Disraeli's early amours, his debts, his dandyism, and his scandalous novels had never quite dissipated. However statesmanlike his demeanor on the floor of the House, he still trailed, to many, the fumes of brimstone.

To make matters worse, he was not a gentleman. Even as leader of the Country party he seemed an opportunist, having only acquired a country estate by mysterious means. While Henry Bentinck worked on reluctant squires, telling Disraeli that he had given up hunting to help settle the leadership deadlock, Edward Stanley seemed unwilling to compromise. In Parliament since 1820 when he came of age, he was of the political generation of Palmerston and Peel although only five years older than Disraeli. Pushy and poor and a late starter, Disraeli had none of the finer instincts that came with privilege and property. Those had to be represented nominally by Herries and Granby.

Paradoxically, one of the Tory die-hards was the editor of the *Morning Herald*, Samuel Phillips, a converted Jew whom Lord George Bentinck had labeled "that circumcised renegade." Phillips even wrote to Disraeli to urge that he "resist the arrangement," as if he had Disraeli's own interests in mind. Turning his coat later, he described the triumvirate as an attempt "to place the leader of the Conservative party like a sandwich between two pieces of bread (very *stale* bread—Herries and Granby), in order that he might be made fit for squeamish throats to swallow."

"Opportunity is more powerful even than conquerors or prophets," Disraeli had written in *Tancred*. Protectionists could choose a chance at power, or disguise their need for Disraeli with impotent figureheads. Even at that, when the bread fell off the sandwich he would be seen as all the party had. Yet he had branded the Conservative Party earlier as an "Organized Hypocrisy," and its behavior toward him reinforced that definition. Whatever its name, he could write to Sarah by February 22, "After much struggling, I am fairly the leader." But it was a party in need of reconstruction, and on a motion in March to examine the burden of taxation on agricultural land, he mustered, in losing, 189 votes (to 280 against), dozens more than could have been expected in 1848. While recognizing in his message to the

Queen that Disraeli was effectively the leader of the Opposition, and "much abler and less passionate" than the emotional Lord George Bentinck, Lord John Russell felt confident that the Government interest, "though not compact," could command "the friends of Sir Robert Peel and the party of Mr Cobden."

Renewed confidence enlivened Disraeli as authority gravitated to him, and it revealed itself in a newly picturesque wit. Years later, George Meredith wrote, "A man related to me that he was in the House one night when the Parliamentary bore Chisholm Anstey [M.P. 1847–52] had been on his legs half an eternity, and he met Dizzy coming down the gangway, and said: 'You turn your back on your supporter?' Dizzy replied: 'I've had enough of that Saracen's Head creaking in the wind.' Saracen's Heads used to be common as Inn-signs, and many a traveller must have heard them creaking through the long night hours. Could any illustration better describe the Bore?"

As Herries and Granby silently fell away, politicians on all sides in the Commons began referring to Disraeli as "leader" and "chief" of his party. "Thus, without any regular nomination or election," Monypenny and Buckle observed, "but by a natural evolutionary process, the lead of the Opposition passed to the fittest." But it was not without price, as Disraeli discovered from a letter dated April 2, 1849. "*Your* position is materially altered," Robert Messer, to whom Disraeli had owed money since at least 1824, wrote, demanding "my just claims." Both he and Thomas Jones had lent money for the disastrous South American mining speculations, with interest now in the tens of thousands of pounds. "I am anxious . . . to avoid legal expenses," Messer threatened, and while Disraeli might edge out of much of the debt as having been assumed when he was legally underage, he could not afford public embarrassment just as he had realized his ambitions in the House. It was a task to try even the ingenuity of Philip Rose.

The reach of longtime creditors that month cost Disraeli the closest friend of his early Parliamentary days. Overwhelmed by his debts, D'Orsay fled to France, the Countess of Blessington following him. "We returned to town on the 16th," Disraeli wrote to her on April 25, "and a few days after, I called at Gore House,

The State of the Nation. Disraeli Measuring the British Lion. *Punch*, July 7, 1849. Following the repeal of the Corn Laws, Disraeli had moved to establish a Select Committee to consider the state of the nation. The motion was defeated by a large majority.

but you were gone. It was a pang; for though absorbing duties of my life have prevented me of late of passing as much time under that roof as it was once my happiness and good fortune . . . , you are assured that my heart never changed for an instant." In truth, his new position had made him timid about being seen at Gore House. He now had a new reason to visit Paris, but Marguerite had a fatal stroke on June 4, before Disraeli could see her again.

"For many years," D'Orsay would write on April 7, 1852, bedridden and forced to use a pencil, "I said there was no power which could prevent you to arrive . . . at the head of the House of Commons. Therefore I let you judge how pleased I was when I saw you in your right place. My sister was also delighted, as she knows I always liked you as a brother." He died that August. It was his last letter to his "best friend."

Suddenly, as the London season began in the late spring of 1849, Disraeli and Edward Stanley were on wary social terms, the upstart adventurer responding warmly to the patrician lord as if there had never been any differences between them. Inviting him to Grosvenor Gate for dinner that June, Disraeli advised that they supped early, at "¼ past seven, so that we may have the pleasure of the sunset & the park while we eat." The satisfactions of the outdoors had never meant so much to him. Involving himself in Hughenden, his own space with his own woods and streams, was part of the high game. The modest three-story house of whitewashed brick, with a loft library already filled with his and his father's books and a terrace looking out over his own vista, kept Mary Anne more and more out of London as she coped with moving in, remaking, and managing the property.

After Sarah visited, Disraeli wrote to her that he had spent several days rearranging the books, most of them on philosophy and religion. "It has quite lost that circulating-library look which you noticed."

Religion invaded Disraeli's public and private life not only because of his past but because of its pervasiveness as a litmus test of Victorian probity. When he proposed a select committee to examine the state of the nation since repeal of the Corn Laws, *Punch* depicted him as a Jewish tailor with tape in hand, measuring a patched and tatty British lion. Again, before adjournment, a "Jew Bill" came up for a third reading in the Commons, inevitably to die in the Lords. Since it had no chance, he chose prudence and a low profile. At the first reading, on February 20, Louise de Rothschild watched from the Gallery as Russell made an "earnest speech," and Gladstone delivered "a fine, silvery toned one in our favour. . . . Disi was silent. . . . Last year he had been our warmest champion, and now!" The diary of Edward Henry Stanley, eldest son of the leader in the Lords—elected M.P. for Lynn at twenty-two, the year before—noted that the bill passed 272 to 206. "Disraeli voted [for it], but kept out of the House until towards the close of debate."

His caution failed to convince his own vicar. With the Commons in session in the early months of his residence at Hughenden, Disraeli could only visit weekends. His movements quickly caused a run-in with the Rev. John R. Piggott. After the Sunday morning service, Disraeli repaired to London, Piggott observing him from the nearby vicarage and sending an unwise note to Grosvenor Gate about the "breach of that commandment which, though not so rigidly enforced as on that people from whom with a natural pride you record your descent, is still not less binding on a Christian."

Disraeli acidly deplored Piggott's "hasty and precipitate spirit." It was his first rebuke in twenty-six years in holy orders, the Vicar confessed, and he prudently began looking for a new place. Once he left in 1851, Disraeli got on well with the Rev. Charles Whishaw Clubbe, his own appointment.

With Disraeli's home life largely now restricted to Hughenden as politics tied up his hours in London often into the small hours of the morning, Mary Anne spent much of her time in Buckinghamshire. Sometimes, because of her health—she was ageing and often ailing—she did not accompany her husband upon country stays with heavy political agendas. At dinner parties in London, also without her, he was usually paired with an attractive lady, and on country house weekends, there were always women eager for the attentions of a celebrity. Mary Anne knew that—she had snared Disraeli herself that way—and suffered fits of jealousy when she absented herself, opening messages to him and reading malign implications into them. At one point, writing as from the Carlton, Disraeli informed Sarah that he had moved to a hotel to escape the wrath of the mistress of Grosvenor Gate. He had returned home, he wrote on July 18, 1849, and "found all of my private locks forced—but instead of love letters, there were only lawyers bills & pecuniary documents." The documents "may yet produce some mischief—but I hope not." Still, there had been "violent temper & scenes."

Apparently there had been some mischief, for he had been claiming visits to Sarah that had not taken place. Whether they

were cover for trysts or for talks about his desperate finances, the
evidence remained hidden. "I said I was going out of town last
Thursday to the Bucks Assizes—but I did not, & Mayer
Rothschild unintentionally let the cat out of the bag." Now
Disraeli was "rather confused & shaky . . . , having had a bad
night in a strange bed," but he was determined on his course. "I
don't know how it will all end: I shall not give up a jot, whatever
[be]tides."

The refusal to "give up a jot" suggested much more than an
overnight amorous escapade, possibly the only time Disraeli was
confronted by his wife with the apparent evidence of infidelity.
He seems to have strayed again, in later years, but as she took
over as mistress of Hughenden she counted upon her possessive
love, which grew even more proprietary, to keep a husband
twelve years her junior—she was then nearly fifty-seven—from
further adventures. One strategy seems to have been to offer renewed trust. "Your letters, & none of mine now, are ever looked
at," he wrote to Sarah on September 7; but he suggested as before, for "absolute safety," the Carlton Club address. Soon Sarah's
letters to her brother at Hughenden, written with studied harm-
lessness, were again being opened, Mary Anne finding nothing
but the evidences of her sister-in-law's pathetic loneliness and
pride in Ben's successes. The first years at Hughenden were difficult when Mary Anne was left alone and sometimes vexing when
they were together, but when visitors came their mutual affection
appeared overwhelming, and it often was.

Parliament ended before the Season did, and the first two
weeks of August were largely spent at the great town houses of
London, except for a day to say farewell to the Metternichs.
Prince Klemens von Metternich, foreign minister of Austria for
nearly forty years, had dominated European affairs after the first
Napoleon as had no one else. Now that the uprisings that forced
his exile had petered out, he was going home.

Disraeli would tell the Earl of Stanhope that had Metternich
"not been a Prince and a Prime Minister, he would have been a
great Professor," and ever afterward he would describe himself as
Metternich's "faithful scholar." What he learned about foreign
policy reinforced his prejudices. Both preferred an aristocratic sta-

tus quo to the instability of democratic institutions, and like Metternich, who had presided over a conglomerate of nationalities and languages, Disraeli saw only prospects of tension in the spread of nationalism and rivalries among the new states it created. The Sidonia in Disraeli would dominate his foreign policy perspectives to the end.*

As Disraeli talked with Metternich for the last time in England, the groom of the chambers announced Lord and Lady Palmerston. "In the stir," Disraeli told Sarah, "we rose and met the Palmerstons in the ante-chamber, [and] exchanged smiles, 'hunting in the same cover.'"

During the long recess, Disraeli continued learning his role as country squire, visiting the judicial proceedings at Quarter Sessions, talking to farmers and foresters, meeting the large landlords in the county. As party leader in the House, his work followed him. "I find the pressure of public life so great," he wrote to Lady Londonderry in declining a visit to Wynyard, "that I have been forced to give up every country house but my own, and have been too much engrossed to ask anyone there. I am surrounded by piles of blue books, and two posts a day bear me reams of despatches, so that my recess of relaxation has combined the plodding of a notary with the anxiety of a house steward. Pleasant—and that is called gratified ambition."

As the new year of 1850 approached, his disclaimers notwithstanding, Disraeli went off upon country house stays that were in large measure political—Missenden Abbey, to visit Baron Carrington; Burghley House and Lord Exeter; Belvoir Castle and the Duke of Rutland. Mary Anne was ill, and Disraeli again went alone, although she was jealous of his being among grand ladies for whom power, she was sure, emanated a sexual attraction. Disraeli's antidote for suspicion was to return as the most dependent of husbands, gratefully awash in uxoriousness.

He expected, Disraeli wrote to Sarah, "a fierce and eventful

*At home in most foreign languages, and a world traveler, Sidonia runs his international financial empire from London because he finds the climate stimulating and English politics congenial. But everywhere he goes he has lieutenants he has planted who are devoted to his service. The Disraelian concept of British Empire has something of Sidonia in it.

session." His goal was to draw more Peelites into the Conservative camp, yet his pragmatism was at odds with the ideological fervor of the Protectionists, especially in the Lords. John Bright, the vigorous Radical M.P. for Durham, a Quaker, penned Disraeli into his diaries for the first time when they met at Bellamy's, the M.P. dining room famous for its pork pies. The Tory leader was a "strange fellow," Bright wrote on January 4, 1850. "Admits Protection gone. Did all he could to prevent squires and farmers making fools of themselves in the recess." Disraeli had to force them "to *do* something," and he made good on his promise when his resolution on agricultural distress and the management of the Poor Laws in rural areas in mid-February, although divided largely on party lines, reduced the government majority to twenty-one. Even Gladstone voted with him. Yet the session was frustrating, as most would be when leading a minority, for it was nearly impossible to propose and carry through anything constructive. "I always . . . deprecated the practice," he said later, ". . . of starting detailed projects in opposition."

Stanley hoped to bring down the Government on foreign policy matters, then induce the Peelites to join him in a new ministry, but Disraeli was a Palmerstonian in such matters, despite some public rows, and quietly failed to cooperate. He was concerned, he noted in a memorandum later, that if Stanley succeeded as Prime Minister, he would bring into his Cabinet the very Peelites whom Disraeli had displaced. "I not only had no experience of high office, but I had positively never held even the humblest office." Yet Disraeli's silence was more than political strategy. He was troubled by bleeding gums, and found no relief, he confided to Sarah on April 13, 1850, even from the application of leeches.

For Peelites themselves, the catastrophic event of the summer of 1850 was the fatal fall from a horse of Sir Robert Peel. His faction reorganized, with Gladstone gaining new strength, and Disraeli made a courteous speech in the House about his late adversary as a great parliamentarian. Peel's death proved no boon to the Protectionists, who were still technically operating under the Committee of Management that Disraeli studiously ignored, even when Stanley wrote to him, "Consult your friends, *including*

Herries." Gladstone was now so cultivated by the Tory leader in the Lords as to suggest to some in the Government that he would soon become Stanley's representative in the other house. With Peel gone, Gladstone was that faction's natural leader, and a neighboring political power, as a Liverpudlian, to Lord Stanley, the uncrowned king of Lancashire. With the tension between Peel and Disraeli gone, some felt that only Gladstone could achieve a reunion of Conservatives.

Disraeli had been at Rosebank on the Thames, where Lady Londonderry was making tea "from a suite of golden pots and kettles." Her husband, restless about news of Peel—he worried about the possible pall in the social season—pressed Disraeli's hand and disappeared. The fete was not yet over when he returned. Lord Londonderry "had actually galloped up to London, called at Whitehall, and galloped back again, while his band was still playing, and his friends still sipping ices." It was "hopeless," he said. "He had done his work," was Bulwer-Lytton's valedictory of Peel. "No man lives who has done his work. There was nothing left for him to do." At the end, his injuries mishandled by his doctors, he had died, so Gladstone claimed, at peace with Disraeli. "I sat next to him [in the House]." He was Gladstone's political father figure as Lyndhurst had been Disraeli's, and when Gladstone had reached Peel's bedside, the former Prime Minister was already dead.

Edward Henry Stanley visited Disraeli after the funeral, finding him breakfasting at Grosvenor Gate "between one and two." He brought up the prospect of "new combinations," including Gladstone, and suggested abandoning protective duties as a way to reunite the Conservatives. That would "raise a mutiny in the camp," said Stanley. Pacing up and down the room, Disraeli remarked about Peel's passing, "What an event! What an event!" It had opened the door to Disraeli, who was already willing to shed some of the party's cherished convictions: He proved it two days later, on July 5, by voting with the Liberals on repeal of the malt tax, which hit the lower classes hardest and symbolized Government's alienation from them. Then on July 29 and again on July 30 came a new attempt by Lionel de Rothschild to claim the seat to which he had been reelected, this time by offering with quiet dignity to swear an oath on the Old Testament. The Clerk of the House refused him, and a new round of acrimony followed, with Rothschild forced to withdraw. The most important constituency in the country, the City of London would be without one of its representatives for years further, even when he was returned unopposed.

The session was anticlimactic after that drama, and dragged to a close with Disraeli no more certain than before as to his prospects in a post-Peel Parliament. He and Mary Anne visited Bulwer-Lytton at Knebworth, then returned to Hughenden September 11, where "two immense chests of George Bentinck's papers from the Duke of Portland" awaited him, he told Sarah, "materials for a memoir, long contemplated." Whether it was delayed reaction to the eventful year or an emotional response to poring over the papers of his lost friend, as Disraeli sat under the russet beeches he loved or took his only exercise, long walks under them, he fell into depression for the first time in many years. He was suffering, he wrote to Sarah on October 12, "a fit of the old illness—wh[ich] the fall of the leaf brings, I apprehend; a sort of equinoctial attack—a great sluggishness and debility." By the end of the month he was arising at seven to read and write, but found that he could not work after dark, and the hours of day were dwindling.

Returning from a round of country house visits, including Knebworth, The Deepdene, and Baillie Cochrane's Lamington, in Lanarkshire, Peelite Q.C. and litterateur Abraham Hayward wrote to Lady Morgan, the popular novelist, his summary of political gossip, and possibly, hopes. "Protection is dead," he declared, "and Disraeli very nearly, if not quite, forgotten. How soon one of these puffed-up reputations goes down. It is like a bladder after the pricking of a pin."

For Disraeli a cure of the ailment (which a later prime minister, Winston Churchill, called "black dog") emerged from events that drew him out of the Bentinck papers and the concerns about his future. Curiously, what refocused his mind was an issue that Parliament thought had been disposed of with Roman Catholic emancipation. A period of relative good feeling existed, and Anglicans could confess their attractions to Roman ritual and pageantry. Disraeli himself thought that both elements were essential to the psyche, the magnet of religion. Then Pope Pius IX named the first English cardinal in centuries, and established a Romish hierarchy in the country. The news completely eclipsed Protectionism as an issue. Englishmen awakened as if invaded, and Lord John Russell saw the uproar as a means of revivifying his moribund ministry. To the Bishop of Durham he wrote a letter, quickly published as he intended, raising the alarm of "a danger within the gates." Unwilling to let Russell appropriate national indignation for the Liberals, Disraeli rushed off a letter to *The Times*, published November 9, blaming Russell for recognizing a parallel hierarchy in Ireland, which was also British soil. Each charge was followed by a countercharge, complicating the question, and Disraeli wrote confidently to Sarah, anticipating the 1851 session, "I think Johnny is checkmated." But Lord Stanley was ill with gout, barely able to get about, and Christmas would pass without any meetings on strategy.

On good days Disraeli walked in his woods in a Tyrolean hat under which he experimented with what William Beresford described in a letter to John Manners as a fierce pair of mustaches. "Now this is very sad," he explained as a party whip, "for he is not the person who ought to attract attention by *outré* dress and appearance, but by his talents. I do trust that this style is only assumed while he is rusticating." Indoors, before a glowing fireplace at Hughenden, Disraeli returned to his memories of Bentinck.

XV

"... WE CANNOT COMPLAIN OF FORTUNE."

1851–1853

IN DISRAELI'S LATE NOVEL *ENDYMION* HE DESCRIBED WHAT NEWSPApers had begun calling, toward the close of 1850, the "Papal Aggression":

The country at first was more stupefied than alarmed. It was conscious that something extraordinary had happened, and some great action taken by an ecclesiastical power, which from tradition it was ever inclined to view with suspicion and some fear. But it held its breath for a while. It so happened that the Prime Minister was a member of a great house which had become illustrious by its profession of Protestant principles. . . . The Ministry was weak and nearly worn out, and its chief, influenced partly by noble and historical sentiment, partly by a conviction that he had a fine occasion to rally the confidence of the country round himself and his friends, and to restore the repute of his political connection,

thought fit, without consulting his colleagues, to publish a manifesto, denouncing the aggression of the Pope
upon our Protestantism as insolent and insidious. . . .
Before the first of January there had been held nearly
seven thousand public meetings, asserting the supremacy of the Queen, and calling on Her Majesty's Government to vindicate it by stringent measures.

Describing his son as "very discreet," Lord Stanley used
Edward Henry Stanley more and more as emissary, to spare his
own gouty legs, and to evade the politicking he found more and
more sordid as the pinnacle of power once predicted for him by
Melbourne seemed to come within his grasp. In mid-January, before Disraeli returned to London on the 20th to prepare for the
opening of a Parliament hot after the Pope, young Stanley visited
Hughenden, taking long walks through the rolling hills about
Wycombe with his host and talking about politics, literature, philosophy, and religion. Although Disraeli knew that whatever he
said would get back to Lord Stanley, all conversation after hours
of intimacy becomes unguarded, and through his son Lord
Stanley discovered much of the real Disraeli.

For what are called rural pursuits ("Shooting, farming, gar-
dening, laying out plantations or roads"), Edward Stanley observed, Disraeli had no taste, preferring his library, but in good
weather he enjoyed walking, talking politics all the while—"his
chief, almost his sole, pleasure." His other favorite topic, indoors
or out, was religion—"I mean by this the origin of the various beliefs which have governed mankind, their changes at different ep-
ochs, and those still to come." On the historical aspects he had
no disagreement, but Disraeli "seemed to think that the sentiment, or instinct, of religion, would, by degrees, . . . vanish as
knowledge becomes more widely spread." Stanley hoped that the
anticipation was "unfounded."

While walking on a cold day through woods belonging to
Lord Carrington, Stanley recalled, Disraeli spoke "with great apparent earnestness," about "restoring the Jews to their own land."
Ignoring the weather, he even paused at the edge of the estate to
outline "the details of his plan." The Holy Land, he explained,

had ample natural resources; all that was needed was "labour, and protection for the labourer." He had it thought out further. The very land

> might be bought from Turkey: money would be forth-
> coming: the Rothschilds and leading Hebrew capitalists
> would all help: the Turkish empire was falling into ruin:
> the Turkish Govt would do anything for money: all that
> was necessary was to establish colonies, with rights over
> the soil, and security from ill treatment. The question of
> nationality might wait until these had taken hold. He
> added that these ideas were extensively entertained
> among the [Jewish] nation. A man who should carry
> them out would be the next Messiah, the true Saviour
> of his people. He saw only a single obstacle: arising from
> the existence of two races among the Hebrews, of
> whom one, those who settled along the shores of the
> Mediterranean, look down on the other, refusing even
> to associate with them. "Sephardim" I think he called
> the superior race.

Disraeli continued in his Tancredian mood, about Judaic achievement and influence, and young Stanley recalled later that he seldom afterward saw Disraeli so excited about anything. "There is no doubt that D's mind is frequently occupied with sub-jects relative to the Hebrews; he said to me once, incidentally, but with earnestness," Stanley added in 1855, "that if he retired from politics in time enough, he should resume literature, and write the *Life of Christ*, . . . intending it for a posthumous work."

From Grosvenor Gate on January 23 Disraeli wrote to Sarah, "I never knew a session about to commence with better pros-pects." Several issues promised to bring down Lord John Russell's ministry. On February 11 Disraeli spoke for three hours on agri-cultural distress, a performance Stanley described as "by the con-fession of all parties" admirable "in point of ingenuity and tact." Next came the debate on Russell's "No Popery" bill, and the first reading of the unenforceable measure on ecclesiastical titles car-ried, 438 to 95. In the lobby Disraeli observed frankly to Spencer

Walpole, M.P. for a Cambridge University seat, "It is curious, Walpole, that you and I have just been voting for a defunct mythology."

On a bill to equalize the borough and the country franchise, Russell lost, largely because of abstentions, and resigned, forcing the Queen to send for Lord Stanley, who was unwilling to form a minority government certain to have a short and difficult life. He preferred to see the Peelites join Russell and would put the other Tories together in a ministry if it seemed to the Queen the only possible solution. Eager to prove that his faction was capable of governing, Disraeli felt thwarted, and in debate in the Commons referred to the Queen's negotiations with Stanley as leaving the door to power still open, which Stanley's son observed in his diary was "contrary to etiquette." According to custom, "Royal conversations are never repeated to third parties without express permission . . . for the Queen especially dislikes having her words quoted or repeated in public."

"D'Israeli," Greville complained in his diary on February 25, "disgusted everybody" and was "without tact or decency," and Lord John Russell [also] "was not very discreet in what he said." To Victoria the episode only validated her dislike of Disraeli. She understood that if a Protectionist ministry came in, he would come with it as leader in the House and a member of the Cabinet, but she told Stanley, "I do not approve of Mr Disraeli. I do not approve of his conduct to Sir Robert Peel." Stanley explained, "Madam, Mr Disraeli has had to make his position, and men who make their positions will say and do things which are not necessary to be said or done by those for whom positions are provided."

"That is true," conceded Victoria. "And all I can now hope is that having attained this great position, he will be temperate. Remember that you make yourself responsible for him!"

Approaching Gladstone, Stanley offered him any appointment but the Foreign Office, even the Exchequer, assuming that leadership of the House could be combined, for Disraeli, with some other Ministry, possibly the Home Office. An avowed Free-Trader like Gladstone could not be offered foreign affairs to administer, and for that post Stanley was prepared to send for Sir

Stratford Canning, the ambassador at Constantinople. Eliminat-
ing any chance of reunion with the Peelites, Stanley made it easy
for Gladstone to refuse any portfolio. Accepting office meant
agreeing to a continued duty on grain imports—an offer he heard
"with an intense sense of relief. . . . Now I had no question at
all." Malmesbury reported to Disraeli that evening—Stanley had
scheduled a meeting at his residence the next day—that they expected to be "confessing ourselves intellectually incapable of
forming a government."

At his cavernous St. James's Place residence, Stanley desperately turned for a cabinet to mediocrities who received what one
called "a very unexpected offer." Terrified by the prospect of responsibility, most declined. "No doubt," young Stanley wrote re-
signedly in his diary on the evening of the 27th, when his father
had given up, "this administration would have been one of the
weakest ever formed." Prince Albert was relieved. "The material,"
he scoffed, "was certainly sad." Only Disraeli was despondent.
The next day Edward Stanley found him "in very low spirits. He
had counted on success, and felt the disappointment keenly." It
was the party's confession of incompetence. Humiliated, he might
retire from politics and return to literature, "leaving those who
had brought him and themselves into this trouble to find their
own way out." To Sarah, he confided, "We cannot complain of
fortune: only of our inveterate imbecility which could not avail
itself of her abundant favours."

Frustrated at having his political fortunes tied to a peer who
feared office, and to a party so packed with second-rate
seatholders that it could not govern, Disraeli seriously contemplated making his living by writing. Could he reproduce the successes of the Young England trilogy if freed from the frustrations
of electioneering? While he understood that giving up the dream
of Downing Street was an act of despair, he also realized that relinquishing an M.P.'s immunity from arrest as a debtor would be
an act of folly. To head that off he wrote to the lawyer representing two of his largest creditors (possibly other creditors
received similar announcements) that he proposed to do something "wh[ich] will surprise the world, but wh[ich] I have long
contemplated"—presumably a departure from politics. Ruefully

referring to his debts, mounting with horrendous interest since his "first, and boyish, embar[r]assment" with borrowed money, Disraeli observed wryly, "Perhaps the most remarkable circumstance of my career, is that it has been so long prolonged." Yet it was debt as much as ambition that had kept him in the Commons, and he warned that any public embarrassment might cost him his parliamentary immunity and his creditors any prospect of repayment. "Blood cannot be got out of a wall—& you may kill the layer of golden eggs."

Negotiations with presumably sympathetic Tory bankers like Thomas Baring went nowhere. Disraeli remained a poor risk, and it was more the possibility of prison than the chances of political success that kept him from the promised "surprise." His career becalmed, he grimly held on to his seat and to the safety it conferred, and the caretaker government of Lord John Russell, the second ministry that Disraeli had brought down, continued in office. There was a fatality about his own career, Disraeli mused. But Lord Stanley reassured him that the Russell regime could not last, and when next the Tories had their opportunity, Disraeli would be at No. 11 Downing Street, adjacent to the Prime Minister, as Chancellor of the Exchequer. In that post he would then have little to do with the hostile Court. And to Disraeli, a chronic debtor who did not even cope with his own household budget, Stanley explained lightly, "They give you the figures."

The Ecclesiastical Titles Bill came up for further amendments, arguments, and divisions through March, Henry Drummond provoking the Irish members when he characterized convents as prisons and brothels. On third reading, the bill threatened no more than a penalty of £100 on the assumption in England of a Vatican title. The vote on March 25 was 414 to 95. After that, the Commons seemed more interested in the distraction taking shape to the west of Park Lane: On May 1, 1851, the Queen opened the Great Exhibition.

Despite the instability of the Ministry, popular talk had turned more to the possible instability of the awesome glasshouse on the edge of Hyde Park—the Crystal Palace. It was widely believed that the Great Exhibition building, designed by a former greenhouse architect, Joseph Paxton, with 293,655 panes of glass, would collapse in the first windstorm, and die-hard Protectionists saw that as a blessing. The World's Fair of technology and manufactures, a dream come true for Prince Albert, was perceived as an advertisement for Free Trade. Disraeli knew what to say about it, as he had to overcome the enmity of Victoria and Albert if he were to get anywhere. He found Protection in any case a losing issue except among ultra-Tories. Hoping that the royal couple would hear of his remarks, he declared the Crystal Palace "an enchanted pile, which the sagacious taste and prescient philanthropy of an accomplished and enlightened Prince have raised for the glory and the instruction of two hemispheres."

The Disraelis went to the Exhibition on Wednesday, May 21, and Ben was so impressed by the spectacle and the exhibits that he urged Sarah, "You must contrive to go, if only for once. . . . Any day you like to come up, Mary Anne will go with you." The Sunday before, the Disraelis were guests at the home of Benjamin Lumley, proprietor of Her Majesty's Theatre in the Haymarket, to meet Jules Janin, French journalist and novelist, and other foreign visitors to the Exhibition. There were many toasts in French, Benjamin wrote to Sarah. "I gave 'Her Majesty's Minister,' at which the foreigners raised their eyes and cried 'Noble! Ah! c'est grand,' &c." Nearby at Gore House and its gardens, where Lady Blessington had so recently entertained, chef and entrepreneur Alexis Soyer, anticipating Great Exhibition crowds, had created, Disraeli had told Sarah earlier on April 16, "a most fantastic paradise of *guinguettes* [outdoor cafés] which I think will astonish and delight the world. Never was [there] such an assemblage of saloons, pavilions, statues, fountains, and all sorts of fanciful creations. Some of the walls are covered with grotesques, in which, among others, your humble servant figures."*

Disraeli would go back for "the last shilling day," on October 3, when some of the exhibitions had already been dismantled. Until then, on cheap days the great, pulsating brass organ labeled a Sommerophone was silent, which he deplored. Music, he suggested to Sarah, "might have a humanising effect on the dog-

---

*Soyer's extravagance would plunge him £7,000 into debt, and the restaurant closed before the Exhibition did.

stealers, cabmen, and coalheavers." That he went on a "Shilling Day" was in part to be among ordinary people—"the millions." It also reflected some rare frugality. Although he had only recently discovered that he might inherit a considerable fortune, he had no idea how much, or when, as the prospective testator, although elderly, was very much alive.

Her name was Sarah Brydges Willyams, and she wanted to meet him at the Crystal Palace, at the fountain. She had written to him from Torquay, and he enclosed her letter with one of his own that August to Philip Rose, asking him "as my best friend" for advice on how to respond. She had written to Disraeli before—without response, she noted—merely as another subject of the Queen commenting upon "your political speeches and your published works." Now she wanted to propose a "private subject," and asked a "personal favour"—that he would be one of the ex- ecutors of the will she was about to make. "I think it right to add that whoever are my executors will also be my residuary legatees, and that the interest they will take under my Will, although not a considerable one, will, at all events, be substantial."

Rose advised caution, but Disraeli was intrigued by more than her unverifiable money. Her Sephardic maiden name had been Sarah Mendez da Costa, and her family had originally come from Spain. "The female Croesus," Charlotte de Rothschild would write some years later to her son Leopold, ". . . has piercing black eyes, wears a jet black wig, with an enormous top knot, no crino- line, is quite a miser, starves herself into a skeleton, . . . keeps nei- ther horses nor carriages, nor men servants—only an enormous watch-dog to protect her and her gold." Her only exercise, accord- ing to neighbors, was to walk, on sturdy leashes, two large and very ugly bulldogs, possibly the origin of the Cerberean legend. A child- less widow, she was in 1851 already past eighty.

On August 2 Disraeli sent his mysterious admirer in Torquay a copy of *Tancred*, which he described as "a vindication, and I hope, a complete one, of the race from wh[ich] we alike spring." Although Mrs. Brydges Willyams never came to London, they would meet on his annual pilgrimages to her estate, Mount Braddon, near Torquay, and Disraeli would be written into her will by a local solicitor rather than by Rose, who prudently declined to represent both parties. Some 250 letters (from Disraeli) later, he came into her inheritance.

In his memoir of his father, he told her, "you will find the name of your family incidentally mentioned." And indeed, on the fourth page of his biographical introduction to *Curiosities of Literature*, writing of the aristocratic Sephardic families which had emigrated to England, he had closed a paragraph with "and the Mendez da Costas, who, I believe, still exist." Now he knew with certainty. He had encountered the very last of the da Costas.

Possibly because of his burgeoning new correspondence with Sarah Brydges Willyams, to whom he was now sending his books, he wrote to Benjamin Lumley—who had been a Levy—on November 10, apropos of Sidonia's fanciful claim, speculating as to whether Mozart, Haydn, or Beethoven could have been Jewish. Reflecting upon what he might do with her money, as he could not confess his enormous burden of debt, he suggested extravagantly in a letter to Torquay that he might endow a scientific college, complete to astronomical observatory.

With the Parliamentary recess, Disraeli returned to the Bentinck memoir, which took a curious turn as he pressed to finish it by year's end. Although he had purchased Bentinck's letters to his political agent in Manchester and had borrowed letters and papers from Bentinck's relatives and colleagues, in earlier chapters he quoted almost nothing from them and used little of the factual minutiae which help to evoke the essence of a life. To Manners in October he described his manuscript, which relied heavily on *Hansard* and Blue Books, as a work which "expands under my pen, since it includes, in truth, every topic of present interest in the political world." Early in December he added a progress report: "G.B.'s life expands into a rather great work. It . . . touches on such vast themes that the pen often pauses to think."

For a work not even as long as most of his novels, Disraeli was finding the task he had given himself more difficult than writing fiction. Calling the work "a political biography" spared him much of the personal detail he preferred not to know, let alone use, yet he was compelled to describe active, living political figures with whom he would be dealing, in real life, for many years more. It was not merely a case of "How was Sir Robert Peel to be turned out?"—the question which got him halfway through the book and would keep readers turning pages afterward to see how it was done. No one in his day, and for decades after, would use the rhetorical question so deftly and so often as a narrative device. (Lytton Strachey would adopt it in 1918 for *Eminent Victorians*, though there it is used more sardonically than dramatically.) But Disraeli was turning more to extracts from letters to fill out the last phase of Bentinck's life, an indirect confession of authorial fatigue.

Twenty-three chapters, which would fill 481 printed pages, brought him to the crucial episode for Bentinck's life and career of the oaths debate on the seating of Lionel de Rothschild. How does one handle a subject so sensitive to the biographer's own life and career? Disraeli began by closing chapter XXIII with the election to the House of "a member who found a difficulty in taking one of the oaths . . . to be sworn preliminarily to any member exercising his right of voting. The difficulty arose from this member being not only of the Jewish race, but unfortunately believing only in the first part of the Jewish religion."

That Tancredian extremity was a position which Disraeli had devised for political reasons of his own and which the Rothschilds accepted with varying degrees of exasperation. He had put it into his novel and again into his speech in the oaths debates of 1848. But what followed as chapter XXIV reads as a completely independent essay possibly drafted earlier as a preface to a reprint of *The Genius of Judaism*, for the posthumous edition of Isaac's works led off by *Curiosities of Literature*. While none of the other books needed such a gloss, *Genius* was a cranky, crotchety polemic. The manuscript sheets of the Bentinck memoir are continuous, including the irrelevant chapter, which is heavily corrected. If its origin were independent of the book, Disraeli rewrote it as he went, to incorporate it into the new work. Yet its linkage to the chapter that follows—a return to Bentinck's political career—is forced. It was an argument that Disraeli wanted to use somewhere, somehow. Whatever the reason for its appearance in a life of Bentinck, there would be no reprinting of *The Genius of Judaism*.

The six thousand words of special pleading in which Bentinck's name does not appear once, remains one of the most peculiar examples of narrative discontinuity in the literature of biography. Instead, readers in 1852 encountered the questions of the divinity of Jesus, the responsibility for the Crucifixion, the post-exile achievements of Jews, the allegedly "inexorable law of nature . . . that a superior race shall never be destroyed or absorbed by an inferior," and the illogic of religious bias. Their irrelevance to the biography was even conceded by Disraeli in the opening sentence of chapter XXV: "The views expressed in the preceding chapter were not those which influenced Lord George Bentinck in forming his opinion that the civil disabilities of those subjects of her Majesty who profess that limited belief in divine revelation which is commonly called the Jewish religion, should be removed."*

Announcing the book's imminent appearance, Disraeli wrote to John Delane at *The Times* asking to nominate his own reviewer, an impertinence which the editor rejected so sharply that Disraeli promptly apologized for the "stupid suggestion." Delane had turned "The Thunderer" into the national newspaper and was a presence increasingly visible at the country seats of the eminent. W. H. Russell, soon to be the paper's famous war correspondent, told the story of Delane's leaving dinner at Stafford House early to return to his office, whereupon Lord Granville asked Disraeli what he thought of the departed guest. After looking around carefully, Disraeli joked, half in earnest, "I observe that Mr Delane has left the room, but I am under the impression that he is still alive and still editor of *The Times*, and so I would rather not answer."

Aside from Delane, there were other early signs of trouble. When the biography appeared, supporters of Lord Stanley, as he was in the book—he had become the 14th Earl of Derby on June 30, 1851, on the death of his father—were indignant because his

---

*In later editions, Disraeli attempted to make the linkage slightly less abrupt. He added softer language prefacing the original opening of chapter XXV, beginning, "It would seem to follow from the views expressed in the preceding chapter, that in communities professing a belief in our Lord, the Jewish race ought not to be subject to any legislative dishonour or disqualification. These views, however, were not those which . . ."

Parliamentary role appeared understated. But to Disraeli, Derby represented the increasingly political liability of both extreme Protectionism and extreme Protestantism. He had been so intran-sigent about the "Jew Bill"—the significance of which to Ben-tinck the biography had dramatized—as to pressure Bentinck to absent himself at the division. The incident was handled in the biography without identifying Derby.

Also, the impassive Tory leader of the Lords had never warmed to the excitable Bentinck, and in 1847 they had split over Stanley's alleged dictatorial tendencies and his attempts to woo Peelites whom Bentinck scorned as disloyal back into the party. "*Nine Peelites,*" Bentinck had written to Disraeli on April 24, 1847, after one such episode, "[and] every man voted dead against Stanley in the H. of Lds. yesterday: *not one with him.*"

To focus upon Bentinck while being Bentinck's successor without adversely affecting his own relationship with the leader of his party was a problem which Disraeli coped with by ignoring Derby as much as possible. Blind to what the author of *Lord George Bentinck* could not publish, William Beresford complained to Derby that the book was "untrue and unjust" in its treatment of him and ultimately "disappointing as biography." As Beresford saw it, "The great hero of the book either openly or by insinua-tion, is the author. In future times, a reader taking it up would consider that Lord Stanley was a secondary personage in the party and the legislature." Gladstone, who hardly came to the book pre-pared to admire it, read it carefully and noted in his diary that *Bentinck* was "a remarkable & interesting work." Few works of nonfiction in its century communicate, despite Disraeli's neces-sary reticences, the flavor of nineteenth-century political life, its complex basis in constituent society, its give-and-take of political bargaining, and its dramas in what have since been called the cor-ridors of power. While Derby—as Stanley—remains shadowy, Peel does not. Other than Bentinck, he is the largest figure in the book and treated with more sympathy than Disraeli ever did from the benches of the House. In life, Peel was in the way of Disraeli's ambition but not in art.

The Times's review was lengthy but unflattering. Disraeli con-soled himself that it was "at least a great advertisement," and

2,750 copies were sold in the first six months. Most of the press was Free Trade in sentiment, which adversely affected other notices, but friends were complimentary. Sarah was enthusiastic, calling it an "exalting" memorial, but despite early expressions of gratitude, the book may have been a time bomb among the Bentincks. In 1854, when Lord Titchfield became the Duke of Portland, he called in the money he had advanced for Hughenden. He had become an eccentric recluse, and Lord Henry Bentinck, more interested once again in hunting than politics, apologized for him but offered no help. Disraeli had to borrow elsewhere at usurious interest, but still attempted to retain ties with Lord Henry. That the effort failed is evident from a note of June 6, 1860. "Lord Henry Bentinck hopes," it read, "that Mr Disraeli will not give himself the needless trouble of calling at Claridge's Hotel tomorrow. Lord H. will not be at home and there is no subject whatever that he has the slightest inclination to discuss with Mr Disraeli."

A draft survives among the Hughenden papers which appeals, "Let me at least know on what ground I am deprived of the friendship which was the pride and consolation of my life." Perhaps Disraeli thought the better of such groveling and failed to send it, the epilogue of his association with the Bentincks.

An event across the Channel as Disraeli was finishing the Bentinck memoir had convinced him that people were not ready for reforms further extending the franchise. Most preferred, he thought, being governed by an authoritarian figure they admired—Why else would they acquiesce in the replacement of the young French republic by what was certain to become a monarchy under an adventurer who called himself another Napoleon? The French constitution had forbidden reelection of the President, but in a coup d'état, Louis Napoleon dismissed the elected Assembly and conducted a plebiscite that kept him in office. Emboldened by that success, he would hold another, as was now freely predicted, to confirm him as Emperor. "The fact is," Disraeli wrote to Lady Londonderry from Hughenden on December 28, "the stroke of Napoleon has changed the whole complexion of politics, and for an English Minister"—he meant Lord John

Russell—"to bring in a reform bill . . . at the present moment is preposterous."

Although Russell's administration was weak, surviving only on the sufferance of factions opposed to Protection, the Earl of Derby was interested in office only under that drooping banner. "I am . . . not prepared indefinitely to maintain a hopeless struggle," he claimed irritably to Disraeli on January 18, as both awaited the reopening of Parliament, "but until the country shall have so pronounced its opinion, I shall maintain my opinion . . . on the grounds of finance and national interests [that] a reimposition of duties on imports, including corn, is desirable." Such rigidity was suicidal for Conservatism, Disraeli feared, but he was not dealing with a contemporary. Little older than his colleague in the Commons, and with a first-class mind, Derby was nevertheless the product of his centuries-old background of immense landed wealth, what would later be called "trickle-down economics," and suspicion of change. Requiring nothing, he appeared impervious to ambition. Still, Disraeli wrote hopefully to a friend, "I think Lord Derby will turn out a better general than the world imagined a few months ago."

When Parliament reassembled on February 4, 1852, everyone in politics knew it would take only an excuse of a division to unseat Russell. Disraeli was ready and broke clear of Derby by inviting leading Tories in the Commons to Grosvenor Gate to discuss the text of the Queen's Speech before it was delivered. His significance in the House had been confirmed by delivery of the text to him as sole survivor of the managerial triad that had never worked anyway. (The Earl invited Tory peers to Derby House in St. James's Square to discuss strategy apart from the M.P. session.) Russell had gambled that he could survive without Viscount Palmerston as his Foreign Minister. The most powerful man in the Cabinet, Palmerston had been acting independently for years and had now alienated the Ministry by granting recognition on his own to Louis Napoleon's usurpation of power. With his magnetic Foreign Minister gone, Russell's shaky coalition fell apart, and the Queen sent for Derby.

With Derby away at a shooting party at Badminton, the Duke of Beaufort's estate, Disraeli dispatched Forbes Mackenzie, a

Tory Whip, with an offer to step aside if Palmerston were willing
to be Derby's leader in the Commons. Waiving his own claim, Disraeli explained, "Palmerston would not like to serve under me,
who[m] he looks upon as a whipper-snapper." Derby hurried back
to London, writing to Disraeli that he would "never forget the generous self-sacrifice," but the wily Palmerston was no longer interested in being someone else's lieutenant. For Victoria, the refusal of
the bait was a relief. "If you do it," she had warned Derby, "he will
never rest 'til he is your master." Disraeli remained leader of the
House, a role now ratified, and became Chancellor of the Exchequer, which brought prestige but about which he had misgivings.
For Derby it brought his colleague "under the same official roof" in
Downing Street, which was a convenience. And for Disraeli it
brought the boon of a large official salary, £5,000—approximately
that of President Millard Fillmore in the United States.

"Here, get on your gown," said Baron Alderson, who was to
swear in the new Chancellor. "You'll find it monstrously heavy."
The black silk robe, lavishly embroidered with gold fringe and
lace, and well-worn, was lying across a chair.

"Oh. I find it uncommonly light," Disraeli bantered as he
tugged on the official robes.

"Well, it's heavy with what makes other things light," said
the Lord Chief Baron of the Exchequer, Jonathan Frederick Pollock.

Addressing an envelope proudly to "The Right Honourable
the Chancellor of the Exchequer," Mrs. Disraeli sent a note to 11
Downing Street: "Bless you, my darling, your own devoted wife
wishes you joy. I hope you will make as good a Chancellor of the
Exchequer as you have been a husband to your affectionate
MARY ANNE." But Charles Pelham Villiers, one of the most
outspoken Free-Traders, took the opportunity of Disraeli's appointment to sneer, "The Chancellor of the Exchequer seems to
be entering upon a career of usefulness, and I would entreat him
not to be deterred by *the novelty of the thing* from pursuing it; and
with his talents"—there were jeering "Hear! Hear!" shouts from
the Opposition benches—"which seem to be *available for any purpose*, I should be really sorry to see him removed from office by
my motion." David Coulton, a journalist for the *Quarterly Review*,

The Protection Giant. *Punch*, March 19, 1852, commenting on the ambiguity of the Conservatives, back in office, on Free Trade. Disraeli is part of the two-headed monster wielding the club of Protection.

wrote to John Murray II, "To be sure there is something of harlequinade in the transformation of Ben, but prescriptive usage does odd tricks with the Exchequer. [George] Lyttleton, the first lord, who scarcely knew how many pence there were in a shilling, was at the head of it once."*

Few of Derby's appointees had any experience of previous office. The Queen's new Privy Council was attended by only three

*George Lyttleton, 1st Baron Lyttleton, a writer who gained a place in Dr. Johnson's *Lives of the Poets*, was a Lord of the Treasury under George II and refused the Chancellorship of the Exchequer under George III.

veteran Councillors. At Buckingham Palace on February 27, the other seventeen had to be sworn in, an episode which Disraeli fictionalized nearly thirty years later in *Endymion*. When the old Duke of Wellington, now very deaf, asked Derby their names, and couldn't catch them, he boomed, "Who? Who?"—and the splendidly titled collection, experienced at entertaining but not at governing, went into memory as the "Who? Who? Ministry."

Beginning badly, Derby in a speech on February 27 announced that he was ready to revive Protection, but he had no majority in the House of Commons to bring it about. For a mandate he had to go to the people, and the cautious session was a preparation for new elections. Disraeli wanted a more activist government than one doing little more than banning Roman Catholic processions, but his major successes were at Court—not in entirely allaying suspicion, but in getting to know the Queen and Prince Albert better. The Prince, Disraeli told Lord Stanley—Derby's son had become an Undersecretary in the Foreign Office under Lord Malmesbury—was "one of the best-educated men he knows, indeed over-educated, something of a pedant and theorist, but a man of talent nevertheless."

Curiously, the fact of being Prime Minister left Derby suspicious of Disraeli's aspirations. "My father," Stanley noted in his diary, ". . . admired his temper, tact, and ability, but seemed jealous lest he should aim at the first place, and sneered at his tendency to extremes of alternate excitement and depression." While Derby had no real concern that his deputy was seeking to unseat him, as Disraeli was a loyal Tory in his acceptance of hierarchical structures, he had put his finger on a problem that dogged Disraeli all his life. He fell easily into despondency, and if Derby's phlegmatic Ministry led to nothing else, it caused Disraeli to ride an emotional roller coaster of hope and despair.

New to managing a burdensome bureaucracy, Disraeli found that learning how to handle a staff and how much he should take on himself absorbed more hours than he had in each day. He wrote to a colleague one Saturday night (May 6, 1852) that he scarcely had the opportunity to scrawl a note. "I have not time for sleep or food," he explained, but he hoped that if the Tories won the crucial divisions to come, "we may, & probably shall, be established for years." In June he was still embattled but happy in the challenges of the Exchequer, seldom, until he assumed the office, the strongest Cabinet post after the Prime Minister. Yet in his groping for control of revenues and expenditures, which he had never managed on his own behalf, he hardly fit the racist stereotype of the money-shrewd Jew.

At least half of the new House would go Tory in the elections now imminent, he anticipated, enough to goad Palmerston into joining a government that could then command a continuing majority—for if he came aboard, Gladstone might follow. It was an outlook that suggested something less than insatiable ambition, for both men were aspirants with Disraeli for the highest office. Later in the year, when questioned by Prince Albert about Disraeli's views, Derby made it clear that his second-in-command was more pragmatist than ideologue. "He did not think," Albert noted, "[that] Mr Disraeli had ever had a strong feeling, one way or the other, about Protection or Free Trade, and that he would make a very good Free Trade Minister."

What he did make was an entertaining Parliamentary reporter. While Derby was matter-of-fact in messages to the Queen, she was intrigued by Disraeli's "curious notes" about what went on in the Commons. "They are just like his novels," she wrote. Unlike other Ministers, he used colorful adjectives and adverbs, and sometimes created dramatic vignettes of the House in action, unafraid to compliment the enemy. Sir James Graham's "great speech" in Opposition was "elaborate, malignant, mischievous" in suggestion that taxing foodstuffs would bring on revolution. "Mr Cobden made one of the cleverest speeches of the cosmopolitan school, and was supported with vigour by Mr Bright." Lord John Russell's speech opposing the Militia Bill "was one of his ablest—statesmanlike, argumentative, terse, and playful; and the effect he produced was considerable." On a resolution by Charles Villiers, "the Debate was very animated and amusing, from the rival narratives of the principal projectors of the demonstration, who, having quarrelled among themselves, entered into secret and—in a Party sense—somewhat scandalous revelations, to the diversion and sometimes astonishment of the House."

Possibly the prize vignette came later, in a report from the session of April 13, 1858, written from the front bench that night. Lord Elphinstone had addressed the House on the Straits Settlements of Malaya, a "strange society" where transported convict labor was crucial. "His enquiry of the Governor's Lady, who never hired any servant but a convict, whether she employed, in her nursery, 'Thieves, or Murderers?' and the answer, 'Always Murderers,' was very effective."

Such "bulletins," Disraeli once apologized, "are often written in tumult, and sometimes in perplexity and . . . he is under the impression that your Majesty would prefer a genuine report of the feeling of the moment, however miniature, to a more artificial and prepared statement." No such documents had ever before reached Victoria.

Parliament dissolved on July 1. The campaign was not joined on the issue of protective tariffs, but Derby never disclaimed hopes for their resuscitation, and some places were lost to Peelites. Disraeli's hopes for three hundred seats fell short by about fourteen, and the government hung together precariously during the recess. When sessions resumed, the final weeks of 1852 were a series of embarrassments and potential embarrassments for Disraeli. Emotionally he had lost some of the balance that had sustained him before. There were problems between the lazy Jem, demanding sinecures from his famous brother, and Sarah, who considered Jem worthless and his life "irregular." Earlier in the year Disraeli had suffered from what he described to Sarah as "the horrors of a torpid liver," and his chief, Derby, had been bedded twice with gout, paralyzing a government already sluggish. Disraeli's own workload at the Exchequer, entirely new to him, when combined with his House leadership activity, left him "neither time to feed nor sleep," and caused difficulties with the neglected Mary Anne. And there was a new problem that he did not seem to know was one, a dubious relationship with a young aristocrat, Henry Lennox.

A younger son of the 5th Duke of Richmond, Lord Henry Lennox at thirty-one was M.P. for Chichester. He had charmed Disraeli into thinking that he was less puerile than he was, furnished his leader with social and political intelligence from sources not often open to Disraeli, and had a retentive capacity for scurrilous jokes. Disraeli lobbied Derby, who was a good friend of Richmond, a Protectionist zealot, into making Lord Henry a junior lord of the Treasury, and it was clear that the leader of the House enjoyed his role as patron of a duke's son. Having come to the Commons later than the gilded Tory youths who did not have to fight their way, he had maintained close friendships before with younger men—Smythe, Manners, and others—and effusive language between men was not uncommon in nineteenth-century correspondences. Yet the use of *dearest* and avowals of affection, even love, appear more in the letters between Lennox and his sponsor in 1852 than at any other time in Disraeli's life.

Although he would continue to attract young disciples throughout his career, no other relationship had the flirtatious dimensions of the Henry Lennox affair, nor was conducted with someone so shallow. Lennox, like Smythe, Manners, Bulwer, D'Orsay, Clay, and other young men who passed through Disraeli's life, were active heterosexuals, even rakes, and often matrimonial adventurers. The relationships seem, from the evidence, including that with Lennox, who became a persistent nuisance, entirely unphysical if marginally homoerotic. Suspicious on occasion of Disraeli's relations with women, possibly with good reason, Mary Anne was never concerned about his loyal young men. The very next year, for example, Charlotte de Rothschild believed that the Duchess of Somerset, whom Disraeli had flirted with when she was Georgiana Sheridan, was "desperately in love with him."

Another sign of Disraeli's lack of balance as 1852 was coming to a close, was his eulogy in the Commons, on behalf of the Government, of the Duke of Wellington, who had died in September and was refrigerated for two months while a grandiose state funeral was arranged. Victorian obsequies were often sentimental orgies, but none exceeded that of the Iron Duke, and Disraeli prepared a speech for the ages. Unfortunately, in shuffling through his notes for the address, he had apparently come across lines quoted by George Smythe in the *Morning Chronicle* in July 1848 which happened to be from an address by Louis Adolphe Thiers nineteen years earlier on the death of Marshal Gouvion Saint-Cyr. On November 15 Disraeli used them, and they were recognized. He was vilified in the press as a plagiarist, and Sir Edward Bulwer-Lytton invented a statement for his old friend to use on the floor of the House, claiming that the long paragraph had been recalled from memory after being read in 1829, and that it was, anyway, only a résumé by Thiers "of brilliant sayings by great [classical] authorities."

Disraeli never had to resort to Bulwer-Lytton's ingenuities, but, seeking consolation, he sent for another young protégé, Lord Stanley, explaining, "I can bear a great reverse, but these petty personal vexations throw one off one's balance."

The worst vexation was yet to come. If the Government were to be defeated, it would come on Disraeli's budget, and the Opposition was ready. His timing could not have been worse. His old crony Louis Napoleon had staged the expected plebiscite in November to confirm his self-elevation to the restored throne of France, and there were fears of a Napoleonic invasion of England. Disraeli's budget had to accommodate new defense expenditures. And on December 2 the onetime exile sheltered in England would declare himself Emperor Napoleon III.*

There was only a thin chance that Derby's ministry would survive the budget proposals, as any single item might provoke a defeat. Seeking additional Parliamentary strength, he tried again to win over Palmerston, and in an audience with the Queen and Prince Albert, Derby proposed having Disraeli, who again was willing to step aside, negotiate the arrangement. Albert was opposed, "considering," he said, "the *laxity of the political consciences* which both these gentlemen have hitherto exhibited. Should Mr Disraeli have to relinquish the lead, Mr Gladstone would be a much fitter successor than Lord Palmerston, for whatever his peculiar crotchets may be, he is a man of the strictest feelings of honor and the purest mind."

When Albert asked again the next day, November 25, why Gladstone could not be asked to lead the Commons, Derby said frankly that Gladstone was (according to the Prince's memorandum) "quite unfit for it; he had none of that decision, boldness, readiness, and clearness which was necessary to lead a Party, to inspire it with confidence, and still [more], to take at times a de-

---

*The numeral recognized that the first Napoleon had sired a son who never reigned in France.

cision on the spur of the moment, which a leader had often to do." Besides, "he could not in honour sacrifice Mr Disraeli."

The budget was delivered on December 3, and agitation built up about it out of proportion to its contents, as it demonstrated the Protection party implicitly disavowing Protection and in effect accepting the policies for which it had gibbeted Sir Robert Peel. The Opposition, nevertheless, was set to sacrifice the Chancellor of the Exchequer and his budget on the sainted Sir Robert's altar. The House of Commons overflowed with Members and visitors. According to Lord Stanley's diary, Disraeli arose to defend his budget at 4:35, "evidently ill." He began by appealing to M.P.s "not [to] become the tools and victims of exhausted factions and obsolete politics." Speaking without animation, despite a profusion of epigrams and sarcasms, he offered dozens of details from daily life. In the pale gaslight, Opposition forces eager to counterattack jotted down notes.

With the revival of railway construction, and 200,000 navvies employed on the beds and trackage making as much as fifteen shillings a day, much of which they spent on meat and bread and beer, farmers had little fear of Free Trade, and Disraeli put no Protectionist pills in his prescription for the improving economy. He even proposed halving the malt tax and lowering the tax on tea, gestures to the working-class electorate. But to make up the difference, and to find new funds for defense against the French, he doubled the house tax and lowered the net of the income tax. Under free trade, he pointed out, compensatory direct taxation was unavoidable. (Macaulay would call it "taking money out of the pockets of people in towns and putting it into the pockets of growers of malt.")

Disraeli closed with a goal for government, and for its taxing powers, borrowed from Francis Hutcheson's *Inquiry Concerning Moral Good and Evil* (1720), that has become a part of political language. His budget, he averred, "has been framed with no other object than to govern the country in a manner that shall most conduce to the greatest happiness of the greatest number."

Speaking for five hours, he received what Stanley called a "fair hearing," but Sidney Herbert, long resenting Disraeli's calling him "Peel's valet," predicted that the budget would earn no adherents from the Opposition because "Jews make no converts."

Suffering from the discomforts of influenza, Disraeli had already left the House. Although Sir Charles Trevelyan, Permanent Secretary to the Treasury and a nonpartisan civil servant, felt that as much as could have been done with a system "so enveloped in obsolete forms" had been proposed, the outlook was bleak unless a dozen or more votes could be wooed to the Derbyite side.

As far as the Prime Minister was concerned, however, Disraeli had embraced the Peelites. The next day Derby wrote to Disraeli that from his seat in the Gallery (he had no place on the floor as a member of the Lords) he heard someone call the budget speech "the eulogy of Peel by Disraeli." If he had shut his eyes he could have persuaded himself that he was hearing the other side rather than an exponent of his rigid Protectionism. "I foresee great discontent among our friends," he deplored, "and great embarrassment." But Disraeli was not concerned about embarrassment and discontent: he was seeking accommodation, not a futile espousal of an obsolete ideology.

The full-dress debate on the budget began on December 10, with Disraeli set to wind it up for the Government, which he began to do at ten in the evening on Thursday, December 16. An unusual early winter thunderstorm raged outside, and some of Disraeli's words were lost. Gladstone noted that the speaker's face was flushed, that he looked as if he had imbibed too much; very likely Disraeli was still feverish with influenza. One by one he mocked the M.P.s who had criticized the budget, Gladstone lamenting that the speech was "disgraced by shameless personalities" yet judging the whole as "grand; I think the most powerful I ever heard from him."

"Yes! I know what I have to face," Disraeli closed. "I have to face a coalition. The combination may be successful. But coalitions, although successful, have always found this, that their triumph has been short. This, too, I know, that England does not love coalitions. I appeal from the coalition to that public opinion which governs the country—to that public opinion whose mild and irresistible influence can control even the decrees of Parliaments, and without whose support the most august and ancient institutions are but"—and quoting from *The Tempest* from memory he got it almost right—" 'the baseless fabric of a vision.' "

A key to that coalition was John Bright, who had visited
Disraeli at his request at Grosvenor Gate the day before. Disraeli
wanted to explain in advance to a Radical power why he had proposed lowering the malt tax, and how tea could not be taxed
without malt. If he could get a majority of just one, he would give
up the house tax after the first reading, but he confessed that defeat remained certain. Even if the Tories "now escaped," he told
Bright, "it was doubtful if they could live till Easter."

Bright was impressed. "This remarkable man is ambitious,
most able, and without prejudices. He conceives it right to strive
for a great career with such principles as are in vogue in his age
. . . but having obtained power, he would use it to found a great
reputation on great services rendered to the country."

In his seat when Disraeli arose the next evening, the M.P.
from Durham was still there three hours later, at 1:00 in the morning, when Disraeli began his peroration. "He fought for his life,"
Bright noted in his diary, "and never man fought more desperately
or with more skill and power. This speech was his greatest speech;
he was in earnest; argument, satire, sarcasm, invective, all were
abundant and of the first class." One by one, Disraeli targeted the
assailants of his budget with taunts that made them cringe. Old
Henry Goulburn, a Peelite veteran of ministries since 1810 and
once a Chancellor of the Exchequer himself, was, for example,
"that weird Sibyl, the member for Cambridge University."

Young George Trevelyan, a schoolboy taken to the House by
his father, recalled that "a sigh of regret went up from his audience" when Disraeli, drained, sat down. Traditionally the Chancellor's was the last word.

While cheers and jeers echoed, Gladstone forced his way to
the Speaker's table, insisted upon replying although he was out of
order, and then riddled Disraeli's budget with festering vindictiveness, rebuking him for having "not yet learned the limits of discretion, of moderation, and of forbearance that ought to restrain
the conduct and language of every member of this House."
Edward Stanley watched Gladstone, "choked with passion," go on
for two hours before an awestruck Commons, unaware that he
had been living in a fever of excitement, spending many of his
evenings when not in the House on the streets accosting London

prostitutes—only the most disturbingly attractive young wom-
en—in order to accompany them to their rooms and lecture them
on their shame, giving them money and often a Bible, and then
returning home, often to flagellate himself. During 1851 and 1852
he waited, tremblingly, for the same woman, Elizabeth Collins,
twenty-five times, finding her on twenty occasions, then scourging himself.* In late 1852 he was handing out copies of *Uncle
Tom's Cabin* rather than his usual Bibles. In his diary he wondered
whether what he was doing was "unlawful," and whether his agonized "rescue" missions were impure temptation, but he lived on
a razor's edge of emotional composure until each next streetwalking expedition. The last opportunity, on December 9, the evening
before the debate had begun, had been followed by scourging after "a conversation not as it should have been," Gladstone recorded. Now, his face livid and distorted with passion, he attacked
Disraeli as a purveyor of political depravity, his agitation finding
release in rhetoric he had only half prepared in his notes.

Disraeli had dramatized the lack of class bias in his budget by
observing, "My own knowledge on the subject is, of course, recent. I was not born and bred a Chancellor of the Exchequer; I
am one of the Parliamentary rabble." Understanding his audience,
Gladstone retorted that, in effect, he *was* so born and bred. He
had learned Peel's great financial management system at the knee
of Sir Robert Peel himself and had no need for the dishonesty
that came from masking inexperience. Invoking Peel over and
over again he made it clear that he was keeper of the fiscal flame
and candidate for the office which Disraeli had discredited.

At 3:00 in the morning, still trembling with emotion, Gladstone sat down. At the division the Tories were beaten, 305 to
286. The Government was lost. The House adjourned at 3:45,
and in the lifting predawn darkness, Gladstone and his followers
walked to the Carlton Club in exhilaration.

"My nervous system was too powerfully acted upon by the

---

*The editors of Gladstone's *Diaries* call the hapless Collins a "protracted rescue
case." In mid-February, less than two months later, Gladstone records that after he
had a conversation at Buckingham Palace with Prince Albert, he set out on a "rescue" mission. "Saw P. Lightfoot & got hold of means of evil wh[ich] after seeing I
burned." It was his second straight day of "rescuing."

scene of last night," he wrote in his diary. He slept only two hours, still excited by "smashing an antagonist across the House of Commons." It was important to begin preparing to assume Disraeli's job, and Gladstone wrote a letter to Stafford Northcote, his former assistant at the Board of Trade, to inquire whether he would be interested in working at the Exchequer.

After a closing Cabinet meeting, Lord Derby took the train to Portsmouth, to be ferried across the Solent to the Isle of Wight. The Queen was spending her Christmas at Osborne House, and his duty was to consult her on the succession. On returning he described the meeting to his son Edward:

> The Queen received him cordially: she seemed grave and anxious: the Prince entered into confidential discussions on many subjects, appearing desirous to take upon them the last opinion that he could receive from his ex-minister. He spoke often of Disraeli, extolled his talent, his energy, but expressed a fear that he was not in his heart favourable to the existing order of things. My Father defended his colleague: said he had been unnaturally kept down for several years, and then suddenly raised to the highest position. "He has better reason than anyone to be attached to our constitutional system since he has experience how easily under it a man may rise." The Prince was glad to hear it, but still thought Disraeli had democratic tendencies "and if that is the case, he may become one of the most dangerous men in Europe."
> My Father, with his accustomed frankness, related the substance of this conversation to Disraeli.

The Prince feared, Derby added, that Disraeli's rise might "raise up a host of inferior imitations." Albert may very well have dreaded a potential Louis Napoleon arising on English soil, and noted, when the outgoing ministers returned their seals at Windsor Castle on December 28, "Mr Disraeli seemed to feel most the loss of office." Yet a curious metamorphosis in his relationship with the Court was already in progress, with Disraeli returning to Albert a state paper late in December with the awkward if fulsome parting words, "I may, perhaps, be permitted to say that the views which your Royal Highness has developed to me in confidential conversation have not fallen on ungrateful soil. I shall ever remember with interest and admiration the princely mind in the princely person, and shall at all times be prepared to prove to your Royal Highness my devotion." And at Windsor, as the warring sides gathered for the transfer of seals, Disraeli, according to a later Cabinet member, John Morley, "with infinite polish and grace asked pardon for the flying words of debate, and drew easy forgiveness." Prince Albert's minute remarked, "We owned that we had been astonished to find them all so *well bred.*"

On January 14, 1853, Lord Stanley saw Disraeli for only the second time in the new year. Baron Stockmar, Prince Albert's old confidant from Coburg, Disraeli said, had come to see him on a mission from Albert, "expressing a wish that communications should be frequent."

Disraeli had to give up not only his office but the furniture he had selected for it and the venerable Exchequer robes, which he believed had belonged to the younger William Pitt. A leader of a minority party that might only attract enough influential adherents to become a majority one by jettisoning him, he may have tasted his sole chance at high office. He wanted to keep the robes, explaining many years later to Baron Pollock, who had presided at the swearing-in, "By the time [the official robes] came to me they were half worn out, and by the time I went out of office they were nearly falling to pieces. I thought I should like to keep the old robes as a matter of curiosity. So I had new ones made at my own expense, and nobly presenting them to my successor, [I] carried off the old ones myself." Turning to Pollock, he added, "Now, should you call that petty larceny or not?"

Pollock could not resist the connection of Disraeli with "Old Clo' " and quipped, "Oh, no! I should call it simply an interesting survival of hereditary instinct."

There was nothing of Petticoat Lane in Disraeli's determination to keep the historic robes. He had no intention of turning them over to his successor because the new Chancellor of the Exchequer was William Ewart Gladstone.

XVI

"... THE BITTER CUP OF ILL SUCCESS."

1853–1856

ONCE ASKED WHETHER SHAKESPEARE'S LINE FROM *AS YOU LIKE IT*, "Sweet are the uses of Adversity," were true, Disraeli retorted, "Yes, if it does not last too long." Dining at the Lionel de Rothschilds in London in his first bleak days out of office, he looked to Anthony de Rothschild's wife, Louise, "perfectly wretched." Unsympathetic with what she considered his less than sincere political pyrotechnics on the Jewish Disabilities Bill and much else, she noted in her diary: "Had Disraeli even wished to carry out any great principle, or to bring forward some truly useful measures, he would not be so cast down, but his elevation having been his only aim, he has nothing to sweeten the bitter cup of ill success."

It made no difference to him that he was now an authentic celebrity, even to enshrinement in Madame Tussaud's, "that British Valhalla," the *Edinburgh Review* mocked, "in which it is difficult for a civilian to gain a niche without being hanged." After forty pages examining his career, the anonymous author decided that Disraeli was not only finished, but had been "a mere vapoury exhalation, or will o' the wisp, raised by an overheated atmosphere from a rank and unwholesome soil." (A biography published by the firm of Richard Bentley in 1854 described Disraeli as a "Hebrew poet" who was "determined not to throw a[ny political] chance away.")

The Exchequer robes went not to Madame Tussaud's in Baker Street but to Hughenden, and Gladstone tried to get them back. The coalition government which Disraeli had predicted included six Peelites, six Whigs, and one Radical, and was headed by the Peelite Earl of Aberdeen, who had only forty seats in the Commons. With party allegiances and identifications still to be sorted out, Aberdeen's adherents were still known as "the friends of Sir Robert Peel," while Disraeli's Tories, again in the wilderness after 305 days, remained "the friends of the Earl of Derby." (Abraham Hayward, of the Peel faction, sneered at the other Tory party as "the Disraelites.") From the former camp, Gladstone on January 21, 1853, sent a polite request to his predecessor offering to pay for Disraeli's office furniture and inquiring about the missing "Official Robes." After more than a month, Disraeli replied that a check for £307/16s./6d. representing what he had not been reimbursed by the Office of Works "would as between us conclude the matter." Gladstone asked again about the robes, a matter which Disraeli ignored, although he later claimed he ordered new attire, with the Chancellor finally writing, "It is highly unpleasant to Mr W. E. Gladstone to address Mr Disraeli without the usual terms of courtesy, but he abstains from them only because he perceives they are unwelcome." Foreshadowed in the exchange was the tone of their future relations.

The only hope for loyalist Tories was a reconstruction of the party in the Commons. First to be swept out by Disraeli was William Beresford, Chief Whip and a feeble war minister in Derby's Cabinet. Having been censured by a House committee for "reckless indifference to systematic bribery," he was an easy target, as was Forbes Mackenzie of Liverpool, another Whip under similar charges. To create an organization to run the party, Disraeli enlisted Philip Rose and his law partner, Markham Spofforth. Since much of the press was Liberal, Disraeli also wanted to fulfil his dream of a newspaper that would be the organ for his ideas. While he had the backing of young Stanley, the Earl of Derby was less interested. "The Captain," Edward Stanley had written frankly of his father, "does not care for office, but wishes to keep things as they are and impede 'Progress.' "

Derby's passive negation, Disraeli knew, was a millstone to his own ambitions and to any constructive aspect to Conservatism. His failed budget, for example, had included a radical proposal to distinguish between earned and unearned incomes in assessing income taxes. A popular newspaper might prod Derby as well as promote Disraeli, for there was only the *Standard* among London papers which could be counted upon as Tory, and that in the worst, bigoted, sense. Among politicians only Viscount Palmerston, now nearly seventy and back in the Cabinet as Home Secretary, had a personal organ, the *Globe*. Canvassing wealthy Tories, Disraeli raised enough funds to begin a weekly he christened *The Press*, to be published at sixpence every Saturday morning, and employed Samuel Lucas, a barrister with Oxford credentials, as editor. For a time, although Derby, the ostensible party leader, remained stubbornly in seclusion at St. Leonards, just west of Hastings, Disraeli was again happy. With few given the opportunity to live an experience over again, he was, now older and wiser, exorcising the haunting memories of *The Representative*.

Newspapers were much on Disraeli's mind as he became involved with one once more. Journalistic irresponsibility became the focus of a speech of his in the Commons on the Aberdeen government's relations with France, and how France—his old friend Louis Napoleon in particular—was being abused by London newspapers. Freedom of the press, abrogated by Napoleon III in his own country, was, in England, Disraeli pointed out on February 18, 1853, "a most perilous privilege." It was not the job of London editors to interfere with the "domestic concerns" of France. It was a matter of "discretion," of "public wisdom," not to indulge in jeremiads that only led to an armaments race. He was not trying to diminish the powers of Parliament, or the press, he said. "My greatest honour is to be a member of this House, in which all my thoughts and feelings are concentred; and as for

The Easter Recess. *Punch*, April 24, 1852, on Disraeli's ambitions. The caption reads, "Oh, no! I'm not Giddy. I should like to go ever so Much Higher."

the Press, I am myself a 'gentleman of the Press,' and I bear no other scutcheon."

The first number of Disraeli's paper appeared on May 7, 1853. He wrote—anonymously—the leading articles in ten of the first eleven issues, and many readers thought they saw his hand, also, in "Letters to the Whigs," in which Bulwer-Lytton echoed Disraeli's style. Too progressive for the more implacable friends of Lord Derby, *The Press* limped along. By the fifth number it had 1,200 subscribers, but never would reach a paying five figures. Another barrister with a flair for writing, Edward Vaughan Kenealy, was recruited as a contributor and recalled talking over the paper's prospects at Grosvenor Gate, where Disraeli's library included a marble bust of himself, commissioned by Mary Anne the year before, and a portrait of Lord George Bentinck. Disraeli looked thin, and in ill health, Kenealy thought. "There is perpetual motion in him. He is wearing out from too much excitement. . . . He has grown less Jewish than when I last saw him and the impression which he leaves is one of pain rather than pleasure. . . . I was sorry to see him so careworn and restless, and wonder why he bothers himself about such miserable cheats as the rewards of political battle."

Kenealy dropped out some months later after disagreements with Lucas and found the law more rewarding, even more conducive to fame, especially after he defended a miserable cheat named Arthur Orton, son of a Wapping butcher, who claimed he was the lost Sir Roger Tichborne. Disbarred for his handling of the trial, Kenealy would open his own newspaper, *The Englishman*, to fight the case in the press.

From his St. Leonards hideaway on May 17 Lord Derby complained to Disraeli that *The Press* was "too little of a newspaper; that we do not give a sufficient quantity of news, and rather too exclusively political. I have mentioned this to Lucas, but, as you are in fact the manager of the machine, I report it to you." Derby seldom came up to London to bother with politics, and it was left to Disraeli to point out in Parliament that Gladstone's first budget resembled in many particulars the one he had passionately condemned only months before. Yet he found in Peelite thinking a continuing hostility toward the landed interest, in which Disraeli saw embodied the institutions which gave the country its national character. The soil was not, he emphasized, "the possession of any exclusive class. The merchant or the manufacturer may deposit within it his accumulated capital, and he may enjoy those privileges which its possession entitles him, on condition that he discharges those duties which its possession also implies." What he saw was the growing dominance of the "great towns" and the inevitable alteration of Britain, changing "a first-rate kingdom for a second-rate republic."

That May, presiding over the Royal Literary Fund, one of the more pleasant tasks he had in midyear, Disraeli told his fellow writers that literature and politics were like night and morning— each had its attractions, and one could not relinquish either. The next month, Derby abandoned his self-exile long enough to entrain to Oxford, where as Chancellor of the University he presided over the awarding of honorary degrees, and twenty years after Isaac had received his honorary doctorate, Ben, who had also not gone to a university, received a D.C.L. in company with Macaulay and Gladstone, Bishop Samuel Wilberforce, historian George Grote, and Bulwer-Lytton. *The Times* described Disraeli as "the lion of the solemnity," but unsolemnly, when he caught sight of Mary Anne in the ladies' gallery, he kissed his hand to her. At a Christ Church banquet to the Chancellor, the undergraduates gathered in Tom Quad in the rain to cheer "Dizzy," and escort him to the gate. "Gentlemen," he told them, "within these classic walls I dare not presume to thank you, but believe this, never will I forget your generous kindness." It felt gratifying not to be discarded, especially by the young.

In the party, however, to be a young Tory aspiring for office meant having family connections and an aversion to change, although the anomaly was the leader in the Commons. Exemplifying the system was the son of a member of Derby's late Cabinet, a product of Eton and Oxford and a Fellow of All Soul's in the year of Disraeli's honors. Then known as Lord Robert Cecil, he would be Viscount Cranborne and in due course the 3rd Marquis of Salisbury. Twenty-three in 1853, a pocket borough was his for the asking—Stamford. He would accept it only after the patron in whose pocket it was, Lord Exeter, assured him that complete distrust of "Mr d'Israeli"—to Cecil a "political charlatan"—was no impediment to being a Conservative M.P.

What he did not know, and would have attributed to Disraeli's vanity rather than his position in the House, was that Disraeli had already written warmly to the new M.P.'s father, "Of Lord Robert I have no hesitation in saying that if he will work, and he has a working look, I will make a man of him."

At Hatfield, the venerable seat of the Cecils and then the residence of the 2nd Marquis, Disraeli would recall about the visit, two years later, in 1855, "We dined every day in a baronial hall in the midst of a real old English park at the time of Queen Elizabeth, interminable avenues of lime and chestnut and oceans of fern, six feet high; golden yew trees and glancing deer." When an ambitious new M.P. in London, Disraeli had been invited to the salons of Salisbury's first wife, "old Sally," whose cordiality he remembered with affection. Now there was a much younger second Marchioness, Mary Catherine, daughter of the 5th Earl De La Warr, and only five years older than her stepson, who found himself with five young half-siblings.

Whether that or other factors provoked his rebelliousness, he was far to the right politically of his elderly father. Disraeli found himself faced with a brilliant, bigoted, churchy, churlish scion of the Cecils and future Marquis whose detestation of him was unconcealed. Nevertheless, when Lord Robert once returned unexpectedly to Hatfield House he found himself in the embrace of his *bête noire*. "Ah, Robert, Robert," Disraeli exclaimed, "how glad I am to see you." No harder task would face Disraeli than the winning of Robert Cecil.

Although Derby's influence had secured Disraeli his honorary degree, the two men remained on uneasy terms. Derby brooded over his failure to recruit Palmerston and Gladstone and knew he could not have them without getting rid of Disraeli. Without Disraeli, however, Palmerston and Gladstone would gobble up the party and alter its directions. With Disraeli, there was always the tension between Derby's reactionary Toryism and his colleague's pragmatism—a recognition that only a dynamic party had a future. In the summer of 1854 they differed publicly on what to do about India, which was still largely governed by the East India Company, over which the Government had only partial control. India had grown too complex for eighteenth-century administration, and while the Aberdeen ministry's India Bill authorized a facade of changes which retained the anomalies, Disraeli and Derby's son proposed amendments to abolish the Company and put India fully under the Crown.

Opposing his father, Stanley wrote a leader in *The Press*, "The Crown or the Company," and Derby, who already saw his son as more guided by Disraeli than by blood ties, used his clout in the Commons to defeat what would be perceived soon as inevitable. Among those voting against the amendments was Derby's Foreign Minister in 1852, Lord Malmesbury, whom Disraeli had looked on as an ally. The backward-looking intervention of Derby was almost his only act of leadership, as he was again complaining of gout, which he nursed at Knowsley, sending Disraeli, so he told Lord Londonderry wryly in September, haunches of venison rather than helpful messages.

With Mary Anne down with influenza—she had spent much of the year ill—it remained for Disraeli to travel to Knowsley alone in December when he received the first invitation of his life to the family seat near Liverpool. Disraeli expected the most luxurious setting in Lancashire. Derby had an annual income in excess of £100,000 and permitted his eldest son £15,000 a year merely to maintain his aviary and menagerie. Disraeli would put the story of Derby's daughter Emily finding at breakfast a birthday check from her father for £5,000 tucked into a napkin into *Endymion*. But Knowsley, Disraeli wrote in wonderment to Hughenden, was "a wretched house, yet very vast: an irregular pile of many ages: half of it like St. James's Palace, low, red, with turrets," set in grounds "almost as large as Windsor." Despite Derby's wealth it was "furnished like a second-rate lodging house, . . . not from stingyness, but from sheer want of taste," although the stables were beautifully kept. "No one has more splendid horses & equipages than Lord Derby."

To reconcile their positions in the Lords and the Commons, Disraeli promised (so Croker learned) "to oppose the principle of [electoral] Reform." His informant, Lord Lonsdale, added, "Dizzy, I understand, promises to be entirely Conservative. . . . He is our only man. He has [the] nerve to face the pelting from the opposite benches." Although Disraeli would have preferred to lead, he was unwilling to be a passive Opposition. "The attacks of my enemies," he told Thomas Jones, "do not disturb me more than the whistling of bullets did Charles [XII] of Sweden in the midst of a battle. He called it 'his music.' " His reputation in debate was now such that he could offer to an opponent he despised "the mercy of my silence." That distinction made him no more acceptable to Tory ultras like Henry Drummond, who railed to Croker on December 19 that the Conservatives could not be united under Disraeli. "You have the most reckless man in the country at the head . . . , who is himself the very model of a destructive." The leader of the House was not merely not a gentleman from Drummond's standpoint but no longer a Protectionist. Corn Law repeal had been "only another wave of that great deluge of democracy," and power was being transferred inexorably to people who had "only a temporary interest in the country."

To call Derby's forces Protectionist was convenient although fewer and fewer Tories believed in the battle cry other than some grandees in both Houses. One of the quirks of the Conservative split was that Peelites and Derbyites both still used the Carlton, making it a logical venue for accommodation. But for a peer of Derby's lineage such places were beneath notice. "I once only saw him at the Carlton Club," Disraeli recalled. "He sat next to me while I was at supper, after the House of Commons [adjourned]." Still, Derby's hope was that if Reform, promoted by the abrasive Lord John Russell, remained the central issue in the Commons, a fissure might open between Liberals and Peelites, a prospect which seemed almost fulfilled when, as Disraeli returned to London, he found that Palmerston had resigned as Home Secretary. Without him the Government tottered.

Eleven days later, on December 26, 1853, having made his point that he was the most powerful man in the ministry and could bring it down single-handed, Palmerston resumed his office. Although Russell would persist in introducing a Reform Bill, it would be withdrawn before the session of 1854 had gone very far. Other priorities had intervened. The country by then was on the brink of war.

In the last months of the old year, the Eastern Question again dominated the newspapers. Russia was finding excuses in the crumbling of the Ottoman hold on the Balkans, eroded by nationalistic agitation among non-Moslems and centuries of Turkish bureaucratic incompetence, to extend its reach toward the Mediterranean, which the British conceived as the lifeline to India. Eager for aggrandizement, Napoleon III put France forward as the protector of Christians in Ottoman lands; and the Kingdom of Sardinia, which already controlled portions of the Italian mainland, coveted more territory, Italian and otherwise. From Malmesbury's estate, Heron Court, in Hampshire, where he was seeing in the new year, Disraeli wrote to Mrs. Brydges Willyams, "The Government seem to have had a paralytic stroke, but they have administered cordials to the patient, and it will linger on awhile. . . . Its alternative is Reform or War. This is a pleasant choice."

While war fever rose in England, Russell went ahead with Reform and Disraeli scoffed in the House, "I thought we were going to make war on the Emperor of Russia, I find we are only going to make war on ourselves." With that he made good on his assurances to Derby, who was still detached from day-to-day affairs. War had not yet been declared, but the Russian ambassador left London on February 7, and in Constantinople, the British ambassador, Stratford Canning, now Viscount Stratford de Redcliffe, was openly pro-Turk. Although Britain had fought no war for forty years and was unprepared to fight one, Aberdeen's government in concert with France issued an ultimatum to Russia to evacuate the Danubian principalities (now Romania) in which the Czar claimed to be protecting Christians persecuted by the Turks.

When Russia took no notice, war became inevitable. A fleet was raised to defend Turkish ports on the Black Sea, then to land troops at Sevastopol, in the Crimea, "the eye tooth of the Bear which must be drawn." Russian aggression was "occasioned by English infirmity," Disraeli told Lady Londonderry. That infirmity—lack of preparedness—meant that no Anglo-French armada would sail until September, although the press and Parliament talked of little else. In the Commons, Disraeli remarked scornfully, "When I heard of the return of our squadron to Constantinople, I could not help recalling the words of a great orator when he was addressing an assembly not less illustrious than this, when he said, 'O Athenians, the men who administer your affairs are men who know not how to make peace or to make war.' "

Once engaged, Disraeli wanted the conflict prosecuted vigorously, the limited war for limited objectives having escalated. The prospects in the Crimean venture, he confided to Lady Londonderry, were "not good," and he predicted, accurately, "a *fiasco*."

He was not eager himself "to precipitate affairs," but he had intimations "from the highest quarter" that if Aberdeen fell, the Tory ministry that might follow "may be under a head, which I never contemplated." He meant himself, and he had been in informal contact with the Court, very likely Prince Albert, the issue apparently being the continuing illness and inaccessibility of Derby. "As for our Chief," his letter to Lady Londonderry of August 7 continued,

> We never see him. His House is always closed; he subscribes to nothing, tho' his fortune is very large; and expects, nevertheless, everything to be done. I have never yet been fairly backed in life. All the great personages I have known, even when what is called "ambitious," by courtesy, have been quite unequal to a grand game. This has been my fate, and I never felt it more keenly than at the present moment, with a confederate always [racing horses] at Newmarket and Doncaster, when Europe, nay the world, is in the throes of immense changes, and all the elements of power at home in a state of dissolution. If ever there were a time when a political chief should concentrate his mind and resources on the situation, 'tis the present. There cannot be too much vigilance, too much thought, and too much daring—all seem wanting.

The 27,000 soldiers shipped from England to the Black Sea in 1854 had almost no reserves behind them, no winter gear as the war would be short, and weapons that Wellington's troops had carried against the first Napoleon. As the news continued bad, and was received at home with indignation, Disraeli wrote to Mrs. Brydges Willyams that in his opinion "the Ministers ought to be impeached." Alma, Balaclava, Inkerman, and the Light Brigade became household words for mismanagement, incompetence, and courage, yet—as often in war—the most ineffective generals were promoted and rewarded.

Perhaps because the 1854 session had been overwhelmed by war, Lord John Russell guessed that he might slip a new Oaths

Bill through a distracted Parliament by dressing it differently. Toward the close of the session he proposed altering the oaths to accommodate any belief, a measure which raised more ill-feeling than one that was specifically intended to emancipate Jews. For Disraeli it posed an awkward dilemma. "Here is a bill," he pointed out from the floor, "in which the word 'Jew' never appears." In effect "the noble lord has prejudiced the Jewish claims," he contended, by a "political convenience." It was a piece of procedural chicanery, he explained in voting against it— and it lost by only four votes in the House, saving the Lords their inevitable veto.

Russell taunted Disraeli with insincerity. "Notwithstanding his great anxiety to see the Jews in possession of these privileges, the right hon. gentleman sometimes stays away, and sometimes votes against them: the political convenience of the hour always seems to overcome his attachment to the cause." Denying the allegations, Disraeli countered, "I never on any occasion have quitted the House—I never absented myself from any division in which the claims of the Jews were concerned; and if I voted against his bill the other night, I tell the noble lord that I do not consider that I voted against a bill which could have benefitted the Jews, but on the contrary, that I voted against a bill which I believe would have been of greater injury to the Jews than any measure ever brought forward."

The excuse was an exaggeration, but he meant that the bill in effect associated Jewish rights with ultra-Protestant fears of Vatican encroachment in England, making it impossible of passage in any case by the other House. "I am quite persuaded," Russell apologized, very likely to Disraeli's surprise, "that the right honourable gentleman had intended to serve the cause of the Jews in the course he has taken." But in the Jewish community the vote cast suspicion upon Disraeli's political motives until two years later, when another, more explicit bill was introduced, and Russell on its third reading described his colleague as "one who, on the peculiar ground of the merit of the Jews, always advocates their cause, and always votes in their favour."

It was not easy to escape the war. On his way with Mary

Anne to visit Mrs. Brydges Willyams in Torquay, Disraeli wrote to his secretary, Henry Williams, on October 3, "Our carriage was stopped, at every stage, with fresh rumors from the seat of war, but beyond the battle [at Balaclava], of which we first heard of on Sunday, all is still doubtful. At least, I am myself a little sceptical of the Tatar in whom, however, all believe."

A stormy December war session of Parliament heard of further scandals and misconduct, with Disraeli attacking the Ministry for anticipating a great war while providing for a small one. Early in the new year of 1855 a resolution by Sheffield M.P. John Arthur Roebuck for a Committee of Inquiry on the War shook the Aberdeen government. In the corridors of the Commons on January 20, John Bright, outraged by what he had heard on the floor, told Disraeli, "I said I wanted *peace,* not to break up a Gov-[ernmen]t, but if they would not make peace, I would make war on them."

Disraeli predicted to Bright that a Derby ministry would come in soon. Bright recalled: "He could not see why I should not join Lord Derby's Cabinet! I smiled, and said I could never lift up my head after such an act—it would destroy me. . . . He thought Palmerston done: 'You may see the breed, but the action and power are gone.' "

Aberdeen's ministers began defecting. The Prime Minister hung on until Bright's plea for an armistice mesmerized the House. "The Angel of Death has been abroad throughout the land; you may almost hear the beating of his wings," Bright declared. "There is no one, as when the first-born were slain of old, to sprinkle with blood the lintel and the two side-posts of our doors, that he may spare and pass on; he takes his victims from the castle of the noble, the mansion of the wealthy and the cottage of the poor and lowly, and it is on behalf of all these classes that I make this solemn appeal."

The Old Testament imagery* captivated Disraeli, who con-

---

*Disraeli sometimes offered his equivalents, in 1858 characterizing the Earl of Shaftesbury as "Gamaliel himself, with the broad phylacteries of faction upon his forehead." The elder Gamaliel, one of the Palestinian masters of Jewish Oral Law, was the grandson of Rabbi Hillel.

gratulated the speaker: "Bright, I would give all I ever had to have made that speech you made just now."

"Well," said Bright, "you might have made it if you had been honest."

"I could not confide the Govt to Ld Palmerston," Victoria noted in her journal about the politician she had despised more than any other in active life, "(though I may yet have to do so)." When Victoria had been a very young queen, Prince Albert had confided to Lord John Russell five years earlier, Palmerston, while a guest at Windsor, "had committed a brutal attack upon one of her ladies in waiting; [he] had at night by stealth, introduced himself into her apartment, barricaded afterwards the door and would have consummated the fiendish scheme by violence had not the miraculous efforts of his victim and assistance rendered by her screams saved her."

Palmerston had then been fifty-three; eighteen years later Victoria still preferred not to have him as her First Minister. When the debate on Roebuck's bill ended on the night of January 29, Aberdeen had almost no Ministry left. The order to clear the Gallery for the division—"Strangers withdraw!"—came at 3:00 in the morning, and when the vote was announced, 305 to 157 for Committee of Inquiry, Count Walewski, the French ambassador, told Count Vitzthum von Eckstaedt, the Minister from Saxony, "In eight days Lord Palmerston will be Prime Minister—that is exactly what we want."

On January 31, with Aberdeen out, the Queen sent for Lord Derby, who asked for time in which to persuade Palmerston to join the Government. "The whole country," he told the Queen, "cried out for Palmerston as the only man fit for carrying on the war with success." Besides, he added, Palmerston was *persona grata* with Napoleon III, a major ally. Yet a memorable declaration by Palmerston in 1848 made him seem safe: "We have no eternal allies, and we have no perpetual enemies. *Our* interests are eternal and perpetual, and these interests it is our duty to follow." And he had no Tory rival for Downing Street. Derby had no interest in being saddled with the mess in which the country had found itself, and Disraeli, helplessly watching his own chance go by, was unquietly furious.

Returning from "rescue" work with two ladies of the street that concluded with prayer rather than the scourge, Gladstone chanced upon Disraeli in the House just after learning that Derby had passed up Downing Street. Impulsively, Gladstone noted in his diary, "[I] put out my hand wh[ich] was very kindly accepted." Gladstone had already told Derby that he would be part of no cabinet that did not include Palmerston, yet in his diary he confided fears that the old man was "in no way equal to the duties which fall upon a Prime Minister." But the Peelites preferred Palmerston to what Gladstone called "the difficulty of Disraeli."

Seeking anyone who could form a government but Palmerston, the Queen sent for Lord Lansdowne, seventy-five and feeble; then she met with the unpopular Lord John Russell, who reported to her on February 3 that none of his essential associates, such as Lord Clarendon, Sydney Herbert, or W. E. Gladstone, would join unless Palmerston were included. Palmerston would only involve himself in a government in which he were chief, yet he was, Derby had told the Queen prematurely, "totally unfit for the task. He had become very deaf as well as very blind, was seventy-one years old, and . . . though he still kept up his sprightly manners of youth, it was evident that his day had gone by."

Derby clearly wanted none of the blame if Palmerston failed, yet he had insisted that no one else was possible. Disraeli told Lord Malmesbury that he was "in a state of disgust beyond all control," and that he had not hesitated to tell Derby "some very disagreeable truths." What he wrote to Lady Londonderry on February 2 suggests the impolitic vein in which he may have given a piece of his mind to Derby:

I was so annoyed and worn out yesterday, that I could not send you two lines to say that our chief has again bolted!

This is the third time that, in the course of six years, during which I have had the lead of the Opposition in the House of Commons, I have stormed the Treasury Benches: twice fruitlessly, and the third time, with a tin kettle to my tail, which rendered the race almost hopeless. You cannot, therefore, be surprised, that I am a little wearied of these barren victories, which like Alma, Inkerman, and Balaclava, may be glorious, but are certainly nothing more.

What is most annoying is, that, this time, we had actually the Court with us . . . and our rivals were Johnny [Russell] in disgrace, and Palmerston, ever detested. The last, however, seems now the inevitable man, and tho' he is really an impostor, utterly exhausted, and, at the best, only ginger beer and not champaign, and now an old painted Pantaloon, very deaf, very blind, and with false teeth, which would fall out of his mouth when speaking, if he did not hesitate and halt so in his talk—he is a name, which the country resolves to associate with energy, wisdom, and eloquence, and will until he has tried and failed.

To Mary Anne, Disraeli wrote about Derby's explanation at a party meeting late in February, "It met everything except the chief point—namely, that we did not accept office because we were afraid and incompetent."

Her alternatives exhausted, Victoria sent for Palmerston, who proceeded to thrive in the job for which he had been aspiring since he had become a Junior Lord of the Admiralty in 1807. Derby left London and joined Malmesbury at Heron Court, the gout that had kept him from governmental duties not an obstacle to his wildfowl shooting. Within days, independent of the changes in the Cabinet, the prospects of peace began to improve. All parties to the conflict were exhausted, and the European winter had been so hard that the Thames had frozen. But Palmerston was even more blessed by fortune. On March 2, 1855, only three weeks after he kissed hands, Czar Nicholas I, whose ambitions had precipitated the war, died suddenly, and was succeeded by Alexander II. When the news reached London by the still primitive telegraph, Disraeli's *Press* urged an immediate armistice and a peace conference.

One of Palmerston's first acts had been to attempt to quash the Committee of Inquiry into the war. Hampered by a speech infirmity, Roebuck could only manage a few sentences of protest, but Disraeli rose to insist that the investigation proceed, and a Sebastopol Committee was activated, with Roebuck as chairman. The results embarrassed the former Aberdeen Government, which so closely resembled, but for Aberdeen himself, the Palmerston Cabinet. Palmerston supporters moved the previous question to shut off the debate. Since newspapers had the Sebastopol Committee's findings, and its recommendation for "severe reprobation" of ministers responsible for the disasters in the Crimea, no one was fooled although after the division no one was officially blamed.

Negotiations dragged, but Napoleon III needed an end to a war as costly and as mortifying to France as it had already been to Britain. He set out on a state visit to Britain in mid-April for discussions on ending the unpopular intervention, and the Disraelis, as an acknowledgment of their position, were invited to Windsor for some of the ceremonies. Disraeli's old friend was forty-seven, short, swarthy, and goateed, but as engaging as ever. "I was very much struck by the smallness of his stature," Mrs. Brydges Willyams soon heard. "He did not seem taller than our Queen." Disraeli was unimpressed by the beautiful Empress Eugénie. "For me she had not a charm. She has Chinese eyes, and a perpetual smile or simper which I detest."

The imperial visit kept public attention on the costly stalemate in the Crimea—"a just but unnecessary war," Disraeli called it, fought in the wrong place for the wrong reasons. Hawkish voices cried for unattainable victory rather than an end to the attrition, and he warned the House on May 24 that invading the vastness of Russia never had worked. "I do not presume to predict what the result of such a struggle would be; but I think few will deny that the hair of the youngest Member present might grow grey before its termination."

Disraeli knew some younger sons of friends who had gone off in expectations of glory, but the fate of only one of them affected him deeply. The Marquess of Londonderry, who had been kind to him in his early days in London, had died while his second son, Lord Adolphus Vane, was at the front, and Frances Anne, Lady Londonderry, was running the family enterprises from offices in

Seaham Harbour, south of Sunderland. The family owned vast coal mines which she had inherited from her father, and railways and factories. Frances Anne ran them all, as well as the employee model villages, in the paternalistic spirit of Disraeli's ideal industrialist Oswald Milbank in *Coningsby*. As the war dragged on she was "in despair" about her son, Sarah Brydges Willyams heard early in September. "The trenches are so near the enemy," Disraeli explained, "that we lose forty [men] *per diem* by casualties! *Casualties*, she says, & truly, what a horrible word to describe the loss of limb and life!"

Sevastopol fell, finally, a few days later, and Lord Adolphus returned on leave, the army unready to let him resume his nominal career as an M.P. He had lost neither life nor limb, but two winters in the Crimea had left him a casualty of a different sort—in the term of a later war, shell-shocked. He would become progressively more eccentric and useless, but that condition was not yet apparent when the Disraelis were invited to welcome him home at Holdernesse House in London, which was "quite dismantled," Mrs. Brydges Willyams learned, although Lady Londonderry "contrived to collect and feed ten agreeable persons."

By the end of the Parliamentary session Lord Adolphus would return and even make a much-applauded open-air speech to his constituents, but Disraeli worried about the dearth of new Tory talent and recognized that Vane would be of little help. The party—and Disraeli—somehow had to survive Derby. It was not that Derby was timid; he preferred the creepingly slow pace of progress and his lack of responsibility. Disraeli talked with the Chief Whip, Sir William Jolliffe, as diplomatically as he could about his frustrations. "I found him very dejected about the prospects of our party," Jolliffe wrote to Derby, as Disraeli hoped he would, on October 23, 1855, "and [I] left him less so; but I, at any rate, find it difficult to contend against his arguments; that it is impossible to exist without a policy, and still less possible for an Opposition to be of the same policy as the Government to which it is opposed."

More and more *The Press* was slipping from Disraeli's direction. Its pacifist articles were being written by young Stanley, who was being courted by Palmerston to change sides and take the

Colonial Office. It was a source of exasperation from his son that the Earl of Derby did not need, as he was already impatient for Stanley to marry and furnish an heir for Knowsley. Derby was also less than happy with his son's assumed burden of social guilt, as Stanley talked often to Disraeli of his democratic sympathies and his desire to divest himself of his wealth and properties. Nothing came of either, but when he rushed to see the Earl, to ask his opinion of the offer of office, Derby—busy at billiards—growled, "What brings you here, Edward? Are you going to be married or has Disraeli cut his throat?"

Disraeli spent the autumn and early winter largely at Hughenden, helpless about affairs, and much of February and March at Grosvenor Gate, for the new session of Parliament, re-turning to the country a week before the Treaty of Paris ending the Crimean War was signed on March 30, 1856. Palmerston took credit for the confluence of factors that had made it possible and ran his Government as if he were his own party. As Derby described him to Malmesbury, "Pam" was "a Conservative Minis-ter working with Radical tools."

The Tory split had hardened into Disraeli and Gladstone fac-tions, impossible of reunion as much on personal as ideological grounds. Happily for his political future, Gladstone was courted by "Pam" as well as Derby. Whatever Derby's overtures, Glad-stone observed in his diary on March 26, "We could not bargain Disraeli out of the saddle, that it must rest with him (as far as we were concerned) to hold the lead if he pleased, that despite my looking to it with doubt and dread I felt he had this right, and that I took it as . . . the question of political junction."

With his future assured in the other party as the reins of Palmerston and Russell began to loosen, Gladstone was pleased with unlikelihood of Tory reunion. Disraeli saw for himself only the small consolations of Opposition status, which had included, during the session, an invitation to dine at Buckingham Palace, where he was viewed now more with curiosity than suspicion. In response to a formulaic inquiry about health, a safe nonpolitical subject, Disraeli observed that he and Mary Anne had been chronic sufferers from influenza over several winters. Victoria ad-vised her regimen of rising early, taking cold shower baths daily, and spending as much time as possible in the fresh air. "She had almost come to defy *catching cold*, . . . the English complaint," he reported to Mrs. Brydges Willyams.

The social season that followed the resumption of peace was more spirited than any in years, and so was the public reawakening to domestic matters. In mid-May the Disraelis had to leave Hughenden for town earlier than anticipated to evade the Sabbatarian disturbances in Hyde Park, just across Park Lane from Grosvenor Gate. Evangelical groups had become more and more rigid and outspoken in their insistence, like the former rector at Hughenden Church, upon a strictly observed Sunday. Although working people had no other day for relaxation, anything resembling enjoyment was inappropriate for the Sabbath, for one of the Mosaic commandments had been to keep the day "holy," yet the Mosaic Sabbath was not even the same day of the week as the Christian one. There were controversies over delivery of the Penny Post on Sunday and about band music in the public parks on Sunday, a clamor which forced the Commissioner of Public Works to discontinue free concerts, one of the few cultural pleasures available to the poor. "What a great man Moses must have been," Disraeli remarked to Mrs. Brydges Willyams, "to have invented a law which should agitate the 19th century, with all its boasted progress!" Characteristically cynical, the Earl of Derby—admittedly a reactionary, but no hypocrite—told Disraeli, "I am not much of a prophet, but there is one thing, I think, I do foresee in this country—& that is a great Ecclesiastical crash."

There was other music available to the better-connected. Disraeli and Mary Anne went to a concert opening the new ballroom at Buckingham Palace, where 1,500 guests gathered one evening, and 500 sat on another evening to listen to an orchestra of 125 play German music, including that of Victoria's and Albert's favorite composer, Felix Mendelssohn.

Among other rigidities, many Evangelical divines had put a strict construction on biblical concepts of creation. Even the great Sir Isaac Newton two centuries earlier had found no intellectual difficulty in accepting the truncated time values suggested in Genesis. But Disraeli urged Mrs. Brydges Willyams to read, as he had, Sir Charles Lyell's 1,600-page *Principles of Geology* (1833).

"I should like to know," he wrote, "whether you think he makes out his case, that the great changes which have taken place in our globe are not the consequence of vast, sudden, and spasmodic changes, but the result of that continual change, thro' countless ages, which is now, as it always has been, going on." Darwin's work in the same spirit would not appear until 1859.

On April 13, 1856, the American consul in Liverpool, a novelist who had earned his post by a campaign biography of the American President, Franklin Pierce, was visiting London with his wife. They looked into Downing Street to see where the Prime Minister lived, and then, just after five, when Members of Parliament were already beginning to conduct the people's business, they walked into the vestibule of the House of Commons. Their guide was Francis Bennoch, a partner in a London wholesale trading firm who dabbled in verse writing. Some M.P.s evidenced a shabby gentility; some were "full of their dignity"; others were clearly country squires; some appeared "aldermanic." The consul guessed that not more than ten in the six hundred "would be missed."

Bennoch pointed out Lord John Russell—"a little, very short, elderly gentleman, in a brown coat, and so large a hat . . . that I saw really no face beneath it," Nathaniel Hawthorne noted in his diary. "By and by there came a rather tall[er], slender person, in a black frock [coat], buttoned up, and black pantaloons, taking long steps, but I thought rather feebly or listlessly. His shoulders were round; or else he had a habitual stoop in them. He had a prominent nose," the author of *The Scarlet Letter* observed, "a thin face, and a sallow, very sallow, complexion, and was a very unwholesome looking person; and had I seen him in America, I should have taken him for a hard-worked editor of a newspaper, weary and worn with night-work and want of exercise; shrivelled, and withered, before his time. It was Disraeli, and I never saw any other Englishman look in the least like him."

Disraeli was a weary fifty-two. Events appeared to be passing him by. His half-a-party, even should it grasp power again, seemed unlikely to be able to hold it.

XVII

"... SO FOND OF MR DIZZY."

1856–1858

IN THE MIDDLE 1850S MARY ANNE WAS OFTEN AILING AND FEELING her age, which publicly was given as four years less than the truth. Having married Wyndham Lewis in 1815 when she was twenty-three, she could easily claim to have been a younger bride. As she approached sixty-four she was obsessed by concerns that her death might not be far off. On June 6, 1856, she wrote a letter which she put aside with her private papers:

> My Own Dear Husband,—If I should depart this life before you, leave orders that we may be buried in the same grave, at whatever distance you may be from England. And now, God bless you, my kindest, dearest! You have been a perfect husband to me. Be put by my side in the same grave. And now farewell, my dear Dizzy. Do not live alone, dearest. Someone, I earnestly hope, you may find as attached to you as your own devoted
>
> Mary Anne

She had mothered him in the fashion of devoted wives who considered their husbands children as well as spouses, and managed his life in all its essentials. Mary Anne kept the family books, oversaw household expenditures, chose Disraeli's clothes, cut his hair, dyed it black as necessary, and arranged the curl over his forehead. Only after her death did her husband discover that she had kept packets of his hair with her personal treasures.

Uneducated and, scoffers would say, underbred—she was very likely a milliner's assistant in Bristol before she became Mrs. Wyndham Lewis—she had picked up what she needed to know through the years and had become Disraeli's private secretary before he had an official one. A writer in *Temple Bar* described from those who knew her "how every morning, when she had settled her household affairs . . . , she would sit down to glance through heaps of newspapers, reviews, and even blue-books, to spare her husband this fatigue. At his ten o'clock breakfast he heard from her all the news of the day, got the pith of the leaders from the *Times,* was told of everything printed in his favour, and often received a useful budget of facts, statistics, and anecdotes, bearing upon speeches which he was going to deliver."

"My own experience tells me," he had written to Lord John Manners in 1851, "that domestic happiness, far from being an obstacle to public life, is the best support of an honorable ambition." Regularity of attendance in the House was related, he thought, to the regularity of one's own house, and he told a friend who had lost his bid for reelection in 1853, "Don't marry until you regain your seat."

His sobriety of dress as befit a Conservative politician he owed to Mary Anne, who turned him from dandy into statesman at the price of a nondescript monotony. His boots were square-toed; his frock coat black, like the cravat he wore tied loose; and as a concession to variety, he was permitted a double-breasted waistcoat of "tabby colour." In summer months he wore a blue frock coat with a velvet collar, tightly buttoned. A contemporary who used the same tailor, Jackson in Cork Street, as did Disraeli in his later years, recalled asking him why he made his illustrious client such ill-fitting clothes. It wasn't his fault, said Jackson. Mrs

Disraeli always received him alone and chose the fabrics and colors, then called in her husband to submit to the necessary measurements, reminding the tailor afterward "not to pay any attention to the way Mr Disraeli stoops, as, she says, he doesn't always stoop, but to make the coat as if for a young man who stands upright! No wonder the clothes don't fit him."

On one occasion early in 1859 her sartorial supervision broke down, as he needed to go from Westminster, in Court attire, to Buckingham Palace. "I have not got my right dress," he wrote in a messenger-delivered note to "My dearest Wife." She was to "Give James breeches, drawers, silk-stockings & shoes. This is the only time you have tripped [up] since our marriage—&, therefore, I send you as punishment, only one kiss."

Mary Anne was a tenacious believer in his attractiveness, and went to the studio of W. P. Frith when she heard that her husband would be in one of the painter's crowded anecdotal canvases. Disraeli's face, Frith recalled, "was certainly not larger than a shilling; and I told Mrs Disraeli, when she called to see the pictures, that I could not think of troubling her husband, and on some excuse or other I escaped showing it to her; as I knew she would be distressed at finding the great man playing so small a part in it."

Frith's friend John Phillip was commissioned by the Speaker of the House, J. E. Denison, to paint a House of Commons scene to include eminent members of the Government and the Opposition. Inevitably the Prime Minister, then Palmerston, was shown speaking. Disraeli had a prominent place on the Tory benches, and came to Phillip's studio for a sitting, then returned to his carriage. But rather than join him, Mary Anne first slipped back inside to Phillip and told him privately, "Remember, his pallor is his beauty!"

On another occasion she accompanied her famous husband to a photographer who had begged for an opportunity. The state of the art required a time exposure for good portraiture, and the photographer brought to Disraeli a pedestal to lean against with dignity, but that prospect was anathema to Mary Anne, who leaped from her seat out of view to push the pedestal away. "Dizzy has never had anyone but me to support him in life," she allegedly exclaimed, "and he shall not be shown with a prop now!"

In a variation of the story, Lady Dorothy Nevill reported Mary Anne's telling her, "The man said he actually wanted him to be taken leaning on a chair, but I soon settled that, for I said, 'Dizzy has always stood alone, and he shall continue to do so!' "

Promoting her husband was her passion, and she would do so even where it was likely to do little good, as Sir Edward Blount described of a visit to Paris. He and the Disraelis were driving along a crowded boulevard, and Disraeli, apparently lost in thought, was sitting back quietly. "Evidently his adoring spouse thought the occasion ought not to be lost, so she roused her absent-minded lord with the words, 'Now do put yourself forward, Dizzy, and show yourself!' "

Sitting once in the Strangers' Gallery with a friend, Mary Anne listened to the debate until it ended, after which the friend gushed, "Mr Disraeli spoke most eloquently tonight. How splendid he is looking just now!"

"Ah, yes," Mary Anne agreed. "You think he looks splendid? Some people think that he is ugly, but he is not: he is very handsome. I should like them to see him when he is asleep."

In a variation on the theme, she listened, in one of the great houses of London, as ladies viewing a large mythological painting commented upon the handsomeness of the nearly nude Greek god. "Oh," Mary Anne scoffed, "you should see my Dizzy in his bath."

Despite the impulsive innocence, she was extremely prudish, once drawing her hand away from a distinguished Frenchman whose method of salutation was not to grasp it, English-style. "*Monsieur, ce n'est par propre,*" she said, drawing her fingers away from his lips. And at a country seat full of paintings splendid enough for the National Gallery, she was alleged to have told her hostess at breakfast the day after the Disraelis had arrived, "I find your house is full of indecent pictures!" To the dismay of the other guests she continued, "There is a most horrible picture in our bedroom: Disraeli says it is Venus and Adonis. I have been awake half the night trying to prevent him from looking at it."

Mary Anne grew more odd as she aged, and she always appeared engagingly eccentric to those who knew her. A penurious housekeeper, she never let her oddities enter into the management of Grosvenor Gate or Hughenden, but when it came to her husband, her unconventionality made her an original. She could turn public and private life inside out, and utter absurdities with such gravity as to foreshadow Oscar Wilde's droll dowagers. "Dizzy has the most wonderful moral courage," she once announced to guests, "but no physical courage. When he has his shower-bath, I always have to pull the string."

Her impromptu remarks, some thought, must have caused Disraeli embarrassment, but he told a friend only that she had never given him "a dull moment." A long rail journey with her was an experience to write home about, literally, as Sir Stafford Northcote did after traveling to Knowsley with the Disraelis. "Mrs Disraeli is great fun," he wrote to Lady Northcote from Lancashire late in 1859, "and we made capital friends in the train, though I could not help occasionally pitying her husband for the startling effect her natural speeches must have upon the ears of his great friends. Still, there is something very warm and good in her manner which makes one forgive a few oddities. . . . What do you say to the idea of asking them to Pynes?* It would complete the astonishment of our neighbors."

One never knew what she was likely to say. One of Disraeli's private secretaries reported that she once told Lady Waldegrave's fourth husband, Chichester Fortescue, that she had heard him much praised. "Where and when?" he asked.

"It was in bed," she said.

Although she lacked the education of most of the ladies she met in society, Disraeli counted upon her as a reader of his novels as they progressed. She knew little about literature. Rosina Bulwer recalled of the early days of Mary Anne's marriage to Disraeli that the subject of Jonathan Swift had come up, and after he had been much praised for his wit, Mrs. Disraeli asked how one could invite the great, and long dead, Dean Swift to one of her parties. The future Earl of Rosebery, Lord Dalmeny as a young man, recalled telling her at dinner that he was about to go up to

*Northcote's estate in Devonshire.

Oxford. "Oh, yes, I love Oxford," she said. "They are all so fond of Mr Dizzy there; they all applaud him so."

Had he received an honorary degree then? Dalmeny asked. "Yes," she said. "He was made a D.T.C.L. or something of the sort."

"Do you care for politics, Mrs Disraeli?"

"No, I have no time. I have so many books and pamphlets to read and see if his name is in any of them, and I have everything to manage, and write his stupid letters."

In her household management Mary Anne's parsimony was legendary, and more than a bit dotty. For a visit of Victoria's cousins the Prince and Princess of Teck she ordered just six rolls for breakfast, Sir Henry Lucy claimed. He noted also that once when Disraeli had to return earlier than expected to London, Mary Anne returned a quarter pound of cheese bought for him to the grocer in High Wycombe. For her London dinners she contracted with a caterer at a fixed price per head, and when Lord Walpole, after his solemn assurances of attendance, failed to turn up, she announced, "He might just as well have made me throw a sovereign into the Thames."*

In an autobiographical memorandum Disraeli confessed his pleasure in walking about Hughenden to talk to woodsmen and groundskeepers. "An old, but very hale, man told me today," he wrote sometime in 1860, "that he was going to be married, & that his bride would not be much younger than himself, but he had lodged in her cottage now for more than a year, & he thought she would do for him." He had been married before, and speaking of his first wife, who had died, he told Disraeli, "I can truly say, from the bottom of my heart, that for fifty years, I never knew what it was to have a happy hour."

Disraeli told Mary Anne, who delightedly made them a wedding dinner.

Not long before, Mary Anne had driven with him to the

---

*A sovereign was a gold coin worth twenty shillings (nearly £2)—a large sum indeed when the annual wages of an experienced cook were £30 and one could have his tailor make a morning coat or have two tons of first-quality coal delivered to one's house in London for the sovereign which Mary Anne paid for a catered dinner portion.

House to wish him well on the final day of a crucial debate. Disraeli was still wobbly from a bout of influenza. Mary Anne leaned out of the carriage to say something to a servant, and before she could tuck her hand in, a footman had slammed the door on it. Her hand throbbed with pain, and she could feel blood oozing through her glove, but she kept up small talk with her Dizzy until they reached Westminster, held out her left hand to him rather than her right, and bade him good-bye. He was not to know—it could upset him just when he needed all his argumentative skills. Flaky when it was unimportant to be guarded, she had self-discipline when she needed it.

She was known to bring him, in a carriage, hampers of food for late dinner when debates in the House ran too long and on occasion to wait for her own dinner at Grosvenor Gate, complete to all her cherished china and silver, until adjournment in the small hours of the morning, so that they could be at the table together. Each lavished attentions on the other in both public and private to encourage the fantasy of a marriage of true love. He had married her for her money, Mary Anne would say, adding proudly, "Dizzy would have married me again for love." And Disraeli did leave the Tory celebration over the Reform Bill of 1867 to return to Mary Anne, who had ordered a steak-and-kidney pie and a bottle of champagne from Fortnum & Mason in Piccadilly. "My dear," he reportedly told her then, "you are more like a mistress than a wife." She was then in her seventies.

Later that year, when the University of Edinburgh conferred an honorary degree on him, he confided to Sir John Skelton how the marriage still thrived despite all the strains upon it. "We were so delighted with our reception, Mrs Disraeli and I," he wrote, "that after we got home we actually danced a jig (or was it a hornpipe?) in our bedroom."

Several versions exist of Disraeli's encounter with his M.P. colleague Bernal Osborne, known as the rudest man in England. "I saw you walking in the Park with Mrs Disraeli, Ben," Osborne began, "and I can't for the life of me understand what sentiment she can possibly inspire you with."

"A sentiment quite foreign to your nature, Bernal," said Disraeli. "Gratitude."

The frustrations of the 1856 session of Parliament had exhausted Disraeli, but as leader of his party in the House he had the awkward duty, considering its fortunes during the year, of the traditional summing-up address. There was little to say for his side. Hopeful anyway, he told Count Vitzthum, "Don't forget to come tomorrow evening to the House. The debate will be interesting as a prelude to the next session." The review was scheduled for Friday evening, July 26, and Disraeli made the mistake of speaking to Palmerston's strength, foreign policy. Given the war and associated matters, he had little choice, but he spoke in Metternich fashion of European stability, which meant opposing the dismemberment, in stages, of the Austrian empire by the unification of Italy and the encouragement of other nationalisms.

With sensitivities in Britain strained over border disputes between Canada and the United States, and suspicion about American expansionism toward the Pacific, Disraeli was also direct and realistic, although that meant ruffling some feathers in the House. The United States, he explained, was still "influenced by colonial tendencies; and when they come in contact with large portions of territory scarcely populated, or, at the most, sparsely populated by an indolent and unintelligent race of men"—such attitudes were entirely typical of the time, and irritated few sensibilities—"it is impossible, and you yourselves find it impossible, to resist the tendency to[ward] expansion; and expansion in that sense is not injurious to England, for it contributes to the wealth of this country."

Richard Henry Dana, Jr., an American lawyer and the author of *Two Years before the Mast*, had been a guest in the Lords to watch the feudal ceremony of James Parke's being received as Lord Wensleydale, including his swearing a series of oaths among which was one abjuring all claims of the long-dead Pretender James III to the throne of England. The Duke of Argyll had then escorted Dana into the Commons, where they watched an obviously tired Disraeli rise for his address. "It was not considered by his friends as one of his best efforts," Dana was told. "The country had been through a war, had got a reasonable peace; no party was prepared to take the Government if the present party were defeated, and he spoke to no practical purpose, and with no hope of result." What Dana did not know was that the party leader or his designate was expected, for better or for worse, to sum up the session, and he was, at the least, "a master of worrying and tormenting satire and invective, being all the while cool and deliberate himself." But Dana thought that Disraeli's closing effort to define Conservatism and the condition of political parties "was a failure," a view he found validated by Palmerston's response "in his usual easy, self-possessed, nonchalant, adroit fashion, with hat in hand, and a drawing room manner."

The session ended early, at about eight o'clock, and both Peelites and Derbyites repaired to their Club, which they still shared uneasily, for refreshment and gossip. For the anti-colonialist, anti-imperialist friends of Gladstone who made up the Peelite party, Disraeli had said all the wrong things—had "made a mess of it," Gladstone himself, loving obscure latinisms, wrote in his diary; "he was vilipended"—disparaged—"in the Carlton at n[igh]t."

"Nervous debility" was the reason Disraeli advanced to Mrs. Brydges Willyams for a sudden and secretive trip to Spa early in August. Taking the waters had never really interested him, but his departure immediately after the Parliamentary session attested to increasing despondency.

"I have not seen a newspaper in any language," he added, "for more than a month, and I did not tell our own household where we were going, so that we have not received a single letter." The lack of curiosity about politics was explained to Lady Londonderry. He had been "so lethargically disposed the whole year, that many things escaped my wearied life. . . . The suppressed gout, at which you laughed, at length, brought me here [to Spa], where, after five weeks, I have found renovation in its bright fountains, and brown baths of iron waters."

Gout was an all-inclusive term in midcentury for whatever physically disabled the limbs of a gentleman, and implied a surfeit of good wine and good food. In reality its cause was an excessive accumulation of uric acid in the body, and its complications beyond the agonizing pain included severe arthritis from deposits of uric acid crystals in the joints to kidney stones and renal failure. To alkalinize urine, Victorian physicians recommended ingesting large quantities of water, often with sodium bicarbonate, and the gouty well-to-do (with rare exceptions the ailment afflicted men) were recommended to watering places where diet could be regulated, baths could soothe aching limbs, and vast amounts of spring water could be imbibed. Railroads, Disraeli explained to Mrs. Brydges Willyams, had made the Belgian hot springs "like a second Pompeii" in the woods of the Ardennes, a place where one could choose society or privacy, as one pleased. A decompression chamber, it regulated the pace of life for the moneyed, and Disraeli lived intermittently as if he had no debts.

Late in September the Disraelis returned to Hughenden, then set out for what had become their autumnal visit to Sarah Brydges Willyams at Torquay. During a quiet autumn at Hughenden they saw only Charlotte de Rothschild and Lord and Lady Villiers, whose son's scandalous behavior and debts Disraeli—sophisticated in such matters—was helping them to work out.* Then he and Mary Anne went off to Paris, where they hoped that Napoleon III, another old friend, would see them. It was "indispensable" for an "imperial policy," he had explained to Lord Henry Lennox (October 31, 1856), to have good relations with France, a feeling he shared, he explained, with Lord Bolingbroke, "and the changes in the world . . . only confirm his prescience. With regard to the Emperor personally, there are many private, as well as public, reasons why I should wish to serve him."

Although Palmerston's pro-French leanings had been politically useful to him, Disraeli hoped to supplant him in the Emperor's affections not only on grounds of long association but by reminding him of the mortality tables. Visibly doddering— Palmerston often needed two sticks to be able to walk—he could not go on, Disraeli hoped, much longer. The trip was also a way

*Villiers would be 6th Earl of Jersey in 1859; Lady Jersey was one of Disraeli's hostesses from his dandy days in London.

DIS—ELI   G—DS—E

The Balancing Brothers of Westminster. *Punch*, February 28, 1857, on the Disraeli–Gladstone rivalry.

to avoid the company of Tory magnificoes who mingled at each other's country manors in the weeks leading up to Christmas and the new year. While to most of them he remained a suspect alien, Disraeli found their ideas close to those of King Canute. "As to Disraeli's unpopularity," Derby deplored to Malmesbury on December 15, "I see it and regret it; and especially regret that he does not see more of the party in private; but they could not do without him."

The Disraelis left for France on November 20, intending to remain through Christmas and into January. The years between visits to Paris seemed to have been, he wrote in a rare letter to his brother James (December 11, 1856) from the Hotel Brighton, "as long as the siege of Troy," and in an image he liked so much that he used it in a number of other letters, he added, "Paris is a beautiful woman and London is an ugly man." Wined and dined by Court and Society, he enjoyed himself as if he counted for something, but soon learned that from Napoleon's standpoint he commanded a very light brigade. At the Tuileries, he told James, "Mary Anne had the honor of sitting on the right hand of our Imperial host and I the scarcely less distinguished post of being next [to] the Empress"—whom he had earlier privately disparaged—"who was very agreeable and sparkled almost as much as her necklace of colossal emeralds and diamonds—as large as the precious stones in Aladdin's cave." The important part of the evening came afterward, when the Emperor invited him privately to converse "on grave matters," their substance left to James's imagination.

In reality there was little helpful substance. Disraeli proved unconvincing about Palmerston's staying power. "Lord Derby has no men," the Emperor said—and he included, by implication, Disraeli. A few months later he explained in confidence to Malmesbury that Disraeli, "like all literary men, . . . from Chateaubriand to Guizot, [is] ignorant of the world, talking well, but nervous when the moment of action arises." Perhaps covertly making his point, he held a grand banquet for Disraeli at the Palais Royal, where his guests met Alfred de Vigny ("the prettiest poet not only in verse but in person in Paris" had become "a corpulent, grey-headed oldish gentleman"), Alexandre Dumas *fils* ("a very handsome man . . . but inclining a little too much to embonpoint"), and Émile de Girardin (now "a white-headed man with large green goggle-eyed spectacles, a hideous guignol").

Late in January, Disraeli recrossed the Channel to prepare for the new session—and to prepare his income tax papers, about which he instructed Henry Padwick of Hill Street, Berkeley Square, not to communicate with him at Grosvenor Gate except in person, and in writing only at the Carlton Club. His income for the year, with that of Mary Anne, he noted for Padwick, was £4,798/11s./10d., and his debts—excluding what had been laid out for him for Hughenden—totaled £27,750.

The new Parliament began grimly for Disraeli. Lord Stanley, his closest associate, was being wooed by the other side, toward which his sympathies ran in any case, and Derby, his father, was, according to Lord Henry Lennox, "As a leader of a party, . . . *more* hopeless than ever! Devoted to Whist, Billiards, Racing, Betting, making a fool of himself with either Ladies Emily Peel or Mary Yorke." On February 2, 1857, Disraeli gathered about fifty Conservatives to review the text of the speech Palmerston had prepared for delivery by the Queen, and alluded mysteriously, Stanley noted, to certain disclosures which could bring down the Government. "By this day fortnight we shall be in office."

Nothing remotely like that happened. Disraeli, and even Gladstone, attacked the budget, suggesting that Peelites and Disraelites were acting in concert to bring Palmerston down, and their seemingly common ground emerged in other domestic areas, leading Disraeli to hope once more for reunion. Even *Punch* suggested that they were acting in concert, cartooning them in acrobat costume side-by-side, the budget between them, as "The Balancing Brothers of Westminster." But Gladstone quenched such expectations in a letter to Derby on February 14, in which he explained again that he and Disraeli could not co-exist in the same party. "I said," he noted in his diary, "that from motives which I could neither describe nor conquer I was quite unable to enter into any squabble or competition with him for the possession of a post of prominence," and he understood besides that Disraeli "could not be thrown away like a sucked orange."

Knowing nothing yet of Gladstone's objections to him, Disraeli began working over Palmerston on foreign policy matters, in particular over the basis for Tory pre-session optimism, which he now revealed to be a secret treaty of 1854 by which England guaranteed Austrian territories in Italy, a promise made to secure Vienna's support during the Crimean War. Palmerston accused Disraeli of "vapouring," but finally had to admit its existence, a success of a sort made possible through information furnished by a young man of twenty-two, Ralph Earle, who worked for the Foreign Office. Earle hoped he could bring the Ministry down, put in Disraeli and Derby, and earn his reward. Governments had fallen before on external embarrassments, but on matters not of mere policy but of war and peace; votes in the House had become close but not yet close enough.

Party strife was briefly suspended on March 4, 1857, when, at Gunnersbury, under the traditional *chupah,* Lionel de Rothschild's beautiful daughter Leonora was married, at nineteen, to her cousin, Baron Alphonse, future head of the French house. The band of the First Life Guards serenaded the couple at the wedding breakfast. The French ambassador offered the first toast. Lord John Russell followed. Then came Disraeli. "Under this roof," he said, "are the heads of the family of Rothschild—a name famous in every capital of Europe and every division of the globe—a family not more regarded for its riches than esteemed for its honor, integrity, and public spirit."

Seated among the wedding guests were M.P.s who continued to vote against seating their host on the benches of the House of Commons.

On the pretext of disapproval of a new military intervention in China to promote British commercial interests carefully not identified as the opium trade, the Government was defeated by sixteen votes, and Palmerston went to the people waving the Union Jack. To the electors at Tiverton, in an address meant for the newspapers, he declared, "An indolent barbarian, wielding authority at Canton, had violated the British flag, broken the engagement of treaties, offered rewards for the heads of British subjects." Disraeli countered with an attack on the "double-dealing" Prime Minister who occupied "a false position" in British politics: "He is the Tory chief of a Radical Cabinet" who masked his lack of direction at home with a "turbulent and aggressive" foreign policy.

While the General Election unfolded late in March, Disraeli wrote to the invisible Derby, "Our party is now a corpse, but it appears to me that, in the present perplexed state of affairs, a *Conservative public pledge to Parliamentary Reform,* a bold and decided course[,] might not only put us on our legs, but greatly help the country and serve the state." Further electoral reform was inevitable; why not promote it in an initiative that would enlarge the party's base? Derby wanted none of it.

Disraeli was returned unopposed, the only bright spot for him in balloting that altered no party alignments but added to

Palmerston's personal following. In a conversation with Stanley, who was more and more alienated from his father, Disraeli despaired of success with the Conservative Party as it was then led. Lord Derby, he felt, "really does not desire office, his health having of late become unequal to its fatigues." And he contended, in what seemed to Stanley a striking paradox, that the House of Lords, because of its passivity, had become "an ingeniously devised contrivance for lessening the power of the aristocracy."

Symbolic of how badly matters were developing for Disraeli was his encounter at the Carlton Club on the evening of May 3, as described by the Earl of Malmesbury, acting leader in the Lords for the ailing Derby. "I found Dizzy last night at the Carlton," he told Derby, "sitting at the table with the Duke of Buckingham. . . . It seems he had come up on business for an hour, and went in to speak to Taylor." (Colonel T. E. Taylor was then Chief Whip.) "You find me poisoned and robbed," Disraeli said. "God has made me blind." Instead of Taylor he had found the Duke, who "forces me to drink a bottle of champagne with him, which always makes me ill, and then borrows £50 of me." Champagne did not always make him ill, but lending money to a duke was difficult for a chronic debtor to stomach.

May was also the month of a left-handed literary compliment to Disraeli. A Post Office civil servant who had managed his first major success in fiction in 1855 with *The Warden*, a slight but entertaining novel about the rivalry for a provincial Anglican preferment, had now emerged with its more ambitious sequel, *Barchester Towers*, lauded as the cleverest novel of the season. It was the beginning of Anthony Trollope's long fictional campaign, both Whiggish and waggish, against the politician who happened to be also the author of *Coningsby* and *Tancred*.* One did not

*Late in 1852 the London firm of Sampson Low published a psychological novel by Herman Melville, *Pierre or, the Ambiguities*, which evidenced striking indebtednesses to Disraeli's autobiographical early novels from *Vivian Grey* and *Contarini Fleming* through *Henrietta Temple* and *Venetia*. Even *The Young Duke* and *Alroy* are mined in *Pierre*, which draws from Disraeli, without parody, characters, situations, and devices in such abundance that the author, had he known of the American novel, would have been flattered. But Disraeli then read few novels, and those largely French—Balzac and George Sand.

have to be familiar with either novel to recognize the author referred to when the ultra-Tory squire Wilfred Thorne considers the
unnamed Tory leader in the Commons untrustworthy and not
quite right to lead "the country party." And even readers of
Disraeli who rejected Trollope's racism were likely to be amused
by the history of Ethelbert Stanhope, the lazy son of the absentee
Barchester vicar who collects butterflies on Lake Como. Young
Bertie Stanhope goes to the Holy Land to convert the Jews, but
instead is converted to Judaism. "He again wrote home to say
that Moses was the only giver of perfect laws to the world . . . ,
that great things were doing in Palestine, and that he had met
one of the family of Sidonia, a most remarkable man, who was
now on his way to Western Europe. . . . This Sidonia, however,
did not take so strong a fancy to him as another of that family
once did to a young English nobleman [Tancred]. At least he provided him with no heaps of gold as large as lions; so the Judaised
Ethelbert was again obliged to draw on the revenues of the Christian Church."

In due course a letter arrives for the Rev. Dr. Vesey Stanhope
"from some member of the family of Sidonia, and politely requested the father to pay a small trifle of £700, being the amount
of a bill discounted in favour of Mr Ethelbert . . . and now overdue for a period of nine months." If Sidonia arrests the insolvent
Bertie, declares the irate vicar, "he must go through the courts."

In the month of May 1857 foreign policy would after all
bring political grief to Lord Palmerston, and from the turbulent
East—an event presaged, so superstitious folk thought afterward,
by the arrival of Brorsen's Comet in the European heavens. It began to be sighted on March 18, faintly visible to the naked eye,
and was confused in the popular press with the great comet of
1556, widely thought to be the reappearance of the great comet
of 1264, which was perhaps that of 975. Extrapolating the
292-year period between the last apparent sightings, it had been
expected in 1848, and when it failed to materialize, John Russell
Hind, a prominent London astronomer who had predicted it, began to offer estimates of gravitational perturbations upon it by
other planets that might have delayed the event, and several hys-

terics began circulating the prophecy that the comet's inevitable collision with the Earth would bring Doomsday on June 13, 1857.

"The world is very frightened about the comet," Disraeli remarked lightly to Sarah Brydges Willyams, "Dr Cumming having declared [that] the last day is certainly at hand; Sebastopol becoming Armageddon, yet it seems that Sebastopol literally means 'blessed city' and the received version of Armageddon is 'accursed plain': so they don't exactly agree." John Cumming, D.D., was an evangelistic Scot whose hellfire preaching had drawn such crowds that his church in Covent Garden had been expanded to seat a thousand. He had published *The Church before the Flood* and *Lectures on the Book of Revelation*, and was a philosopher, Disraeli scoffed, who had shocked the ladies who paid high pew rents for the privilege, "by his scientific announcement that the world has already been destroyed 27 times; that, reasoning by analogy, it must be destroyed again and probably often."

If the predicted catastrophe did not occur, Disraeli joked, he and Mary Anne would visit late in July, but "the misty tail of the comet would, if it touched us, pour forth an overwhelming deluge—so in 4 & 20 hours we may be shrivelled or drowned."

While Disraeli took theology more lightly in private than in public, he never undervalued religious feeling. Religion itself remained to him little more than the symbol of his heritage, as he explained, apparently to a clergyman, in a letter of which he preserved the draft at Hughenden. "For myself," he wrote, "I look upon the Church as the only Jewish institution that remains, and irrespective of its being the depository of divine truth, [I] must ever cling to it as the visible means which embalms the memory of my race, their deeds and thoughts, and connects their blood with the origin of things." Whatever his ambivalence toward Roman Catholicism, which he saw darkly as conspiratorial yet warmly as the conservator of useful ritual, he confessed "a certain reverence" for it as he had "for all churches which recognise the divine mission of the House of Israel." It was a paradox that he would be forced by politics to turn more and more to anti-ritualistic declarations, positions required by his party and his Queen.

High Church practice, allegedly aping the Church of Rome,

"sought refuge," he would claim in an 1870 preface to a new edition of his novels, "in medieval superstitions, which are generally only the embodiments of pagan ceremonies and creeds." Yet he admired the changelessness of the Roman Church, which remained close, he thought, to the ceremonials of the last Temple in Jerusalem—a link not to theology, but to an imagined racial aristocracy. Christianity in Dr. Cumming's apocalyptic form was merely vulgar and exploitative, while its Anglican form had a social, if not spiritual, value for gentlemen and ladies. But each, he argued, "owed its existence to a Jew," reason enough to respect the people of the source.

Another key to Disraeli's attitudes was his admiration for Joseph-Ernest Renan's *Vie de Jésus* (1863), which explained away as embellished natural events biblical miracles attributed to divinity. "I should like to know, from your bright mind & glowing pen," he wrote to Charlotte de Rothschild (August 21, 1863), recommending the book, "what you think of this work."

The advent of the new comet had prompted Dr. Cumming to prophesy, on the basis of his readings in Revelations, that the world would end in 1867, which was more encouraging than sometime in that June of 1857. But even nonbelievers were concerned, as it streaked faintly across the sky, that something almost as threatening to the status quo was already happening across the world in India, where on May 10 (people in England heard, finally, on June 26), a mutiny among Indian troops had erupted. Soon after came the news that General George Anson, military commander in India, was dead. To the long history of army mismanagement, incompetence, penuriousness, irresponsibility, and indifference, already the source of embarrassment in the Crimea, were added, in India, guilt on the scale of the subcontinent.

Under the cloak of a merchant company, Britain had, since the reign of Elizabeth, exploited teeming subject races in southern Asia. The East India Company, prospering under its feudal royal charter, was landlord and tax collector, and paid the bills for the army—made up of native troops and British officers—that maintained order. A cabinet minister in London oversaw the company directors, and its appointee, the Governor General, was actually designated by the Government, a confusion of ultimate authority which Disraeli had vainly tried to clarify only a few years earlier.

The mutiny arose when sepoy troops heard rumors that their new Enfield rifles used cartridges greased with beef fat—or, even worse, pork fat—to save farthings over the prescribed, and largely acceptable, mutton fat. Troops rejecting the defiled equipment—offensive to both Hindus and Muslims—had been court-martialed for insubordination, and other soldiers tried to free the men in fetters. The few English officers were incapable of keeping discipline; many were murdered, as were their families in military stations across India. Few of the facts were known as the first reports came over the long distances not yet linked by cable and telegraph, but Disraeli recognized the fruits of maladministration. "The rise and fall of empires," he declared in the House on June 27, "are not affairs of greased cartridges."

Nothing disturbed the sanctity of "the season." Fetes every night, Disraeli wrote to Mrs. Brydges Willyams, and illuminations in the park. Prince Frederick of Prussia was in London to visit his fiancée, Princess Victoria, "and young Princes and Princesses require balls." At first no one was aware of the death of Anson in India, and since he had been known as "the finest whist player in Europe," when the news came that the last of the Moghul monarchs, Bahadur Shah Zafar, had been put back on his throne in Delhi by the mutineers—he had been moved to a tame "Court" in Calcutta—"I said that for my part I had confidence in George Anson, because he had seen the Great Mog[h]ul so often on the ace of spades that he would know how to deal with him. All the world laughed very much, and Mrs Anson sent off the joke to the General. Alas! Alas!"

The Disraelis were still in London late in July. Thomas Carlyle took a Sunday carriage outing in Regent's Park on the 25th, to see the crowds—a hundred thousand, he estimated—forsaking Sabbatarian zeal to enjoy a "People's Band" playing from a conical tent ("vile opera trash, I suppose," he wrote to his wife). "Men, women, and children, all in their Sunday clothes, and quiet tho' lively, were moving, minutely incessantly, far and wide, on their green floor under the sky: poor souls, after all!" He approved of their success in finding a little band music to enjoy, whatever it was, since on a Sunday "all else was denied." In Kensington Gardens "Dizzy and his old Wife crossed me, out taking an after-dinner drive; they looked content, 'perfectly sated with revenge and food'. . . ."

Not realizing the extent of the Mutiny, as it came to be called, Palmerston took it at first casually. "I have many things I could say, if we were in your boudoir," Disraeli wrote to Lady Londonderry on July 31, "but India is a whirl-pool in which all merges, great or small. The season is over, but the Parliament will last a long time. Everybody is alarmed and shocked at the private tone of the government, which is flippant. Her Majesty [is] sorely oppressed."

In the Commons, he called for a new relationship between the people of India and "their real Ruler and Sovereign, Queen Victoria," and the end of the East India Company, and for "respect for their laws, their usages, their customs, and, above all, their religion, . . . and you will do as much as all your fleets and armies can achieve."

The Disraelis spent September and October at Hughenden, from which he told Lady Londonderry that he took "a gloomy view of affairs." They did not see Mrs. Brydges Willyams until November, India—rather than the comet—having intervened. A round of country houses followed while Palmerston's government belatedly prepared a bill to reform the administration of India, and troops sent from home as well as from China stations began to quell the uprisings.

One country squire unvisited was George Smythe. Withering away from tuberculosis, his legs and arms, he wrote to John Manners, "not larger than slate-pencils," Smythe died on November 9, at thirty-nine, while the Disraelis were in Torquay. The once fast-living Smythe had succeeded as Lord Strangford, a distinction that did him little good, and had married his mistress on his deathbed, giving her, Disraeli wrote, "The Coronet for a legacy." To his old Young England crony Smythe left a cup of Derbyshire spar,* about which Disraeli said to Sir William Fraser years after-

*Castleton "blue john" (from *bleu jaune*) fluorite.

ward, "It is not a great thing: but for a man to remember one at all at such a time is most gratifying."

As 1858 began, politics, even the passage of the India Bill, gave way to the wedding celebrations for the Princess Royal, a bride of seventeen, and her Prussian prince of twenty-seven. There were festivities in and out of Court, with guests in splendid accoutrements. Lord Stratford de Redcliffe, Disraeli told Lady Londonderry, "had on the finest coat that was ever seen since Joseph's jacket." And at Lionel de Rothschild's estate, Gunnersbury, at a different kind of royal gathering, the Disraelis met "all the illustrious exiles of France" and guests appropriate to them, including Cardinal Wiseman. The banquet could not have been surpassed in splendor at Windsor, and it was, Disraeli confessed to Lady Londonderry, "rather curious to dine with a Cardinal at Gunnersbury!" The revels continued for a week after the wedding on January 25. At a reception at St. James's Palace the Secretary of the American legation, Benjamin Moran, a student of the then fashionable pseudoscience of phrenology, stood next to Disraeli, "who has a much better head than I had supposed. Ideality is large, but he seems to lack analysis."

The India Bill had a majority of 145 on its first reading on the evening of February 18, 1858. Such majorities, and his return in the General Election, had made Palmerston careless. His Ministry was soon in bad odor because of the appointment of a friend of Lady Palmerston as Lord Privy Seal. The Marquess of Clanricarde lived his scandalous domestic life in public—a matter of small consequence during the Regency. Since Victoria's accession, Evangelicalism in the country and the tidying of morals at Court by Prince Albert had made a difference. The Prince Consort (as he now officially was) privately labeled Clanricarde "a reprobate." To make matters worse, after a failed attempt on the life of Napoleon III by an Italian who employed a bomb made in Birmingham, Palmerston demonstrated his solidarity with the Emperor by asking for sweeping conspiracy legislation that outraged his Whig and Radical supporters. On February 20, the bill was defeated by nineteen votes although 146 Conservatives of Peelite and Disraelite persuasion voted with Palmerston, who promptly resigned.

Despite the Tory votes that had nearly saved him, the Prime Minister was out, and from Buckingham Palace came an invitation to Lord Derby, who still hoped to evade Downing Street. That Saturday evening, after seeing the Queen, Derby sent a note to Disraeli explaining that since he had no majority in the House, she might wish to refuse acceptance of the government's resignation. Either way, he explained, "we have not declined office."

On Sunday, February 21, Victoria summoned Derby. Disraeli was again Chancellor of the Exchequer.

XVIII

"... THE FIELD OF BATTLE."

1858–1862

"THE HOUSE IS WILD AND CAPRICIOUS AT THIS MOMENT," DISRAELI reported to the Queen as he returned to his regular bulletins as leader of the Commons. Since she had asked, when he was last in that position, for what she "could not meet in newspapers," he was sending her "these rough notes, written on the field of battle."

The metaphors of March 1858 were appropriate, as the new Ministry began in acrimony—to which Disraeli contributed, making light of it when he could. Of an attack on the Government by Bernal Osborne, who had spoken rarely while his side was in power, the Chancellor of the Exchequer wrote on March 22 from his front bench that "after five years' silence" on Bernal's part, "his weapons were not as bright as of yore." Yet "the House, which was very full, became much excited. The Ministerial benches were in high spirit."

Contentiousness was unproductive for legislation, and there were arguments about India (Palmerston's bill was withdrawn and replaced), Ireland, France, Italy, a bill to permit marriage with a deceased wife's sister (attacked by the Church), and another to allocate funds for cleaning up the stench of the polluted Thames (which had made Westminster barely tolerable as the weather warmed). Disraeli's budget address in April suggested good-humoredly a group of small stamp taxes made palatable by the popularity and ubiquitousness of the Penny Post. "Now, so far as I can form an opinion on the subject from conversation with men of business, there is no mode of taxation more popular than the application of stamps to various operations of commerce. No one feels the burden of it. . . . People like to see vast results accomplished by slight means." To him that was Conservatism metamorphosed from principle into practice.

With spring, also, came what *The Times* had called the "annual pastime" of the Parliament in rejecting an oaths bill to permit the seating of Jews. Lionel de Rothschild had not been the only M.P. denied his seat. In 1851, David Salomons had been elected Whig M.P. for Greenwich. He refused to take the prescribed oath but insisted on his seat, and there he made a maiden speech for which he was fined £500 and was ejected. (On completion of the new Houses of Parliament in 1860, Salomons arranged to buy the seat that had proved so expensive. He put it in his billiards room at Broomhill.)

When Salomons was elected Lord Mayor of the City of London in 1855, an office over which the House of Lords exercised no jurisdiction, it was clear that change was inexorably coming to Parliament as well. Derby remained the barrier, inexplicably telling Disraeli that dropping the ban would lead to Jews in the Cabinet, and that he would not feel comfortable with a Jew as Chancellor of the Exchequer.

Disraeli himself had voted against bills that he thought amended the oaths process in an underhanded manner, earning opprobrium from some of the Rothschilds who felt that he had done Jews a disservice. In 1849, 1851, 1853, 1856, and 1857, he had voted for bills that explicitly removed Jewish disabilities. In 1858 he saw compromise with the Lords possible in the assertion of the Commons that it had the right to determine its own membership.

A new oaths bill had been passed in the session and promptly emasculated by the Lords, which eliminated the operative clause that would have seated a Jew. The Commons under Disraeli struck back by creating a committee to establish rationale for its restoration, and placing Lionel de Rothschild, reelected but still unsworn, on it. As a rearguard measure to cover his retreat, Derby proposed, and pushed through, a resolution which declared:

Without imputing any disloyalty or disaffection to Her Majesty's Subjects of the Jewish Persuasion, the Lords consider that the Denial and Rejection of that Saviour, in whose Name each House of Parliament daily offers up its collective Prayers for the Divine Blessing on its Councils, constitutes a moral unfitness to take part in the Legislation of a professedly Christian Community.

While some in the Lords might be excused in the light of contemporary thinking that non-Anglicans should not legislate upon matters relating to the Established Church, Parliamentary seats had already gone to Romanists and others. Even antediluvian reasoning required some logic, and rationalizations were fast fading, but for the intent to deter the Crown, if only a little longer, from creating the first Jewish peer. What the resolution accomplished in the summer of 1858 was to end resistance in one House to the determination of the other. On July 1 Derby announced his support of a proposal by the Earl of Lucan, who represented Disraeli and Russell in the matter, to give each House the authority to alter its own oath. According to Greville, the Prime Minister supported the compromise "sulkily and reluctantly," and resorted to "all sorts of paltry shifts and pretences . . . to make the sacrifice of their old prejudices somewhat palatable, or rather less painful and mortifying to his Party." Even so, many of Derby's colleagues refused, barely enough of them joining the Opposition to secure passage. It was not an edifying spectacle for the leader of the Lords and Prime Minister, but he headed a party long pledged to resisting legislation.

Disraeli's inability to carry more than a few grudging Conservatives with him remained an embarrassment. When "Mrs Dizzy" dined at the Mayer de Rothschilds, Lionel wrote on July 18 to Charlotte (then in the country) that Mary Anne insisted upon "how much Dizzy had done for us and how angry he was because we wouldn't believe it."

"For eleven years," said Charlotte in relief, "we've had the M.P. question screaming in every corner of the house." Now the die-hards had been bypassed, and on July 26, 1858, her husband was quietly sworn in, shaking hands with Disraeli on his way to his seat. He would be followed by David Salomons in 1859, Sir Francis Goldsmid in 1860, Nathaniel de Rothschild and Frederick Goldsmid in 1865, and Julian Goldsmid in 1866. None represented Disraeli's own party, which would not elect a Jew until Saul Isaac sat for Nottingham in 1874.

Overcoming the inertia of his party was Disraeli's perennial problem. Even the annual summer stench of the Thames, now worse than ever and attributed by some to the newest comet discovered by Giambattista Donati—the brightest of the six associated with the Florentine astronomer—did not move Parliament to action until the thermometer moved above eighty degrees, which was tropical for London. *The Times* reported on July 3 that "the Chancellor of the Exchequer . . . with a mass of papers in one hand and with his pocket handkerchief clutched in the other, and applied closely to his nose, with body half bent, hastened in dismay from the pestilential odour, followed closely by Sir James Graham, who seemed to be attacked by a sudden fit of expectoration; Mr Gladstone also paid particular attention to his nose." The aroma of the sewers finally guaranteed Disraeli bipartisan support for a bill to clean up what he described in introducing it as the "Stygian pool reeking with ineffable and intolerable horrors." The bill authorized the Metropolitan Board of Works to raise rates—always a politically sensitive matter but now less sensitive than Parliamentary noses—to finance a comprehensive drainage system. The task, causing chaos in London traffic, would take until the mid–1870s to complete and inspire future calls for early adjournment.

To Tory Whip Sir William Jolliffe, Henry Drummond—a

Neanderthal to the end—complained, "Lord Derby and Mr
Disraeli have led the Conservative Party to adopt every measure
they opposed as Radical ten years ago. They have made their
party the tool of their own ambition. . . . I do not think it cred-
itable to the intelligence or honour of the Country Gentlemen of
England to vote black to be white, or white to be black at their
bidding."

Apart from personal animus and the prompting of
ambition—Palmerston and Russell, the Opposition leaders, were
now hoary with age—it was not difficult to see why Gladstone resisted yet another effort to draw him into the Conservative orbit.
This time—it was prior to the final "Jew Bill" debates—Disraeli
was less than helpful. Seconding Derby's invitation to Gladstone
to "assume at this time a commanding position" in the party and
the Ministry, Disraeli wrote (May 26, 1858), "Thus you see, for
more than eight years, instead of thrusting myself into the foremost place"—he was suggesting that he might have ousted Derby
on grounds of incapacity—"I have been, at all times actively prepared to make every sacrifice of self for the public good, which I
have thought identical with your accepting office in a Conservative Government. Don't you think the time has come when you
might deign to be magnanimous?" The question struck a harsh
note, although Disraeli would tell Bishop Wilberforce in 1862, "I
almost went on my knees to him." But that genuflection was not
to Gladstone's ambitions. Disraeli had already made it clear that
if he relinquished his leadership in the Commons "to overcome
all difficulties," it would only be to a third party, Sir James Graham, whose parliamentary skills he admired, but who, most im-
portantly, was not Gladstone.

To Disraeli, Gladstone responded vaguely yet negatively the
same day about "the handsomeness of your conduct," but seeing
no likely arrangements that would make his crossing the aisle
"worth a trial." Confessing less than the truth he added, "You
consider that relations between yourself & me have proved the
main difficulty in the way of certain political arrangements—will
you allow me to assure you that I have never in my life taken a
decision which turned upon them." To Derby he replied only that
he saw "no public advantage" in his changing sides "single-

handed," and Derby could find no approach, he explained to Disraeli, "which should not be either an insult" to Gladstone "or a degradation to us." Approaches to Aberdeen and others to join with Gladstone failed, and the only solution Derby and Disraeli could think of was to thrust Gladstone out of harm's way— physically. They would offer him, appealing to his deep interests in Homer's Greece, the post of Lord High Commissioner of the Ionian Islands, a British protectorate since 1815 and rife with agitation for union with Greece. The idea had been that of Bulwer-Lytton, who had accepted the Colonial Office under Derby and considered Gladstone's appointment a "masterstroke." But his offer of constitutional reform was spurned by the islanders, and he would return in March 1859 to further overtures from Derby, all of which he rejected.

Gladstone now had a new reason to distrust any government in which Disraeli was involved. Having filched papers that embarrassed Palmerston, a young man named Ralph Earle was the Chancellor of the Exchequer's new private secretary. Ambitious, ingratiating, and possessed of a conspiratorial view of politics much like that of his chief, Earle at twenty-two was a Vivian Grey figure mirroring Disraeli at the same age. Unable to learn from his own experience, Disraeli would even send the young intriguer off on a delicate mission to Napoleon III.

Early in the next year, writing about his shaky Government and the services of Ralph Earle, Disraeli told Mrs. Brydges Willyams, "No language can convey to you the absorbing character of my life. It is that of a general in the field, and the sense of responsibility prevents one from doing anything but what is a fulfillment of pressing and immediate duty. I have two excellent private secretaries, both young men, and very good-looking and clever. The first secretary, Mr Earle, has been returned to Parliament [from Berwick], tho' he is only 23, but a man in matured thought and power of observation. Without his assistance I could not get thro' my work." The other secretary was Charles Ryan, officially a Treasury clerk and, as Disraeli would discover, more reliable than Earle.

Seeing foreign affairs as his own route to the top at a time of new tensions with France over Austria and Italy, Earle pushed

Disraeli into interfering beyond his cabinet office, straining relations with Derby and Malmesbury. Disraeli also promoted an India Bill to allay the Queen's concerns that royal prerogatives
would be undermined. It was a beginning, he assured her in language foreshadowing the imperial decade of the 1870s, "only the
ante-chamber of an imperial palace," and in future, he urged,
"the name of your Majesty ought to be impressed upon their native life" through "institutions, forms and ceremonies."

A means of enlarging the electorate in a Conservative direction, Derby had been brought to think, would be a new reform
bill, but in consultations with his own faction and the Opposition
over a "moderate" extension of the franchise, he found little
agreement. Although the Bill of 1859 would be derided as
"change without progress," it did offer the vote to possessors of a
modest amount of personal property, to university graduates, to
various previously excluded professionals. It also disintegrated
Derby's Cabinet, as Tories who preferred no change and no progress resigned. Some, like Bulwer-Lytton, used the excuse of
health, and Disraeli already knew when he and Mary Anne went
off to Torquay and Sarah Brydges Willyams over the Christmas
holidays that his days in Downing Street were again numbered.

His final visit of the ministry with Victoria and Albert was
a long weekend at Windsor, with work in the mornings, audiences in the afternoons, and, Disraeli wrote to Sarah Brydges
Willyams on January 21, 1859, "a band at dinner, bagpipes after
dinner, and a complete orchestra in the evening." Victoria and
Albert were hosts "who have the art of conversation, and who, as
they know everything that is interesting, can entertain without
compromising their dignity." What Disraeli evaded saying was
that their public dignity required a stiff morality that would have
delighted Bishop Wilberforce and would have been gloomy even
for Gladstone. Among the guests was the exiled duc d'Aumale,
with whom Disraeli had last dined at the Lionel de Rothschilds.
In a letter to Mrs. Brydges Willyams, Disraeli described the duke
and Albert as "the two most cultivated minds I ever met, & men,
too, of great abilities." Chatting with the Prince, the duke mentioned Julius Caesar, and was full of superlatives. "The most complete character of antiquity," d'Aumale claimed excitedly,

forgetting that to the dour Albert, Caesar had dallied, at the very least, with Cleopatra.

"But a very debauched man," deplored the Prince Consort.

For Mrs. Brydges Willyams, her eminent correspondent, the closest thing to a foster son she had, was her entrée into the lives of the high and mighty.

Disraeli interleaved tales of courts and castles with vignettes of the Hughenden Manor she would never see. The most vivid pictures of life at Hughenden come from Disraeli's letters to her: his arising at seven to work before breakfast, his walks in his beloved woods—while he would plant trees, Gladstone spent his own leisure at Hawarden chopping down trees—his delight in the peacocks which flaunted their plumage on his terrace, his repairing to his library to indulge a love of books almost as intense as his father's, his entertaining grand political friends and those like the Rothschilds he liked to think were almost family.

The link that had led Sarah Brydges Willyams to him, and a subject that arose often in their letters, was their Jewish ancestry, which both claimed from Spain, Disraeli imaginatively—a wish-fulfilment fantasy for which his evidence was the Lara family, linked to his own, but not to him. His elderly admirer also had a Lara connection and preferred to think that it related her to the Spanish—yet Jewish—aristocratic house of the Laras. That allegedly shared heritage was, Disraeli intimated, "the mysterious sympathy wh[ich] now binds us together," and such speculations gave some zest to her isolated life in Torquay, leading her in 1859 to request Disraeli's help in having a coat of arms embodying her heritage authorized by the College of Arms. She even dropped her married name in favor of her Sephardic one, sending him a French biography of Napoleon inscribed, "The Right Hon. B. Disraeli, from his devoted friend Sarah Mendez da Costa."

Indulging her, Disraeli communicated with the Spanish and Portuguese ambassadors to determine the heraldic symbols borne by the Mendez da Costa and Lara families. The months of negotiations turned into years, and on March 20, 1862, he wrote to her that he could do no more. Content with the results, she responded three days later that she hoped that on her death, as her proper heir, he would assume the names—and arms—of both Lara

and Mendez da Costa. Although country gentlemen and the nobility had often added to their names, or even changed them, as
a stipulation of inheritance, Disraeli understood that in his case
it would be political death. He decided to ignore the matter.

Neither Mrs. Brydges Willyams nor Disraeli had much use
for theology, but they shared an interest in how religion impacted
upon people. Their letters often touched upon the subject. Writing about a harvest festival at Hughenden attended by farmers
and their families, and even by Rothschilds, Disraeli would make
light of the Anglican connection. "The Clergy are at the bottom
of this movement; it connects the harvest with religion, & the
Church," he explained to her. "Even a *dissenting* farmer can
scarcely refuse to walk in the procession on such an occasion.
Unconsciously, all [such fetes] are reviving pagan rites & restoring the Dionysiac festivals!" A "great Roman Catholic lady," he
wrote on another occasion, had asked him why, since so many ordained clergy were incapable of stirring a congregation, actors
were not employed to preach. "You know," he confided, "I
thought her remarks [were] unanswerable—& I did not much
care to prove she was wrong."

Early in February, the Cabinet decided upon packaging Reform in two bills, so that each would not prejudice the other.
While the mild proposals dragged through the Commons toward
inevitable defeat, Derby was again away nursing his gout. Another General Election in May settled nothing, as a gain of
twenty seats barely kept the minority Conservatives in office.
Charges of ballot-buying gathered more newspaper columns than
did the campaigns or candidates. According to Malmesbury the
French Minister to London, the duc de Persigny (the "Duke of St
Angelo" in Disraeli's *Endymion*), helped subsidize the friends of
Lord Palmerston. Derby himself contributed an alleged £20,000 to
the Conservative funds, suggesting that despite his earlier diffi-
dence he now liked being Prime Minister. Later in the Lords he
explained that parties customarily assisted impecunious candidates, a revelation to Disraeli, who had never received such funds
in the days when he did not run, as now, unopposed.

It was a trying time for him, and he suffered from insomnia
until Mary Anne located some laudanum (a tincture of opium) to

help him relax. It soothed his head, he acknowledged to her from his front bench in the House. Tenuously, the Tories remained in office until Lord John Russell found a combination to bring them down. Disraeli reported to Victoria on June 11 that the "majority against your Majesty's servants" was thirteen. That Saturday morning Derby resigned.

The night before the crucial division, unaware that Russell and Palmerston had cut a deal that each would serve under the other, depending upon whom the Queen might choose, Disraeli came up with a last-resort strategy to save the Tories. He and Derby would both retire in favor of Stanley, who was Liberal-minded beyond what each of his seniors conceived, and who might bring Liberals and even Radicals into a Government more stable than any in decades. Only thirty-three and without the ambitions of a younger Pitt, Stanley claimed unreadiness for high office, and Victoria reached for Palmerston. At Derby's request she signed a warrant to give Disraeli a pension. Derby received the Garter, Malmesbury the Grand Cross of the Bath, and other friends of Derby pocketed outgoing peerages and baronetcies. Disraeli could claim a parting patronage appointment that was an indirect acknowledgment to Art. Out of respect for the historical painter Benjamin R. Haydon, who had committed suicide in 1846, his son Frederic, who had left the Navy for the Civil Service, was named subinspector of factories at Halifax in Yorkshire. The elder Haydon, Disraeli knew, had never cared much for him.

Palmerston's new Ministry included, in Disraeli's former post, the eager Gladstone. The appointment implicitly recognized his status as heir-apparent of a Liberal Party now firmly amalgamated with onetime Whigs, Peelites, Radicals, and dissident Derbyites. The politics of the future was in place.

As usual when Parliament went into autumn hibernation, Disraeli returned to Hughenden, this time to console himself in the bosom of his woodlands and shelves of books. There were also country houses to visit, including the necessary trip to Derby's gloomy pile, Knowsley, and then by rail to Manchester, to address an audience of six thousand in the Mechanics' Institute, in the familiar Free Trade Hall, on the values of education. Every man, he declared, had to make it his business in life to be prepared to seize his opportunity when it came. He might have added, using his own case, to be ready, if that failed, for the next opportunity, and then the one after that.

Nearly fifty-five, Disraeli felt more spent than his years. Almost his only real happiness out of office was his increasing closeness with the Rothschilds, who accepted the political necessity of his peculiar views and admired his tenacity and courage. Lionel de Rothschild and his family not only visited, but spent two days at Hughenden, bringing with them from France, Disraeli told Mrs. Brydges Willyams, "a dessert from Paris," made with peaches and melons. "I gave a dinner to the neighbourhood the second day, that he might meet the notables—& [eat] his dessert."

After a visit to Pynes—the Northcotes had determined to have their neighboring notables meet the memorable Mary Anne—the Disraelis went to London, where Baron de Rothschild was entertaining the Austrian and French ambassadors. They returned to Hughenden just in time to be summoned to the bedside of Sarah D'Israeli. Not expecting to find Sarah dying, Mary Anne

The library at Hughenden.

went to St. Leonards ahead of Ben, then sent for him. Sarah had suffered an apparent stroke. "Language cannot describe what this sudden, & by me never contemplated catastrophe has meant," he wrote to his brother Ralph. "She was the harbor of refuge in all the storms of my life, & I had hoped she w[oul]d have closed my eyes!" In September at Hughenden she had appeared frail and failing. With the death of her father and Benjamin's reliance on Mary Anne, purpose had drained from existence. Like another Sarah close to her brother, she was a bystander at another's life, but Mrs. Brydges Willyams had already experienced a life of her own.

Failing, after the *Hartlebury* co-authorship venture with Ben, to find any direction, from poetry and fiction to biblical explication for children, Sarah D'Israeli had settled into being editor and amanuensis for her father, then into moving aimlessly from place to place. She would see various Rothschilds on visits to Grosvenor Gate and Hughenden, and once, in 1858, Charlotte de Rothschild had sent Sarah, then at Ledbury in Herefordshire, a religious work of her own, *Addresses to Young Children: Originally Delivered in the Girls' Free School, Bell Lane*, sermons that would have been described then as of "an improving nature." Sarah responded, "I have read your little volume with sympathy & admiration; the tone of tenderness which pervades the Addresses & their devout and elevated feelings must touch the hearts of all of every creed. I had the gratification to read one aloud last Evening (on the holiness of the Sabbath) & its piety and eloquence deeply touched my auditors"—who, she went on to explain, put aside their farming implements in the long early autumn twilight to listen. The picture of the Baroness de Rothschild's *Shabbat* prayer being read by a D'Israeli, however Christianized, to Herefordshire farmers, encapsulates the alienation of the lonely Victorian spinster, dead and almost unmourned at fifty-seven.

To Lady Londonderry, on December 12, Disraeli had described arriving at the bedside, in Twickenham, of his "nearest & dearest relative," who was "soon, most unexpectedly and suddenly, to be lost to us!" For Sarah there had been only Ben and Mary Anne. She had disapproved of James's "irregular" life, and he and Ralph had drifted away. She had been "a person of great intelligence and charm"—wasted assets in her milieu—doomed (although her brother did not intend that meaning in his words) to be only "the soul of a house and the angelic spirit of a family." On the 17th, he wrote to Mary Anne, whose place he had taken at the deathbed, that Sarah was conscious "but seems dozing," unaware that she was "sinking fast." Two days later she was dead. The anxiety left Mary Anne, ten years Sarah's elder, with a severe attack of sciatica and unable to attend the interment at Willesden Cemetery, Paddington.

On Christmas Day, 1859, writing on black-edged mourning paper, Disraeli thanked Lord John Manners for his expression of sympathy. Sarah had been, he said, his "first & ever-faithful friend!" He had played out his life for her in his letters, and she had responded that he was "the only thing in my life that has never disappointed me." She had seen her brother's idealization of her in the Miriam of *Alroy* and the Eva of *Tancred*, and their "mystical" relationship would be celebrated in the Myra of *Endymion*. On a visit to the house "where we lived so long together, and so fondly!" Myra confides, "All I have desired, all I have dreamed, have come to pass, Darling; beloved of my soul, by all our sorrows, by all our joys, in this scene of our childhood and bygone days, let me give you my last embrace." Twenty years after her death, it was, through the medium of fiction, Benjamin's last embrace of Sarah.

Later, Sarah's role in the splintered family was made clear in a letter to Ralph. "We have never had a line from you since yr visit here," Benjamin wrote on December 5, 1860, "—& of course, we never hear from James. This is not the way to keep the family together—poor darling Sa's last hope and prayer."

On January 24, 1860, barely a month after Sarah's death, Parliament went back into session. Disraeli had been at Grosvenor Gate for nearly three weeks, preparing the politics of Opposition and discovering how peripheral his role would be. Seeing no practical way of unsettling the new alignment, Derby agreed informally not to contest Palmerston's dominance. To Disraeli went instructions, on January 12, 1860, to "keep the present men in and resist all temptations to avail ourselves of a casual majority." Disraeli protested that "you cannot keep a large army in order without letting them sometimes smell gunpowder."

No passable reform bill seemed likely from the other side. Too many politicians in the new Government were at ideological odds, and Palmerston himself seemed to Disraeli a Tory in Whig clothing. The promised legislation, he told Mrs. Brydges Willyams on March 24, resembled Isambard Kingdom Brunel's great iron ship, 693 feet long and five times the size of the biggest vessel then afloat, nearing completion at the Isle of Dogs in the Thames: "The New Reform Bill is like 'The Great Eastern' & sticks in its stays. It will not be launched, & if it ever do[es] float, I think it will founder."

Although the mighty vessel did get to sea and laid the first Atlantic telegraph cable, it was a financial loss for its backers, who included Napoleon III. The Reform Bill of 1860 was less successful, but its failure did not quell doubts about Disraeli's own generalship. In the influential *Quarterly Review* for April 1860, Lord Robert Cecil continued his attacks on Disraeli, already begun venomously in July 1858, when he announced, "There is no escape on earth for man from taxes, toothache, or the statesmanship of Mr D'Israeli." His party's leader, he charged, supported the dangerous creed of democracy, in which "two day-labourers shall outvote Baron Rothschild" (who, unlike Cecil, supported electoral reform).

Inured to personal abuse, Disraeli told journalist Francis Espinasse on March 6, 1860, "My life, since I emerged from the crowd, has been passed in a glass house, tho' its windows have often been broken." The new *Quarterly* was a rock through yet another window, Cecil characterizing Disraeli as a failed leader. "He had never led the Conservatives to victory, as Sir Robert Peel had led them to victory. He had never procured the triumphant assertion of any Conservative principle, or shielded from ruin any ancient institution." Instead, he had made "any Government, while he was in opposition, next to an impossibility," and his political tactics were "shameless." Cecil's father, 2nd Marquis of Salisbury, had berated him for his invective, and Lord Robert had replied (July 26, 1859), "I have never concealed my opinion of Mr D'Israeli. . . . So far as I have been able to ascertain by conversation

I do not think my opinion is at all singular on our side of the House of Commons." Why he wrote at all for money, and in a sensational style to attract attention, he had explained earlier. His father had disapproved of Robert's marriage and refused to support his son's family in Salisbury style. He had "no other means of gaining money on which I have any ground for relying except writing," and he had to produce what he could "sell."

His daughter (and biographer) attributed his manic-depressive nature to "hereditary infirmity," but its anti-Semitic aspect had more to do with his milieu and his ultra–High Church leanings. On Easter Day, 1861, he wrote to a Parliamentary ally, Lord Carnarvon, that "Dizzy" seemed, during the current session (despite the new *Quarterly* article that charged otherwise), "converted from evil ways. . . . I am beginning to incline to the belief that he really has been baptized."

Seeking a Parliamentary strategy, Disraeli had written to Malmesbury in February 1861—when the Earl was acting in the Lords again for the ailing Derby—that the best Conservative cause in domestic politics would be to maintain the primacy of the Established Church. That alone may have moved Cecil a few inches in Disraeli's direction. Conflicts between the Anglican clergy and the burgeoning, activist Dissenting churches had been growing, especially over the education of the young and the taxation of non-Anglicans to support parish churches from which they dissented. Despite such highly visible Anglican adherents as Gladstone, Liberals were also the defenders of other faiths. Disraeli saw political benefits in being the party of the Church. But Malmesbury told Ralph Earle, if the conspiratorial private secretary is to be believed, "We shall never get on until we get rid of Disraeli."

The "noisy Parliamentary fights," Disraeli told Mrs. Brydges Willyams, were merely "sham battles." Reform had been shelved by Palmerston, and the Conservatives agreed, Greville charged in his diary, only in "their undisguised dislike of their leader." That perception was lost on Mary Anne, who told Sarah Brydges Willyams on May 6, 1860, that except for Lord Robert Cecil, who remained angry "because Dizzy did not give him office," her husband "never was so popular with his party." Yet its representatives were no longer bothering to be present in Parliament. Lord Stanley noted in his diary: "Talk with D[israeli]; he lamented the apathy of the country gentlemen, said it was impossible to induce them to attend, even where their own interests were concerned." Little had changed, Disraeli admitted. Except to go hunting, "many men of large income . . . seldom stirred beyond their estates."

Considering the reactionary views of most old Tories, Stanley thought, their absence was "not much to be regretted. Nevertheless, it is unsatisfactory to see the opposition benches completely bare, except the front bench, from 7 to 10 every night, unless an important party division is likely. . . . The real work of the House is done by less than 200 out of 654 members; and of these the majority are either liberals of the middle class, or officials past and present." The only Conservative without a party position who attended regularly, he noted, was Richard Spooner, "now 80 years of age: and he is a banker, not a squire."

As Derby, at sixty-two and in increasingly poor health, not only failed to lead the party but, when he did, failed to recognize the temper of the times, his son worried about the stagnation of the party and of his own future. Stanley saw himself as unambitious, and "the only other possible chief is Disraeli, with whom I have been long allied: . . . old habit has drawn us together, and I admire his perseverance not less than his talent; but how can I reconcile his open ridicule, in private, of all religions, with his preaching of a new church-and-state agitation? Or how can I help seeing that glory and power, rather than the public good, have been his objects? He has at least the merit, in this respect, of being no hypocrite." As for other Tories who had held office or aspired to it, Stanley saw little more than mediocrity, a view in which Disraeli concurred, observing to Mrs. Brydges Willyams that although the country was "thoroughly Conservative," it had "little confidence in Conservative statesmen."

Stanley's musings of November 30, 1861, were set down as the Disraelis were on their annual late autumn round of visits, the most important to Frances Anne, Marchioness of Londonderry, now sixty-one. Life for her had gone very sour with the death of her husband and the war neurosis of her son, who was now beyond recovery. From Seaham Hall on December 8 Disraeli wrote to Torquay about the remarkable woman who ran her mines and blast furnaces and steamships on the edge of the North Sea. Although she had a "palace in a vast park," Wynyard, twenty miles to the west, Lady Londonderry preferred to transact business "with innumerable agents" from the office building that flew her flag—"and I remember her five-and-twenty years ago, a mere fine lady; nay, the finest in London! But one must find excitement, if one has brains."

While the Disraelis were traveling south from Seaham, newspapers were reporting the dread news that Prince Albert was dying. That summer the Prince Consort had seemed pale and unwell as he presided over ceremonies to which the Queen, still mourning the death of her mother, the Duchess of Kent, in March, felt unequal. "Am ill, feverish, with pains in my limbs, and feel very miserable," was a typical entry in Albert's diary at the time, and he had told his brother Ernest, the Duke of Coburg, the previous year that he would soon be dead. Before his contracting, so his doctors declared in early December, typhoid fever, he had told Victoria, *"Ich hänge gar nicht am Leben."* He did not "cling to life," and if he came down with severe illness, which he apparently knew he had, he would "give up at once." He may have recognized the symptoms of inoperable cancer, to which the pneumonia or typhoid he suffered at the end was only secondary.

In a darkened room at the Castle on December 14, the Prince's life ebbed away. Concerns about the Civil War in America—averting English intervention in the conflict had been among Albert's last efforts—faded temporarily from London newspapers. The news reached Disraeli at the home of Mrs. Brydges Willyams. He wondered about "into whose hands" the unreliable Prince of Wales might fall and about the future of the Queen, who had "long shown indications of a nervous and excitable disposition." Victoria had long been dependent upon Albert's advice on matters "small or great," Disraeli knew. "I have myself . . . heard him at dinner, suggest to her in German to enquire about this, that, and the other: and the questions never failed to follow. . . . The worst consequence possible is one, unluckily, not unlikely: that without being absolutely incapacitated for affairs, she may fall into a state of mind in which it will be difficult to do business with her, and impossible to anticipate what she will approve or disapprove."

Hurrying back to London, Disraeli saw the Saxon ambassador, Count Vitzthum, to whom he confided: "With Prince Albert, we have buried our Sovereign. This German Prince has governed England for twenty-one years with a wisdom and energy such as none of our Kings has ever shown." Albert had foreshadowed the possibilities of modern monarchy, Disraeli thought. "If he had outlived some of our 'old stagers' "—Disraeli may have had Palmerston and Russell in mind—"he would have given us, while retaining all constitutional guarantees, the blessings of absolute government."

In weeds and widow's cap, the hysterical Queen had been hurried off to Osborne, the funeral in Wolsey's Chapel at Windsor held without her. Mourning fittings everywhere exhausted supplies of black drapery throughout the kingdom, with fresh shipments of cotton from America doubtful as a result of the blockade of Confederate ports by the Union. Christmas was darkened, but the new session of Parliament was not delayed. It was now vital to open both Houses with addresses to the late Prince's memory, and both sides—through Palmerston, Derby, Granville, Russell, and Disraeli—gave expression "in a becoming manner" as Count Vitzthum put it "to the feeling of irreparable loss." Palmerston observed that it was no exaggeration to say that if the word *perfect* could be applied to any person, given acknowledged human imperfection, the Prince Consort had earned that description.

Disraeli's address pointed to the Prince's long, failed battle in Parliament over the rank to which his status entitled him, ended finally by Victoria with her own Letters Patent. It was a paradox, said the leader of the Opposition, that Albert had been "the prime councillor of a realm the constitution of which did not recognise his political existence." Albert, he added, had also contributed to national culture not only in detecting its absence. "He resolved to supply it," said Disraeli, thinking in particular of the Great Exhibition of 1851, a revolutionary event in the transmission of technology and culture.

The Prince Consort was no mere facade, Disraeli concluded. "His contributions to the cause of the state were far more powerful. . . . He gave to it his thought, his time, his toil; he gave to it his life." And turning to the members of the House who had worked on "great undertakings" with the Prince, he asked, "without fear of a denial, whether he was not the leading spirit, whether his was not the mind which foresaw the difficulty, his not the resources which supplied the remedy; whether his was not the courage which sustained them under apparently overpowering difficulties; whether everyone who worked with him did not feel that he was the real originator of those plans of improvement which they assisted in carrying into effect."

After reading the texts of the addresses, Victoria asked her private secretary, Sir Charles Phipps, to compliment Lord Derby on his words in the Lords. Then Phipps added, "The Queen would be glad that Mr Disraeli should also be made aware of H.M.'s grateful sense of his testimony to the worth and character of the Prince—perhaps as discriminating in the characteristics pointed out, and certainly as eloquent in the language employed, as any of those beautiful and glorious orations."

To Sir Charles, Disraeli conveyed his thanks to the Queen on February 9, 1862. "What I attempted to express on Thursday night," he wrote, "I deeply felt. During those conversations with which, of late years, the Prince occasionally honored me, I acquired much, both in knowledge and in feeling, which will ever influence my life." In implicit reply, Victoria sent him engravings of herself and the Prince.

Two weeks later, talking to Lord Stanley, Disraeli raised, when the Princes's name came up, a favorite image—he liked to find links to his mythical connections to Venice—about weak republics under a weak nominal ruler. "A few years more [under Albert], and we should have had, in practice, an absolute monarchy: now all that is changed and we shall go back to the old thing—the Venetian constitution—a Doge."

THE
HIGH
GAME
1862–1874

XIX

"... MIRAGES THAT RISE UP BEFORE THE POLITICAL EYE."

1862–1866

"I KNOW THAT IN OPPOSITION, MEN DO INDULGE IN DREAMS," Disraeli recalled in Parliament in 1879. "I have had experience of Opposition, and I hope it has left me it may be a wiser even if a sadder man. I know that there are mirages that rise up before the political eye which are extremely delightful and equally decep-tive." In the early 1860s he saw mirages of new ministries, and he dreamed of opportunities beyond Palmerston, who seemed, as he approached eighty, ageless and immortal, and beyond the gout-disabled Derby, who threatened almost daily to betake himself of his deathbed. The House of Commons, where Tories appeared to be a perpetual minority, was an unsatisfying stage, and Disraeli looked forward to each retreat to Hughenden. "I am an actor without an audience," he told Mrs. Brydges Willyams, now past ninety and also apparently immortal.

In Parliament his allies were few. He was blamed for Derby's apathy, for the failure to recruit Gladstone, for being his alien self. Yet, while the Tory squirearchy disliked him for not being like them, his party enemies detested him because as leader he represented them. "We have not an idea in common," the eponymous hero of Disraeli's Lothair (1870) would say of the squires he felt obligated to invite "to slaughter his grouse." Yet lumping him with the fox-hunting, deer-stalking, fowl-shooting aristocracy whose pursuits disgusted Disraeli, John Ruskin railed ignorantly to Charles Eliot Norton in Massachusetts that while innocent Americans were being gunned down in the civil war then tearing the nation apart, "the guiltiest—Derby and d'Israeli, & such like—are shooting grouse."

In truth some of Ruskin's favorite people were supporting the South, and slavery, while Disraeli attempted, at worst, to remain neutral. A few outspoken royalists felt that since the American colonies had rebelled against their king in England, the states of the new Confederacy were giving the Republic its just comeuppance. Some—the idea briefly tempted Disraeli—rejoiced in the failure of republican institutions, and saw in the South the remains of a squirearchy of English vintage. Disraeli, who would quickly recant such notions, at first saw the early Confederate military successes as "tell[ing] immensely in favour of an aristocracy." Many in both parties, especially those from the industrial Midlands, viewed Britain's need for Southern cotton as more crucial than the immorality of the slave system behind its production. Also, the Northerners were protectionist, while the largely agricultural South needed free trade, and was no rival to the commercial supremacy of Britain. Further, the North seemed to have continuing designs upon Canada and would be weakened by disunion to the benefit of Britain's huge colony, which shared a border of three thousand miles.

Ignoring his elevated moral posture on most other matters, Gladstone, at a public dinner in Newcastle, embraced the slave-owning South and declared of its President, "Jefferson Davis had made an army, had made a navy, and what was more, had made a nation." Had he made his gaffe as a private citizen it would have been shortsighted enough, but he was Chancellor of the Exchequer and third-ranking member of Palmerston's Government. (Decades later he confessed that he had committed a "gross impropriety," but even then ignored the issue of slavery.) Lord

Stanley noted that privately—if a dinner on November 21, 1862, attended by Members of Parliament can be called private— Gladstone made "no secret of his views as to a separation. He thought Virginia must be divided between the two federations, and probably Tennessee likewise." Earl Russell, the Foreign Secretary—he had been elevated to the Lords in 1861—was also pro-South, despite his impeccably Liberal record. "The North," he claimed, "was striving for empire and the South for independence." Palmerston held his tongue.

An outspoken friend of the Union, John Bright, had been surprised at Disraeli's reaction—"more favourable to the North than I expected," he noted in his diary. When he considered the difficulties of the North and the "awful emergency" it had met "manfully and courageously," Disraeli had told the House, he thought it became England, in its relations with the United States, "to extend to all which they say at least a generous interpretation, and to their acts a liberal construction." Still, Disraeli foresaw, "whenever the waters have subsided, a different America from that which was known to our fathers"—the likelihood of frequent turbulence, rival states, unstable cabinets. An influential member of the governing party, he told the House on February 5, 1863, had confided to him that "the Lord of Hosts was on the side of the Southern states." What Disraeli wanted was more silence and less meddling, while Derby approved of mediation, which was tantamount to recognition of the South. The mills of Lancashire needed cotton.

Lord Robert Cecil and A. J. B. Beresford-Hope, with other Tories, went even farther, organizing a Southern Independence Association which, by December 1862, had died of its puerile espousal of innocent Southern womanhood and "the preservation of property." Its public concern was for "strict neutrality," which was code for assisting the South by building its blockade-runners in English shipyards and lending the money to pay for them.

The Civil War had initiated the era of the floating ironclad, and with France also experimenting with iron ships, Disraeli spoke out powerfully in Parliament against naval rivalry and, in language that foreshadowed British high seas doctrine for generations to come, for supremacy. Further, he wanted not merely more tonnage, but vessels that would be technologically without rivals. "Our navy is not to be equal to France," he said from the floor on June 3, 1862, "but it is to be greatly superior. It is a necessary condition of our geographical position and our political power that our navy be as superior to the navy of France as the army of France is superior to ours." Then he warned about hasty expenditure on some "apparent novelty" that is taken at the moment to be "the type and model of perfection." He wanted neither false economies nor rash expenditures but the best equipment that could be planned for in a time when years elapsed between letting a contract and delivery of a ship.

At the official sequel to the Great Exhibition of 1851, held as planned in mid-1862 despite the death of Albert, Disraeli and Gladstone met, coldly, and although they were in the same Parliamentary group, turned their backs to each other. Theater proprietor John Hollingshead, strolling through the Exhibition with Thackeray, with whom Disraeli had not spoken since the novelist's cruel *Codlingsby* in 1847, observed Disraeli walking toward them. "They saw each other," Hollingshead recalled, "but showed no signs of recognition."

With the Crystal Palace already moved to a site south of the Thames in Sydenham, and re-erected with a revised roof configuration, the new London exhibition space was a temporary building on a plot facing Cromwell Road since occupied by the Natural History Museum. The widowed and reclusive Queen did not attend; the hall had none of the excitement of Paxton's glass palace. (Asked by Victoria about the differences between the two exhibitions, Disraeli told her that the earlier one was a woman, the successor a man.) The emphasis upon peaceful pursuits—so attractive in 1851 but out of place after the Crimean War and the tensions with a Napoleonized France—had been replaced by shows of armaments and crassly commercial wares that gave the building the derisive label, "the Palace of Puffs." "This," Disraeli wrote to Mrs. Brydges Willyams, grossly exaggerating the few steps from his town house to Hyde Park, "is not so fascinating a one as that you remember when you made me an assignation by the crystal fountain, which I was ungallant enough not to keep, being far away when it arrived at Grosvenor Gate."

With Palmerston having his way in the Commons, Disraeli turned for interest to foreign affairs, hosting the Grand Duke of Saxe-Weimar at Grosvenor Gate with exotic dishes brought in by Mary Anne from caterers; renewing acquaintance with Napoleon III, who was visiting the Exhibition; and meeting Count Otto von Bismarck for the first time. His old friend Louis Napoleon, he wrote Mrs. Brydges Willyams, was "a true Bonaparte in mind & visage . . . and all his charlantry of manner and expression." Bismarck, who would be appointed President of the Prussian Ministry on September 21, 1862, told Disraeli frankly of his plans. At a party given by Baron Brunnow, the Prussian ambassador, Bismarck was in a mood of alcoholic expansiveness. "I shall soon be compelled," he said, as if he had not been intriguing for the post, "to undertake the conduct of the Prussian Government. My first care will be to reorganise the army, with or without the help of the Landtag." When the military commanded respect, he went on, "I shall seize the first best pretext to declare war against Austria, dissolve the German Diet, subdue the minor States, and give national unity to Germany under Prussian leadership. I have come here to say this to the Queen's Ministers."

"Be careful about that man!" Disraeli warned Count Vitzthum. "He means what he says."

The surprise of Disraeli's summer came on his return to Hughenden from political business in London. Confidently expecting to live to see greater things for her husband, Mary Anne at seventy had been consulting with architects about adding to the house, which had insufficient entertainment space. Outdoors she was planning new gardens, Disraeli wrote their London neighbor Lady Dorothy Nevill, then in the country. Mary Anne "has more than twenty navvies at work, levelling and making terraces." While about it she planned a surprise for him, which he described delightedly to Baroness de Rothschild. In a gossipy letter to Leonora and Leopold that August, Charlotte relayed the news, in her usual unawed fashion, about "the great Disraeli, who rhapsodizes about the enchantments of his dear country home, the silver river, where rose-coloured trout disport themselves, the ever-growing, ever-improving and really beautiful trees, and 'though last not least a monument to my father, raised by my wife, and in my absence. It is quite finished and really, whether I consider the design, the execution or even the material—I think it one of the most beautiful things in England.' How pleased Mrs Dis must be with the success of the secretly planned monument."

With Hughenden no more than twenty miles from any of the Rothschild country homes, exchange visits were frequent. Constance de Rothschild, daughter of Sir Anthony, who lived seventeen miles away at Aston Clinton, recalled Disraeli "in his velveteen coat, his leather leggings, his soft felt hat, and carrying his little hatchet, for relieving the bark of trees from the encroaching ivy," in his role as squire. The day before he went to Aston Clinton to accompany Sir Anthony to the Aylesbury assizes, Disraeli and Mary Anne bade farewell to the last of the Hughenden guests who for all or part of ten days had enjoyed the strutting peacocks on the terrace, the swans—Hero and Leander—on the pond, the woodland setting in the Chiltern Hills, and the suspense as to what Mary Anne might do or say. "The only fault of our party," Disraeli wrote to Charlotte, "was that it contained no Rothschilds—but that was not our fault, for we tried not only the English, but the French & Austrian dynasties, but in vain."

In the waning weeks of 1862 and into 1863, the Disraelis made the usual round of social and political visits, staying at Seaham Hall with Lady Londonderry. Her health, Disraeli was distressed to see, was beginning to fail. The occasion was the unveiling, in Durham Market Place, of an equestrian statue of her late husband in his dashing maturity, as he appeared, imaginatively, in the sculpting of Gaetano Monti of Milan. After the ceremony on December 2, 1862, Disraeli spoke at a luncheon, crediting his old friend as a man of "enlightened mind" who understood that the aristocracy had a leadership role to play in the country's commerce. In general Disraeli felt that the well-born were born to lead, not to luxuriate in their good fortune. When, that winter, it became clear, as Parliament was about to resume, that Lord Stanley was being courted by the Greeks, desperate for a competent king, Disraeli observed to Mrs. Brydges Willyams, whom he and Mary Anne had just seen in Torquay, "This beats any novel. I think he ought to take the crown, but he will not. Had I his youth, I would not hesitate, even with the earldom of Derby in the distance. . . . Life becomes like a fairy tale, & our intimate acquaintances turn into Sovereign Princes, who, the day before, were M.P.'s, & guardsmen, & foxhunters."

With the exception of the fuss over purchasing for the nation the South Kensington site of the Exhibition of 1862, Parliament's attention remained focused upon foreign affairs. The Queen wanted the area utilized for the national collections of science and art, a concept derided as "Albertopolis" by the frugal-minded. Stanley derided the "Court dictation" and the "waste of money." It was a rare occasion when both Gladstone and Disraeli were on the same side, yet the vote at first was lost. As was often the case, the Queen turned out to be right.

Victoria was also exercised about European matters from which her Parliament preferred to remain distant. Palmerston was eager to cede the unruly Ionian Islanders to Greece, to keep aloof from Russia's heavy-handed suppression of the Poles, and to take no sides in Prussia's forcible absorption of Schleswig-Holstein, long claimed by the Danes. The Queen was imperial-minded, Russophobic, and torn over Prussia and Denmark. Her eldest daughter was married to an heir to the Prussian throne, and her eldest son, her own heir, was about to marry Princess Alexandra of Denmark.

The royal wedding, on March 10, 1863, was the social event of the decade. Disraeli assumed that his invitation, when so many other dignitaries were excluded for want of seating room in St. George's Chapel at Windsor, was due to Victoria's interest in him. He never knew that Palmerston had asked that the leader of the Conservative Party in the House be among the guests as he had supported funding the Prince of Wales's "establishment." Disraeli recalled "rage, envy, and indignation"—even "hysterics of mortification"—on the part of the uninvited, which made the pageant seem even more impressive. Yet the rituals were muted by the Queen's insistence upon her continued mourning for Albert. She sat out the ceremonies in the Royal Closet, visible to everyone in her black silk and crêpe. Upon her widow's weeds she pinned the Prince Consort's own Garter badge with blue ribbon, and a miniature of Albert set with diamonds, worn as a brooch. That made it possible for him—since the sum of her theology was a belief in a hereafter in which she would be reunited with her husband—to see the wedding. Lord Granville told the Duchess of Manchester that when the chorale composed by Prince Albert and sung by Jenny Lind began, Victoria "gave a look upwards, which spoke volumes."

"I had never seen the Queen," Disraeli recalled, "since the catastrophe, and ventured, being near-sighted, to use my glass. I saw H.M. well, and unfortunately caught her glance." Scolded by her frown, he did not repeat the error.

The postwedding breakfast—by the time all five hundred gathered it was a late lunch—was followed by chaos at the Windsor railway station. Departing ladies in their jewels and swirling gowns, separated from their husbands, tried to squeeze into the crowded railway cars. Disraeli managed to rescue Countess Apponyi, the wife of the Austrian ambassador, swathed in sables and blue velvet embroidered in gold, and assist her aboard. "I think I had to sit on my wife's lap," Disraeli remembered. "When we got to Paddington [Station] in the rain there was no ambassadorial carriage; but ours was there, and so we took home safe this brilliant and delightful person."

On April 22, 1863, invited to a personal audience with the Queen, an event now rare for persons outside the Government, Disraeli was at first delayed by the arrival of Earl Russell, who had brought with him reports on the Polish insurrection. Disraeli conversed as best he could with the rather innocent young Prince and Princess of Wales. The next morning, after breakfast, he was led by an attendant down a long gallery into what had been Prince Albert's study, still kept as he left it. Now it was Victoria's room for meeting special guests. It appeared to Disraeli, with one change, as if the Prince "had resided in it yesterday." A chair had a plaque attached, identifying it as the one in which Albert sat until 1861. When the Queen materialized through a door opposite, Disraeli bowed deeply and remained standing, appropriate protocol with the Sovereign, and they talked about affairs as if he were still her Minister.

H.M. expressed her conviction that, whatever happened, the American Union could not be restored. She
spoke fully about Poland, nor was it difficult to
recognise that the insurrection alarmed her from its possible consequences on the state of Germany. H.M.,
however, it was quite clear, was sanguine that the Russians would suppress it by the summer.

She asked me frankly whether I thought the present
Ministry would get through the session. I said they were
weak, but there was no desire to displace them unless a
stronger one could be established. She said she hoped
no crisis would be brought about wantonly, for, in her
forlorn condition, she hardly knew what she could do.
I said H.M.'s comfort was an element in all our considerations, and that no action would be taken, I felt sure,
unless from commanding necessity.

She said, "Lord Palmerston was grown very old." I replied, "But his voice in debate, Madam, is as loud as
ever."

"Yes!" she exclaimed with animation. "And his handwriting! Did you ever see such a handwriting? So very
clear and strong! Nevertheless I see in him a great
change, a very great change. His countenance is so
changed."

Then H.M., turning from public affairs, deigned to
say that it had given her great pleasure to observe that
I had been chosen Trustee of the British Museum. . . .
At last she asked after my wife, and hoped she was well,
and then, with a graceful bow, vanished.

Disraeli returned from Windsor just in time for the debate in
the Commons on a resolution for supplementing by £50,000 the
£60,000 already raised by private subscription for a memorial to
Albert and spoke about the need to mark "a sublime life and a
transcendent career." It was a Thursday night; on Saturday morning he received from the Queen a copy, bound in white morocco,
of a book of the Prince's speeches, and a letter from Victoria
thanking him for words in Parliament that were "soothing to her

broken heart." Disraeli replied fulsomely. Although he had been treated with suspicion by Albert at the start, Disraeli had sincerely admired his intelligence and integrity. "The Prince is the only person whom Mr Disraeli has ever known," he asserted, "who realized the Ideal. . . . The only character in English History that would, in some respects, draw near to him is Sir Philip Sidney: the same high tone, the same universal accomplishment, the same blended tenderness and vigor, the same rare combination of romantic energy and classic repose."

The relationship between sovereign and subject ripened from that series of exchanges, but Disraeli proved of little use in Parliament when the matter of Government purchase of the Exhibition building came up again. Allegedly it was ugly and useless, and only its size had some dubious value. Again the rare cooperation between Disraeli and Gladstone came to nothing.

European rivalries were the main preoccupation of Parliament through the year. Italy struggled for union, Prussia to consolidate its influence over minor German states at Austria's expense, France to fulfill imperial ambitions in the direction of Italy and the Rhineland, Russia to put down internal agitation and seek distractions abroad. Disraeli preferred broad solutions through peaceful commerce of mutual benefit rather than by territorial aggrandizement. Each case, he told Mrs. Brydges Willyams on October 17, 1863, was "a diplomatic Frankenstein." Peace was best preserved "not by statesmen, but by capitalists," he felt, and in Sidonia fashion he visualized beneath events "secret societies" and "millionaires." ("Of course," he would declare to Lord Stanley on November 4, 1863, "life is conspiracy & extortion.")

On November 5 he explained further that various untoward alliances might assist Austria to regain Silesia, France to acquire a piece of the Rhineland, a unified Italy to seize the Adriatic coast around Venice, Galicia to go to a restored Poland. How much she cared, in her nineties, about the future of Europe was of no concern to Disraeli. She was his opportunity to think aloud, and he poured out his thoughts with a frankness he offered no one else.

Whatever Disraeli's long-delayed financial expectations from Sarah Brydges Willyams, he seldom mentioned money matters to her, but a year earlier, on November 23, 1862, he had written that the estate of Sir James Viney, Mary Anne's long-dead uncle, had been settled after twenty-five years in Chancery, and his properties sold after their mortgages were paid. "We now are clear of it," he told her, "with something in our pockets." Something always seemed to turn up to rescue Disraeli from his debts. Sarah had left almost everything to him three years earlier. After his second tenure at the Exchequer he had been entitled to an annual pension of £2,000, and at the time of the Viney settlement a Yorkshire bachelor with a large estate, Andrew Montagu, had offered to help the Tory cause financially and was invited to buy up Disraeli's debts and charge him a lower-than-usurious interest. Through Philip Rose and Lionel de Rothschild, Montagu discharged all debts Disraeli made known to him in return for a mortgage on Hughenden at three percent. Disraeli had been paying about £6,000 a year in interest on about £60,000 he still owed, some of that representing huge accretions of interest. Now he could manage to pay interest of £1,800 from his Ministerial pension.

While his financial outlook was the best it had been since he was twenty, his political prospects seemed to him bleak. From Hughenden on October 21 he had written to Baroness de Rothschild that Mary Anne, nearly finished redecorating some guest rooms, had named a suite for Charlotte, "so that, now that you have a vested interest in Hughenden, I trust that yr visits will be more frequent, & not so brief." Then he explained his state of mind. "For my part," he began, "were it not that it deprives me of seeing you, and yr [London] hearth, I should not much care if I always remained here. I don't think one is much wanted now in the House of Commons."

A week after his long foreign policy lesson of November 5, 1863, to Sarah Brydges Willyams, now ninety-four, the Disraelis learned of her sudden and alarming illness, and rushed off to Torquay, "but too late," Charlotte wrote to her son Leopold, "to receive her blessing. The old lady expired at the age of one hundred and two and none of us could wish to live longer. . . . I put down my pen," she added—it was November 13, 1863—"to take it up again and write to Mrs Dis a letter which sincerity prevents me from making one of condolence, and which from motives of feeling and delicacy cannot be one of congratulations, I wish the Emperor of the French would give me some of his epistolary talent."

Two weeks later she informed Leo that Sir Hugh Cairns, "who was out with the Rothschild hounds on Thursday, told Sir Anthony that he thought that the legacy of Mrs Willyams might jeopardize Mr Disraeli's pension . . . , as the legislature had never contemplated pensioning rich men." But, she added, "For once in my life I have talked to some purpose. . . . I have this fortnight been repeating what is the truth, namely that the inheritance will do nothing beyond paying the great and illustrious adventurer's debts. This is now generally believed." Charlotte had seldom if ever lobbied her husband's powerful friends, but she preserved Disraeli's pension. A line in the will would have validated her loyalty—that the legacy to Disraeli by Mrs. Willyams was "in testimony of her affection for him; and in approval and admiration of his efforts to vindicate the race of Israel: her views respecting which he is well acquainted with; and which no doubt he will endeavor to accomplish."

Lionel, too, had written to Leo. His letter the day before (November 30, 1863) noted that "the Dizzys" had dined with them and described the interment at Hughenden and the inheritance. "They are in the black," said the Baron. Disraeli was more in the black than he wanted most people to know. After bequests and settlement of debts, he had been left £40,000, much of which would go to the improvements already underway at Hughenden. But to James Buller he fudged on November 13, "She left many legacies, chiefly to her god-children. . . I am obliged to undertake the management of her affairs. . . . Your daughter is left a legacy of £500."

By no means had Disraeli become a rich man. As he entered his sixtieth year, his joint family income after the renovations to the house and lands had climbed to £9,000. About half of that was Mary Anne's.

At sixty-five the Earl of Derby dozed off at meetings and had difficulty walking and even standing. At audiences the Queen ignored his distress and left him longing for a chair. Yet the ailing

Derby continued privately to indulge his hobby of projecting imaginary Tory cabinets. His son Edward found the tinkering idiotic, but a disgruntled group in the Commons would have been glad to see Disraeli replaced on the floor and in Derby's fantasies by General Jonathan Peel, War Secretary in the last Tory cabinet and brother of the sainted Sir Robert. While Peel had no such ambitions, the discontented twenty-five thought his name might rally former Tories. Their alternative to the diffident general was Edward Stanley. Conceding the inability of substituting for Disraeli—who remained the wrong sort—a Tory M.P. in the ultra faction deplored unsportingly in sports metaphor, "Our team is the Gentlemen of England, with a Player given."

Disraeli dismissed the efforts to oust him as unlikely to benefit the party. Neither the Government nor the Opposition had clearly opposing policies, and no likely division would unseat the Prime Minister, he told Stanley glumly when they met on February 1, 1864. Only three months before, Disraeli had heard that Palmerston, who was already twenty when his adversary was born, had been accused of "imprudence" with a clergyman's wife. There was still life in the old roué, and when stuffy Tories proposed publicizing the allegation, Disraeli counseled silence, lest Palmerston sweep the country. Even if Palmerston were out of the picture, Disraeli warned Derby's heir, who was as lacking in eagerness for Downing Street as he was for the throne of Greece, the Government was unlikely to collapse. "Russell and Gladstone could carry on affairs."

For the new session of Parliament, Disraeli's advice, born of the hopeless party outlook, was "criticise, but suggest nothing." It was a far cry from his earlier dictum: "You cannot keep a large army in order without letting them sometimes smell gunpowder." In keeping with circumstances, however, Disraeli criticized, charging Palmerston with bungling British involvement in the Schleswig-Holstein affair. "A little scene," Gladstone noted laconically in his diary on February 22 about his own sarcastic response. Disraeli would arise regularly to criticize foreign policy matters, rousing Palmerston on March 3 with an accusation, largely aimed at Earl Russell, of "diplomatic rubbish." The Prime Minister, cranky because of a gouty hand and a severe cold, shouted back, "There is also such a thing as parliamentary rubbish."

Despite the party warfare, some of it a facade, when the Queen's annual review in Hyde Park took place on a sunny Saturday morning in late May, Mary Anne Disraeli had a *grand déjeuner* at Grosvenor Gate for politicians whom she invited to see the spectacle across Park Lane from the Disraeli windows and roof. Since Baroness de Rothschild had her own guests for strawberries and grapes (cooking was not done on the Sabbath), including two Russian ladies who evaded another Sabbath ban by going up to the roof six stories over Piccadilly to smoke cigars, she could not attend. Charles Villiers, who never missed a party and went to both, filled Charlotte in. "All the most distinguished persons in the realm," she in turn lightly exaggerated to Leopold, then at Cambridge, "honored Mrs Dis—the Conservatives, of course, but also the Bishop of Oxford . . . , the Dean of Westminster, Dr Stanley, and—but you will never guess—Disraeli's great and illustrious rival, the incomparable Gladstone." Gladstone's diary for May 28, 1864, indicates only that he was at "Mr Disraeli's, on the roofs."

Skirmishing in the Commons continued through June and into July, when Disraeli moved, on the 4th, for a vote of no confidence in the Government on the grounds that they had "failed to maintain their avowed policy of upholding the integrity and independence of Denmark," and in so fumbling its opportunities "[the Government] has lowered the just influence of this country in the capitals of Europe, and thereby diminished the securities for peace." There was no question that Britain had been idle while Denmark, badly mishandling the succession for the duchies, had been overpowered in Schleswig and Holstein by Prussian military forces nominally assisted by Austria.

"Some of the longest and most disastrous wars of modern Europe," he began, "have been wars of succession." And he went on for two and a half hours to outline the dispute and the violated treaties, and the threatened shifts in the balance of power that would impact upon England.

In the Lords, Disraeli received no help from Derby, who was again ill, and no Tory alternative had his persuasive powers. In the Commons, Gladstone followed Disraeli to answer for the Ministry in a speech, he noted in his diary, that took "1 hr 35 m—I threw overboard all my heavy armament: & fought *light.*" The motion, he charged, was little more than the echo of a few obscure newspapers in Germany that criticized its government. Britain, he claimed, had since used "prudence and patriotism" in a "difficult negotiation" with Prussia which kept Denmark from dismemberment, as the disputed duchies were never part of the kingdom proper.

The recognized funny man of the Commons, Bernal Osborne, refused to condemn Palmerston, since despite his years, "panting time toils after him in vain." He had been "paternal, but stationary" in domestic policy, and "the apostle and minister of peace" in foreign affairs. His cabinet was "a museum of curiosities" but there would be no gain for the nation if he were replaced. Palmerston, his vigor ebbing at seventy-eight, responded weakly, claiming that Disraeli's motion was "a gratuitous libel," and that England stood as high as ever in the councils of Europe.

As mover of the motion, Disraeli rose to close the debate after four nights of argument, but he came up eighteen votes short. After five years in office, beginning with a slender majority of thirteen, Palmerston was hanging on through Tory defections. At least five voted with the Government; other sympathetic Tories stayed away, which was just as effective.

Parliament was prorogued on July 29, 1864, with the Conservatives no closer to power than they had been at the start of the session. The no-confidence motion had been a sham fight in any case. Disraeli had not wanted intervention against Germany, which would only make France "mistress of Europe." England's policy had to remain one of having no dominant nation on the Continent, but he saw no other means than the embarrassment of Palmerston to get his minority party into Downing Street.

Retreating in frustration to the country, Disraeli found a gift from a South American admirer of a pair of what Charlotte de Rothschild described as large emerald birds with long tails. He asked her where she thought their stuffed plumage would best be displayed, and she named every location in Hughenden she could think of, from Disraeli's library to the hall. "I know not where to put them," he said, finally. "May I send them to you?"

"We never look a gift horse in the mouth," said her daughter Evy.

At Knowsley, where the Earl of Derby had spent most of the Parliamentary session nursing his ailments, politics continued to have a low priority while the leader of his party, it became known, worked on his translations of the *Iliad.* "What will Dizzy write?" Charlotte asked Leo, her Cambridge scholar, on October 16. "The History of the Jews if he would undertake it," she ventured, "would suit his genius, and give meaning to the many months of quasi-solitude which he enjoys at Hughenden." She had visited with Evy the month before to see the completed renovations, and a look into Disraeli's library may have inspired the idea. It was a history he could write from his own and his father's books, but he preferred to write the history of his own time, and to do so as fiction.

Although he did write something on a religious subject soon after, it was very different indeed. He had been asked to speak at a Diocesan Society conference chaired by the Bishop of Oxford, Samuel Wilberforce, and discussed the new trends in biblical scholarship with cautious political correctness. It was at the Sheldonian Theatre at Oxford on November 25, 1864, that he made the celebrated remark most associated with him and yet least characteristic of his real thinking. Disraeli was not about to commit political suicide by discussing religion as frankly as he had often done with Sarah Brydges Willyams. "The discoveries of science are not, we are told, consistent with the teachings of the Church," he said. "Now, I am sure there is not one in this theatre who is not prepared to do full justice to the merits of scientific men, and who does not appreciate the discoveries of science which have added so much to the convenience of life and the comfort of man." But, he said, while it was "fashionable and modish" to interpret the Bible scientifically, he would leave that to the Church, and he was on the side of the angels rather than the apes. To believe otherwise was "foreign to the conscience of humanity." Bishop Wilberforce did not deviate from his support of Gladstone, but Disraeli felt that he had done himself no harm.

Dressing for an Oxford Bal Masqué. *Punch*, December 10, 1864, satirizing Disraeli's Oxford speech on November 25, 1864. Caption: "The Question is, is Man an Ape or an Angel? (A Laugh) Now, I am on the side of the Angels. (Cheers)"

For reasons both personal and public, Disraeli was largely silent in the first months of 1865. He preferred to let the other side make mistakes and even chose not to respond in the Commons to the traditional Address from the Throne opening the new session. In her continued seclusion the Queen would have the speech, prepared by the Government in any case, read in her absence, and as he wrote to Derby from Hughenden on December 12, he did not feel that it was useful "to show our cards."

Not until March 13, 1865, did Disraeli rise in the House,

choosing a debate on Canada, which under the pressure of the American war was moving toward the security of confederation. Times had changed, American Legation Secretary Benjamin Moran noted from the Gallery. As late as June 23, 1864, although it was clear that the South could no longer win its war for survival, Gladstone had spoken angrily of the "negrophiles" of the North who would sacrifice three white lives to free one black man. Now Moran saw from the Government side—he expected it from Disraeli—a "tone of respect" toward Lincoln and the United States "in wonderful contrast to the jeers, the sneers and the disrespect common in that House . . . two and three years ago." Yet Disraeli had also observed, to push a government reluctant to spend money on anything, that if it did not invest in making Canada both independent and secure, a United States emboldened by its victory over the rebel South might seize its opportunities for expansion.

On April 3, Moran was back in the Gallery for the expected eulogies of the great Radical M.P. Richard Cobden, who had just died. It was five in the afternoon, and formal business had been quickly declared over. Once Palmerston spoke of the great national loss occasioned by Cobden's passing, Disraeli made, Moran noted in his diary, "the best speech I ever heard in the House of Commons. . . . He said that death had been busy in that Parliament . . . but the great men who had been snatched away were still there in spirit, and would be quoted and be respected, and have their influence, regardless of the caprices of constituencies. He thought Mr Cobden the greatest man his class had produced in England."

A month later, after the murder of Lincoln, Moran was again in the Gallery. Official notice had arrived from the State Department that on May 1, officials were to begin wearing crêpe on the left arm for six months. Moran was appropriately armbanded as he sat listening to what seemed a distinct lack of grace among the M.P.s, in which, due to the absence of Palmerston, who was ill, Sir George Grey, speaking for the Government, began innocently by asserting that the majority of the British people had always been on the side of the North, and was met embarrassingly by cries from the Liberal benches of "No, no!" and "Hear, hear!"

Concluding, Disraeli used the divisiveness to effect. "Sir," he observed, addressing the Chair, "whatever the various and varying opinions in this House, and in the country generally, on the policy of the late President of the United States, on this, I think, all must agree, that in one of the severest trials which ever tested the moral qualities of man, he fulfilled his duty with simplicity and strength. . . . Whenever such crimes are perpetrated the public mind is apt to fall into gloom and perplexity; for it is ignorant alike of the causes and consequences of such deeds." But he looked for hope rather than despondency, that from the "awful trials of the last four years, of which not the least is this violent demise, the various populations of North America may issue [forth] elevated and chastened; rich in that accumulated wisdom, and strong in that disciplined energy which a young nation can only acquire in a protracted and perilous struggle."

With Disraeli's seconding of the Address to the Crown on a message of sympathy to the new American President, Andrew Johnson, over, Moran pushed through the crowds to get to the Lords for its parallel motion, arriving in time to hear the Earl of Derby, "who showed a small mind in his remarks," repeat the discredited phrase of Earl Russell about the North fighting for empire and the South for independence. Curiously, Moran went on with three others from the legation to see a burlesque by music-hall queen Marie Wilton before donning their full mourning "crépe and black," English-style.

In the aftermath of the Confederate surrender, Disraeli would make only one gesture that could be interpreted as pro-South. Judah P. Benjamin, Secretary of War and then Secretary of State in Jefferson Davis's government and highest-ranking Jew in the Confederacy, had escaped to England, where he hoped to establish himself at the English bar. "Mr D'Israeli," he reported to his nephew in New Orleans that September, ". . . wrote to a friend of mine expressing the desire of being useful to me when he should arrive in town." By 1870 Judah Benjamin was a Q.C.

For Disraeli the major event of the dying Parliament was the government attempt to make an election issue of the new Reform Bill. To keep his Conservative base he had to step back from democratic compromises he would have made when last in office

and defend what he contended was the proven efficacy of tradition. Sitting once more in the Strangers' Gallery, Moran was impressed by how Disraeli closed the debate for the Opposition. It
was "a statesman's speech," Moran thought. "Indeed, his was the
speech of the evening and showed him to be a great man."

British subjects had "unbroken order and complete freedom," Disraeli claimed, yet such gains had been made under an
aristocratic sanction. The nation was fortunate in its unique, if
apparently undemocratic, advantages:

> [It] is not governed by force; it is not governed by
> standing armies; it is governed by a most singular series
> of traditionary influences, which generation after gener-
> ation cherishes because it knows that they embalm cus-
> tom and represent law. And, with this, what have you
> done? You have created the greatest Empire of modern
> times. You have amassed a capital of fabulous amount.
> You have devised and sustained a system of credit still
> more marvelous. And, above all, you have established
> and maintained a scheme so vast and complicated of la-
> bour and industry, that the history of the world affords
> no parallel to it. And all these mighty creations are out
> of all proportion to the essential and indigenous ele-
> ments and resources of the country. If you destroy that
> state of society, remember this—England cannot begin
> again.

On May 10, the Earl of Shaftesbury, who opposed Disraeli on
most issues, wrote to him to applaud the idea that the franchise
should be extended only if it were not degraded in the quality of
those who would exercise it. "England rests entirely on her institutions," he agreed. Social, civil, and religious liberty, he thought,
could be jeopardized by "pure democracy." The bill was defeated
in the House by seventy-four votes, and John Bright cried treachery. "Mr Disraeli," he charged, "is a man of brains, of genius, of
a great capacity of action, of a wonderful tenacity of purpose, and
of a rare courage. He would have been a statesman if his powers
had been directed by any ennobling principle or idea."

Palmerston was still not up to the rigors of active politics and was absent at the division. Rumor had it that he was dying and that Gladstone would take his place, with the old man elevated at least briefly to the Lords. But Palmerston's popularity remained undiminished, and the General Election which followed the dissolution of Parliament on July 6, 1865, gave him twenty-five additional seats, although at the price of Gladstone's at Oxford, lost to a young Conservative, Gathorne Gathorne-Hardy. "A dear dream is dispelled," Gladstone wrote on July 17: "God's will be done." But he scurried about to find a new seat, still a rather easy proposition when all elections were not held on the same day, and at Newton—a lesser eminence having withdrawn for him—he scraped into third place in a three-seat constituency.

Both Disraeli and Gladstone, as family friends, had been on hand on July 7, 1865, when Lionel de Rothschild married off his second daughter, Evelina, to Baron Ferdinand de Rothschild, her cousin and son of the head of the Vienna branch of the banking empire. The ceremony was at Lionel's vast town house at 148 Piccadilly, overlooking Hyde Park and Green Park. Fourteen bridesmaids represented many of the most venerable names in the English aristocracy. As the cantor was about to chant his blessings over the couple, Lionel called out, "Ben, there are so many of you Christians present that our *chazan* wants to know whether he should just read the prayers or sing them as in the synagogue?"

"Oh, please let him sing them," Disraeli said. "I like to hear the old-fashioned tunes." As usual at a Rothschild wedding, he gave a post-nuptial toast—this time after the Austrian ambassador and, representing the party in power, the First Lord of the Admiralty. (Eighteen months later, Evelina died in childbirth at twenty-six. The family's grief was profound. Devastated, Baron Ferdinand never remarried.)

Brooding in isolation at Knowsley, Derby predicted to Disraeli about the July election results that neither of them would ever hold office again. Even making allowances for the artificial modesty appropriate to the sender in the circumstances, Disraeli's response from Hughenden on August 6, 1865, conceded his failure. "I am quite aware," he wrote, "that I have had an opportunity in life to which I have not been adequate; still, having led a portion of the House for seventeen years, I am disinclined, in the decline of life, to serve under anybody in that assembly; and as no one but yourself would offer me its lead, and as we both agree that such a combination would not succeed, I look upon my career in the House of Commons, so far as office is concerned, to have concluded." He was ready, he indicated, to retire from politics if Derby could recruit a replacement who could bring to their side sufficient members to make a majority. "The leadership of hopeless Opposition," he confessed, "is a gloomy affair."

Disraeli had made that offer before. Derby again shook it off. Neither of them could accept less, he responded on August 12, than "a *bona fide* Conservative Government." Both were thinking of, without identifying, Derby's diffident son Edward as a rallying point for the Conservatives if they were to resume office. Disraeli would have accepted him, but Derby would not. His son, who had failed to marry and provide an heir, and who regularly shrank from traditional Toryism, was not really Derby's kind of politician and would have been happy, but for the pressures of family connection, to join Gladstone. Chief promoter of Edward Stanley, and influential because of the venerable Cecils she represented by marriage, was Mary Catherine, Lady Salisbury. Her stepson Robert, who had succeeded his dead elder brother as Lord Cranborne, detested Disraeli as a Jewish adventurer. Hatred of Disraeli was one of the few matters about which Robert and his stepmother agreed. Stanley had long been involved with Lady Salisbury, five years his elder but far younger than her aged husband, and she was his self-appointed patroness. With old Salisbury's complaisance, Stanley had made Hatfield his second home.

More flexible politically than the Earl, Disraeli understood the need for reforms that were anathema to Derby. But Derby could hardly countenance his son—with whom he was on correct, rather than congenial, terms—as his political successor. Other party elders still hoped for anyone other than Disraeli.

It did not improve Disraeli's political outlook when he was elected at long last to Grillon's, the elite men's dining club. Derby and Gladstone had been members before they were thirty. Sheer bigotry had kept Disraeli out until he was past sixty. It seemed almost a parting salute, and he could not greet the achievement with any enthusiasm. Gentlemen's dining clubs were an eighteenth-century atavism, a collection of "prigs and bores," he explained to Hugh Cairns a few years later, "whispering to their next-door neighbors over a bad dinner in a dingy room." Disraeli preferred the company and the conversation of interesting women.

Palmerston died on October 18, two days before his eighty-first birthday. Earl Russell was his inevitable successor as Prime Minister, as was Gladstone as party leader in the Commons, putting him directly opposite Disraeli for the first time. A week later, visiting Hughenden, Stanley found his host with visions of "renewed political life." With the next session of Parliament months off, their talk of politics as they explored the indoor and outdoor improvements at Hughenden was only perfunctory. The "old and plain" house, Stanley observed, "is now recased, and really handsome; the garden enlarged, new paths cut through the woods, fresh plantations made. . . . D enjoys this place thoroughly, and is never happier than when showing it to a friend."

With new Liberal leadership forthcoming, Disraeli made more trips to London from Hughenden than were usual for him in autumn and winter, to plan the bringing down of what he saw as an interim ministry. He was also, at long distance, a candidate for another office, that of Rector of the University of Edinburgh, an honorific post competed for on literary as well as political grounds, as his opponent was Thomas Carlyle. Ironically, the rector whose term was ending was Gladstone. Edinburgh students, who made the nominations as well as voted upon them, knew *Sartor Resartus* and Carlyle's *Cromwell* and *Frederick the Great,* and considered the one-time student who had left without a degree in 1814 the foremost living Scot.

Normally diffident about honors, this one was something special to the crusty culture hero, now nearly seventy. Disraeli's candidacy was almost quixotic, and his agreeing to run induced Carlyle to accept. There were few in politics he disliked more than Disraeli. "A Jew is bad [enough]," he had written to Monckton Milnes years before, "but what is a sham-Jew, a

Quack-Jew? And how can a real Jew . . . try to be a Senator, or even citizen, of any country except his own wretched Palestine?"

The election took place early in November. Disraeli lost, with 310 votes to Carlyle's 657.

One of several occasions to mark the fiftieth anniversary year of Waterloo was to be the placement of a huge block of gray Cornish granite at a site on the late Duke of Wellington's estate at Strathfieldsaye, near Reading, as base for a bronze statue by Baron Carlo Marochetti, the Queen's favorite sculptor. Disraeli, traveling as he often did now without Mary Anne, but employing their Upper Grosvenor Street neighbor, Lady Dorothy Nevill, as companion, was to speak on the occasion. However there was no occasion. The granite base was almost as much of an engineering problem as had been the Duke's funeral car in 1852, so ponderous that it became mired in the mud of unpaved London streets. The granite block could not traverse bridges en route to the site until these were strengthened. Meanwhile the welcoming party arrived, including the sculptor and William Howard Russell of *The Times*, who found nothing he could report. There were noble lords and ladies, and nothing to toast but themselves.

That they did exactly that was clear from Dorothy Nevill's letter to Lady Airlie early that December. "It would have made you laugh to see the [2nd] Duke [of Wellington]—Dizzy—Ld Stanhope, etc, dancing a new dance, which consists in running in a ring, jumping and singing,—'What have you for supper, Mrs Bond?—Ducks in the garden, geese in the pond, etc, etc.' " Disraeli was obviously happier than in years, and Lady Dorothy gossiped about the unstatesmanlike jollity in a letter to ultra-Tory Lord Ellenborough, who responded on December 14 that he was amused that "the chief guest, the Pillar, did not arrive. . . . I always doubted their being able to get it there; and I think when the Duke asked you all for this season he must have speculated on a frost or on snow on which it might travel on a sledge."

The dance, he speculated, must have had its origins in the festivals of Pan and Bacchus, "only, as you do not mention it, I suppose the Roman precedent was not fully followed, for the Saltatori were naked. Perhaps D[israeli] in his excitement proposed this to Lord Stanhope, who would have entered into a long disquisition [upon] . . . the Lupercalia."

"Dizzy was in great force after dinner," Russell noted. "Talked of Tycho Brahe, Copernicus, Kepler, Galileo, the Ptolemaic system, etc. to our wonder till [William] Calcraft suggested he was lecturing and John Hay shrewdly hit on the real fact that he was only repeating part of the speech he would have made had he been elected Rector of the University of Edinburgh. He does not shoot and does nothing at all but spy into books— flat-footed, bad-legged creature." Disraeli, who would not have prepared a rectorial address in advance for a post he knew he could not win, was fascinated by astronomy, and would even put an astronomer in his next novel—which he probably did not yet know he was going to write. John Hay, twenty-seven, who had been a private secretary to the late President Lincoln, was visiting from Paris, where he was Secretary of the American legation. Russell, who had been a Civil War correspondent for *The Times* and had met Hay in Washington, knew very well that the Conservative leader in the Commons did much more than "spy into books," but he had his paper's suspicion of Disraeli. And Hay, a passionate republican with an antipathy to Tories, felt that electoral reform in England would not stave off the demise of the monarchy once Victoria was gone.

When the new session opened on February 6, 1866, it was with Victoria present, in widow's cap and flowing black tulle veil, to open Parliament for the first time since the Prince Consort's death, and that event, and the necessary eulogies of Palmerston, delayed partisan acrimony. Seated upon a throne draped with the robes of state she refused to wear, the Queen stared rigidly ahead while the Lord Chamberlain intoned the Address she refused to read. It was not exactly an end to her seclusion, but she had been driven to Westminster in a carriage with windows on both sides open, so that she could be seen. The exorcism of Albert was still far from complete.

The Queen had never trusted Palmerston but had grown to recognize his popularity across all classes. He had been the quintessential English gentleman. In his eulogy, Disraeli, who had once derided Palmerston as a "painted pantaloon" (in his old age he

concealed time's ravages with rouge), lamented "the disappearance of such a character from the scene—of so much sagacity, of
so much experience, and, I may say, of so much fame." And he
trusted that "the time may never come when the love of fame
shall cease to be the sovereign passion of our public men."

At a meeting of Conservatives to prepare tactics for confronting the expected new Reform Bill at Lord Salisbury's London
home on March 3, Derby advised saying as little as possible until
the Government's entire plan was laid out. Robert Lowe, one of
the most ambitious, yet conservative, of the Liberals, had sent
Spencer Walpole a note suggesting that Disraeli take over, even
that he attempt to bring down the Liberals, who might not follow
Gladstone. That no one else, not even Disraeli, spoke, Stafford
Northcote noted in his diary, seemed evidence that Derby was
not ready to retire from the leadership. But Lady Salisbury pulled
Northcote aside to suggest that Derby's heir, to whom it was no
secret that she was devoted, be cultivated by the party as alternative to Gladstone.

Informed by Northcote, Disraeli brushed aside the idea as
"dreams of princesses in fairyland. . . . It won't do." Disraeli
thought that "W.E.G. and S." sounded appropriate enough as opposing party leaders. "One is a man of transcendent ability; the
other, though not of transcendent ability, has considerable power.
But neither of them can deal with men. Stanley is a mere child
in such matters. The other, though more experienced, is too impetuous and wanting in judgment to succeed as a leader."

Not until March 12 did Gladstone bring in his bill for more
equitable representation in the Commons. A compromise measure recognizing the variety of views among the Liberals, it satisfied almost no one. Only the most reactionary among Disraeli's
partisans were as concerned about the alleged venality and ignorance of the working class voters whom the bill would enfranchise
as were the forty or so in the faction led by Lowe, the quarrel-
some, visually impaired albino who sat for the borough of Calne.

Members on both sides, from ultra-Tories to the Lowe cabal
of the Liberals, were alarmed by the unpredictability of the new
voters to be enfranchised. Traditionally safe seats might be swept
away, and the social fabric frayed. John Bright disdainfully labeled

the Lowe faction on his own side of the aisle the "Cave of Adullam" after the place where the biblical David, as a fugitive from King Saul, had once hidden himself, where "everyone that was discontented gathered themselves unto him."* Lowe wanted to be a power in the country. Keeping his Adullamites together to vote as a bloc with the Conservatives, he was not permitting his dislike of Disraeli to interfere with his opportunism; and Ben was not the first of the D'Israeli family with whom Lowe had tangled. As a schoolboy he had bullied the younger James D'Israeli and was as pugnacious as ever.

The Government won a preliminary skirmish, on an amendment, by only five votes. On May 10 came the collapse of a major banking house, followed by a slump in the stock market and a rise in interest rates to 10 percent. The Government's own stock was faltering but Disraeli, listening too much to his eager private secretary Ralph Earle, made some strategic blunders that delayed a Liberal defeat. On another amendment moved for its divisiveness, Disraeli finally came within seven votes of overturning Gladstone. Keeping his own counsel, Lowe wanted his bloc to be the swing votes which would determine the next government, and he wanted to determine the character of the coalition.

If Gladstone's bill passed, Disraeli wrote to Henry Liddell, "the aristocratic settlement of this country will receive a fatal blow." On June 18, an amendment on how much annual rent or property taxation would make a voter eligible lost by nine votes, but Lowe's faction wanted the more malleable Stanley rather than Derby or Disraeli. Lord Clarendon, an old Palmerstonian minister and ambassador who knew nearly everyone and everything, wrote to Delane at *The Times*, "Disraeli and Derby are *wild for office*, and I know from the best authority that Derby though coy will not be found reluctant." Even the ministries were already parceled out, he contended. "The loot is, I believe, all distributed."

Finally, on June 26, although it took a speech of two hours to make Russell's intentions clear, Gladstone announced the Cabinet's resignation. The next day Victoria sent for Lord Derby, rec-

*1 Samuel 22:2.

ommending that he include the Liberal dissidents to build a working majority.

It took only a few days for talk of coalitions to subside. Only one Liberal would accept office, a minor post. Derby would not throw Disraeli overboard to suit Lowe and would not step aside in favor of his son. Disraeli's advice since the early 1850s had been that it was fatal to a party to refuse office, and Derby, assuming that this opportunity would be, by all odds, his last, took Disraeli back with him to Downing Street. Yet there was no one else for the Foreign Office but Derby's son, and Stanley, ever the defeatist, arranged to borrow an appropriate house in London for diplomatic entertainment, explaining in his diary that he expected that the life of a Derby-Disraeli administration would be short. The arrangement "puts an end to one of my difficulties, since to take and furnish a house for a few months would be absurd, and I do not suppose our tenure of office will last longer."

On that note of melancholy from one of the key men in the new Government, the Derby-Disraeli partnership resumed office for the third time.

XX

"... A REVIVING TOUCH OF NATURE IN ONE OF HER MOST POPULAR AND AGREEABLE FORMS."

Ralph and Kate

"HE IS LONGING FOR THE REFRESHING FOLIAGE OF HIS SPLENDID BEECH trees—for repose at Hughenden—," Charlotte de Rothschild wrote of Disraeli to her son Leopold in the summer of 1864, "but Mary Anne wants a continuation of London and the world." At seventy-two, even with Hughenden enlarged and refurbished, Mary Anne did not want to be isolated in the country when each social season might be her last. Yet "in the brilliant world," Charlotte added in a report to Leo two years later that seems almost a postscript to the earlier letter, "Mrs Dis ... soon grows weary and dissatisfied because men and women listen to her great husband and pay little attention to her." As a result, "she says odd and startling things to arrest the eyes and ears of men and women."

Depressed by his party's stagnation and the possibility that his political career was stalled just short of 10 Downing Street, Disraeli at fifty-nine may have needed more than the consolation of his beeches and his books. While Mary Anne complained of exile in Beaconsfield, he had to continue his frustrating daily rounds to Westminster. Conditions were right for him to have sought the accessible arms of the liveliest of his friends in London, Dolly Nevill, twenty-one years younger, who lived diagonally across Upper Grosvenor Street. But did he?

At thirty-eight, Lady Dorothy Walpole Nevill was vivacious and youthful, with three children and a largely absent husband, and a reputation for flouting convention that had followed her from girlhood. Writing scrappy autobiographical vignettes in the early 1860s, Disraeli described her as "without absolute beauty" but "wild and bewitching."

To Disraeli, Dorothy's family had become "very strange" since the towering figure of Sir Robert Walpole, the first English prime minister. After the celebrated Horace Walpole, the squire of Twickenham and creator of the battlemented pseudo-castle Strawberry Hill, Dorothy seemed the most remarkable member. The Earl of Orford, Dorothy's father—a friend of Isaac D'Israeli— had resided at the time of her birth on April Fool's Day, 1826, at 11 Berkeley Square, the town house in which his illustrious forebear, one of the liveliest correspondents to use the English language, had died in 1797.

Disraeli was a political ally of her brothers Horatio and Frederick. Horatio (Lord Walpole until 1858, when he succeeded his father as earl) was characterized by Disraeli as his "greatest friend" after the exiled Henri, duc d'Aumale, the intellectual son of Louis-Philippe to whom *Lothair* would be dedicated. Much younger than her brothers, Dorothy as a petted teenager already had a reputation as a free spirit, and the Bishop of Oxford, Samuel Wilberforce, chaffed her as *"Semper Vividis."* Charles Dickens described her to William Macready as "extraordinarily free and careless" in her youth. "It is not her fault if Scandal ever leaves her alone," he remarked after her most notorious escapade, "for such a braver of all conventionalities never wore petticoats." Pretty and clever, carrying one of the great family names in England, she was sought after by young aristocrats and shook most of them off while acquiring wide notoriety for being fast.

Her debut in society was delayed by family absence on the Continent, but when it came—in 1846, when she was twenty—it was memorable: a cycle, she claimed, of sixty parties, fifty balls, thirty-five breakfasts, and thirty "drums"—large evening socials for which rival hostesses "drummed up" attendance, competing for elite guests. At one she overheard someone ask, "Who is that young lady who looks as if she had come out of a picture of George III's time?" The inquirer was Disraeli, who hadn't seen her since she was a child. "You are dear Walpole's sister," he said, introducing himself, "and I must know you."

Among her talents she possessed an aptitude for heraldic art and before long asked Disraeli for a favorite quotation to emblazon. He gave her some lines from his Manchester Athenaeum speech of 1844 (delivered less than two years before) beginning "Knowledge is the mystic ladder in the patriarch's dream." She worked it in embroidery, and Disraeli added his signature.

Dorothy's ladylike—even bluestocking—side turned few admirers away although she had come into the marriage market late. One suitor was George Augustus Frederick Percy Sydney Smythe, elder son of a career ambassador, the 6th Viscount Strangford, and at twenty-six brilliant, handsome, and irresponsible. Although he had turned his coat, leaving Disraeli's Young England faction for Peel, Disraeli liked him, and Smythe probably met Dorothy at a breakfast at Grosvenor Gate. His affections, she discovered, even when distributed among several amorous targets, were not easily shaken off. In the summer of 1846 (her debut year) he came calling at the Earl of Orford's country estate in Hampshire, after which events become confused. On August 29, he retreated hurriedly to France. Fortunately for his constituents (he held a seat for Canterbury), Parliament was not in session, but his return for its opening seemed in doubt.

Still abroad on November 3, he wrote dolefully to Lord John Manners that he had become one of those "whom English hypocrisy has banished & proscribed." To Disraeli, Smythe claimed that daughters of great houses failed to interest him because he was impatient with the social niceties. "Family I don't care in the least for: [I] would rather marry into a rich vulgar family. Madness no objection. As for Scrofula why should I care for it more than [does] a king?" If low tastes eliminated him as potential husband for Lady Dorothy, her certain lack of any share in the Walpole

inheritance—she was after all a daughter—would have been a further disincentive to the fortune-hunting Smythe. When it came
to dalliance he was less particular, but marriage to a daughter of
the Walpoles seemed out of the question. Yet would he have any
choice? Resisting family pressure to marry Dolly Walpole, Smythe
would have to meet her elder brother, Lord Walpole, to discuss
his sister's future.

In the scandal press, reports circulated, abetted by the family
but treated with skepticism, that Lady Dorothy had done nothing
more than fall down a flight of stairs while visiting friends in the
country, necessitating the care of a Norwich surgeon. That the
surgeon may not have been treating the results of exactly that
kind of fall was suggested in a letter from Lord George Bentinck
to Disraeli. Although it had not appeared in print, "the talk in
the Clubs is that Lord Walpole has had Smythe out & shot him
in the wrist. —The scandalous say he has enjoyed the favours of
both the married and unmarried [Walpole] sisters & of the sister
in law also. —It is much discussed whether Smythe will be received in Society after such an outrage as getting an Earl's daughter with child (if she be with child) & then casting her off &
refusing to marry her. —This is quite a modern description of
profligacy reserved for a Member of Peel's moral Government, the
contagion of its political bad faith spreading into private life."

Whether or not there was a duel with Dorothy's brother,
Smythe did fight the last duel on English soil, at Weybridge in
1852. He had charged his opponent, Frederick Romilly, who held
the other Canterbury seat, with election tampering, and they had
it out at Smythe's expense. Although he did not lose his life, he
lost his seat.

Such risk-taking was typical for Smythe, who was sometimes
undone by his own charm and what he thought it enabled him to
get away with. When Disraeli transformed him into "Waldershare" in Endymion late in life, he described him, as kindly as he
could, as "profligate but sentimental; unprincipled but romantic,"
and possessed by a "versatile nature [that] becomes palled even
with the society of duchesses." The Orford version of Dolly's fall
became literal rather than figurative, her encounter with Smythe
a case of mistaken identity. Smythe had indeed come to Hamp-

shire on a visit, the Countess of Orford wrote to Mary Anne, *"unsanctioned by* either Lord O. or myself," and had put up in a small hotel nearby in Andover, where he took up with a local female "of bad character" misidentified as Dorothy, went walking and riding with the young woman, and was discovered with her—literally—in a summerhouse folly. The "calumnious stories" that followed, linking Dorothy with Smythe, were, the Countess contended, untrue, as when Smythe had arrived, he had allegedly been asked "to quit the neighbourhood."

Since their daughter was such a favorite of the Disraelis, her mother entreated Mary Anne, "Do tell me if these atrocious stories are still going on and you need not fear telling me what you hear as nothing can be worse than what we have already heard." She did not need to say that rumors ranged from seduction to abortion, the latter allegation resulting from what the Orfords explained as a "slight accident" in which Dorothy had "hurt her back" and been attended by a physician who "ordered leeches to be applied . . . and a warm bath every other night for a fortnight."

The episode assured that Lady Dorothy would never again be received in the prudish Court of Queen Victoria, whom she had to outlive to be invited once more to Windsor. Her banishment raised concerns that Dorothy would never be able to find a husband of appropriately elevated station and venerable family—or any husband at all.

Smythe remained abroad until March, indulging, he boasted to Disraeli, in "affairs of debauch." Dorothy remained in parentally imposed exile even longer, at Wolterton in Norfolk, while her family made quiet efforts to find her a husband. For the summer of 1847 they took a house at Sidmouth in Devon, transferring Dorothy there. A visitor that August was Reginald Nevill, a Walpole cousin and grandson of the first Earl of Abergavenny. He was assumed to be a confirmed bachelor, but on September 29, 1847, after he went to London with the Countess to be looked over at breakfast by the Disraelis at Grosvenor Gate, and then paid a visit to his lawyer's office, the Orfords announced Nevill's engagement to their daughter. Reggie Nevill was forty, Dolly twenty-one. He hardly resembled the eager young swains whom

Dorothy had been leading on, but he could afford her, and Disraeli was relieved that she would be safely established. To a letter of congratulations from him, Dorothy replied, "I am so glad you approve of my choice of a husband. I assure you, I could never have found another so well suited to me. He is so good[,] so devoted to me[,] it will be my own fault if I am not happy."*

Announcing that she saw "nothing to be ashamed of in being married," Lady Dorothy was wed to Reginald Nevill on December 2, 1847, with a Walpole cousin performing the ceremony. The Earl of Orford was overcome with happiness and relief. Nevill had, Disraeli knew, "a good £8,000 a year," and it was a perfect match because he provided almost everything and desired almost nothing. But the marriage failed to end gossip about Dorothy and Smythe. The scandal sheet *Chit-Chat* on April 16, 1848, some months after the wedding, punned on the name of Dorothy's flown friend, "Lady Dorothy Nevill is always quite struck when passing a smith's shop. The working of the *bellows*, the glowing *fire*, the subdued *roar*, and the rapid *hammering*, suggest recollections which are not *forge-eries* upon the imagination."

The evidence of the calendar, nevertheless, was that Dorothy's firstborn, a daughter, was surely Reggie Nevill's. She then furnished him with an heir, Edward Augustus Nevill, and Reggie provided her with the town house she wanted, across Upper Grosvenor Street from the Disraelis. Nevill preferred the country, and purchased Dangstein in Hampshire, more than a thousand acres situated twenty-two miles from the nearest railway station at Godalming. There Dorothy discovered a passion for horticulture while Nevill hunted, bred horses, and indulged his hobby of coaching—a curious sport in which gentlemen dressed as coachmen and drove their own equipages. Dorothy would see less and less of him in London, but since she regarded him in the early 1860s as a "Palmerstonian" imbecile while she was a Disraeli devotee, she did not encourage his further interest in politics or in London. In his long absences she "naturally became great friends"

*Most letters, as convention demanded, would be between the two wives—134 survive from Dorothy to Mary Anne. Nevertheless, she and Disraeli continued a separate correspondence over four decades.

with her famous neighbor. In some later letters she referred to herself as "Mouse" and to Disraeli as "Lion."

When her second son, Horace, was born (two others would die in infancy), Dorothy asked Mary Anne to be the godmother. Unusual among aristocratic mothers, Dorothy nursed the child herself, which was almost as scandalous as some of her other pursuits, like smoking cigars and drinking whisky.

In the country she raised silkworms, constructed an elaborate apiary, aviary, and arboretum, and as a botanist became so adept at insect fertilization of orchids that Darwin asked for samples and she was mentioned in the scientific literature. She even contributed to it herself by translating and abridging a small book from the French of F. E. Guérin-Meneville, *The Ailanthus Silkworm and the Ailanthus Tree* (1862). According to Disraeli she was the equal as a botanist of the famed Professor Sir Joseph Hooker of Kew Gardens, and "without doubt the creator of the finest pinetum and conservatories and collections of rare trees in the world—all formed and collected . . . by herself at Dangstein." Her gardens turn up imaginatively in the closing pages of Disraeli's *Lothair,* written in 1869, where Lady Corisande creates one in which, "in their season, flourished abundantly all those productions of nature which are banished from our once delighted senses," and where "bees were busy in the air . . . and you might watch them labouring in their glassy hives."

Although, to Disraeli, Lady Dorothy was more interesting for herself than her avocations, he talked the language of her interests in their letters, valuing most her succulent strawberries. Since she also cultivated the eminent of her time and collected their letters and crested letterheads, Disraeli waited on one occasion until he was a weekend guest at Windsor Castle to thank his "Dearest Dorothy" for a shipment to Grosvenor Gate of Dangstein strawberries. On notepaper with a royal device he praised them (April 11, 1858) as "fresh, & delicious, as yourself, & [they] came to me at a welcome moment when I was spiritless and feverish. Their revival was a welcome touch of nature in one of her most popular and agreeable forms." And he was, to "dearest Dorothy," "your friend, whose affection for you requires no proof."

They understood each other, and Disraeli would sometimes confide in her outside the code of botany. "Ah, dear Dorothy," he wrote in 1858, a particularly trying time when he hung onto office by his fingertips, "it is not my politics they dislike! It is myself." Dorothy realized that more than his brand of Toryism was involved—there was a taint of anti-Semitism. But he was nothing like the Rev. Joseph Wolff, husband of her Aunt Georgianna, the eccentric German-Jewish apostate who had become a Christian missionary and self-promoting adventurer. Wolff had entered Bokhara in central Asia in surplice and college cap, reading the Anglican service aloud, saving his life that way because the inhabitants took him for a madman, but losing all his canonicals to bandits as he trekked six hundred miles through Afghanistan to safety. Back in England he seldom removed his clothes (and seldom washed), the Earl of Orford, his brother-in-law, growling that Wolff was concealing, that way, the phylacteries he had sewn into his trouser legs.

Disraeli was different, an authentic gentleman, although Dorothy remembered his metamorphosis from curled and ringleted dandy into sober statesman. Now that he was a powerful Member of Parliament he was able to return some of the family's earlier favors, even helping to arrange for a seat in the Commons for her brother Frederick.

Late in March 1864, Mrs. Disraeli was unwell, a situation no longer unusual at Grosvenor Gate, and Lady Dorothy inquired sympathetically, promising some of her famed strawberries from the country. On April 21, Disraeli himself thanked her for the first fruits of the season, boasting that they had made, in one serving, an entire meal. "When are you coming to town?" he asked, "and how do your *Coniferoe* and all their graceful companions flourish?" Disraeli remained in London until July 29, when the dismal Parliamentary session ended. By then Lady Dorothy was back at 29 Grosvenor Street, without her husband, who clung to the rustic distractions at Dangstein.

A possible clue to Disraeli's state of mind emerges in a reminiscence by political journalist T. E. Kebbel, who visited Hughenden overnight early in October 1864. One of the guests for dinner was Henry Lygon, Viscount Elmley (later 4th Earl of

Beauchamp). The other was a Buckinghamshire country gentleman whose pride was his herd of Alderney cattle. Over drinks in
the drawing room after Mrs. Disraeli had retired, their conversation turned to the virtues of claret and burgundy over the "deeper
potations" that the first Georges had introduced from Hanover.
The owner of the Alderneys praised the wine cellar at the King's
Arms, at Berkhamsted, and Disraeli confessed that he did not recall the inn.

"You must remember the house, sir," the country gentleman
protested. "There was a very handsome barmaid there—
monstrous fine gal—you must have been in the King's Arms, sir."

"Perhaps," said Disraeli, "if I had been in *her* arms I might
have remembered it.'

"Mr Lygon," Kebbel wrote, "looked grave."

Ralph Nevill, Dorothy's third surviving son, born on March
4, 1865, was almost certainly conceived in London in June 1864.
A granddaughter of Dorothy's youngest brother "was brought up
to believe" (according to Guy Nevill, a cousin) that Ralph, who
"appeared to be a cross between his grandfather, Lord Orford, and
Disraeli," was Disraeli's child. (Bulwer-Lytton's son described
Ralph Nevill as looking like "an over-cooked snipe.") As an old
woman, Dorothy told young Edward Cazalet, "Why, I have seen
Dizzy in his night-cap, I have known him ill, I have known him
in every possible way." If Ralph were Disraeli's child, he went unacknowledged, as was certainly necessary. He had a legal father in
the absent, eccentric Reggie Nevill, with whom, on the rare occasion when he was seen in London, Disraeli was friendly, until
Nevill died in 1878. Lady Dorothy got over the loss quickly. Outside the family she never mentioned him.

Unlike Disraeli's letters to other women, those to Dolly often closed with "your affectionate D." She was also one of the
rare individuals whom he addressed by first name. Yet in his first
letter to her after Ralph's birth, barely a month after her confinement, although congratulations were in order, he did not even allude to the event. Instead, from Hughenden on April 17, 1865,
he described, in a letter to Dorothy, his first trip into Buckinghamshire by carriage and horses in many years. "How delightful
after railroads! We baited at Gerrard's Cross, twenty miles from

town, and then strolled into Bulstrode Park to see the house the
Duke of Somerset is building . . . amid the old pleasance which I
described thirty years ago in *Henrietta Temple*; for Bulstrode, then
mansionless and deserted, was the origin of Armine. Excuse this
egotism, the characteristic of scribblers when they had left off
work. Adieu, dear Dorothy."

Her vivacity exercised its spell over Disraeli, as the
Strathfieldsaye episode of dancing in a ring that December would
demonstrate (see page 414). Ralph was then nine months old and
at home. In Mary Anne's fading years, and after, Dorothy would
often accompany—*chaperon* hardly seems the appropriate verb—
Disraeli to town and country houses, until his health and august
status required the attendance of his private secretary. Only when
Disraeli had to relinquish 2 Grosvenor Gate did regular visits to
29 Upper Grosvenor Street end. "I well remember my mother
telling me as a child," Ralph wrote of the Grosvenor Gate days,
"to say 'How-do-you-do' to him. Dressed in a shabby old paletot,
he sat looking at me as if I were some strange little animal, but
with no unkindly expression on his inscrutable old face he shook
me by the hand."

Having cared little about her earlier brood, Dorothy became
a doting mother to Ralph, not only nursing him but carrying him
about to her friends and even mounting one of his baby teeth
in a brooch she designed. "He inherits the blood of the Walpoles
and the Nevills and might be a credit to them," she explained to
A. H. Sayce, "so I am taking care to make him see as much of
men like Darwin and Tyndall, and to know what sensible conversation means." But he was never much good at science and may
have been too coddled to be good at anything.

If Ralph had an intimation that he was not Reggie's son he
kept it to himself. "My father, however," he once wrote, "—his
well-known and active interest in agriculture serving as an
excuse—generally managed to avoid [people and London]."
Ralph hardly knew him. He seldom mentioned—even avoided
mentioning—Disraeli. "As a small child," he wrote, "I was frequently taken out by Lady Beaconsfield in her brougham—she
was my brother's godmother, and very kind to children." His earliest memories were of newsboys in 1870 shouting about Sedan,

"Great slaughter of the French! Capture of the Emperor!" A delicate child, he had few playmates, preferring his thousand tin soldiers. Like his mother he had no interest in religion and a particular horror of Christmas.

Lady Dorothy resumed her myriad enterprises when Ralph, appropriately for his class, went to boarding school and then to Eton, where he was when Nevill's death left her only an annuity of £800 a year. Ralph was thirteen. Dorothy had to sell her properties and her specimens. Many of her prize plants and trees left England to grace the estates of the King of the Belgians and the Prince of Monaco. In London she found a smaller house in Charles Street, off Berkeley Square, where she added a greenhouse. In the early 1880s she would be one of the founders of the Primrose League, named for Disraeli's allegedly favorite flower and supporting his brand of "Tory democracy." The year after, having overlooked Lady Dorothy, the League amended its charter to include women.

Left an income by Nevill, Ralph went up to Oxford in 1883, and by the later 1880s was living the unstrenuous life of an unattached gentleman of leisure. Through his diplomat uncle, Sir Henry Drummond Wolff, son of the eccentric missionary, he secured honorary attaché posts at Tehran in 1888 and Madrid in 1892 and traveled widely—as far as Japan—fulfilling interests he described as "collecting and anything amusing." A lifelong bachelor and clubman (he even wrote a book about London clubs), he got into publishing largely by editing and arranging five often overlapping volumes of his mother's gossipy, letter-littered, rambling memoirs—"the tangled remnants of my brain," she confessed. He turned out nearly thirty books of his own, including *Floreat Etona* (1912), an anecdotal history of his school, and such light evocations of the late Victorian years as *Piccadilly to Pall Mall* and *Fancies, Fashions and Fads*. Like Disraeli, he found Byron's *Don Juan* and *Childe Harold* delicious reading when a boy, but they did him less good.

When the war began in 1914 the first volunteer work he was able to find was at a field glasses distribution depot. He transferred to a job as a censor of letters, then moved to the Military Permit Office in Bedford Square, which evaluated requests for

out-of-country travel, an assignment that enabled him to claim
that he worked for Navy Intelligence. After 1918 Nevill lived
mostly in Paris, where he produced *Mayfair and Montmartre* and
two other books about his adopted city. Although *The Times*
thought him worthy of an obituary, none of his works are remembered.

While Dolly remained close to Disraeli all his life, her relationship to Mary Anne was such that no cause for suspicion was
ever awakened. When her concerns about Disraeli's attractiveness
to other women caused squabbles, few in their circle knew about
them. Affairs among the well-placed could not always be hidden,
but conspiracies of silence were common, and only one's solicitor
knew everything (or almost everything). Besides, few thought
that the ageing Disraeli, however much his exoticism and his political power evoked their own appeal, remained attractive to
women after his dandy days.

Ralph died in June 1930, seventeen years after his long-lived
mother. He never managed to emerge from Lady Dorothy's overwhelming shadow and would have been a disappointment to
Disraeli.

In the year of Ralph Nevill's birth, a woman—we may never
know who she was—conceived a child who, when she came of
age in the later 1880s, looked in a surviving photograph strikingly
like Disraeli, and would be sent out of sight to Australia with a
husband of no great promise and an income of mysterious origin.
Sir Philip Rose, Disraeli's attorney and confidant who drew up his
friend's last will in 1878, would note privately to Sir Nathaniel de
Rothschild, the other co-executor of the estate, at the time of
probate, that the will made no provision for the "infant beneficiary" ("infant Tenant" in another paragraph), but if said minor
child brought an action against the estate requiring an allowance
he thought it would be granted. (The young woman in the picture claimed that her father, so she told her granddaughter, provided financial support, however indirectly, until his death and
that it was continued even beyond that.)

Was that young woman the minor child carefully left out of a will that Disraeli knew would become public, yet who was discreetly under the wing of his designated trustees? The Rothschilds burned their most confidential papers and were so assiduous at it that, although some letters escaped the pyre, trunks of Disraeli's business correspondence with Baron Lionel and his son Natty were incinerated, and Natty's son Nathaniel Charles was permitted to keep only a Disraeli envelope for his personal autograph collection. Rose was the most discreet of lawyers as well as Disraeli's confidant over decades of delicate service. The only solid clue that survives seems to be his revealing advisory opinion to the future Lord Rothschild. Natty had been described by Disraeli (to Lady Bradford) as "N. Rothschild who knows everything"—and it seems certain from Sir Philip Rose's memorandum on the will that he understood the reference to be to Kate Donovan or someone like her. Following the secretive methods of the firm when it came to confidential matters, Rothschild committed much to his retentive memory. (Disraeli once remarked that when he wanted any date in history, he asked Natty.)

Catherine ("Kate") Donovan—as she was on her birth certificate—was aristocratic in manner beyond her "paper" parents. She would tell a very few in her family that she was Disraeli's daughter by an unknown mother whom she took to be both French and of the Jewish faith. Kate had little more than her looks and the curious upbringing she remembered to bolster her contention.

According to the record, Kate was born to John Vincent Donovan of Hackney, twenty-one, and his wife, Mary, twenty-three, on March 13, 1866—little more than a year after Ralph Nevill—and christened Catherine Mary. Apparent conception, if the birth certificate accords with reality—registration was a month later—would have been approximately mid-July, 1865. That summer, Parliament was dissolved on July 6 and elections held almost immediately after. Disraeli was returned unopposed on July 13, making only one campaign address for himself in Buckinghamshire. On July 19 he made a political speech in his home county in behalf of a Tory candidate at Newport Pagnell. It was a quiet time and his freedom of movement for social visits was considerable. There is no telling, if he were responsible for

Kate, when she was actually conceived or born, as given the infant mortality rate at the time, she may have been documented,
when an appropriate certificate became available, with the name
of a legitimate child who died in early infancy, with the family
compensated for use of the identity. (Census records show that
the first Donovan child to survive and live with the family in its
domicile was Agnes, born in June 1867.)

Possibly premature, Kate told Dorothy, her daughter, that she
was so small at birth that she could have "fitted into a quart milk
jug." Her granddaughter, Catherine, remembered hearing the
same story. John Vincent Donovan, whose brood burgeoned to at
least ten yet who had no children at the time of Kate's arrival,
was a compositor for Hansard, the parliamentary reporting publisher, and may have been known to Members who arranged to
have printer's proofs of their speeches as taken down by short-
hand reporters altered or corrected.

The address from which Catherine's birth was registered
at no time listed an occupant named Donovan. The house in
Lower Kennington Lane, south of the Thames, was that of
Thomas Bacon, a furniture seller, who lived there with his large
extended family. It may have been an address of convenience for
young Kate's registry, or the Donovans may have been temporary
dwellers with Bacon in their working-class district of brush makers, piano tuners, and coffee roasters. Kate did not recall being
brought up there at all but rather with a sophisticated and well-
to-do family in the London countryside by someone who called
herself Kate's "grandmother." It was not uncommon for a well-
connected Victorian country family to bring up a ward; and Kate
would not have been an object of special curiosity.

Kate recalled having horses and once giving ale to a horse
that proceeded to kick the stable door down; and she spoke of
peacocks in the garden screaming when a threat of rain was in
the air. Yet her upbringing remains shadowy. The family with
whom she lived also had a town house, and at one time or another, Kate claimed, as a child, to have met there various persons
of importance, even the Prince of Wales, who allegedly called her
"my little Katy." Her favorite was Baroness Burdett-Coutts, whom
she spoke of, Kate's granddaughter recalled, "with the greatest af-

fection," and who invited her often for Sunday tea. Kate spoke of the Rothschilds "with great esteem and an air of intimacy. She seemed to think higher of them than of royalty itself." She apparently knew Leopold, whom she referred to as "Leo." Kate remained, in her quiet way, a great snob about such claimed connections all her life.

She was petite and fine-boned, with wavy black hair not as ringleted as Disraeli's, yet her great pride. Like Disraeli, she kept it dyed a deep black nearly all her days. Her handwriting was well schooled and elegant, and her reading belied Lower Kennington Lane. She had flawless English, some knowledge of other languages, and believed that a family in France whom she visited often as a girl were "cousins" related to her unacknowledged mother. A father-figure not Disraeli took her to see the Egyptian obelisk, "Cleopatra's Needle," being brought gingerly up the Thames in 1878, and she spoke to her daughter and granddaughter about visits to Continental places—to Paris, to Salzburg, to Pompeii, and to Venice, a city she had been taught particularly to value. "There was something deeply Italian—Venetian—in her background," her granddaughter thought.

Kate claimed that in the later 1870s her "father" gave her a porcelain figurine purchased as a souvenir in Germany. Her family concludes that the comic, Italianate, one-man band with all his instruments was chosen because of its vague resemblance, from hair to nose to pointed goatee, to Disraeli. Perhaps the gift can be linked to his attendance at the Congress of Berlin in 1878. Disraeli did collect Dresden china, which he displayed in a black wooden cabinet at Hughenden. Kate prized the figurine all her life as a link with her past, and it remains with her family.

One of her claims was to have crossed the Atlantic as a girl to see Niagara Falls—hardly the holiday of a working-class daughter, but also not substantiated. The Falls were legendary by the later nineteenth century, everyone's dreamed-of wedding trip; and in 1882 Oscar Wilde had declared the cataract as "one of the earliest, if not the keenest, disappointments in American married life." She may have read about that. Yet her experiences of London itself were beyond the resources of Kennington Lane. She remembered being taken to see Sarah Bernhardt perform, and

Gilbert and Sullivan operettas in the newly electric-lit Savoy Theatre in the Strand. She received piano lessons and later saw to it that her children were musically educated—voice, piano, cello, violin, flute.

Although Kate's birth certificate located her in a Roman Catholic family, she was raised as an Anglican and married in 1888 at the Presbyterian Church of St. Andrew in Marylebone. Except for her wedding, however, she was never known as an adult to enter a church. She would read only the Old Testament, bridled at any veneration of Jesus as deity—she chastened her second husband for teaching "Gentle Jesus, Meek and Mild" to her granddaughter, Kate. For a time she even kept meat and milk dishes separate, and she lit Sabbath candles as a young woman as part of her claim to be Jewish. Yet by Jewish religious law that claim could only be validated by a Jewish mother and hardly by a baptized Jewish father, as was Benjamin Disraeli.

Kate offered no evidence that she had ever met Disraeli, who died when she was fourteen, but who was concerned, she felt, about her happiness through the quiet employment of intermediaries. That there was also some Donovan connection beyond the birth certificate seems likely. Kate's daughter remembered meeting, on a visit to Australia, red-haired "Dardy," or Frederick, described by her mother as a brother. "How?" Dorothy asked. "There were two families," Kate said in a way that did not encourage further questions, but might have meant that her mother had a legitimate family at a later time, and even that Mary Donovan herself was involved somehow, before she began a legitimate family. After the mysterious Kate, it is clear that the Donovan ménage included a Frederick who bore no resemblance to Kate, and was born in Lambeth in 1869. Was the family connection a common mother, or merely the technical one of a document relating her to the Donovans?

Did Disraeli have any proved relationship with the Donovans? Other than a possible link through Hansard, a December 1863 letter to an agent handling some of Disraeli's complicated financial matters indicates that until that date he had been renting stables at Grosvenor Gate to a "Mr Donovan." (With dozens of Donovans in London, this is not a persuasive connection to John

Vincent Donovan.) Kate married Henry James John Stacey of Marylebone in 1888. Could it be sheer coincidence that the Disraeli estate in 1892 was "letting . . . part of Coombe's Farm and two cottages to Messrs Stacey," an arrangement handled by Rose's firm?

Kate emigrated to Australia with Stacey and bore him two sons before she abandoned him in Sydney, charging him with alcoholism. She then established an irregular union with George Peter Styles, a watchmaker. In Brisbane she bore him a daughter, Dorothy, in 1901. The family believed that Kate named her for Dolly Nevill although there is no evidence that one knew the other. Despite her gossipy nature, Lady Dorothy knew how and when to be discreet.

From Brisbane, after the birth of their daughter, Kate and Styles embarked for the North Island town of Napier in New Zealand, where they established a jewelry shop. While she managed the sales counter, Styles repaired watches in a back room. A Wellington firm of diamond merchants, Rothschild and Rothschild, no relation to the banking dynasty, offered a line of credit on the strength of some unknown guarantee that cannot be traced and was intended to remain so.

Both of Kate's children by Styles were born before he became, legally, her second husband in 1915. Louis, born in New Zealand and later an optometrist there, was known to intolerant Napierites as "the Jew boy," a tag brought upon him by Kate's practices if not her pretensions. In England she had been a young woman of charm and intelligence. Down Under, those attributes, largely stifled, made her waspish. It was not a place for Paris gowns, which she once had worn, and there were few to appreciate the milky white skin and ebony coiffure that had been her pride when she visited Baroness Burdett-Coutts, the only great lady she ever spoke about with warm affection. Dorothy, the elder of her Styles offspring, was allowed to play only with the children of the Levy family in Napier, after one of whom, Esther, Dorothy's daughter was given her middle name. To Dorothy, Kate imparted some of her confidences. Catherine Esther, as a child, received some as well, Kate explaining about religion that she believed, above all, in a Day of Atonement, a special day to right the year's wrongs. Young Kate remembered, too, a copy of Disraeli's *Coningsby* displayed prominently when she was too young to read it.

Disraeli, who had not acknowledged the first Catherine, and never to anyone's knowledge made himself known to her, fast disappeared into family myth as his self-styled daughter aged and became more secretive. She lived into her nineties still quietly claiming to her children her pride of ancestry.

Kate's great-grandson, formally Jewish by conversion, had named his son Benjamin before he ever heard the Disraeli story from Dorothy, distant still in New Zealand. In her own eighties, she possessed little more than her memories of her mother's cryptic tales of a vanished life, and the circumstantial evidence among her photographs that the comely young woman who had resembled a distaff Disraeli had weathered in her old age into a Mediterranean-looking matron. Nearly as long-lived as Kate, Dorothy died on March 23, 1992, at ninety, having requested the Reform Jewish ritual at her funeral. In her last months, perhaps linking Ralph and Kate, she confided to a close friend, "There wasn't one child; there were two children—a boy and a girl. From two different mothers."

The evidence for Disraeli's paternity is plausible without being conclusive. By Victorian standards his behavior would have been acceptable for a gentleman of rank. His society was one in which women were often left to bear both the children and the burden. In the case of Ralph and Kate one child had a legal father and inheritance; the other was apparently provided for. Could Disraeli have betrayed his ambitions, and the reputations of the mothers, one the daughter of an earl, by acknowledging his children—if, indeed, they were his? The surviving clues tantalize but the jury on Ralph and Kate is still out.

XXI

"... THE MINISTRY BY HIMSELF."

1866–1868

DISRAELI DETERMINED TO MAKE SOMETHING OF THE THIRD DERBY AD-ministration. Dismissed in advance as another caretaker government, it proved more effective than anticipated. But for the selection of the elderly Lord Chelmsford as Lord Chancellor, Disraeli got his way about key Cabinet appointments. He detested Chelmsford, who had been one of the most stubborn opponents of the Oaths Bill over many sessions, but bided his time.

The immediate domestic issue inherited by the Tories was the question of the limits of free speech in public places. They feared that mass demonstrations could lead to riots, and mobs to much worse, even republican insurrection. Agitation over electoral inequalities had been keeping the Metropolitan Police busy in Hyde Park, and the worried Queen would soon urge "wretched Reform" upon Derby and Disraeli. Even more disturbing was that on the day that the new Cabinet was sworn in at Windsor, July 5, 1866, news came that Austria, its army overwhelmed at Sadowa, had asked Prussia for an armistice. The war which Bismarck sought had been short and decisive, and Victoria's son-in-law, Crown Prince Frederick, had been a hero. But with Austria out, the balance of power in the German Confederation was gone. Prussia dominated central Europe. Disraeli knew it would happen: Bismarck had told him so when they had met in London.

Whatever Disraeli's concerns about Europe, his immediate goal as the Derby government examined its priorities was to defuse acrimony over demonstrations in Hyde Park and Victoria Park. When John Stuart Mill "delivered a speech hardly worthy of a philosopher, but rather more adapted to Hyde Park," the Leader of the House reported to the Queen, "the C[hancello]r of the Exchequer ventured to tell him this, & then the matter died off." He explained to Victoria that mass meetings in the parks were the acceptable price of a free society. "Public meetings are the recognised, & indispensable, organs of a free constitution. They are safety-valves. It is desirable . . . that there should be some public places provided where the great body of the people, like the Comitia of the Romans, should have the right to assemble, & discuss, & express their opinion."

The Queen had urged some restrictions upon use of parks deemed Royal, but Parliament shrank from closing the safety valves, especially as adjournment approached. The House's "pulse is very low," Disraeli told the Queen on July 26, "but extreme unction will not be administered, I believe, until Friday." Reform agitation had already overwhelmed the police at Hyde Park on July 23, and protests continued for two days further, a mob breaking down the railings near the Marble Arch, trampling the flower beds and heaving stones at the windows of the well-to-do off Park Lane. Soldiers were dispatched to protect the area, and with duty keeping him at Westminster, Disraeli relied on bulletins from his new private secretary, Montagu Corry. Sending news by messenger at 6:40 P.M., Corry noted from Grosvenor Gate, "The soldiers have moved away to the Marble Arch, and Mrs Disraeli wishes me to add that the people in general seem to be thoroughly enjoying themselves, and I really believe she sympathizes with them."

Monty Corry had met Disraeli the year before at Raby, the Duke of Cleveland's estate. A young solicitor, Corry was the dapper, black-bearded second son of Henry Corry, Secretary to the Admiralty in the previous Tory administration. At Raby he had been the life of the house party one rainy afternoon, dancing with the younger women and singing comic songs. Knowing that Corry was seeking some minor office, Disraeli told him privately that evening, "I think you must be my impresario."

To make room, Disraeli named the ambitious Ralph Earle to be Secretary of the Poor Law Board under the Home Office. Although the salary was excellent, it seemed to Earle not enough of a promotion. He quickly became a rebel, then left the government for private business. Corry thrived. "The relations between a Minister and his secretary are, or at least should be, among the finest that can subsist between two individuals," Disraeli wrote in *Endymion*. "Except the married status, there is none in which so great a confidence is involved, in which more forbearance ought to be exercised, or more sympathy ought to exist." (Disraeli had forgotten—or could not mention—Philip Rose, who had long been unique as confidential agent and solicitor.)

From the front bench on July 30 Disraeli penned a note to the Queen about the latest demonstration for Reform. "Mr Mill entered the House this evening, about ten o'ck, & then I knew that the great meeting was really over. He had not been seated ten minutes before he sank into profound slumber, from wh[ich] nothing could rouse him. It was a great contrast to his usual demeanour: his bright, ultra-vigilant face, with almost too much tension of interest, & air of unflagging duty. A philosopher, who, past middle life, becomes Member for Westminster, & attends monster meetings at Islington, may be pardoned if for a moment, he confesses the weakness of exhausted nature." The term "Tory Democracy" would later be associated with Disraeli. Its reality is validated by his sympathy and respect for political opponents like Cobden, Bright, and Mill, whose radical views about social and economic change he respected and wanted the Queen to understand.

"London is clearing fast," John Delane reported to his deputy at *The Times*, G. W. Dasent, on August 7. "The Lords today mustered only three on one side and one on the other, Granville saying it was all very well when he was paid [as a Minister] but he could not listen to Westmeath *gratis.*"* In the Commons only a few undersecretaries remained to cope with adjournment. No one wanted to be near the fetid Thames at Westminster while work on the new Embankment affected the sewer system. Delane heard, nevertheless, that the Tory whitebait dinner at Greenwich had been "great fun, Derby and Dizzy being there in high spirits, and the Chancellor [of the Exchequer] pouring forth a perfect avalanche of puns. It was very long since they had a chance."

It was clear as Parliament adjourned that when it met again it would have to take up Reform; rumors even arose that legislation on some form of Household Suffrage—a vote for each head of a household who paid rates and taxes—was being secretly drafted. In actuality Derby and Disraeli had no idea what extension of the electorate their party would accept which would be enough, besides, to attract enough other votes for passage. Addressing his Buckinghamshire constituents, Disraeli admitted, "We are sometimes taunted with not having a policy." But the Conservatives did have one, he contended—"to uphold our constitution in church and state. It is to bring in all those measures and to pursue in every respect that policy which will secure to this country the continuance of prosperity and peace."

With such broad ambiguities, Disraeli kept the door open for anything. Peace meant external as well as internal balancing acts. A reunited America had sued for damages wrought by the Confederate raider *Alabama,* built in a British shipyard. There were concerns about Irish-American ex-soldiers crossing the Atlantic to increase unrest in John Bull's other island. Europe was incubating new wars in which Britain had no desire to become involved. As always, Disraeli had his own intelligence service via the Rothschilds, who seemed, Sidonia-style, to know everything. (Lionel, in turn, expected reciprocal information and received it.) In December Disraeli told Stanley, the Foreign Minister, that the Rothschilds had confided "alarming news as to the state of France. It was thought that people were getting tired of the empire." Citizens were indeed weary of the Emperor Napoleon's cir-

---

*General T. J. Nugent, 8th Earl of Westmeath, was notorious for his evictions of his Irish tenants and, at eighty-one, crankier than ever.

cuses without bread—a climate of civil and military corruption and an economy artificially propelled by grandiose building schemes to beautify Paris. When France collapsed on a push from Bismarck, Disraeli was not surprised.

His other high-level source of information was the Queen, who had him to dinners and overnight stays at Windsor, where trivia necessarily predominated while he was seated at her table and the significant was exchanged only while he stood opposite her chair in Albert's study. At one dinner in November—he went on business without Mary Anne, to whom he jotted notes on crested Windsor paper—he sat next to Princess Louise, "very good looking, & vivacious. 'It's a great many years since we met,' she said. . . . 'I meant old days. I was one of the little girls who had to knock when you were talking with my father, & dinner was waiting.' "

From Oxford, Balliol don Benjamin Jowett wrote to Florence Nightingale that month that with Russell feeble, the Liberals Gladstone and Lowe "divided against themselves," and Derby "a schoolboy of magnificent proportions," the nation was being run by "a wandering Jew." He offered her an "immoral sentiment" as he called it: "Don't you wish for a Bismarck?"

Derby's ministers met through the recess, and after Christmas began preparing the Queen's Speech to open the new session. In cautious language they suggested measures which, "without unduly disturbing the balance of political power, shall freely extend the elective franchise." Although Disraeli preferred to have the specifics emerge from consensus in Parliament, Derby was being pressed by Victoria to end, quickly, sixteen years of failed efforts to enlarge the voting population. Republican sentiment was growing, in part because of unheard cries for reform, but also because Victoria had been in mourning and seclusion too long. In her absence the Speech was duly read by a functionary, and a cartoon—"Where is Britannia?"—depicted the empty Royal robes draped upon the empty Parliamentary throne. Reform within a constitutional monarchy, it implied, also required a visible monarch.

"Of all possible hares to start," Derby proposed, "I do not know a better [one] than the extension to household suffrage."

Yet he and Disraeli intended to hedge it with enough qualifications as to limit the outcome while claiming Conservative credit
for the principle. Evidence for the claim was already in print,
Disraeli having published that January his *Speeches on Parliamentary Reform*, which established his interest as early as 1851 in extending the vote to more of the working class and his contention
that there was no "finality" in the grants of franchise in the Reform Bill of 1832. By 1857 he had called at Aylesbury for "a bold
and decided course" of Reform. Household Suffrage in February
1867 was a runaway locomotive that almost seemed to be hurtling
in all directions at once. Despite its momentum, there was no obvious mandate for any position, and Disraeli needed all of his Parliamentary skills to keep from being overwhelmed by liberalizing
proposals and counterproposals. "I have had enough of it," he
confided to John Bright in the House lobby on March 1. "I have
had thirty years, and twenty years as leader of a party. I am sick
of it, and if I can get this thing done, then I shall go away."

"Devouring ambition—not to preach and act the truth, but
to distinguish himself," Bright scoffed in his diary, would keep
Disraeli going. " 'We come here for fame!' he said to me many
years ago. And he distinguished himself, but on a low field."

There was no collusion between the broad-hatted, unsmiling
Quaker and Disraeli, but Bright promised not to indulge in opposition for its own sake. "I told him that people said that he and
I always fought with gloves on, but sometimes I had been tempted
to take them off." Disraeli agreed that there had "always been
something of sympathy" between them, which Bright thought was
true, "tho' our course and aims have been so different." As they
talked, the Opposition Whip, Henry Brand (a future Speaker),
walked past them and Disraeli quipped, "He will think it is a Coalition."

When they separated to go to their opposite benches, Disraeli pressed Bright's hand and said, "Well, whatever happens,
you and I will always be friends."

On March 18, 1867, Disraeli brought in his much worked-
over bill, while Gladstone on one side tried to qualify it by a
minimum payment of rates and Lord Cranborne—Robert Cecil—
tried to negate it altogether with crippling amendments. Neither

side wanted many working-class voters enfranchised. Conservatives worried that too much democracy might leave them in a permanent minority, while Liberals were concerned that laborers might vote against the middle class. They would go, assuredly, according to the genetic code of the time, into one party or the other, as a character would explain in Gilbert and Sullivan's *Iolanthe* (1882):

> *I often think it's comical*
> *How Nature always does contrive*
> *That every boy and every gal*
> *That's born into this world alive,*
> *Is either a little Liberal*
> *Or else a little Conservative!*

Certain that deals with potential Liberal defectors would strip the safeguards from the bill, the Earl of Carnarvon, Derby's Colonial Secretary and the only member of the Cabinet more reactionary than Cranborne, sent his resignation to Downing Street with the threat that it would be followed by that of Cranborne and of the Minister of War, General Jonathan Peel. Of the brother of the late Sir Robert, Disraeli remarked that on hearing the words *Household Suffrage* the General's eyes "lit up with insanity." On the morning of February 25, awakened by the delivery of a message from Derby with Carnarvon's letter, Disraeli knew he was right. "The enclosed, just received, is utter ruin," Derby had scrawled. "What on earth are we to do?"

It was a "stabbing in the back," Disraeli replied, although expecting it, and summoned the Cabinet to a meeting that afternoon. From the agonized session he sent Mary Anne a bulletin— "The ship floats; that is all." Two hours later he was in the House, explaining his new compromise package, put together so hastily that it became known as the "Ten Minutes Bill." So complex, in order to patch over Tory differences while appealing to defectors from the Opposition, it led, startlingly to Disraeli, to demands for a simpler and more sweeping bill, regardless of the discontented in the party, as ultras had nowhere else to go. And it led, too, to further attempts by Gladstone to derail legislation that might go even farther in liberality than Liberals wanted, both because the electoral impact remained unpredictable and because the credit would go to the Conservatives.

"All I hear and observe," Disraeli wrote to Derby on February 28, "more and more convinces me that the bold line is the safer one, and, moreover, that it will be successful." Cranborne, Carnarvon, and Peel formally resigned on March 2, which simplified strategy for Derby and Disraeli. Cranborne had bolstered his arguments against Reform of any degree with dire statistics projecting a permanent Tory minority, and when Derby happened to meet Lady Cranborne he asked her lightly, "Is Robert still doing his sums?"

"Yes," she said, referring to the Cabinet, "and he has reached rather a curious result—take three from fifteen, and nothing remains." While a clever gibe, it was completely wrong. On March 4, Disraeli withdrew the "Ten Minutes Bill" and announced that he would bring in a fresh measure. M.P.s on both sides copied Cranborne with their own fanciful estimates as to which party would benefit from redistributions of seats between city and country, and from a variety of qualifications on the voter. Emphatically, Disraeli declared to wavering Tories that under no circumstances would the Government support undiluted Household Suffrage. Nor, he claimed, were they merely mitigating the inevitable, preventing the bad from becoming worse.

His impossible former colleague, Disraeli understood, was too fastidious and too little of a tactician to command a resistance movement among the most reactionary Tories. There was no young Disraeli on the Conservative back benches to reenact the mutiny of 1846 against Sir Robert Peel. Nor was a Cecil likely to cross the floor to the Liberals. While he considered Disraeli an unprincipled "rogue," Cranborne was certain, as he wrote to his brother, that Gladstone was "a lunatic." The Liberal leader's "rescue" activity with pretty prostitutes did not need to get into the newspapers to be widely known. Gladstone even arranged to have one striking beauty, Miss Summerhayes—described in his diary as "no common specimen of womanhood"—to pose for the portraitist William Dyce. Meetings with Miss Summerhayes continued in 1867, by which time Gladstone was involved with a new threesome of smart and sophisticated courtesans (one he described as "at the very top of the tree"), as well as with a notorious demimondaine, Laura Thistlethwaite, who claimed a prior Anglican conversion. Although no religious "rescue" was necessary in her case, she remained close to Gladstone for years.

For straitlaced Tories, the Liberal leader's public rectitude was at variance with his less-than-secret other life. The Earl of Carnarvon speculated in his diary on June 9, 1866: "Gladstone seems to be going out of his mind. Northcote has just told me that Gladstone's latest passion is Mrs Thistlethwaite. He goes to dinner with her and she in return in her preachments to her congregation exhorts them to put up their prayers on behalf of Mr G's reform bill." (She once filed a Gladstone letter with the notation, "Oh how madly I love.")

In his diary the usually circumspect Gathorne-Hardy used the initials M.O.G. for "Mad Old Gladstone," and a despairing Liberal asked an anti-Disraeli Conservative—so Benjamin Jowett wrote to Florence Nightingale in June 1867—"Will you take our madman in exchange for your rogue?" The rather timid Lord Stanley observed in his diary about Gladstone's unabashed attraction to Mrs. Thistlethwaite that it was "characteristic of him to be indifferent to scandal." His open religious fervor seemed to immunize him from political harm, whatever his fevered pursuit of "fallen" women, while the pitch at which the obsession often kept him seemed to add passion to his pronouncements in the Commons. "The right honorable gentleman," Disraeli responded after one energetic attack over Reform, "gets up and addresses me in a tone which, I must say, is very unusual in this House. Not that I at all care for the heat he displays, although really his manner is sometimes so excited and so alarming that one almost might feel thankful that gentlemen in this House, who sit on opposite sides of this table, are divided by a good broad piece of furniture."

In unwittingly masturbatory language, Gladstone explained his need for Mrs. Thistlethwaite in a curious letter to her in 1869, in which he confessed his "selfish" life away from his family. "From morning to night all my life is pressure, pressure to get on, to dispatch the thing I have in hand, that I might go onto the

next, urgently waiting for me. Not for many years past have I
written except in haste a letter to my wife. As for my children,
they rarely get any." Yet Gladstone by 1867 had become the retiring Russell's designated heir, the next prime minister should
the Liberals be returned to office.

To backbenchers on both sides, whenever Gladstone was
compared to his rival, everything else paled before one overwhelming Disraelian disability. It was clear enough in the Chancellor of the Exchequer's appeal to a friendly Tory peer, "If you
could soften Jem Lowther it would greatly serve us." As Lord
Houghton (Monckton Milnes) reported to his wife, "There is a
mot of James Lowther's going the round of the town, that he did
not see how he could meet his constituents after having refused
a moderate measure from a good Christian and taken an extreme
measure from a bad Jew."

Putting the best face on his proposals for even the most conservative of Conservatives, Disraeli claimed in the Commons on
March 18, 1867, that the bill was "prudent" rather than "democratic." He trusted that "it will never be the fate of this country
to live . . . under a democracy." On March 26 he declared that
the vote should be conferred only upon those "competent to fulfil
a trust." Yet in committee and on the floor Disraeli patiently permitted legislation by amendment and by amendment of amendments which threatened to undermine both Gladstone and the
original Tory bill, as the vital thing was to extract a bill from the
House, not to win a gladiatorial contest.

On April 8, a "tearoom revolt" led by James Clay ensured
eventual passage of Reform by keeping enough votes from Gladstone to prevent his mutilating the bill with crippling restrictions.
Meeting in the tearoom of the House, Radical and Liberal M.P.s,
numbering about fifty but claiming to represent more votes than
those present, were united only in opposing Gladstone's tactics.
Before they told him that they would not support his amendments to Disraeli's bill, he expected to block Reform by about
forty-five votes.

On the crucial division only seven Conservatives supported
Gladstone. Forty-five of his own party voted against him. Eight
tearoom Liberals and twenty others abstained. It was, Disraeli re-

ported dramatically to the Queen, "a collapse perhaps unequalled in party and political history, and the result is [that] your Majesty's Government is not only immensely strengthened, but with no fear of subversion; the bill, in all its good and necessary provisions, [is] safe." In his diary Gladstone confessed, "A smash perhaps without example."

While Disraeli credited "your Majesty's determined support" of the bill, the rebellion had been managed by Disraeli's old companion of 1830–31. Clay had sailed the Mediterranean from Malta with Meredith and Disraeli. Now a Liberal from Brighton, Clay had given up woman-chasing, settled down with the daughter of one of Wellington's generals, found a safe seat in the House, and written a book on whist that made him England's expert on the game. (In 1873, when at sixty-eight Clay lay dying in London, Disraeli visited him every day.)

Since more efforts by Gladstone were expected to amend Household Suffrage to death, Disraeli assured the House on April 12, "The men to whom the measure will open the franchise will, it seems to me, be actuated by higher motives than those for which you give them credit, will adapt themselves to the altered circumstances with which they will have to deal, and will not allow their rights to depend on any mere accidental arrangements." In language that sounded more like Bright than anyone else in the Commons, Disraeli described the artisan and mechanic classes as citizens "whose virtue, prudence, intelligence, and frugality" earned them the right "to enter into the privileged pale of the constituent body of the country." Unpersuaded but submitting to necessity, Gathorne-Hardy spoke up in the House—that "constituent body" to which his leader had referred—to support a transfer of power in which he did not believe. "As I went out," he confided in his diary, "men said much was owing to me. I doubt such effects of a speech on such a question. Well there we are but how much further are we to get? It is one thing to break up a Ministry but could I again serve under so unscrupulous a man as Disraeli?"*

*Reading his words later, Hardy added, "I think I misconceived much in writing thus. This seems too strong."

The Derby, 1867. Dizzy Wins with "Reform Bill." *Punch*, May 25, 1867, quotes a skeptical Mr. Punch on Disraeli's securing a majority of 21 on the bill's first division in the House: "Don't be too sure; wait till he's WEIGHED."

The division that Friday evening gave the bill a majority of twenty-one, virtually assuring that unless some external event upset calculations, reform legislation would get through before the end of the session. Excited Conservatives gathered afterwards for a late supper at the Carlton Club. When Disraeli looked in on his way home, Sir Matthew Ridley interrupted the self-congratulations by proposing a toast: "Here's the man who rode the race, who took the time, who kept the time, and who did the trick!" Using the same racing metaphor, *Punch* would cartoon the

event as "The Derby, 1867. Dizzy Wins with 'Reform Bill,' " depicting Disraeli jockeying in his horse a length ahead of the competition, but captioning a suggestion of chicanery: "Don't be too
sure; wait till he's WEIGHED."

Pressed at the Carlton to stay, Disraeli declined. He owed it
to his wife to share the success and walked home to his Fortnum
and Mason pie, and bottle of champagne.

Concerns about mob misrule could still cut into the thin victory margin. More votes were to come, and few M.P.s would vote
any alleged mob the franchise. In early May, after the Easter
recess—"almost like in July," Stanley observed in his diary—a
demonstration in Hyde Park went on, to the surprise of most,
fairly peaceably. To Matthew Arnold, watching from a balcony
overlooking the park as railings gave way to the press of crowds,
and flower beds were again trampled, it was "anarchy" manifest-
ing itself, yet the windows across Park Lane went unscathed and
the begonias would blossom again. All that was being manifested
was a desire to have a share in the park and thus in the nation.

Derby and Disraeli had decided not to oppose the gathering
unless there were violence. Spencer Walpole, misunderstanding
his signals, first sternly forbade the demonstration and then ignored it when it happened, contributing to the appearance that
the Government was indecisive and vacillating. Indignation
flared in Downing Street, but not at the people in the park,
and Gathorne-Hardy was named to replace Walpole at the Home
Office.

The significance of the May 6 gathering, called a riot by
some who failed to perceive that it could have been far more dis-
orderly, and that no one marched to nonexistent barricades, was
not lost at Westminster. Unlike their Continental counterparts,
the English had shown over years of sporadic agitation that they
were not prone to popular revolution.

At a Conservative meeting in mid-May, Disraeli's bill was
agreed upon, with M.P.s pleased that they were being consulted
rather than presented with the decisions of leadership. Yet they
were caught in the momentum which Household Suffrage had
gathered, as was the Opposition. "This offspring is a stolen child,"
Bernal Osborne complained. "The right honourable gentleman

has stolen it, and then . . . he has treated it as the gipsies do stolen children—he has disfigured it to make it pass for his own." The son of a career-minded convert from Judaism, Ralph Bernal Osborne—on his marriage he added his mother-in-law's name— had discreetly employed a gypsy rather than a Jewish metaphor. *Punch* had no such sensitivities and pictured "Fagin's Political School," with an exaggeratedly Semitic Disraeli in Cockney rags, teaching his cronies how to pick the pocket of a gentleman carrying a rolled-up "Reform Bill."

Ruefully, Gladstone admitted later about Household Suffrage, the Government "bowled us down by the force of the phrase." He saw the adoption of liberalizing amendments brought in by the Radicals after the Easter recess, which Disraeli accepted to get Reform through, as "the sole act of Mr Disraeli," who put the most Conservative twist he could to the bill by inviting the great statistician of the day, Sir John Lambert, to explain to Tories what the new voters could mean to the party's future.

Reform would double the electorate. Communities under 10,000 in population would lose their second seats for redistribution to larger cities, and the urban household franchise would involve no financial qualifications. Although the bill bore no resemblance to proposals offered earlier by Disraeli, he maintained that his strategy had been to let the legislation evolve by consent. "I had to prepare the mind of the country," he would tell a crowd in Edinburgh early in November, "and to educate—if it be not arrogant to use such a phrase—to educate our party . . . on the question of Reform." In all, before the final division, Disraeli would speak on the bill in the Commons, sometimes at length, on occasion to respond to questions, 310 times.

The *Tomahawk* satirized Disraeli's success as if conceived in concert with Bright, who wrote, in imaginary congratulations to the leader of the Commons, "We have had a very hard struggle to carry our Bill," which despite "one or two blemishes," promises "to effect our object by transferring power from those who may be clever enough to see through us, to the hands of those who are sure to take us at our own valuation."

Needing someone to share his satisfaction, Disraeli walked to Piccadilly Terrace on May 26 and found Charlotte de Rothschild

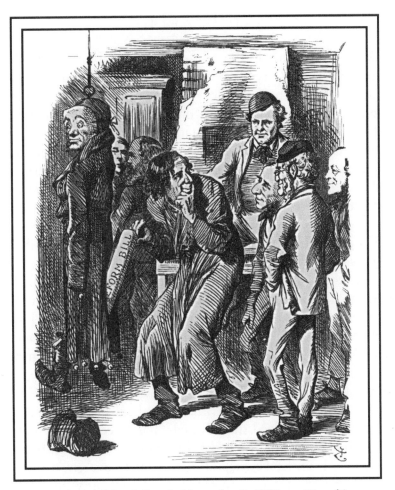

Fagin's Political School. *Punch*, November 9, 1867, on Disraeli's strategy of stealing the Opposition's ideas and claiming them as his own.
The anti-Semitic innuendo needs no comment.

home. On the heavy, black-bordered stationery she was still using
eleven months after the death of her daughter Evelina, she wrote
to Leo that "Dis" had visited without Mary Anne, "and in my
opinion was so brilliantly eloquent, and so wonderfully agreeable,
that I was quite sorry to be his only listener; when dear Papa
came back from Gunnersbury, I made the great man repeat his
anecdotes, but a twice-told tale loses much."

Now confident that Household Suffrage was proceeding
through its readings with inevitability, Disraeli responded to fears
of mob rule: "I do not believe that the country is in danger. I

think England is safe in the race of men who inhabit her." After sitting in the Gallery to hear what seemed to him a reborn Disraeli, John Lothrop Motley wrote to his daughter Lily that American politics could engage only scant attention when England was confronting "the new-fangled radicalism of the Derby-Disraeli Cabinet. There are to be malignant and benignant demonstrations tonight and tomorrow night in the House of Lords. . . . The Peers will denounce the Reform Bill fiercely, and then mildly vote for it, comforting themselves with the conviction that chaos is really come again. . . . Meantime they dare not really oppose the popular verdict which Dizzy has so craftily and audaciously exploited to his own benefit."

Another American in London at the climax was John Hay, returning from his diplomatic stint in Paris and watching in wonder from the Strangers' Gallery as the M.P.s doffed their hats to speak, then clapped them back on. "Nothing could be clearer or finer," he thought, recalling the relatively anarchic Congress in Washington, "than Disraeli's and Gladstone's manner of stating their points." At the home of the American Minister, Charles Francis Adams, in Mansfield Street, Portland Place, the talk was political. Adams judged that Disraeli "has forced the present bill on the Tory party, that he had led them the devil's own rigadoon of a dance. If so, I take back all the credit I have given them for shrewdness and sagacity and transfer it all to Dizzy himself."

Motley put the enactment of Reform into a Civil War comparison that he tried on his wife. Having "jockeyed his party" into supporting a bill "far more liberal than anything Bright would have ventured to propose," although at such cost as the secession of stalwarts like Cranborne, Disraeli had accomplished a "metamorphosis . . . almost as great as if Jeff Davis, [Robert] Toombs, and the rest of the slavery party, instead of going in for rebellion, had met Lincoln's candidacy for the Presidency in 1860 and his platform by a programme abolishing slavery." What Motley did not note was that while Disraeli had sought milder reform, he knew that the Conservative Party was dead unless he brought in real reform. (And that he was seventy votes short on a party vote.) After that, the Conservatives would have to convince the new electorate that England was secure in Tory hands. Why not make the masses a Conservative asset rather than evolve parties of the rich and the poor? It was a necessary gamble, confessedly, to Derby as it passed its final reading in the Lords on August 6, 1867, "*a leap in the dark.*"

"Oh, Mr Disraeli, I haven't seen you since you ruined the country," Lady Cowper said to him brightly when they chanced upon each other in London.

"I assure you," he said, "if that is so, it is your fault."

"Why?" Lady Palmerston's daughter-in-law asked in surprise. "I had nothing to do with it."

"No," said Disraeli, "but I called several times in St James's Square to take your Ladyship's advice on political affairs, and it is to my never having found you that I attribute any defect there may be in the Bill."

He could afford to quip about Reform. Lionel de Rothschild told Charlotte, who wrote to Leopold, that "Dizzy" was radiant with the success, while "Mrs Dis beams like the disk of the sun." But Disraeli conceded his exasperation at Derby, who, after recommending a baronetcy for the new Lord Mayor of London, professed relief that despite his biblical name, Thomas Gabriel was not a Jew. "Such is gratitude," Charlotte snapped, from a Prime Minister who "may be said to owe tenure of office to the genius of an Israelite." While prejudices died hard, an article on the Talmud in the *Quarterly Review* offered some amelioration. Disraeli told her that it "proves that everything gentle and sublime in the religious code of the New Testament is a mere transcript from the so-called oral law of the Jews."

The long session continued into the traditional period of recess, ending on August 21. To the most extreme Conservatives, the Reform Bill was a betrayal. Cranborne in the *Quarterly Review* sulkily titled his jeremiad "The Conservative Surrender." Carlyle prophesied catastrophe for the country in "Shooting Niagara"— his equivalent to Derby's "leap in the dark." Tory versifier Coventry Patmore of "Angel in the House" fame decried 1867 as

The year of the great crime,
When the false English nobles, and their Jew,

By God demented, slew
The trust they stood twice pledged to keep from wrong.

Disraeli responded to the "gloomy imagery" by labeling "these Edinburgh and Quarterly Reviews" as honored relics of a vanished past, "first-class post-houses" for carriage travelers in the days of fast railways. "Things are altered," he noted in a banquet speech. ". . . In a progressive country change is constant, and the great question is not whether you should resist change which is inevitable, but whether that change should be carried out in deference to the manners, the customs, the laws, the traditions of the people, or in deference to abstract principles and arbitrary and general doctrines."

Months earlier, when Reform was taken up by Disraeli with every intent to pass some sort of bill, Abraham Hayward, a Tory die-hard, had seen the strategy as a move toward the succession. With Derby often incapacitated by illness, "the odds are that he will soon retire. Disraeli is playing for the Premiership, but I think it will end in the Duke of Richmond as nominal head." Beresford Hope, a staunch Tory who preferred Gladstone to a Jew, vowed "never [to] fall down and worship the golden image set up in the deserts of Arabia," and that he would, "with whole heart and conscience, vote against the Asian Mystery."

Sir John Skelton, a Scottish literary critic, saw such hopes of evading Disraeli's claims as futile. "Whig or Radical or Tory don't matter [to him] much, perhaps; but vision fascinates him. . . . England is the Israel of his imagination, and he will be the Imperial Minister before he dies—if he gets the chance." During the recess, Skelton saw Disraeli in Edinburgh with Mary Anne, who had aged into one of "the witches in Macbeth. . . . The potent wizard himself" was a figure to inspire awe although not admiration, "with his olive complexion and coal-black eyes, and the mighty dome of his forehead (no Christian temple, to be sure), . . . unlike any living creature one has met. . . . The face is more like a mask than ever, and the division between him and mere mortals more marked. I would as soon have thought of sitting down at table with Hamlet, or Lear, or the Wandering Jew."

Although the Disraelian package for Reform was far more

generous than Gladstone had vainly fought for not long before, he took it as a defeat. Defending his own bill in 1866, Gladstone had exhorted with Evangelical fervor, "You cannot fight against the future. Time is on our side." But it was Disraeli who was fighting the calendar. He was in his sixties and might not have another chance at making history. By standing for change more sweeping than his Liberal adversary wanted, Disraeli had bested him with votes from Gladstone's own party. Bernal Osborne, no more than Gladstone a champion of Disraeli, declared "without any innuendo respecting his sincerity," that he had always considered Disraeli "the greatest Radical in this House. He has achieved what no other man in the country could have done. . . . He has converted these Conservatives into Radical reformers. In fact the Chancellor of the Exchequer is the Ministry by himself, for it could not exist a day without him." Similarly, General Grey, the Queen's private secretary, remarked to Victoria that Disraeli, not Derby, was "the directing mind of the ministry." The Chancellor of the Exchequer was the party leader with whom Gladstone, in and out of the Commons, had to deal, and in their communications each was cold and correct. When Gladstone had built a new library at Hawarden connected to the spacious old drawing room, he had false book backs attached to the connecting door, among them four volumes sardonically titled *"An Israelite without Guile, by Ben Disraeli, Esq."* They revealed volumes about Gladstone's animosity, which had intensified with both men's ambitions.

As 1867 waned, Disraeli was effective head of the government. Derby's ailments were now so acute that at Knowsley he had to be carried up and down the stairs, and he found it difficult to grasp a pen. Foreign affairs were keeping Disraeli busy from Hughenden, and there were more Fenian terrorist outrages in England. At the beginning of the session the Queen's Speech had contained a warning to King Theodore of Abyssinia about British captives he held. To C. Rivers Wilson—then a young Exchequer aide, later a knighted financial expert—Disraeli felt comfortable enough to quip, "Abyssinian campaigns will hardly comport with financial experiments." And he observed wryly of Irish matters that relevant papers were to be directed to Lord Mayo at Dublin Castle, as he was "at this moment, de jure as well as de facto (he is always the latter), the Government of Ireland, for Lord Abercorn"—the Lord Lieutenant—"has retired to his palatial retreat at Baronscourt, the Chancellor has gone to Scotland, the Atty Genl to Switzerland, and the U. Secy is dead, or nearly so, of Fenianism."

Running Downing Street in the absence of Derby, Disraeli had to abandon any serious concerns with Ireland but for employing spies as infiltrators into the Fenians, among the politically active priesthood, and as ostensible tourists. With the Abyssinian situation no better, he ordered an expedition from India to effect a landing on the Horn of Africa and employ force. Affairs required an unusual November Parliamentary session to cover matters foreign and domestic which had been neglected during the long Reform Bill process. Derby remained in Lancashire, contemplating quitting office, as he had confided to Disraeli in a letter on September 10.

By no means certain that his own party would permit him to succeed Derby, Disraeli replied that he was "selfish" in hoping that the Prime Minister would stay on, "as my career will terminate with yours." Whether or not Disraeli believed that, the grandees who represented the party's traditional power structure could insist upon one of their own to replace the Earl, an aristocrat with a venerable title and appropriate religious credentials. As Bishop Wilberforce, one of the most influential of churchmen, put it, not entirely in admiration, "The most wonderful thing is the rise of Disraeli. It is not the mere assertion of talent, as you hear so many say. It seems to me quite beside that." After meeting Disraeli early in October, at Blenheim Castle, he added (to another correspondent), "He is a marvellous man. Not a bit a Briton, but all over an Eastern Jew."

Derby's friends knew that his days were over and had already gathered at Lord Lonsdale's Lowther Castle in August to ponder a new leader—anyone but the Jew. But their host, the Lord Eskdale of *Coningsby*, reminded the die-hards that "Ben Dizzy," as they called him, had long before left those who tried to shout him down hoarse, and that flowered waistcoats, "unsuitable to a fledging member of the House of Commons, were permissible in a leader"; further, that no other Tory could hold his own "against the devastating eloquence of Gladstone and the cunning of the Whig aristocracy." Disraeli remained "the only man among them who could carry the horn and rally the hounds."

In Disraeli's political and social rounds of country seats in the early autumn and in several speeches he gave to large audiences, including the major address in Edinburgh, his welcome belied private discomfort about his acceptability. In acting like an inevitable prime minister he had shed much of what had been perceived as abrasiveness, yet the tension of waiting was draining him, and he had already waited through what seemed an excruciatingly long apprenticeship. That he was straining to avoid saying or doing the wrong thing at the wrong time was clear from Baroness de Rothschild's report of a weekend at Gunnersbury when the Disraelis were the last to leave. Writing to Leopold on Monday, November 5, 1867, she described "the laborious exertion* of speaking to the Chancellor of the Exchequer and his consort from 10 in the morning till 12 at night. The illustrious cabinet minister was most amiable but he was not at all amusing, and endeavoured to make others talk while he listened. . . . Mrs Dis, pale, thin and wrinkled[,] was in admirable temper. . . . Her wig was irreproachable, adorned with sky blue velvet folds and gold butterflies and chains, which were not ridiculous, but very becoming."

A few days later, Mary Anne, now seventy-five, fell seriously ill. Even Gladstone, who was back for a November session of Parliament, visited Grosvenor Gate to pay his respects. There was apprehension in London that the end was near, and he genuinely liked Mrs. Disraeli. The traditional dinner hosted by the Leader of the Commons at the beginning of a session went on as scheduled, but Disraeli absented himself. Still deep in her morbid widowhood, the Queen inquired after Mary Anne, and Disraeli as usual reported on the reopening of Parliament on November 19, noting that he was "very touched" by an allusion to his wife by Mr. Gladstone. "This morning all seemed dark," he told the

*Charlotte had also been hobbled by a painful foot infection and was about to leave for Jews' Hospital in London that Monday for treatment.

Queen, "and he was told to hope no more; but within three hours of this there was a change, and everything became hopeful."

The strain of the session and of Mary Anne's illness led to Disraeli's own collapse ten days later. From his bed, and in pencil, he confided to Corry, who relayed his instructions: "I have still faith in my star." A bundle of messages survives, labeled by Mary Anne, "Notes from dear Dizzy during our illness, when we could not leave our rooms."

By the end of December both were recovering, and Disraeli was meeting again with his Cabinet, but as the new year of 1868 began the Earl of Derby still remained ill at Knowsley. Business with the Queen had to be transacted, and accompanied by Corry, Disraeli went to Osborne. The substance of his audience became clear in advance when General Grey came to his rooms. Derby would soon resign and Victoria intended to name Disraeli. As the two men, who had long respected each other's abilities, talked politics in the royal setting, the historical irony was not lost on the Chancellor of the Exchequer. When a too-young lieutenant colonel, thanks to the clout of his father, then Prime Minister, and boasting no background for the position but his name, Charles Grey had run for a seat in the Commons from Wycombe, the impertinent adventurer he had bested had been a dandified Disraeli. Choosing the Royal secretariat over elective ambitions, Grey had risen as courtier while his rival had taken the only avenue to office open to him. Now both would be, thirty-six years later, at the pinnacle of their professions, with the son of the 2nd Earl Grey, as servant of the Queen, deferring to the soberly clad grandson of a Jewish immigrant from Italy. Disraeli knew that he had reached what he called "the top of the greasy pole."

XXII

"... THE GREASY POLE."

1868

ONLY A FEW TANTALIZING DAYS REMAINED UNTIL DISRAELI COULD move next door into 10 Downing Street. Lying "like a useless log" in Lancashire on February 9, Derby was secretly—he thought—negotiating for parting peerages for loyalists and arranging other political dispositions. The next day he was assured by his successor, as if Disraeli knew nothing, that "at this critical moment, . . . all shall be done on my part which perfect devotion can accomplish, to maintain, unimpaired and unsullied, your interests and influence." Finally, Derby confirmed that he was resigning office and had recommended Disraeli to the Queen. When Disraeli replied on February 20 that he would not "shrink from the situation," the delicate dance was over. Only the formalities remained, and Disraeli wrote graceful thanks to Derby for what had "happened so rapidly and unexpectedly." He had "never contemplated or desired it," he added—another diplomatic untruth. "I was entirely content with my position, and all that I aspired to was that, after a Government of tolerable length, and, at least, fair repute, my retirement from public affairs should have accompanied your own." It was consistent with what he had said to Derby before, but Disraeli was plainly pleased, as much for Mary Anne as for himself. She had lived for the day as much as had her husband, and had earned it.

Corry knew, but Disraeli had to prepare George Barrington, who had been a private secretary at the Exchequer, to move with him. Viscount Barrington and his wife had become Disraeli's close friends. "I am much touched by all your fidelity and sympathy with me, now and always," he added in a note on February 24, closing effusively, "I always loved you." Disraeli was profoundly moved by his elevation, more so than he could confess to himself or to others, but his emotions spilled over as the day neared.

So did Mary Anne's. "By the time this reaches you," she wrote hurriedly to Charlotte de Rothschild, "Dizzy will be Prime Minister of England! Lord Stanley is to announce this in the House of Commons today!" And she remarked to another friend, "You don't know my Dizzy, what great plans he has long matured for the good and greatness of England. But they have made him wait and drudge so long! And now time is against him."

More than the calendar year seemed hostile. J. E. Denison, the Speaker, recalled that when Lord Stanley rose at 4:30 on February 25 after the usual notices of impending motions to announce that his father had resigned on grounds of health, and that Mr. Disraeli would be in consultation with the Queen about forming a successor administration, "The announcement was received in silence . . . not broken by any expression of opinion, one way or another." Disraeli, by tradition, was not in the House, and not a witness to the lack of enthusiasm.

In an exchange of letters the next day, he accepted office. "He can only offer devotion," he told Victoria. And he expected "the benefit of your Majesty's guidance" in the "management of great transactions." Even had she not been gifted with "great abilities," he declared, "which all acknowledge," her experience gave her advantages in judgment "which few living persons, and probably no living prince, can rival." Victoria responded that she only wished that "her beloved husband were here now to assist him"—Disraeli—"with his guidance." The invocation of Albert made it clear that the most urgent task of any prime minister remained what it had been since the Prince Consort's death. Victoria had to be extricated from the comfortable shadows of her mourning. More and more perceived by the public as malingering, she had to be restored as an active queen. The invisibility of the monarchy, except when the Queen needed incomes voted by Parliament for her children as they came of age or married, was the best possible propaganda for republicanism.

Disraeli arrived at Osborne House at seven in the evening on February 28, and almost immediately was ushered in for his first audience in his new role. "You must kiss hands," Victoria said, holding out her right hand. In the tradition of centuries past, Disraeli knelt before her and, taking her plump hand in both of his, promised, "In loving loyalty and faith."

"The present man will do well," Victoria assured her daughter Vicky, the Crown Princess of Prussia, "and will be particularly loyal and anxious to please me in every way. He is very peculiar, but very clever and sensible and very conciliatory." Just before his arrival she had described him to Vicky less like a Household servant than the begetter of Household Suffrage—"a man risen from the people," whose "real talent" and patient "good temper" had brought about the Reform Bill. On the same date Vicky, like her late father a Liberal in sympathies, had written to the Queen that the "vain and ambitious" Disraeli very likely owed his position less to his talents than to "the dearth of clever men in the Tory party." She had no "aristocratic prejudice" against him, Vicky claimed on March 3, "on account of his being a Jew and an adventurer. A person that rises to a high place by his abilities has surely as good a right as anyone to be your Prime Minister."

One of Disraeli's most implacable enemies, Lord Clarendon, sneered to the great ladies of his acquaintance about what a "bitter pill" the new Prime Minister was to the Tory establishment. He had no need to convert Lady Salisbury, who privately took her stepson Robert's view of Disraeli rather than her elderly husband's. Without "one single element of a gentleman," Clarendon declared, "the Jew" had somehow "ingratiated himself with the Missus"—Victoria. Packed with even more malice, much the same letter went to the Duchess of Manchester. "It is rather fun,"

Clarendon contended, "to see the Tory magnates scraping off of
Dizzy & eating & pretending to like all the dirt they have thrown
upon him during the last 10 years, but as the alternative of this
operation was loss of power they of course did not hesitate for a
moment." He had no objection to someone, by his own exertions,
reaching "the top of the ladder," and he even thought the better,
he claimed, of English institutions for making it possible, "but
then I desire that such a man shd be honest & well principled &
have some consistency & some perception of the difference between right & wrong, in all of wh[ich] the Jew is notoriously deficient, & the keeping himself in power will be the sole motive &
guide of his conduct." Clarendon expected a long tenure of office
for Disraeli, "for success is nowadays the only divinity adored &
he has all the Jews & all the press on his side."

The Earl of Shaftesbury claimed no bigotry in his own invective. "Disraeli Prime Minister! He is a Hebrew; this is a good
thing. He is a man sprung from an inferior station, another good
thing in these days, as showing the liberality of our institutions.
But he is a leper, without principle, without feeling, without regard to anything, human or Divine, beyond his personal ambition." From the Birmingham Oratory, Father John Henry
Newman (a Cardinal only in 1879) wrote to Sir Frederic Rogers,
"Does not Disraeli's elevation show that, when you open the
highest places to mere talent, you must not hope to find in them
nobility of mind?" Gladstone, he thought, was "too religious" to
compete effectively with the new Prime Minister. To her estate
agent at Melbourne Hall, Lady Palmerston wrote from Park Lane,
"We are all dreadfully disgusted at the prospect of having a Jew
for our Prime Minister." John Bright described Disraeli's elevation
much as had Victoria's daughter—"A great triumph of intellect
and courage and patience and unscrupulousness, employed in the
service of a party full of prejudices and selfishness and wanting in
brains. The Tories have hired Disraeli, and he has had his reward
from them." But Lord John Manners, kept on as Commissioner of
Works, came to congratulate him and was "fairly embraced"—and
to Dorothy Nevill, Disraeli confided, "It is all well and good
now—I feel my position assured."

It was assured enough for him to replace the seventy-four-year-old Baron Chelmsford as Lord Chancellor with the younger and more effective Hugh Cairns, created a baron the year before by Derby. Furious, Chelmsford demanded nothing less as a sop, Disraeli observed to the Queen, than "to be made . . . an Earl! . . . It seems impossible that your Majesty can entertain such preposterous claims."

The other major change in the Cabinet was the new Chancellor of the Exchequer. The hulking, efficient Ward Hunt, forty-three, had been Financial Secretary to the Treasury and M.P. for the northern division of Northamptonshire. Hunt had, Disraeli explained to Victoria, no title whatever in a Cabinet with three dukes and two earls, "but he has the sagacity of the elephant, as well as the form."

Writing to the Queen often in that vein, Disraeli entertained as well as informed, sometimes furnishing vivid personality sketches as well as revealing quotations. "She declares," one of Victoria's closest friends, Lady Augusta Stanley, wife of the Dean of Westminster, informed Lord Clarendon later in the year, "that she never had such letters in her life, which is probably true, and [that] she never before knew *everything*." Even worse to Disraeli haters at Court, General Grey had commented that the Prime Minister's letters to the Queen "were the most statesmanlike he had seen for years."

On March 5, 1868, the new Prime Minister entered the House to Conservative cheers less hearty than if he had been nearly anyone else, but he had started the session off well before his elevation by proposing a bill amending the Corrupt Practices Act of 1854. He knew the costs and frustrations of bribery in elections, and while his bill was only as strong as the votes he thought he could get for it, it did empower judges in a constituency to hear petitions rather than a possibly biased committee in the Commons. Newly enfranchised working-class voters might be more susceptible to bribes, and in effect the legislation was a follow-up to Reform about which even Gladstone spoke in support. It appeared to be a good beginning.

On that Thursday afternoon Mrs. Disraeli was in the Gallery for the first time. The next day she told Speaker Denison that she

Rival Stars. *Punch*, March 14, 1868.
MR. BENDIZZY (HAMLET). " 'To be, or not to be, that is the question:'—
Ahem!"
MR. GLADSTONE *(out of an engagement)*. [*Aside.*] " 'Leading busi-
ness,' forsooth! His line is 'General Utility!' Is the Manager mad? But no
matter-rr—a time WILL come—"

had resolved long before never to attend a session until she could
see her husband take his seat as Prime Minister. Mary Anne was
thrilled by her new status. Later in the year, when she offered to
show the visiting Queen Sophia of the Netherlands (consort of
William III) the new state buildings—the Foreign Office and the
India Office—Mary Anne asked, "Would her Highness like to see
these?" The Queen wondered what might be a convenient time,

and Mrs. Disraeli laughed, "Oh! Any time your Highness pleases. You know, they *all* belong to me!"

Less than two weeks later, all good feeling evaporated as Gladstone rose to retrieve the initiative he had lost to Disraeli over Reform. According to the passionately hostile Lady Cranborne, whose husband had wanted no reform whatever, Gladstone found that Disraeli now "meant to outbid him by bringing in a more sweeping Irish Reform"—more a reactionary fear than a reality—and struck first. What Gladstone proposed, shrewdly, was the elimination of state support of the Church of Ireland on the logical grounds that it had few adherents, large up-keep costs, and little reason to exist. The Anglican Establishment in Ireland, he charged, was an anomaly feeding discontent. Whatever the language of the Act of Union, it failed to justify endowing an unrepresentative religious body.

With Fenian outrages still vivid—prison breakouts, assassination threats, bombings, invasion alarms—Gladstone played upon a variety of fears that retrieved not only the Catholic vote but that of strayed Low Churchmen. Two hours later, with March 16 winding down and midnight approaching, a tired Disraeli followed with a rambling reply, emphasizing legalisms and loyalty, that went on until 1:30. Gladstone, he charged, was involved in a conspiracy which united "the High Church Ritualists, of whom the right honourable gentleman is the representative . . . , and the Irish followers of the Pope." Masquerading as Liberals, they were "in secret confederacy . . . to seize upon the supreme authority. They have their hand on the Realm of England." And he added darkly that even "the Crown" was in danger.

Disraeli's conspiratorial hyperbole betrayed his realization that he had been outflanked and badly wounded, and sounded desperate even to the most passionate adherents of the stepchild Church of Ireland. "Disraeli ambiguous and his manner laboured," John Bright noted, "giving the idea that he was the worse for the brandy and water he drank before he rose and during his speech." George Smalley, the American-born reporter for the *New York Tribune*, was indignant in print about the "drunken speech," and alleged that Disraeli left the House at 3:30 A.M. "blind drunk" and did not recover his senses until noon. "Indeed," he charged, "how can you contradict what 600 eye-witnesses testify to? . . . England is disgraced by Mr Disraeli, but the often praised elasticity of her Constitution has not yet enabled her to throw him off."*

Disraeli's "life-long hypocrisy" was code to Smalley for the Prime Minister's Jewishness. The *Tribune* newsman's radical politics also included republicanism and Fenianism, leaving him a less than reliable source on Tory matters. Other observers noticed that Disraeli had drawn a pitcher of a liquid that seemed not entirely water as he spoke, and had fumbled his reply—very likely because Gladstone's legislative surprise had left little with which to counterattack. Gladstone suggested slyly afterward that the flailing response was "delivered under the influence of"—and he paused for effect—"a heated imagination." The innuendo struck home.

When Disraeli compounded his difficulties by choosing the defeatist Lord Stanley to answer for the party, the noble lord confessed, to the dismay of his own father, that "considerable modifications might be made" in the status of the Church of Ireland. Gathorne-Hardy, a High Churchman, confided to his diary that "anything so disheartening . . . never was heard," and the Queen wrote to Vicky on March 25, "There is great excitement about this Irish Church question, and Mr Gladstone has done immense mischief. The old religious feuds will return with great fury and bitterness."

Gladstone had chosen his issue with cunning. It fit his high moral tone about religious equality and coalesced support from a variety of political camps. Since adherents of the Church of Ireland were few and often absentee, the proposal rankled no one whose vote he needed. The Irish Church was a cause popular almost entirely with ecclesiastics who benefited from appointments to its nearly empty churches. As the Duke of Argyll, a close associate of Gladstone, admitted frankly, "There was really no other way of getting Dizzy out of office."

---

*Disraeli would quaff a considerable amount of brandy and water while speaking for three hours in Manchester in 1872, the elixir possibly contributing to one of his greatest addresses (see p. 501 below).

Unsurprisingly, another voice in outspoken opposition was the ultra-Tory Lord Cranborne. Disraeli had tried unsuccessfully to win him back into the Cabinet to reconcile all bands of the Conservative spectrum, even the author of a diatribe which had accused the Prime Minister of surrendering to Radicalism. Sir Stafford Northcote, Disraeli's emissary, was dismissed with the snub, "I have the greatest respect for every member of the Government except one,—but I do not think my honour is safe in the hands of that one." Lady Cranborne told Lady Augusta Stanley that "nothing could equal Dizzy's *lies*," but that Disraeli had an ally at Court in Princess Helena, whom Lady Augusta described as "wild about Dizzy. . . . I think he must have spread his butter very thick."

In the Commons, Cranborne had help from his reactionary counterpart on the Liberal benches, Robert Lowe, about whom Disraeli said, "When the bark is heard on this side of this House the rt. hon. member from Calne emerges, I will not say from his cave,* but perhaps from a more cynical habitation. He joins immediately in the chorus of reciprocal malignity."

Defeated in the House on April 4 by forty-eight votes, Disraeli evaded resignation by declaring an Easter recess after which, he knew, resolutions of censure would be brought to force him to dissolve the Government. He went to Osborne to seek the Queen's covert assistance, but more significant help came from the mortality tables. Old Lord Salisbury died. Cranborne succeeded as 3rd Marquis, moving his malignity out of the Commons and into the House of Lords. Unfortunately, his father's widow was now free to exercise her blandishments more openly upon Lord Stanley, toward whom Disraeli's loyalties remained blindly excessive. To Baron Sandford, the new Marquis predicted that "the Jew" would offer the Queen a resignation arranged in advance to be refused pending dissolution of Parliament and new elections. "Matters seem very critical—a woman on the throne, & a Jew adventurer who found out the secret of getting round her."

---

*A pun on the "Cave of Adullam," the cabal of conservative Liberals (see p. 417 above).

Too politically sophisticated to believe in either party yet loyal to the Liberals because they had literally proved more liberal, Nathan de Rothschild wrote to his mother, Charlotte, from Paris, "From what I can hear, the Liberal party is not likely to be more united about the Irish Church than they were last year about Reform, and by fair means or foul Dizzy will tide over this session." Natty's father felt more positive, not realizing how Irish disestablishment would tie up the political agenda. "Dizzy," he suggested to Charlotte, "may propose Liberal measures, and he then will be supported by the public who are always fond of a man of talent." While the Rothschilds would continue to share foreign policy intelligence with Disraeli,* often through Stanley, they would be proved, as rarely happened, wrong on Disraeli's securing Liberal defections as he did the year before. Irish issues were normally a quagmire, but Gladstone would find it easy to unite his camp against an institution as unpopular as the Church of Ireland.

Party whips suggested that Disraeli display some apparent control by hosting a grand reception marking the new Ministry. The obvious venue was the impressive new Foreign Office overlooking St. James's Park, which was graced on the evening of Wednesday, March 25, not only by the Prime Minister and "Mrs. Dizzy" but by the Prince and Princess of Wales and Mr. and Mrs. Gladstone. Leading bishops turned up in resplendent dress, and Church, Crown, and State mingled as if no disagreement involving their offices existed. When the queue of carriages left in the small hours, the political armistice was over.

Parliament resumed with Victoria's agreement that Disraeli should stay on until new elections. At Osborne he had presented the Queen with the collected edition of his novels, and she offered him a signed copy of her *Leaves from the Journal of Our Life in the Highlands*. Although her book was instantly popular in the bookshops, the mean-spirited claimed its appeal was less out of affection for the Queen and what she revealed about her life with

---

*And sometimes military intelligence. A letter on increasing Prussian army expenditures, sent from Berlin in April 1868 to Lionel de Rothschild, begins, "Tell your friend that . . ."

Albert, than for its references to her gillie John Brown. Whether or not Disraeli said it, Lady Palmerston was quick to relate—she had close connections to several of the Queen's Ladies-in-Waiting—that the Prime Minister prefaced a remark after accepting the Queen's book, "We authors, Ma'am, . . ."

Victoria understood as a result of Disraeli's visit that early dissolution of Parliament would require an election under the existing register of voters. The new register broadening the suffrage under the Second Reform Act was a complex mechanism only likely to be ready for use late in the year. Her Ministers, she wrote in an exchange of letters on May 2, "have done nothing to forfeit the confidence she has reposed in them." Although Gladstone could gamble on a mandate from the old register by forcing a premature ballot, his chances of success were less by that route. As Lord Houghton explained from London to his wife in the country, "Gladstone is the great triumph; but as he owns that he has to drive a four-in-hand, consisting of English Liberals, English Dissenters, Scotch Presbyterians, and Irish Catholics, he requires all his courage to look his difficulties in the face."

With the threat of early elections paradoxically keeping him in office, Disraeli hoped to check, before dissolution, the erosion in the Conservative position. Invective against him, however, ran high from Radicals like Bright to ultra-Tories like Salisbury and conservative Liberals like the ambitious, albino-tufted Robert Lowe. "All the men who spoke against Mr Disraeli," he wrote on May 4 in the traditional third person to the Queen, "were expectants of high office. They were bitter and chagrined. Principally among these, Mr Lowe, and Mr Bright. The first most violent and bitter; he positively raised his crest, and hissed, like an adder."

Bright denied ambition, but he became a member of the next Liberal Cabinet as President of the Board of Trade. In Anthony Trollope's *Phineas Finn* (1869), which deals with political life during the Household Suffrage agitation, Bright is Turnbull, a demagogue with "a moral skin of great thickness," while Disraeli is Daubeny, usually shortened to "Dubby," the leader of the Conservatives in the Commons, who would "give his fingers and toes" to remain in power, and owes his place to "skill rather than principle." Trollope told John Blackwood, successor to his father in the publishing firm, "You think exactly about Dizzy as I do; you *know* you would be very glad to hear he had been up for—for shoplifting."

The ambitious Gresham, who leads the assault on the Irish Church in the sequel, *Phineas Redux,* is the barely disguised Gladstone, now Daubeny's political rival. Accused in the *Daily Telegraph* of not being "gentlemanlike" in his malicious depictions of political enemies, Trollope responded that he had only used their ideas, not their persons. For example, his "turbulent" Turnbull was nothing like Bright "in manners, in character, in mode of life." Nor, he fudged, were any of the others. Bright's real-life position in 1868, as he dramatized his break with Disraeli, was that the leader of the House was using the Queen as his political shield. No longer a friendly opponent, he charged, "A Minister who deceives his Sovereign is as guilty as the conspirator who would dethrone her." Because Disraeli had claimed that Irish disestablishment violated the Coronation oath as well as the flag in which the religious symbols of the kingdom were united, Bright added that the Prime Minister was "guilty of a very high crime and a great misdemeanor against his Sovereign and against his country." Disraeli challenged the M.P. from Birmingham to come down from the back benches to turn his insinuations into specifics. "Let him prefer those charges; I will meet him; and I will appeal the verdict only of gentlemen who sit on the same side of the House as himself!" Bright cautiously remained in his seat.

In foreign affairs, events were going better for Disraeli although Parliament did not always see things his way. England had steered clear of European involvements despite increasing instability across the Channel, and had freed its hostages in Abyssinia after an expedition by troops from India under Sir Robert Napier. On April 13, the inland fortress of Magdala was stormed, the proud Emperor Theodore shooting himself to avoid capture with a pistol that in more placid days had been a gift from Queen Victoria. As soon as a messenger could get to a telegraph, the news was dispatched to the Secretary for India, Sir Stafford Northcote, but it arrived at the India Office in the small hours of a Sunday morning, when the addressee was in attendance on the Queen at

Osborne. Northcote's son waited until a discreet 11 o'clock to carry the intelligence to Disraeli, whom he found at Grosvenor Gate still in a dressing gown, with a turban swathed around his head. (Mary Anne may have been dyeing and dressing his hair.)

On returning, Sir Stafford found everyone delighted—"that is, except the Liberals." Two precepts of Gladstonian Liberalism were an aversion to colonial adventures and a reluctance to spend money; Disraeli had violated both. Although £2,000,000 had been voted for the assault, it required sending supplies and troops both from England and India, and the construction of rail trackage from the coast into the mountains. In the Commons the actual cost of £8,600,000 was deplored. Disraeli retorted that "money is not to be considered in such matters: success alone is to be thought of."

Since Gladstone was a friend of Napier, when Disraeli proposed on July 2 a vote of thanks to the general's forces, the resolution passed easily; Napier was awarded a peerage with an "of Magdala tag," as was the tradition on the happy conclusion of one of the Queen's little wars. When he returned to claim his honors he loyally visited Hughenden.

While stalling dissolution, Disraeli had a second burden to bear. The Queen's obsessive interest in Church appointments, and the political and social pressures elsewhere for preferment, hardly suggested grounds for retaining an Established Church in either of John Bull's islands. "Nothing gives me more trouble than the Episcopacy," he later wrote Lady Bradford. "There are so many parties, so many 'schools of thought' in the Church." Victoria privately professed almost no theology. Religion to both the Queen and the Prime Minister was not necessarily true or good, but a social institution to regulate conduct. Vacant clerical livings, from archbishop to canon, were debated, and offered, on grounds upon which dogma had little part, as Sir Henry Irving, who played in command performances for the Queen in the 1870s and after, confirmed when he took a young clergyman who was a relative to see Disraeli (in his second ministry) for advice. The rather new curate at Windsor had been deputed, in the absence of more senior men of the cloth, to preach the following Sunday. "If you preach thirty minutes," Disraeli warned, "Her

Majesty will be bored. If you preach fifteen minutes, Her Majesty will be pleased. If you preach ten minutes, Her Majesty will be delighted."

"But," said the curate, "what can a preacher possibly say in only ten minutes?"

"That," said the Prime Minister, "will be a matter of indifference to Her Majesty."

The Queen preferred personable men who invested an occasion with dignity shorn of ritual: Princess Louise knew "a sensible, liberal-minded" man of the cloth; a peer's clerical younger son needed employment; the Prince of Wales's ex-tutor needed an income and change of air; an "object of the Queen's favour" had a large family. Disraeli tried proposing, for the highest offices, professors of theology who were "sound Churchmen." Victoria had other uses for the Church, and other definitions of *soundness*. It left him almost relieved that soon the ecclesiastical reward system would be in the hands of another prime minister—as he had no hopes of turning his minority party, further fractured by Reform, into a majority.

The Queen recognized that Disraeli would be leaving office when, in the fall, she presented him with a portrait of Prince Albert ("that gifted being," Disraeli responded). From Perth, as he entrained alone to attend the Queen at Balmoral, he wrote to Mary Anne, his sense of mortality now close since her near fatal illness the year before, "I was greatly distressed at our separation, and when I woke this morning [I] did not know where I was. Nothing but the gravity of public life sustains me under a great trial, which no one can understand except those who live on the terms of entire affection and companionship like ourselves."

In November, as elections approached, Disraeli resigned himself to the Queen's latest choices for Church preferments, often made in consultation with Dean Wellesley of Windsor. "Mr Disraeli has behaved so well towards your Majesty, in all these Church appointments," Wellesley conceded, "that the Dean greatly regrets [only] that he had not some more fixed principle about them than the merely political bias they may have one way or another."

Seeking attractive young candidates who could represent the

future of the Tory party, Disraeli had a difficult time filling ballots in constituencies which seemed hardly worth contesting. One was the county of Middlesex, largest two-seat district in Parliament and long held by Lord Enfield, whose tenure dated back to Whig days, and Henry Labouchere, a feisty Radical. Someone suggested Lord George Hamilton, son of the Duke of Abercorn, then Disraeli's Lord Lieutenant of Ireland. Hamilton was conveniently nearby as an ensign in the Coldstream Guards. He took the invitation lightly until Colonel T. E. Taylor, the Conservative Whip, went to see him. Low Church voters who sympathized with the Government's Irish policy, Taylor said, would vote Hamilton's way. He should talk to Disraeli himself.

At Downing Street, Hamilton was questioned to see if he had "any wits or ideas." Disraeli then asked how old he was. "Twenty-two," confessed the slight young Guardsman.

"Really!" Disraeli said. "You look about eighteen." He patted Hamilton on the cheek and sent him on with "All right, little David—go in and kill Goliath." But he campaigned alone. Not even a nominal aspirant could be found for the second seat, and Delane of *The Times* excoriated Disraeli for putting up ignorant young aristocrats who were entirely unrepresentative for urban constituencies. Hamilton would defeat Labouchere and at twenty-seven become Undersecretary for India.

Gladstone's party campaigned in November as if political and social reform mattered very little. The appeal was to Dissenting interests, and on divisive religious grounds. With the Catholic and Evangelical vote securely his while the rest divided, the Liberals doubled their majority, but one aspirant their sweep did not pull in was Anthony Trollope. Not satisfied by writing what was almost fiction about politics, he had wanted to experience the real thing, and ran for the Yorkshire constituency of Beverly employing an agent who knew the East Riding well. As Trollope described his campaigning in his *Autobiography*, his agent warned him that it would be expensive, instructive, and unsuccessful:

"You don't expect to get in!" he said. . . . I would not, I said, be sanguine, but nevertheless I was disposed to hope the best. "Oh no!" continued he, with good-humoured raillery, "you won't get in. I don't suppose you really expect it. But there is a fine career open to you. You will spend £1000, and lose the election. Then you will petition, and spend another £1000. You will throw out the elected members. There will be a commission, and the borough will be disfranchised. For a beginner such as you are, that will be a great success."

Everything happened as predicted. Beverly lost its borough status on petition, and the corrupt winners were denied seats, but so was Trollope, who had been at the bottom of the poll. He recycled his adventure into the novel *Ralph the Heir,* where Sir Thomas Underwood—Trollope elevated himself—stands for Percycross, as bribe-ridden a borough as Maidstone and Shrewsbury had been for Disraeli.

Through General Grey, Disraeli informed the Queen on November 23 that he was prepared to resign without waiting for the new Parliament to meet, but he wanted one mark of favor from Victoria. As retiring Prime Minister he could have asked for an earldom. Instead, he entreated the Queen, "Might her husband then hope that your Majesty would be graciously pleased to create [Mrs. Disraeli] Viscountess Beaconsfield, [after] a town with which Mr Disraeli has been long connected and which is the nearest town to his estate in Bucks which is not yet ennobled?" He explained that she had an independent income to sustain a peerage in her own right and that the elder William Pitt had established the precedent when his wife was created Baroness Chatham.

Disraeli at sixty-four was unready to leave political life. Mary Anne was a frail seventy-six. While the Queen was disposed to grant the peerage, General Grey advised cautiously that although Disraeli deserved whatever was at Victoria's disposal, "attacks, and even ridicule, . . . would surely follow the creation of Mrs Disraeli [as] a peeress in her own right." Rather than let him face "endless ridicule," Grey proposed making Disraeli a Knight Commander of the Bath, which would not keep him out of the Commons, while the spouse of Sir Benjamin would be addressed as

Lady Disraeli. "But then comes the doubt whether he would be satisfied."

Two days later Mary Anne learned that she would be Viscountess Beaconsfield. Orders went out immediately for monograms and coronets to validate the title, and on the 26th she thanked the Queen for a kindness which she knew reflected her Majesty's "appreciation of Mr Disraeli."

Even the usually venomous *Punch* offered "homage sincere" in verses "affably" recognizing "the triumph she honours and shares"—which

> *acknowledged what ne'er can be paid,*
> *Earnest devotion and womanly aid.*
> *Long may the gems of that coronet flame,*
> *Decking her brow who's more proud of his fame.*

From Calcutta, Lord Napier of Magdala wrote to Sir Henry Durand in Bombay that he wondered why people were surprised that the Prime Minister did not cling to his office until Parliament had reassembled. He did "just the thing he ought to have done. Why will they be surprised when he does anything well? His ecclesiastical appointments have been unexceptionable. The Reform Bill was a good measure, and it so puzzles one to find the Liberal Party alarmed at its extent, that it is hard to believe that the Party names mean anything. My own confidence in the mass of the people is very great; they will educate themselves up to their position."

On December 1, 1868, the outgoing Prime Minister went to Windsor for, as he put it to Stanley, "the coup de grace," and General Grey telegraphed to Hawarden to find out where the inevitable letter to Gladstone should be personally delivered. Pleased with his own elevation, Gladstone closed a formal letter to his predecessor about the Speakership with the line, "I also beg of you to present my best compliments on her coming patent to (I suppose I must still say, and can never use the name for the last time without regret) Mrs Disraeli." The mutual detestation stopped short of Mary Anne.

XXIII

"BUT NOW THEY HAVE TURNED ME OUT OF PLACE."

1869–1872

ON FEBRUARY 7, 1869, LORD STANLEY CALLED UPON DISRAELI AT Hughenden for the second time since they had left office, and found him reluctant to discuss politics. There was "nothing to be done for the present." Instead he talked amusingly of being taken out hunting in Yorkshire and acquitting himself well although he did not ride, shoot, or fish. While he had been away, recognition of a sort had arrived. The first issue of *Vanity Fair,* on January 30, included a full-page cartoon in color, "the Right Honourable Benjamin Disraeli." Easily recognizable, he was in long black overcoat, top hat and cane, with too-long trousers tumbling over his shoes, thanks to Mary Anne's measurements, and a head too large for his body. That the inaugural cover portrayed a defeated politician out of office was a remarkable index to his fame.

Vanity Fair's recognition would soon be an index to social success, largely because of the skill of Carlo Pellegrini, who signed himself "Ape," in capturing character. Everyone who counted wanted every cartoon, and *Vanity Fair* became a social habit.

As for Mary Anne, who was now a Lady by royal patent, friends began receiving coroneted notes from her signed "Beaconsfield." Even to her husband she was no longer, on paper, merely Mary Anne.

While the Disraelis were country-house visiting through the winter they learned that James D'Israeli was dying. As they prepared to spend Christmas with Lord Beauchamp, word came that James had indeed died. Ben found himself executor "without the slightest hint of such an office," he wrote, explaining his delay to Beauchamp. James was buried next to Mrs. Brydges Willyams at Hughenden, and Disraeli set to winding up his brother's tangled affairs. James's housekeeper, Mrs. Bassett, turned out unsurprisingly to have been his mistress. Disraeli did not discover that the pair had a child until Annie Bassett wrote to him ten years later that while she was attending a girls' school at Lewisham, Sarah D'Israeli had overseen her care.

Mrs. Bassett received £6,000 in James's will, with Benjamin acquiring the residuary £5,300 after expenses. Left nothing, Ralph came grudgingly to the funeral, "which was most distasteful to me," he complained to his brother. It was a new grievance for Ralph, who preferred to forget that he owed his Parliamentary sinecure to Benjamin's influence. His wife, the former Kate Trevor (a relation by marriage to Olivia Basevi, his and Ben's aunt), had given birth to what would be their only son, and Ben's only nephew, in April 1867. Looking ahead to his brother's will, Ralph had named his son Coningsby, designating Ben as godfather. Disraeli acknowledged the baptismal sponsorship but begged off attendance, fearing, he hinted to Ralph, that the sensitivities of the ailing and childless Mary Anne would be bruised by anything that suggested an implicit heir—"our matter," he described it. For the moment, young Coningsby was promised nothing.

When Lord Stanley again dined at Grosvenor Gate on March 15, 1869, political talk was less about Irish Disestablishment, against which opposition seemed "hopeless," than about the continuing ceremonial absence of Victoria. As Prime Minister, Gladstone spoke to her, she once complained, as if she were a public meeting, which did not help draw her out of seclusion.

The prestige of the monarchy would fade, Disraeli worried, if people discover "they can do as well without a Court."

On March 23, 1869, the Irish Church Bill was given its second reading in the Commons. Stafford Northcote, once Gladstone's private secretary at the Exchequer but now a Conservative, attacked Disestablishment as being compounded of robbery and bribery—robbery of the Established Church and bribery of Irish Catholics to conciliate the population. Gladstone brushed the words off. He knew that Disestablishment would pass sweepingly.

Late in the session, as debate on the third reading closed, Disraeli, who had said little, rose to remind the House that certain enthusiasms were irresponsible misjudgments only likely to encourage strife. The Members knew well, he recalled for them, going back a hundred years, "that when Benjamin Franklin's [London] mission was rejected, there was loud and continued cheering, and lords of the privy council waved their hats and tossed them in the air. But that was the commencement of one of the greatest struggles this country ever embarked in; it was the commencement of a series of the greatest disasters England ever experienced."

On the division there was a majority of 114 for Disestablishment and Disendowment, and the measure went on to the Upper House. Gladstone described the outcome as a vote for religious equality in Ireland.

Despite his concerns for religious forbearance, in July 1869 Gladstone filed among his papers a broadside in coarse black ink on cheap paper which apparently gave him joy. It was titled "DIZZY'S LAMENT":

> *Oh dear! oh dear! What shall I do?*
> *They call me merry Ben the Jew,*
> *The leader of the Tory crew,*
>   *Poor old Benjamin Dizzy;*
> *I'd a great big house in Buckinghamshire,*
> *My wages was five thousand a year,*
> *But now they have turned me out of place,*
> *With a ticket for soup, in great disgrace. . . .*

I've got the sack, what shall I do?
They call me a converted Jew. . . .
I never thought they'd turn me out,
For well I knew my way about.
So pity poor Benjamin Dizzy.
Oh, if I could Bill Gladstone thump,
I'd burst his nose, and kick his r——p,
If like Jack Heenan* I could fight,
I'd wallop both him and Johnny Bright.

As the Irish Church debate moved to its close, Disraeli quietly embarked on a novel about religion in which political and religious agitation in Ireland figured, although only as a side issue to larger struggles involving Continental politics and Roman Catholicism. Writing it kept him busy when he and Mary Anne were not entertaining at Hughenden or being entertained elsewhere during the recess. With Mary Anne failing, they traveled less.

Lord Derby, who had never resumed his leadership in the Upper House, died on October 23. His son, now 15th Earl of Derby, was free to marry the ambitious dowager Marchioness of Salisbury. More than a shift in titles was involved, as a new opportunity glimmered to oust Disraeli and return the Tory party to its traditional grandees. Earl Cairns had succeeded reluctantly to the leadership in the Lords. He was eager to step down, and the reactionary Carnarvon, meeting Gathorne-Hardy to discuss the private Derby obsequies, was "very anxious for entire reunion in the party & looking for Salisbury as leader when & if the impediment"—meaning Disraeli—"can be removed." The new Marquis of Salisbury was already positioning himself to succeed the late 14th Earl of Derby as Chancellor of Oxford, and was the choice of the ultras to lead the Lords. Disraeli hoped to head off the extreme wing by promoting the new earl to be leader in the Upper House after a transition period when someone safe would

---

*John C. Heenan, a bare-knuckled prize-fighter from California, fought the Pimlico pugilist Tom Sayers to a draw in 1860 after two hours and six minutes and thirty-seven rounds.

fill the gap. Even that was more of a risk than Disraeli realized, as he had no idea how much Mary Catherine, now Lady Derby, disliked him and dominated her husband.

The Disraelis were at Blenheim just before Christmas, returning to host Derby at Hughenden on December 23. During long walks through the beeches, he and Disraeli felt each other out about politics as they went. Disraeli sensed the mood among Conservative powers to force his retirement. "He admitted to me," Derby noted in his journal, "that though still willing to exert himself for the benefit of the party if necessary, his interest in it was diminished, he had obtained his object, and if he never held office again, he should not feel that his life had been a failure. He had often doubted whether he should go on with the leadership in the Commons; the fatigue was considerable: but he saw no one in whose hands he could leave it, and that circumstance had decided him [to stay]."

With the possibility looming that his counterpart in the Lords might be an enemy who had just described him, in the Autumn 1869 *Quarterly Review*, as a "political gamester," Disraeli let it be known that Salisbury was a man without a party, not a Conservative, however much he pontificated on "Conservative Policy." In February 1870 the Duke of Richmond, a safer choice, succeeded Cairns in the Upper House. Hardly a leader, he merely watched over a session in which the Liberals were overwhelmingly dominant. Helplessly, Disraeli watched, too, as Fenian violence and what Gladstone deplored as "agrarian crime" followed Irish Church Disestablishment, the act that was to help ease the situation. All he could do was to speak out in the Commons against Gladstone's Irish Land Bill, intended to prevent landlord evictions without compensation for "unexhausted improvements." Disraeli wanted freedom of contract rather than mandated stipulations. His amendment was defeated by seventy-six votes, but tenant refusal to pay rents to largely absentee landlords continued to agitate Ireland.

The great measure of Gladstone's Ministry was the Education Act of 1870, which established access to elementary education for every child, paid for by local rates. It would cause a leap in the literacy level of the population, but not until haggling over religious teaching in state-supported schools was settled by the requirement that the Bible was to be read and explained without distinctive sectarian formulas. Disraeli objected to the explaining, which would create "a new sacerdotal class," the lay schoolmasters. Few others seemed concerned, and the bill passed.

Although Ireland had little to do with Disraeli's novel *Lothair*, which he began on leaving office, it did precipitate its conspiratorial element, which involved Fenian cells in London and demobilized Americans seeking post–Civil War excitement. Lord Stanley had told Disraeli at the time of a series of Irish outrages in 1867 that an informant spoke of "155 Fenian and republican clubs in London alone." A Fenian rising, Disraeli confided to a friend in 1880, had been aborted when he, Lord Mayo, and Gathorne-Hardy "succeeded in stopping it" by seizing the revolutionary adventurer Gustave Paul Cluseret, a shady former French officer who had been on the other side of the barricades in 1848, fought in the Crimea, then in Sicily under Garibaldi, then as a major general with Fremont and McClellan for the Union in 1862–65. Joining the International in France, Cluseret linked up with the Fenians. "We had [him] watched in his London lodgings," Disraeli recalled, "and as he was on the point of starting for Ireland to take the command of the rebellion he was neatly stopped." An American citizen by naturalization, Cluseret was quietly deported. Returning to agitation against the Second Empire, he would be involved in the Paris Commune of 1871. In *Lothair* the passionate Garibaldian soldier of fortune Captain Bruges echoes the colorful Frenchman.

Another kind of conspiracy furnished the anti-Popery romance that became the springboard of the novel. On Christmas Eve, 1868, within weeks of the Disraeli government's relinquishing of power, the young 3rd Marquess of Bute, heir to some of the richest properties in Britain, was, to the shock of the aristocracy, received into the Roman Catholic Church. The event became the central intrigue of *Lothair*.

Since *Tancred*, twenty-three years earlier, Disraeli had eschewed fiction. His political life was full, and at any time during the unstable years since the toppling of Peel, he might have been summoned into office. Now in 1869, although the Lords had not sustained Gladstone on the Irish Church Bill until Cairns engineered a secret compromise with Granville, it appeared that the Liberals would be in power for a long time. For Disraeli, fiction was again an alternative forum for his ideas.

Until he had completed *Lothair*, even Monty Corry did not know of it. When Thomas Longman announced that publication in the traditional three small volumes* was set for May 2, 1870, for one of the highest sums ever paid for a novel, Anthony Trollope and Monckton Milnes (now Lord Houghton) wagered on the amount, which Houghton fantasized as £10,000. Only Dickens was worth that, Trollope insisted. The contract actually specified £1,000 on signing, with royalties then to begin after sales of two thousand copies. Over the first six years, Disraeli would earn more than £7,500. "There is immense and most malevolent curiosity about Disraeli's novel," Houghton wrote eagerly to his friend Henry Bright. "His wisest friends think that it must be a mistake, and his enemies hope it will be his ruin." Clearly not among the former was J. T. Delane of *The Times*, who, on seeing the Longman announcement, sent a note to his deputy, George Dasent, no literary critic: "Would you like to write a review of Disraeli's new novel *Lothair* as soon as it comes out? I should not like to be hard on the old fellow, but I can't help thinking that it must be some old material he has had on hand, and which he has now worked up."

Among the speakers at the Royal Academy banquet on April 30 were Dickens and Disraeli to represent authors, and Gladstone as Prime Minister (although he had just published a Homeric study, *Juventus Mundi*). The Prince of Wales, who neither wrote nor read books, also spoke. Dickens rose last, responding to the toast, "Prosperity to the Interests of Literature," and acknowledged Disraeli's "tardy return to it." However tardy, his position guaranteed him considerable, if not necessarily respectful, attention. Evenhandedly, *Punch* caricatured Disraeli and Gladstone, their backs to each other in a bookshop, examining each other's new titles with disdain. John Tenniel's cartoon appeared on May 14. On May 18 Gladstone noted in his diary that

*Lending libraries earned more that way as books were rented by the volume.

"Critics." *Punch*, May 14, 1870. Gladstone's treatise on Greek myth appeared in the same season as Disraeli's best-selling novel. *Punch's* dialogue:

MR. G–D–S–T–NE: *"Hm!—Flippant!"*

MR. D–S–R–LI: *"Ha!—Prosy!"*

he had read "a spice of *Lothair*." After keeping at it daily, on the 25th he recorded, "Finished *Lothair*."

Disraeli's past strategy of fictionalizing recognizable contemporaries guaranteed *Lothair* a large readership. Gladstone did not find himself in it, but Samuel Wilberforce—"The Bishop" in the novel—was furious. "My wrath against D. has burnt before this so fiercely," he confessed to an old friend, "that it seems to have burnt up all the materials for burning and to be like an exhausted

prairie fire—full of black stumps, burnt grass, and all abomina-
tions." Henry Edward Manning, who had a more significant and
more vicious role as Cardinal Grandison, handled his notoriety
with the worldly aplomb of his character in the novel. In a gesture toward Roman Catholics, Disraeli when Prime Minister had
offered to charter a Catholic university in Dublin, and had, he
thought, Manning's support and that of Irish bishops. He was
even assured that there would be no opposition from Gladstone's
side. Since Gladstone had his own schemes to employ Irish causes
to unseat Disraeli, the promised support to the Conservatives
failed to materialize. Disraeli felt that the Archbishop of
Westminster—he would not become a Cardinal until 1875—had
used him, and Manning paid the price.

In *Lothair*, Cardinal Grandison is a suave Machiavellian prel-
ate with ascetic pallor and fragility. Prior to his conversion to
Rome, he had been named one of the two guardians of the immensely wealthy but orphaned Lothair, Marquess of Muriel. The
other guardian is Lord Colloden, a dour Scottish Presbyterian. A
third influence to enter Lothair's life represents an aspect of religion personalized in the beautiful women who attract him—Clare
Arundel, Lady Corisande, and Theodora Campian. Clare is asked
to sacrifice her desire to become a nun to the ensnaring of
Lothair, but he is even more captivated by the mysterious
Theodora. Twelve years his senior—a hint of Disraeli's own age
disparity to his wife—she is, unknown to the fashionable society
that adores her, the patroness of the secret "Mary Anne" societies, revolutionary cells suggesting the First International. Unattainable to Lothair except as a living icon to worship, Theodora
is married to a courtly, self-exiled former Confederate colonel.

The year is 1867. Revolution is unsettling the old order in
Europe from Ireland to Italy and the Balkans. The struggles are
mirrored by religious rivalries, the competing claims of a reactionary Vatican, a stodgy Anglican Church, and new sciences, from
astronomy to zoology.

The signal event of young Lothair's life, sheltered as was
Lord Tancred's, is scheduled to be the festival at Muriel Towers to
mark his twenty-first birthday. The ceremonies are romantically
feudal in the extreme, with impossible numbers of loyal retainers,

from farm families to the lower nobility, thronging the grounds in the numbers of a Crystal Palace exhibition, and religious ceremonies of every Christian variety performed, with everyone feted and fed in happy and good order. Aesthetically the event is a triumph; between the lines one can perceive Disraeli's audacity at portraying the serene late afternoon of a shallow culture of social parasites. It is a society in which no one works or even thinks, its raison d'être fading in a world remorselessly changing under pressure of political, scientific, and social revolutions.

While the celebrations of Lothair's majority go according to plan, almost nothing else does. Ideological terrorist organizations like the Fenians lurk everywhere; Lothair inadvertently finds himself in a revolutionary movement, and soon is magnetized by its spiritual leader. An earlier proposal of marriage to the quiet Anglican beauty, Lady Corisande, has failed on grounds of his youth and inexperience; and his flirtation with the Roman Catholic Church and its selfless devotee, Clare Arundel, becomes almost catastrophic. The birthday pomp fails to deflect him from following the charismatic Theodora to fight for her native Italy. The gesture is romantic; Lothair has never known anything squalid. The reality of popular revolution proves sordid and confused. In the prevailing amateurishness his role as Captain Muriel is exactly right, but on the *campagna* near Rome he suffers a head wound and is taken prisoner by Vatican forces, who exemplify moral squalor, even to the naive Lothair.

Theodora, in soldier's garb, dies in the clash, but not before she has explained to her acolyte her ideals about freedom of conscience. She also has him vow not to succumb to the blandishments of the Papacy, an illiberal force in the world and the particular enemy of Italian unification, the cause for which she has paid with her life. Earlier, in England, walking with her in the moonlight, Lothair had asked her about "true religion," and her response puzzled him. "I worship in a church where I believe God dwells, and dwells for my guidance and my good: my conscience." It is as close as Disraeli would come—and here indirectly, through a character whose ideas were meant to be valued, even venerated—to suggesting a personal faith.

Under house arrest by Roman clerics who plan to announce

Lothair's conversion as a propaganda coup, he slips away on another moonlit night and wanders, still somewhat dazed from his head wound, into the ruins of the vast Coliseum. There, Theodora continues to direct his destiny by appearing to him in a vision one might explain as the product of his injury. He imagines her saying only one word: "Remember!" And he falls to the ground, unconscious.

Father Coleman, who had followed him, carries Lothair back to the ecclesiastical palace where he is nursed tenderly by the saintly Clare Arundel. The relentless proseltyzing Monsignor Catesby has spread the false story, promoted as miraculous, that the Blessed Virgin herself, a halo about her head, had guided the devout Englishwoman to her stricken and dying compatriot. Lothair is horrified by the invention of the cleric easily recognized by readers as based upon the unscrupulous Monsignor Capel, who had converted the Marquess of Bute.*

Catesby's faked miracle is intended not only to frustrate the Italian Risorgimento but to create a sensation in England, capped by Lothair's conversion, which will dramatically sway English opinion toward Romanism. The implications for poor Lothair, manipulated as he knows he is by Catesby, are grim. He plans another escape. Harking back to memories of his Mediterranean experience of 1830–31, the seminal episodes of his life, Disraeli has Lothair flee by hiring several fishermen early one morning to set sail for Malta. There, through the long arm of fictional coincidence, he encounters acquaintances from England who have a yacht, the entourage of the fashionable painter Gaston Phoebus, who represents what he describes as "Aryan" principles of aesthetics, yet is en route to Jerusalem on a lucrative painting commission.

Phoebus, who carries Arnoldian intellectual fastidiousness to absurd extremes, is a foreshadowing of the Aesthetic movement. Based on the society painter Frederic (later Baron) Leighton, he

---

*Robert Capel was already a figure in England of greatly magnified influence who years later would be involved in financial scandals and allegedly "grave moral offences" that required him to leave England for California. Once, in error, in the first printing of *Lothair*, Disraeli wrote "Capel" for "Catesby."

is a wealthy exponent of Greek art and tastes who is not above painting seductive mythological nudes as an evasion of Victorian prudery. Commercially successful, contending that critics are "men who have failed in literature and art," he is Disraeli's caricature of Hellenism in conflict with the Hebraism that instinctively attracts Lothair to the Holy Land. Drawn to read Matthew Arnold's writings by Sir Anthony de Rothschild's wife, Louise, a friend of the critic, Disraeli was responding to *Culture and Anarchy* (1867). There, Arnold excoriated the individualism preached by Liberals as leading toward a selfish and inevitably heartless society, advocated a caring state as the fount of authority, and promoted "Hellenism" over "Hebraism"—valuing the culture of what he called "sweetness and light" over moralistic Evangelical emphasis upon industry in all its forms.

Phoebus's opposite materializes to Lothair on the Mount of Olives, where he has gone to visit the cradle of his faith. A venerable Syrian, Paraclete—Disraeli's equivalent to the Sidonia of the 1840s novels—confronts Lothair's priggishness and innocence, both of which have survived his experiences nearly intact, with a perspective that conflates mysticism and science. Earlier, the revisionist view of the universe that science had provoked took the form of Professor Gozelius, whom Lothair encountered at the villa of Theodora and her husband. "Baron Gozelius agrees with your celebrated pastor, Dr Cumming," Theodora had said on introducing the astronomer to Lothair, "and [he] believes that the end of the world is at hand."

Gozelius explains that the planet is always in danger of destruction: "If I were a public office, I would not insure it." And he describes cataclysmic events occurring in the heavens as part of the cycle of creation and extinction. "I have seen a world created and a world destroyed. The last was flickering ten years, and it went out as I was watching it."

"And the first?" Lothair inquires.

"Disturbed space for half a century; a great pregnancy. William Herschel told me it would come when I was a boy, and I cruised for it through two-thirds of my life. It came at last, and it repaid me."

John Herschel, the son of the great astronomer, was then

studying the heavens from the southern hemisphere, where *eta Carinae* was discovered. A cluster of very massive, rapidly evolving stars with bizarre variability behavior, it had brightened by 1843 to be the second-brightest star in the sky. Declining in brightness slowly, and then precipitously, it was barely visible by 1860.* Yet it had not "died" in a supernova fashion, leaving behind a dense neutron star, or a black hole—beyond the science of Disraeli's day. For the novelist, what was important was that science had become, in effect, the new Book of Revelation, yet without excluding a sense of the ineffable in lives that would be the richer for an element of mysticism.

"It is science," Lothair complains to Paraclete, having failed in his innocence to grasp Gozelius, "that by demonstrating the insignificance of this globe in the vast scale of creation, has led to this infidelity [to religion]."

Paraclete disagrees. Science can demonstrate the insignificance of the globe on which man resides but not man, he contends, for it is man who has discovered design. "There must be design, or all we see would be without sense, and I do not believe in the unmeaning."

Reluctant to drop the bottom out of Lothair's world, Paraclete compares the concept of an omnipotent and omniscient God with "natural forces, unconscious and irresistible," seeing little difference. And he cites Goethe's concept (playing on Leibniz) "that in the centre of space we might find a monad of pure intelligence," the irreducible entity from which the universe began—an idea strikingly foreshadowing "Big Bang" theory of the later twentieth century with its initial "singularity." Is that any more persuasive, asks Paraclete, who is willing to see "design" in religious metaphor as well, than the belief, "first revealed to man amidst these everlasting hills, that God made man in His own image?"

That was what Lothair, and, undoubtedly, Disraeli's potential reading audience, wanted to hear. "I have often found in that assurance a source of consolation," he concedes. And he leaves—in the Syrian's words—the "so transcendent, so various, so inex-

*Curiously, it began reawakening about 1950.

haustible" vistas of Jerusalem for England, returning to confess to Lady Corisande, "I have committed many mistakes, doubtless many follies, have formed many opinions, and have changed many opinions." He had been constant, however, in one of them, his love for her—and, presumably, the Anglican gentility of her world.

The fairy-tale ending concealed a host of heresies that were a clue to the real Disraeli beneath the politically necessary fictions. That someone as high in political life as a former Prime Minister who aspired to reclaim the office would write so outrageously is only one index to Disraeli's risk-taking in the novel. Lothair's earnest progress to apparent wisdom, maturity, faith, and love is the narrative from which a more subversive subtext about politics, science, and religion may be drawn. The novel's immediate success was predicated upon a public which would accept what was on its face a merrie England in which there would be class harmony and cooperation if only the religious and political troublemakers were kept out or kept in their places. Lothair inspired a song, a waltz, a ship, a street, a perfume. Corisande was equally popular, especially after Baron Mayer de Rothschild's filly of that name won the Cesarewitch stakes. On the Monday of publication, Mudie's Circulating Library, the major commercial lending establishment, was, Thomas Longman wrote, "in a state of siege." The firm had ordered only fifteen hundred copies, and quickly sought seven hundred more. Two thousand subscribers were waiting, and footmen sent from the great London houses had queued ahead of everyone else to secure the first books.

Lothair seized the interest of both the upper classes and the middle classes. The first felt flattered by the golden glow shed over the landed aristocracy when apparently seen at its best—its patrician sense of duty to the nation and the attractiveness of its leisured way of life. The middle classes were eager for colorful details about how the aristocracy lived, what its denizens discussed with each other, how reassured one might be that its continued existence was in the national interest at a time of republican agitation. Lothair was a compulsive reading experience, offering suspense, conspiracy, villainy, violence, heroism, romance, and sparkling, epigrammatic, dialogue the likes of which would not appear from another author until Oscar Wilde published *The Picture of Dorian Gray*—itself indebted to the earlier Disraeli.

Fictional vignettes of the famous again provoked the guessing game of identities and pleased everyone but a clutch of critics and one or two disgruntled prototypes. An "Oxford Professor" in the book, who may have been based on Goldwin Smith, an unforgiving Peelite who considered Disraeli an "oriental trickster," became the most notorious character in the novel because Smith foolishly identified himself, accusing the author of "the stingless insults of a coward." Archbishop Manning prudently said nothing about "Cardinal Grandison," nor did Monsignor Capel about "Catesby." While Disraeli could not permit art to follow life by having Rome prevail upon Lothair, as that would have been unacceptable to his public, the Roman Catholic hierarchy in England obviously understood the political necessities and seemed flattered by Disraeli's melodramatic exaggeration of its powers and influence. When, on April 16, 1872, the Marquess of Bute was married in London at Brompton Oratory, the ceremony was performed by Manning, with Mass celebrated by Capel. Only five witnesses were present at the wedding, one of them Disraeli.

Always attracted to the dignity and color of Catholic ritual, even as evidenced in *Lothair*, Disraeli was nevertheless excoriated from pulpits in Ireland with priestly maledictions about his novel's paganism. The more knowledgeable understood. In *Robert Orange* (1900), a romantic novel by "John Oliver Hobbes" (Mrs. Pearl Craigie), a Catholic convert, the author, who idolized Disraeli, made her eponymous hero, modeled upon Disraeli, a Roman Catholic.

Although some of the major characters, like Lothair himself, seemed to lack flesh and blood, Disraeli's supporting cast pulsated with life, figures like Mr. Ruby, the Bond Street jeweler, who advises letting pearls of the quality he purveys "lie on a sunny bank in the garden, in a westerly wind," to "maintain their complexion." (Disraeli did exactly that for Mary Anne's pearls on the terrace at Hughenden.) And there is Mr. Pinto, a stocky Portuguese beloved for his unique English and absurd epigrams, as well as St. Aldegonde, heir to a wealthy dukedom but "a republican of the reddest dye," opposed to all privilege except that of dukes, "who were a necessity." Only the hero and his ultimate heroine, Lady Corisande, lack interest. One has little more than his innocence, the other not much more than her gentility. Leslie Stephen complained in a review that Lothair was a "passive bucket" into which a variety of teachers pump ideas, leaving him "unpleasantly like a fool." What Stephen may have seen without realizing it was the key to Disraeli's novelistic subversion. What Lothair learns to the greater glory of his audience's predispositions was suspect in exact proportion to the noble lord's lack of intellectual depth in a society with no purpose but its own preservation. How lucky it was for Disraeli, Carlyle once remarked, that most of his Tory colleagues never read a book.

Possibly the reader who best appreciated the novel was James Clay, Disraeli's crewmate of 1830–31, who then shared his new friend's cynicism and wanderlust. "You are a wonderful fellow," he wrote to Disraeli, "to have retained the freshness and buoyancy of twenty-five." Perhaps Disraeli's greatest disappointment about the novel's reception was his experience, confided to Dolly Nevill, that he was once getting into a hansom cab when the driver opened the trapdoor behind him and called down, "I know who you are, sir, and have read all your books, except *Lothair.*"

The outbreak of the Franco-Prussian War during the summer of 1870 temporarily slackened demand, but in November Longman led off a six-shilling-per-volume collected Disraeli edition with a reissue of *Lothair* and interest regenerated. Ironically, the war distracted France from the defense of Rome, and the battle at Mentana lost in 1867, in which the fictional Theodora dies, had its outcome reversed, with Rome falling to the forces of Mazzini's united Italy. In Germany, with its war going well, a novel of European intrigue was an immediate best-seller for Baron Tauchnitz, and in the United States the firm of Appleton sold eighty thousand copies by October. Across the Atlantic, *Lothair* became one of the great publishing successes of its time.

Critical acclaim and copies sold bear no direct relation to each other, and *Lothair* proved the point. In technique it was old fashioned. Disraeli had read few novels since completing his own *Tancred* and learned nothing from contemporary example. His stylistic oddities were graceless to critics familiar with new fiction, and even his foreshadowings of a Meredith or a Wilde in his epigrammatic prose and quirky characters were unacceptable to fashionable reviewers. Some critics, in fact, were also political enemies or writers with other accounts to settle. Anthony Trollope called it Disraeli's "worst" novel, "falser even than *Vivian Grey.*" In the still influential *Blackwood's Magazine,* Sir Edward Bruce Hamley condemned the book as a "jest" upon the reading public by "a madman in plush breeches." But, Hamley predicted nastily, Disraeli was only preparing readers for the sequel, in which celebrities from Count Bismarck and General Robert E. Lee to Ferdinand de Lesseps, builder of the just completed Suez Canal, would turn out to be secret Jews. The struggle between Roman Catholicism and Protestantism in *Lothair* would prove to be only preliminary to the conversion of the hero to Judaism and the celebration of the Passover at Muriel Towers. Disraeli, Sir Edward alleged, was setting himself up as a new messiah.

The scurrility of the attack was so pronounced that *Blackwood's* felt compelled to follow it with a long, defensive, "Note" a month later (July 1870) quoting derogatory extracts from other reviews to prove that its indictment was in keeping with the general tone of the press. Yet the *Daily Telegraph* had called Hamley "a literary assassin," and while *The Standard* observed that *Blackwood's* had only "taunted [Disraeli] with his Jewish descent," *Bell's Weekly Messenger* labeled it "an attack of offensively personal character." "Nothing could be more brutal or blasphemous than this," the *Sunday Times* said of Hamley's messiah gibe.

Aggrieved at the attacks, *Blackwood's* retorted, "Do they suppose that nobody agrees with us in our estimate of *Lothair?*" And it went on to quote critical opinion allegedly in its favor, although largely dealing with novels that Disraeli had written a generation earlier.

In the even more influential *Fortnightly Review* (June 1870), Positivist philosopher Frederic Harrison described *Lothair* as a "political event" as well as a "brilliant" and amusing novel. It was not up to Balzac as fiction, or in wit up to Voltaire, but its art was more French than English—"quite as good as a first-rate Parisian feuilleton,* and there are few things better." But he was not "blind in praise," as he found "clumsy phrases," "gross solecisms," and "outrageously absurd" plot devices. Since Disraeli was too masterly a speaker and writer to be guilty of it all, he suggested that "the busy statesman . . . employed assistance." The real problem of the novel, he quoted a friend as saying, was not in the writing, but that "the selfish vagaries of a besotted caste" were "fawningly belauded." That was taking Disraeli's aims too seriously, Harrison concluded. "The object of a novel is to amuse. . . . Here we have a picture of a state of society, more or less true to life; there is much that is very diverting, and [that] presents us with human nature. The public likes to hear of the great." *The Times*'s review was so positive, despite Dasent's charge from his editor, that Disraeli wrote to Delane to express his "gratification" and ask that his appreciation go to the "accomplished critic," obviously "a writer of thought and taste and literary culture."

In *Macmillan's Magazine* (June 1870) Disraeli's old enemy Abraham Hayward called the novel's hero "a painted mannequin" and its style "a profusion of tawdry ornaments." The anonymous critic of the *New Monthly Magazine* (August 1870), on the other hand, saw "wonderful freshness and vigour" in the novel, the work "of a supreme mind." It was superior, he judged, to George Eliot's *Romola*. Less praise came from the Tory-minded *Quarterly Review* (July 1870), which faulted Disraeli's failure "to respect all creeds" and the "lack of passion" in what purported to be a love story. Lothair's character was "weak and silly," and Corisandewas "an aristocratic doll which has been taught to speak and walk."

Since Henry James later (1878) set a scene in *Daisy Miller* in a moonlit Coliseum to which a defiant young person has escaped watchful elders, his review in the *Atlantic Monthly* (August 1870) has the interest of establishing that he read *Lothair*. It was clever and amusing, he thought, but needed "firmer handling." Still, he found great interest in the "frequent betrayal of the possible inno-

*Then the columns of European newspapers containing fiction, criticism, and satire.

cence of one who has been supposed to be nothing if not know-ing." James was approaching close to Disraeli's ruling strategy.

Another American expatriate in London, the writer of amusing romances of the frontier West, found Disraeli's characters as a delicious subject for satire and produced a small book aping Thackeray's *Codlingsby*. The hero of Bret Harte's *Lothaw* "was ex-tremely rich. The possessor of seventeen castles, fifteen villas, nine shooting-boxes, and seven town houses, he had other estates of which he had not even heard." His stables near Oxford "occu-pied more ground than the University." And the divine Theodora, "slim, but shapely as an Ionic column," offers Harte his happiest opportunities. "Her face was Grecian, with Corin-thian temples." And when Lothaw goes to see the dying woman after the battle, "she was already a classic ruin—as wrecked and yet as perfect as the Parthenon." Her husband, the General, is an American out of Harte's absurd West. "She wants to see you be-fore she dies," he informs the hero. "Here is the key to my lodg-ing. I will finish my cigar out here."

Another book published in 1870 but destined to make much smaller waves was the *History and Literature of the Israelites* by Louise and Anthony de Rothschild's daughters Constance and Annie, then in their middle twenties. Since the Jewish Free Schools taught only the Torah, the first five books of the Bible, they determined to deal with the others, and sent one of the first copies to Disraeli, who paid them the compliment of reading it critically rather than returning an empty compliment. She de-scribed, in an "animated and picturesque" style, he wrote on July 17 to Constance, "the great story of our ancestors, and have treated with force and feeling their immortal annals." But he questioned the "propriety" of introducing "historical criticism" into what was essentially a narrative, as had been done with "Ja-cob's Blessing." The meaning of Jacob's insistence on being blessed by his angelic wrestling opponent before he will release him remains a matter of controversy, perhaps because of Jacob's failure to relinquish the blessing he had fraudulently taken from Esau.

When the second volume—Annie's—appeared later in the year he wrote to her approvingly of the lack of "disturbing criticism which would have marred the harmony of the general scheme." Annie de Rothschild had dealt with the prophets and the poets, and Disraeli regretted how little of that literature had survived, some of that "rewritten for a particular purpose." For her, too, he had a critical concern—that she used the "conventional and conventicle title" of "The Lord" in her translations rather than "the real name of the God of Israel, which would have given more clearness and meaning to the narrative." And he confided, paradoxically, that he wished Ernest Renan, author of the untraditional *Vie de Jésus*, would do a study of Ecclesiastes (which Renan would do in 1882).

As Disraeli savored his popular success with *Lothair* he found that his triumph had exacerbated Conservative discontent with him as their leader. The new collected edition made matters worse, for the early novels suggested even more that Disraeli was more a Jewish literary man than a Tory statesman. Again his rivals, overt and reluctant, were sounded out about succeeding him. Disraeli's refusal to oppose with vigor Gladstone's educational and other reforms while Salisbury opposed everything on grounds that every reform aided the poor to rob the rich, suggested him as the logical successor. Disraeli's patient advice was to let Gladstone become the victim of his own temperament.

While Northcote and Manners were among the few to remain loyal, Disraeli knew he would need the others later and bore no grudges. As he put the political situation to Dorothy Nevill on May 3, 1871, "Humpty-Dumpty has had a great fall, but I hope we shall get him on the wall again."

With Mary Anne increasingly ill, Disraeli was also distracted through much of 1871. She was clearly failing from inoperable disease—it was stomach cancer—but each pretended not to know how serious her condition was. They paid visits when they could, and in September 1871 even held their annual harvest home at Hughenden, an event that caused him great embarrassment because he used the occasion for a mishandled address.

Bad teeth, long neglected, had affected his speechmaking and left him in discomfort. The dentures could not wait for the close of a session, and Lord George Hamilton recalled Disraeli replying to the defense of an Irish bill with "a twenty minutes' speech of the most scathing invective and ridicule," when suddenly he stopped in the midst of an epigram, put his handkerchief, which was in his right hand, to his mouth, and turned behind him to Lord John Manners as if to ask a question. Then he took up his speech at the very word he had left it, only those near him hearing his whisper to Manners, "It is all right." When he finished, he received "uproarious applause" from the Tory benches.

At dinner two days later with Alderman Lawrence, a Radical M.P., Hamilton was surprised to hear Lawrence say, "Your Chief is a wonderful fellow."

"I am glad you think so," said young Hamilton.

"Would you like to know what happened the other night when he turned to John Manners? Well, in the best part of his speech and in the middle of a sentence his teeth fell out. He caught them up with extraordinary rapidity in his right hand, turned round apparently to ask a question of his neighbour, put them in, and resumed his speech at the exact word where he had left it off."

A week before the harvest home, Charlotte de Rothschild was at Hughenden, where she was warned off the event by Disraeli, who joked that there would be too many bishops present. Writing about the visit to Leopold she noted the new look of "the illustrious Caucasian"—her jesting but not unaffectionate term for Disraeli. Incongruous as usual, Mary Anne was "in youthful muslins, profusely decorated with blue and yellow ribbons." Disraeli wore "a suit of pearl grey, a soft hat, a new set of teeth, and a new collection of curls." He had kept, she wrote Leopold, who was in Switzerland, "the double-headed monster" at bay—the vicissitudes of the world and old age.

Whether the embarrassment of his informal talk at Hughenden was a mental slip of ageing that newly dyed curls could not arrest, or the undisciplined new teeth, Disraeli used a badly chosen word that journalists took down avidly but which only one newspaper had the bad taste to quote. It was known from vague reports in the Court Circular that the Queen, at Balmoral, had been ill. The ailment was not the fatigue she usually claimed to maintain her seclusion and her mourning, already in its tenth year, but what appears to have been (reading between the lines of her physician's coverup) a severe staphylococcus infection that had spread to the soft tissue behind the throat. Her doctors evaded the use of the term *quinsy*, the label at the time for peritonsillar abscess, a life-threatening infection that had spread from lymph nodes to throat. She was ill enough to need the surgical services of the renowned Dr. Joseph Lister and took two further months to recover.

Not knowing quite how sick she was, Disraeli in his harvest home talk defended the Queen from charges of malingering, claiming that she had been broken in health by the ceremonial demands upon her, and was "morally and physically incapacitated" from performing her duties. But, he quickly added, her role went beyond mere pomp and show, and her other state duties continued to be performed "with a punctuality and a precision which have certainly never been surpassed, and rarely equalled, by any monarch of these realms." She retained, he claimed, "complete control over the political tradition of England," in "a reign which has been distinguished by public duty and private virtue."

Seizing upon "morally," the Gladstone-backing *Daily Telegraph* charged that Disraeli had contended that the Queen was unfit to reign. One of the less employed meanings of *moral* was to refer to psychological rather than physical effects, and all that Disraeli had been doing was to refer to the Queen's emotional and physical incapacities, but he was forced to rush off an apologetic letter to Victoria's physician, Sir William Jenner. The Queen remained deeply offended. "Disraeli has done her & the country a left-handed service," Gladstone wrote happily to Granville, now his Foreign Minister, assuming that the Tory leader had permanently discredited himself with the Queen, the Conservatives, and loyal Englishmen in general.

Another illness paradoxically reversed perceptions. The Prince of Wales at his estate at Sandringham came down with what was unquestionably typhoid fever, and in early December was privately given up by his doctors. Wherever "God Save the Queen" was sung, concerned audiences added "God Bless the Prince of Wales." *Reynolds' Newspaper*, a republican organ backing the outspoken antiroyalist Sir Charles Dilke, described the dramatic event, as public as the Queen's own nearly fatal illness had been concealed, a "sham panic got up for the occasion to serve a political end." The philandering, spendthrift Bertie was so little regarded that his mother had told intimates that she hoped to outlive him, as he was not fit to be king. But the possible death of their future king galvanized popular loyalty, and Disraeli, inviting Lord Henry Lennox to Grosvenor Gate for a private dinner with him and Mary Anne, began on December 13, "We are in town absorbed in this dreadful sorrow. My bulletin 9 o'clock from Sandringham this morning is dark. The ray of hope of last night seems flickering."

Lennox's reply began, "What a sell for Dilke this illness has been!"

A few days later the Prince was declared out of danger, and the Queen asked Gladstone to prepare a public thanksgiving. He recommended St. Paul's "in conformity with unbroken usage." Victoria objected to a Cathedral service as "false & hollow," Gladstone noted after an audience with her. "She considered that no religious act ought ever to be allied with pomp or show." But he saw political opportunities in what he described as "great national acts of religion," and wore down the Queen's objections by suggesting that "this great occasion" would counter republican feeling in the country and create affection for the unloved Prince of Wales.

Pressing for as early a date as Bertie's physicians might permit, Victoria chose February 27, 1872, close enough to the opening of Parliament for her to evade that duty on grounds of conserving her strength for the Prince's Thanksgiving. Needing the partisan lift likely from any spectacle for the masses, Gladstone gave in, hoping all the while that the Prince would be up to his occasion.

For Victoria, a London February was little more than a Balmoral summer. She rode in an open carriage, wearing a black silk dress and bonnet, and was seated next to the wan Prince, who was up to little more than lifting his hat to acknowledge loyal cheers. Observing the enthusiastic crowds, the Queen may have wondered about the fuss over her alleged seclusion and unpopularity. During her convalescence she had read two books about the horrors and excesses of the Paris Commune that had followed the defeat and departure of Napoleon III. Such news of France's agonies as had reached England had already dampened the ardor of all but the most resolute radicals. Other agonies also seemed to have their positive side. Had the successive near fatal illnesses of the Queen and the Prince of Wales been part of a calculated strategy, they could not have been improved upon as a means of rescuing the monarchy from opprobrium and reversing any drift toward republicanism. Yet Albert Edward was no better a future king when he recovered, nor was Victoria a more accessible queen.

The first signs of a turn in Disraeli's own favor had been his election the previous autumn, over John Ruskin, as Lord Rector of Glasgow University. But the procession to St. Paul's was a demonstration in the center of things. Both Gladstone and Disraeli as leaders of their parties had accompanied the Sovereign and Prince in separate carriages. Crowds greeted the Prime Minister with indifference at best, while Disraeli encountered continuing ovations not only from the City to Waterloo Place, but along Regent Street and Oxford Street and thence to Grosvenor Gate to drop Lady Beaconsfield off, and finally to the Carlton Club.

Sir William Fraser recalled seeing Disraeli at the Carlton ostensibly listening to a colleague but with an expression "as that of one who looks into another world." Afterwards Fraser figured it out: "He was thinking that he will be Prime Minister again."

XXIV.

"THE AGE OF RUINS IS PAST."

1872–1874

THE OUTPOURING OF POPULAR SUPPORT FOR DISRAELI AT THE PRINCE of Wales's Thanksgiving came when he needed it most. On February 1, 1872, five former members of Disraeli's cabinet met Earl Cairns and the Duke of Marlborough at Burghley, the country seat of Lord Exeter, to reconsider the Tory leadership. Gathorne-Hardy confessed that he did not prefer Derby to Disraeli, "but that it was idle to ignore the general opinion." Yet no one present, he noted in his diary on February 3, "could or would undertake such a task" as telling Disraeli that he had to go. With Manners and Northcote dissenting, the Burghley cabal agreed, cautiously, in Gathorne-Hardy's words, "that Disraeli has not as far as appears the position in House & country to enable him to do what the other might." The "other" was the current Lord Derby, whose name, according to the Chief Whip, Gerald Noel, might shift "40 or fifty seats." Disraeli also had such marginal seats in mind when, in 1870, he appointed the shrewd John Eldon Gorst (knighted as a Liberal in 1885) to head a Conservative Party office in London and set him to work to revive party branches in the constituencies.

While the prickly personality of Gladstone had begun to erode his following, "Dizzy" was becoming a celebrity beyond party. Recognizing an opportunity, he took on Gladstone in the Commons on the evening of the 27th. Ireland, Disraeli realized, would become a bone in the Prime Minister's throat, as Gladstone insisted on his solutions even at the price of Liberal harmony. "The right honourable gentleman persuaded the people of England," Disraeli remarked, "that with regard to Irish politics he was in possession of the philosopher's stone. . . . After all his heroic exploits, and at the head of his great majority, [he] is making Government ridiculous."

Disraeli also prodded his counterpart in the Lords, the Duke of Richmond (father of Lord John Manners), to be more cooperative with the Commons. Disraeli wanted an Opposition that opposed, especially when there were issues that clearly separated the parties. The Duke turned to Earl Cairns, his predecessor as leader, for advice, and Cairns complained that it was Disraeli who had been unnaturally quiescent—"down in the mouth." Now that party prospects were "looking up," Cairns carped, "awakening himself, [Disraeli] turns round and insists that everyone else is asleep."

To demonstrate that Disraeli was indeed awake to Tory opportunities, John Gorst, capitalizing upon the positive auguries of the procession to St. Paul's, contrived an invitation to the Free Trade Hall in Manchester. An efficient organizer, Gorst arranged for a vast parade on April 2 of the Conservative Associations of Lancashire, with representatives, identified by banners, from more than two hundred Lancashire boroughs, divisions, and townships. On the reviewing platform were Disraeli and the wan but courageous Lady Beaconsfield.

In the crowded Free Trade Hall the next day, fortified by two bottles of brandy and water, Disraeli spoke for three and a half hours. Every major newspaper covered the event. It was a spacious speechmaking era, paralleled in the theater by programs which included a one-act "curtain-raiser" to extend the evening, and in the concert hall by performances which featured two symphonies prefaced by an overture and padded with shorter works. On the lecture platform the speaker, however expansive, was usually introduced by several preliminary orations. In Manchester, Disraeli elaborated upon his standard speech, unchanged except in particulars since Shrewsbury in the 1840s. (The Conservatives were the guardians of tradition, the basis of the nation's rights, liberties, and prosperity.) But he knew that on social issues, with the Liberals seen as the party of extremes, he could appeal to the material interests of the working class by recommending cautious reforms which would not frighten the middle class nor appear to rob the upper class.

Memorably, Disraeli characterized the Gladstone government and its "subsiding energy" with a fanciful geography he had never encountered (nor had anyone else): "As I sat opposite the Treasury Bench the minister reminded me of one of those marine landscapes not very unusual on the coasts of South America. You behold a range of exhausted volcanoes. Not a flame flickers on a single pallid crest. . . . There are occasional earthquakes, and ever and anon the dark rumbling of the sea." The metaphor mocked Liberalism in office too long, letting fall into decay those political institutions which should be ensuring English prosperity by bringing "increased means and increased leisure, . . . the two civilisers of man."

"The age of ruins is past," Sidonia had asserted to Harry Coningsby in Disraeli's novel of 1844. "Have you seen Manchester?" In 1872, cities like Manchester were burgeoning still, but despite the supposedly benign dominance of Liberalism, all were suffering from the urban blight that made living and working in them much less than utopian. For Disraeli and the Conservatives, their own age of ruins seemed behind them. A new lease on Downing Street, backed this time by a majority in Parliament, seemed possible for the first time since the Tories began fragmenting in the very year of *Coningsby*.

Briefed by Sir Charles Adderley on public health concerns, Disraeli offered a memorable Conservative promise, that "the first consideration of a Minister should be the health of the people," which he defined as "pure air, pure water, the inspection of unhealthy habitations, [of] the adulteration of food." Conservatives would put them all on the legislative agenda, Disraeli committing the party to social progress while committing the party to him. The Burghley House revolt was over. "Oh! Dizzy, Dizzy, it is the greatest night of all!" Mary Anne cried as she rushed to him when the speechmaking was over. "It pays for all!"

To make certain that Disraeli was recognized as in control of the party, Gorst arranged a second widely covered address, this time for London and the south, to be delivered at the relocated Crystal Palace in Sydenham on June 24. The audience was the National Union of Conservative and Constitutional Associations, which included delegates from working men's Conservative clubs. In the chair was the Duke of Abercorn, widely assumed to be the model for the Duke in Disraeli's *Lothair*, the father of the fair Corisande.

As in Manchester, Disraeli cultivated a modernized image for the party, positive rather than defensive, with a readily grasped sense of direction. Helpfully, Sir Charles Dilke, one of the most radical of Gladstone's supporters, focused Disraeli's mind by delivering a speech at Newcastle on the obsolescence of the monarchy fiery enough to precipitate riots. A second stimulus came by way of a letter from Lord Napier, who was still commanding the Indian Army from Calcutta. "I consider it a duty," he wrote on April 26, "to try and cause every Native, high or low, to look upon us as friends, and be ready to take an interest in all that affects their welfare or happiness."

Comparing Conservative and Liberal principles as he saw them, Disraeli restated Tory interest in "elevation of the condition of the people, . . . reduction in their hours of labour . . . to humanise their toil." Responding to Dilke's charge at Newcastle that the Royal Family cost taxpayers a million pounds a year, he observed that the revenues of the Crown estates went into the public exchequer, more than compensating for Civil List outlays. His point was *that there is no sovereignty of any first-rate state which costs so little to the people as the sovereignty of England.* Using the United States as basis, because European monarchies were allegedly so spendthrift, he added about the position he had filled in 1868 that the President of the United States and the Prime

The Conservative Programme.
"Deputation below, Sir.—Want to know the Conservative Programme."
Rt. Hon. Ben. Diz. *"Eh?—Oh!—Ah!—Yes!—Quite so! Tell them, my good Abercorn, with my compliments, that we propose to rely on the Sublime Instincts of an Ancient People!!" Punch,* July 6, 1872. Lord Abercorn chaired the Conservative rally at the Crystal Palace.

Minister of England "are paid at much the same rate—the income of a second-class professional man."

Then Disraeli turned to an imperial theme which he described as a thoroughly Conservative one. Over the entire history of the party calling itself Liberal, he charged, its energies have gone "to effect the disintegration of the Empire." Rather, the jewel in the crown of England that was India, and the other colonies for which the nation was "trustee," should become "the source of incalculable strength and happiness in this land." A party of Little Englanders, he contended, was unfit to govern a worldwide community of English settlement. Although Britain had not even been fulfilling its European responsibilities, withdrawing into itself under Gladstone, it was Disraeli's "confident conviction" that never was there "a moment in our history when the power of England was so great and her resources so vast and inexhaustible."

He was also convinced "that the great body of the working class of England [would] utterly repudiate such [Little England] sentiments," for raw materials and markets for manufactures meant jobs in Manchester and Birmingham. While he spoke in terms of "greatness," his audience understood that he meant prosperity. He also appealed beyond material well-being to national pride. "The issue is . . . whether you will be content to be a comfortable England, modelled and moulded upon Continental principles and meeting in due course an inevitable fate, or whether you will be a great country—an Imperial country—a country where your sons, when they rise, rise to paramount positions, and obtain not merely the esteem of their countrymen, but command the respect of the world." The challenge brought the 2,500 faithful to their feet. A theme had been sounded and the Conservative Party released from its malaise. Dramatically contrasting the timid, tuppence-minded Liberal attitude with the imperial mystique, Disraeli had articulated values that would govern Britain as far into the future as World War II.

Few specific proposals emanated from Disraeli during the session itself. He was biding his time, while his party, seeing by-elections go in their favor, chafed. He expected Gladstone's tactlessness in handling his own coalition to do him in. Conservative impatience is obvious in Gathorne-Hardy's diary. The entry for May 7, 1872, reveals another aspect of Disraeli's continuing problems with the ultra-Tory side of the party, toward which he could never make himself acceptable. "Dr Lee," Hardy noted, ". . . shewed me a remarkable letter of Newman." Frederick George Lee, who was extremely High Church, was actively promoting reconciliation with Rome, and Father Newman saw no hope as long as Disraeli and Gladstone were able to tamper with the Anglican Church: "Disraeli is a man of the world, a politician, and in thought and in belief as much a Jew as he is Christian. On the other hand he is the representative of all the old notions which Tories used to cherish and the Pope at this time represents, while Gladstone is the leader of a mixed multitude, who profess a Babel of religions or none at all. I never can feel respect for Mr Disraeli's self—I never can hold fellowship with Gladstone. . . . And I don't think that, when it comes to the point, Disraeli will do any thing for you—he will use you and throw you over. What does he care, for instance, for the Athanasian Creed?"

The Disraelis returned from the Crystal Palace triumph exhausted. Although Mary Anne hid her emaciation under extravagant dresses, she could not conceal her failing condition. As her stomach could no longer tolerate most drugs, they had to be discontinued, and she lived in pain. Under the tension, Disraeli was first to collapse. Sir William Gull blamed the worsening of the bronchial asthma that had become chronic.

Hughenden in the summer was now impractical. Doctors were remote, and Mary Anne could only be pushed in a chair, indoors and out. In London her condition remained grim. Disraeli put the best face upon it in a letter to Sir Anthony de Rothschild on September 10, thanking him for "cases of Parisian pears and peaches." Ordinarily they would have been sent, in the post-Parliamentary months, to the country, but the Rothschilds were aware of the situation. "We are still here," Disraeli acknowledged. "That tells our sad tale, but my wife insists . . . that I am to say nothing depressing to her friends. . . . We were never in London during this Season before. Our situation gives us some compensation in trees and visited bowers. We try to believe that the Park is not called Hyde, and to forget that the bowers are the bowers of Kensington."

On good days Mary Anne had callers, but her decline was clear to those who had seen her at a Foreign Office reception on June 19. The young 5th Earl of Rosebery (the former Lord Dalmeny) noted, "Lady Beaconsfield [is] in wonderful spirits, although I am afraid she is very ill. I took her through the rooms, and she insisted on introducing me to the Burmese Ambassador as her son!" Cancer had invaded her brain, and she was not always rational.

The last time that she appeared in public was at a reception given by the Countess of Loudoun on July 17. Mary Anne had to be carried out, and guests marveled that she had managed to come. "To see her weaker and weaker every day is heartrending," Disraeli had minuted to Montagu Corry, but until the session ended he repaired briefly each afternoon to the Commons, writing to her from there such notes as (on July 25), "I have nothing to tell you, except that I love you, which, I fear, you will think rather dull." Natty Rothschild, then M.P. for Aylesbury, "was very affectionate about you, and wanted me to come home and dine with him . . . but I told him that you were the only person now, whom I could dine with; and [I] only relinquished you tonight for my country."

She was asleep when he returned, and asleep when he left for Westminster the next day. Awakening, she sent a note to him at the Commons: "I miss you sadly. I feel so grateful for your tender love and kindness." She signed it proudly, "Your own devoted Beaconsfield." In date it is the last of her letters he preserved and probably her last.

Insisting that a change of air would do her good, she asked to return to Hughenden, very likely because she preferred dying there. Their "hegira from Grosvenor Gate," as Disraeli put it, took place in the closing days of September. "It tears my heart to see such a spirit suffer, and suffer so much!" he wrote to Lord Cairns, adding, "The buoyancy of her spirit is so remarkable," that if she only had "a desire for sustenance," her condition might improve. As in London, even what he called in a letter to Corry (October 13) "the feats of Lionel [de Rothschild]'s *chef,*" sent hopefully for Mary Anne, went untouched. To Lord Barrington, Disraeli wrote on October 16 that she had been "for many years a helpmate as it has been the lot of few men to possess"—a description suggesting that she was already being mourned.

Her last house party, at which she was a quiet spectator, took place from November 21 through November 25. Lord John Manners and his wife, Lord Rosebery, William Vernon Harcourt, and Lord Ronald Gower were present, all pretending to be jocular, but

Disraeli told Gower, a look of woe crossing his face, "She suffers so dreadfully at times." On December 11 Disraeli's deputy Gathorne-Hardy noted in his diary, "I fear the long suspended blow is about to fall."

In her last days she asked for Corry. "She says she must see you," Disraeli wrote to London, where Corry was handling Downing Street business. "Calm, but the delusions stronger than ever." Monty came, and so did a clergyman, whom she dismissed. She explained to Corry, "He told me to turn my thoughts to Jesus Christ but I couldn't. You know Dizzy is my Jesus Christ." At the end, pneumonia took hold and addled her brain further, and, Rosebery was told, "she denounced Disraeli to Monty Corry— [with] Disraeli shedding tears by the door."

The end came at noon on Sunday, December 15. Struggling to breathe, she refused her bed and died upright in her chair. Although her death certificate gave her age as seventy-six, she was eighty.

Before the day was out, the Queen had sent Disraeli her "heartfelt sympathy." She understood "the unbounded devotion and affection which united him to the dear partner of his life, whose only thought was him." For Victoria the date held almost mystical significance. "*Yesterday*," she wrote, "was the anniversary of her great loss." The consolation she offered, which meant more to her than to the new widower, was "the blessed certainty of eternal reunion." Even Gladstone, who recalled that he and Catherine were "married in the same year," sent his sympathies, recalling that he had enjoyed Mary Anne's "marked but unmerited regard." Disraeli responded that he was "touched" by the kind words.

On December 20, 1872, a bleak, cold, rainy Friday, Disraeli watched Hughenden tenants carry the coffin to its place in the church vault next to James D'Israeli and Sarah Brydges Willyams. One space now remained. When Philip Rose, Monty Corry, and Mary Anne's doctor left the churchyard, Disraeli stood bareheaded and alone in the rain and wind for another ten minutes, then returned to the house.

Deluged with tributes and with sympathy, Disraeli followed tradition by responding on notepaper edged with black which he continued to use the rest of his life. To do otherwise would seem to be forgetting her. He had once thought such sentiments in the Queen were morbid, he later told Lady Bradford. Yet when he had been "on the point sometimes of terminating this emblem of my bereavement, the thought that there was no longer any being in the world to whom I was an object of concentrated feeling overcame me and the sign remained."

One letter of sympathy came from Dorothy Nevill, whom he would lose as neighbor, for Mary Anne's death meant that the lease of 2 Grosvenor Gate would now revert to Wyndham Lewis's family. Hughenden, he wrote to Dorothy on January 31, 1873, was now his only home, but he had to continue his labors in London somehow, and somewhere. "I feel quite incapable of the duties, but my friends will be indulgent to a broken spirit." Among the outpouring of condolences was a message from Queen Sophia of the Netherlands, whom Mary Anne had escorted about London. "It is given to few to have a character like hers," the Queen wrote, perhaps with more truth than intended.

When a note of sympathy came from Juliana de Rothschild, wife of Baron Mayer, the squire of Mentmore, Disraeli responded that Mary Anne "often said that the intimate relations with your family formed one of the greatest sources of her happiness." It was not an exaggeration. The Rothschilds were more indulgent toward her eccentricities, which they recognized as an element of her warmheartedness, than were the rigid Tory ladies on the periphery of her husband's party. They also understood her solicitous care of her "Dizzy." Visiting Anthony and Louise de Rothschild soon after—which was not "going into society" while in mourning, as the Rothschilds were family—Disraeli chose Constance, then twenty-nine, to talk to after dinner about his loss. "Sympathy," he assured her, was the quality indispensable to a happy marriage. "Sympathy goes before beauty or talent. Sympathy—and that is what I have had!" He spoke to no one else the rest of the evening, her father appearing concerned "that I might grow vain or conceited at such a distinguishing mark of friendship from so great a personage." But she was still unmarried—she would wed Cyril Flower in 1877—and Disraeli was offering advice while talking out his grief.

"When I tell my coachman to drive 'Home,' " he confided to Lord Malmesbury, "I feel it is a mockery." Home, arranged by Monty Corry, became Edward's Hotel in George Street, east of Sloane Square, rooms once occupied by Lady Cowper before she married Lord Palmerston. They were, he told friends, "a cave of despair," but he had lost about £5,000 a year in Mary Anne's income from Wyndham Lewis's estate, and had no idea whether Opposition politics and reduced means made a lease on a town house practical.

At Hughenden, Disraeli was visited by Cairns and Gathorne-Hardy on January 20 to discuss the new Parliamentary session, and Hardy called twice in London. On February 7, the day the Queen's Address would be read, he found Disraeli "in a dressing gown of bright & many colours," preparing notes for his response. There would be nothing dramatic in it, and he expected a session without serious incident, which suited his desire for seclusion—or at least a professed desire for seclusion that was at odds with the loneliness he quickly complained of in his hotel.

Three days into the session, as Disraeli discovered when he arrived at Lionel de Rothschild's Piccadilly mansion, a crisis atmosphere turned the Liberals frantic. Expecting only "a family circle," he found Charles Villiers, Bernal Osborne—both friends of Lionel's—and Lord Cork and Lord Houghton. All Liberals, they were eager for his opinion on "the Bill," which *The Times* had got hold of, and Delane had shown to Rothschild. A *Punch* cartoon had caricatured Gladstone as a jockey catapulting a steeplechasing horse labeled "Liberal Majority" at a formidable stone wall identified as "Irish University Bill." In the background were two jumps already accomplished, "Irish Land Bill" and "Irish Church Bill." The caption was, "Would he clear it?"

A professing Catholic in Ireland could not enter Trinity College, Dublin. Other than seminaries, only the secular Queen's University colleges at Belfast, Cork, and Galway were open. Disraeli earlier had offered state chartering of a Catholic university in Ireland, but no public funds. It was all that he saw likely to pass in a largely Protestant Parliament. Gladstone offered to settle what he called the "last social and religious grievance" of Ireland by making the University of Dublin the central institution, affiliating the existing colleges with a new religiously neutral college implicitly Catholic in teaching personnel. Very little public money was promised.

The proposal alienated the Protestant vote without satisfying the Catholic faction. Irish M.P.s rebelled, and the bill was nibbled to death by hostile amendments. Gladstone had been permitted four years of "confiscation," Disraeli told the Commons. No one now was "certain of his property," and no one was the better for it. "The Irish Roman Catholic clergy were perfectly satisfied while you were despoiling the Irish Church. They looked not unwillingly upon the plunder of the Irish landlords, and they thought that the time had arrived when the great drama would be fulfilled, and the spirit of confiscation would descend upon the sacred walls of Trinity College . . . and endow the university of [St.] Stephen's Green."

Gladstone's quarter loaf satisfied no one. On a second reading 274 votes were cast for it, most merely to keep him in office; 287 were recorded against it. Having guaranteed that he would leave Downing Street if the bill failed, he kept his pledge, and on March 13, 1873, announced that the Queen had accepted his Government's resignation.

Sent for by Victoria, Disraeli refused to form yet another minority Ministry. It would play into Gladstone's hands, as such a government could be embarrassed on any vote the majority Opposition chose. The Conservative leadership, anticipating such a move, had already determined to let Gladstone simmer, but Edward Horsman, John Pakington, and Edward Bouverie, all anti-Disraeli in any case, urged Gathorne-Hardy to support a ministry under the unwilling Derby. In the Lords, the Duke of Richmond declared that Tories were not rejecting power, but declining powerlessness. Gladstone was forced to return, with Disraeli hoping that Liberal disarray would enhance Tory prospects when a General Election was held.

"Well, we have gone through our crisis," Gladstone claimed to his brother Robertson on March 21, "and I fear nobody is much the better for it." There was no reason for the Tories to reject power, he thought, but for the reluctance of the other side to be "educated" again by Disraeli. "The Conservative Party will never assume its natural position until Disraeli retires; & I some-times think he & I might with advantage pair off [in retirement] together."

Mourning and seclusion became difficult under the heated political circumstances. It seemed that beyond his notepaper and the mourning band round his hat (which he retained the rest of his life), Disraeli had little opportunity to feel sorry for himself, yet when he returned at midnight to Edward's Hotel, he knew he was alone. Throughout the session his friends tried to keep him from solitary dining at the hotel. His black-edged letters are full of diplomatic refusals of invitations—there were more than he could cope with, and he awaited the relief of the Easter recess and escape to Hughenden. Once there, going through Mary Anne's papers and possessions, he found that almost every scrap of his notes to her had been saved, and even his hair clippings. And he found her touching letter of June 6, 1856, with the admonition, "Do not live alone, dearest. Some one I earnestly hope you may find as attached to you as your own devoted Mary Anne." Since political business kept him in London, he could not complete go-ing through her papers until August, when, he told Corry, "she died for me 100 times."

The year was an emotional roller coaster. Intimations of mortality collided with new female interests that rejuvenated the increasingly gouty and asthmatic widower of sixty-eight. At least two ladies of his acquaintance wasted little time in trying to turn Mary Anne's posthumous hope into matrimony. Monty Corry, much out of London because of the illness and death of his father, was a rare intimate aware of it until one lady let the world know her version. "Saturday alone with my Countess," Disraeli had written Corry about February 18, 1873. The cryptic tag identified the eccentric Countess of Cardigan, forty-nine, widow of the Cri-mean War hero who had sent the Light Brigade to its doom. Adeline de Horsey had been, publicly, the general's mistress, be-coming chatelaine of Deene Park after the death of Cardigan's first wife. Rich and fast, she was eager to become the consort of a Prime Minister, as she was certain Disraeli would again be, ap-proaching him with an offer to work as his unpaid private secre-tary, an opening that led instead to several private dinners. Then

the Countess turned amorous, telling Disraeli that she had received, since becoming a widow, twelve offers of marriage, but
was interested only in him.

Lady Cardigan would be, Disraeli understood, catastrophic to
his reputation. A draft note by him that June suggests that "at
present it w[oul]d be better that we sh[oul]d not meet"—
apparently a reply to her proposal of marriage. It would be, she
had written unevasively, the "union which would to me secure
happiness, comfort & the realization of my most ambitious
hopes." All their "*real* friends," she added, realizing that she was
a social pariah, would understand a marriage of "the greatest man
we have in genius & intellect with the wealthiest relict of the
staunchest Conservative peer that ever lived."

Later she claimed that after her elderly uncle, Admiral
Henry John Rous, who wrote a column on the turf for *The Times*,
had warned her, "My dear, you can't marry that damned old Jew,"
she happened upon the Prince of Wales while riding and asked
his advice "about a proposal of marriage I had just received from
Disraeli." He cautioned her that the union would not be "a very
happy one." To Disraeli's further disadvantage, she alleged—
suggesting some intimacy—that he had bad breath. The charge of
halitosis is unproven; however the Countess's frank offer is preserved in the Hughenden papers. As for the Prince, when as
Edward VII he was told about the Countess's *My Recollections*,
published in 1909, he did not deny the encounter but only that
she misrepresented what he had said. It would have been a tem-
pestuous marriage.

A second interested lady was the richest woman in England,
Angela Burdett-Coutts, heiress to a banking fortune and a baron-
ess at fifty-seven, in 1871. A lady of multiple philanthropies, she
was an old friend of Disraeli's and one of the few, if we accept
Kate Donovan's story of her childhood, close enough to Disraeli
to befriend his unadvertised daughter. That he never considered the
Baroness the marrying kind is clear from a mocking comment in his
letter to Lady Bradford of July 19, 1874, about a reception for the
Crown Princess of Germany he had to attend as Prime Minister.
"The guests were all the quizzes in London," he wrote—*quiz* the
term then current for an eccentric person—"except the romantic

Baroness and [her companion] Mrs Brown." It was clear that Lady
Bradford had been privy to Angela Burdett-Coutts's offer. From
1837, when Angela was twenty-three, she had been mistress of her
own town house at 1 Stratton Street, Berkeley Square, and a great
and well-connected lady. But there would be no marriage with Disraeli.

On August 29, 1873, he confided his relief from the importu-
nities of the aggressive Adeline—but not yet those of the eager
Angela—to Lady Bradford. To the Countess, who had been Selina
Forester of Shropshire when he first met her in the distant 1830s,
early in her reign as a society beauty, he noted without naming
names that he "had received from the lady an announcement of
the immediately impending event—'as you have always taken so
kind an interest in my welfare.' One can scarcely congratulate, but
may sincerely wish her every happiness. It sounds very bad."
Disraeli, the code indicates, was already sufficiently intimate with
Lady Bradford to have gossiped about the Countess of Cardigan's
courtship, for what he was quoting was the impulsive Adeline's letter informing him that since he had failed her, she was marrying,
instead, the Comte de Lancastre, a Portuguese aristocrat.

Disraeli was not altogether rid of the Countess—she pressed
him unsuccessfully to have her received at Court—but he was
already finding safer solace in the friendship of Lady Bradford
and her elder sister, Anne, the long-widowed Countess of Chesterfield. A visit that summer to Bretby, Lady Chesterfield's country house, renewed Disraeli's relationship with Selina, fifty-four,
married to a Tory sporting peer, and already a grandmother. Anne
was two years older than Disraeli, but although nearly a septuagenarian himself, he fell in love with the slender Lady Bradford and
was determined to be her *cavalier servente*. Physical passion had
little if anything to do with it: Disraeli had been used to decades
of sharing intimacies with devoted women, and, while flattered by
the admiration of the great man, Lady Bradford accepted his attentions with more patience than ardor. In any case, the 4th Earl
of Bradford was more interested in his racing stud than in Selina.
Before the long correspondence closed, Disraeli had written more
than eleven hundred letters to Lady Bradford and over five hundred to Lady Chesterfield.

August and September were months of comparative solitude at Hughenden. With the exception of Arthur Helps, an emissary from the Queen, Disraeli wrote to Charlotte de Rothschild on September 14, "I have neither seen, nor spoken, to a human being." Hoping to continue a quiet life to repair his health, with a light diet—"a spare radish," he put it to Lady Bradford—he then sought the sea breezes at Brighton. On the first evening he encountered his friends the Sturts. To enjoy Gerard Sturt's talk ("his wondrous rattle is as good as champagne") he agreed to have dinner with them, but then Charlotte Sturt fell ill at the table, fancied the cause was the Brighton air, and insisted on entraining immediately for London. The next day Disraeli was recognized in the street by Baroness Brunnow, wife of the Russian Ambassador. She insisted on his dining in their suite, where he found a feast served by five footmen and messengers arriving with tallies of the by-election at Dover. (The Baron was excited about English politics, which bore no resemblance to the czarist variety.) At ten, to celebrate the results, a local group gave him a serenade, although he thought he had arrived incognito—"the most beautiful thing I ever heard," he gushed to Selina.

The next day he strolled into the Aquarium, then went to hear the Christy Minstrels, who took off their hats to him and "made him a low ceremonious bow," young Reginald Brett (the future Lord Esher) was told by Disraeli. Then Disraeli met the Marquis of Clanricarde and Lady Clanricarde, who could not be dissuaded from offering him a Scot-style dinner, and he did not want to offend their tastes. "One does say foolish things sometimes," he admitted to Brett, "but if there is one thing I never eat, it is roast mutton, and one thing I never drink, it is dry sherry; so I dined on Seltzer water."

The morning after, he escaped homeward, then on to Glasgow, where University students had voted him Lord Rector, and afterward to Weston, the Shropshire seat of the Bradfords. At Glasgow he told students that two kinds of understanding were crucial for success in life, self-knowledge and a perception of the spirit of the age. "It is singular," he observed, "that though there is no lack of those who will explain the past, and certainly no want of those who will predict the future, when the present is concerned—the present that we see and feel—our opinions about it are in general bewildered and mistaken."

While in Scotland he visited Lamington, the home of his Young England friend Alexander Baillie-Cochrane, now 1st Baron Lamington, and in the tradition of marking the visit of a distinguished guest, he planted a tree, first throwing (again as tradition required) a shilling into the pit prepared for the sapling: "To bring fortune to the family." For Young England there was, by 1873, Smythe excepted, good fortune. All the by-election signs now suggested a Conservative spring. For one successful effort, that of Lord Grey de Wilton at Bath, Disraeli released an open letter which accused Gladstone's regime of a negative activism, harassing every trade, profession, class, institution, and "species of property" in the country. It was "civil warfare" that, he contended, "outraged public opinion" and stumbled into "mistakes which have always been discreditable, and sometimes ruinous." Although the Liberals seemed "quite proud of it," Disraeli predicted that the country "has, I think, made up its mind to close this career of plundering and blundering."

As in earlier days with Mary Anne, Disraeli passed his late autumn and early winter in the country seats of his friends— Gunnersbury (Rothschilds), Ashridge (Lord Brownlow), Sandringham (Prince of Wales), Blenheim (Duke of Marlborough), Hemsted Park (Gathorne-Hardy), Trentham (Duke of Sutherland), and finally Crichel (Baron Alington, then H. G. Sturt), where at last he found, once more, the adored Lady Bradford. Since Disraeli could seldom bring himself to ride, hunt, or fish, and played whist in the evenings only when he craved the company, his weeks at magnificent manors and miles-broad estates were employed in walking, talking, and writing. He preferred "amusing people" to serious political talk in such venues. "I would rather hold a good [political] council," he assured Lady Bradford, "without the paraphernalia of pheasants and the conventional finery of second-rate women." She, however, was different. Anticipating Crichel early in January 1874 he told her, "I shall stay . . . exactly as long as you do. Who our companions may be is a matter of perfect indifference to me; so long as you are present I should rather prefer persons I dislike, as they would not require any attention."

Expecting dissolution and a Conservative victory, Disraeli, when at Hemsted Park on December 19, asked Jane Gathorne-Hardy to have him and Corry driven to nearby Bedgebury, the seat of A. J. Beresford Hope, to see Lady Mildred, Hope's wife, who was a Cecil—Lord Salisbury's sister. Disraeli wanted to forge a link to the stubborn Marquis, to broaden his possible Cabinet. Returning to Hughenden from his round of visits in the second week of January, Disraeli planned to remain, but for a business weekend in London, until the new session began early in February. On Friday, January 23, he checked in at Edward's Hotel, then repaired to the Carlton Club for the latest political news. The likely Liberal candidate for the county seat in Lincolnshire, he learned, had decided, in view of Conservative prospects, not to stand. Also, the Conservative mediocrity who was only someone's son-in-law had stepped aside for "a most powerful and popular candidate," Disraeli wrote to Lady Bradford. "I think we shall walk over the course."

Realizing that if he did not hurry the balloting he would lose more seats, Gladstone made a surprise decision to hold a General Election that would pre-empt the opening of Parliament. Disraeli only learned of it when he read his *Times* in bed at his hotel on Saturday morning. Columns detailed Gladstone's statement, including a pledge to abolish the income tax. Deliberately timing his announcement for a quiet weekend, he hoped to catch the Opposition unprepared, but Disraeli telegraphed every power in the party he could find for a strategy session in London. Then he cobbled together a statement for release in London papers recapitulating his Manchester and Crystal Palace manifestos.

Members flocked into the Carlton on January 25, a Monday, Gathorne-Hardy's diary recording the scene as "excited, great writing of [election] addresses, telegraph sending, &c." Among Disraeli's other priorities—actually Corry's—was to locate a house to lease, and 2 Whitehall Gardens, just off Horse Guard's Avenue and overlooking the Embankment, was found. It was a few minutes' walk from Parliament.

Polling began on February 1, a Sunday, with elections spread over nearly two weeks. It was the month that serialization began—each number a shilling—of Anthony Trollope's sardonic

Paradise and the Peri. A peri in Persian folklore is a supernatural being descended from fallen angels and excluded from Paradise until
penance is accomplished. The caption in *Punch* (Feb. 28, 1874) is:

> "Joy, joy for ever! My task is done—
> The gates are passed, and Heaven is won!"—*Lalla Rookh*

For the first time, Disraeli had a majority with him in Parliament.

new novel, *The Way We Live Now*, in which the swindler Augustus Melmotte, a foreigner of suspect origins who buys his way into
Parliament, is "not the first vulgar man whom the Conservatives
had taken by the hand, and patted on the back, and told that he
was a god." Disraeli was too preoccupied to read it. He was chagrined at having his own seat in Buckinghamshire contested—"No danger," he told Lady Bradford, to whom he wrote

several times a week, but it seemed an attempt to distract him from campaigning for distant constituencies. Yet John Gorst had done his job, finding strong candidates and furnishing them with funds raised by local associations and—from the Central Office—by traditional backers of the Conservatives, the landed proprietors. Even the Reform Bill had turned out well this time, as it was clear that many votes came from humble households. A new Home Rule Party in Ireland also drew votes from the Liberals and was seen almost as a perverse Gladstone legacy.

The tally for the country gave Conservatives 350 seats, Liberals 245, Home Rulers 57. "My own election for Greenwich, after [Thomas White] Boord the distiller," Gladstone acknowledged in his diary on February 8, "is more like a defeat than a victory, though it places me in Parliament again." In a two-seat constituency, the Prime Minister had placed second to a Tory exploiter of the demon of drink. To the Lord Lieutenant of Ireland, Lord Spencer, Gladstone falsely blamed the Liberal losses on having been "swept away, literally, by a torrent of beer & gin." Campaign funds from the distillers and brewers who found the Dissenting vote generally against them had openly gone to the Conservatives, but they had not created the decisive tilt away from the Liberals.

On the same day, as election tallies were confirming the extent of the Tory sweep, Lord Salisbury, returned to the fold, had dinner with his stepmother Mary (now Lady Derby) and her husband, noting afterward, "I gathered that they had not quite given up the idea of his having the first place." While Disraeli looked upon the stocky Lancastrian with affection, Derby's ideas were closer to those of Gladstone. Except on Church questions, where Salisbury was both High and committed, Disraeli was ideologically closer to his former antagonist, who still worried that his rapprochement would turn out to be a "nightmare."

At home in Carlton Gardens, Gladstone was gripped by the notion that he could call back the old Parliament in order to have it appropriate away the five-million-pound surplus he had accumulated. Otherwise Disraeli gained access to the funds. To his family Gladstone explained how delaying his resignation while he reconvened his own majority might thwart Disraeli, but he found only one supporter. "Is it not disgusting," the gentle

Mrs. Gladstone complained to her eldest son, Herbert, "after all Papa's labour and patriotism and years of work to think of handing over his nest-egg to that Jew!"

With some country votes still to be counted, Disraeli learned on February 12, "from high authority," he confided to Lady Bradford, "that the crisis is at hand and that G's colleagues will not support him in his . . . idea of meeting Parliament." Gladstone and the old Liberal Parliament were out. On February 17 the Queen dispatched Sir Henry Ponsonby, who had replaced the late General Grey, to deliver the expected invitation to form a Government. In his seventieth year, Disraeli had secured, at last, real power.

At thirty minutes past noon the next day, he presented Victoria with his proposed Cabinet of six from the Lords and six from the Commons. Some had been with him before—Derby, Malmesbury, Northcote, Hardy, Hunt, Manners, Richmond, and Cairns. His candidate for the Home Office was Richard Assheton Cross of South Lancashire, "an able man, much respected," the Queen agreed. For Financial Secretary to the Treasury, a sub-Cabinet post, Disraeli recommended another M.P. who had made good from modest beginnings, W. H. Smith of railway bookstalls fame, "a rich and most respectable clever man," she noted, "who always maintained that the working classes were *not* republican." The real coup was the Secretary for India, the testy Lord Salisbury, "who had readily consented to join the Government," Victoria noted happily, thoroughly pleased with the return of Disraeli and the broad spectrum of Conservative politics he had harmonized from the ruins of Peel's party. "He repeatedly said," she wrote in her memorandum of the meeting, "*whatever I wished SHOULD be done*, whatever the difficulties might be."

On the 20th, Disraeli had a further audience with the Queen, reporting progress on unsettled posts, including that of Sir Michael Beach, "a rising man," as Secretary for Ireland. Inevitably, as one of the appointments to the Queen's Household, Disraeli recommended Lord Bradford as Master of the Horse, "and Selina will ride in Royal carriages," the new Prime Minister wrote exuberantly to her sister Anne, "and head the line even in the entrée and gallop over all Her Majesty's lieges."

"After all," he would confess two years later to Lady Bradford, "it is affectation to talk of the bore and bother of patronage and all that. The sense of power is delightful. It is amusing to receive the letters I do, especially since Deaneries were in the market. I had no idea that I was an object of so much esteem, confidence, public and private, and respectful affection—and as nobody in the world, were I to die tomorrow, would give up even a dinner-party, one is sensible of the fun of life."

Following some further business with "the Faery," as he called the Queen privately after Edmund Spenser's Elizabethan _Faerie Queene_, shaking off one Household appointment, Disraeli kissed hands, romantically declaring, so Victoria recorded, "I plight my troth to the kindest of _Mistresses_." From Dolly Nevill came an expression of happiness "at your great success. The only drawback to you must be that Lady Beaconsfield is not here to see it." Despite his ebullient lines to Selina he was more honest to Dolly. "Power has come to me too late. There were days when on waking I felt I could move dynasties and governments but that has passed away."

The last official to see Gladstone at Downing Street, Sir William Boxall of the National Gallery, found him preparing to entrain for Windsor at 5:10 to formally resign his Ministry. His face, Boxall remembered, looked "perfectly demoniacal." The incoming Prime Minister had arrived at Windsor at 2:45. At 6:00, Gladstone appeared to return his seals of office, "very grave, and little disposed to talk." He would take the opportunity to rest, he confided, and was not, in the Queen's words, "inclined to take part in the ordinary discussions in Parliament." He maintained stoutly that the "greatest intelligence" was still to be found in the Liberal ranks, however infected by "self-seekers." For the moment, he conceded "greater cohesion" among the Conservatives.

If on moving back into 10 Downing Street Disraeli took with him a copy of his _Coningsby_, he rediscovered it as a manual of modern politics. In part the novel concerned the fall of a ruling party and resignation of the Government. Since 1844, Disraeli had survived a generation of Tadpoles and Tapers, and found their philosophy of pragmatic politics as good as a primer. Tadpole had advised, "The time has gone by for Tory Governments; what the country requires is a sound Conservative

Government—Tory men and Whig measures." That had worked in 1867, but in 1868 Gladstone had discovered the divisive political potential of Ireland. Disraeli understood that if he were to have a meaningful tenure at the top of the greasy pole, he had to reopen the pages of *Coningsby* and hearken to Tadpole.

THE
ELYSIAN
FIELDS
1874–1881

XXV

"I LIVE FOR POWER AND THE AFFECTIONS."

1874–1875

FAME CAME TO THE PRIME MINISTER IN 1874 IN A VARIETY OF WAYS. "Captain [Sir Fairfax] Moresby, commanding H.M.S. *Basilisk*," he reported to Lady Bradford, "writes me dated 'The Java Seas,' and says that in surveying the coasts of New Guinea he has discovered a mountain nearly as high as Mont Blanc, and that he has named it Mount Disraeli!" (There would be a Disraeli in Quebec, and a Hughenden in Queensland, and in Putney a Disraeli Road.) And Arthur Sullivan, the rising composer, had written music to lyrics which the Prime Minister had penned long before, beginning, "My heart is like a silent lute"—Captain Armine's song from *Henrietta Temple*.

Symbolically, the first major event of Disraeli's premiership was his being awakened at 6:00 A.M. on February 27 with the news that General Sir Garnet Wolseley's forces had captured the Ashanti capital of Coomassie (now Kumasi in Ghana). Much of Disraeli's Ministry would be consumed by foreign affairs, welcome and unwelcome. He had claimed for Britain a continuing imperial

future and, where her interests were directly or even indirectly involved, a role in Europe. Disraeli would have a surfeit of both.

The new regime had its official entertaining to initiate, and
without Mary Anne to oversee such things, Disraeli had Gunter's
of Piccadilly arrange for his own banquet. To assist the leading caterer in London, he told Lady Bradford, "Baroness Rothschild
sent me six large baskets of English strawberries, 200 heads of gigantic Parisian asperges, and the largest and finest Strasburg foie
gras that ever was seen. All agreed that the change of nationality
[to Germany] had not deprived Alsace of its skill."

Although Disraeli could stomach little of the rich fare of a
season of banquets for and by members of the new Government,
he acted up to his role. One of his new majority in the House was
Lord Randolph Churchill, son of the Duke of Marlborough, a
member of the 1868 Cabinet who now declined Disraeli's offer of
the Viceroyalty of Ireland. Newly married to a lovely American
heiress, Jennie Jerome of New York, Lord Randolph was establishing himself on the social circuit without demonstrating any political ambition. At one gathering, after Disraeli had devoted
himself to Jennie, the Prince of Wales asked her, "And tell me,
my dear, what office did you get for Randolph?" Though her husband sought none, Jennie invited the Prime Minister to dinner,
and toward the end of the evening his host offered him more
wine. "My dear Randolph," said Disraeli, "I have sipped your excellent champagne; I have drunk your good claret; I have tasted
your delicious port; I will have no more." After the guests had departed, Randolph mentioned the encomium to his wife. Jennie
was amused at the courtesy. She had observed that Disraeli drank
only a little weak brandy and water.

Often still, he was seen at receptions attended also by Gladstone, although the two seldom exchanged a word. At one event,
when Disraeli's carriage failed to arrive, Gladstone was first to offer him a way to Whitehall Gardens, but a cab turned up to the
relief of both men. At dinners each radiated a different kind of
appeal, Jennie recalled: "When I left the dining room after sitting
next to Gladstone, I thought he was the cleverest man in England. But when I sat next to Disraeli, I left feeling that *I* was the
cleverest woman!"

"Good-bye!" *Punch*, January 30, 1875.
D—SR—LI. "*Sorry to lose you!—I* BEGAN *with books; you're ending with them. Perhaps you're the wiser of the two.*"
Gladstone had formally resigned as Liberal leader, ostensibly to write.

While Disraeli plunged back into politics and society at the highest level, Gladstone announced that he would leave the leadership of his party, presumably forever. Yet curiously, as he withdrew from politics (without giving up his Parliamentary seat), he began reading Disraeli's *Vivian Grey*, dipping into it daily and noting, finally, on March 9 in his diary, "Finished *Vivian Grey*. The first quarter extremely clever, the rest trash." (The author himself called it "puerile." He was hardly more than a boy when he wrote it.) Why Gladstone spent his time while he was involved in extricating himself from Liberal affairs in reading his rival's prentice book is a mystery. Perhaps the defeated Prime Minister had wondered if the work explained anything about what drove Disraeli.

Operating from the Lords once Gladstone made good his resignation, the Marquess of Hartington, heir to the Duke of Devonshire, would be the Liberal leader. Although addicted to women, horses, and cards, "Harty-Tarty" was, in the tradition of the privileged families which had governed England for generations, clever and capable. Even his morning devotions in the boudoir of the beautiful Louise, Duchess of Manchester, failed to keep him from afternoons and evenings in Parliament—when he was not at the race course or the card table. "I said to Hartington," Count Apponyi, the Austrian ambassador, told Disraeli (who in turn reported it to Lady Bradford), "what with whist, the turf, & what I delicately called 'morning visits,' I wonder how you can find time for politics."

"I wonder too," Hartington had conceded.

At a reception, Gladstone observed to the Princess of Wales, so he noted in his diary, "D[israeli] complained of my absence: said they c[oul]d not get on without me." It was easy to see why.

When Easter came, early in April, Disraeli spent ten days at Lady Chesterfield's estate, Bretby, to which ministerial red boxes kept arriving with the government's business, including messages from "Her," as he identified the Queen. As usual, Disraeli was accompanied by Dolly Nevill—her husband Reggie at Dangstein hardly mattered—yet it may have been then that he broached to Anne the possibility of marriage, which he followed up discreetly in a letter of May 25, 1875, reminding her yet again that they were both lonely after losses of their spouses, and united by their love of another person. To be offered matrimony in exchange for access to her sister was hardly Lady Chesterfield's idea of mellow romance. Although Disraeli's elder, she hardly needed a near-invalid to care for, even a prime ministerial one. Their friendship survived the offer, which made its way to Lady Bradford, and into family gossip.

Only on his return did he begin again to experience the

symptoms of mortality that would rein in his effectiveness. Gout invaded his left hand, which was soon swathed in flannels. The ailment would affect, at various inopportune times, all his limbs. Asthma would add to his discomforts, waking and sleeping. Still, he determined to savor Downing Street. "Life, at least so much of it as may remain to me," he confided to Lady Bradford, "is far too valuable to waste its fragrance on the desert air. I live for Power and the affections." He insisted early in the next year (February 2, 1875) that "the political world was never more amusing." But he knew that neither he nor the country were up to grand new designs after the divisiveness of the Gladstone years.

Gladstone's most constructive legislation was still in the process of becoming operative, in particular the Education Act of 1870. While some of Disraeli's colleagues wanted a broad program of progressive Conservatism, he preferred a quiet assimilation of reforms already in place, with modifications to improve their efficacy. The first Queen's Speech to be drafted, Richard Cross, the new Home Secretary, later recalled, required queries to the Cabinet to see whether anyone had any ideas to contribute. "I had quite expected," he recalled about Disraeli's request for suggestions, "that his mind was full of legislative schemes."

When the Cabinet offered its proposals, some of them following up Disraeli's own philosophy as laid out in the Manchester and Crystal Palace addresses of 1872, he backed them, even when they had hard going in the Commons because special interest groups found the bills either too modest or too sweeping. Further, there was the Queen's agenda. High on her legislative list was a ban on allegedly Romanist practices in the Established Church. She also pressed Disraeli to appoint less ritualistic clergy. Victoria, the Prime Minister observed, not entirely in jest, required a Cabinet department all to herself.

Measures framed in the first months of the new Ministry were debated and passed in some form in the 1875 session, with only a few incurring unexpected opposition held over into 1876. "Disraeli's mind," Cross complained, "was either above or below (whichever way you like to put it) mere questions of detail. When the House was in Committee he was, comparatively speaking, nowhere." The Earl of Carnarvon, the returning Colonial

Secretary whom Disraeli genuinely disliked despite his being Lady Chesterfield's son-in-law, seldom saw his chief except at Cabinet meetings, largely dealing with Monty Corry, who, he carped, was the real Prime Minister. But Disraeli expected his staff, from minister to menial, to do the staff work, while he occupied himself with tactics and with his personal department of the Queen.

However Disraeli's Parliamentary accomplishments came about, they did come. The Artisans' Dwelling Act made cheap government loans available to municipalities for construction of working-class housing. Other acts gave labor unions more legal standing, including their right to picket peaceably, their freedom from suit because of a member's unauthorized behavior, and their equal footing with employers in negotiating contracts. The Public Health Act modernized the sanitary codes nationwide. Although Sir Charles Adderley at the Board of Trade bungled oversight of the bill, the Merchant Shipping Act, attacked by Liberal M.P. Samuel Plimsoll for not going far enough, established load lines and other safety regulations for commercial vessels. The Peace Preservation Act pushed through by Gladstone to police Ireland was liberalized to eliminate the summary suppression of newspapers and night curfews in "proclaimed" districts. The Agricultural Holdings Act gave tenant farmers in England rights already granted in Ireland to claim compensation from landlords for improvements "unexhausted" at the end of a contract.

Legislation to improve the quality of life continued to be introduced in the 1876 session and beyond, including the Rivers Pollution Act prohibiting the fouling of rivers and streams with solid matter or harmful liquids and making manufacturers and other polluters legally responsible. Another act consolidated factory legislation, from limiting hours of labor and otherwise protecting women and children to mandating sanitary facilities for all workers on the job. One Food and Drugs Act created quality standards, while another established medical licensing requirements to reduce the prevalence of quackery. The Friendly Societies Act protected savings of small investors, and other social legislation forbade the enclosure of common land except for the public good, such as the creation of free public playgrounds. To get many of the bills through a Tory Parliament, Disraeli had to accept permissive rather than compulsory law, explaining that in a "free country" one had to "trust to persuasion and example," which in practice worked better in municipalities where voters used their power of the ballot.

Under Disraeli's implicit policy of making existing legislation work better before attempting further innovation, Gladstone's Education Act came up for review. Viscount Sandon, who was running the Board of Education, told the Commons that the need was not for more laws but for raising the level of attendance. Although Conservatives shied away from compulsion, there was no way of getting children to school other than by forbidding any employment of children under ten, mandating a standard of achievement or school attendance for any employment after that, acting against parents who neglected the education of their children, and empowering boards of guardians to pay fees for poor children. Liberals who had done nothing about compulsion when in power complained that Disraeli's Ministry was doing too little, while Conservatives wanted no incentives that cost money. But the Education Act of 1870 was made more effective except where there was foot-dragging on the local level.

Campaigning early in 1874, Disraeli had confessed, "I have, for forty years, been labouring to replace the Tory party in their natural and historical position in this country. I am in the sunset of life, but I do not despair of seeing my purpose effected." In office he did not promise a utopian program of comprehensive reform. He knew that politics was the art of the possible, and carried the message of *Coningsby* and *Sybil* as far as the climate of the 1870s permitted. Disraeli's "legislative schemes" had been gestating since the Young England novels and were in the process of being realized.

The Public Worship Regulation Act of 1874 was Disraeli's most aggravating and least useful bill. It was an act, he admitted in the House on August 5, 1874, "to put down Ritualism," to prevent a "small but pernicious sect" from promoting what the Queen considered Popery. High Church politicians like the Marquis of Salisbury were outraged. Disraeli privately agreed, writing to Lady Bradford that the bill was "Church nonsense." Salisbury, on the other hand, told his wife that when it came to Anglicanism, Disraeli was "sublimely ignorant." To the Prime Minister, the crucial point was that Victoria, railing against what she considered to be the Italianizing of the Protestant communion, wanted the legislation. It was an urgency communicated by a flurry of letters and telegrams, sent by "the Faery" from Osborne, Windsor, and Balmoral, which suggested that her Established Church was endangered by the emphasis upon vestments, trappings, and nuances of liturgy rather than upon how the faithful should live. What concerned Disraeli more than ceremony was the movement among Dissenting and Presbyterian preachers to impose strict Sabbatarianism upon everyone's lives. For John Manners to be Minister in Residence to the Queen at Balmoral beginning on May 25, 1874, Disraeli quipped to Lady Chesterfield, Manners would have to travel on a Sunday, "which is perilous in Scotland; and probably he may be tied to the stake by a Calvinist congregation before he reaches the Palace."

Two days earlier Disraeli had written to Lady Bradford, ostensibly about a lengthy telegram he had just received from Balmoral, "giving me a great deal of trouble; but in so feminine a manner that it was delightful. I must say that I feel fortunate in having a female Sovereign. I owe everything to woman; and if in the sunset of life I have still a young heart, it is due to that influence." He was more under the influence, however, of Lady Bradford's reception at her town house on Belgrave Square the evening before. The memory of her graceful figure "peering over the balustrade" and watching the departing guests descending the staircase "with—at least on my part—unwilling steps," still haunted him. "If my letters during the last few months to my three fair correspondents"—he included the Queen and Selina's sister, Anne—"were collected," he confessed, "they would make as much as [all] three volumes of *Lothair*." He never owned up to his many letters to Dorothy Nevill.

When he wrote to Victoria, the extravagant phrases were incidental to matters of business. When he wrote to Lady Chesterfield, it was either because he was receiving few responses from her sister or was diplomatically furnishing a numerical equity. He valued, he told Lady Bradford, whose interest in political and intellectual matters was minimal, her "sweet serenity." Having sat next to Victoria's eldest daughter, the Crown Princess of Germany, at dinner at Hatfield, seat of the Cecils, he told Selina on July 12 that Vicky made "one of her grandest displays—aesthetical, literary, philosophical; a very great contrast to your conversation, my Lady. And which do you think pleased me most?"

Disraeli was unembarrassed by the confession because infatuation had blinded him to the reality that he was a gouty, often ill widower five months short of seventy, writing tepid love letters to a married woman of modest intellectual gifts who responded with little more than sympathy and patience. Her willingness to indulge Disraeli and to permit him his bliss of occasional nearness was enough to effuse his life with an autumnal glow. A very different kind of passion animated his letters to Lady Henrietta Sykes in the middle 1830s; now devotion was enough, if gently reciprocated.

In the years just preceding World War I, and then for some months into it, another Prime Minister—one married although his very much younger correspondent was not—wrote in even greater volume and with impulsive indiscretion on the edge of unrequited rapture. But H. H. Asquith had a clever wife, Margot, who looked the other way. Lady Venetia Stanley knew that a moneyed marriage was more useful than another trunkful of love letters. She accepted Edwin Montagu, of Asquith's cabinet, even going through a less than heartfelt conversion to Judaism before the wedding. The letters stopped. Asquith was dismayed, but once spared from letter writing, he was no better a premier than he had been when he penned passionate lines to Venetia during his cabinet meetings.

Lady Chesterfield read Disraeli's books and recalled passages in her letters. "Selina," he told Anne, somewhat unfairly, "has read very few and does not remember a line she has read." Yet in order to have something to say beyond domestic trivia and diplomatic queries about him, Lady Bradford perused several of Disraeli's early novels. He was pleased because they were "reproductions of my own life and feelings," and curious how his romantic earlier self in them "affect[ed] the person who most interests myself." Although she was no Héloïse to his Abelard, he enjoined

her, "Pray never think of altering your style of writing. It has inexpressible charms to me; being natural and graceful and often
picturesque." Her letters, but for a few innocuous notes, do not
survive. Retrieved by her from Disraeli's trustees, she apparently
destroyed them. But she preserved his.

Only Disraeli himself could have been persuaded by the constructive dimension he claimed for his epistolary passion. "When
you have the government of a country on your shoulders, to love
a person and to be in love with a person," he explained to Lady
Bradford (November 3, 1874), "makes all the difference. In the
first case, everything that distracts your mind from your great purpose weakens and wearies you. In the second instance"—his own
relationship to Selina—"the difficulty of seeing your beloved, or
communicating with her, only animates and excites you. I have
devised schemes of seeing or writing to you in the midst of stately
councils, and the thought and memory of you, instead of being an
obstacle has been an inspiration." It was a paean to the powers of
unreturned adoration.

Somehow England survived Disraeli's separation from reality.
Lady Bradford took up less of his attention than he preferred to
imagine. More serious were his constant companions, gout, bronchitis, and asthma. Even the Queen's doctors could suggest little
more than sea air as a relief from London soot and fog. From his
convalescence in Bournemouth he wrote to Lady Bradford on
Christmas Eve, 1874, "with mustard on my throat," that if he did
not see her before returning to Downing Street, "all the Physicians in the world will do me no good." As possessive a lover as
if he were a real one, three days earlier he had begun a letter to
Selina—punning on *Selene,* Goddess of the Moon—"It is not a
slice of the moon I want; I want all." Yet he knew she recoiled
from such declarations, and he had to explain, more reasonably,
in another letter, "I require sympathy; but male sympathy does
not suit me and I am fastidious as to the other sex. You suit me
exactly for you have quickness of perception and tact." On occasion he had to force himself to realize that he was beyond even
a paper passion.

Cabinet members came and went through December as
Disraeli remained at windy, chilly, even snowy, Bournemouth.

With Derby he mulled over New Year's honors, and inevitably another went to Lady Bradford's husband—the Lord Lieutenancy of Shropshire. It almost made the wintry resort tolerable to be able to use political position to reward one's friends, and to have friends who could make the locale more habitable. A Rothschild son had occupied Disraeli's rooms previously, and had the hampers of food and drink shipped from Gunnersbury continued for the Prime Minister; and bread, butter, and turkeys came from Lady Chesterfield at Bretby, in addition to twenty pheasants from the Prince of Wales at Sandringham. His Cabinet dined well because of the hotel's reputation for bad food.

At Lady Derby's suggestion, Disraeli offered New Year's recognition to two writers, neither of whom liked him. Derby thought that it would be "a good political investment." A baronetcy for the Poet Laureate, Alfred Tennyson—it was a step above mere knighthood—would also make the Queen happy. She actually read his poems, and he had dedicated his *Idylls of the King* to Prince Albert's memory. Although Tennyson preferred his honors to come from Gladstone, he would have accepted a higher hereditary title even from Disraeli, a barony rather than a baronetcy. When it was not forthcoming, Tennyson decided to wait it out. Disraeli was puzzled by the constant reaching after rewards he thought beyond reason. A colonel of little importance had, not long before, turned down a title, and the Prime Minister had observed to Derby, "I am sorry that Society persists in cheapening a simple knighthood. It satisfied Sir Isaac Newton & Sir Walter Raleigh."

Thomas Carlyle, who disliked both party leaders, had once remarked, "Dizzy is a charlatan and knows it. Gladstone is a charlatan and does not know it." As for "the Philosopher of Chelsea," Disraeli reported to Derby from Bournemouth, he should not receive honors merely equivalent to that of a lawyer or a statesman, or be "disturbed by common cares." The offer, Carlyle confessed to his brother in Dumfries, was "a pan of hot coals for my guilty head!" He was "gratified a little within my own dark heart at this mark of the good will of high people." But such compliments, he responded to Disraeli, were out of keeping "with the tenor of my poor life." No longer in need of money after years of frugality, yet "never degrading poverty," at eighty his funds, he conceded, were now "amply abundant, even superabundant." Yet the cranky old prophet did not remain grateful very long. His pleasure at being offered the Grand Cross of the Bath and a pension by a man he had publicly excoriated for decades wore off in due course. At first it was "magnanimous of Dizzy." Two years later Disraeli was "a cursed old Jew, not worth his weight in cold bacon."*

Disraeli's shattered health, and the Queen's desire to keep him alive and well enough to remain her Prime Minister, gave him special clout at Court. To Lady Bradford he wrote about his reception at Osborne in August 1874, "I really thought she was going to embrace me. She was wreathed with smiles, and, as she talked, glided about the room like a bird. She told me it was all owing to my courage and tact, and then she said, 'To think of your having the gout all the time. How you must have suffered!' " Taken ill while at Balmoral the next month, he wrote Lady Bradford (September 12, 1874), "the Queen paid me a visit in my bedchamber." In every possible way the Queen made it clear that she was grateful to have him at her side again, and that she would not easily let him go.

Victoria indeed required a Cabinet portfolio. Disraeli's letters and memoranda recorded nearly daily telegrams and letters from her, and often twice and thrice daily. She required frequent audiences, wherever she happened to be, and ministers cringed from attendance at distant, often dreary, Balmoral. She also required unfailing patience. "I have just come up from Windsor," Disraeli would write to Derby on one occasion (April 9, 1875). ". . . I had a long audience on nothing but disagreeable subjects—& in addition she had a headache." But if the monarchy as an institution were to survive, Disraeli felt that he had to draw her more into the mainstream of public life; and he worked at it.

To the Queen his "courage" meant that he would undertake, even if reluctantly, to see her pet measures through Parliament,

*Curiously, Derby, who was more traditionally religious than his chief, would propose, eight months later, a baronetcy for Charles Darwin, as "Right or wrong, his reputation is European." Apparently wary of repercussions from church factions, Disraeli shied away.

including the divisive and ultimately unenforceable Public Worship Regulation Act. He recognized that although she was delighted not to have Gladstone about—he would have denied her the Ritualism bill and been difficult in every other way—certain Queenly enthusiasms had to be indulged, whatever the cost, to secure her cooperation when he needed it. Trade-offs meant mediating among legislative factions, and to get Salisbury and Hardy and other High Church champions to concede her Ritualism bill, he watered it down, offering her more rhetoric than reality.

Disraeli found the contagion of Ritualism even within walking distance of Hughenden Manor. He had assisted financially in the rehabilitation of the local church, after which the Rev. Henry Blagden, the vicar, held a High Church reopening. There, Disraeli told Lady Bradford, nearly a hundred clergymen turned up in surplices and "parti-coloured scarves. . . . Everything was intoned." A luncheon followed, at which he dampened the sacerdotal ardor by expressing the hope that "the beauty of holiness" could somehow be combined with the Protestant faith. In the Commons itself he declared that it was quite proper for Roman Catholics to practice every element of their religion, but not for Anglicans to ape Romanism—"Mass in masquerade." Victoria loved the line, but the outcome embittered the faithful of nearly every persuasion just enough to cost Disraeli votes he needed in crucial tests ahead.

"You ought not to stand now," Victoria once cautioned him at Osborne as he swayed on his gouty legs. "You shall have a chair!" And in private audiences thereafter he sat. "Only think of that!" he confided to Selina. "I remember that Lord Derby, after one of his illnesses, . . . mentioned it to me as proof of the Queen's favour, that Her Majesty had remarked to him how sorry she was that she could not ask him to be seated, the etiquette was so severe."

Shortly before that, gout forced him to appear in the Commons "in a black velvet shoe of Venetian fashion," borrowed from a costume for a masked ball. Bronchitis and asthma dogged him at day's end, and he had trouble breathing at night. Yet an old addiction manifested itself at times, and he confessed to Lady Bradford early in January 1875 that he had suicidally smoked "a harmless segar."

His greatest grief came from his campaign to draw the Queen out into playing her symbolic role, and she took advantage of her promises to do so to get her way wherever possible. When her yacht *Alberta*, with Victoria aboard, collided in the Solent with the schooner *Mistletoe*, the nominal commander was the Queen's nephew, Prince Ernest Leopold Victor of Leiningen, but the deck officer had been a Captain Welch, who was clearly derelict. Two on the schooner drowned, but inquests and inquiries, intimidated by the Queen's too obvious interest, gingerly failed to reach verdicts. Finally the Admiralty, anticipating questions in Parliament, reprimanded Welch after Disraeli intervened to silence Victoria. Where the Queen was concerned, Derby deplored in his diary, "he is too submissive & given to flattery."

During the autumn of 1875 another collision caused embarrassment. Two battleships rammed each other in the Irish Channel and one of them, the *Vanguard*, sank. It was the same season as the drawn-out struggle over the Merchant Shipping Bill, and Disraeli joked to Salisbury, "Water I trust will not be fatal to the Government. . . . We seem to be in a leaky state."

Disraeli's own "leaky state" at seventy included frailties he could no longer conceal. Long myopic, he had used a single eyeglass on his better eye, as he saw double with his left eye. It was less obvious than a Venetian shoe, and about as effective. He had regretted to John Murray III, grandson of his father's publisher and son of his own, in July 1874, that he had not seen him at a meeting about a memorial to Lord Byron, "but I am so nearsighted that I am obliged to ask even my intimate friends to address me." Finally, Lady Derby, whom he still miscalled on occasion Lady Salisbury, took him to an oculist in Albany Street, a recent German émigré, who wrote out a prescription for corrective lenses. At Hughenden he had "enjoyed the pleasure of watch[ing] the sunbeams on the binding of the books" in his library, a phenomenon enhanced by his defective vision. Late in 1875 he could read them again.

One pleasure he had looked forward to was Gladstone's oft-announced retirement to his own library, to ruminate among his

Homeric studies and biblical exegeses. "Only those who are acquainted with the malignity of Gladstone through a rivalry of twenty-five years," he told Lady Bradford, could appreciate his pride in having surmounted it. There were a few moments of mutual generosity even then, but their relationship was seldom warmer than correct. Only a year largely out of the limelight and remote from his rescuing opportunities, Gladstone longed to be back. "Instead of retiring to Mount Athos," Disraeli scoffed to Lady Chesterfield, "[he] has taken another house in Carlton Terrace; so I suppose he has had enough of spiritual things." An anonymous article in June 1875 attacking his policies, Disraeli guessed to Lady Bradford, was "certainly Gladstone. . . . His style is so involved, so wanting in both melody and harmony, that it always gives me a headache."

Living alone but for his country house visits—often to Bretby and Lady Chesterfield—he found, as always, that the Rothschilds remained his family. Mayer had died early in 1875, leaving Mentmore to an ailing wife, and inevitably to his only child, Hannah, but Disraeli had never been close to him. His friends were Anthony and Lionel, their spouses, and now their grown children. He worried about Lionel, who was clearly failing. Inviting himself regularly to Rothschild family dinners, he explained to Lady Chesterfield, "I cannot endure my solitary dinners and evenings."

After one dinner with Lionel de Rothschild, in August 1874, Disraeli commented that he had been obliged to sacrifice pleasure to business while Parliament lasted. When the Baron later mentioned that to Charlotte, she wondered whether the sacrifice included the "hours and hours at the feet of Lady B," who had captured his "septuagenarian heart." It was neither an affair of state nor an affair. He saw Selina less than his friends imagined, but Disraeli's devotion was the talk of London. One evening in May 1874, dining *en famille* in the Baron's Piccadilly house, Disraeli learned from a telegram to Lionel of the fall of the latest revolving-door French Cabinet. Although he was always grateful for news obtained through the firm, he complained via Derby to his ambassador in Paris about the embassy's sloth. He understood

that the House of Rothschild had "peculiar opportunities for ob-
taining information," but, he reminded his diplomats, "Divisions
do not take place in the French Chambre at night, and on Saturdays."

Disraeli's proudest foreign affairs coup occurred through the
good offices of the Rothschilds, and in the same season as one of
his chanciest gambles. The Prince of Wales wanted to junket to
India, a possible diplomatic catastrophe. "Scrapes" with women
seemed inevitable, and his entourage of playboy friends made the
trip seem additionally risky. Disraeli talked the Queen into it on
grounds that if Bertie were out of England *under supervision* for six
months, it would be worth the price, and if he learned something
about the Empire, that would be a bonus. Somehow Disraeli extracted £112,500 from the Admiralty and the Treasury, and another £100,000 from the Government of India. The party
embarked on the *Serapis*, a troopship converted luxuriously for
the royal progress, Bertie stoutly resplendent in his field marshal's
uniform—an unearned rank to which his mother had raised him
on his last birthday.

The Prince understood the efforts taken in his behalf and
wrote to Disraeli, "I am fully alive to the importance of my trip
to India and hope that neither you [n]or anyone else in my land
will have cause to regret that the honour of my country has been
placed in my hands whilst in India. Am I saying too much in stating this?"

The *Serapis* took the shortest route, through the new Suez
Canal. On November 8, 1875, the Prince's thirty-fourth birthday,
the ship entered Bombay harbor. The Queen dispatched cables to
him almost daily urging him to be careful, and with newspaper-
men limiting his opportunities for wenching, Bertie busied himself dispatching enormous quantities of game, from wild pigs to
elephants, that were beaten into his range. For Disraeli's government the success of the trip would emerge in unexpected ways.
The Prince had wide press coverage, which limited his liberties to
be himself, yet called attention to the subcontinent in ways that
would be useful to the Crown. And he had made very public passages through the Canal, seen now as a link to India.

Disraeli had sailed past the Isthmus of Suez while traveling from the Holy Land to Egypt in 1831, long before Ferdinand de Lesseps had conceived his feat of engineering. The Turkish territories the Canal bisected in 1869 had remained significant to him when other Englishmen, remembering the fiasco of intervention in the Crimea, preferred to let the feudal and mismanaged empire fall apart. Yet Turkey not only lay astride land and sea routes to India; it had long been the "Sick Man of Europe" and a major if festering presence in the Balkans between a paranoid Austria-Hungary and an expansionist Russia. From the week of Disraeli's return to Downing Street, exchanges of cables with the embassy in Constantinople had apprised him of Turkey's slackening grip upon its disintegrating European domains. The "Eastern Question" would simmer into 1875.

On taking office, Disraeli had begun discreet inquiries about purchasing for England some of the French-owned shares in the Canal. Four-fifths of the traffic through it was British, shrinking weeks off the Cape route to East Africa and India. Secretly sending Natty de Rothschild, Lionel's eldest son, to Paris to negotiate, Disraeli had tried to buy de Lesseps out. The French government preferred to keep the Canal in its control despite a financial squeeze that had caused de Lesseps to try to raise passage fees—a move blocked by Khedive Ismail Pasha's threat of military action. The fee structure was regulated by the company's concession agreement. But the profligate Khedive, nominally under Turkish suzerainty, needed money himself to pay an installment due on the large Egyptian debt and began negotiations with competing French syndicates to raise as much as £4,000,000. (Egypt owned 176,602 ordinary shares of the 400,000 in the Suez Canal Company.)

Disraeli found out about Ismail Pasha's straits on November 15, two days after the offer to sell had been made. One source, direct to Disraeli, was Baron de Rothschild. Banker Henry Oppenheim also knew, telling Frederick Greenwood of the *Pall Mall Gazette*, who then contacted the Foreign Office. Derby telegraphed his Consul General in Cairo, who confirmed the Khedive's overtures and added that Ismail Pasha preferred to sell to

Britain in order to prevent a near-monopoly of Canal ownership by the French.

Urgently summoning his Cabinet, Disraeli found his Ministers—with Parliament in recess—timid about acting on their own. Northcote at the Exchequer was reluctant to commit a very large sum without Bank of England authorization, and Derby, despite his having run down the lead all the way to Cairo, typically preferred to keep clear of foreign entanglements.

The Queen's enthusiastic interest also put the Foreign Secretary off. Disraeli had only recently come through one serious difference of opinion about her with Derby. Victoria was impetuous and interfering, and Derby was not going to let her run his office. The issue, earlier in 1875, had been Spain, where Carlist, Bourbon, and Republican factions had created chaos for decades. A shaky Republican regime was being challenged by both royalist parties, and the Bourbons had proclaimed young Alfonso, son of ex-queen Isabella, as King. Impatiently, Victoria wanted him recognized, but her Minister to Madrid, Austen Henry Layard, excavator of Nineveh, nephew of Disraeli's old patrons the Austens, and son-in-law of Lady Charlotte Bertie, was loyal to the tottering Republic.

Disraeli was pushed both ways. For the Queen, Sir Henry Ponsonby demanded that the able Layard be fired from the diplomatic service rather than merely replaced. Layard wanted to keep "doing us harm"—so Victoria claimed she had learned from her personal intelligence network—because of his "admiration for the charms of the Duchess de la Torre." He was "not to be trusted" and once, she charged, "went by the nickname *Lie-hard.*"

Derby was furious and threatened to quit. Shrewdly, Disraeli cautioned the Queen that Layard, if removed, would have to "retire with honour and credit to himself," implying a distinguished new position and possibly a knighthood. It would be a heavy price for pique.

On March 21, with the Queen showing signs of yielding, Disraeli addressed her delicately to dramatize the importance to him personally of retaining a loyal Derby. The Earl had sat through two hours of the Prime Minister's failed persuasion in "icy" silence. The "necessary gulf between a Sovereign and her Ministers," Disraeli urged her, need not be a bar to "confidence and sympathy," without which public affairs could not be carried on. He needed to demonstrate both, he implied, and so did the Queen, and by way of example he described his parting with Derby.

Rather than leave Downing Street in bitterness, Derby had offered, taking Disraeli's arm still in silence, to walk with him to Whitehall Gardens. At the door, Disraeli invited him in for lunch. It was two o'clock. Speaking for the first time, Derby replied that he "never lunched." It got in the way of work. Then he offered the Prime Minister his hand, "which is not his habit"—Derby was a very withdrawn individual—and said, "Good-bye, old friend."

As Disraeli described to Victoria the tense scene between friends finding their paths beginning to separate, he prayed that Derby's scheduled audience with the Queen "might happily bear fruit." He did not want to lose him. To make certain, he minuted his Foreign Minister after his meeting, "As I do not think you ought to bear all the brunt of the fray, I have written to the great lady, I think, conclusively on the matter." Derby remained; Layard remained; Alfonso hung onto his throne, and his son Alfonso XIII married a granddaughter of Victoria in 1906. Layard would leave Madrid only when he was promoted in 1877 to Ambassador to Constantinople, where he became a central figure in the ongoing "Eastern Question" and persona grata once more at Buckingham Palace.

Eight months later the Queen was alerted by Disraeli to the other end of the Mediterranean, with the Suez offer left deliberately vague. Although France controlled more than fifty percent of the shares, if the purchase succeeded, Britain would secure a substantial role in the Canal's management. While he permitted the Cabinet to debate the matter, saying little in five meetings while he tried to reach a consensus, Disraeli had already received assurances from Lionel de Rothschild that his firm would advance the money.

As usual the decision was Lionel's. Sir Anthony, who largely kept aloof from day-to-day transactions, was dying. In hopes that sea air might be salubrious, a ship had been chartered for him in Southhampton Water. As early as July 18, when Disraeli had called on his old friend, he was too ill to see anyone. "I am sorry—very—for Sir Anthony," he had told Lady Bradford; "a thoro[ugh]ly good fellow, the most genial being I ever knew, the most kind-hearted and the most generous." He died aboard ship on January 4, 1876, and Disraeli wrote Louise: "One of the best of men has left us."

With time running out, the Khedive on November 23, 1875, agreed to accept the proffered four million, and the next day, with Disraeli's package arranged, his Cabinet agreed. Monty Corry was sped to the Rothschild offices at New Court, St. Swithin's Lane, and on November 26 the shares were deposited with the Consulate in Cairo.

"I am today in a state of prostration—coma," he told Lady Bradford. "It is just settled: you have it, Madam," Disraeli wrote to the Queen. "The French Government has been outgeneraled. . . . Four millions sterling! and almost immediately. There was only one firm that could do it—Rothschilds. They behaved admirably." She had "the entire interest of the Khedive," he explained. Most people in England, excited by the daring coup, assumed that the entire interest in the Canal had been purchased. Misunderstanding too, Gladstone noted his concern in his diary about a "purchase outright of the Suez Canal Shares. . . . I fear grave consequences: & I am not in the least degree moved by the storm of approval wh[ich] seems to be rising."

When it became clear that rather than securing a British monopoly, Disraeli had prevented a French one, Gladstone and Lowe turned instead to objecting to Rothschilds' 2½ percent commission on the funds advanced, as if the firm were a nonprofit concern and Britain a charity case. Yet Rothschilds had no security for the loan except the shares, which could have been a doubtful asset, and Lionel had to do Disraeli the favor of breaking family tradition by concealing the negotiations from Paris until the arrangements were complete. Each branch of the firm was intensely loyal to the nation in which it operated, and Disraeli later explained to the Prince of Wales that Rothschilds "could not appeal to their strongest ally, their own family in Paris, for Baron

"Mosé in Egitto!!!" *Punch*, December 11, 1875. Pleased with himself after arranging the purchase of Suez Canal shares, Disraeli, holding a key reading Suez Canal with a ribbon identifying it as the key to India, contemplates a Sphinx which has an uncanny resemblance to Benjamin Disraeli.

Alphonse is *si francese* that he would have betrayed the whole scheme instantly."*

Suez captured the public imagination, and helped move the

---

*The Rothschilds earned in the five months before the loan was repaid a 2½ percent commission and £53,000 in interest. Because of fluctuations in the money market, particularly in the price of gold, the firm risked paying out funds that could have been repaid in cheaper money. It was part of the merchant banking business to take such risks with secrecy and with speed—and to take the profits from them when they worked.

Palmerstonian *Daily Telegraph*, which had supported Gladstone, over to Disraeli. In the month of Suez, the former Prime Minister, who had seemingly retired from the Liberal leadership, wrote ruefully to Edward Levy-Lawson, the future Lord Burnham, "I fear you and I are diverging rather widely . . . on a great matter recently brought into the public view; but you have probably at least the advantage of having 999 of every thousand on your side." In its columns "the man of disgraceful jibes and sneering sophisms" who had been "the Disraelian windbag of surfeited acrimony and undigested platitude" suddenly acquired "unrivalled polemical gifts of rhetoric, sarcasm, invective, ornament and governed passion."

Writing in her journal on November 24, Victoria noted with satisfaction that the purchase "gives us complete security for India. . . . An immense thing." For Disraeli the occasion evoked Sidonia in the world of *Alroy*, as he offered to go to Windsor to tell Victoria "the whole wondrous tale." Did he recognize that he was quoting the subtitle of his Eastern novel? From the Queen's standpoint, her Prime Minister's vision of Britain coincided with her own. To Theodore Martin, the biographer of her beloved Albert, she wrote, "It is *entirely* the doing of Mr Disraeli, who has *very large ideas*, and *very lofty views* of the position this country should hold. His mind is so much greater, larger, and his apprehension of things great and small so much quicker than that of Mr Gladstone."

Although Victoria regularly gave Disraeli grief on Church preferments, refusing "zealous pious men" in favor of ecclesiastics with "social qualities" and with "intellect to grapple with the dangers of Atheism and Catholicism," she demonstrated in personal ways her special relationship with him. Disraeli thought that he got more than he gave although, as the Layard affair had shown, she bargained hard and not always by the rules. At a dinner given by Disraeli early in February 1876 for Tory powers and their spouses, Derby drew Monty Corry aside to talk about the Queen, as he saw "all his chief's correspondence." Corry, he recorded, "*thinks there is no flaw anywhere in her intellect, which is shrewd & acute: but that she is selfish & despotic beyond measure:*

that if her power were equal to her will, some of our heads would not be on our shoulders."

To Matthew Arnold, whom Disraeli first met at Louise de Rothschild's in 1864, Disraeli had confessed, "Everyone likes flattery, and when it comes to Royalty you should lay it on with a trowel." Yet Disraeli knew that the Queen was too astute to misperceive it. Rather, she relished the roles each played: monarch and courtier in a never-never land that was a unique dimension of their regard for each other. When he received a delicate wooden box with the Queen's name on it, and inside it "three miniature bouquets—two of primroses and one of snowdrops," he told Lady Bradford (February 25, 1875) he wrote to "the Faery" that he had hosted a banquet that evening, and

> amid my stars and ribbons, some snowdrops on my heart proved that I was also decorated by a gracious Sovereign. Then, I said, that I had been awakened in the night and fancied it was all a dream, or that they were magical flowers sent me, perhaps, by another Sovereign—Queen Titania, who had been gathering flowers with her Court in a soft and sea-girt isle, and had sent me some blossoms which, according to the legend, deprived the recipient of his senses. I said I certainly should lose my head were not my sense of duty to my Sovereign stronger, I really believed, than my conceit. Something like this, only a little more polished.

On April 23 he again thanked the Queen gratefully "for your Majesty's delightful present"—further flowers from the Isle of Wight. "He likes the primroses so much better for their being wild: they seem an offering from the fauns and dryads of the woods of Osborne; and camellias, blooming in the natural air, become your Majesty's Faery Isle." No wonder that, on one occasion, when he bent to kiss her hand, he told Lady Bradford (February 26, 1876), "she actually gave me a squeeze." The courtier was an ailing seventy-one and the Sovereign, short and stout and still in her widow's weeds, was fifty-seven.

XXVI

"WHAT'S THE USE OF POWER IF YOU DON'T MAKE PEOPLE DO WHAT THEY DON'T LIKE?"

1875–1876

THE APPARENT GIFT OF THE GATE TO INDIA LED TO THE REVIVAL OF Victoria's ambitions to have an imperial title reflecting her sovereignty over England's expanding empire. Disraeli himself had raised the matter in Parliament years before, just after the Sepoy Mutiny and during the debates over revising the political link between Whitehall and the subcontinent. Suez, the Queen told Disraeli in audience at Windsor, was "a blow to Bismarck." Not only was she annoyed by what Disraeli confided to Derby were the Iron Chancellor's "insolent declarations that England had ceased to be a political power," which the Canal shares coup had exploded, but by Bismarck's arrogant dominance of the German monarchy. The doddering William I, father-in-law of Crown Princess Victoria, was an emperor in style alone, and the Queen received litanies about Bismarck's brazen abuse of power in letters from her unhappy daughter in Berlin.

The eastern Mediterranean trembled under an unstable peace, but Derby as Foreign Minister preferred no English initiatives. Only Disraeli kept him from recommending Gladstonian retrenchments worldwide. Costly colonies seemed to Derby good for national pride alone, and they mired England in expensive little wars that he preferred to avoid, even if it meant that other flags would fly from the deserts and jungles and islets that were earning peerages for their conquerors. If the Prince of Wales and his mother agreed upon anything, it was that Britain should be significant in world affairs, and Disraeli, prodded by the Queen, kept a wary eye on the *Dreikaiserbund,* the informal linkage of the interests of the emperors of Germany, Austria-Hungary, and Russia. It seemed more the business of Britain after Suez than before, and Britain's traditional interest—here Disraeli was the clear inheritor of the Palmerstonian outlook—was to permit no power on the Continent to become dominant.

It had long irritated Victoria that the thrones of the *Dreikaiserbund* were technically "imperial." When Vicky succeeded with Crown Prince Frederick to the throne of Germany, she would be "Empress" and have titular precedence over her mother, a mere "Queen." Apart from her personal pride, her nation's place in the world seemed involved. Suez had called attention to the anomaly, and early in 1876, estimating that her timing was opportune, Victoria announced to Disraeli that she intended to open Parliament in person in February. Since Albert's death she had done so only when she wanted something from the two Houses, and again this was the case. As early as January 1873 she had questioned Sir Henry Ponsonby, her intermediary with Gladstone's government, "I am an Empress & in common conversation am sometimes called Empress of India. Why have I never officially assumed the title?" Although she owned an inscribed copy, she had almost certainly never read *Tancred,* in which in 1847 Disraeli had an Emir suggest that the Queen of England should transfer the seat of her sovereignty from London to Delhi, after which "we will acknowledge the Empress of India as our suzerain." The novelist had probably forgotten the dialogue himself, but with Disraeli at Downing Street, and the Suez coup still fresh, she dampened any elation about her presenting her own Address by asking him to introduce legislation to formally create her "Empress of India."

Cautiously, as his first soundings were negative, Disraeli responded that he could not mention a revised Royal Style in Her Majesty's gracious opening speech—only a paragraph on the Prince of Wales's ongoing and successful voyage to India. Englishmen—especially Gladstonian Liberals—felt that there was no grander title than Queen of England, and they saw no connection between empty social precedence and European politics. Disraeli foresaw a distasteful fight and did not have the stomach for it, but he felt obligated to the Queen to press her case.

India in the month of Suez had offered Disraeli an opportunity to honor a late friend. Edward Bulwer-Lytton, a crony of the tumultuous 1830s, had died at seventy in 1873. His son Robert, a minor poet under the name Owen Meredith, had chosen a diplomatic career and in November 1875 at forty-four was minister at Lisbon. India needed a new Viceroy, and the post—"superb, but awful," Disraeli described it to Derby—was offered to Lord John Manners, then to the 3rd Earl of Powis, who when M.P. from North Shropshire in the 1840s as Edward James Herbert was part of Young England. Distance and climate dissuaded both, and Disraeli turned to the son of his old companion, who was also a relative by marriage of Lady Derby. It was another avenue to recognize old loyalties, and before Lord Lytton left for his assignment, Disraeli asked him to accept as his aide young Harcourt Rose, son of Sir Philip Rose. By Disraeli's arrangement, Captain Rose had been serving on Lord Napier's staff in India. But on arriving in Calcutta, Lytton found young Rose suddenly unavailable. He had been "invalided" to England, the Viceroy reported to the Prince of Wales, "in consequence of an extraordinary accident: the bite of a donkey had reduced him to a condition that would be a very appropriate qualification for employment in any Oriental Court. . . . The story is a strange one and I am quite unable to understand how the donkey could have perpetrated such an assault on the Captain."

Somehow the son of Disraeli's solicitor recovered sufficiently to join the viceregal court at Simla. Edith Lytton, the Vicereine, described the convalescent Rose as "such a muff* but a very good whist player."

Initiating her unannounced campaign to be Empress of India, the Queen rode in state to Parliament on February 8, 1876. Enthusiastic Londoners lined the route, the Prime Minister managing with difficulty to slip in to take his place; in thanking her for graciously being present he observed "what an immense influence Your Majesty's occasional appearance can produce." Yet once the business of the Commons began, Disraeli was faced with carping from Gladstone and Lowe about the Suez shares, and then about the Queen's proposed supplementary title. Debate was lengthy and acrimonious. Lowe even warned that adding the title ignored the possibility of losing India. "The right honourable gentleman is a prophet," said Disraeli, "but he is always a prophet of evil." And the Prime Minister enunciated a reason for the legislation that went to the core of a rank-conscious society: "It is only by the amplification of titles that you can touch and satisfy the imagination of nations; and that is an element which governments must not despise."

A month later, to further promote her aspirations, Victoria emerged in public once more, this time for a progress in her carriage through the East End. On a windy day in early March she went out, accompanied as always by Princess Beatrice, to open a new wing of London Hospital, just below Whitechapel Road. Civil servant Arthur Munby, humorless as usual, noted in his diary, "The Queen was badly drest, and looked red and blowsed & commonplace; and not amiable either." (A few days later he observed Disraeli, on foot in Green Park, "looking worn and gaunt.") Victoria, who had not seen the mournful Mr. Munby, wrote to Vicky in Berlin that the crowds were cheerful and immense, and displayed "really touching inscriptions," several to the "Queen and Empress" and the "Empress of India." The title was popular among the people, she contended, but was "as, alas, almost everything is, a party thing."

"Party" was an oversimplification. The tag of *Emperor*, the

Muff: a nineteenth-century term for one who is awkward or stupid in some physical sport.

3rd Earl Grey deprecated, had a "tawdry grandeur," and he and others pointed to the dethroned Napoleon III, the deposed and executed Maximilian of Mexico, and tribal sovereigns in Africa, while Victoria, as the Duke of Somerset put it, was "first Queen in the world." A meeting in Oxford appealed to her "not to assume any other title" after one don involved in the discussion blamed the agitation on Disraeli, "who is not English in race, sentiment, or character." Objections to the bill occupied the House far longer than he had anticipated, and George Meredith wrote to the Liberal politician and editor John Morley late in March that he fancied Disraeli "was heartily sick with the task his Imperial Mistress imposed on him at a moment when he did not know the English people so well."

Radicalism, Morley responded, would have "nothing to regret at the passing of the Bill," as public hostility to it would be "a stimulus to political reform." With his own party unenthusiastic, Disraeli was wary of bringing matters to a division. "We had 260 men in town, but we could not flog them up," he wrote wearily to Lady Bradford on March 29. On April 2 he assured Lady Chesterfield that he would not give in: "It would be an act of weakness, not of conciliation. . . . If you want to govern the world you must know how to say Bo[o] to a goose. And what is the use of power if you don't make people do what they don't like?"

Anne Chesterfield must have caught the teasing reference to her likely reading tastes. Charlotte Yonge in her romantic novel *Countess Kate* (1864) had a character chide, "Dear me, Mary, can't you say bo[o] to a goose!"

Two months later he was able to crow to Selina, "Generally speaking there is no gambling like politics"—a quip he had acquired from Lord Palmerston—because he had caught his Opposition risking a high card. Robert Lowe, who was alternating with the still unretired Gladstone in managing the attack on the bill, inadvertently assisted Disraeli by announcing in an Easter recess speech at East Retford his "conviction that at least two previous [Prime] Ministers have entirely refused to have anything to do with such a change. More pliant persons have now been found. And I have no doubt the thing will be done."

The effect on the House was electric. Although he was

Lowe's closest political colleague, Gladstone repudiated the charge with reference to himself. He would have had more to disown had word leaked out then—it took until the *Bradford Chronicle and Mail* revealed it on January 21, 1880—that when he sent a telegram of congratulations to the Ameer of Afghanistan in the Queen's name as Prime Minister in 1869, "the Queen's title was amended by adding *Empress of India."*

On May 2, Disraeli rose, stung by the allegation that he was a pliant Prime Minister, and he was well prepared to embarrass the enemy. Had there been, he asked, any "unconstitutional and personal influence" wielded by the Sovereign? He could answer for the late Earl of Derby, and Gladstone had answered for himself. That left—he ignored his own case—only the venerable Earl Russell, then seventy-eight, and the venerated Palmerston. To respond to Lowe he asked leave to introduce the Queen's name in the debate. Then he read a message from Victoria asserting "not the slightest foundation" for the "calumnious gossip" which, Disraeli deplored, had come "from the mouth of a Privy Councillor, and one of Her Majesty's late Cabinet Ministers."

On May 5, a pleased Prime Minister reported to Lady Bradford, "Lowe appeared in a white sheet last night, holding a taper of repentance." To Lady Chesterfield he added, "He is in the mud, and there I leave him." Right or wrong, Lowe was politically finished. By a majority of seventy-five, 209 to 134, the Royal Titles Bill passed its third reading and Victoria was authorized to style herself "Queen and Empress." Latinizing the designations in the traditional fashion, she began closing her letters with "Victoria R & I."

The Eastern Question continued to simmer through the spring of 1876, and the Queen and Disraeli, both of whom had been Russophobic for decades, took the unpopular course of tilting toward the un-Christian Turks. Contending with a divided Cabinet, Disraeli ordered elements of the Royal Navy into the waters off Constantinople not, as he put it in a memorandum to Victoria, "to protect Christians or Turks, but to uphold your Majesty's Empire."

Victoria's concerns about Britain's role in Europe were validated on May 12, 1876, when the governments of Russia, Ger-

many, and Austria, in response to uprisings against the Turks in
Bosnia and Hercegovina, issued a joint statement from Berlin demanding an armistice—which would liberate territories that had
been Turkish since 1389—and the creation of a mixed tribunal of
Christians and Moslems to reform alleged abuses. Armed intervention was threatened if the Sultan refused. It was a weekend,
sacrosanct in Victoria's domains, a diplomatic excuse given later
for not consulting Whitehall. "They have begun to treat England
as if we were Montenegro or Monaco," Disraeli growled to Baron
Brunnow, the Russian ambassador, and he refused to recognize the
Dreikaiserbund's note, in effect encouraging Turkey to resist, which
it did, even more strenuously when the rebellion spread to Bulgaria and alleged "volunteers" arrived from Russia to confront the
Turks.

Few Englishmen cared to protect the Islamic overlords of the
Balkans, but Disraeli claimed a geopolitical interest for Britain.
He had been forced to convene Cabinet meetings "under this
roof," he wrote to the Queen from Whitehall Gardens on May
18, as he was "suffering much from gout." To Derby he observed
on May 25 that what was taking place in Turkish waters was "unprecedented. All the navies of Europe assembled . . . & England
with a naval force which she has never tried in battle."

On June 23, while the Turks dealt with the uprisings in their
centuries-old fashion, the *Daily News,* a Radical paper, published
an account of alleged Ottoman outrages in Bulgaria which
eclipsed in graphic content anything published before. Disraeli
impatiently dismissed the stories as "coffee-house babble," a response which only fed indignation. Forced to do something dramatic, and in concert with other interested parties, he recalled
the respected ambassador in Berlin, Lord Odo Russell, for consultation on Eastern affairs, and Russell offered his estimate that Bismarck would prefer to see neither Russia nor Austria dominate
more of the Balkans and would side with England. Relieved, the
Queen noted in her journal after seeing Russell at Windsor on
July 5 that "Mr Gladstone's policy had really made it appear as
though England would never hold her old place again."

On July 8, still gouty and working mostly from home,
Disraeli himself managed an hour's audience with Victoria, ven-

turing out to Paddington Station and Windsor on a mild summer day to listen to the Queen complain (he told Lady Chesterfield), "of the sweltering climes of the realms she rules." He was always cold now, while Victoria, whose lifelong hyperthyroidism kept her feeling too warm, longed for escape to less sultry Scotland. His return express had to depart at 5:05, leaving their conference begun only at 4:00 insufficient time for the usual agenda, which—given their terms of comfortable familiarity—was short on business and

"New Crowns for Old Ones!" *Punch*, April 15, 1876. Quoting from "Alladin," Disraeli offers Victoria the title he had pushed through Parliament for her, Empress of India.

long on lesser matters, and Victoria engaged as always in unqueenly informalities. "We talked so long and so agreeably," he continued to Anne, "that the clock in the Closet struck 5! . . . I was obliged to jump up"—he now always sat with her—"and tell the truth. 'Run away, run away directly,' she said with many smiles—and so at an audience, instead of being dismissed, I dismissed my Sovereign!"

Cheerful as his account seemed, Disraeli, increasingly enfeebled by illness, was less and less able to defend his Ministry on foreign affairs questions in the House. Earlier in the year he had noted to Selina (January 20, 1876) that to judge from the "general mien" of his cabinet colleagues as they discussed the Burials Bill about to come before the Commons, they thought the legislation was "rather a fitting subject for their chief." He had "turned the corner," he insisted then; he was now always turning further corners, in and out of sickbeds. Concerned about his condition, the Queen dispatched one of her own physicians, Sir William Gull, to attend to him. The occasionally competent Gull, "tinkering" for a week, Disraeli told Lady Bradford, prescribed, for a patient whose complications included kidney trouble, a regimen of port wine, from which he had kept away for ten years, "and which nearly killed me. . . . I really thought, and not for the first time, that it was all over."

Concerned that he would have to step down, Victoria raised the possibility of relieving him of some of the regimen of Downing Street by removing him to the Lords. As early as March 6, Disraeli had mentioned that option to Derby, but confessed that he did not want to thrust the leadership of the Commons "into confusion," and even talked "of retiring altogether." That outcome, Derby thought, "cannot be, unless his health were so far to break down as to make his continuance in public business impossible." The strain of shepherding the Royal Titles Bill, followed by the stress of the revived Eastern Question, made the attractions of the Lords more inviting, for what might have been a distant foreign atrocity to officially deplore was becoming a domestic religious issue. And in a Britain where the Bible was much more than a book, Bulgaria had reached not only a press that pivoted upon sensation, but pulpits in remote counties.

Newspaper dispatches were heating up the hottest summer in years by printing gruesome details of Turkish barbarities against Bulgarian Christians of the sort that usually prompted readers to turn to the police news about headless corpses and violated virgins. To Disraeli's further distress the evangelical alarmist Lord Shaftesbury was convening public meetings, pledging the country, Disraeli wrote the Queen, still from Whitehall Gardens, "to give no aid to Turkey either moral or material. Lord Shaftesbury is always ready to place philanthropy at the aid of faction." Gladstone and his surrogates also emerged in the interest of oppressed Christians, charging that Disraeli was holding British foreign policy hostage to his Jewish sympathies. Russian oppression of Jews in its "Pale of Settlement" and in satellite countries like Romania was notorious, while Turkish toleration of Jews over the centuries, however inconsistent in various regions, had been relatively benign. Disraeli ignored the slanders in order not to give them publicity. He had troubles enough.

Tactical errors, possibly due to Disraeli's low state of health, were also contributing to his difficulties. On July 12, answering a question in the House about reports of the massacre of 25,000 Bulgarians, he agreed that there had been "atrocious" occurrences, but claimed, accurately, that the slaughter had been exaggerated. Yet thousands had died, and the nauseating accounts were not altogether nonsense—even the tales of torture, which he dismissed by observing that Turks "seldom resort to torture but generally terminate their connexion with culprits in a more expeditious manner."

As a joke it was in poor taste, and his seemingly callous approach was perceived as another attempt to keep Moslem Turkey in Christian Europe. Whatever his sympathies, Disraeli was a realist; a few weeks later he confided to Derby that England could not defend the territorial integrity of the Ottoman Empire, but only its own imperial interests. That meant encouraging rivalries among the three "Northern" emperors and seeking, in the event of the dismemberment of Turkey, a British protectorate over the Indian lifeline. "Constantinople with an adequate district should be neutralized and made a free port," he suggested, "in the custody and guardianship of England as the Ionian Isles were." Such

The last visit of Lord Beaconsfield to the House [of Commons], August 1875. *Drawn from life by Harry Furniss.*

speculation was prompted by a coup in the capital in which an insane sultan had been replaced by his half-brother in what did not seem the last of such events. Disraeli was recognizing that the old order—or disorder—in the eastern Mediterranean was gone, and that something short of a big European war had to replace the crumbling status quo.

Struggling to run his Government from one sickbed after another—his appearances in the Commons were now brief—he recommended to the Queen that he resign the premiership, or retain it while easing the strain by going to the Lords. The leadership of the Commons would have to go to Hardy or Northcote.

On June 27, Cairns had hinted to Hardy that Disraeli might make the move "after the session," but on July 12 Hardy noted in his diary that Disraeli had already been urged by the Queen, before she escaped for the summer to Balmoral, that he move to the Lords rather than "retire altogether." Disraeli told Hardy he had been weakened by what he called "bronchial gout," but his most acute problems were asthma and one of the consequences of gout, Bright's disease, or nephritis, which had become chronic and debilitating.

Since Victoria had offered an earldom to Disraeli as early as 1868, when he was outgoing Prime Minister, the idea was not new. She had again proposed the move once he had been taken ill at Balmoral two years earlier, but, Disraeli explained to Derby, "As I have no heir, I was unwilling, in the decline of life, to commence a new career in a House of Parliament in which I had no experience." With his health deteriorating further, the Lords was his only alternative to leaving office.

While the Queen did not want to lose Disraeli as head of her Government, especially to the passive and isolationist Derby, who did not share her anti-Russian sentiments, she did not know that Disraeli had already sounded out his deputy—whom he described to Lady Chesterfield as inhibited by "salutary apathy"—on the succession. According to Gathorne-Hardy, Derby had "utterly scouted the idea . . . , that he could never manage H.M., that he did not think he could lead his colleagues on Church questions, in short nothing on earth would make him take the post." Hardy was not surprised. Derby, he felt, "withdraws more and more and feels his unfitness to lead men." Yet Disraeli's ability to respond to events was questionable, given the lethargy caused by his ailments. Even the Queen reacted with "horror" to the reports of Turkish atrocities which had galvanized the press and wondered to Disraeli why he did not deplore them sufficiently to prevent partisan furor. Disraeli, in turn, complained to Derby that the Foreign Office had misled him about Bulgaria— that the press had more information than he was receiving. However unsympathetic to his chief's policies, Carnarvon fidgeted to Derby that Disraeli would throw it all up and retire, which would be "political suicide" for the Conservatives.

With small wars and rebellions against Turkish rule in the Balkans continuing, and religious questions more important to the public than political ones, only the punishment and dismemberment of the immoral and godless Ottoman Empire, the Liberal press argued, would solve the problem. That outcome, Victoria understood, would only strengthen Russia and endanger overland communications with India. Disraeli would have to remain to see the crisis through, as she saw no one else available whom she could trust. The solution remained a peerage, and the titles of rank were waiting. The legendary Edmund Burke, one of the greatest of Parliamentarians, had been expecting to be created Earl of Beaconsfield when he died in 1797. The territorial title remained unused.

On August 11, 1876, Disraeli made his last speech in the Commons, a reply to charges that he had played down the extent of Turkish atrocities, or was even pro-Turk. His duty, he reiterated, was "to maintain the Empire of England." At the close of business he walked to the Bar to survey what had been his political home since 1837, and then left to shake hands with those in the lobby who knew he was not to return. He had not waited until the 16th, the last day of the session, but had deliberately underplayed his exit.

On August 12, the next morning, newspapers reported that he had been created Earl of Beaconsfield and Viscount Hughenden. *Punch* published a cartoon with the caption "New crowns for old ones!"—showing Disraeli in vizier's garb, offering an Imperial crown to Victoria in exchange for his peer's coronet. From Osborne the Queen wrote to Crown Princess Victoria that she "will have been surprised at Mr Disraeli's well-earned elevation to the Peerage—but it was entirely on account of his health which at 72, and not robust, cannot stand the anxiety and responsibility in addition to the lead of the House of Commons and the late hours. Sir S. Northcote succeeds him . . . in the H. of C. while he takes it in the H. of Lords. He is immensely popular in the country." How much that popularity had been eroded was not the Queen's concern. For her, as she explained to Vicky, "his retirement would be a very serious calamity."

Empress and Earl; or, One Good Turn Deserves Another. *Punch,* August 26, 1876.

LORD BEACONSFIELD. *"Thanks, your Majesty. I might have had it before! Now I think I have* EARNED *it!"*

How Disraeli felt about his title became clear from his correspondence with Selina. *"I am quite tired of that place,"* he had hinted to Lady Bradford about the House of Commons on August 8, and on August 10, just before the news was released, he confided, "The Faery insists upon my changing my name at once—and my principal colleagues agree with H.M. I thought it might have been postponed for some months. There is one person to whom I shall never-change my name and to whom, I trust, I shall ever be, Hers sincerely, D." On August 22 from Hughenden, the session over, and a visit to the Bradfords also over, he wrote a bread-and-butter note to Selina about the crowds at every railway station from Birmingham southward collecting to offer "vociferous ejaculations and congratulations to the 'noble Hurl of Beaconsfield.' " And he signed it "Ever your devoted Beaconsfield."

XXVII

"I AM DEAD, DEAD BUT IN
THE ELYSIAN FIELDS."

1876–1878

WHILE HIS TITLE WAS STILL NEW, THE EARL OF BEACONSFIELD WAS surprised by a bow from a lady he myopically failed to recognize. "Who is she?" he asked Monty Corry, on whose arm he leaned. "Lady Sebright," his private secretary said, referring to the pretty wife of the High Sheriff of Hertfordshire. Turning back toward Olivia to atone, he observed her turning round also, and saying, "How do you do, Mr. Disraeli?— Oh, I beg pardon, Lord Beaconsfield!"

"Of what use is my coronet to me, my dear lady," said the Prime Minister in his most courtly manner, "so long as Sir John is alive?"

Disraeli had few such moments in which to savor his new dignities. Such popular recognition as represented by the Beaconsfield Arms in Bridlington and the Earl of Beaconsfield pub in Plaistow very likely escaped his notice. Foreign affairs would overwhelm the Beaconsfield segment of his premiership, and his worst moments would come from the less-than-retired

Gladstone, whose interest in foreign matters had always been minimal. Disraeli viewed the southern Balkans, where only a truncated Greece had escaped into independence, as Turkey's Ireland, a problem of diverse customs and religions to be solved internally. He also saw only strong, large nations as bulwarks against Russian expansionism.

From Hawarden, Gladstone viewed the growing public concern over Turkish atrocities in putting down a Bulgarian insurrection in April and May as an opportunity to exploit politically his rigid convictions in religion and morals.

Waiting until August to gear up his outrage, he gave three hectic days to writing his emotional and mischievous *The Bulgarian Horrors and the Question of the East*. Published on September 6, while his ostensible successor, Hartington, was happily killing grouse at Bolton Abbey—he sent Disraeli four brace—the pamphlet sold in the tens of thousands. A masterpiece of opportunism, it ignored czarist oppression and misrule while focusing upon the plight of Christian Slavs. Some of the horrors were real, reported by government observers; others anticipated the fictitious Belgian butcheries that would galvanize anti-Germanism in 1914. Disraeli rushed back from Hughenden.

At Downing Street on September 9 he found, he wrote Lady Bradford, "Gladstone's pamphlet, which he had the impudence to send me, . . . quite as unprincipled as usual though on the surface apparently not so ill-written as is his custom . . . because it is evidently dictated, so it is not so involved and obscure; but more wordy and more careless and imprudent." It encouraged Russia, he felt. Disraeli was encouraging Turkey if only by a naive belief that the new sultan, whose misrule—which at first seemed like reform to Disraeli—would "turn out trumps." With Russia mobilizing, expansion-minded Serbia and Montenegro at war with Turkey since June, and Disraeli's emissary, Salisbury, shuttling among European capitals to repair the peace, Derby fired off futile telegrams from the Foreign Office to restrain Austrian and Russian eagerness to partition European Turkey. The Prime Minister felt isolated at home. Only the Queen sounded belligerent, pressing Disraeli to keep the faith with her Russophobia but remaining away in Scotland.

Looking between the lines of Gladstone's shrill pieties, Disraeli saw one aim as essentially "Christian"—as he put it to Lord Barrington (September 11) and others, that, "for ethnological reasons, . . . the Turks, as a race, should be expelled from Europe." The behavior of "that wicked maniac" was "treasonable," he told Lady Chesterfield, as Turkey's collapse would "weaken" England in relation to other powers, but more than political and theological motives were behind Gladstone's sanctimonious pillorying of the Disraeli foreign policy. As he explained delicately to Lady Bradford, "There may be more infamous men but I don't believe there is anyone more wicked. And millions believe he is a virtuous, moral, even transcendent being! Abandoned in his private life, *criblé de dettes* & the willing votary of every delusion that might bring him favor!"

The line was deliberately cryptic but in the waning months of 1876 its meaning became an open secret. The French for "over one's ears in debt" was not meant literally: Gladstone was a wealthy man. And the term *votary*—devoted admirer—had nothing to do with religious delusions. In London completing the revisions on his *Horrors* pamphlet and reading proof sheets, Gladstone had managed dinner and the theater with Laura Thistlethwaite and several emotional "rescue" assignations. After one he noted in his diary, "I might put down much." He read a life of Madame DuBarry with avidity—"most repulsive & most instructive" was his diary reaction. Soon, amid Gladstone's relentless speechmaking on the Eastern Question, while the Balkans shuddered through violence, armistice, recriminations, and more violence, Gathorne-Hardy as War Minister saw the Queen at Balmoral and learned more from her about Gladstone as votary than he had heard from Disraeli.

"The Queen," Hardy noted in his diary on October 29, "was . . . strongly Anti-Russ[ian] & still more Anti Gladstone." (Victoria "knows all about" Mrs. Thistlethwaite, Disraeli had told Lady Bradford.) She spoke of Gladstone with horror, of his consorting "with a Russian female spy, about wh[om] there is much gossip." He had renewed his friendship with Olga Novikov, notorious as "the M.P. from Russia"—the charming wife of a member of the Russian General Staff—and from October through December saw her or wrote to her nearly daily. On one October day (the 27th) he was with Madame Novikov and Laura Thistlethwaite separately, dining with Mrs. Thistlethwaite and then going with her to a Gaiety burlesque. He continued in the company of both women, and at one rally on the Eastern Question he sat Olga Novikov on the platform, from which he personally escorted her afterward. Mrs. Gladstone as usual was far off at Hawarden.

While Madame Novikov was tempting Gladstone, the new Russian ambassador, Count Shuvalov, a practiced seducer, tried to work his charms on Lady Salisbury, assigning his wife to the upright, High Church, Marquis—both efforts destined for failure. What success Olga Novikov had with Gladstone other than in reinforcing his Russophilism is untraceable, but it was clearly another moment in his turbulent emotional life when he had lost control. The Liberal diplomat Robert R. D. Morier, Minister to Lisbon 1876–81, later used his trenchant pen to explain Gladstone and Novikov to Sir Louis Mallet, a Liberal civil servant who worked under Salisbury as Permanent Undersecretary of State for India. Examine the psychological background of Gladstone's behavior, Morier urged Mallet on May 20, 1880, to interpret "a word or a sentence dropped here or there which only the initiated can comprehend." One had to observe the influence which "that strumpet Madame Novikoff . . . has over him and the way quite unconsciously to himself that he sees everything through *her* eyes." What Morier saw motivating Gladstone, perceived similarly although in different terms by both Disraeli and Victoria, he identified as "suppressed priapism." Morier maintained that much of "human action" was determined by how much sexual satisfaction a person needed, and gratified. Gladstone was "a case of too little [gratification]. I am convinced that he came into the world with the most tremendously virile powers, that his strongly ascetic religiosity has kept them down—that Mrs G has been the only flesh he has ever tasted!" As a result "there is even at his time of life a lurking desire within him seeking unconsciously to himself to be assuaged. Madame N. who is an extremely accomplished whore will have seized this at a glance. She will have been far too cunning to play on this instru-

Benjamin Bombastes. *Punch*, August 4, 1877. *Punch*'s caption about
the Prime Minister's challenge to Russia:
"Who dares this pair of Boots displace,
Must meet Bombastes face to face!—
Thus do I challenge all the human race!"

ment directly but she will have known exactly how to utilize her
knowledge."

For Disraeli it was an exasperating dilemma. He was convinced that Gladstone—"the greatest Tartuffe of his age"—knew
what he was doing, and that his crusade against Islamic oppressors
of Christians was not only contrary to Britain's geopolitical interests but masked other less savory personal motives. One unsavory
aspect of the agitation was strident anti-Semitism, some of it em-
anating from Gladstone's favorite historian, the Radical Edward

Freeman, who wrote about backward, semibarbarous Russia to James Bryce, "There is a nation in the freshness of a new life, burning to go on the noblest of crusades and one loathsome Jew wants to stop them."

From the platform upon which both Gladstone and Olga Novikov sat, Freeman wondered (about Disraeli) whether "the Jew in his drunken insolence" would also "fight to uphold the independence and integrity of Sodom." Gladstone himself went back to *Tancred* and looked for evidence in its "crypto-Judaism" of anti-Christian bias, while editor T. P. O'Connor searched Disraeli's novels for evidences of "this strong feeling of the [racial] kinsmanship of the Jew and the Mohammedan, and their bond of hate against the Christians," which he found "innumerable." History made it difficult, he charged, "to distinguish the follower of Moses from the votary of Mohammed." Gladstone would read O'Connor's biography of Disraeli (through 1846), in which O'Connor charged, "The sublimity of the stakes cannot exalt the meanness of his passions." In his diary, Gladstone commented "*very* remarkable." Young Reginald Brett, an admirer of Disraeli who thought that he was the "perfect captain of a side," noted in his diary (August 30, 1876) receiving a letter suggesting that the Prime Minister's ambitions for an earldom came from "his desire to glorify the Hebrew race by admitting one of the chosen people to the hitherto untasted honours of the English peerage."

Sir William Harcourt snapped to Sir Charles Dilke (October 20, 1876), "Gladstone and Dizzy seem to cap one another in folly and imprudence, and I don't know which has made the greatest ass of himself." Although a radical and even a republican, Dilke responded impatiently, "If Gladstone goes on much longer, I shall turn Turk." Later he told his constituents that he preferred Turkey to Russia at Constantinople. "The Turkish is in ordinary times a less stifling despotism than the Russian. . . . The Turks let any man go to church and read any book, the Russians do not." Gladstone, nevertheless, had effectively convinced a vocal segment of the electorate that to support Christianity one had to side with the Czar.

As often happens in such causes, the intellectual Left adopted the apparent oppressed, and there was curious coalescing of far Right and far Left opinion. Attacking Disraeli, Carlyle wrote his last letter to *The Times*, and the nonbelieving William Morris, who became Treasurer of the Gladstonian Eastern Question Association, one to the *Daily News*. Swinburne wrote a satiric anti-Turk poem, and George Meredith professed a similar bias, as did William Michael Rossetti. Edward FitzGerald of *Rubiyat* fame used the anti-Semitic device of the apostrophe, writing that "D'Israeli's" writings were like his politics—"showy and shallow," that he was—again pointedly identifying him as "D'Israeli"—"a very clever Quack, whose statesmanship is as flashy and superficial as his Novels." (Gladstone, on the other hand, was "honest.") And Henry James, writing from Paris to a friend in the United States, offered his fervent "*Delenda* Constantinople now. I must say she deserves it." Yet he added, an indication of where Disraeli's support would be coming from in the face of concerted hysteria, "I must say too that my own sentiment in the matter is one of satisfaction at seeing England being, and counting for, something in European politics."

The Russian threat as seen from Whitehall was not limited to the eastern Mediterranean but applied to other approaches to India. Disraeli instructed the Viceroy to shore up relations with the Khan of Khelat, ruler of Baluchistan, between Persia and India, and with the Ameer of Afghanistan, who controlled the mountain passes between Bukhara and Samarkand and between Rawalpindi and Srinagar. Every perceived menace from Albania to Afghanistan seemed to have a relationship to India, crown jewel of the Empire. Even matters more remote geographically became victims of the preoccupation with the Eastern Question, as when a message reached the Colonial Office on September 20, 1876, that the Afrikaners in the Transvaal, Dutchmen who decades before had trekked north from the Cape, were in economic "*extremis*" and that it would be an opportune time to federate the interior with the Cape Colony. Carnarvon sent a note to Disraeli asking whether to intervene if "the crisis . . . makes this in any way possible." Busy with Turkey, the Prime Minister unwisely scribbled a note, "Do what you think wisest."

To cool off the Balkan situation while considering military options, Disraeli agreed late in November to send a representative to a multipower conference at Constantinople. Preparing for it, he queried the War Office on Russian movements and intentions, finally writing in exasperation to Corry, "The Intelligence Dept must change its name. It is the department of ignorance."

That Disraeli had hopes of success is clear from his instructions to Lord Salisbury, his plenipotentiary. His confidence in the head of the India Office—and for Disraeli, India loomed in the background—had grown as he learned to lean on the Marquis's intellect and to rely less on Derby's indecisiveness. A memorandum of November 10, 1876, to Salisbury can be read as a forecast of who would be the next Conservative Prime Minister. Britain suffered, Disraeli observed, from "a feeble and formal diplomacy" that inhibited honest exchanges of ideas between the powers and left relations in a "slough of despond." Significantly, he added, "Also, personally for yourself, I wish it. This is a momentous period in your life and career. If all goes well you will have achieved an European reputation and position which will immensely strengthen your future course." While an anti-Turk "National Convention of the Eastern Question" organized by Gladstone was promoting what Disraeli considered destabilizing solutions and offering them as philanthropic ones regardless of their political repercussions, they received no sympathy in Downing Street. Coercion of Turkey through a foreign occupation of Constantinople that might easily become permanent seemed not in England's interest. He authorized Salisbury to go no farther than "friendly influence and persuasion."

Such Disraeli loyalists in the cabinet as Earl Cairns were only strengthened in their opposition to the dismemberment of Turkey by the open alignment of Gladstone with the Russians. Being "in bed with the enemy" seemed more than metaphor to the Lord Chancellor, who was so irate at the presence of Count Shuvalov and Madame Novikov on the Eastern Question platform, where the ambassador congratulated Gladstone on his "grand triumph," and at Gladstone's simultaneous and equally public involvement with Laura Thistlethwaite, that he exploded to Disraeli, "Could not *The World* or some such paper be got to publish this?" Yet Gladstone's reputation for rectitude continued to protect him from the scandal columns, and the apparent hypocrisies which nauseated Disraeli left him immovable on the key issue. A minute by Lord Barrington about an October 23 conference with Disraeli put the matter succinctly. The Prime Minister "is determined that the Russians shall not, directly or indirectly, become possessed of Constantinople." Barrington agreed that would undermine the Empire.

At the Foreign Office, after "fresh telegrams" from Salisbury on December 14, the pacific Derby conceded that "any force not under the control of the Porte," even a Belgian gendarmerie, "will likely be resisted, . . . which applies to every form of interference with the internal affairs of Turkey." Meetings would drag on, but on January 20, 1877, the Six Powers withdrew without agreement. Concerned about keeping his head while Turkish mobs reacted to foreign demands with religious fanaticism of their own, the Sultan dropped any semblance of compromise. "Christian" soldiers patrolling Islamic Constantinople would have been an explosive nonsolution, and the crisis dragged on toward war.

Almost everything seemed to be going badly in the months following Disraeli's earldom. Foreign affairs overwhelmed any domestic agenda, and an index of discontent was the by-election in Buckinghamshire to fill Disraeli's seat. The Conservative candidate, handpicked by the Prime Minister, barely squeaked through. To Derby it had been "folly on our part" to push the Royal Titles Bill, which satisfied only Victoria and encouraged her obstinacy. Expressing her satisfaction at Christmas, when Disraeli remained alone at Whitehall Gardens, the Queen sent him a Christmas card and a sumptuously illustrated folio volume of Goethe's *Faust* with a letter hoping that it was worthy of a place in the library at Hughenden. Both were signed "V.R. et I." It was the first time she had used her new style. Disraeli responded with a thank-you in his most fulsome vein, assuring her of "his respectful devotion, & the entire devotion of his life & heart."

On January 1, 1877, the Queen was proclaimed Empress of India at a sun-scorched *durbar* in Delhi stage-managed by Lord Lytton. At Windsor, with the countryside so awash with winter floods that invitees had difficulty getting through from London, Victoria presided at a celebratory dinner, startling her guests, including Disraeli and Lord George Hamilton, the Undersecretary for India, by wearing masses of jewels given to her by Indian princes and maharajahs. On the Queen's short, stout figure the baubles were incongruous, but the display demonstrated how much the title meant to her. Eventually she would have a "Durbar Room" annex built at Osborne to house her Indian artifacts, bringing her as close to the subcontinent as she would ever get.

While a conciliatory faction and a war faction competed for the Czar's backing in St. Petersburg, Victoria kept urging firmness upon Disraeli, Derby, and Salisbury. Derby she thought hopeless, kept in the Foreign Office because Disraeli needed to placate his moderate ministers. Salisbury seemed to fluctuate between his High Church sympathies and what she perceived as the national interest. "Mawkish sentimentality" for the Russians, "who hardly deserve the name of Christians," she warned Disraeli, would cause them to misinterpret British priorities.

With Disraeli more ill than ever, confined to Whitehall Gardens or, worse still for management of affairs, to Hughenden, the Government drifted. The short walk to Downing Street was no longer possible. Disraeli went by carriage. And news in his red boxes continued to be frustrating. "What a Satanic Society!" he exclaimed to Derby about a dispatch from Belgrade. Every entity in Europe that impinged upon Turkish territory was greedy for spoils, and just as Serbia was eager to expand at Turkey's expense, Austria was making its own arrangements with Christian rebels in Bosnia and Hercegovina, the two half-Moslem provinces along the Adriatic that had been Turkish since 1463, to "protect" them. (Complete annexation came in 1908.)

Via the Rothschilds, Disraeli discovered double-dealing and deception on the part of all the countries involved, and on January 10, 1877, Lionel asked for English good offices on behalf of Romanian Jews under Russian control, "who are being tormented in the usual way." Despite Eastern Question pieties, czarist religious ideals had certain limits.

With the Prime Minister obviously failing, rumors surfaced in the press that he would resign and be succeeded by the Duke of Richmond as a compromise choice. Disraeli reportedly would keep only his title of Lord Privy Seal, which had a salary but few duties, and afforded precedence over "all ordinary Peers." Derby speculated in his journal about what would happen to the "vacant post," vowing that he would never serve "under a junior"—especially his wife's ambitious stepson, Salisbury. Encouraged by Mary, Derby began to covet the position, and Lady Derby was encouraged by the affectionate Shuvalov, to whom, to undermine Disraeli, she loyally furnished confidential cabinet information. With her help, the Earl of Beaconsfield's Eastern strategy was in confusion. Derby (with Shuvalov in the background), Salisbury, and Carnarvon continued to act according to High Church priorities at odds with the Russophobia of the Prime Minister and the Queen. It was no encouragement to Disraeli's pro-Turk policy that as Parliament was about to resume, with the Empress of India present to dignify the occasion for the new leader of the Lords, *Truth* published a squib on January 25: "An eminent West End divine has announced his intention to preach a sermon . . . upon 'Israelites in Egyptian bonds.' Is this meant sarcastical?"

Parliament was opened on Thursday afternoon, February 8, with the Earl of Beaconsfield in his peer's robes of scarlet and ermine at Victoria's left hand, holding the Sword of State. When the business of the Lords began at five, his patent of nobility was read, and he was conducted to "the Dukes' bench," where he had the right to sit as Lord Privy Seal. He was greeted formally by the Lord Chancellor, Earl Cairns, and then, divested of his robes, took his place as leader of the House of Lords, to which he adapted with easy grace. Afterward Lord Aberdare asked him how he found the new setting. "I am dead," Disraeli said, "dead but in the Elysian fields." To many it seemed that illness had indeed drawn much of the life from his sallow basilisk face, in which an eyelid had begun to droop, but his cold sarcasm and refusal to be ruffled were unchanged from the House of Commons.

There was good reason to be ruffled as the pamphlet offensive unleashed by Gladstone went on unabated, much of it blatantly bigoted. In the profusely illustrated, seventy-page *Benjamin D————: His Little Dinner*, the Prime Minister was "among us—not of us . . . , for Little Ben was an Israelite, and understood not the ways of the Gentiles." *Dizzi-ben-Dizzi, the Orphan of Bagdad*, professed to be about "How Little Ben, the innkeeper, changed the sign of the Queen's Inn to the Empress Hotel Limited and what was the Result." In *Truth*, which printed a canto of "The Song of Big Ben" nearly each week, the Prime Minister was, "though coroneted, . . . the same old crafty Dizzy."

While Victoria exhorted Disraeli to keep his Cabinet firm, he was in reality almost isolated within it. Although he brought sixty peers together to dine with him the evening before Parliament opened, he wished, he told Lady Bradford, "they would always attend the House of Lords in equal numbers." In the Commons, where Sir Stafford Northcote now led, the debates began early on how much the Great Powers should press Turkey for what were called reforms but were concessions of territory and autonomy. The Duke of Argyll was spokesman for the Opposition in the Lords. In the Commons the official Liberal leader, Hartington, so Northcote wrote to the Queen, was "statesmanlike" in comparison to Gladstone, whose attack "really was in parts like the speech of a madman."

With the fissures in his Cabinet wide, Disraeli remained reticent in Parliament on the Eastern Question, speaking only once in the 1877 session on the subject. On February 20 he spoke in the Lords on the need for stability in the Balkans, and the likelihood of continuing confrontations if Turkey were reduced to a "cabbage garden" around Constantinople. He was supposed to have lost the confidence of his colleagues, he said, because none had publicly risen to his defense despite attacks from the platform and from the press. "I dare say I have had as many leading articles, mainly of a vituperative nature, written against me as anyone ever had," he admitted, and he appreciated the "humanitarian" considerations behind many of them. But his determination "to maintain the empire of England" remained his first priority, and the Eastern Question deeply involved that.

Depressed by painful gout, which often required Cabinet meetings at home, and by the hold on public opinion which the anti-Turk movement had generated, Disraeli could hardly depose Derby. The leader of the opposition in his own Cabinet was the link with possible compromise, and—Disraeli told Victoria—Derby's "personal honour" was involved. In any case, Disraeli's own Ministers seemed closer to Derby than to him. In defeatist language Salisbury explained to Lytton in Delhi on March 9, "the

old policy—wise enough in its time—of defending English interests by sustaining the Ottoman dynasty has become impractica-
ble." England needed "a *pied-à-terre* in place of that which we
shall infallibly lose at Constantinople." But Disraeli was unwilling
to relinquish Constantinople and vast Asian and Balkan territories to the Russians—which his Cabinet preferred to a new Crimean War involving England. His approach, which Salisbury
described to Carnarvon as "rolling down the incline," was to occupy, with Turkey's permission, Gallipoli, in order to secure the
Dardanelles from Russia, returning it on the conclusion of a European settlement.

Disraeli found little support for what amounted to a military
intervention on the Turkish side to deter the Russians. When the
Cabinet objected that it would insure war, Disraeli offered on
March 21 the most timid the opportunity to resign. They did not,
urging instead that Disraeli reexamine partition of Turkey as the
only way to preserve what would be left of it. The Balkan Christians had to be saved, Carnarvon argued, but the visiting Count
Ignatiev, Russian ambassador to Constantinople, assured both Disraeli and the Queen that it could be accomplished through
negotiations: "The curtain has not yet fallen; there will be peace."
All that Disraeli could do was to transfer Layard from Madrid to
Constantinople to better represent his own voice there, and Russia
claimed pacifically that it would begin demobilizing. It was a typical Russian deception, and Lionel de Rothschild, rarely so naive,
wrote to Disraeli rejoicing prematurely "at the success of a patriotic and just policy. Owing to your great firmness and statesmanlike views we have arrived at a point where we may confidently
expect to congratulate you on the prospects of a general peace."

To his Ministers on April 16 Disraeli proposed a preemptive
Dardanelles occupation, as he suspected the Russians, however
talking compromise, to be preparing a drive south. In six weeks
they could be in Gallipoli. Few in the Cabinet were swayed.
Disraeli blamed "false religionism." Derby was for "doing nothing," Disraeli reported to the Queen, and Salisbury—he might
also have added Carnarvon—"evidently is thinking more of raising the Cross on the cupola of St Sophia, than of the power of
England." As the Cabinet next met, on April 21, the Russians

crossed Turkish frontiers in the Balkans and in Armenia, and Disraeli confided to his Ministers a private note from Victoria claiming that she would abdicate rather than kiss the feet of the Czar. Three days later Russia officially declared war, but the Prime Minister could extract from his Cabinet only a weak authorization to send deploring notes and (on April 28) a declaration of neutrality contingent on Russia's not threatening the Dardanelles. "A Government can only die once," he warned: "It is better to die with glory, than vanish in an ignominious end. The country would still rally round British interests: [but] in three months British interests would be in the mud." Derby felt that the country was unwilling to pay for retrieving someone else's chestnuts from the fire, particularly an unworthy someone.

With gout crippling his hands and feet and asthma clogging his lungs, Disraeli had to leave affairs to subordinates and hope that events, or pressure by the Queen, would move them. "Be bold!" she exhorted him, and she approved a devious communications arrangement that evaded their official channels during the anxious spring and summer. But while largely restricted to Whitehall Gardens, Disraeli could not risk an affront to the American government by failing to host on June 21 what he described to Lady Chesterfield as a "colossal" banquet for former President (and General) Ulysses S. Grant, then on the first leg of a world tour. Grant, who sat at the Prime Minister's side, proved "more honorable than pleasant," and the evening grew more and more difficult. The room was crowded with forty guests, from whose strong male effluvia Disraeli was protected by vases of fragrant white stephanotis. In time the "strong perfumes, . . . mixing with the fumes of tobacco, did not at all benefit my bronchial tubes. . . . I felt so overcome I escaped as soon as possible."

Wherever the Queen was, Ponsonby was with her, supporting Gladstone's foreign policy positions. Derby remained disloyal in the Cabinet. Whether Victoria was at Windsor or Balmoral, she resorted to Jane Ely, a lady-in-waiting, as a courier, while young Prince Leopold was given a key to the Queen's red boxes—"as one of your private secretaries," Disraeli put it.

"I have never known the country so excited upon any question," Gladstone wrote to Arthur Gordon (later Lord Stanmore).

No small portion of excitement finds its way to me personally, in the shape of an idolising sentiment among the people such as I never before experienced. . . . I have watched very closely [Disraeli's] strange & at first sight inexplicable proceedings on this Eastern Question: and I believe their fountainhead to be race antipathy, that aversion which the Jews, with a few honourable exceptions, are showing so vindictively towards the Eastern Christians. Though he has been baptized, his Jew feelings are the most radical & the most real, & so far respectable, portion of his profoundly falsified nature.

Although the Russian advance was swift until Osman Pasha held at Plevna in mid-July, Disraeli found no sympathy in the Cabinet for requesting credits from Parliament for military preparations. "Lord Derby seems for peace at any price," he wrote to the Queen in frustration, "& Lord Salisbury seems to think that the progress of Russia is the progress of religion & civilisation." It did not help that on July 29, after a month's illness, the First Lord of the Admiralty, Ward Hunt, died. Disraeli got W. H. Smith to take the job although Victoria was opposed to "a man of the Middle Class" and cautioned that he "must not *act* the Lord High Admiral which is offensive to the Service." Smith would prove a strong appointment as well as the inspiration for Gilbert and Sullivan's "Ruler of the Queen's Navee" in *H.M.S. Pinafore*— which Disraeli found in poor taste—two years later.

Although he remained in poor health through the summer and early autumn, a drumfire of telegrams and notes to Hughenden kept him vigilant to the Queen's views. She was for intervention rather than a "milk-and-water, peace-at-any-price policy," but Derby sent word to Layard in Constantinople that the Turkish government could expect no more than neutrality. "It maddens the Queen," she responded to Disraeli, "to feel that all our efforts are being destroyed by the Minister who ought to carry them out." Through Layard, Disraeli arranged for the military attaché at Constantinople to advise Turkish army engineers on strengthening fortifications on the Gallipoli peninsula—

"Power and Place"—The Earl of Beaconsfield, K.G., and Mr. Montagu Corry, P.S. "Spy" in *Vanity Fair*, December 16, 1879. According to the accompanying text, "The Private Secretary, upright, fresh, and smart, marches erect and alert, as though he were the pillar of physical strength of the partnership; the Knight of the Garter, leaning lightly on his arm, with shoulders still broad and held back, with eyes no longer keen and feet no longer swift, shows like the depositary of surviving brain-power in a frame worn and weary."

defenses the British would then fail to breach in 1915. And in England the gritty Turkish resistance at Plevna began to turn popular feeling around to the point that Gladstone had to write to Shuvalov to ask for "even a few verified cases of barbarity" to invigorate his movement.

At Woburn Abbey, seat of the Duke of Bedford, Disraeli told

Lady Derby what he apparently hoped would be communicated to the Russians. There were "six parties" in his Cabinet, Disraeli said: "The party of war at any price: Hardy, J. Manners, Hicks Beach. The party who are for declaring war if [the Russians] threaten Constantinople: Cross, Smith & Cairns. The party who are for letting the Russians go to Constantinople but not stay there: Lord Salisbury. The Party who are for having Christian service in St Sophia—Lord Carnarvon. The party of peace at any price—Lord Derby. The party who are for reconciling all these parties & standing by our international engagements—the Queen & myself." He had omitted the Duke of Richmond, Derby noted, who would follow Disraeli anywhere, and Northcote, "I suppose as undecided." Perhaps for Shuvalov, he copied the list into his diary.

"Dreadfully infirm," according to the papers, Disraeli, while waiting to consult a new doctor, who, he told Lady Bradford, "like all untried men, is a magician," retreated to Brighton, seeking sun and warmth. At his hotel he had his first experience of being elevated to an upper story by a lift—"a charming machine; and when I take my place in it either to mount or to fall, I often wish it would never stop." According to Henry Labouchere's weekly, *Truth* (October 25, 1877), "The Asian Mystery," leaning heavily on his Private Secretary's arm, was "now a puppet, worked by Monty Corry." Brighton had been chosen, *Truth* suggested, because of its Jewish clientele:

> *See, close behind this couple comes a band*
> *Of chosen people from the Promised Land.*
> *In fact the List of Visitors transcribes*
> *A large proportion of the ten lost tribes.*

The next month, *Truth* alleged (November 22, 1877) that "a tacit conspiracy has, for more than a year, existed on the part of a considerable number of Anglo-Hebrews, to drag us into a war on behalf of the Turks" because of "affinity of race and feeling between the Jews and the Turks," and because, it confessed, the "intolerance and injustice" with which Jews were treated by "Russians, Servians, and Roumanians." It left no doubt that the Prime Minister was a co-conspirator.

Edmund Yates, editor of *The World*, encountered Disraeli on the Brighton esplanade, huddling in a long greatcoat and curly-brimmed hat. He was at the seaside, Disraeli explained, because he had just been in "the middle of the country, where the fall of the leaf made everything very dreary." They discussed the retirement of John Delane of *The Times*, Charles Dickens, and whether men with a reputation for clever talk ever lived up to their reputations. "I can easily understand that you, or any other clever man," Disraeli said, "finding yourself in the company of a professional writer, and having a smart thing on the tip of your tongue, might hesitate to give it utterance, saying to yourself, 'If I say that, this damned fellow will put it in his article.' "

Returning from Brighton, Disraeli moved from Whitehall Gardens into Downing Street, setting a precedent for future Prime Ministers. "I have been ill and continue very ill," he wrote to Lady Bradford, "and am quite incapable of walking upstairs; gout and bronchitis have ended in asthma. . . . Sometimes I am obliged to sit up all night, and want of sleep at last breaks me down. . . . I have managed to attend every Cabinet. . . . I can't walk at present from Whitehall to Downing Street, but am obliged to brougham even that . . . , which I once could have repeated fifty times a day." He had been planning the change for a year, negotiating with the Treasury over what was personal expense and what was public necessity, using the precedent of Number 11, which had long been the official residence of the Chancellor of the Exchequer. The main reception room took £1,042/10s. to redecorate. The private apartments, unused for thirty years, remained dilapidated, and it took all of 1878, and an additional £2,350, to rehabilitate them, including a bath with hot water and an Axminster carpet, twenty-three by twenty feet, that cost the Treasury £140. Until then it was a spartan existence.

On November 1, Disraeli had seen Dr. Joseph Kidd for the first time. The Prime Minister's firmness in foreign affairs might have been up to the Queen's expectations had his health not been undermined by her doctors, especially Sir William Jenner and Sir William Gull. Earl Cairns had pressed him to try a homeopathic physician. Although looked down upon by traditionally trained doctors, Dr. Kidd was reputedly effective in treating bronchial cases. On examining Disraeli, now nearly seventy-three, Kidd found that his patient's ailments had long been aggravated by the quackery which had passed for medicine. He eliminated remedies he thought ignorant, especially the doses of ipecac, from a root named for its causing vomiting, prescribed for Disraeli's asthma. Its properties were powerful: it stimulated nausea, diarrhea, and heavy perspiration, enervating him without relieving his symptoms. Since Kidd felt that perspiring was necessary to reduce the strain on the kidneys to eliminate fluid, he recommended warm nightclothes and flannel sheets, and exposure to a heat lamp. "You say you want me to perspire," Disraeli objected. "I never did since I was born. I have had a dry skin all my life." But he followed instructions.

Kidd's alternative dosage was potassium iodide, which had few side effects. He forbade Dr. Gull's favorite specific of port wine, and recommended a lighter claret. He cut out "steel"— liquids prescribed for their iron content, which only aggravated Disraeli's gout—and ordered light suppers "of one course, without pastry, pudding, or fruit." He did not want sugar to stimulate his patient in the evening and keep him sleepless, and moved the primary meal to early afternoon. Also, he prescribed "a mild course of arsenic," to clear the bronchial tubes "without any subsequent nausea."

One did not recover from either asthma or his other afflictions in the current state of medicine, Disraeli understood, but he might begin functioning more effectively. He claimed to Lady Bradford that he was "curable," and while arsenic was more liberally administered then, it might have furnished, in the wrong dosages, a more permanent cure.

At the traditional Lord Mayor's banquet at the Guildhall in November, Disraeli was marginally up to offering the expected address. As soon as he finished, Corry took him home to Downing Street.

On December 10, the Turks at Plevna crumbled, and Disraeli determined to put the military on a war footing regardless of misgivings in the Cabinet. The Queen reminded him that people were thoroughly "alarmed" about Russia and more sympathetic toward the Turks, "who are defending their home and hearth."

Further, few would want England to slip timidly into "a second-rate power." Lady Salisbury reported, apparently from her husband's Cabinet discussions, that Victoria "had lost control of herself, badgers her Ministers and pushes them toward war!" Yet she was also aware of the public mood, which had found Gladstone's sanctimony increasingly hollow. Militants stoned his windows. In December 1877 a music hall boast in a song by G. W. Hunt, bellowed by the "lion comique" Gilbert Hastings Macdermott, gave a word to the language:

> We don't want to fight, but by Jingo, if we do,
> We've got the ships, we've got the men, we've got the money too.
> We've fought the Bear before,
> And while Britons shall be true
> The Russians shall not have Constantinople.

Although *Constantinople* made a poor rhyme, the song helped forge a mood as much as reflect it. It was the moment for the Queen to back her embattled Prime Minister by the long-promised occasion of her presence. On December 15, Victoria, Beatrice, Ponsonby, and a lord-in-waiting, Colonel du Plat, went by train from Windsor to High Wycombe (a trip of about forty minutes), and thence by open landau, drawn by four horses, to Hughenden Manor. The Earl of Beaconsfield, with Monty Corry, greeted the Queen at the thronged, beflagged station and led the Queen's party to Hughenden in another carriage. In the Italian garden, which recalled that of Benjamin D'Israeli, the Prime Minister's grandfather, Victoria and Beatrice each planted a tree; then the Queen and Disraeli talked politics in the library before luncheon, Victoria urging him "strongly" to "bring things to an issue." By 3:30 it was all over. After plucking a statuette of Disraeli from the library as a souvenir, Victoria was on her way back to High Wycombe station, where she and her Prime Minister parted. The afternoon had been brief, yet its symbolism reverberated to rally Disraeli's forces and pluck up his nerve. Gladstone's tame historian, Freeman, wrote of the Queen's "going ostentatiously to eat with Disraeli in his ghetto," but not since dining with Melbourne at Brocket had Victoria visited her Prime Minister.

With events turning public opinion around, Disraeli began pressing for an armistice and mediation before the Russians got anywhere near Constantinople. Lady Derby kept at Carnarvon to resist "the wonderful chief," and Derby himself needed little persuasion. A new bias had entered his vocabulary via Mary and Shuvalov. In an almost Gladstonian message to Salisbury, Derby professed nothing but "friendship and goodwill" toward Disraeli but added, "He believes thoroughly in 'prestige'—as all foreigners [do]." Suddenly the Prime Minister, to one of the most genuinely tolerant of men, had become a "foreigner."

Derby was reacting to Disraeli's frank statement in the Cabinet, "The country is asleep and I want to wake it," but Plevna had already done that. Its siege had dominated the news for weeks and its importance was clear. Although the town in Bulgaria (now called Pleven), just south of the Danube, was remote from the straits, the Turks had no defenses behind it on the road to Adrianople, the last stronghold before the capital. The Turks would be forced in any settlement to relinquish more if they lost more. Meanwhile, thirty thousand Turkish prisoners from Plevna were prodded northward through Romania, poorly clothed and fed, and in subzero weather. Nearly half of them died.

Whether or not a war would be, as Derby warned, "unpopular and unprofitable," Disraeli felt that only a realistic expectation of English intervention would stop the Russians, and the Czar's regime was aware that dissension among Disraeli's closest Ministers still left armed involvement remote. Through Mary Derby, every argument raised in the Cabinet found its way to St. Petersburg. Unaware how little sympathy Salisbury had for warlike moves to prop up what was left of Turkey, as he saw no crisis as yet affecting English interests, Disraeli reminded him that "the great culprit"—Lady Derby—kept Whitehall from being taken seriously by Russia. "Mischievous gossip," he warned, was causing their every decision to be "betrayed," which made it impossible to convince the Russian military of his determination.

Since the "culprit" was Salisbury's stepmother, and the culprit's husband, the most unreliable member of the Cabinet, had been almost a surrogate son to Disraeli, the leaks continued into the new year, now with an added fillip. The congenial Shuvalov

Neutrality Under Difficulties. *Punch*, August 5, 1876. The pro-Turkey (or anti-Russia) Prime Minister attempts official indifference toward Ottoman outrages in the Balkans. *Punch*'s caption: Dizzy: "Bulgarian Atrocities! I can't find them in the 'Official Reports'!!!"

had become a frequent visitor at the Stratford Place home of Liberal stalwart Sir William Harcourt, who fancied himself a future Prime Minister. Through Mary Derby and the ingratiating envoy of an unfriendly power, the Opposition was receiving details of secret Cabinet discussions. Derby recognized his disloyalty, but the enticements of his wife were overwhelming, and he was now drinking heavily. Although on the edge of breakdown, he remained Foreign Minister as long as Disraeli was unwilling to pay the political price of letting him defect to Gladstone.

Disraeli made no secret of his intention to send the fleet to hold Gallipoli if the Russians only pretended to consider peace talks while relentlessly advancing on Adrianople. The anti-Turk Ponsonby told Carnarvon, who shared his views, "So I went to Church with a curious heart, and joined in the war psalm 'Let God Arise' including the words 'there is little Benjamin their ruler.'" Ponsonby's Gladstonian bias is clear from his apparently deliberate misquotation of Psalm 68, which includes a line relating to the hierarchy of the tribes of Israel, "There is little Benjamin *with* their ruler, the princes of Judah." The tribe of Benjamin, youngest son of Jacob, was the smallest and least powerful.

Derby took to his bed from alleged overwork, although his work largely had been that of conduit to Shuvalov through Mary. The Queen again pressed for his resignation and urged Disraeli to take the job himself as no one else could be trusted. "Lord D will *do nothing, originate nothing,* and besides is indiscreet & leaves our Ambassadors *abroad* without instructions.... What can be the *cause* of Lord Derby's incredible conduct?"

Although Victoria suggested names to reconstitute the Cabinet after the expected pacifist defections, on January 26, 1878, Disraeli backed down and again ordered the British flotilla away from Constantinople. The Queen despaired. Disraeli would open a Cabinet meeting by quoting a stern message from her that they stand firm, and remind Russia "that any advance on Constantinople would free us from neutrality," but he was without a majority of his own Ministers. Aware of every sentence uttered in Cabinet, Gladstone considered Victoria's conduct unconstitutional, and "an outrage." It was a paradox that the Queen visible to her public was not the one who administered wiggings to her Ministers but the reclusive widow in a bonnet who went for carriage rides in the Highlands with her ladies.

Early in 1878 Disraeli was beginning to recover from his physicians. It was just in time. On January 2 his Colonial Minister, Carnarvon, made a speech undercutting his own government by declaring that any repetition of the Crimean War would be "insane." Both Disraeli and the Queen reprimanded him, normally an invitation to resign, but both Salisbury and Derby urged him to stay. Still playing both sides, Salisbury urged Carnarvon on January 8, "Providence has put in our hands the trust of keeping the country from entering on a wrongful war. Do not renounce such a task on account of a rude phrase by a man whose insolence is proverbial." In the Salisbury-Disraeli relationship over the years since the Marquis was only Robert Cecil, the insolence had been entirely on his side, but Carnarvon preferred to believe the untruth, and announced that he would remain so as to promote his views.

Disappointed, the Queen, in order to back up her hesitant Prime Minister, offered him, as symbolism, the Garter. In the circumstances it would have looked bad, he realized. He declined in a letter she described as "beautiful." As for the Czar's people, she exploded to him, "Oh if the Queen were a man, she would like to go and give those horrid Russians whose word one cannot trust such a beating."

Parliament opened on January 17, earlier than usual, to vote Disraeli £6 million in military credits, and at the price of Carnarvon's resignation, the authority to send Admiral Sir Geoffrey Hornby's fleet into the Dardanelles. The decision also prompted Derby to resign, his first move beyond apathy in weeks.

Just as Disraeli thought he had taken control of events—he had even received the Queen's blessing to replace Derby with Salisbury—everything unraveled. The excuse for sending in the ironclads had been that Russia had "excluded" the straits from the agenda of a proposed congress to settle the Eastern Question, but a decoding error was discovered which had inverted the operative word from *include*. Disraeli had to recall the fleet, which gave Derby an excuse to return. The Queen was outraged. Disraeli had to write to explain that his war credits were otherwise in jeopardy. Yet both Derby and Carnarvon, who also returned to the Cabinet, were only back to block any bellicose action. It was Disraeli's most embarrassing moment in public office. He appeared weak and unable to project a policy. But in the Cabinet itself, power had begun to shift. The two returnees were almost without portfolio. No one consulted them. Salisbury, seeing his future assured if Disraeli came out of the crisis honorably, and recognizing that playing into the hands of the excitable Carnarvon and the broken Derby would bring him down as well, decided that Britain's interest might be at least as important as that of the Balkan Christians.

"I expect to hear shortly of a disgraceful peace," Disraeli had prophesied to Lady Chesterfield, and indeed on January 31, bereft of any support whatever by British indecisiveness, the Turks signed an armistice at Adrianople that foreshadowed the harsh terms of a future settlement. At the Corn Exchange in Oxford, Gladstone crowed that his object in eighteen months of passionate campaigning had been achieved—to "counter-work as well as I could what I believe to be the purpose of Lord Beaconsfield."

With Monty Corry in nervous collapse from overwork, Disraeli was almost on his own. The Elysian Fields seemed much less blissful. "The mask has fallen," Disraeli wrote to Lady Bradford (February 1) about Gladstone. Beneath the "pious Xtian" was a "vindictive fiend." A few days later the Commons was convulsed by a false report that the Russians had occupied Constantinople, and war seemed imminent. Tension faded once the rumor was scotched, yet the armistice quickly was violated by the Russians, who exploited the military helplessness of the Turks. The news strengthened Disraeli's hand in the Cabinet, as did the harsh terms exacted by the Russians, details of which were leaking out of San Stefano, where the negotiations were taking place. "The Queen is as violent as anyone," Derby noted in his diary on February 10, and felt "that her Ministers had deceived & misled her." After the next Cabinet meeting on February 14 Derby was "ill-pleased & despondent," yet "relieved" by a visit from "Shou," the familiar and tireless Shuvalov, who had come to pry the details from him.

The altered situation, Shuvalov told Derby, was "as bad as it can be," as war fever in England had begun to overwhelm Gladstone's exhortations. Still, three times in February Disraeli instructed the fleet to steam into the straits, ostensibly to protect British lives and property, only to withdraw the orders on assurances from Russia that it would not encroach upon the waterway. In Constantinople, rude posters in the guise of an advertisement materialized on city walls, one even affixed to the door of the British Embassy: "Lost: between Besika Bay and the Sultan's Palace, a fleet of six fine ironclads, bearing the English flag. Anyone communicating to Lord Beaconsfield information as to their whereabouts will be suitably rewarded."

While the public may have thought that Disraeli was practicing a game of bluff, the reality, well known to the Russians, was continued division in Whitehall. With no allies and collapse imminent, the Turks signed an abject peace treaty, full terms of which only reached London on March 23. The clauses left Turkey only a fingernail in Europe across the Dardanelles; they also created a swollen Bulgaria (a Russian puppet) extending south to the Aegean Sea, and ceded to Russia fifty miles of Black Sea coast in Asia. Confident of backing by Austria and Germany, the Russians agreed to a congress in Berlin to afford the great powers an opportunity to ratify the *diktat*.

The Queen was not only alarmed; she was furious, especially after Derby rose in the Lords to confirm the Government's continuing passivity. "This *really* is *too serious*," she told Disraeli, "and he *ought* to go. You *injure* the Government *most seriously* if such things happen; *all confidence* in our conduct and *intentions* is completely shaken." It was more than an indirect tongue-lashing of Derby; Disraeli knew it was meant for him. She had seen his "strong, firm, determined tone" disappear, and warned, "Remember[,] *vacillation* and *delay* will be *ruinous* to the country, not to speak of the Government. Lord Derby *must* go, for HE is believed abroad to be THE person who *acts* and NO ONE trusts him! What use is there in keeping him?"

With public as well as Court pressure to protect British interests, the ailing Disraeli finally secured Derby's second and final resignation—Carnarvon had already gone—on March 27 when the Cabinet voted to call up reserves and to send troops from India to Malta in readiness to occupy Cyprus and Alexandretta (now Iskendrun), on the southern Turkish coast east of Cyprus. The German Crown Princess, one of Victoria's ears to Continental intelligence, congratulated her on Derby's exit, and reported that it had changed perceptions about how far Russia would be permitted to extend its power.

Employing the Indians and making the orders dramatically known, Disraeli explained to the Queen on April 12, were intended to have a European impact. "After all the sneers of our

"Going to Congress." *Fun*, June 12, 1878. Parodying Millais's *The Huguenot, Fun* shows Disraeli bidding good-bye to an unhappy Gladstone and departing for Berlin.

not having any great military force, the imagination of the Continent will be much affected by the first appearance of what they will believe to be an inexhaustible supply of men." What he did not add was that drawing on "native" soldiers also alleviated fears at home that Russophobia could cost British lives. But in the Lords, Derby announced his departure with dire warnings about unidentified warlike conspiracies. Inviting a tart rebuke from the Queen, he duly received one; yet, having drawn a large attendance in the Lords, he was pleased that "there can be no more talk," he wrote on April 8 in his now erratic journal, "of my being incapacitated by health," or of "failure of nerves." He thought, he added six days later, that he had "gained by resignation," and indeed he had gained the good opinion of Gladstone, whose party he would eventually join. He praised his own "moral courage" and described Disraeli, his friend of thirty years, as "utterly without scruple." In the reconstitution of the Cabinet, with Hardy—a man of substantial means—moving to the Lords as Earl of Cranbrook, Frederick Stanley, Derby's brother and heir, was named to the War Office. Derby despised him—and Disraeli had twisted the knife.

Ostensible war preparations went on, this time with popular support. Henry James, now living on Bolton Street, just off Piccadilly, wrote to an American friend, "London smells of gunpowder, and the tawdry old Jew who is at the head of this great old British Empire would like immensely to wind up his career with a fine long cannonade." (From the distance of Paris, imperial aims for Britain had seemed worthwhile, but now, closer to the bellicose crowds in the streets, James found the cause of the Turks "a shabby one," and resorted to reflex anti-Semitism.) Speaking in Manchester before eighteen hundred delegates of provincial Liberal organizations on April 30, John Bright lapsed into uncharacteristic bigotry, fulminating against a Prime Minister who was preparing to shed English blood when he had "not one single drop of English blood in his veins." *Punch* on the other hand offered a "parody for the prudent," claiming, "We don't want to go to war; for, by jingo, if we do, we may lose our ships, and lose our men, and what's worse, our money too."

Elevated from the India Office to the Foreign Office, Lord Salisbury expected in June to head the British delegation to the Berlin Congress agreed upon by Russia and the prostrate Turks. Victoria did not want Disraeli to go on grounds that he was "far from strong." Still, he urged his own presence on grounds of his clout. If the German delegation were to be headed by Bismarck, he felt that he had to appear, and the Prince of Wales argued that only Disraeli's presence would prove "that we are really in earnest." Besides, Disraeli wanted to go. Unlike Metternich, to whom he had played pupil, he had never been involved in an international conference, and saw Berlin as the last possibility in his lifetime to star on the world's stage.

As was the practice, much of the outcome was prearranged. Salisbury's Christian sentiments coincided with the suspect pieties of Shuvalov in pressing the Turks to agree to station no troops, during the period of the Congress, anywhere in Rumelia, the southern sector of Bulgaria where massacres had occurred. From the Porte, Salisbury also obtained agreement to cede Cyprus—to protect Turkey's flanks as well as provide Britain with a base to defend Suez.* As a gesture of good will, although there were few Christians in the Sultan's Asiatic domains, he promised the Powers that they would be protected. And while all arrangements were subject to ratification at Berlin, they were all communicated in advance to Bismarck as president of the Congress, enabling him to set a date in mid-June. Only the question of exactly how much of the Ottoman Empire would survive seemed in suspense.

Traveling with Monty Corry and several aides, but no physician, Disraeli took four days and three nights for his journey, sleeping at Calais, Brussels (where he dined with Leopold II), and Cologne. At eight on the evening of June 11 he arrived at the Kaiserhof in Berlin, where a message awaited that Bismarck hoped to see him that evening. Seventy-three and exhausted despite the leisurely pace of his journey, Disraeli pondered making excuses, then thought the better of it, and turned up at 10:30.

Bismarck had recalled little about Disraeli from their only meeting, in London, accepting his reputation as a "romantically oratorical semite" whose honor and reliability were questionable. Count Münster, his ambassador in England, filled him in with a report describing the Prime Minister as "very vain and enfeebled by age," but still capable of "illuminating and brilliant ideas." He also reported the open anti-Semitism of Disraeli's "own colleagues and former ministers," who were heard to say that "a British minister would never have done that." It was the first time, Münster

---

*Before leaving for Berlin, Salisbury joked to Northcote (June 6, 1878) about an "imaginary calendar of events" in which the Daily News, discovering the cession of Cyprus, "conclusively proves that the idea of taking Cyprus could only have occurred to the Semitic instincts of the Prime Minister."

said, that the Prime Minister's Jewish descent was being used against him within his own government. What Disraeli knew about Bismarck came from Lord Odo Russell, his envoy in Berlin, and from the Queen and her daughter Vicky, the German crown princess. Both women detested Bismarck as an egomaniacal intriguer with a gigantic appetite for food and drink—and power.

"Not unsatisfactory," Disraeli telegraphed to Victoria. "It was sixteen years since we met," he wrote to Lady Bradford. "I should not have recognised him. Then, he was a very tall man with black hair, a puggish nose and pallid face and a waist like a wasp. Now, he is a giant, his face ruddy, his locks and head [and broad mustache] silvery-white, and enormously stout; on the whole, a very effective appearance." They talked for an hour and a quarter. After that the days of the Congress became long ceremonial ones of receptions and dinners, punctuated by large-scale meetings at which agreements were ratified and preceded by private talks at which they were provisionally made. Germany was still in its first decade as a unified nation, and the regime was eager to demonstrate that it could do things on a Great Power scale.

But for Bismarck, Disraeli overshadowed the other participants, and he was content to be regarded in his host's country as an equal. The amorous Count Shuvalov had also come to Berlin, leaving Madame Novikov behind in England to sustain anti-Turk sentiment. At the Congress his superior was Prince Gortchakov, at eighty still the Czar's chancellor, and to Disraeli "an old coxcomb." The able and shrewd Count Andrassy represented Austria, and for France, recovering from defeat and the chaos (in Paris) of the Commune, Georges Waddington presented the Republic's claims to a continuing interest in the Middle East in the face of such affronts as the British encroachment upon Suez. Representing the Sultan, Pasha Carathéodory had the unfortunate role of ratifying the amputations of Turkish territory and hoping to survive his return home.

Disraeli made his opening address in English, Russell having convinced him not to use his inelegant French. The myths about his "catastrophic" French are many, yet Disraeli had spent many months over a lifetime in France, and while he was no Talleyrand, he could manage the language. But Odo Russell, ever the diplomat, observed that the assembled plenipotentiaries would be disappointed if he did not use the language in which he had distinguished himself. "They know that they have here in you the greatest master of English oratory, and are looking forward to your speech in English as the intellectual treat of their lives."

Lord Beaconsfield fixed his glass to his eye, a gesture employed to gain time for thought, and said, "There is much force in what you say. I will consider the point." If he saw through the flattery, he kept that to himself.

A week into the Congress, Salisbury complained to his wife about Disraeli's incapacities, into much of which can be read his annoyance at being upstaged. A great burly bear of a man, balding and full-bearded, he was a physical counterpart to the older Bismarck, but the frail Prime Minister was the focus of interest. Baron Tauchnitz had all of Disraeli's novels for sale in Berlin's many bookshops, and the rental libraries ran out of their stocks. Berliners followed Disraeli's entourage and searched for stories about him in their newspapers. Irritated, Salisbury wrote, "What with deafness, ignorance of French and Bismarck's extraordinary mode of speech, Beaconsfield has [only] the dimmest idea of what is going on, understands everything crossways and imagines a perpetual conspiracy." Yet Disraeli's French was adequate, and his rapport with Prince Bismarck—he had been elevated—was taking hold. As Bismarck told Count von Radowitz, "In spite of his fantastic novel-writing, [Disraeli] is a capable statesman. It was easy to transact business with him: in a quarter of an hour you knew exactly how you stood with him, the limits to which he was prepared to go were exactly defined."

On one evening they dined almost alone. "He was in the bosom of his family," Disraeli wrote Lady Bradford, "the Princess, a daughter, 2 sons, and a married niece. . . . After dinner he and I retired and smoked. It is the last blow to my shattered constitution, but had I refrained from smoking I should have made no way. So we spent a couple of memorable hours." Among other things they discussed Gladstone, who Disraeli prophesied, relaxed by the Chancellor's brandy and cigars, would die in a monastery or in a madhouse. Bismarck guessed that when Gladstone felt politically played out, he would create a sensation by "going over" to Rome, and that if he became a widower, the Pope would create him a Cardinal. After the Congress, Bismarck remained an admirer of Disraeli. In his office he would point out to visitors, "There hangs the portrait of my Sovereign; there on the right that of my wife; and on the left, there, that of Lord Beaconsfield."

Disraeli, so Bismarck realized, remained the one with whom to do business. Not only was he the ultimate authority, he was the embodiment of British Russophobia, to which the Congress had to answer, while Salisbury's record showed him to be more pro-

"Façon de Parler!" *Punch*, June 22, 1878. Bismarck and Disraeli parleying in Berlin.

Christian than pro-Turk. On details, however, it was Salisbury who counted—Disraeli had never been interested in them, and his lassitude made them now impossible. Once, when he dozed off and someone commiserated about the exhaustion of the conference, he quipped, "Oh, no! It is time that tires me."

Time, in the presence of the past, also materialized in Berlin. The once-widowed Lady Charlotte Guest, who had attracted the dandyish Disraeli of bachelor days, was there, remarried, as Lady Charlotte Schreiber. On June 17 he "subsided into an armchair beside me," she wrote in her diary, "where he remained a long time, and, until someone was brought up to be introduced, we talked of old times, of Spain, of the East." She found a Tauchnitz edition of *Alroy* and two days later had finished it and began Goethe's *Wilhelm Meister*, which she did not know had been one of the inspirations for Disraeli's *Contarini Fleming*.

Disraeli's priority in the afternoon plenary sessions around the horseshoe table in the Radziwill Palace was to retain for Turkey as much of its European territory as furnished a defensive buffer for the Dardanelles. Greece eyed the Aegean coast of Thrace, awarded to Bulgaria but at Britain's insistence returned to Turkey. Disraeli told Bismarck's *vortragender Rat*, Lothar Bucher, coldly, in German, "Greece is a young state, and when you're young you can"—and he shifted to English for emphasis—"*afford to wait.*"

There was no contiguous Turkish territory for Bismarck to seize, enabling him to remain above the battle, and when France wanted something for its involvement, Salisbury suggested "protecting" the loosely held Ottoman sheikdom across the Mediterranean, Tunis. "Do what you like there," said Salisbury in a burst of Christian generosity akin to his feelings about European Turkey. "You will be obliged to take it. You cannot leave Carthage in the hands of the barbarians."

When Waddington reported the "offer," Salisbury denied it, telling Disraeli, "He makes me talk of Tunis and Carthage as if they had been my own personal property, and I was making him a liberal wedding present." But he conceded that the "general tenor" was accurate. By 1881, Tunis was under the Tricolor.

Toward the close of the Congress, the Russians gave in to

Disraeli's refusal to permit Bulgaria access to the Aegean but insisted that the Sultan could not garrison what would remain of Turkish Bulgaria. Disraeli had only just survived an asthmatic collapse—possibly brought on by Bismarck's cigars—that had kept him to his bed and prompted Corry to call Dr. Kidd from London. Despite his shaky condition, Disraeli threatened to walk out and asked Corry to summon a special train. Realizing that Disraeli was not bluffing, Bismarck leaned on the Russians. Whether Corry had called for the train before the Czar yielded or only before the concession arrived from St. Petersburg is irrelevant. Turkey retained its rump of the Balkans.

Alexander II would speak bitterly of the Congress as "a European coalition against Russia, under Bismarck," but the Chancellor felt that he had saved Russia from a disastrous war which might have ended in revolution and the end of the line of czars. Ironically, Austria's gain of Bosnia and Hercegovina, a transfer of vassalage, would, in 1914, ignite an even greater war and the end of monarchies in Austria and Germany as well as in Russia.

Although Disraeli had not won on the issue of keeping Turkish areas on the eastern shore of the Black Sea from the Russians, he was able to claim to the Queen that he had kept Russia out of the Mediterranean. Strategically, it was far more significant than the acquisition of Cyprus, news that leaked out before the signing to embarrass Disraeli at home. He would make something of Cyprus anyway as a shield for Suez, and Bismarck predicted to him, "It will be popular: a nation likes progress." Despite territorial gains, Russia had been thwarted, and Turkey, in a fashion, resuscitated, without a reprise of the Crimean War. Every Christian had not been plucked from the Sultan's sway, but the Balkans and the Caucasus over the centuries had become, through conversion, intermarriage, and the movement of peoples, an ethnic muddle that would leave, whatever the political boundaries to come, intermingled Muslims and Christians chafing under each other's rule.

Returning by train and Channel steamer to Dover, Disraeli stepped onto a platform at Charing Cross station that had been red-carpeted and bedecked with flowers in one of the few efficient operations by Lord Henry Lennox as First Commissioner of

Works. Cheering throngs, including such dignitaries, Disraeli wrote to Lady Bradford, as "the Romantic Baroness," Angela Burdett-Coutts, watched each carriage until he exited on the arm of Lord Salisbury, and others craned from hotel and office windows in the Strand as the dignitaries emerged. It was the largest and most enthusiastic gathering of Londoners since the ceremonies of thanksgiving for the recovery of the Prince of Wales. And in a way it was another thanksgiving.

In a bigoted barb, "Tay Pay" O'Connor remarked, "These multitudes of free English Christians [were] cheering the man who had given back more than a million of Christians to the most degrading slavery, as if he had conferred an everlasting honour upon the name of England, and had most at heart the interests of Christendom." What further convicted the noble Earl, he claimed, was that he was seen to grasp the hand of a frail old man of ninety-five who had been brought forward to greet him by Lennox—Sir Moses Montefiore. It proved to O'Connor "the triumph of Judea, a Jewish policy, a Jew. The Hebrew, who drove through those crowds to Downing Street, was dragging the whole of Christendom behind the Juggernaut car."

The "Juggernaut" was the open barouche in which the Prime Minister, still in his gray traveling coat, rode with Salisbury to Whitehall. At 10 Downing Street, Sir Henry Ponsonby waited to do his duty, a congratulatory letter from the Queen in his hand. Brandishing it, Disraeli assured cheering crowds, sharing the glory, "Lord Salisbury and I have brought you back peace—but a peace I hope with honour."* Making sly fun of Britain's gain, Bernard Shaw's *Caesar and Cleopatra* (1898), the subtext of which is Victorian England, has Caesar offer the Queen's brother, Ptolemy, "a present of Cyprus" in lieu of Egypt. "But Cyprus is of no use to anybody," Ptolemy's chancellor protests. Caesar shrugs, "No matter; you shall have it for the sake of peace."

"Peace with honor," explains Caesar's English slave, Britannus, slyly, "*anticipating a later statesman.*"

*Almost certainly Disraeli intended to recall Lord John Russell's unlucky remark in a speech in September 1853, on the eve of the Crimean War, in which he said, "If peace cannot be maintained with honour, it is no longer peace."

Even more artfully, Shaw had earlier ended his sardonic comedy *Arms and the Man* (1894)—about a Balkan war yet to take place, impoverished Bulgaria's successful defense against Serbia in 1885–86—with the pompous Major Saranoff contending admiringly of the businesslike Swiss soldier-of-fortune, Captain Bluntschli, "What a man! Is he a man!" It may have been covert parody. Only an aficionado of the British Museum Reading Room would have known that J. C. Bluntschli had written a critique of the Congress of Berlin, *"Die Organisation des europäischen Staatenvereines"* in *Die Gegenwart (The Present Time)* in 1878. And in Berlin, word had quickly emerged about Bismarck's surprising praise of Disraeli, *"Der alte Jude, das ist der Mann!"*

XXVIII

"EVERYTHING, THEY SAY, COMES TOO LATE.
IT IS SOMETHING IF IT COMES."

1878–1880

IN THE MONTH OF HIS GREATEST FAME, DAZZLED BY ADULATION YET exhausted by his frailties, Disraeli made the crucial error of his long Ministry. Parliament then could exercise authority for seven years; the Conservative Government still had two and a half years of its mandate. Had he called for new elections on his triumphal return from Berlin, his mandate would have been renewed with enormous majorities. On August 10 the idea was discussed in the Cabinet—and rejected. Few could see any shadow looming in the high noon of Tory prestige.

At the Queen's invitation, Disraeli traveled to Osborne soon after his return from Berlin to receive her thanks and furnish details about the conference and its participants. Victoria was particularly interested in the almost mythic Bismarck, "who talked very loosely and carelessly about everything." The Prime Minister was now willing to accept the Garter if Lord Salisbury were similarly invested. In his diary on July 16, 1878, Carnarvon complained that Salisbury had been "completely effaced by Disraeli and patronised by him—a very curious spectacle." Their ovations, Carnarvon preferred to think, were "very much the result of the hatred of Gladstone."

Berlin infused Disraeli with new confidence. Reporting to Parliament on his mission, he began, "My Lords, in laying on the table . . . , as I am about to do, the protocols of the Congress of Berlin"—but while he spoke, marshaling his details from only a half-sheet of notepaper, the table remained bare. Realizing that the sheaf of official documents was actually on the bench at the Prime Minister's side, the Marquis of Salisbury tugged at Disraeli's coattail to remind him to pick them up, but he saw them only as he concluded and sat down. Taking up the tape-tied packet, he rose again and tossed it erratically onto the table, narrowly missing Lord Redesdale.

Irked by the climate of praise, Gladstone wrote to Disraeli on July 30 to protest his referring to the notorious Corn Exchange attack at Oxford—quoted in *The Times*—as a speech in which "I described you as a dangerous devilish character." Also, *The Times* had quoted Disraeli as charging that Gladstone had heatedly "indulged in criticisms complete with the most offensive epithets." He demanded the evidence, and Disraeli promptly responded that Gladstone had claimed that "the great name of England" was "degraded and debased" by the Prime Minister. "In the same spirit . . . at Southwark, Lord Beaconsfield was charged with 'an act of duplicity of which every Englishman should be ashamed.' With regard to the epithet 'devilish' which Lord Beaconsfield used in the House of Lords, he is informed that it was not Mr Gladstone at Hawarden who compared Lord Beaconsfield to Mephistopheles but only one of Mr Gladstone's friends, timidly inquiring how they were to 'get rid of this Mephistopheles'; but, as Mr Gladstone proceeded to explain the mode, . . . Lord Beaconsfield may perhaps be excused for assuming that Mr Gladstone sanctioned the propriety of the scarcely complimentary appellation."

Gladstone's gorge rose at the cold, third-person form in which the reply was couched as well as at the evidence presented, "and [he] follows to his regret," he wrote, "his Lordship's example in laying aside the mode of address which had been honoured between them." His "impressions," Gladstone contended, related "to policy and not to character." But he admitted using "strong language," alleging in return that in 1854 Disraeli had accused the Earl of Aberdeen, then Prime Minister, "individually to be the cause of the Crimean War just declared." Further, "it has always been the study of Mr Gladstone to speak freely on public measures," and he observed that Lord Beaconsfield had followed that practice as well. Disraeli put the matter aside, not even mentioning Gladstone's charges about "the most deadly mischief which *that alien* would drag [us] into"—that Disraeli was "going to annex England to his native East & make it the appanage of an Asiatic empire." The wild accusations had appeared in the August 15, 1877, and May 27, 1878, issues of *The Nineteenth Century.*

For the public, the events abroad overshadowed, for some months, hard economic times at home. Demand for industrial products slumped and, although bad weather had reduced crops, agricultural prices fell. Even the usually hostile Father John Henry Newman confided to Lord Blachford that, perhaps for the first time in his life, he was "much dazzled" with Disraeli's "fine work" at Berlin. "It is a grand idea[,] that of hugging from love the Turk to death, instead of the Russian bear, which, as a poem or a romance, finds a weak part in my imagination."

Having, as a young man, written an anti-Semitic diatribe against Disraeli in the guise of a novel critique for the *North American Review,* James Russell Lowell, after a career as a poet, had become a diplomat, and in July 1878 was soon to move from Minister to Spain, where he had been friendly with Layard, to the American legation in London. To Charles Eliot Norton in Massachusetts, commenting from Madrid on the Congress, he wrote, "I think if Beaconsfield were not a Jew, people would think him rather fine. But they can't get over an hereditary itch." And to Thomas Hughes in England, author of *Tom Brown's School Days,* Lowell wrote later in the year, "I am satisfied that Dizzy's policy has done a great deal to restore the prestige of England. . . ; and as I back the English race against the field, I am not sorry for it." (He also liked the Turks when compared to the "barbarism" of the Russians.) "And then I think a good deal of the prejudice against Beaconsfield"—he had apparently got over his own—"is

Figures from a "Triumph" (A Relief—on the Road to Berlin). *Punch*, June 15, 1878. Lord Beaconsfield and Lord Salisbury (the Foreign Secretary) on their way to expected triumphs at the Berlin Congress.

mediaeval, of a piece with the enlightened public opinion which dictated the legend of Hugh of Lincoln."* Further, he suggested that Disraeli's rise to Prime Minister was "a modern version . . . of the story of Joseph."

Even the famed cutlers of Sheffield—in one of the industries affected by depressed prices and unemployment—demonstrated their appreciation, presenting the Prime Minister with a pair of carving knives. " 'Peace with Honour,' is engraven on the handles," *Vanity Fair*, which published a "Spy" caricature of Disraeli

---

*The first invention of "ritual murder" was to explain the disappearance of William of Norwich in 1244. An apostate Jew claimed that William had been killed by local Jews to reenact the Crucifixion and to provide blood for the baking of Passover matzohs. When the unmolested body of the boy was found, Jews already arrested were released, but William was canonized anyway, and a shrine erected to him, the beginning of centuries of similar allegations across Europe and the Middle East, usually at Easter. When Hugh of Lincoln disappeared in 1255, ritual murder was again claimed, and a vividly imaginative narrative by Matthew Paris, a Benedictine chronicler, of the alleged killing stirred up massacres of Jews and led to the expulsion of the survivors from England in 1290, a royal directive that remained in force until rescinded by Oliver Cromwell in 1658.

and Corry titled "Power and Place," observed. "It is only natural to suppose that the gift is an expression of admiration by the donors for his Lordship's artistic vivisection of Turkey."

There was a rush of Disraeli mugs, jugs, and octagonal plates, including one with his scene of triumph at Berlin. Painters vied to do his portrait, and James McNeill Whistler, who like Disraeli had been immortalized by *Vanity Fair*, and had produced a remarkable canvas of Carlyle, traveled to Hughenden in September to ask the Prime Minister to sit for him. Henry Graves, a publisher of prints with a gallery at 48 Pall Mall, had offered a thousand pounds for a portrait from which he could make a plate. "Everything was most wonderful," the painter told Alan Cole. "We were the two artists together—recognising each other at a glance! 'If I sit to anyone, it will be to you, Mr Whistler,' were Disraeli's last words as he left me at the gate. And then he sat to [John] Millais!"

It was understandable. Visually, the figure in *Arrangement in Grey and Black, No. 2*,* with tired eyes looking out over the craggy, worn face, is Carlyle to history. But Whistler had required so many sittings, and so many daubings-out and new sittings, that Carlyle had escaped and let a model pose in his long black cloak. Disraeli had no time for that kind of adulation.

The pictures of the period, and the photographs, show an impeccably dressed and coiffed Disraeli who understood that a public figure was always sitting for his portrait. With Mary Anne gone, he now wore a frock coat that was a perfect fit, and had his hair attended to in London by a fashionable hairdresser who re-dyed his locks—there was hardly now more than the one atop his head to curl—and gummed and shaped the imperial on his chin. When the Prime Minister retired, he tied a large handkerchief over his precious curl to keep it in place.

In the aftermath of Berlin, Sir Eric Barrington of the British delegation wrote to Constance Rothschild Flower, who had married Cyril Flower (later Lord Battersea), "Lord Beaconsfield . . . has been a great lion here: the *Lion of Judah!* Though Austria may be the only country really satisfied with the decisions of the Con-

*No. 1 was "Whistler's Mother."

gress there is no doubt that he will have made England pre-eminent among the nations." Almost certainly choosing his timing to coincide with the Congress's preservation of Asian Turkey, the anti-Semitic Gyösö von Istóczy spoke in Austria's Hungarian Diet in Budapest (June 24, 1878) to promote the idea of a Jewish state in Turkish Palestine which would accept allegedly unassimilable Jews from eastern Europe and reconnect them with a land which needed the economic stability they would bring. Political conditions, he felt, were becoming ripe for a restoration of the state "from which they have been expelled for 1,800 years." Istóczy looked to European statesmen of Jewish "race"—such as Disraeli—to take the initiative.

If Disraeli received reports of the speech, as was likely, it may have awakened memories of his own prophecies. He was too old and ailing for initiatives of his own, but not for employing his good offices for enterprises of others, as he did when Laurence Oliphant proposed a utopian scheme to help solve at least part of the Eastern Question. Oliphant wanted to capitalize a company under a grant of authority from the Sultan to build roads and railways in Palestine. He also wanted the Sultan to permit Jews of the troubled areas of eastern Europe to settle agricultural communities there. Oliphant had approached the Prince of Wales and Princess Helena (Princess Christian of Schleswig-Holstein since her marriage), and it was the Princess who wrote to Disraeli on November 11, 1878. Later in the month the Prince held a house party at Sandringham to give Oliphant an opportunity to talk to the Prime Minister, the Foreign Secretary, and the Austrian ambassador, Count Beust. In January 1879, armed with letters of introduction from Disraeli and Salisbury, Oliphant left for Beirut, hoping to convince the Ottoman authorities that a Jewish homeland under British protection would benefit their empire and further block Russian encroachment. With Ambassador Layard's help, Oliphant was able to talk to the Sultan about a concession, but his Ministers objected. The idea was dropped when Gladstone returned to office and interest from Downing Street disappeared, only to be reawakened a generation later when the plan found its Sidonia in the Rothschilds.

Layard told his friend Lady Augusta Gregory that Oliphant

"didn't think I had given him enough support, but he himself put a stopper on it by telling the Sultan's secretary that he was seeking to fulfil the [prophecy in] Scripture that the end of the world was to come when the Jews were restored to their native land; and his Majesty had no desire to hurry that event."

Disraeli could hardly call public attention to Jewish interests, as printers of scurrilous diatribes seemed to be working overtime. *Ben-Dizzy the Bold!* emanated from the London firm of R. Buckmaster of 46 Newnington Butts. At threepence for a fifteen-page pamphlet it was expensive, but the listed price may have meant nothing if it were distributed by a political client. Ostensibly "By a True Briton," it charged,

> *The chief of the clan still nurtures a plan*
> *of a Palestine free as of yore.*
> *A Palestine free! and its Emperor, HE!*
> *the wonderful strategist Ben:*
> *To all which we say, Good luck to the day!*
> *we fervently wish it. Amen.*

Gladstone's diary records his enjoying a similar scurrility. Written in mock-biblical prose, *The Book of Benjamin* was a tuppence pamphlet published by Charles Watts of 84 Fleet Street:

> Now it came to pass in the six-and-thirtieth year of the reign of Victoria, and in the fifth month of the year,* that Benjamin of Israel . . . went down unto his house to rest. And as he lay on his couch meditating upon things past and things to come, he fell into a trance. And in the trance he heard as it were a voice speaking unto him, but beheld no man. . . . And the voice said: Arise, then, awake from thy sleep, O Benjamin, for thou art chosen to bear a message unto the people of this land. And Benjamin answered and said: Who am I, and what is my father's house, that this should be given

*Since Victoria became Queen in 1837, the "dream" is placed in May 1873, the year before Disraeli became Prime Minister for the second time.

unto me? And behold, now, I am not of their race and religion; peradventure they will not listen to my words—yea, they will scoff at my teaching, as in days that are gone. (For aforetime Benjamin had stood forth as a prophet among the people; but they had rejected him and despised his teachings.) . . .

And the voice appeared and said: Fear not, Benjamin, for I am with thee. And lo, the people shall be smitten with blindness, so that they shall not see clearly the thing that is. Then, shall they, being blind, turn upon the man Gladstone, whom thou hatest, and shall drive him from his place, and thou shalt reign in his stead.

The Book of Benjamin went into at least five editions through 1879 and was followed by an even more snide sequel.

Another pamphlet, this one illustrated, parodied Sir Joseph Porter's song in the new hit *H.M.S. Pinafore*. In "The Pretty Little Coronet and Great Big B!" the hero sings,

When I was a youth I plied my pen,
(It's five or six years, I think, since then)
And blessed with a modest prophetic mind,
In a vacant mood I have oft designed
Upon my blotting pad in a hand so free,
A pretty little coronet and a great big B!

After many verses and choruses the saga concluded:

I feel that Providence kindly sent
Me to re-model the Parliament,
Where in tones so modest I hum this song,
That I am the only man who can't go wrong!
For this is the motto of a good To-ree,
A pretty little coronet, and a great big B!

Its mood was almost genial compared to the sneering anti-Semitism of most indictments.

A penny pamphlet, *Lord Beaconsfield Interviewed*, printed by John Heywood of John Dalton Street in Manchester and 18 Paternoster Square in London, invented what it described as a "Remarkable Statement of His Lordship." It "proved" Disraeli's fidelity to "the ancient faith" by having him explain, "Now tell me: in Europe an English or French prince who wants a throne never hesitates to change his religion. *Why should I be more nice? I am of that religion which gives me a scepter.*" And it implied that, like the family of his Sidonia and other Aragonese, Disraeli and his ilk "*secretly adhered to the ancient faith and ceremonies of their fathers*—a belief in the God of Sinai, & the rights and observances of the laws of Moses."

A broadside printed by James Robertson of Glasgow dated March 19, 1880, was titled *Imperium et Libertas?* and eschewed religion for accusations of "despotic power" and "wild war schemes." It attacked "Ben's mystic show," in which, with "trickster's skill," he misled a "Jingo rabble" with visions of "Imperial glamour." Britannia, it charged, "wears a Dizzy bauble."

Gladstone put it among his papers, along with another, printed by Robert Seager of Ipswich and dated the next day. It was a single-sheet philippic:

THE SONG OF KING BENJAMIN: A BALLAD FOR THE TIMES
As Benjamin sat on his vice-regal throne,
Surrounded by ensigns of Victoria's [he] won,
Behind and before flowed a river of gore,
From the victims of rapine and murderous gore.

Each verse (one to "Bonnie Dundee") was set to a familiar song, and one had King Benjamin himself exhort his benighted followers in rather unimaginative rhyme,

"Let parsons and publicans, Bible in hand,
Remain in firm phalanx all over this land
My reign to support, and the world shall soon sport
At the ruin my policy everywhere wrought!"

Also among Gladstone's papers is another penny polemic printed by Charles Watts:

LORD BEAKY'S LIES
AND ENGLAND'S ALLIES

The cover of the leaflet quoted Carlyle's malign description of Disraeli as "a superlative Hebrew conjuror, spell-binding all the great Lords, great Parties, great Interests of England . . . and leading them by the nose, like somnambulant cattle." The text excoriated the "witches' cauldron" stirred by "Beaconsfield, Salisbury, and Levy"—the latter was Edward Levy-Lawson, proprietor of the *Daily Telegraph*, a Gladstone supporter who had defected to the enemy. Page 41 described Disraeli as a Fagin, but the previous page eclipsed all the other diatribes in Gladstone's collection. "Chateaubriand described Talleyrand as a lump of dirt in a silk stocking," it observed. "Do we not, unfortunately, know a Hebrew *nobleman* to whom the same words might be applied, minus the silk stocking?"

From the diplomatic standpoint, Disraeli would have been pleased to be lumped with Talleyrand. From the Queen's perspective, the results of the Berlin Congress seemed concrete evidence that her imperial ambitions were succeeding, yet elements of the Empire were already unraveling. There were too many places to defend, and defense seemed to require even more acquisition—a lesson of Empire almost impossible to grasp. India appeared always to need shoring up somewhere, and the Great Game of hegemony over the buffer states between India and Russian dependencies in central Asia seemed only exacerbated by the settlement in Berlin. Toward the end of July, as Disraeli gossiped at Osborne with Victoria, a Russian mission was in Kabul working at turning the Ameer of Afghanistan against the British.

Lytton asked London's permission to counter with a British mission, and received telegraphed authority on August 3 to proceed to Kabul through Kandahar. Emboldened by his success in preparing troops to be sent to Malta, the Viceroy wanted further confrontation with Russia, which seemed intent on making Afghanistan a vassal state, and informed Sher Ali that he had to dismiss the Russians. Although the India Office warned Lytton that he was exceeding his authority, he ordered troops off anyway, under command of General Sir Neville Chamberlain, and sent them by an unapproved route, the Khyber Pass. As soon as the General was stopped by the Afghans at the border, war became certain. "When V-Roys and Comms-in-Chief disobey orders," Disraeli growled to Hardy, now Lord Cranbrook, "they ought to be sure of success in their mutiny. Lytton by disobeying orders had only secured insult and failure."

Lytton sent the Ameer's "insolent reply" to London, where Disraeli read it with a sinking heart on October 19. The Viceroy insisted that he was not a "reckless military fire-brand," but that his generals were, and that Chamberlain had already pushed off from Peshawar. Lytton extended his insubordination with an ulti-matum to Sher Ali on November 2, claiming it was his response to an affront to the British Crown. Three columns were already advancing into the hills when in Parliament on December 11 Disraeli lamely defended the policy his appointee had made for him. Sir Sam Browne, a V.C. in the Mutiny and the originator of the sword belt that bore his name, commanded a column, Gen-eral Sir Thomas Biddulph another, and General Frederick Roberts of later Boer War fame, the third. Roberts' operations sent the Ameer fleeing into Turkestan, and the British negotiated a pro-tectorate with his son, Yakub Khan, whom the Ameer had kept in prison.

Disraeli explained with some embarrassment about the son of his old crony. "His policy is perfectly fitted to a state of affairs in which Russia was our assailant. But she has sneaked out of her hostile position." Fortunately, Russia was also busy elsewhere, bringing in the harvest of the Berlin Congress. It seemed that the accidental Afghan policy had worked, and Disraeli would write loyally to Lytton a few weeks after a treaty was signed on May 31, 1879, that "it will always be a source of real satisfaction that I had the opportunity of placing you on the throne of the G[rea]t Mogul."

The race of the western European powers to seize segments of Africa had accelerated in the 1870s. Disraeli had been content, but for India and some assorted islands, to federate and manage largely empty and white-settled Canada, Australia, and New Zealand. Africa presented hostile environments as well as populations less than eager for the civilization of missionaries and traders. To operate the best-located coaling station on its pre-Suez trade routes, Britain had taken the Cape Colony from the Dutch East India Company and declared its seizure permanent in 1806. When slavery was outlawed throughout the Empire in 1834, the Dutch farmers ("Boers"), who spoke a patois they called Afrikaans, had hauled their wagons into the interior, taken new slaves, and worked land over which there was no "European" flag but their own. That had changed in 1876 when Carnarvon as Colonial Minister federated the Transvaal into a British South Africa that also included the Zulu lands abutting Natal to the east as far as the Indian Ocean. Sir Bartle Frere in Cape Town had recommended it to the Colonial Office—there were rumors of gold finds beyond the Vaal. Although Disraeli no longer had Carnarvon on his hands, he had the consequences.

In "Cape affairs," he wrote to Lady Bradford on September 27, 1878, ". . . every day brings forward a new blunder of Twitters"—Disraeli's name for his worry-prone former colleague. Bringing the independent southern African kingdoms under British suzerainty had first appeared to be a good thing—some tribes even needed and wanted protection from the Boers, who seemed grim medieval throwbacks. Zulu chieftain Cetshwayo did not, and resisted. The rearrangement looked good on paper but would not work out as hoped.

On eleven sheets of paper, on the last of which he signed "Beaconsfield," Disraeli validated his last will and testament on December 16, 1878, in the law offices of Sir Philip Rose's firm at 6 Victoria Street, Westminster. In his major bequest he left, for use during his lifetime, Hughenden Manor and its grounds to his nephew, Coningsby Ralph Disraeli.* He left to Montagu Corry all his letters, papers, and manuscripts, with authorization to dispose

---

*The very novel, Coningsby, had just been read, at long last, by Victoria—"a very remarkable, strange book" she noted in her journal on October 31, 1878. She recognized his "democratic conservatism" in it, his "large, patriotic views," and his "love for, and faith in, the Jews."

or destroy any of them as he saw fit. And other than his direction that he be buried "in the same Vault in the Churchyard of Hughenden" as his late wife, there was no mention anywhere of religion, and no directions for his funeral except that it be "conducted with the same simplicity as hers was." Appointed as his executors were Sir Nathaniel Mayer de Rothschild, eldest of Lionel's three sons, and Sir Philip Rose.

Baron Lionel's role in the interlocking family firm had been dominating, but in December 1878, at seventy, the stocky, trim-bearded financier was dying of heart disease. Disraeli considered Lionel his closest friend, the one he saw more often than anyone else in London. After Mary Anne's death, there was no address at which he could be found more often than the Rothschild home at Piccadilly Terrace, at which he needed no invitation to dine. In July 1873, newly widowered, he had written to Charlotte to ask for a present of Lionel's portrait. "My lost, or my absent friends are assembling around me in my solitude, and it pains me that the countenance of one of my dearest should be wanting."

He had hoped to have Lionel to take over the management of the Khedive of Egypt's confused finances after the Suez loan, but the suggestion was diplomatically turned aside because of concerns about offending France. Otherwise the familial relationship continued. When Hannah de Rothschild, Lionel's niece and Mayer's sole heir (after her mother), married the Earl of Rosebery on March 20, 1878, she asked Disraeli to stand for her father and give her away. (The first Rosebery child, born the next year, was named Sybil, after Disraeli's heroine.) Hannah's aunt Charlotte would not be at any of the wedding festivities. She had suffered a mental breakdown in 1877, at the time her husband became seriously ill, and when Lionel died on June 3, 1879, she could not comprehend what had happened. Disraeli, who knew she did not always take him seriously, had doted on her wit and charm, and that she meant more to him than any of the other ladies in his life was clear from a line in a letter to her in 1869, "There is no one I love more than you." There had been weeks in London during Parliamentary sittings when he had visited her nearly every day, first inquiring in a handwritten note delivered to Piccadilly Place to find out whether she was alone.

Disraeli was at Hughenden when he heard the news about Lionel and sent Corry immediately with a letter of condolence to "My Dearest Children: . . . I am quite overwhelmed—and cannot trust myself to say more. I send this by a faithful messenger who will bring back to me how you are, in this the most trying moment of your lives!"

Natty, thirty-nine and now central to the firm, had been in Paris on business when the end came. He wrote to Disraeli afterward, "The loss we have all sustained is so great, I may say inexpressible, and the sudden blow has so stunned us all that we can do nothing but think of the best and kindest of fathers. . . . I admired and appreciated . . . the greatness of his judgment and the lucidity of his mind. He always laid the greatest store in your love and friendship and hoped and trusted it would be extended to his sons."

Disraeli remained close to all three sons—Nathaniel Mayer, Alfred, and Leopold. Liberals by family tradition, they were in practice Disraeli Conservatives, Natty once warning Disraeli—in March 1879—of a Liberal vote of censure to be sprung by Sir Charles Dilke following the debacle in Natal. The Rothschilds' link with Gladstone, cemented over decades of Liberal politics, was tried during the Eastern Question tensions, but remained unbroken although Natty's parting salutation in a letter of December 30, 1879, suggests his personal bias. Reporting Liberal irritation with the fanaticism of Gladstone, he closed a letter to Disraeli, "That he will do you good and himself harm is the wish of ever yours. . . ." And in another, Disraeli was one "whom I hope I may be permitted to call my dearest friend." How sincerely that affection was reciprocated would be seen in Disraeli's last novel, which he had already begun.

Since Cetshwayo's tribesmen were perceived by colonists in Natal as a menace—the Europeans were importing Indian laborers because Zulus would not be domesticated—the Cape administration determined to pacify them with modern weapons. Cetshwayo was first sent a list of humiliating demands, one of which was that he dismantle his proud army. When he refused, troops were assembled under the 2nd Baron Chelmsford—Frederick Thesiger had just succeeded to his father's title—who had served under Napier. Early in 1879, he set off with five thousand Europeans and eight thousand Kaffirs in three columns, intending to unite at Ulindi, the Zulu capital, sixty miles into the hinterland. By January 22 his main force was camped near a hill called Isandhlwana, from which patrols slipped out to locate the Zulus. Then Chelmsford moved out his main force to follow. Toward noon the next day a Zulu *impi,* or field army, surprised the remaining six companies of the 24th Regiment. Of the 1,800 men, more than half of them English, only 355 escaped. Zulus took no prisoners.

The news dismayed England. "The terrible disaster," Disraeli wrote to Lady Chesterfield, "has shaken me to the centre and what increases the grief is that I have not only to endure it, but to sustain others and to keep a bold front before an unscrupulous enemy." He meant not Cetshwayo but Gladstone, who disapproved of imperial adventures and was out in any case to embarrass the Tories. Over the objections of the Queen, Disraeli made Chelmsford pay the political price. Sir Garnet Wolseley, the hero of the Ashanti wars, was sent to take over. "It is quite true that Wolseley is an egotist and a braggart," said Disraeli. "So was Nelson."

Reinforcements had to be dispatched and quickly, and the young, exiled Prince Imperial of France Louis Napoleon, twenty-three and trained at Woolwich, asked to go. His widowed mother, former Empress Eugénie, now a great friend of Victoria, was eager to see him secure a little glory to embolden the Bonapartists. Disraeli was opposed on political grounds. It would be "injudicious" to offend the French government. With the connivance of the army chief, the Duke of Cambridge, a mediocrity but the Queen's cousin, the matter was arranged by the royal ladies.

"I am quite mystified about that little abortion, the Prince Imperial," Disraeli wrote with exasperation to Salisbury on February 28. "I thought we had agreed not to sanction his adventure? Instead of that he has royal audiences previous to his departure . . . and is attended to the station by Whiskerandos himself [Lord Napier], the very general who was to conquer Constantinople. . . . What am I to say on this? H.M. knows my little sympathy with the Buonapartes."

Technically, Louis Napoleon went out only as an observer,

but, Disraeli told Lady Chesterfield, "I fear . . . that some indiscreet friends, in very high places, gave him privately letters to Ld
Chelmsford, begging that General to place the Prince on his
staff." On June 1, on a reconnaissance with several companions
who fled for their lives, the Prince was ambushed. Unable to re-
mount his frightened horse, he was speared by Zulu *assegais*.

With no cable as yet to the Cape, the news was slow to
reach London. On the afternoon of June 19, Disraeli was handed
a message at the opening of an exhibition at the Grosvenor Gallery. "This is terrible news," he said. "Yes," agreed G. W. E. Russell, an M.P., "and I am afraid that the French will accuse our
people of having deserted him and left him to his fate."

"I am not so sure they will be wrong," Disraeli agreed.
"Well! My conscience is clear. I did all that I could to stop his
going. But what can you do when you have to deal with two obstinate women!"

In tears, Princess Beatrice brought the Queen the cable delivered by John Brown, and they wept together. Still "Baby" to
Victoria, Beatrice and her mother had nursed the dream of a revived Bonapartist France with the Princess as the Prince Imperial's consort. Court gossip had linked him to Beatrice, fixing as
one of his reasons for intruding into the Zulu wars his need to
prove himself acceptable to the British public.

Despite a new attack of gout, Disraeli hurried to Windsor as
soon as he was free from his bed and his sofa to offer his condolences to the Queen. "A very long audience—nearly an hour and
a half," he told Lady Chesterfield, "and H.M. talked only of [the]
one subject which seems greatly to have affected her." He may
not have realized how important Louis Napoleon had been to
Victoria or why his body was interred with a measure of pomp
that could not have gone over well with the Republic. "I have
just got a telegram from the Queen," Disraeli wrote ruefully to
Anne Chesterfield on July 1, "who has returned to Windsor and
who seems highly pleased at all that occurred at Chislehurst this
morning. I hope the French Government will be as joyful. In my
mind, nothing could be more injudicious than the whole affair."

The death of the Prince Imperial raised for the Queen further questions about British unpreparedness in South Africa and

the need to convince a penurious Parliament to raise tax revenues for the military. "Our great lesson is again taught us," she lectured Disraeli, "but is never followed. NEVER *let the Army and Navy DOWN so low as to be obliged* to go to *great expense* in a hurry." It had happened before, she reminded him, in the Crimean War. "We were *not* prepared. . . . If *we are* to *maintain* our position as a *first-rate* Power . . . we must, with our Indian Empire and large Colonies, *be prepared for attacks and wars*, somewhere or other, CONTINUALLY. And the *true economy* will be *to be always ready.* Lord Beaconsfield can do his country the greatest service by repeating this again, and by *seeing it carried out.* It will *prevent war.*" The Queen did not understand the hazards of appealing to an electorate hostile to paying any taxes whatever.

Disraeli complained to Lady Bradford that while the military remained a plaything of the aristocracy it would be inefficient, however modern the cannons and cruisers. "The Horse Guards," he said, referring to the Duke of Cambridge's offices, "will ruin this country, unless there is a Prime Minister who will have his way, and that cannot be counted upon." The case of the Prince Imperial was evidence enough. "I tremble," he added, "when I think of what may be the fate of this country if, as is not unlikely, a great struggle occurs, with the Duke of Cambridge's [choice of] generals." The Duke had held his position since 1856 and would hang on to it for thirty-nine years, leaving a broad gap between the Queen's principles and her practice.

General "Little Bobs" Roberts was not one of the Duke's protégés. The son of an Indian Army general, he returned as a cadet to England in 1852, rising on ability thereafter, in the Mutiny, in the Punjab, in Abyssinia. After the Afghan War had ended, he was in India when Major Pierre Louis Napoleon Cavagnari, the British envoy in Kabul, was murdered with his staff in July 1879. Cavagnari was a naturalized Englishman knighted for negotiating the treaty that had ended the war, and his death seemed more than the act of a few mutinous Afghans. With Disraeli's backing, Lytton sent Roberts into the hills on a punitive expedition, dispensing with the mediocre senior officers who had been rewarded for their blunders the year before. Moved up in responsibility were such young officers with a future as Ian Hamilton and Hector MacDonald. Before the campaign the Viceroy sent Disraeli his acid opinions of the Indian Army generals he would not use, and from Downing Street a note went to Salisbury on September 9, "And these are the men whom only a few months or weeks ago he commended for all these distinctions. I begin to think he ought to be tried by court martial himself; but I have confidence still in his energy and resource."

The Opposition at home singled out Lytton for attack: the murders and the costly campaign to redeem them were his ulti-mate responsibility. But Kabul fell on October 13, and Roberts hanged some plausible, perhaps even guilty, Afghans. The news arrived in London in time for the Lord Mayor's Dinner, the major political occasion for the waning year.

The annual dinner at the Guildhall was traditionally a time for grand statements of principle. Newsworthy tidbits were also saved for it, which made the Prime Minister's appearance loom each November as more of an event, and the entire assemblage arose when his carriage arrived three-quarters of an hour past schedule. His hosts, aware he was ailing, were used to his appearing late and disappearing early. "My present physicians," he had written to Lady Bradford, "are, Dr Solitude, Dr Silence, Dr Warmth, and two general practitioners, Regular Hours and Regular Meals."

At Hughenden, as he described his life away from Downing Street to her, he was in his study in the morning and his library in the evening. ("Books are companions even if you don't open them.") The first post came at seven and the second at noon— "which always disturbs me, for it brings the newspapers which are fortunately dull enough but which must be looked at." His sub-stantial meal of the day was served at two, and to assist digestion he paused lengthily between courses, catching up on his reading. (He reached first for the *Revue des deux mondes*, which he consid-ered the best magazine in the world. And he returned to his fa-ther's favorite authors—Homer, Virgil, and Horace.) He took a walk in his beloved woods before dark and then resumed his work. The relaxed routine prepared him for the Guildhall ordeal, but it did not help that his valet, Mr. Baum, had injured himself a few days earlier and was on crutches.

"I verily believe," New York Tribune reporter George Smalley cabled home about the wait for Disraeli, "the guests would rather have gone without their dinner than without this sauce to it . . . ; the applause is deafening. . . . It was a common remark that Lord Beaconsfield was looking uncommonly well. . . . The condition of this great man's health is an affair of State." But his apparent vigor was a pose, Smalley contended. "When he made his entry into the Library of the Guildhall, I stood near the door. I could see him pull himself together and compose the muscles of his face till the desired expression was attained. . . . A strange fire burned in his eyes. The jaw and lips were set fast. For those two minutes no man's face was more full of energy, no step firmer than his." At seventy-four—he would be seventy-five in a month—and with a General Election looming, Disraeli was determined to look the leader.

He had some help from the Queen. "He wore his Windsor uniform of dark blue with embroideries in gold, with pendent sword, and on his breast that matchless and priceless star of diamonds inclosing the ruby cross of the Garter which fills all meaner breasts with envy." Republics, Smalley suggested, lacked something in color and ceremony.

In the Banqueting Hall, to which the Earl escorted the Lady Mayoress, he made the awaited postprandial address. The old man, Smalley wrote, was husbanding his strength. "But you could not listen to a sentence without perceiving that he had a consummate knowledge of the art of speaking in public, and consummate cleverness in making the most of his knowledge. . . . He says to the English people: Mind your own business; plant and reap; stick to your lasts, to your furnaces and looms, to ships and factories; leave politics to your betters; I will govern you."

When he came to the murder of the English emissaries in Kabul, and the swift reprisal, Smalley saw "excellent mimicry of pathos," but—the correspondent for all his wry admiration of the Prime Minister was a Gladstone sympathizer as the closest thing to a republican—not "a genuine sorrow." What Disraeli had said was that during Britain's efforts "to establish tranquility" in Central Asia there had occurred "a dark calamity, which even in this scene at this hour we cannot recall without emotion. A great nation can endure the loss of a pitched battle with dignity and self-control. They may even find consolation under such circumstances in the consciousness of a good cause, and in the heroic acts of their countrymen, though defeated. But calamities that commence with treachery and are consummated by assassination and massacre—where the victims are youth and genius, unrivalled courage and the highest patriotism—those are the incidents that rend the hearts of nations." Lord Lytton, Disraeli claimed, had shown "firmness and constancy in difficulty and danger." Peace had again been restored.

While to Smalley the lines were too lofty to have been sincerely felt, he conceded that "what is genuine in the man is his intellect and his courage; together with his scorn for men whose intellect is kept in subjection to settled convictions."

Later in the evening Sir Stafford Northcote spoke on finance. Disraeli struggled to listen, but "the cheeks grew hollow, the tint of his skin waxlike, the lips relaxed, the cavernous jaws fell slightly apart, the carefully trained curls on the left of the brow slid out of place, the fire sank low in his eyes." Then he revived to "fresh serenity," and conducted the Lady Mayoress to the drawing room. The faithful Corry brought his cloak, "a romantic garment of cloth, very short and lined with fur," and guests waited for the cry, "Lord Beaconsfield's carriage coming up!" Corry followed his chief into the coffee-colored interior, and carriage and horses and footman and coachman vanished in the direction of Downing Street.

Concluding his address, Disraeli had prophesied that the next year he would again have the honor of being spokesman for his Cabinet, a statement that elicited what a reporter called "much amusement," as Gladstone was tearing rhetorically through the country. The Prime Minister recognized the reality privately, and had already begun thinking about parting honors for loyalists. The young 6th Duke of Portland succeeded to the title on December 6, 1879, when his childless cousin, the 5th Duke (a nephew of Disraeli's late friend Lord George Bentinck) died. Disraeli waited until just after the funeral at Welbeck Abbey on the twelfth to invite the young man, who had been mere William John Arthur Charles James Cavendish-Bentinck, to Hughenden to discuss a possible title for his stepmother in recognition of the unforgotten debt to the Bentincks. At Paddington Station the Duke met Corry on the platform as directed, and was conveyed to Disraeli's carriage, where he found the Prime Minister huddled in a back Inverness cape with a "wide-awake" hat pulled down over his face. The "Siberian clime"—as he described it to Lady Bradford—had been too much for his failing lungs. He held out a lean hand and said, "I am so very glad to make your acquaintance: how do you do? I am afraid I cannot talk to you now, as I am an old man, not in the best of health, and it fatigues me to converse in the [moving] train. No doubt dear Monty will make up for that; and I'm sure you already know that he is very pleasant and agreeable, especially to young people."

At High Wycombe, two closed carriages drew up, and the Duke was escorted into one with Disraeli, immediately feeling as if he were with the Lower Master at Eton. At Hughenden, Disraeli, the Duke, and Corry were the only diners; the meal seemed eerie as the host ate slowly and in silence. When the table was cleared, Disraeli settled into his explanation. "I am a man of many faults," he began, "and many failings like everyone else, but perhaps I have one redeeming quality. I mean, that the feeling of gratitude is very strong within me; and I believe I owe any success that may have been mine in my long life mainly to two people. One was of course my dear wife; and the other was your relative, Lord George Bentinck. When I was a young and struggling man, Lord George held forth the hand of friendship to me, and we became not only political allies but very sincere friends. I had a great affection and admiration both for him and for his brother Henry, and so I shall only be too glad to be of some service to you. Now, I hope, you will understand why I was anxious to make your acquaintance; and I trust that I may be able to pay back a small part of the debt which I owe to the Bentinck family." The Duke's stepmother, Mrs. Bentinck, would be created Lady Bolsover.*

Disraeli remained at Hughenden through the "Merrie Xmas"

*The Duke's story has been much distorted in anecdotage, often with Disraeli's silence at dinner described as some form of symbolic punishment of the Portlands for withdrawing the Hughenden loan.

he told Lady Chesterfield that he "never believed in," with affairs, foreign and domestic, brought to him in his red boxes. The only news that elicited a smile was a dispatch from Lord Odo Russell in Berlin which quoted a newspaper report that Prince Bismarck on winter holiday at his vast estate at Varzin was "reading over again all Lord Beaconsfield's novels." The costly colonial wars which Disraeli had tried to put in a better light at the Guildhall, and the agricultural bankruptcies which Northcote, following him, had to explain, made it a gloomy December, spent largely alone, brooding over the embers of the dying Ministry.

Ill as he remained, and uncertain as were his political prospects, he nevertheless began pressing the Queen to open Parliament in person, in state "as splendid as might be convenient to your Majesty," to help revive the appeal of the Government. The relentless attacks on Disraeli remained beyond the understanding of Mary Ann Evans—novelist George Eliot—whom Edith Simcox found reading her newspapers alone on Boxing Day, "disgusted with the venom of the Liberal speeches from Gladstone downwards." Disraeli, she said, was no fool, "and so he must care for a place in history, and how could he expect to win that by doing harm?"

Gladstone had railed about the subjugation of the Zulus and the annexation of the Transvaal, that it was a country "where we have chosen most unwisely, I am tempted to say insanely, to place ourselves in the strange predicament of the free subjects of a monarchy going to coerce the free subjects of a republic." The Afrikaaners had enslaved or driven out the black peoples whose lands they had appropriated, but Gladstone went on, in his pre-election jeremiads, to single out the British. "Remember the rights of the savage, as we call him," Gladstone exhorted in a rally at Dalkeith, and he deplored yet again the Empress of India title he had at least once employed himself* as one of the visible excesses of imperial ambition, a thing of "theatrical bombast and folly." Still, a by-election at Southwark in February gave the Con-

*Disraeli's young Undersecretary for India, Lord George Hamilton, had discovered the evidence in the India Office files. Gladstone filed the newspaper story about it.

servatives a surprisingly large majority, encouraging the Queen about Tory prospects after dissolution. On the same day, February 14, 1880, in response to her greeting card, Disraeli sent her from Downing Street a message in his vintage style:

> He wishes he could repose on a sunny bank, like young Valentine in the pretty picture that fell from a rosy cloud this morn—but the reverie of the happy youth would be rather different from his. Valentine would dream of the future, and youthful loves, and all under the inspiration of a beautiful clime! Lord Beaconsfield, no longer in the sunset, but the twilight of existence, must encounter a life of anxiety and toil; but this, too, has its romance, when he remembers that he labours for the most gracious of beings!

Lord Chelmsford—with his relief by Sir Garnet Wolseley, now Disraeli's Governor of Cyprus, announced—was not about to hand the laurels as well as his South African command to the hero of the Ashanti wars. Just as Wolseley landed at Durban, having shipped through Suez, Chelmsford's regrouped forces were surrounding the royal kraal at Ulundi. Outgunned, the Zulus threw themselves suicidally upon the traditional British armed square, four deep, from which, through a gap, cavalry charged, impaling Cetshwayo's warriors with lances, slashing them with sabers, and trampling the wounded underfoot. Cetshwayo was taken prisoner and eventually brought to England for an audience with the new sovereign of his fragmented and subdued domains.

The Afrikaaners were less easily reconciled to imperial rule. While their Orange Free State north of the Cape Colony remained quiescent and undisturbed, the Transvaal, on the high veld to the north, had been claimed for the Union Jack during Carnarvon's colonial watch. Rejecting annexation, Paul Kruger, leader of a Boer triumvirate, ritually reconstituted the Republic in a ceremony on the Rand, later the great goldfield. Forming into guerrilla units, the Dutch farmers continued their marauding, and Gladstone's policy of retrenchment abroad appeared more and more persuasive to the public, who, in economic straits themselves, had no stomach for expensive ventures in overseas prestige that despite each victory seemed no bargain.

Dissolution of Parliament could not be put off in hopes of better times, and Disraeli hurried it forward to March, telegraphing to Windsor to explain that the longer he waited, with agricultural distress increasing, the larger the majority would be against him. He could not confess that his health was making it impossible for him to continue. "I came back very bad from Windsor," he wrote to Lady Bradford on February 28. "I believe [it is] the consequence of having to pace so often that terrible corridor—the Palace of the Winds."

The campaign was bitter. As Earl Granville explained politely to the Queen, "Lord Beaconsfield and Mr Gladstone are men of extraordinary ability; they dislike each other more than is usual among public men. Of no other politician Lord Beaconsfield would have said in public, that his conduct was worse than those who committed the Bulgarian atrocities. He has a power of saying in two words that which drives a person of Mr Gladstone's peculiar temperament into a great state of excitement." Gladstone was not opposing the Queen, Granville claimed, little realizing how much Disraeli's Russophobic policies were Victoria's.

Gladstone spoke to thousands, often in the open, about "the sanctity of life in the hill villages of Afghanistan," about which he knew very little, and about the aspirations of other peoples in other climes to live their lives without the collision of geopolitics with what he perceived as Christian ethics. In the frosty air of the Midlothian district in which he was campaigning for a seat, and in other venues, his voice rang out thrillingly against Disraeli's "immoral" bullying of the innocent of every religion and hue for rapacious imperial interests. Electorally attractive high moral ground, it ignored the power vacuum which would inevitably be filled by rival nations themselves claiming sanctimoniously to be carrying Christianity and civilization to people who wanted neither boon. He also touched the sensitive pocketbook nerve, as colonies could not be maintained on the cheap.

Curiously, Disraeli now seemed to have not only Cardinal Newman but Cardinal Manning, prototype of his manipulative

Prince of the Church in *Lothair*, on his side. "I am no politician," Manning had told Disraeli modestly in December 1879 as Gladstone campaigned up and down the island, "but it is clear to me that, having an Empire, we must either give it up or keep it up. To give it up would be our extinction as a power in the world; to keep it up seems to me to demand, and even to dictate, the policy you have pursued. And Englishmen must give up trembling at dangers and puling about taxes." Disraeli thanked him, as "the voice of patriotism from one so eminent as yourself will animate the faltering and add courage even to the brave."

Manning confessed his enmity toward Gladstone, who had once been to him the paragon of politicians but now was a fierce old man enjoying the passions he was evoking from his audiences. "I thought," Disraeli replied, "he had always been an Italian in the custody of a Scotsman."

As Gladstone's appeal to the masses burgeoned, he seemed to be losing the support of intellectuals appalled at his demagoguery, but these represented few votes. "Lord Beaconsfield's foe," George Meredith wrote to James Thomson on March 16, was "an old-fashioned godly man, with a fast faith in his godliness, and superior eloquence, when he selects an enemy," but he now sounded so lacking in judgment that "the devil would not be in us if the enemy did not become popular."

Arriving in England late in the winter to take up his diplomatic duties, James Russell Lowell dealt formally with Salisbury and saw Disraeli only once, at a reception. A letter to his sister-in-law in Boston reflects the Prime Minister's failing health and Lowell's perception of Gladstone's hatred, as Disraeli appeared to him "uglier than the wildest dream of Gladstone could picture him." Ever the shrewd diplomat, he nevertheless made friendly contacts with Gladstone, who appeared, with a General Election imminent, destined to be the next occupant of 10 Downing Street.

Parliament's business was rushed through in the last weeks of winter. On March 20, a Saturday, Gathorne-Hardy, now Earl of Cranbrook, caught up with Disraeli as he left the chamber, "and had a long saunter with him on the sunny side of the India Office sheltered from the West wind. He was cheerful about our prospects but had his doubts about [the Home] Counties, which surprised me. He often has means of judging wh[ich] others have not." Publicly, the Prime Minister had put a better face on their prospects than was the reality. He expected to lose.

Those with seats in jeopardy hoped for a delay. "If Disraeli dissolves this Parliament at all, we will not put him in Bedlam," Sir William Fraser vowed, "nor in Hanwell; we will keep him for a very small cell in Colney Hatch!" But Dissolution came, an index to Disraeli's exhaustion as well as to his sense of the public temper.

Victoria went off to Baden on family business, which required the travel of a Minister in attendance. Disraeli tried to send W. H. Smith, as a culminating honor should the Government go out, but Smith, a family man who did not want to spend Easter away, pleaded that "an ornamental peer" substitute for him. Needing more than that, Disraeli asked Sir Michael Hicks Beach, who requested advice on coping with his assignment. "First of all," Disraeli said, "remember she is a woman."

The election returns were grim. Gladstone's diary notes for March 31, "By 11 P.M. the doom of the Govt came in view." Not all results came in on the first day, but by April 4 he could write, "It seemed as if the arm of the Lord had bared itself for a work He has made His own." "I have been longing for the fall of the Disraeli Government as I did for the fall of the Second Empire," old Abraham Hayward wrote a friend happily. Napoleon III had already gone. "Now my second wish is about to be gratified."

While at Baden the Queen learned of the Liberal landslide—a majority of 108. "Your Majesty," Disraeli telegraphed her on April 7, "must not be unnecessarily hurried or agitated at this moment. . . . I take the responsibility myself." She had expected it, having written to Vicky, "People ignorant and unreasoning think a change of Government will give them a good harvest and restore commerce." She answered Disraeli the same day in a rare first-person message: "What your loss to me as a Minister would be, it is impossible to estimate. But I trust you will always remain my friend, to whom I can turn and on whom I can rely. Hope you will come to Windsor in the forenoon on Sunday, and stop all day, and dine and sleep."

Before that dreaded Sunday she pondered the alternatives to

Gladstone—including abdication, she informed Ponsonby, "rather than send for or have any *communication* with that *half-mad firebrand* who wd soon ruin everything & be a *Dictator*. Others but herself *may submit* to his democratic rule, but *not the Queen*." His ranting had demonstrated, she told Ponsonby, who remained an admirer of Gladstone, "a most unpardonable & personal hatred to Ld B who had restored England to the position she had lost under Mr G's Gov't."

Although Disraeli and his Sovereign both knew that his departure from Downing Street was forever, Victoria hoped, she told him, that his period out of office "would only be for a short time." His relations with her, he telegraphed back, "were his chief, he might say his only happiness & interest in this world." In return, she conferred upon him once more the privilege of writing to her in the first person, for "when we correspond, which I hope we shall on many a *private* subject & without anyone being astonished or offended, & even more without anyone knowing about it—I hope it will be in this easy form. . . . You must not think it is a real parting. I shall always let you know how I am & what I am doing, & you must promise me to let me hear from you & about you." And she proposed—she had done so before—to bestow a peerage on his nephew and heir, Coningsby, now thirteen. Again Disraeli refused: it had not been earned.

Disraeli did have a delicate and awkward request to make for a peerage. Monty Corry had become more than a private secretary; he was a surrogate son. And he was nearly everything else for Disraeli, from male nurse to Minister without Portfolio. Other titles, honors, and sinecures had been proposed for him before, including Keeper of the Privy Purse for the Queen, yet Corry insisted on remaining with Disraeli, who truly needed him. On the day the electoral defeat became certain, Disraeli wrote to Corry's wealthy, widowed aunt, Lady Charlotte Lyster, who was childless, telling her that his scheme to elicit a barony for Monty depended upon her making provision for him of inheritable income and property to sustain a peerage. Disraeli then proposed Monty to the Queen as Baron Rowton of Rowton Castle in Shropshire, which he would possess on his aunt's demise.

Victoria had hesitated earlier about creating Mary Anne Viscountess Beaconsfield. He persuaded her this time by pointing out that Gladstone's ostensible democrats coveted more titles than Disraeli's Tories. The Queen knew that the Liberals in any case would find ways to poke fun at the peerage, but Corry might have received honors earlier in some of the roles he had refused in order to serve Disraeli. She gave in, and inevitably there were snide reminders in the press that Caligula had made his horse a Roman senator.

Disraeli wound up his business, sometimes beset by "pesterers of the 11th hour," more often with matters of transition from power, and left Downing Street for the last time on April 25, two days before a farewell audience with the Queen. "A most dreary life & labor mine!" he confessed to Lady Bradford. "Winding up a Government is as hard work as forming one, without any of its excitement." He expected, once the "beggars mournful and indignant" were gone, "utter neglect & isolation." Concluding dignities went to Cross, Northcote, Manners, and Baillie-Cochrane, but Disraeli was persuaded not to insist upon further honors for Lord Henry Lennox.

Since the Queen hoped to find some way to keep Gladstone from Downing Street, Disraeli advised her, realizing as Victoria did that it would be in vain, to send for Hartington, who was still titular leader of his party. But "Harty-Tarty," well aware that he was not the one who had led the Liberals back into office, declined to serve without Gladstone, who refused office under anyone else. On April 23 she was forced to name him Prime Minister—and he insisted further on being his own Chancellor of the Exchequer. He was, she emphasized to Vicky, "a most disagreeable person—half-crazy, and so excited."

Two days earlier, Disraeli met his Cabinet for the last time, and thanked them for the harmony in which they had worked— there had been a new spirit after the departures of Carnarvon and Derby.* "All assented heartily to the expressions of good feeling," Cranbrook noted, and Salisbury observed, somewhat imaginatively, "that there had never been a cloud between him and the Prime

*In a letter to *The Times* on March 15, Derby announced his shift to the Liberal Party.

Minister through all their arduous work." On April 25, Disraeli left Downing Street. He no longer had a place of his own in London and for two weeks remained with the Beauchamps in Belgrave Square, leaving them once for his farewell audience at Windsor.

At Hughenden he possessed, briefly, what he wanted—"a dose of solitude." Yet he could not keep from brooding over what he took as a personal electoral defeat. What the Opposition had labeled "Beaconsfieldism"—the emphasis upon Empire—had pushed aside the domestic dreams, since *Coningsby* and *Sybil*, of meshing, through Tory democracy, the "Two Nations." Rather than point to the political cycles, Disraeli, in a letter to Lord Lytton, now to be an Earl, blamed the cycles of Nature.

> Whatever philosophers may say, there is such a thing as luck & fortune—& the reverse—& that it should have fallen to my lot to govern England for a series of years with a decaying commerce & the soil stricken with ste- rility presents an issue which, I believe, no calculation could have foreseen or baffled.
>
> The distress of this country is the cause & the sole cause of the fall for the government over wh: I presided. Had the dissolution been postponed for a few months the consequences wd have been still more serious, for we shd have lost all our counties. . . .
>
> At the solicitation of the Queen & the unanimous entreaty of our party, Lords & Commons assembled at Bridgewater House, I have consented to relinquish my purpose of retiring at present from public life. It is not in my humor ever to leave my friends in adversity but I think, tho' generous, they err in still wishing me to represent them. The situation requires youth & energy. When they are found—& they will be found—I shall make my bow.

It was flattering to be wanted, still, as leader, but Disraeli knew he was, as he told Lytton, "in the sunset of life—or rather I sh'd say the twilight of existence," and there were still things he wanted to finish. One was a novel.

XXIX

"I HAVE HAD A GOOD INNINGS AND CANNOT AGREE WITH THE GREAT KING THAT ALL IS VANITY."

1880–1881

OUT OF OFFICE, THE EARL OF BEACONSFIELD WAS NOT OUT OF MIND at Windsor Castle. For Victoria, to accept Gladstone was dismaying. To lose Disraeli was much like a bereavement, as she told him in unqueenly language. "I often think of you—indeed constantly; and [I] rejoice to see you looking down from the wall after dinner," she confided. "Oh! if only I had you, my kind friend and wise counsellor and strong arm, to help and lean on! I have *no one.*" But she could not cultivate loneliness; Disraeli could, and used it at Hughenden to complete a novel.

Endymion was already well along when Disraeli quitted Downing Street. He had begun it before he returned to office in 1874, and had kept it secret—almost.

The novel was in the planning stages in 1872 when Disraeli wrote to the Duchess of Somerset (Lady Seymour in 1839) to ask whether she retained any souvenirs of the Eglinton Tournament, the great social and spectator event of its year. He wanted his novel's hero to be part of that central experience of early Victorian England, the symbolic revival of medieval-ism.

Conceived and hosted by the 13th Earl of Eglinton, a wealthy sporting peer, the pseudo-medieval reenactment had been staged at Eglinton Castle in Ayrshire, near Glasgow, on August 28, 1839, the Wednesday following the close of the Parliamentary session. Thirteen knights in authentic-looking costume and armor jousted with real lances, and a Queen of Beauty—Lady Sey-mour—awarded a trophy to the champion.

Tens of thousands of aficionados of chivalry had journeyed by steamboat and railway to the site, crowding the temporary grandstands and the grassy slopes. The rains came as the ceremo-nies began at 3:00 in the afternoon. In the downpour, the colorful procession of knights, retainers, and ladies struggled through the mud, then scattered. The crowds and the marchers looked to one observer like a vanquished army in retreat. The tilting itself—the pièce de résistance of the occasion—was abbreviated. Fewer lances were brandished than umbrellas.

Unwilling to give in after a year's preparation, Lord Eglinton postponed the jousting and the concluding banquet to the first dry day, which turned out to be August 30. Following the final melee, captained by Lord Waterford on one side and Lord Alford on the other, a repast medievalized by a conspicuous boar's head was served, and two thousand determined guests danced under the Earl's rehabilitated marquee.

Since Disraeli had been married in London on August 28, 1839, he had missed the spectacle although not the rain, shel-tering with Mary Anne far from Scotland in Tunbridge Wells. The Duchess, once Jane Georgiana Sheridan, one of the reigning beauties of Disraeli's bachelor days, had nothing saved from the Eglinton Tournament "except a coloured print which I will send you. I had all sorts of relics, [including] points of splintered spears with the colours of the Knights, but a stupid old house-maid considered them as 'rubbish' as she said and burnt them." For authenticity, Disraeli had to search elsewhere.

In the nostalgia-drenched England of his "Montfort Tourna-ment" in *Endymion*, "The sun shone, and not one of the breath-less multitude was disappointed."

Monty Corry's recollection that his first glimpse of the novel came when the unfinished manuscript was locked away in the new strong room at Hughenden on October 15, 1878, is precise without being accurate. On November 19, 1877, accompanied by Corry, Disraeli had entrained for St. Albans, where Lord Verulam's carriage was waiting to take them to Gorhambury. A descendant of Francis Bacon (the first Baron Verulam and Viscount St. Albans), the ruins of whose house still remained on the property, Verulam was an agreeable aristocrat. Lame and using two crutches, he guided guests about his park, showing them Bacon's observatory, the old "Kissing Oak" under which Queen Elizabeth reputedly embraced her host, and his house filled with Baconian relics.

One of Verulam's visitors was travel writer and memorist Augustus Hare, who recalled Disraeli explaining why he never carried a watch: "I live under the shadow of Big Ben." He also noted in his diary about November 20, 1877, that the Prime Minister "seemed absorbed. . . . Scarcely noticed any one, barely answered his hostess when spoken to." Apologizing for Lord Beaconsfield, "Corry said that his chief declared that the greatest pleasure in life was writing a book, because 'in that way alone man could become a creator': that his habit was to make marionettes, and then to live with them for some months before he put them into action. Lately he had made some marionettes; now he was living with them, and their society occupied him entirely."

When Disraeli began thinking out his marionettes is unclear. It may have been soon after he completed *Lothair*. The name of Disraeli's autobiographical protagonist, Endymion Ferrars, may be a clue to the actual writing. Although the satirist William Aytoun had published a burlesque of Disraeli's "Ixion in Heaven" in 1842 entitled "Endymion," Disraeli had almost certainly forgotten it. The mythological Endymion, the handsome son of Zeus and the nymph Calyce, was the object of the desperate love of Selene, the Moon goddess. One story about their relationship is that Endymion was lying asleep in a cave one night when Selene gently kissed his closed eyes, after which Zeus gave him eternal youth at the cost of his never awakening. Disraeli's epistolary courtship of Selina, Countess of Bradford, dates from 1873, and his christening his hero Endymion seems to link the author with his own Moon goddess.

When he put the manuscript away for safekeeping in 1878, not expecting to complete it, if ever, until he left office, he explained to Corry that there were about a hundred pages to go. In the box he left notes on how the plot was to be worked out in case Corry would have to finish it—or publish it as it was. Settled into Hughenden after the summer Parliamentary recess, he set to work completing it while Corry negotiated with Thomas Longman, publisher of *Lothair*, on the basis of the novel's imminent completion. Corry, now Lord Rowton, wanted at least as attractive a contract for *Endymion* as for *Lothair*, pressing for £7,500 for all rights. Partly it was a matter of pride, partly of pounds, as Disraeli did not want to linger indefinitely at Seamore Place despite the generosity of Alfred de Rothschild.

Longman's first offer, on July 20, was unsatisfactory to Corry. On August 4 the publisher reconsidered—although neither he nor Corry had read a single page of the book. It was, after all, a three-volume novel by a successful writer and statesman who was probably the most eminent man in England. Turning up in the Lords late in the day while the Liberal leader in the Upper House, the Duke of Argyll, was speaking, Corry first sat impatiently at Disraeli's side, then got up briefly and returned with a note:

> There are things too big to impart in whispers! so I leave your side, just to write these words—Longman has today offered *Ten Thousand Pounds* for *Endymion*.
>
> I have accepted it! I cannot tell you what a pleasure it is to me to see my ardent ambition for you gratified!
>
> And you have an added honor which may for ever remain without precedent.

Longman followed up the offer to Corry with a formal one in which he asked Disraeli to judge for himself whether the commercial possibilities of the work were up to that advance. On August 7, Disraeli accepted "with pleasure," adding, "I would not do so, unless I had a conviction that you would have no cause to regret the sales price." It was a very large sum for 1880, one of the highest offers, then, in the history of authorship. Dickens had brought in £9,000 for *Dombey and Son*, of which he retained three-quarters. George Eliot had earned from all sales on *Middlemarch* about £8,000, and about £9,000 for *Daniel Deronda*. The highest sum that the envious Anthony Trollope had garnered for a single novel had been £3,525 for *Can You Forgive Her?* (1864), not one of his more esteemed works. (The usual retail price then for a three-volume novel, upon which royalties would have been computed, was thirty-one shillings.)

Disraeli asked Corry to read the manuscript through, to validate that it was "fit to publish." Then he was to read it a second time "to see if it be in English." On still a third reading he was to check spelling and punctuation. Invited to Hughenden to discuss details of publication, Longman delivered a portion of the advance and received an invitation to return on September 14 to collect the pages. Accepting the check, Disraeli told Corry, was "magic."

Longman worked quickly. By September 18 he estimated that to fit his three-volume format, the novel, somewhat longer than *Lothair*, would need one extra letter on each line and one extra line on each page. Proofs would be sent in secrecy to provide for the most possible surprise value.

Disraeli worked equally fast, finding only one error in a character's name, *Jowett* for *Jawett*, which he worried might be seen "as a slur on the celebrated Oxford Don." Given Disraeli's ailments and poor eyesight, proofreading well over nine hundred pages was a tremendous task, but by October 6 he had passed all the pages. By November 5 the sheets were at the binders, with press and presentation copies promised for the 23rd. Disraeli intended to send the Queen a special copy, "in more stately garb," he instructed Longman, bound in dark green morocco. As release date neared, Longman worried about a possible special session of Parliament to pass Gladstone's Irish Coercion Bill, writing Disraeli that the "awful condition of Irish affairs is absorbing more of public attention than the publisher of *Endymion* cares about. I fear it will affect the sale." The 26th was the official release date, and Mudie's ordered three thousand copies for its subscribers—"unprecedented," Longman told Disraeli, for a work of fiction. The first printing was 7,000 copies, and 10,500 were in print by December 3. Press interest was so great that Disraeli received from Longman 110 notices and reviews from British and Irish papers alone.

The first was the most troublesome. The *Standard* had somehow secured an early copy, summarizing the plot in its issue of November 23, guessing at the identity of the major characters, and deploring that the political narrative had "less dramatic interest than almost any of the novels . . . of Lord Beaconsfield." Its editor, Disraeli explained to Longman, was a friend of the republican-leaning Liberals Charles Dilke and Joseph Chamberlain, although the paper had supported Disraeli when he was in office. The leak may have damaged sales, but reviews in general were positive, and what pleased Disraeli most was that the *Revue des deux mondes*, "that capital periodical," liked it, and appeared to be "the only notice, out of the hundreds wh[ich] we have received in which the critic has read the book he reviewed."

Lady Dorothy Nevill, who read Disraeli again and again with "a renewal of sentiment," she told Edmund Gosse, pored over *Endymion* almost as personal history. "What a charm," she declared, "after the beef and mutton of ordinary novels." She knew more of the originals of Disraeli's characters, from the amiable Waldershare, a much-laundered George Smythe, to the chatelaines of the great houses, than anyone but the author himself. Still, Disraeli told Lord Beauchamp, *Endymion* was the first novel he had ever published "without the preliminary advantage of a female critic." He said much the same thing to Emma de Rothschild, Natty's wife, in presenting a copy "from her friend Beaconsfield," and she responded, after some praise, "If I might venture to allude to a shadow amongst so much light, I would ask why your hero, possessing every quality likely to ensure a success, should be partly indebted to the worldly and prosperous position of a sister?"

While fixing upon the weakness of Disraeli's protagonist, Lady de Rothschild failed to notice, nor did her husband, the little private joke about Sir Nathaniel that had been slipped into the book. Natty, who never forgot anything, was the one to whom Disraeli went when he needed a date in history. Midway through the novel a character confides to Endymion, "I like reading encyclopedias. The 'Dictionary of Dates' is a favorite book of mine." Of a younger generation than the author, Emma was even less able to recognize that among the personal and political debts Disraeli was paying through his characters was the overwhelming one he owed to Sarah. In *Endymion* she has the great marriage denied to her in life and the impact upon the hero's career which her pathetic real-life role made impossible.

Beginning in 1827 with Canning's death, the career of Endymion Ferrars encompasses thirty years of English politics. Young Ferrars is the son of a failed politician who has retired to a country house much like Bradenham. Since the family cannot afford upscale schooling for Endymion, he leaves Eton at sixteen for a government clerkship. His ambitions are modest, but the "irresistible will" of Myra, his twin sister, and that of older women who enter his life as sponsors of his career, move him upward. In the politically turbulent years culminating in the Reform Bill, Endymion's mother dies suddenly and his father is a suicide. The young man's prospects are dim, but he has attracted notice because he is obviously clever and of good family, and because Mr. Vigo, whose trade is the dressing of gentlemen, offers him credit, and advice to avoid the "shabby genteel" look. Vigo tells Endymion, "No man gives me the trouble Lord Eglantine does; he has not made up his mind whether he will be a great poet or prime minister. 'You must choose, my lord,' I tell him. 'I can not send you out looking like Lord Byron if you mean to be a Canning or Pitt.' "

Dress is crucial, for this is the grand London world of Disraeli's rise, and the novel is his elegiac backward glance at it. Endymion inhabits the great political salons of rich and regal women, attends the Eglinton Tournament, meets lively and enterprising young men who have useful connections, and—although he is a slow learner—they teach him something about the real world. He observes the reigns of George IV and William IV give way to that of a buoyant young Queen; he matures in the age of Chartism and railway shares mania; and he enters politics in the era of Sir Robert Peel, experiencing the stage fright of young Disraeli on making his maiden speech in the Commons.

It is given to the novel's Metternich figure to enunciate Disraeli's racial loyalties, observing that "Semites now exercise a vast influence over affairs through their smallest though most peculiar family, the Jews. There is no race gifted with so much tenacity, and such skill in organization. These qualities have given them an unprecedented hold over property and illimitable credit." "In another quarter century," he predicts, "they will claim their share of open government."

Their representative in the novel is recognizable, but is not burdened with a faith awkward to the plot. Myra, Endymion's twin, becomes companion to Adriana, the only child of the head of the Neuchatel banking family, Swiss in origin in the novel but clearly the Rothschilds. Adrian Neuchatel is a version of Baron Lionel, and the banker's country seat, Hainault, is much like Gunnersbury, although east rather than west of London. Myra's connection with the Neuchatels is as valuable as is her brother's relationships with influential London hostesses. While the ladies have their network of highly placed people, Neuchatel himself becomes Endymion's informal university. Among other things he recommends reading foreign newspapers. "The most successful man in life," he says, "is the man who has the best information." He prefers private business to elective politics, reminding Endymion, "A public man is responsible, and a responsible man is a slave." While the electorate can make the elected its pawns, "it is private life that governs the world." But the public pose, he understands, is always crucial. "Nobody should look anxious, except those who have no anxiety."

If there are echoes of Lionel de Rothschild in the shrewdness of Adrian Neuchatel, there is affectionate reminiscence in the portrait of his wife, Emily, who is much like Charlotte. Warm and witty, she is a tireless news-gatherer and letter-writer to her daughter, a benefactor to "her schools," a zealot for rare solitude, indifferent to elegant cuisine and elaborate ceremony, and prizing guests for their intellect, yet a gracious hostess for her husband to ambassadors and cabinet ministers.

Endymion, who has trouble finding a purpose for himself,

comments early in the novel to the ambitious Radical Job Thornberry that his rural life must be a pleasant one. "Yes," agrees Job, "but life should be more than pleasant; an ox in a pasture has a pleasant life." He would like to go into politics and replace feudalism with "the commercial principle." Curiously, his name deflects direct identification with either Cobden or Bright, as Job Thornberry was the leading character in the younger George Colman's stage masterpiece, *John Bull,* produced at Covent Garden in 1803, the year before Disraeli was born.

At Somerset House and other government bureaus, Endymion meets a variety of personalities adapted from Disraeli's experience. "St. Barbe," jealous, ambitious for success as a writer, and a satirist of snobs who is a snob himself, is Thackeray, repaid for his *Codlingsby;* "Gushy" the sentimentalist is Dickens. "Waldershare," good-hearted, romantic and capricious, represents the best in the often unprincipled Smythe. "Count Ferrol" is the younger Bismarck, and "Baron Sergius" is Metternich, and their counsel is almost a manual on how European foreign affairs were transacted in the first half of the century. "You will find it of the first importance in public life," advises Ferrol, "to know personally those who are carrying on the business of the world; so much depends on the character of an individual, his habits of thought, his prejudices, his social weaknesses, his health. Conducting affairs without this advantage is, in effect, an affair of stationery; it is pens and paper that are in communication, not human beings."

The novel is rich in the wry wisdom of Disraeli's six decades in political and fashionable life. Critics who saw apothegms pilfered or inverted missed the point that he was representing what he knew, what he heard, and what he found more true when turned into its opposite: "As a general rule, nobody has money who ought to have it." "What is the use of diamond necklaces if you cannot help a friend into Parliament?" "Marriage is a mighty instrument." "Life is a masquerade." "Desperation is sometimes as powerful an inspirer as genius." "As for religion generally, if a man believe in his Maker and does his duty to his neighbor, in my mind that is sufficient." "It is not good taste to believe in the Devil." "A little knowledge of the world is a dangerous thing, especially in literature." "I prefer the society of a first-rate woman to that of any man." "Never dine out in a high[-necked] dress." "Only let a man be able to drive into Bamford on market day, and get two or three linendrapers to take off their hats to him, and he will be happy enough, and always ready to die for our glorious Constitution." "The most precious stone . . . must be cut and polished." "Without tact you can learn nothing. Tact teaches you when to be silent." "I think life would be very insipid if all our lots were the same." "No one can be patient who is not independent." "Every procession must end."

Having soured on Gladstone, Cardinal Manning is rewarded by a gentler image than his Machiavellian one in *Lothair*, becoming Nigel Penruddock, a convert to Rome who rises to Papal Legate to England and Archbishop of Tyre. He is also given lines that Victoria told Disraeli she found the most amusing in the novel, the young priest's panegyric, "The Athanasian creed is the most splendid ecclesiastical lyric ever poured forth by the genius of man. I give every clause of it implicit assent. It does not pretend to be divine; it is human, but the Church has hallowed it, and the Church ever acts under the influence of the Divine Spirit. St Athanasius was by far the greatest man that ever existed." The lines carry an irony the novelist never knew, as he could not have read Cardinal Newman's private letter questioning what Disraeli thought of the Athanasian creed; and in a double irony, the dialogue is given to the churchman modeled upon the man whom Newman most disliked, Manning.

"Lord Roehampton" is an urbane cabinet minister patterned upon Lyndhurst as well as Palmerston, and who confesses "the feelings of youth and the frame of age." He marries Myra, giving Endymion a boost among the Whigs; on Roehampton's death she marries the former Continental exile she had known as "Colonel Albert," now the amiable King Florestan. A sanitized Napoleon III, he is given an island nation much like Sardinia, which had furnished troops to assist the West against Russia in the Crimean War.

Adriana Neuchatel (with something of Hannah de Rothschild—heiress to Mayer's millions—in her) is denied her chance at marriage to Endymion, but not her opportunity to manipulate his life. Her anonymous gift of £20,000 in bonds, a trifle to her, enables him to finance—in effect, purchase—a Parliamentary election. His open political sponsors are older women, especially the beautiful, domineering, Berengaria, Lady Montfort, who combines elements of Lady Cowper (Palmerston's wife), Mary Anne Wyndham Lewis (whose husband's death was to Disraeli's advantage), and Lady Londonderry, the energetic, lion-hunting hostess Disraeli admired. "Everything in this world depends upon will," Lady Montfort exhorts Endymion. "I think everything in this world," he claims, "depends upon woman." And for him it does.

Lady Montfort's husband (a version of Sir Francis Sykes and a like-minded complaisant husband) conveniently dies, leaving Berengaria a fortune and the opportunity to marry her protégé in a romanticized version of the Wyndham Lewis affair. Montfort had not been meanly heartless, as "he had no heart. He was good-natured, provided it brought him no inconvenience," for he had "a contemptuous fine taste, which assured him that a gentleman should never be deprived of tranquility in a world where nothing was of the slightest consequence."

Pressed earlier to propose marriage to Adriana, Endymion had shrunk back, claiming not that he was already magnetized by Lady Montfort but that at twenty-five he was unready. "Great men," his sister scolds him—she means potentially great—"should think of Opportunity, and not of Time. Time is the excuse of feeble and puzzled spirits." Agreeing with Berengaria, Myra warns that Time cannot accomplish what ought to be achieved by Will. Although in her wit, her resolve, and her ambition, Myra Ferrars is the true Disraelian figure ("You are myself," she tells Endymion), the novel is ultimately about a female political dimension that remained crucial in a culture where office, and even the ballot, were denied to women—when their political fulfillment came in nourishing male ambition. "If we cannot shape your destiny," Myra tells her twin, "there is no such thing as witchcraft."

Unable to wrest Endymion from Lady Montfort, Adriana marries the charmingly cynical Waldershare, who is given the Disraelian lines in the novel inappropriate for the rather prim Endymion. "Sensible men are all of the same religion," Waldershare observes; when he is asked, "And pray what is that?" he quips, "Sensible men never tell."

At the end of the novel the Earl of Aberdeen's government has fallen—it is the period of the Crimean War—and Endymion Ferrars, who has advanced from clerk, to private secretary (as Disraeli was to Lyndhurst), to M.P., and then to the Cabinet, becomes Prime Minister—a Whig one at that.

What puzzled readers and critics as much as the Whig milieu in which the Tory novelist's hero makes his way, was the old-fashioned outlook, attuned as it was to the old-fashioned prose. To evoke the vanished London of his youth, Disraeli was writing in his early manner, and when Ellery Sedgwick in *The Nation* attacked the novel as dated by fifty years, he failed to recognize that it had been the author's intention. Like other critics, he also saw the weakness of *Endymion* in its malleable hero, who has "no real struggle" and is "fatally successful." (Unlike his creator, the protagonist has to be pushed into being ambitious.) Writing anonymously in the *Quarterly Review*, Alfred Austin recognized Disraeli's strategies, writing, "What he did at twenty-five [in *Vivian Grey*], he is doing at seventy-five, only doing it better." But now, Austin noted, Lord Beaconsfield was the only person writing political novels from the inside, "and the only person who, by the very conditions of the case, could have written them."

Most of the more favorable notices were nevertheless on the edge of being unkind, the *Edinburgh Review* calling the novel "a satirical picture of life, with the transformations of a Christmas pantomime." From Washington, the Anglophilic Henry Adams, mining his anti-Semitic vein, wrote to Charles Milnes Gaskell, "I have read *Endymion*, with stares and gasps. There is but one excuse for it; the author must be in a terrible want of money; his tenants have paid him nothing, and Mr Gladstone has docked his pension. If he has not, he should. *Endymion* is a disgrace to the government, to the House of Lords, the Commons and the Jews."

It took the Queen nearly two months to finish *Endymion*, but she read all of it and questioned, on February 7, 1881, "Were you not thinking of the Duchess of Manchester in Lady Montfort, and of Mr Bright in Job Thornberry? But *who is* Endymion taken after? How is it that your hero should be a *Whig?*"

Three days later Disraeli responded in the last long letter he wrote, explaining "what I would admit to no one else, that I think there are features of Lady Palmerston in her youth in that representation, and some traits of devotion drawn from someone else." If a delicate allusion to Lady Bradford, it suggested that he could only wed Selina in fiction. "Indeed," he assured Victoria, "I had no intention or desire to draw any living characters." As for Thornberry, he explained, "I have endeavoured to convey my impression of the style of Mr Cobden as an orator. All the rest is typical: traits, perhaps of Mr Bright, but the catastrophe of the family occurred literally to Mr [John] Potter, the Socinian Mayor of Manchester, and M.P., who, having made his fortune, sent his two sons to Oxford to make them gentlemen; but they only became Roman Catholics."

Endymion, Disraeli explained, "was not intended for a hero any more than M. Gil Blas by Le Sage." In Alain-René Lesage's *Gil Blas* (1715), the hero is a rather passive student pushed by circumstance into a series of adventures—fleeced by a swindler, carried off by brigands, but eventually ingenious enough to succeed by his wits in a variety of professions and even, twice, in marriage. Endymion was not intended to be interesting in himself, Disraeli added; thus he was given "no imagination and very controlled passion: but he has great patience, perseverance, judgement, and tact, which qualities, with good looks, have, before this, elevated men in your Majesty's Councils. He is in fact rather a plodder, and I thought quite good enough to be a Whig."

He feared it was "too long a letter," Disraeli closed. "It is like an Address in answer to the gracious Speech from the Throne." But it was the most revealing private letter he had ever written about his fiction—and his last.

What critics overlooked was the mellow charm of the narrative, a political fantasy spun about the author's friends and enemies of a lifetime, and embodying his appraisal to Lady Bradford, "I have had a good innings and cannot agree with the great King that all is vanity." With no serious pretensions or sermonizing to slow it down, *Endymion* nevertheless examines how society and politics were interlinked in the aristocratic milieu in which he challenged the norms. A world which the rising bourgeois political powers of the 1880s saw as well lost, it was never as sunny as Disraeli painted it, yet in some ways it was more hospitable than his fiction. An outsider like Disraeli could never have penetrated Endymion Ferrars's society, not even its lowest rung.

"I don't give my mind at all to politics," he had written to Lady Bradford on September 10, for "the A.V."—the Arch-Villain, Gladstone—"has carried everything before him." Yet in the leisure between his completion of *Endymion* and the arrival of Longman to pick the pages up, he discussed his favorite subject, politics, with Lord Ronald Leveson-Gower, a Scottish M.P. of thirty-five who dabbled also in painting, sculpture, poetry, and boys, and would be the model for Lord Henry Wotton in Wilde's *The Picture of Dorian Gray*. (His elder brother, the 3rd Duke of Sutherland, was a Disraeli ally in the Upper House and a crony of the Prince of Wales.) Gower had been to Hughenden once before, eight years earlier, when Disraeli posed for a statue, seated, with arms folded (now in the National Portrait Gallery). Proudly, Disraeli showed Gower the changes since. A portrait of Byron by William Westall hung at the landing. On the staircase were pictures of personal and political friends and the Queen's portrait by Heinrich von Angeli that was her gift. Some of the painters—he mentioned Stuart Wortley and Augustus Lumley in his diary—Gower dismissed as "amateurs," but kept that to himself. The tour of the manor was a review of Lord Beaconsfield's rise, from the portraits of his mother and father to two of his grandfather Benjamin—"the real D'Israeli," said Gower's host.

In the library while they examined Hughenden's treasures, including Isaac's books and manuscripts and presentation books from Victoria, Disraeli picked up a volume Gower described as on "Solomon's writings," and spoke of religion in the vein of his novels. "I would indeed be very ungrateful to speak ill of Christianity," he said, "which has caused half the civilised world to worship a man and the other half a woman, both of my race." He spoke of his early travels to Spain and the East, and after dinner, at which Disraeli ate little—"only some venison and a little of a cabinet pudding (which I thought an appropriate dish)"—they sat in the library. Despite an asthmatic cough, Disraeli smoked a forbidden cigarette, dismissing his ailments with the thought that he was likely to live only two years more at most, though he had prophesied to the Queen a fanciful twenty.

Although Mary Anne had been dead eight years, Disraeli referred to her as "my dear wife." She had been, Gower thought, "his good angel." Her portraits were prominent in the house, Disraeli's favorite a flattering enlargement of a miniature showing a youngish Mary Anne whom he, and perhaps no one else, ever knew. At 11:00 he rose to go off to bed, and was up at 7:30 for breakfast before his guest was awake. After Gower's breakfast they examined further Hughenden treasures and looked in at the rooms used by the Prince of Wales earlier in the year. As the peacocks cried, they walked down the slope to the churchyard, where at the east wall were the graves of Mary Anne, Sarah Brydges Willyams, and James D'Israeli.

After lunch, they went on a long walk in the bright sun down to the trout stream—the Hughen—and through the beeches to the high road, where a pony cart waited to take them further. It was market day in Wycombe, and when the pair dismounted and walked among the crowds, people bowed to their famous neighbor. The next morning, a wet one, they sat in the smoking room, dominated by a portrait of Lord George Bentinck, and again talked politics, largely about Disraeli's desire to leave its burdens altogether. He had asked, he confided, to have Salisbury replace him as party leader. And he excoriated Hartington for lack of courage in deferring to Gladstone when the Marquess could have been Prime Minister. The post arrived just as Gower was leaving in the rain, Disraeli's carriage taking him to Wycombe Station. With the mail was *The Times*, which included a letter from Gladstone thanking the public for its prayers during his recent illness. "Did you ever hear anything like that?" Disraeli said, glancing at the letter with disgust. "It reminds one of the Pope blessing all the world from the balcony of St Peter's."

Two months later, on November 8, Gower was back. It was a golden autumn day, but Disraeli, sunning himself on his veranda among the shrill peacocks, was huddled in a fur-lined coat that reached nearly to his feet, one of which was slippered after a sharp attack of gout. He rejoiced in his gout, Disraeli claimed, for it had driven away his bronchitis. After lunch, as they sat by a blazing fire in the library, he accepted what he claimed was the first cigarette he had smoked since Gower's last visit, and was "full of the past, and his youth." He described the three Sheridan sisters in the flower of their beauty and dinners they graced, where the wit and humor flowed "more copiously by far than the claret." Gazing into the fire he murmured, "Dreams! dreams! dreams!"

"Life," he sighed, "is [either] an ennui, or an anxiety." For the person born with position and means, with little to strive for, he explained, existence could be a burden and a bore. For the self-made man, life was full of troubles and anxieties—to achieve position and then to hold on to it. "My idea of a happy future state," he mused, "is one of those long midsummer days, when one dines at nine o'clock."

"I believe he is engaged in writing something," Gower guessed, "but this he didn't tell me." Something in Disraeli's conversation suggested it, but Gower and almost everyone else learned of it only when the fragment was published in *The Times* in 1905. Before becoming too ill to carry it further, Disraeli had only reached the tenth chapter. Since called *Falconet* after the likely leading character, it begins among the spacious brick residences surrounding Clapham Common which housed pious merchants and magnates who preferred a quieter life than that of the Mayfair aristocracy. That the father of the first leading figure is named Wilberforce Falconet suggests the Evangelical ambience, and indeed there was a Clapham sect earlier in the century. Its religious and philanthropic ideals motivated Shaftesbury and Macaulay (whose father, Zachary, was a Claphamite), and inspired Thackeray's satiric view of Clapham in *The Newcombes* (1855). Falconet's daughters are pretty and pious, and two of his five sons are assiduous in the family counting house. Another enters the clergy, and the black sheep chooses the army. The youngest, Joseph Toplady Falconet, a brilliant Oxford scholar but deficient in a sense of humor and disputatious in nature, is eager to be "a lay champion of the Church. . . . A seat in the House of Commons seemed to be indicated."

"What's the use of cutting up the A.V.?" Disraeli wrote to Lady Bradford on November 2, 1880. ". . . I see no chance of [political] salvation unless he really goes mad, but he is such a hypocrite that I shall never believe that, till he is in Bedlam." Yet Disraeli was cutting him up in a way that seemed feasible only for a writer drifting out of politics. He would dissect Gladstone's hypocrisies in his novel—and the "Arch Villain," seen as a political climber, is young Falconet.

Critics have found a sardonic combination of names in Disraeli's coinage. Joseph Surface was W. B. Sheridan's scheming hypocrite in *The School for Scandal*, while Augustus Montague Toplady was the anti-Wesleyan divine who was the hymnist of "Rock of Ages." It is possible, too, that Disraeli intended some ironic sexual innuendo in the name—a suggestion of what Gladstone never accomplished in his relations with demimondaines, and possibly the source of his manic intensity. It was well known that Gladstone in 1839 had Latinized "Rock of Ages," and was already imposing what to Disraeli were the irrelevant perspectives of religion upon the practical business of politics. Seething at the "A.V." during the Eastern crisis, he had written to Lord Derby in October 1876, "Posterity will do justice to that unprincipled maniac Gladstone—extraordinary mixture of envy, vindictiveness, hypocrisy and superstition; and with one commanding characteristic—whether Prime Minister, or Leader of the Opposition, whether preaching, praying, speechifying or scribbling— never a gentleman."

The lineaments of Joseph Toplady Falconet were laid out long before the writing was begun, and when Disraeli, at a Royal Academy view, saw the Millais portrait of Gladstone, he remarked that there was one element missing in the face—the vindictiveness. In what we have of *Falconet* the Gladstone figure is still too immature for that, but already visible is the Joseph Surface side. Gladstone, so Disraeli wrote to Lady Bradford, was "a ceaseless Tartuffe from the beginning." Was *Falconet* beneath the dignity of a former prime minister to write? It may be that Disraeli did not intend to publish it in his lifetime, but that he began it at all suggests how much he thought a corrective to Gladstone's aura of sanctity was necessary. His version was intended as a Gladstone for the ages.

The opening pages suggest the high noon of the Claphamites, a period of expansive optimism, but Disraeli juggled time and set *Falconet* in the recent past. Optimism, but for the Falconet family, is almost gone. The experience of the Eastern Question had left its mark on Disraeli, and he was unconvincing, even to himself, when he had insisted to Victoria on October 28, 1880, that he was neither a pessimist nor "a disappointed politician." Bleakly, he added, "I gratefully recognise that I have had my fair chance, & share, of serving my Sovereign & my country, but with nearly a half century of experience in public life, I wish not to deny that the present condition of affairs fills me with anxiety, & even gloom." "I am not a pessimist," he maintained to Lady Chesterfield on December 22, while admitting, "the present state of affairs makes me tremble. Old England seems to be tumbling to pieces. . . . I receive letters every day asking me to write a manifesto and make a speech; that I am the only man who could do so with effect; and all that. Why should I?" Yet he was answering his own question in fiction, the medium for his argument that either the political processes had failed or that humanity itself had failed its opportunities.

The name Falconet, Sarah Bradford suggests in her biography, "may have been inspired by Gladstone's appearance; to admirers he resembled an eagle, to Disraeli a bird of prey." Like Joseph Surface and Augustus Toplady, however, the only Falconet of any fame also derived from the later eighteenth century. Peter Falconet was a portrait painter, but in the novel it is Falconet's own portrait that is to be limned. Not much of it was drawn in the few chapters in which Falconet appears, although he is seen passionately attacking the revival of the slave trade in the Red Sea. There is no truth to the allegation, yet his audience is electrified and it suffices to prove Falconet's readiness for the seat that falls vacant when Lord Gaston, son of Earl Bertram's first marriage, resigns it. But, advises the Earl, a cabinet minister much like Palmerston, the issue so eloquently raised was unsuitable for the House of Commons. "I think I would leave the Red Sea alone. It was a miracle that saved us from being drowned in it before." Once in the Commons, however, Falconet perceives "the fund of Religionism in the House," and takes up Sabbatarianism. He is "essentially a prig, and among prigs there is a freemasonry which never fails. All the prigs spoke of him as the coming man."

While the Earl is as vivacious and paradox-loving as Oscar Wilde's later lords, Gaston is the last of Disraeli's disillusioned young men. There is an undeveloped suggestion that Gaston is hopelessly in love with his still-beautiful stepmother, carrying through to the close Disraeli's sense that the ideal mate for an ambitious young man is an experienced older woman. The world disappoints Gaston. Not merely Parliaments, which are "worn out," but "even this little planet." If it has a future, he contends, it is not for the human race. "The mistake which our self-conceit has always made has been to suppose that this planet was made for man. There was never any foundation for such belief, and now we know it is mere folly."

He is "capable of devotion," Gaston insists—but only "to the happiness of my species. For that reason I wish it to become extinct."

Another disillusioned young gentleman, seen earlier in *Lothair*, is Hugo Bohun, whose wretchedness is of a different order. At a ball he dances with Lady Bertram's daughter, Ermyntrude, and gushes that she had made the night one of the happiest of his life. "Do you know, I think it wonderfully kind of you to dance with such a miserable wretch as I am."

"One meets with so many happy people," Ermyntrude assures him. "I rather like sometimes to meet a miserable wretch."

"What other miserable wretch do you know except myself?"

"I know several wretches," says Ermyntrude, in lines that anticipate Wilde's Cecily and Gwendolen in *The Importance of Being Earnest*. "But I am not at all sure they are miserable wretches."

"Well, what's your idea of a wretch?"

"I think a man who is discontented with his lot in life is a wretch."

"Everybody is discontented with their lot in life."

"I thought just now you said you were most happy."

"So I am when I am with you."

"Then, after all, you are not a real wretch."

"Do you think Gaston is?" Hugo asks.

"His wretchedness is on so great a scale that it amounts to the sublime."

"I should think you were contented with your lot in life," asserts Hugo.

"I have not yet considered that question so deeply as it deserves," says Lady Ermyntrude, observing that a dance seemed the wrong place for such reflections. And she reaches for the hand of a passing young man to return to the floor.

"Now," mourns Hugo, "I feel this is the most miserable night of my life."

More serious characters are introduced in the early chapters, but they remain undeveloped. The Hartmann Brothers banking family is still another variation of the Rothschilds, with the firm's future dependent upon an only daughter. The present head, recruited from the German branch, is a devotee not of Falconet's religion of hymns and tracts but of Spinoza and Kant, whose portraits hang in his library. And there is a Buddhist philosopher from Ceylon, Kusinara, who apparently thinks in parallel with Lord Gaston. Arriving as a missionary because his understanding is that the English were "rapidly renouncing, not only their own religion, but their religious principles altogether," he is surprised by the Sabbatarian zeal, which "could only have been equalled in old Jerusalem." Their narrowness of outlook vexes him. "True religion," he contends, "would secure repose for every day." To Kusinara, "the great remedy which can alone cure the evils of the human race" is its elimination. "Death," he explains, "is the only happiness, if understood."

His mysterious companion—they had met on the boat from Rotterdam that brought them to England—is eager to meet with Hartmann, while Kusinara carries a letter of credit to Falconet and Company. The unnamed traveller, "high-bred" and "in the prime of middle age," is as cynical as young Lord Gaston, and, it proves, as nihilistic as the German financier, whose name echoes that of Leo Hartmann, a Nihilist conspirator whom the Russians had vainly tried to extradite from Paris early in 1880. Yet the suggestion by Disraeli's biographer G. E. Buckle that the Nihilist angle was influenced by the assassination of Alexander II in St. Petersburg on March 13, 1881, places the writing of the novel fragment at a time when Disraeli was already beyond authorship.

"If anything is to be done in this world," the mysterious stranger assures Hartmann, "it must be done by visionaries; men who see the future, and make the future because they see it." To him the terms Liberal and Conservative mean little—"different names for the same thing." The only solution to human misery, he asserts, "is the destruction of the species. . . . We differ only in our estimate of the time required. . . . You think that centuries must elapse before the consummation. . . . All that is happening in the world appears to me to indicate a speedier catastrophe." He sees in the "immense armies" assembling in Europe, and the "new-fangled armaments," inevitable depopulation not from "the slaughter of battles" they make inevitable, but from the "disease and famine" that would follow.

Hartmann doubts that the "comparatively slight means" of destruction represented by armaments could result in the elimination of humanity. "Not so slight as you may imagine," the stranger contends. "Besides we must accept all means. Destruction in every form must be welcomed." If "creeds are falling away," he muses, "cannot our principle of experimentation be clothed in a celestial form?" There is nothing to be compared to the stimulus of the "religious principle," the stranger contends, "except the influence of women."

His sardonic view may mesh somehow with the loss of faith, but Disraeli leaves no clue as to how the feminine factor is to influence the argument, or how the gentle Kusinara's Buddhism is to clash—or mesh—with the destructive element. To complicate matters, Kusinara is by birth, Mrs. Falconet finds, "half a Christian." She resolves "that he should become a whole one." There, one paragraph into Chapter X, the fragment stops.

How Disraeli could have integrated his social comedy with the political drama of progress thwarted by religiosity, with the further implications of new secular creeds like Communism and Nihilism, and with forebodings about man's suicidal exploitation of his planet, cannot be guessed at. The manuscript breaks off too soon. Yet it is a provocative last testament, a frank summing up by a pragmatic politician freed from an active politician's constraints. It would have taken all of Disraeli's genius to bring it off.

Autumn and winter at Hughenden had not been easy. He saw few visitors, and on grounds of health turned away his brother's offer to visit. Both knew that even a robust Ben had little interest in Ralph or even in Ralph's son, despite his status as heir to Hughenden. On occasion, braving what he described as "the black fogs of Westminster," Disraeli entrained to London, either for political business or to see Dr. Kidd, staying in the suite of rooms kept for him in Seamore Place. He could travel only in the interstices between attacks of gout that kept him on crutches at Hughenden, where Baum and Mrs. Baum carried him up and down the stairs. The affliction, he confessed to Salisbury, was "the Devil on two sticks." To Ralph he explained that if his doctor's house calls to Hughenden had continued, "I shd have had to mortgage my estate." But there were good days. On December 21, which had been bright and sunny, he wrote to Victoria that he had managed a walk of three miles with his dog.

On Christmas Day came an outpouring of gifts from the Queen, to which Disraeli responded with a note prefaced, "Oh! Madam, & most beloved Sovereign!" Most of his correspondence with Victoria since his leaving office had been conducted outside formal channels, with Monty Corry delivering messages to John Brown. In return, letters and packets came through Brown—even salmon from Balmoral. It was an unguarded exchange between sovereign and subject, ranging the gamut from formal to friendly, from grave to gossipy, with perhaps the most amusing from Disraeli's side being his comments on the forthcoming marriage between Baroness Burdett-Coutts, then sixty-six—she had several times proposed marriage to him—and William Ashmead-Bartlett, who was nearly young enough to be her grandson. It was, Disraeli remarked, "the greatest scrape" since the British embarrassments in Afghanistan. "I thought Angela would have become classical, & history."

With the 1881 Parliamentary session to begin earlier than usual, on January 7—Gladstone wanted to rush through his Irish Coercion Bill—Disraeli left the solitude of Hughenden on December 31. He would never see it again. Until Christmas the late autumn weather had been kind to his ailments. He felt ready to return to politics. By the time he left Wycombe Station for

Paddington the east winds had become severe, carrying with them bitter cold and snow. As his carriage brought him to Alfred de Rothschild's house he was near collapse, unable to breathe. The Baums saw him to bed, and he remained indoors at Seamore Place until the sessions began, braving the frost daily to go to the Lords, and to the dinner parties at which he was now, but for the Prince of Wales, the lion of each occasion. Other than Victoria and her heir, he remained, in or out of office, the most eminent individual in England.

Going out at all, however, remained hazardous. His asthma was aggravated by smoke-filled rooms, and Dr. Kidd observed that increasing uremia left Disraeli drowsy at times and affected his hearing and his sight. Sir William Fraser remembered seeing him in the Carlton Club and looking vacantly about. "I know you wish someone to speak to you," ventured Fraser, a former M.P. "I am very much obliged to you," said Disraeli. "I am so blind; I come here; I look round; I see no one; I go away." Often, still, the old wit and ebullience returned, and he could act the party leader—as was necessary. Salisbury, whom he had singled out as his successor in the Lords, refused to return from his winter home on the Riviera for the early debates, feeling that Gladstone had the majorities to have his way.

While the Burdett-Coutts nuptials irritated Disraeli as the extremity of bad taste, he was looking forward to another marriage, that of his host's brother. Leopold de Rothschild, younger brother of Natty and Alfred and the inheritor of Gunnersbury Park, was one of the richest bachelors in Britain. Leo had vowed not to marry until he found a bride "as beautiful and accomplished" as Louise Sassoon, of a notable Italian-Jewish family. Arthur Sassoon introduced him to his young sister-in-law, Marie Perugia, eighteen to Leo's thirty-six. "I have always been of opinion," Disraeli had congratulated him from Hughenden on December 11, 1880, "that there cannot be too many Rothschilds."

On January 19, 1881, a wind-whipped snowstorm kept Disraeli from the wedding at the Central Synagogue, Great Portland Street, although he managed to get to the reception at Arthur Sassoon's spacious house at 2 Albert Gate in time for the cutting of the bridal cake, which weighed 180 pounds and was adorned with orange blossoms. In the first residence he had ever been in illuminated by what he called "magical" electricity, nec-essary indeed as the snow blanketed London, he proposed the health of the Prince of Wales in champagne which Dr. Kidd did not permit him to drink. Prince Bertie in turn toasted the bride and groom.

Four days earlier, Disraeli had moved from Seamore Place to 19 Curzon Street, a house in Mayfair upon which he had taken a seven-year lease on the income from *Endymion*. Though Alfred de Rothschild was "the best and kindest host in the world," Disraeli told Lady Chesterfield, if he were to participate at all in Parliament, he required his own domicile; Monty Corry had found him one. Albert Gate, just above Lowndes Square at Hyde Park, was only a short carriage ride from Curzon Street, but get-ting to the snowbound wedding breakfast had left him, he wrote to Anne Chesterfield several days later, "in a state of stupor and only capable of lying on a sofa by the fire."

The move was responsible for a signal mark of Disraeli's fame, the *World* reported, one that would disappear when the mo-tor vehicle replaced the horse a generation later. "A crossing sweeper," it observed, "has just established himself in front of Lord Beaconsfield's newly acquired house in Curzon Street. . . . That crossing sweeper is a symbolical personage. His broom is to the ex-Premier that which the cloak of Sir Walter Raleigh was in the matter of that memorable puddle to Queen Elizabeth. . . . Lord Beaconsfield may be out of office but he will never be out of the English mind."

As a private entrepreneur depending upon tips from the walking public, the sweeper would have some rewarding weeks, but the eminent occupant of 19 Curzon Street seldom chanced going out himself. His last letter to Lady Chesterfield, on January 26, apologized for not calling—"but the moment I breathe the air, even in furs and a close carriage, the asthmatic seizure comes on." He had tried, and had to return.

"Asthma," Dr. Kidd noted, "is a most peculiar disease. . . . From the first, asthma followed Lord Beaconsfield in Curzon Street. After a week in the close small bedroom, . . . a small stuffy

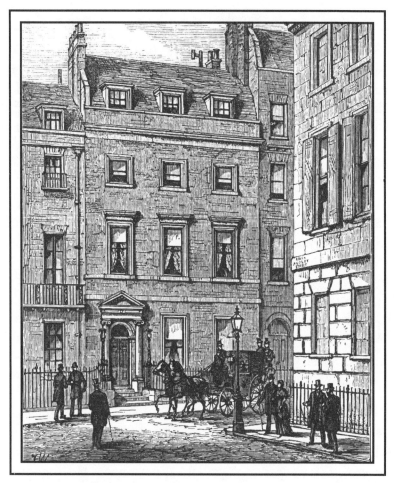

Lord Beaconsfield's house at 19 Curzon Street, Mayfair, where he died in April 1881.

one with fluffy paper and old-fashioned curtains . . . , the bed was moved out into the airy drawing-room with great benefit."

It was an optimistic assessment. As the weather briefly moderated, Disraeli again appeared in the Lords, attacking the Government's Afghan policy; he entertained once at Curzon Street, leaning on a cane and taking to his bed afterward for two days, "having inhaled some of my poison in the form of a cigarette." He dined twice at Alfred de Rothschild's bachelor mansion that had been his temporary home (Alfred had a natural daughter, Almina, but never married). And on the last day of February he visited Windsor Castle for dinner, remaining overnight into

March 1. The morning before he arrived, the Queen had received a telegram informing her of the humiliating rout at Majuba Hill in the Transvaal, where the road from Pietermartizburg to Pretoria crossed the Natal-Transvaal border. A small force of 180 Boers had killed, wounded, and captured many times their numbers of Gordon Highlanders, convincing Gladstone to back away from further adventures in South Africa as he was also withdrawing from the Indian frontier. "Dreadful news," she noted in her journal. "Another fearful defeat." Disraeli agreed: Empire meant imperial responsibilities which could not be shortchanged.

On March 15, Disraeli pushed himself to Parliament to offer words of condolence to the Queen and to the Russian Government on behalf of his party after the assassination of Alexander II two days earlier. A few days afterward, at a dinner party at which he could eat almost nothing, he confided to Lucy Goschen, whose husband George, a Liberal M.P., was on temporary assignment by Gladstone to Constantinople, "I am blind and deaf. I live only for [warmer] climate and I never get it." After dinner she and Lady Northcote were chatting when Disraeli came up to them and applied his eyeglass to better make them out. When Lady Northcote offered her chair he said, "No, I won't take that, but if Mrs Goschen will allow me, I will sit on the sofa between you." They had him to themselves until Lucy Goschen arose to leave, and Disraeli said that he was leaving as well. "I *live* early," he explained, ". . . I am like the birds, alive all day but must rest early—I am dead at half-past ten and buried by twelve." To her husband she wrote that Disraeli "has lost his old spirit and is very aged . . . , very blind and seemed to me to see nothing with one eye."

The weather was at its worst for him—a sleety east wind—when he returned from another reception. He took to his bed with bronchitis, emerging from his bedroom only for a political meeting at his home on March 26, a Saturday, with Salisbury, Cairns, and Hardy, who wrote in his diary of "an interesting talk on the Transvaal disgrace." Disraeli was very feeble, but his feelings were roused by such family tragedies as that of Lord Hawarden, who had lost an only son through botched battle tactics that had led to nothing for the survivors but ignominious surrender. "If I could only give expression to the indignation I feel," he said, "but it is of no use."

The Tory leadership had come to Curzon Street reluctantly, Salisbury later told the Queen, because they did not think that Disraeli was up to transacting any business, but he had insisted on it. "He could not bear to be absent when a matter affecting the national honour was being discussed."

Skeptically, Hardy noted in his diary that "the chief had been poorly & feels weak & ill but his servant & Barrington thought him really better." George Barrington, a close friend, was standing in for Rowton, again called abroad because of his sister's serious illness. Rowton had no idea that Disraeli was dying. Baum and Barrington knew more than they intimated.

With Monty away, Disraeli had been dealing with Thomas Longman himself about book business—the sensitive matter that *Endymion* had not earned back its record advance. Longman's strategy had been to exhaust the luxury (three-volume) market before advertising a one-volume edition, and he had just released the novel at six shillings. Only two days before Disraeli's Curzon Street meeting with Opposition leaders, Longman had been able to report that the cheap edition was "making good start" with eight thousand copies sold. Still, Disraeli offered to return three thousand as yet unearned pounds, and Longman refused, saying that the firm's offer had been made "with eyes open," and that they expected that the arrangement would answer their expectations.

As March closed, politicians and old associates continued to visit at Curzon Street, ostensibly on business but clearly because they sensed that Disraeli would not recover. Why else would Sir Charles Dilke, an old opponent, be brought in by Barrington, or George Hamilton, a youngish ally? Even Socialist proseltyzer Henry Mayers Hyndman applied for advice, Disraeli telling him, "Britain is a very difficult country to move, Mr Hyndman, a very difficult country indeed, and one in which there is more disappointment to be looked for than success."

Philip Rose learned what Disraeli understood of his condition on March 29, only a week after he had taken to his bed. "Dear friend," he said to the man who knew more about him than anyone else, "I shall never survive this attack. I feel it is quite impossible." Two days later when Rose was back, Disraeli told him, "I feel I am dying. Whatever the doctors may tell you, I do not believe I shall get well."

The Queen remained anxious and sent a Household aide, Captain Fleetwood Edwards, to consult Dr. Kidd and ask whether royal physicians might intervene—a professional complication since Victoria's doctors did not recognize a homeopathic physician. Sir William Jenner, in fact, first objected but at the Queen's orders would see Disraeli three times. As late as March 20 Disraeli had been able to write a note to her, a brief scrawl for which he apologized, "I am ashamed to address your Majesty not only from my [bed]room, but even my bed." She responded with daily inquiries to Barrington and on March 30 she sent by messenger from Windsor "some Osborne primroses. . . . I meant to pay you a little visit this week," she added, "but I thought it better you should be quiet and not speak. And I beg you will be very good and obey the doctors and commit no imprudence. . . . Everyone is so distressed at your not being well."

The last publisher's proofs that Disraeli would see also arrived on March 30, his remarks in *Hansard* on the death of the Czar. When his doctor worried that the effort to work on them might be too much, Disraeli took the sheets, insisting, "I will not go down to posterity talking bad grammar."

The idea that the Queen might visit, and see him at his worst, was firmly yet wittily rejected. "No, it is better not," he said. "She would only ask me to take a message to Albert." When he received the last letter from her that he knew about, dated April 5, with instructions that it should be read to him if he were not able to read it himself, he held it before him, then decided, "This letter ought to be read to me by Lord Barrington, a Privy Councillor."

Possibly the last letter he was shown of the many messages of support and concern, some with suggestions for "infallible" cures, was a postcard. According to Kidd it delighted his patient. Signed by "A British Workman," it read, "Don't die yet; we can't do without you."

"I followed his illness from day to day with great anxiety," recalled Winston, the young son of Lord Randolph Churchill, "because everyone said what a loss he would be to the country and how no one else could stop Mr Gladstone from working his wicked will upon us all." Liberal Roman Catholic historian John Acton wrote to Mary Gladstone from Cannes on April 2 "under the shadow of Disraeli's illness." The last accounts he had heard were "very threatening," and he confessed that he liked him "better than the mass of his party. . . . He, at least, if he had no principles or scruples, had no prejudices or superstitions or fanaticism. . . . With a few allowances a good deal may be said for the Tory leader who made England a Democracy."

Rowton returned on April 7, by which time Kidd had called in two additional doctors on his own, both from Brompton Hospital, Richard Quain and Mitchell Bruce, who shared with Kidd attendance through the night. Disraeli was now totally bedridden and understood the gravity of his condition. Offered an air cushion to lie on, he rejected it with, "Take away that emblem of mortality!" But he accepted a padded "fracture couch" raised and lowered mechanically as more comfortable than his own bed, for the dry coughing that wracked his chest and his choking inability to expel mucus kept him in nearly constant pain. Knowing of the mass arrests of revolutionaries in Russia following Alexander II's murder he quipped wryly, "I have suffered much. Had I been a Nihilist, I should have confessed all."

Like most mortally ill patients, he wanted the truth from his doctors but did not get it. Every night at 11:00 they composed a work of fiction for the morning papers, suggesting more than actually written, and soon they added a morning bulletin for the afternoon papers. "You have given a good report," Disraeli once told Dr. Bruce, "but your face looks anxious." Each bulletin was posted in the hallway for visitors, and throngs—often entire families—came to read the latest news on Disraeli's condition and to write their names and good wishes in the visitors' book in the hall.

During one of the 11 o'clock consultations about a text for the morning editions, the Prince of Wales and Prince Alfred, the Duke of Edinburgh (whose wife was the daughter of the murdered Czar), came to Curzon Street on returning to London from the funeral in St. Petersburg and asked anxiously about the illustrious patient. Gladstone called several times to read the latest bulletin, once writing piously in his diary about his old adversary, "May the Almighty be near his pillow."

While it was as clear to most of the public as to the patient himself that he would not recover, the usual conspiracy of silence on the subject persisted until broken by Edmund Yates, who speculated in the *World* on April 6, "One may be quite sure that the end, which of all others, Lord Beaconsfield would desire for himself, is [Lord] Chatham's. To sink back on the Treasury Bench, in the middle of his denunciations of the pusillanimity of Liberalism, and to expire surrounded by all the great officers of State, would be an appropriate termination for his career." There was no reason to conceal the paper—or any paper—from the patient; he was beyond seeing any of them.

Although Lord Rowton had returned from his sister's bedside in Algiers on the 7th, Disraeli would not see him until the 10th. Monty could not fathom whether the reason was pique at his dereliction or concern as to how his chief appeared *in extremis*. Finally, Monty simply walked in as if he had nothing but Parliamentary affairs to transact and realized that such bulletins as "Lord Beaconsfield's strength is maintained" were nonsense. Armed also with good news, he told Disraeli that Thomas Longman had reported "that his firm had just turned the corner, & was beginning to make a profit out of the bargain" for *Endymion*. After that, "the Chief" was beyond business.

Only what Disraeli called "the little demon"—a powder of saltpeter and stramonium which filled his chest with vapor to break up the mucus—gave relief, although with harsh aftereffects. And the more frequently the doctors had recourse to it, the worse Disraeli's exhaustion. Further, as his kidneys were more and more obstructed, his uremia became acute. He was ready to turn his face to the wall.

As Disraeli's condition deteriorated there were more daily bulletins, each more dishonest than the last. One, on April 15, in purple ink and dated "Good Friday Morning, 10:15 a.m.," lied, "The only change to report is Lord Beaconsfield's condition this morning is one of slowly progressive improvement."

Lord Cairns asked Kidd, "With so near a prospect of death, can you not get Canon Fleming to visit him?" Kidd broached such subjects as Christ and the Redemption, and Disraeli shook the suggestions off. He wanted no clergyman present. A rumor would surface, nevertheless, that he had called for Father Clarke, S.J., of the Jesuit Church in Farm Street, nearby, but that with Clarke away in Liverpool another Jesuit father hastened over to receive Disraeli into the Catholic Church. Another story was that at the end, Disraeli held the hand of Philip Rose and murmured, "There is—one God—of Israel!"—the traditional *Shema Yisroel* declaration that is the central statement of Judaism. More likely, Disraeli died as he had lived, a confirmed skeptic in the tradition of his father.

On Easter Monday morning, April 18, the physicians posted their usual purple-ink bulletin reporting that "Lord Beaconsfield had been rather more restless and taken rather less nourishment. As a consequence there has been no material gain of strength." In reality he had become incoherent in speech and gradually, through the day, comatose. Rowton remained at the bedside with Kidd and Bruce. "At one o'clock [on the 19th]," Kidd wrote, "we summoned Dr Quain, Lord Barrington, and Sir Philip Rose to witness the end. Lord Barrington was the first to arrive, and at once joined Lord Rowton in a loving clasping of Lord Beaconsfield's right hand; his left hand was laid in mine. Soon afterwards Dr Quain arrived. It touched us all deeply to see the dying statesman rise up in the bed and lean forward in the way he used to do when rising to reply in debate; his lips moved but no sound came. He fell back on the pillows, and in about ten minutes, without suffering or distress, his spirit passed away." The end had come at 4:30 in the morning. Benjamin Disraeli was seventy-six.

XXX

"EVERY PROCESSION MUST END."

1881

"AS HE LIVED, SO HE DIED—ALL DISPLAY, WITHOUT REALITY OR GEN-uineness," Gladstone complained to his secretary, Edward Hamilton. The display was in its absence. Disraeli wanted neither a clergyman at the close, nor a show funeral thereafter, and the quiet simplicity irked the Prime Minister. The Roman Catholic *Nation* in Dublin would go even further. "Priest or parson, book or prayer, cross or crescent, symbol or sign of faith, there was nothing to tell whether the dying man thought of Moses, or Mahomet, or Christ. . . . Lord Beaconsfield died as dies a horse."

Faithful John Brown was in tears when he came to tell the Queen what she had long anticipated, and she wrote to Rowton, "I feel deeply for *you*—who loved him and devoted yourself to him as few sons ever do! . . . I hardly dare trust to speak of myself. The loss is so *overwhelming*. . . . Never had I *so* kind and devoted a Minister and very few such devoted friends." Dropping third-person speech, as she had done so often with Disraeli, was indic-ative of her emotional state, and Lord Rowton came to Windsor to share his grief with the Queen, bringing with him Disraeli's will to assure her that a private interment at Hughenden had been his wish. Preceding Monty was a message from Dean Stanley of Westminster which had deeply moved her. Rowton or Barrington, the Dean wrote, would describe to her "the striking appearance of Lord Beaconsfield, when at the last he raised himself as if to make one of his great speeches—and then bowed down and passed away."

While the Queen deplored what she described to Salisbury as "the gloomy pomp of a so-called public funeral and the dismal dreariness of a grave in the great Metropolitan Abbey," she asked through Lady Ely whether Disraeli's body could be publicly transported to Hughenden so that ordinary people could express their sorrow. Rowton consulted the executors, Sir Philip Rose and Sir Nathaniel de Rothschild, reporting to Victoria that the executors had decided against a procession. Should even the time of removal be made known, Rowton explained, it would be "a difficult matter to control the hundreds of thousands who would gather to do him honour. And so they have resolved that the removal shall be made at night, the time being kept quite secret. When the sun rises tomorrow the coffin will rest in the room at Hughenden where hangs the picture of his *dear Queen*."

Before 1 o'clock in the morning on Sunday, April 24, with the crowds that had gathered each day in Curzon Street gone, Alfred de Rothschild arrived at the darkened house and gazed on his friend's face for the last time. Then he assisted at closing the coffin. If he had gone there also to perform some Jewish rite over the remains, that may never be known, although it is significant that the body was not moved until after the Jewish Sabbath was over, a day when religious law forbade such ceremony. He and Baum saw the coffin placed on a special train at Paddington, and Baum remained with it to Wycombe, where Nathaniel received the body.

The funeral at Hughenden took place on the 26th, a Tuesday. In Wycombe at the inn portico where Disraeli's political career began, the venerable red lion had black crêpe draped about its neck. In the crowded manor, three of Victoria's sons—the Prince of Wales, Prince Arthur (the Duke of Connaught), and

Prince Leopold, the Queen's personal representative—led the aristocratic mourners. The ambassadors from France, Germany, Russia, and Turkey were present, as well as peers and politicians of both parties, even the apostate Earl of Derby. The absent Gladstone had pleaded the press of public business.

On the coffin lay a wreath of "Osborne primroses" from Victoria, the card inscribed in her own hand. On the terrace the peacocks screeched, and someone remarked that a peacock feather might have been a better symbol of the departed than the primrose. Carrying a crimson velvet cushion with the Earl's coronet and insignia, Baum walked before the coffin as it was wheeled by Disraeli's tenants down the hill to the churchyard. Behind walked the chief mourners, Ralph D'Israeli and his son Coningsby, a Charterhouse schoolboy, followed by Rowton, Barrington, Rose, and Natty de Rothschild. (Coningsby, at fourteen the heir of Hughenden, would have no male issue.)

Behind the dignitaries came the common folk of Buckinghamshire and the curious from farther off. The coffin was placed between those of Sarah Brydges Willyams and Mary Anne, and the vault closed. The invited guests—Natty ordered cards printed—returned indoors for the traditional reading of the will, after which they crowded into carriages for the special train from Wycombe at 5:30.

Protocol kept the Queen from attending a funeral of a subject. Victoria made a private trip by carriage from Windsor on April 30. From the manor she walked down the slope, tracing the steps of those who had followed the body of her friend. The vault at Hughenden Church was reopened so that she could see the coffin, on which still lay her primroses. "Could hardly realise it all," she wrote in her journal, "it all seemed so sad, and so cheerless. I placed a wreath of china flowers." Then, under her portrait in the library, sitting in the chair that in 1877 had its legs shortened by an inch-and-a-half to accommodate her five-foot frame, she took tea as she had at the height of the Eastern crisis, only this time with Disraeli's shade. "I seem to hear his voice, and the impassioned, eager way he described everything."

For Hughenden Church the Queen ordered a marble monu-

"Peace with Honour." *Punch*, April 30, 1881. Death had turned *Punch* respectful about Disraeli.

ment, "placed by his grateful and affectionate Sovereign and friend, Victoria R.I." The "I" was Disraeli's gift. The last line was a quotation she had chosen from Proverbs, "Kings love him that speaketh right."

Gladstone's absence had prompted public scorn. His secretary, Edward Hamilton, defended the apparent snub in his diary by remarking that the Prime Minister would have been accused "of being a humbug" had he attended, and that the "private character" of the funeral made his presence unnecessary. To make amends was not easy for Gladstone. At the annual Royal Academy dinner on the evening of the Queen's visit to Disraeli's grave, the Prime Minister found the unfinished portrait of Lord Beaconsfield by Sir John Millais looking down at him in the foyer. Millais had managed only two sittings from his subject, and the gaunt, sorrowful features of the face, the most finished part, suggested mortality. Although the submission date had passed and the work abandoned, Victoria asked that the canvas be exhibited, and that Millais prepare it as much as possible for showing. Each speaker in turn referred to it. When Gladstone arose he felt that he had to allude to the picture and remarked, unfeelingly, "It is, indeed, an unfinished work. In this sense it was a premature death."

On Sunday, May 1, a memorial service was held in Westminster Abbey. Every place was filled, and congregants had to sit on the altar steps to hear an even more curious address by Dean Stanley, who selected a text from Judges 16:30, "So the dead which he slew at his death were more than they which he slew in his life." As if he were creating a cartoon for *Punch* he coupled the Earl of Beaconsfield with the live but embarrassed Gladstone, calling them the "Great Twin Brothers." The oft-postponed memorial addresses in both Houses were scheduled, finally, for Monday, May 9. Contemplating his on Friday, Gladstone remained in bed all day with a sharp attack of diarrhea. He called in his doctor twice. On Monday he prayed for guidance, and while he failed to say that Disraeli's death was a great loss to the nation, he recognized Disraeli's "consistency of purpose" and "great parliamentary courage." The address was admired, and the entire ordeal of oratory lasted only an hour.

Most reactions to Disraeli's passing, public and private, referred to the courage in adversity that sustained his sense of purpose. An exception was Dorothy Nevill, who, writing to Lady Airlie, was "more than ordinarily sad. . . . For twenty-one years we lived near each other, and how much happiness and brightness I had then." Salisbury, whose detestation of Disraeli over two decades, before they began working together, had been passionate, spoke in the Lords as Gladstone was addressing the Commons, of how "anxious and difficult times" reveal the character of men. Salisbury was well aware of "the social difficulties which opposed themselves to [Disraeli's] early rise"—like others of his class he had contributed to them—and he recalled "the splendid perseverance by which they were overcome." He congratulated his fellow peers, among whom would soon sit the first Lord Rothschild—Natty rather than his late father—that the man they were memorializing "exemplified that open career to all persons, whatever their initial difficulties may be, which is one of the characteristics of their institutions of which they are most proud. . . . If the genius and the perseverance are there, the most splendid position and the widest influence are open to any subject of the Queen." Opinions would differ about the Earl of Beaconsfield's policies, he concluded, but beyond controversy one fact remained undeniable. *"Zeal for the greatness of England was the passion of his life."*

Preaching the University Sermon at Oxford, the Bishop of Liverpool avoided politics and "simply drew two grand lessons from his career," Charles Dodgson (Lewis Carroll) reported: "One, the courage of going forward *alone* in the course one feels to be right, 'without waiting helplessly, as we are so apt to do, for some one to join us.' The other, perseverance under defeat and discouragement. 'No man ever led a minority as he did.' In this he seems to stand in contrast with his great rival. I don't think he could *ever* have brought himself, as Gladstone did, to retire from the leadership of his party directly after they were beaten, and then, as soon as they had recovered themselves, put himself at their head again."

There were others—there would always be others—who refused to see Disraeli as a British statesman, but always as the ultimate outsider. "His *Semitic* politics of course were genuine enough," Wilfrid Scawen Blunt conceded to Wilfrid Meynell, a Disraeli biographer. "For his avowing these I hold him in esteem—for a Jew ought to be a Jew—and I enjoy as a *tour de force* his smashing of those solemn rogues the Whigs, and his bamboozling of the Tories. Our dull English nation deserved what it got, and there is nothing funnier in our history than the way he cajoled our square-toed aristocratic Party to put off its respectable broad-cloth, and robe itself in his suit of Imperial spangles, and got our fine ladies after his death to worship their old worldweary Hebrew beguiler under the innocent form of a primrose."

Blunt was offering at least a half-truth. Since Disraeli could not escape his origins, he made the most of them, with an authentic pride. Also, however, he brought the Conservative Party within reach of the twentieth century, and carried—despite Gladstone's fierce opposition—one of the two crucial reform bills of the nineteenth century. He helped preserve constitutional monarchy by drawing the Queen out of perpetual mourning into a new symbolic national role and created the climate for what became "Tory Democracy." He articulated an imperial role for Britain that would last into World War II and brought an intermittently self-isolated Britain into the concert of Europe. In the process he raised the level of Parliamentary debate, invented the political novel, and created in himself an enduring personality. As Oscar Wilde wrote in an essay he never published, "Lord Beaconsfield played a brilliant comedy to a 'pit full of kings,' and was immensely pleased at his own performance." Whether or not he would be "spoken of on Parnassus," Wilde predicted that he would be "quoted in Piccadilly." Perhaps Disraeli's political and personal achievements suffice for both Parnassus and Piccadilly.

Sources

The center of Disraeli studies is the Disraeli Project at the Queen's University, Kingston, Ontario, Canada, which is producing the multivolume *Benjamin Disraeli Letters*. The General Editor is now Professor M. G. Wiebe. All letters quoted from have been checked, where extant letters or photocopies exist, with the Project's files. The Project also has a library of Disraeli-related publications second to none.

Significant published studies begin with the full yet discreet six-volume *Life* (1910–19) by W. F. Monypenny and G. E. Buckle. The first radical reshaping of their story was by B. R. Jerman in *The Young Disraeli* (1960), which was followed by a new complete biography by Robert Blake, *Disraeli* (1966). Additional light was thrown on the life by Sarah Bradford in her *Disraeli* (1982), which utilized the first volume of the *Letters* and early Project discoveries, as well as overlooked English documentation. The emergence of other diaries, journals, and letters since, including the meticulously annotated *The Gladstone Diaries* (1968–), edited by M. R. D. Foot and H. G. C. Matthew, has enormously enlarged the data base.

Some publications have been cited in the text itself. Others not obvious from the context are cited in the notes to each chapter; citations are abbreviated after the initial reference.

The sources for the brief quotations at the head of each chapter occur in the chapters themselves or, in a few cases, an earlier one.

I. 1837

Details about Maidstone in 1837 are from P. D. Rowsby, West Kent Archives Office, Maidstone. The Maidstone *Gazette* covered the campaign minutely, printing Disraeli's remarks. Gansevoort Melville's diary was published as *1846 London Journal and Letters from England, 1845*, ed. Hershel Parker (New York, 1966). The story in the *World* about Mrs. Wyndham Lewis's offer of financial aid to Disraeli appeared on January 30, 1889.

II. 1804–1817

Brit milah instructions for London Jewry as the new century began appeared in *Jewish Ritual: Or the Religious Customs and Ceremonies of the Jews, Used in their Publick Worship and Private Devotions* (London, 1753). Zachary Citron, Administrator of Bevis Marks, showed me the circumcision chairs in the synagogue in July 1990. *The Bevis Marks Synagogue* by Richard D. Barnett and Abraham Levy (Plymouth, 1970) is an illustrated history of the congregation and building. Disraeli's (hereafter BD) own colorful family reminiscences, "On the Life and Writings of Mr Disraeli by his Son," was prefaced to Isaac's posthumous *Collected Works*, and although useful, is in places as accurate as BD's spelling of his father's surname. The story about the neighboring grandfathers of BD and Cardinal Manning is told by Lady Dorothy Nevill in her *Under Five Reigns* (London, 1910); undoubtedly she heard it from BD himself. The April 22, 1760, suit in Chancery involving the elder Benjamin D'Israeli and associates is Add MS 36191, British Library (hereafter BL).

III. 1817–1824

Disraeli's letters and autobiographical fiction are the sources of much of what is known about his life at the time of his formal and informal schooling. Beatrix Potter's reminiscence of Dr. Cogan's daughter is in her *Journal*, ed. Leslie Linder (London, 1989), entry for May 30, 1885. John Murray's own account of his relations with Isaac and Ben, including their letters, is in *Memoirs of John Murray* (London, 1891). BD's own account is in *Disraeli Reminiscences*, ed. H. M. and M. Swartz (London, 1975). *Rumpel Stiltskin* existed in only two hand-produced copies (1823) until the Roxburghe Club published an edition in 1952 (Mospik collection).

IV. 1824–1826

BD's account of the Flanders/Rhineland journey in Monypenny and Buckle is supplemented by additional extracts from his diary in C. L. Cline's "The Unfinished Diary of Disraeli's Journey to Flanders and the Rhineland (1824)," *Studies in English*, Department of English, University of Texas (Austin, 1943). The second part of *Vivian Grey* further supplements the account, although with fictional embellishments. The Jewish ancestry of Robert Plumer Ward is detailed in Ellen Moers, *The Dandy* (New York, 1960). A copy of *Lawyers and Legislators; or, Notes on the [South] American Mining Companies* (London, 1825) is in the Pattee Library, Penn State. *The Life of Paul Jones, from Original Documents in the possession of John Henry Sherburne, Esq.* (London, 1825) has an unsigned five-page preface by BD. There is a copy in the Mospik collection.

V. 1826–1830

BD's letters and autobiographical fiction are again the major sources for this period. Jerman in *The Young Disraeli* quotes at length from letters from the Austens, and is also a major source for documentation of the relationship with the Boltons in this and subsequent chapters. Edgar Allan Poe's borrowings from BD are cited by Ruth Leigh Borden in "Poe and Disraeli," *American Literature*, 8 (1937). I have consulted pharmacologist Eliot Vesell, Hershey College of Medicine, Penn State, about the early uses of digitalis. The route of the Thames Coach from London was described by BD to Samuel Carter Hall in a letter dated by the Disraeli Project as September 23, 1832 (Mospik collection).

VI. 1830–1831

BD's letters are the key source for his grand tour. *Contarini Fleming* was largely written in the final stages of the journey and includes vivid accounts based upon BD's travels. Much historical and geographical background for BD's travels appears in Robert Blake's *Disraeli's Grand Tour* (London, 1982). Additional background, and links with BD's fiction as late as *Lothair* (1870), appear in Donald Sultana's *Benjamin Disraeli in Spain, Malta and Albania, 1830–32* (London, 1976). The graphic medical details about William Meredith's death, and much else, were excised from BD's letters by Ralph D'Israeli in his editions of *Home Letters, 1830–31* (1885) and *Lord Beaconsfield's Correspondence with his Sister* (1886).

VII. 1831–1833

Isaac's letter to Austen on his honorary degree is dated June 16, 1832, BL Add MS 45908. His *The Genius of Judaism* was published by Edward Moxon in 1833. It was pillaged from by BD for the long and irrelevant chapter in *Lord George Bentinck*. BD's fifteen closely printed pages of "Notes to *Alroy*" include a number of reminiscences of his Eastern journey not recorded by him else-where. Also there are references to historical works he consulted, many of them Judaica from his father's library. A reference to "the erratic pages of the Talmud" suggests his reading of Isaac's *Genius of Judaism* before it appeared in print. The basic source for the period is, again, Disraeli's own writings: speeches, letters, fic-tion, travel accounts.

VIII. *1833–1834*

Helen Blackwood's story of Ben and Isaac was told to Sir William Fraser in a letter from her son, the Marquess of Dufferin and Ava, and quoted in its entirety in Fraser's *Disraeli and His Day* (London, 1891). Helen Blackwood, when Lady Dufferin, told John Lothrop Motley the story of Mr. Norton's wine and Disraeli's retort, re-ported in Motley's letter to his wife, Mary, of June 6, 1858, in *The Correspondence of John Lothrop Motley*, ed. G. W. Curtis (New York, 1889). Lady Charlotte Bertie's journal is quoted in *Lady Charlotte* by Revel Guest and Angela V. John (London, 1989). The fullest account of the Henrietta Sykes saga is in Jerman's *The Young Disraeli*. A copy of *Velvet Lawn* is in the Royal Archives, Windsor Castle. Identification of *A Year at Hartlebury* was a Disraeli Project discovery, reprinted with background appendices by Ellen Henderson and John P. Matthews (Toronto, 1983). Benjamin R. Haydon's diary entry on Disraeli is dated February 27, 1833, pub-lished in *The Diary of Benjamin Robert Haydon*, ed. Willard Bissell Pope (Cambridge, MA, 1963). BD's letter of September 2, 1863 (copy at the Disraeli Project), suggesting that even princes benefit from sowing wild oats before marriage was written to Lord Derby.

IX. *1834–1837*

Chapter I takes up part of the 1837 narrative; its notes are rele-vant also to this chapter. Benjamin Austen's letters to BD are in the British Library, as are Sarah D'Israeli's letters to him. BD's scrappy diary, much mutilated either by him or his heirs, is published in full in the *Disraeli Letters*, I, as Appendix III. Sydney Smith's letter to his daughter, Mrs. Holland, appears in *Letters of Sydney Smith*, ed. Howell C. Smith (London, 1953). A list of the books still in the Hughenden library, with their annotations, usually by BD, was prepared for the curator, David Gordon. Where possible it also lists their provenance. The designation *Hughenden Papers* refers to those documents now archived at Oxford.

X. *1837–1841*

George Augustus Sala's recollection of BD at Lady Blessington's is from *Sala* by Ralph Straus (London, 1942). Carlyle's wry reaction to the anonymous BD's writing "extravagantly in my manner" is from a letter to Alexander Carlyle, January 10, 1838, in *Collected Letters of Thomas and Jane Welsh Carlyle*, ed. C. R. Sanders (Durham, 1985). Macready's diary entry of March 26, 1839, about BD's play *Alarcos* is from *The Diaries of William Charles Macready, 1833–1851*, ed. William Toynbee (London, 1912). The malicious gossip on BD's political dinners is in *The Satirist*, January 26, 1840, and the verses "An M.P." appeared in *The Satirist* on January 26, 1840. The alleged extracts from an 1805 book by a Moldavian ex-rabbi were published in *The Satirist* on June 28, 1840, and in the same issue under "Chit-Chat" appeared the "cut of one" couplet. BD's alleged "Hebrew accent and dialect" was noted on August 2, 1840. Nathaniel Montefiore's letter of January 8, 1840, about Mary Anne is quoted in Lucy Cohen's *Lady de Rothschild and Her Daughters* (London, 1935). The "Jerusalem pony" story was told by Fraser in *Disraeli and His Day*, where Fraser also quotes George Tomline as recalling to him BD's "mites crawling about a cheese" statement.

XI. *1841–1844*

Letters by and to John Wilson Croker are in *The Croker Papers*, ed. Bernard Pool (New York, 1967; abridgment of the 1884 edition). The only book on the brief spring of "Young England" is the book of that title by Richard Faber (London, 1987). A still useful discussion of the Judaic dimension in *Coningsby* is Chapter VI of Cecil Roth's *Benjamin Disraeli* (London, 1952). John Gibson Lockhart's letters about Disraeli (also in XII) are found in Andrew Lang's *The Life and Letters of John Gibson Lockhart* (New York, 1897). Hannah de Rothschild's letter to her daughter-in-law Charlotte is in *Dear Lord Rothschild: Birds, Bees and History* by Miriam Rothschild (London, 1983). Carlyle's letter of March 17, 1844, to Monckton Milnes is in the *Collected Letters of Thomas and Jane Welsh Carlyle*, XVII, ed. Clyde de L. Ryals (Durham, 1990).

XII. *1844–1846*

The Mary Anne–George Smythe story is in *Mary Anne Disraeli* by James Sykes (London, 1928). A copy of William North's *Anti-Coningsby* (London, 1844) is in the Mospik collection. Further letters from Hannah de Rothschild are in *Dear Lord Rothschild*. The dedicatory poem in the new edition of *Alroy*—to Israel as "My County!"—is first seen in BD's letter to his publisher, Henry Colburn, August 31, 1845, number 1436 in the published *Letters*, IV. *The Letter-Bag of Lady Elizabeth Spencer-Stanhope*, ed. A. M. Stirling (London, 1913), contains her letter about seeing BD at Fryston. The *Young England* newspaper prospectus is in the BL Peel Papers, Add MS 40556. Charlotte's long letter to Louise de Rothschild of September 10, 1845, on Mary Anne's impulsive visit is in *The English Rothschilds* by Richard W. Davis (Chapel Hill, 1983). Dickens's attacks on BD and "that Dunghill Lord" are in a letter to John Forster, July 5, 1846, *The Letters of Charles Dickens*, IV, 1844–1846, ed. Kathleen Tillotson (Oxford, 1977). For the adventures of the Chartist poem submitted to BD, see *The Life of Thomas Cooper, written by himself* (London, 1882). Lord Broughton's diary extracts are from his *Recollections of a Long Life* (London, 1911). Gladstone's notes on reading *Sybil* (1845) are in BL Add MS 44792, folios 149–50. Lady Palmerston's letters are in *The Letters of Lady Palmerston*, ed. Tresham Lever (London, 1957).

XIII. 1846–1847

BD's remark to Gladstone, "Your last word was *revolution*," is from *Disraeli and His Day*. His remark about "lying in wait for points" is from Augustus J. C. Hare's *The Story of My Life* (London, 1900). Hare is quoting a veteran photographer, a Mr. Eddis. Isabel Burton's enthusiasm for *Tancred* is established by her writings quoted by Edward Rice in *Captain Sir Richard Francis Burton* (New York, 1990). Carlyle's slur on *Tancred* as "Jewish jackasseries" occurs in a letter to Monckton Milnes quoted at length in T. Wemyss Reid's *The Life of Lord Houghton* (New York, 1891). Charles Kingsley's fictional borrowings from *Tancred* are described by Brenda Colloms in *Charles Kingsley: The Lion of Eversley* (London, 1975). Robert Blake sums up the early political hostility between Disraeli and Gladstone in a published lecture, *Disraeli and Gladstone* (Cambridge, 1969). Beresford's letter to Lord Stanley (later Derby) "prefer[ing] a Christian to Jew or infidel" is in the Derby papers, Liverpool, where much of Stanley's correspondence is archived. BD's recollection of Lyndhurst on Evolution and the observation about Christianity's paradoxical usefulness to Jews are both in the BD *Reminiscences*, sections 48 and 56. Palmerston's correspondence with Queen Victoria on Disraeli is quoted in *The Letters of Queen Victoria*, ed. A. C. Benson and Viscount Esher (New York, 1907). Lord George Bentinck's new suits of clothes are noted by BD in *Reminiscences*, section 71.

XIV. 1848–1850

The awkwardness of BD's relations with Charlotte and Lionel de Rothschild in 1848 at another peak in the Oaths debate is described by Richard Davis in *The English Rothschilds*. The letter to the editor in *The Morning Post* on "the fragrant tribe of Hebrews" requiring a "de-odourizing" of Parliament was dated March 8, 1848. Gladstone's recollection of his remark to Lord John Russell during the debate is from John Morley's *The Life of William Ewart Gladstone*, III (London, 1903). Disraeli's letters to Lady Londonderry here and elsewhere after 1848 are from *Letters from Benjamin*

Disraeli to Frances Anne Marchioness of Londonderry 1837–1861 (London, 1938). Isaac's description of his library is in BD's memoir of his father introducing the collected edition of ID's works. With a copy of Disraeli's will in the Rothschild Family Archive is a list, dated October 5, 1881, of "Books sold from Hughenden" after BD's death. It consists preponderantly of Judaica presumably of no interest to Coningsby or to Ralph D'Israeli. Hannah Arendt and others have pointed to BD's "racial" claims for Jews as fuelling later anti-Semitism. Few writings by later bigots like Houston Stewart Chamberlain spent many lines, if any at all (as in Chamberlain's influential *Foundations of the Nineteenth Century*, 1911), on allusions to such remarks in Disraeli's writings. In the U.S., Henry Ford's notorious *Dearborn Independent* (issue of December 18, 1920) claimed the remarks of the fictional Sidonia as evidence of the validity of the anti-Semitic forgery *The Protocols of the Elders of Zion*. BD's letters to and from Lady Blessington (with some to and from D'Orsay) are quoted by R. R. Madden in *The Literary Life and Correspondence of the Countess of Blessington* (London, 1855). A copy of Robert Messer's letter of April 2, 1849, dunning BD for overdue debts is in the Disraeli Project files. BD's observation that weak governments are often more durable than strong ones is in the diary entry by Lord Brougham (John Cam Hobhouse) for July 22, 1848, in his *Recollections of a Long Life*. BD's meeting with Thomas Love Peacock is recorded by Lord Broughton in his diary for December 22, 1848 (MS BL). BD's letters to Lord Stanley (Derby) are in the Derby papers, Liverpool. Copies of BD's letters to Sarah D'Israeli from the Hughenden papers are in the Disraeli Project files. George Meredith's anecdote about BD's reaction to the M.P. bore Chisholm Anstey is in the *Collected Letters of George Meredith*, ed. C. L. Cline (Oxford, 1970), letter of December 19, 1902, to Lady Ulrica Duncombe. BD's relations with Prince Metternich, including both sides of their correspondence, are found in Alan Palmer's *Metternich* (New York, 1972). The Demosthenes-Cicero story about BD and Metternich appears in Anonymous, *Notebooks of a Spinster Lady* (London, 1919). BD's praise of Metternich as "a great Professor" is from the Stanhope MSS 690 (6) 1, a letter of February 12, 1864, to the Earl of Stanhope.

XV. 1851–1853

Robert Stewart's *The Politics of Protection: Lord Derby and the Protectionist Party, 1841–1852* (Cambridge, 1971), J. B. Conacher's *The Peelites and the Party System, 1846–1852* (Hamden, CT, 1972), and Wilbur D. Jones's *Lord Derby and Victorian Conservatism* (Athens, GA, 1956) update in detail BD's own narrative of events in *Lord George Bentinck* (London, 1851). Gladstone's diary entries are supplemented by his notes and correspondence in BL Add MS 44778. Copies of BD's letters to and from Mrs. Sarah Brydges Willyams are in the Disraeli Project files; these are more reliable than the letters extracted in Monypenny and Buckle, upon which most previous biographies depend. BD's speculations about whether Mozart, Haydn, or Beethoven could have had Jewish origins appears in a letter to Benjamin Lumley, November 10, 1851, quoted as item 43 in Christie's auction catalog of the March 27, 1985 sale. Dasent's *John Delane* (New York, 1908) includes many letters dealing with BD *in extenso*. Spencer H. Walpole's quotation of Disraeli on "a defunct mythology" is from André Maurois, *Disraeli, A Picture of the Victorian Age* (New York, 1928). BD himself reported Lord Elphinstone's remark in the Commons, "Always Murderers," to the Queen on April 13, 1858. Palmerston's correspondence with the Queen, 1837–1865, is in *Regina vs Palmerston* by Brian Connell (New York, 1961). Benjamin Moran's *The Journal of Benjamin Moran*, ed. Sarah Agnes Wallace and Frances Elma Gillespie (Chicago, 1948), is full of references to Disraeli into the later 1860s. Moran was American legation secretary. *Melville's Reading* by Merton M. Sealts, Jr. (Columbia, SC, 1988) sums up the striking Disraelian dimension of *Pierre* first elaborated upon by Henry A. Murray in his 1949 edition of the novel.

BD's "I have not time for sleep or food" appears in a letter dated May 6, 1852 (Mospik collection). Gladstone's diaries document his obsession with "rescuing" streetwalking prostitutes. He used codes for a "rescue subject," for his personal employment of a scourge, and for "rescue work done this day" which he chose not to detail. George Paston's *At John Murray's* (London, 1932) quotes the deprecation as financial managers of both Lyttleton and BD. BD's finding the Exchequer robes "uncommonly light" is in Wilfrid Meynell's *The Man Disraeli* (London, 1927), while the story of BD's refusal to pass the robes on to Gladstone is in Gladstone's diaries and letters, his letters from BD (BL), and the version by Judge Pollock reported in *Notebooks of a Spinster Lady*.

XVI. 1853–1856

BD on adversity is from *Disraeli and His Day*. Louise de Rothschild's recollection of the downcast BD, dated January 11, 1853, is in *The English Rothschilds*. The anonymously authored *The Right Honourable Benjamin Disraeli, M.P.: A Literary and Political Biography* (London, 1854) described BD as "Hebrew poet" turned "Marylebone Radical" when there appeared the chance of a London seat. It was reviewed at great length in *The Times* on January 17, 1854. See notes above for the Exchequer robes affair, for which the BL file is Add MS 44374.

BD's relations with the young Henry Stanley, afterward Lord Stanley, and then the Earl of Derby, are detailed from Stanley's diaries in *Disraeli, Derby, and the Conservative Party*, ed. John Vincent (New York, 1978). Stanley kept an extensive journal (much utilized here and throughout) now among the Derby Papers, Liverpool. The only reliable biography of Robert Cecil (Lord Salisbury), rich in documentation, is the nevertheless highly partisan account by his daughter Gwendolen Cecil, *Life of Robert, Marquis of Salisbury* (London, 1921).

BD's association with the Tory organ *The Press* is covered very fully in Monypenny and Buckle, but for E. V. Kenealy's role, see Arabella Kenealy's *Memoirs of Edward Vaughan Kenealy* (London, 1908). Entries from John Bright's diaries are from *The Diaries of John Bright*, ed. R. A. J. Walling (New York, 1931).

Drummond's diatribe to Croker on BD as "the model of a destructive" is December 19, 1853, in the Croker Papers. BD's claim to Thomas Jones, January 28, 1854, that attacks did not disturb him is from an extract in a Sotheby catalogue, item 291 in the March 10, 1964, sale. Nathaniel Hawthorne's observation of BD in the Commons is from his *English Notebooks,* ed. Randall Stewart (New York, 1941).

XVII. *1856–1858*

Anecdotes about Mrs. Disraeli appear in Sykes's *Mary Anne Disraeli* and in Monypenny and Buckle. The Cork Street tailor story appears in Julian Osgood Field's anonymously authored *Uncensored Recollections* (Philadelphia, 1901) and Lady Dorothy Nevill's several memoirs include other anecdotes of Mary Anne (hereafter MA) including MA's expostulation about throwing the cost of an uneaten dinner (a sovereign coin) into the Thames and her refusal to permit her hand to be kissed. Disraeli told a number of them himself, sometimes to Baroness de Rothschild, whose letter to her sister-in-law about MA was quoted in an earlier chapter. The story of the Hughenden groundskeeper is in BD's own *Reminiscences,* part 63, dated 1860. A BD letter in the Hughenden Papers (January 22, 1859) requests MA to furnish the forgotten Court dress. *The Man Disraeli* includes the story of BD posing against a pillar, and W. P. Frith's *A Victorian Canvas* (London, 1957 repr.) has the "pallor" story. The Paris story is from Sir Edward Blount's *Memoirs 1815–1902* (London, 1902). The *Venus and Adonis* story is from *Disraeli and His Day.* Field, as well as Lady Augusta Gregory in *Seventy Years* (London, 1976), report the "gratitude" retort to Bernal Osborne, a remark that appears in many memoirs. There are many versions of MA's stoic response to her hand injury; I have used the one by Lord Redesdale in his *Memories* (New York, 1916). BD's advice to Lord John Manners on marriage as support of "an honorable ambition" is dated March 25, 1851. Lord Dalmeny's account is from Robert Rhodes James's *Rosebery* (London, 1963).

The diary of House of Commons Speaker John Evelyn Denison, Viscount Ossington, is *Notes from My Diary when Speaker of the House of Commons* (London, 1899). The diary of Sir Stafford Northcote (Lord Iddesleigh) is in *Life, Letters and Diaries of Sir Stafford Northcote, First Earl of Iddesleigh* (London, 1890). BD's reports of the Court of Napoleon III are many: One account is that of December 11, 1856 to James D'Israeli (Mospik collection). The account in his own *Reminiscences* refers to the Emperor's contention that Derby had "no men." The letter to his accountant, Henry Padwick, (copy at the Disraeli Project) is dated January 27, 1857.

BD's report of the comet to Mrs. Willyams is in a letter of June 7, 1857. Many of his letters to her dealt with aspects of religion. Details on Brorsen's Comet are from Brian G. Marsden (April 8, 1992) of the Smithsonian Astrophysical Observatory. BD's letter forwarding a copy of Renan's life of Jesus was August 21, 1863 (Rothschild Family Archives). Benjamin Moran's phrenological description of BD is from his diary for January 30, 1858. Richard Henry Dana, Jr.'s very different American observation of BD is from *The Journal of Richard Henry Dana, Jr.*, ed. Robert F. Lucid (Cambridge, MA, 1968), entry for July 25, 1856. Gladstone's diary entry following that day's session has the same date. Carlyle's spiteful letter about BD in the park was written to his wife on July 26, 1857. Fraser in *Disraeli and His Day* recalled being shown the cup bequeathed by Smythe and noted BD's remark.

XVIII. *1858–1862*

Many communications to Queen Victoria from BD are not in the nine volumes of the Queen's *Letters*, which is both selective and discreet on both sides of the correspondence. Those extracted here which are not published in the *Letters* come from a microfilm furnished to the Disraeli Project from the Royal Archives and are utilized with the permission of the Royal Librarian, Oliver Everett. Lionel de Rothschild's comment about MA comes from a letter in the Rothschild Family Archive. The Wilberforce biography with diary and letter references to BD is A. R. Ashwell's *Life of Right Reverend Samuel Wilberforce, D.D.* (London, 1880). The best analysis of Ralph Earle is G. B. Henderson's "Ralph Anstruther Earle," *English Historical Review*, 58 (1943). The letters to Mrs. Willyams in this section come from the early 1860s as well as 1858–59 and are quoted here to focus on their religious content. BD's correspondence with Gladstone in May 1858, including Gladstone's drafts of his responses, are in BL Add MS 44389. BD's taking laudanum as an aid to sleep is noted in his letter to MA of June 7, 1859, Hughenden Papers.

Sarah D'Israeli's letter to Baroness de Rothschild is in the Rothschild Family Archive. Letters on the death of Sarah are in the Hughenden Papers, the Lady Londonderry *Letters*, and the letter to John Manners is in the files of the Disraeli Project (copy). Lord Robert Cecil's diatribes against BD are quoted in his daughter's *Marquis of Salisbury*. BD's letter to Francis Espinasse is at the Massachusetts Historical Society. The reports of Count Charles Frederick Vitzthum von Eckstaedt, to whom BD often confided, are in his reminiscences, *St Petersburg and London in the years 1852–1864*, ed. Henry Reeve (London, 1887).

XIX. 1862–1866

Ruskin's letter inventing Disraeli's grouse-shooting is to Charles Eliot Norton, August 28, 1862, in *The Correspondence of John Ruskin and Charles Eliot Norton*, ed. J. L. Bradley and Ian Ousby (Cambridge, 1987). Gladstone confessed "gross impropriety" in his pro-South Civil War statements in Lionel Tollemache's *Talks with Mr. Gladstone* (Brighton, 1984). BD's Exhibition snubbing of Thackeray and the novelist's staring past BD was reported by John Hollingshead in the *London Chronicle*, March 25, 1899. Baroness de Rothschild's letters to Leopold and Leonora are from the Rothschild Family Archive, as are BD's letters to the Baroness. BD's letters to Mrs. Brydges Willyams are from microfilm copies at the Disraeli Project. His letter of November 13, 1863, to James Butler, about the legacy to his daughter, is at the Firestone Library, Princeton. Baron de Rothschild's own letter to Leopold (November 30, 1863) about the Disraelis being "in the black" is also from the Rothschild Archives.

BD's letter to the Queen about Albert (April 29, 1863) is from the Royal Archives, Windsor. His conversations with Lord Stanley are from Stanley's published journal, including the gossip about Palmerston's improprieties. Judah P. Benjamin's letter alluding to BD's assistance is quoted by Robert Douthat Meade in *Judah P. Benjamin, Confederate Statesman* (New York, 1943). BD's visit with Lady Dorothy Nevill is described in her memoirs, in the diary of W. H. Russell as quoted in Alan Hankinson's *Man of Wars: William Henry Russell of the Times* (London, 1982), and in *Letters of John Hay* (Washington, 1909). Lord Clarendon's letter to Delane is from *Delane of the Times*.

XX. Ralph and Kate

Ralph Nevill edited five books of his mother's memoirs, which often overlap: *Leaves from the Notebooks of Lady Dorothy Nevill* (1907); *Reminiscences of Lady Dorothy Nevill* (1906 and 1910); *My Own Times* (1912); *Under Five Reigns* (1912); and *Life and Letters of Lady Dorothy Nevill* (1919). A number of Lady Dorothy's letters to BD were also published in the *Anglo-Saxon Review* IV (1899–1901) as "Some Letters and Recollections of Lord Beaconsfield and Others." Guy Nevill's supplementary data from family papers is in his *Exotic Groves* (Lymington, 1984). Other Dolly Nevill references are BD's published and unpublished letters, many of these in the Mospik collection. Her botany book and all of Ralph Nevill's books are in the BL. T. E. Kebbel's reminiscence of BD in October 1864 is from his *Lord Beaconsfield and Other Tory Memories* (London, 1907). Gossip about the Nevill-Smythe affair is in *The Satirist,* April 9 and 16, 1848. Charles Dickens's comment on the scandal appears in a letter to Macready, October 24, 1846, in the Pilgrim edition of Dickens's *Letters.* Ralph Nevill's memoir is *Unconventional Memories* (London, 1923); his Eton history/reminiscence is *Floreat Etona* (London, 1911). Lady Dorothy's references to her son's editing her memoirs, to her lack of religion, to her dislike of being a "recluse" in the country with Reggie, and to BD's novels, are from Edmund Gosse's *Lady Dorothy Nevill: An Open Letter* [to Lady Burghclere] (London, 1930; edition limited to 30 copies).

Documentation about Kate Donovan—including the recounting of her conversations about her past—comes from letters and photographs in 1991–92 sent to the author by her granddaughter, Catherine Esther Styles, and from her son, Peter Aaron Sayers, as well as from conversations with Peter Sayers. BD's will is in the public record at Somerset House. Sir Philip Rose's notation to his co-trustee about the existence of a minor child beneficiary unmentioned in the will is in the Rothschild Family Archives, which also has a copy of the will to which it is attached. Kate's birth certificate is in the public record, and her marriage in 1888 to Henry James John Stacey is entered in the register of St. Andrew's, Marylebone. The address given by the bride for the wedding certificate is 28 Coburg Buildings, a block of flats in Westminster where she very likely did not live; it was then the Donovan residence, where the Census did not list her. (She appears never to have lived with the Donovans although she was in occasional contact with them.) Stacey gave his address as 71 Wells Street, Marylebone, which was actually the residence of the Vicar of St. Andrew's, the Rev. Charles George Griffinhoofe, who married the couple. The implication is that each was concealing an actual address. (The Donovan family can be traced in the Post Office Directory and in Census records, which note each resident by name and age.) A letter to BD's solicitor and financial agent (he had several of each) William Lovell, December 18 [, 1863], BL Add MS 37502, folio 134, confirms BD's rental of stables at Grosvenor Gate to a Mr. Donovan through an agent named Grogan. The Rothschild Family Archives document the rental of Hughenden (BD Estate) properties—"part of Coombes Farm and two cottages"—to "Messrs Stacey" (otherwise unidentified) on July 28, 1892.

XXI. 1866–1868

Jowett's letter to Florence Nightingale, November 1866, is in *Dear Miss Nightingale*, ed. Colin Prest and Vincent Quinn (Oxford, 1987). BD's letter to the Queen (Royal Archives), July 27, 1866, on agitation in public parks, is not in the published correspondence. BD's reference to Princess Louise ("Princess Christian"—an allusion to her husband) is in a letter (Hughenden Papers) to MA, November 25, 1866. Lord Stanley's (Derby's)

journal remains a crucial source for the Tory years in power,
1866–1868. BD's relations with Bright are from Bright's diaries.
Gladstone's encounters with demimondaines are documented and
coded (by him) in his published diaries; the letters from Mrs.
Thistlethwaite and Gladstone's own letters are extracted from the
editor's notes and introduction. Carnarvon's diary is in the BL;
Hardy's is published. Hayward is quoted in a letter to his sisters,
February 13, 1867, from *Mr Hayward's Letters*. Beresford Hope's
slur is quoted from *The Man Disraeli*. BD's appeal to square James
Lowther, March 29, 1867, is in the Mospik collection; Miles's on
Lowther's *mot*, either May 20 or June 20, 1867, is quoted in the
Life of Lord Houghton. Charlotte de Rothschild's mourning-
banded letter to Leopold, May 27, 1867, is in the Rothschild
Family Archives. Motley's letter to his wife on the Reform Bill,
July 17, 1867, is in his *Correspondence*; John Hay's letter of the
same period is from his *Letters*. Patmore's "1867" is quoted in
Disraeli and His Day. Skelton is quoted from Blake's *Disraeli*.
Gladstone's false-backed books defaming BD are described in
Richard Shannon's *Gladstone* (Chapel Hill, 1984). Disraeli's letter
to Charles Rivers Wilson, September 1, 1867, is in the Mospik
collection. His letter dated October 22, 1868, financing a spying
mission in Ireland was sent to "Col. W. Fielding," BD's misspell-
ing for W. H. A. Feilding, who was agent for the spies. It is privately held. Wilberforce's letter of October 14, 1867, is from the
Life of Bishop Wilberforce. The "bundle" of messages exchanged by
BD and MA is in the Hughenden Papers. BD's letter to Gladstone thanking him for his expressions of sympathy when MA
was ill is dated November 20, 1867, and is BL Add MS 44413, folio 242 in the Gladstone Papers. The Lowther Castle gathering to
derail "Ben Dizzy" is described by Lord Esher, whose father was in
Disraeli's first Cabinet, in *Cloud-Capped Towers* (London, 1927).

XXII. 1868

BD's letters to Derby on accepting office are in the Derby Papers,
Liverpool. BD's effusive note to Barrington is in the BL
Barrington papers. The Queen's letters to her daughter Vicky are

from the multivolume series edited by Roger Fulford. MA's invitation to the Dutch queen, Sophia, is reported in *Notebooks of a Spinster Lady*. Clarendon's letter to the Duchess of Manchester is in *"My Dear Duchess": Social and Political Letters to the Duchess of Manchester 1858–1869*, ed. A. L. Kennedy (London, 1956). Lady Palmerston's letter of February 1868 to Fox, her agent, is from *The Letters of Lady Palmerston*. Father Newman's letter to Rogers is in vol. XXIV of *The Letters and Diaries*. The allegation about a brandy-laced speech is in Bright's diary and in George Smalley's dispatch to the New York *Tribune*, published May 7, 1868. His "life-long hypocrisy" charge appeared in the issue of December 5, 1868. Lady Augusta Bruce Stanley is quoted from an undated 1868 letter in *Later Letters of Lady Augusta Stanley*, ed. Dean of Windsor and Hector Bolitho (London, 1929). Cranborne (Robert Cecil; later Lord Salisbury) is quoted from Lady Gwendolen Cecil's biography of him. Nathaniel de Rothschild is quoted from *The English Rothschilds*. Napier's request to visit Hughenden is from an MS note in the Mospik collection. Trollope's comment to Blackwood about BD is quoted in *Trollope: Interviews and Recollections*, ed. R. C. Terry (Basingstoke, Hampshire, 1987). Henry Irving's clergyman story is from *My Memories of Eighty Years* by Chauncey M. Depew (New York, 1922). Lord George Hamilton's explanation of how he was induced to run for Parliament is in his *Parliamentary Reminiscences and Reflections* (London, 1916).

XXIII. *1869–1872*

John Vincent's edition of Lord Stanley's 1849–1869 diary, *Disraeli, Derby and the Conservative Party*, concludes with Stanley's accession to the earldom. It is one of the most valuable documentary records of the two decades of BD's rise. "Dizzy's Lament" is BL Add MS 44421, folio 229 in the Gladstone Papers. The friend to whom BD confided the Cluseret story was Lord Ronald Gower, who noted it in his memoirs. Details on the heavenly body (actually *eta Carinae*) attributed to "Baron Gozelius" were furnished by astronomers Peter Usher, Richard Wade, Eric Feigelson, and David Weintraub. Bret Harte's satire was *Lothaw: The Adventures* of a Young Gentleman in Search of a Religion by "Mr Benjamins" (London, 1870). BD's reaction to the biblical retelling by Connie and Annie de Rothschild is from Lady Louisa de Rothschild and Her Daughters by Lucy Cohen (London, 1935). The tale of BD's losing his new teeth in the midst of an address is from Lord George Hamilton's memoir. BD's letter to Manners about the gloom over the Prince of Wales's illness is dated December 13, 1871 (Mospik collection).

XXIV. 1872–1874

From the later 1860s until the end, much inside political information appears in the diaries of Gathorne-Hardy, citing comments by Cairns, Northcote, Carnarvon, and others. The entries parallel those of Lord Stanley (Derby). Lord Napier's letters to Disraeli are in Letters of Field-Marshal Lord Napier of Magdala (Norwich, 1936). Father Newman's letter to F. G. Lee, April 5, 1872, is from The Letters and Diaries of John Henry Newman, XXVI, ed. C. S. Dessain and Thomas Gornall (Oxford, 1974). BD's letters to members of the Rothschild family are from The English Rothschilds. His letters to Viscount Barrington are in the BL Barrington papers. Corry's recollections of MA's death are in Monypenny and Buckle. Rosebery's diary notes are quoted in Rhodes James's Rosebery. BD's letters to the Countess of Bradford and the Countess of Chesterfield are from The Letters of Disraeli to Lady Bradford and Lady Chesterfield, ed. Marquess of Zetland (London, 1929). The Countess of Cardigan's My Recollections (London, 1909) includes her account that Admiral Rous, her uncle, cautioned her against marrying "that damned old Jew." BD's letter to Sir Anthony de Rothschild, September 10, 1872, about MA's last days, is in The English Rothschilds. Gladstone's quixotic attempts to hang onto office after the electoral defeat in early 1874 are detailed in his Diaries. Boxall's last visit to Downing Street in Gladstone's administration is described as Lady Gregory remembered it being told to her in Seventy Years, ed. Colin Smythe (New York, 1976).

XXV. 1874–1875

The MS score of the Sir Arthur Sullivan song to BD's words is in a private collection. Lady Randolph Churchill's story of BD at dinner is from the *Reminiscences of Lady Randolph Churchill* (New York, 1908). Gladstone's reading of *Vivian Grey* is from his *Diaries*. Paul Smith's *Conservatism and Social Reform* (London, 1967) is valuable for its analysis of the inner workings of BD's long Ministry. Gathorne-Hardy's diaries dramatize the events from the standpoint of a participant, as do the new Lord Derby's diaries (Liverpool). W. H. Smith's diaries and letters, published in Viscount Chilston's *W. H. Smith* (London, 1965), offer another Cabinet member's perspective. Richard Assheton Cross's papers are BL Add MS 51265. The question of giving Carlyle and Tennyson New Year's honors is debated in Lord Derby's manuscript diaries; the Stanley/Derby archives also include BD's letters to Derby on other Cabinet matters. These include BD's letter to Derby of October 9, 1874, on a simple knighthood satisfying a Newton or Raleigh. Carlyle's refusal of honors is explained to his own satisfaction in his letter of January 1, 1875, to his brother, Dr. Carlyle, in *New Letters of Thomas Carlyle*, II, ed. Alexander Carlyle (London, 1904). Carlyle's "charlatan" quip is quoted by Gladstone's private secretary, Edward Hamilton, in his diary entry for May 7, 1883, in *The Diary of Sir Edward Walter Hamilton, 1880–1885*, ed. D. W. R. Bahlman (Oxford, 1972). The involvement of Bulwer Lytton's son in Disraeli's government is detailed in *The Lyttons in India* by Mary Lutyens (London, 1979). The shift of the *Daily Telegraph* from a Gladstonian organ to a Disraelian one is described by Lord Burnham in *Peterborough Court* (London, 1955). Charlotte de Rothschild's reference to BD's "septuagenarian heart" and his infatuation with Selina Bradford is in her letter of August 3, 1874, to Leonora and Leopold de Rothschild (Family Archive).

The Layard affair is best seen in unpublished exchanges (Royal Archives) between the Queen (sometimes with Ponsonby as intermediary) and BD. It is Ponsonby who quotes Victoria as characterizing Layard as "Lie-hard" and alleging his being influenced by a Madrid seductress (February 15, 1875). BD's warning that the Queen would have to grant Layard parting honors she begrudged is in a note dated February 20, 1875, that apparently caused her to back off. The Suez shares purchase has become the stuff of myth and legend, as with Baron Lionel's alleged peeling of a grape before responding to Corry. The actual facts are seen in Derby's MS diaries (Liverpool), BD's letters to the Queen, in the Rothschild papers, and shrewdly summed up in Lord Rothschild's *"You have it, Madam"* (London, 1980). Many letters and speeches attest to the misunderstanding of what percentage of control was actually purchased and how much profit was made by the London branch of the Rothschilds on the transaction: this is best seen in Gladstone's letters, diaries, and Parliamentary speeches.

The death of Sir Anthony de Rothschild, and BD's letter of condolence to Louise de Rothschild, are reported in *The English Rothschilds*, which quotes BD's entire letter of January 5, 1876.

XXVI. *1875–1876*

The events about Lytton's appointment and actions as Viceroy of India are documented in *The Lyttons in India*. These include the Rose episode. Arthur J. Munby's sour look at BD is from his diary of "a few day's later" than March 7, 1876, in Derek Hudson's *Munby: Man of Two Worlds* (Boston, 1972). Victoria's claim that Suez was "a blow to Bismarck" was reported by BD to Derby, who noted it in his diary. Cabinet discussions are reported in BD's letters to the Queen, in Gathorne-Hardy's diaries, and in the MS diaries of Lord Derby. Gladstone kept a cutting of the *Bradford Chronicle and Mail* report of his using the *Empress of India* title in 1869 in his files (BL Add MS 44480). BD's formal proposal to Victoria that he "go to the House of Lords" was made in his letter to her of July 25, 1876 (Royal Archives).

XXVII. *1876–1878*

The encounter by the new earl with Lady Sebright appears in *The Man Disraeli*. BD's letters to Lord Barrington are in the

Barrington Papers (BL). The wily operations of Madame Novikov and Count Shuvalov are reported in the Gladstone and Derby diaries. Moirier's letter positing a sexual basis for Gladstone's behavior is quoted at length, from a copy of the MS at Balliol College, Oxford, in a footnote to Gladstone's published diary. Reggie Brett's diary entry is from *The Journals and Letters of Viscount Esher 1870–1903*, ed. Maurice V. Brett (London, 1934). Cabinet matters are reported by Gathorne-Hardy (who often quotes Cairns), Derby, and (to the Queen) Disraeli himself. BD's exchanges with Salisbury appear in the Gwendolen Cecil *Life*. A copy of *Benjamin D———: His Little Dinner* (London, 1876) is in the Pattee Library, Penn State. *Dizzi-ben-Dizzi* is in the Mospik collection. BD's deliberately leaked information (or disinformation) to Lady Derby was reported to her husband and recorded in his MS diary. Edmund Yates's Brighton interview with BD on October 7, 1877, was recalled in full in his *Memoirs of a Man of the World* (New York, 1885). Dr. Kidd's early treatment of BD was detailed in his article, "The Last Illness of Lord Beaconsfield," *Nineteenth Century*, 26 (July 1889). Lord Carnarvon's treason to BD in the Cabinet is validated in the Derby diaries and in the Carnarvon Papers (BL Add MS 60910-12, 60763-66, 60817-19). The standard studies of the Turkish problem in BD's time, utilized here, are W. N. Medlicott's *The Congress of Berlin and After: A Diplomatic History of the Near Eastern Settlement, 1878–1880* (London, 1938; repr. 1963); Richard Millman's *Britain and the Eastern Question, 1875–1880* (Oxford, 1979); and R. T. Shannon's *Gladstone and the Bulgarian Agitation, 1876* (London, 1963). Henry James's change of tune appeared in a letter to Mrs. John Rollin Tilton, April 3 [1878], in *Henry James Letters, II, 1875–1883*, ed. Leon Edel (Cambridge, MA, 1975).

XXVIII. 1878–1880

Gladstone's complaint to BD about being misquoted is in draft form, accompanied in the Gladstone Papers (44457) by BD's prompt but undated reply. James Russell Lowell's letter to Thomas Hughes, November 17, 1878, is in *The Letters of James Russell*

Lowell, II, ed. C. E. Norton (New York 1894). Whistler's complaint to Alan Cole about BD's failure to sit for him is dated September 19, [1878], in *The Life of James McNeill Whistler* by E. R.
and J. Pennell (London, 1911). Father Newman's letter to Lord
Blatchford about BD's Berlin triumph, dated July 22, 1878, is in
vol. XXVIII of the *Letters and Diaries*. Sir Eric Barrington's letter
of July 12, 1878 from Berlin is in *The English Rothschilds*. Istóczy's
speech to the Hungarian Diet is quoted by Robert Wistrich in
The Jews of Vienna in the Age of Franz Joseph (Oxford, 1989). BD's
"pre-Zionist" relations with Laurence Oliphant are detailed in
Anne Taylor's *Laurence Oliphant 1829–1888* (Oxford, 1982). *Ben-
Dizzy the Bold!* is in the Mospik collection, as are *The Pretty Little
Coronet* and *Lord Beaconsfield Interviewed. The Book of Benjamin* is
in the Gladstone Papers (BL), as are *The Song of King Benjamin*
and the scurrilous *Imperium et Libertas?* and *Lord Beaky's Lies.*
BD's expression of affection for Charlotte de Rothschild (Family
Archives) is dated March 28, 1867. His condolence note to
"Natty" and Sir Nathaniel's response are quoted in *The English
Rothschilds*. The evasion of BD's strictures about exposing young
Prince Napoleon to danger and the results are described in greater
detail in Stanley Weintraub's *Victoria* (New York and London,
1987). The Guildhall dinner is described at length by George
Smalley for the New York *Tribune* and reprinted in his *London
Letters*, I (New York, 1891). The dinner visit of the young 6th
Duke of Portland is described in his *Men, Women and Things*
(London, 1937). It has been garbled in some retellings to seem
cruel rather than—as it was—kind. Cardinal Manning's Decem-
ber 1879 letter to BD is quoted in Robert Gray's *Cardinal Manning*
(New York, 1985). Lowell's letter to his niece is dated April 4,
1880. George Eliot's letter to Edith Simcox is in Gordon S.
Haight, *George Eliot* (New York, 1968).

XXIX. *1880–1881*

The role of Lady Seymour in the Eglinton Tournament and BD's
inquiry to her are found in Mark Girouard's *The Return to Cam-
elot: Chivalry and the English Gentleman* (New Haven, 1981). Au-

gustus J. C. Hare quotes from his diary in *The Story of My Life* about BD's absorption in his novel. Corry's negotiations with Longman and the novel's publishing history, including material from the archives of the Longman Group, is thoroughly detailed in Annabel Jones's "Disraeli's *Endymion*," in *Essays in the History of Publishing*, ed. Asa Briggs (London, 1974). BD's letter of November 21, 1880, to Lord Beauchamp is extracted from a Disraeli Project copy. Emma de Rothschild's reaction to the novel is quoted in *Dear Lord Rothschild* by Miriam Rothschild. Henry Adams's letter to C. M. Gaskell, January 1, 1881, is in *Letters of Henry Adams, 1858–1891*, ed. W. C. Ward (Boston, 1930). BD's letter to the Queen on *Endymion* is in the collected Victoria *Letters*.

Lord Ronald Gower writes about his last visits to Hughenden in *My Reminiscences*. The November 2, 1880, letter to Lady Bradford on the "A.V." was not printed in the two volumes edited by the Marquess of Zetland; it is found in the Bradford Papers, Staffordshire County Record Office. Sarah Bradford's suggestions about Joseph Toplady Falconet and Gladstone appear in her *Disraeli* (London, 1982). BD's using John Brown as a conduit for private letters to the Queen is documented in the Hughenden Papers and the Royal Archives. BD's effusive thank-you to the Queen, written Christmas Day, 1880, is in the Royal Archives, as is his wry letter on the marriage of Baroness Burdett-Coutts. Dr. Kidd's medical comments—which may be self-serving—are from his "The Last Illness of Lord Beaconsfield." Fraser's last encounter with BD is described in *The Man Disraeli*. Disraeli's wedding note to Leopold de Rothschild is in the Family Archive. The crossing sweeper story is in "The Recluse of Curzon Street," *The World*, February 9, 1881. Lucy Goschen's letter to her husband in Turkey about meeting BD is printed in *Lord Goschen and His Friends*, ed. Percy Colson (London, 1945).

Hyndman's story of visiting the dying BD is in *The Record of an Adventurous Life* (London, 1911). Winston Churchill's reminiscence is from his *A Roving Commission* (New York, 1930). Florence Arnold-Forster reports her family's visit (among many) to sign their names in the dying Disraeli's visitors book (entry of April 3, 1881) in *Florence Arnold Forster's Irish Journal*, ed. T. W.

Moody, R. Hawkins, and M. Moody (Oxford, 1988). Lord Acton's letter of April 2, 1881, is in *Letters of Lord Acton to Mary Gladstone* (London, 1904). Gladstone not only called but received purple-ink bulletins about BD's condition (BL 44,469). Rumors about the religious state of the dying man proliferated in his final days. Dr. Kidd claimed in "The Last Illness" that Disraeli spoke twice "on spiritual subjects, in a manner indicating his appreciation of the work of Christ and of the Redemption." The operative words suggest Kidd's fashioning something out of nothing. *The Londonderry Standard* (quoted in *Pall Mall Gazette*, May 19, 1886) alleged that BD "begged one of his friends to go for Father Clarke." No priest was summoned, and none came. Rowton allegedly told William Stone (*The Squire of Piccadilly* [London, 1951]) that BD went "on the Day of Atonement to the Bevis Marks synagogue"—an impossibility as he was too familiar a face in London—and J. O. Field (*Uncensored Recollections*) reported the Philip Rose story uncorroborated anywhere else—certainly not by Rose. John R. Robinson's *Fifty Years of Fleet Street*, ed. Frederick Moy Thomas (New York, 1904), alleges "according to an influential member of the Jewish community" that "Lord Beaconsfield on his death-bed sent for a Rabbi and made a declaration of faith in the Jewish form"—apparently an embroidering of the version attributed to Rose. Almost certainly none of the tales of an edifying religious end are true.

XXX. 1881

Gladstone's absenting of himself from the funeral, much condemned, was explained by his private secretary, Edward Hamilton, as not from "unworthy motives" (*Diary*, May 4, 1881): "If he *had* gone to the funeral, of course they would have accused him of being a humbug." Gladstone's illness while preparing his memorial address is documented in *The Gladstone Diaries*. Dorothy Nevill's undated letter [April 1881] to Lady Airlie is in Nevill's *Life and Letters*. Dean Stanley's sermon on BD, and the "curious text" he chose, are commented upon by Lady Knightley in a diary entry of May 1, 1881, published in *The Journals of Lady Knightley of*

Fawsley, ed. Julia Cartwright (New York, 1917). "Lewis Carroll's" letter to Mrs. V. Blakemore, April 25, 1881, on the University Sermon at Oxford is in *Letters of Lewis Carroll*, I, ed. M. N. Cohen and R. L. Green (London, 1959). W. S. Blunt's opinions of BD are in a diary entry for September 30, 1903, in *My Diaries, Being a Personal Narrative of Events, 1888–1914* (London, 1919–1920). Wilde's "pit full of kings" quotation is from an unpublished MS review of the Ralph D'Israeli edition of BD's *Letters*, William Andrews Clark Library, UCLA.

Acknowledgments

For revelations about his feverish early manhood, I and other Disraeli biographers since the early 1960s are indebted to the late B. R. Jerman, author of *The Young Disraeli* (1961). Barney Jerman was my colleague when I first came to Penn State in the middle 1950s, and his sleuthing into Disraeli's early years appeared to eliminate any chance that I would ever write on his subject. Later he ran into much bad luck, but his book stands as the beginning of modern Disraeli studies. Although there was much documentation unavailable to him than that has enriched this book, I stand on the shade of his shoulders.

The major new data source is the Disraeli Project, editorial umbrella for the ongoing publication of *Letters of Benjamin Disraeli*, at Queen's University in Kingston, Canada. No one alive knows more about Disraeli than the Project's director, M. G. Wiebe. My indebtedness to Mel and his staff is profound. A prince among private collectors of Disraeliana is Donald R. Mospik. No other collection matches his, and this book is the better for my having access to Don's cabinets and shelves. I am grateful, too, to Jacob, Lord Rothschild, and to Simone Mace, curator, for access to the Rothschild Family Archive, which has added a special dimension to this biography. Previously unpublished Rothschild material is used here with the authorization of the Family Archive.

My chief library resource, as always, has been Penn State's Pattee Library, its Special Collections curators, Charles W. Mann and Sandra Stelts, and its Interlibrary Loan chief, Noelene Martin. Many library collections have furnished valuable material, from Oxford and Colindale (British Library) to Pasadena (Huntingdon) and Los Angeles (UCLA). My source notes acknowledge documentary sources in detail where relevant. I owe special debts on both sides of the Atlantic also to Lucy Addington, Doris Alexander, Richard Atkins, Karl Beckson, Erella Brown, Charles T. Butler, Zachary Citron, Ralph Condee, Mark Curthoys, the Earl of Derby, Vivian Elliot, Eric Feigelson, David Gordon, Gladys Greenfield, Emily Grosholz, Baruch Halpern, Alan Hanley-Browne, Eileen Hanley-Browne, Mark Hanley-Browne, Heinz Henisch, Philip Jenkins, Nicholas Joukovsky, Richard Kopley, Heinz Kosok, Brian G. Marsden, Mary Millar, Inge Miller, Delores Mospik, Michel Pharand, Shirley Rader, Susan Reighard, Peter Aaron Sayers, Catherine Esther Styles, Peter Usher, Elliot Vesell, Richard Wade, Daniel Walden, Thomas R. Wartik, David Weintraub, Rodelle Weintraub, and Philip Winsor.

INDEX

[Bold type indicates illustration and caption in text pages.]

Abercorn, Duke of, 456, 473, 503, **504**
Aberdare, Lord, 573
Aberdeen, Earl of, 100, 248, 328, 329, 333, 336, 339–40, 342–43, 375, 601
Acton, John, 1st Baron, 656
Adams, Charles Francis, 452
Adams, Gen. Sir Frederick, 96
Adams, Henry, 639
Adams, John (cobbler), 14
Adderley, Sir Charles, 502, 530
Addresses to Young Children (Rothschild), 381
"Adventures of a certain Mr. Aylmer Papillon in a terra incognita, The" (BD, 1824), 46, 80
Age, The, 61, 138
Agricultural Holdings Act (1875), 530
Ailanthus Silkworm and the Ailanthus Tree, The (Guérin-Meneville), 425
Ainsworth, William Harrison, 237
Airlie, Lady, 414, 663
Akiba, Rabbi, 171
Alabama (ship), 440
Alaman, Don Lucas, 52
Albert, Prince Consort of England, 168n, 185n, 201, 232, 252, 256, 304, 306, 337, 340, 368, 397–400, 415, 460, 469, 535
 BD on, 316, 376–77, 386–88, 400
 on BD, 317, 325–26
 and Gladstone, 320–21, 324n, 325–26
Alberta (yacht), 538
Alderson, Baron, 314
Alexander II, Czar of Russia, 342, 596, 647, 653, 656
Alexandra, Princess of Wales, 397–98
Alfonso XII, King of Spain, 542, 543
Alfonso XIII, King of Spain, 543
Alford, Lord, 629
Alfred, Prince, Duke of Edinburgh, 656–57
Allotment of Waste Lands Bill, 231
Almack's (club), 154
Alroy, David, 82, 98, 138
Alroy, or The Prince of the Captivity (BD's novel), 77–78, 93, 96, 101, 103–105, 104n, 120, 151, 262, 263, 362n, 546, 595
 dedicated to Sarah, 142–43, 382
 and Jewish background, 111–13, 115, 223, 280
 new preface, 245–46

Alroy, or The Prince of the Captivity (BD's novel) *(cont.)*
  published, 135–43
  written, 111–12, 121
Andrassy, Count, 592
Angeli, Heinrich von, 641
Anglo-Mexican Mining Association, 51
Anson, Gen. George, 282, 365, 366
Anson, Isabella Forester (Mrs. George), 282, 366
Anstey, Chisholm, 290
Anti-Coningsby; or, The New Generation Grown Old, 223
Anti-Semitism, xi–xii, 23–24, 113, 190–92, 196, 216n, 219, 220, 222–25, 247, 248, 273, 276, 277, 280n, 384, 426, **451,** 453, 602n
  barred from Parliament, 112–13, 116, 267, 274–78, 337–38, 371–73
  and BD as Prime Minister, 519, 567–68, 601–602, 605
  and BD elected to Grillon's, 412–13
  and BD in House of Commons, 190–92, 197, 321
  and BD's becoming Prime Minister, 446, 454–57, 461–462, 466, 467
  and BD's leadership of Conservatives in House of Commons, 288–89, 412, 426, 446, **450, 451,** 453
  and BD's publications, 138, 220, 221–25, 492
  and BD's quest for seat, 4–5, 11–13, 113, 116, 161–62
  and BD's schooling, 36–37
  and Eastern Question, 367–69, 590–91, 601, 605–608
  and *Endymion*, 639
  Gladstone's, 435, 567–68, 576, 601, 605–608
  and Rectorship of Edinburgh, 413–14
  and university, 134
Apologie de Spinosa et du Spinosisme, 280
Apponyi, Count, 528
Apponyi, Countess, 398
Argyll, Duke of, 355, 466, 574, 630
Arms and the Man (Shaw), 598
Arnold, Matthew, 449, 487, 547
Arthur, Prince, Duke of Connaught, 660–61
Artisan's Dwelling Act (1876), 530
Arundell, Isabel, 270
Ashley, Lord. *See* Shaftesbury, 7th Earl of Shaftesbury
Ashmead-Bartlett, William, 649
Asquith, H. H., 533
Athenaeum Club, 116, 228
Atlantic Monthly, 493
Aumale, Henri, duc d', 376–77, 420
Austen, Benjamin, 53, 66, 67, 72–73, **75,**
  82–83, 85, 116, 118, 121, 134, 135, 149, 150
  letters from BD, 78–79, 82–83, 89, 94, 95, 98, 114, 129, 152, 158, 160, 170
Austen, Sara, 53, 66–79, **74,** 82–83, 86, 89, 116, 118, 150
  letters from BD, 67, 84, 99, 130, 131
  letters to BD, 67, 69–71, 80, 83
Austin, Charles, 181
Avigdor, Henri, 248
Aytoun, William, 630

Bacon, Francis, 56, 630
Bacon, Thomas, 432
Baillie-Cochrane, Alexander (1st Baron Lamington), 203, 204, 206, 207, 209, 212, 228, 516, 626
Ballantyne, James, 58
Balzac, Honoré de, 362n
Barber, Francis, 25
Barchester Towers (Trollope), 362
Baring, Sir Thomas, 129, 132–33, 281, 305
Barnes, Thomas, 163
Barrington, Sir Eric, 603
Barrington, George, Viscount, 460, 654, 655, 658, 661
  letters from BD, 507, 565, 571
Basevi, Naphtali (grandfather), 27, 30
Basevi, Olivia (aunt), 477
Basevi, George, Jr. (cousin), 12, 60, 91n
Basevi, George (uncle), 11, 12, 51
Basevi, Nathaniel (cousin), 12, 38, 38n
Bassett, Annie, 477
Bassett, Mrs. (mistress of James D'Israeli), 477
Baudrand, Gen. Marie de, 205
Baum, Mr. (BD's valet), 616, 649, 650, 654, 660, 661
Baylis, Mrs. M., 240
Beach, Sir Michael Hicks. *See* Hicks Beach
Beaconsfield Arms, 563
Beaconsfield, Earl of (pub), 563
Beaconsfield, Earl of. *See* Disraeli, Benjamin
Beaconsfield, Viscountess. *See* Disraeli, Mary Anne
Beadon, Edwards, 162
Beatrice, Princess of England, 551, 582, 614
Beauchamp, Lord (*formerly* Elmley Lygon), 477, 633
Beckford, William, 127, 135
Bell's Weekly Messenger, 29, 492
Belzoni, Giovanni Battista, 40
Ben-Dizzy the Bold! (pamphlet), 605
Benjamin, Judah P., 409
Benjamin D———: His Little Dinner (pamphlet), 573
Bennoch, Francis, 347
Bentinck, Lord George, 159, 251–53, 255–59,

269, 272, 273, 275–77, 280–84, 289,
   290, 298, 299, 331, 618, 619, 642
BD's memoir of, 308
death, 285–86
letters to BD, 423
Bentinck, Lord Henry, 284–89, 312
last letter from BD, 312
Bentinck, Mrs. *See* Bolsover, Lady
Bentley, Richard, 135, 150, 151, 233, 328
Beresford, William, 281, 299, 311, 328
Beresford-Hope, A. J. B., 393
Berkeley, Augustus Fitzhardinge, 181
Berlin Congress (1878), 590–97, 600,
   602–604, **602,** 608, 609
Bernal, Ralph, 116
Bernhardt, Sarah, 433
Bertie, Lady Charlotte (*later* Lady Charlotte
   Guest and Lady Charlotte Schreiber),
   141, 144, 149, 542
Beust, Count, 604
Bevis Marks Synagogue, 17–19, 22, 30, 116
Bibliotheca Judaica, 280
Biddulph, Gen. Sir Thomas, 609
Bismarck, Count Otto von, xii, 395, 437–38,
   441, 548, 590–92, **594,** 595, 596, 598,
   636
on BD, 593, 598, 620
Blachford, Lord, 600
Blackwood, Frederick, 139
Blackwood, Helen (Marchioness of Dufferin),
   139–40
Blackwood, John, 470
Blackwood's Magazine, 57, 228, 492
Blagden, Rev. Henry, 537
Blake, Robert, 103
Blake, William, 80, 279
Blessington, Marguerite, Countess of, 11,
   125–26, 153, 154, 158, 160, 168, 183,
   194, 238, 283, 290–92, 306
letters from BD, 157–58
Blount, Sir Edward, 351
Blunt, Wilfrid Scawen, 664
Bluntschli, J. C., 598
Bolingbroke, Lord, 206, 357
Bolsover, Lady (Mrs. Bentinck), 618, 618n
Bolton, Clarissa "Clara," 84–85, 87, 117–19,
   131, 134–36, 143–46, 153
Bolton, Dr. George Buckley, 83–84, 114,
   117–19, 131, 143
Bonaparte, Lucien, 154
Bond, Effie, 113
Book of Beauty, Heath's (Blessington), 11,
   158, 165, 166n, 194
Book of Benjamin, 605–606
Book of Joel, 280
Boord, Thomas White, 519
Borthwick, Peter, 210
Botta, Paul Emile, 109
Bouverie, Edward, 511

Boxall, Sir William, 521
Bradenham House, **170**
father buried at, 278
leased, 80–81, 258
Bradford, 4th Earl of, 514, 520, 533, 535
Bradford, Selina Forester, Countess of, 65,
   151, 431, 471, 516, 520, 539
and *Endymion*, 630–31, 640
letters from BD, 509, 513–21, 525, 526,
   528, 529, 531–34, 536, 537, 539, 544,
   547, 552, 553, 556, 561–62, 564, 565,
   574, 579, 580, 581, 587, 592, 593,
   597, 610, 615, 616, 619, 622, 626,
   641, 643–44
letters to BD, 534
Bradford, Sarah, 180n, 645
Bradford Chronicle and Mail, 553
Brand, Henry, 442
Breidenbach, Herr, 201
Brett, Reginald (Lord Esher), 515, 568
Briggs, Samuel, 106
Bright, Henry, 482
Bright, John, 296, 317, 339, 393, 416–17,
   439, 442, 447, 452, 462, 469, 470,
   479, 636, 639, 640
on BD, 323, 410, 442, 465, 590
British Museum, BD as Trustee, 399
British Quarterly Review, 225
Brorsen's Comet, 363–64, 365
Brown, John, 469, 614, 649, 659
Browne, Sir Sam, 609
Browning, Elizabeth Barrett, 228, 250
Browning, Robert, 250, 268
Brownlow, Lord, 516
Bruce, Mitchell, 655, 657
Brunel, Isambard Kingdom, 182, 383
Brunnow, Baron, 395, 515, 554
Brunnow, Baroness, 515
Bryce, James, 568
Bucher, Lothar, 595
Buckingham, Duke of, 362
Buckingham and Chandos, Duke of, 195,
   232, 362
Buckle, G. E., 214, 288, 290, 647
Bucks Gazette, 132–34
Bulgarian Horrors and the Question of the East
   (Gladstone), 564–65
Buller, James, 402
Bulwer, Edward Lytton (Sir Edward Bulwer-
   Lytton), 87, 114, 116, 126, 130,
   135–37, 177, 192, 279, 283, 297, 298,
   319, 320, 330, 332, 375, 376, 427,
   550
letters from BD, 98–99
letters to BD, 279
Bulwer, Henry, 87, 205, 230
Bulwer, Rosina (*later* Lady Lytton), 99,
   123–24, 128–29, 352
letters from BD, 171

Burdett-Coutts, Baroness Angela, 229,
432–33, 435, 513–14, 597, 649, 650
Burials Bill (1876), 556
Burke, Edmund, 560
Burton, Richard, 270
Bute, 3rd Marquess of, 481, 486, 490
Byron, George Gordon, Lord, 30, 39, 42, 43,
46, 67n, 68, 72–73, 82, 90, 94–96,
120, 127, 128, 136, 158, 169, 206,
429, 538, 641

Cabinets, BD's
BD's first, 467
BD's second, 517, 520, 529–30, 574–78,
583–89
under Derby, 313–26, 376, 437, 443, 452
Caesar, Julius, 34, 376–77
Caesar and Cleopatra (Shaw), 597
Cairns, Earl (*formerly* Sir Hugh), 402, 413,
463, 479, 480, 482, 500, 501, 510,
520, 559, 570, 573, 578, 580, 653,
658
letters from BD, 507
"Calantha" (BD, poem), 165
Calcraft, William, 415
Cambridge, Duke of, 613, 615
Cambridge University, 33, 45
Campbell, Sir John, 176–77
Canning, Sir George, 55–56, 58
Canning, Sir Stratford (Viscount Stratford de
Redcliffe), 304, 336, 368
Can You Forgive Her? (Trollope), 632
Capel, Monsignor Robert, 486, 486n, 490
"Captain Swing" protest, 228 and 228n
Carathéodory, Pasha, 592
Cardigan, Adeline de Horsey, Countess of,
512, 514
Cardigan, 7th Earl of (and General), 512
Carlton Club, 9, 164, 170, 188, 189, 253,
256, 335, 356, 362, 448–49, 517, 650
Carlyle, Alexander, 178
Carlyle, Thomas, 119, 153, 178, 221, 237,
256, 267–69, 366–67, 392, 413–14,
453, 491, 603
on BD, xii, 270, 413–14, 535–36, 569, 608
Carnarvon, Earl of, 384, 443, 444, 445, 479,
529–30, 559, 569, 573, 575, 579, 582,
583, 586, 588, 599–600, 610, 621, 626
"Carrier-Pigeon, The" (BD, 1835), 154, 158
Carrington, Lord, 154, 159, 295, 301
Carroll, Sir George, 177
Carter, John, 132
Catechism on the Corn Laws (Thompson), 12
Catholic Emancipation (1829), 177
Cavagnari, Maj. Pierre Louis Napoleon,
615–16
Cavendish, Charles Compton, 271–72
Cazalet, Edward, 427
Cecil, Lord Robert (*later* Viscount

Cranborne; *afterwards* 3rd Marquis of
Salisbury), 332–33, 383–85, 393, 412
Cellini, Benvenuto, 79
Cetshwayo, Chieftain, 610, 612, 613, 621
Chalon, Alfred Edward, **144,** 153, 194
Chamberlain, Joseph, 633
Chamberlain, General Sir Neville, 609
Chambers, Robert, 260
Chandos, Lord (*see also* Duke of Buckingham
and Chandos), 160, 168
Chapman, Thomas, 258
Charles X, King of France, 117
Chartists, 186–88, 227, 228, 236, 238–39,
243, 634
Chatham, Baroness, 474
Chelmsford, Frederick Augustus Thesiger,
2nd Baron, 612–14, 621
Chelmsford, Frederick Thesiger, 1st Baron,
437, 463
Cherry and Fair Star, 150–51
Chesterfield, Anne Forester, Countess of,
528, 530, 533, 535
letters from BD, 514, 520, 532, 539, 552,
553, 555–56, 559, 565, 574, 587, 613,
614, 620, 645, 651
Childe Harold (Byron), 39, 73, 94, 115, 120,
127, 429
Chimes, The (Dickens), 224
Chit-Chat, 424
Church before the Flood, The (Cumming), 364
Churchill, Jennie Jerome, 526
Churchill, Lord Randolph, 526, 656
Churchill, Winston, 186, 298, 656
Church of England (Anglican), 31–32, 36,
134n, 207, 267, 298, 371, 506
BD and, 364–65, 378, 384
BD on, 406
Victoria and, 471–72, 529, 531–32, 537,
546
Clanricarde, Marchioness of, 515
Clanricarde, Marquis of, 368, 515
Clapham Sect, 643–45
Clarendon, Lord, 341, 417, 461–63
Clarke, Father, 658
Clay, James, 94–96, 98, 100, 101, 103–104,
106–108, 114, 136, 319, 446, 447
letters to BD, 491
Cleveland, Duke of, 438
Cloud-Capped Towers (Esher), 682
Clubb, Rev. Charles Wishaw, 293
Cluseret, Gustave Paul, 481
Cobden, Richard, 217, 229, 255, 290, 317,
439, 636
BD on, 408, 640
Cobden, William, 207, 234
Cochrane, Alexander Baillie. *See* Baillie-
Cochrane, Alexander
Cockburn, Alexander, 87

Codlingsby (Thackeray), 222, **222,** 223, 394, 494, 636
Cogan, Rev. Eli, 33–34, 36
Cohen, Meyer, 5
Colburn, Henry, 66, 68–70, 76, 77, 80, 83, 85, 86, 93, 97, 124, 135, 138, 155, 156, 165, 219, 225, 237, 245
Cole, Alan, 603
Coleridge, John Taylor, 59
Coleridge, Rev. William Hart, 32
Collins, Elizabeth, 324, 324n
Colman (the younger), George, 636
Colombian Mining Association, 51
Confessions of an English Opium Eater (De Quincey), 42–43
Coningsby, George, 5th Earl of Essex, 154
Coningsby, or The New Generation (BD, 1844), 14n, 93, 119, 154, 188, 242–43, 246, 269, 344, 362, 436, 502, 521, 531
  continuation, 227, 260
  sales and reception, 220–26, 229–31, 240
  written, 211–19
  Victoria on, 610n
Conroy, Sir John, 186
Conservative Associations of Lancashire, 501
Conservative party (Tories), xii, 96, 98, 125, **504**
  BD emerges as leader, 281–98
  BD leads, as Chancellor of Exchequer, 313–26, **315,** 370–88, 418, 437–58
  BD leads, as Prime Minister, 459–75, 531, 559
  BD leads, under Aberdeen, 328–39
  BD leads, under Gladstone, 475–81, 495–521
  BD leads, under Palmerston, 340–47, 355–69, 383–88, 391–418
  BD leads young, 202–203, 205–19
  BD's impact on, 665
  BD's opposition to Peel, 233–35, 249–58
  BD's pamphlets supporting, 163
  BD's political philosophy and, 43–44, 129–30, 132, 134, 136, 159–60, 199, 207–208, 371
  BD's unpopularity with, 384–85, 391–92, 401, 403, 411–13, 426, 463, 500–501
  and *Coningsby,* 212–13
  elections of 1834, 159–60
  elections of 1835, 161–62
  elections of 1837, 3–16, 168–71
  elections of 1841, 196–97, 200
  elections of 1847, 273
  elections of 1859, 378–79
  elections of 1865, 411
  elections of 1868, 472–73
  elections of 1874, 518–20
  elections of 1880, 622–27
  Gladstone as leader, 296–97

and Jews oath, 275–78, 371–73
  newspaper founded, 329–31
  and Reform Bill, 439–55
  split between Peelites and Derbyites, 14, 16, 328, 335, 345, 356
"Conservative Surrender, The" (Cranborne), 453
Constantinople, conference of 1876, 569–70
"Consul's Daughter, The" (BD, 1836), 153, 166n
Contarini Fleming (BD, 1832), 20–21, 29–30, 36–40, 43, 63, 67–70, 79, 92, 96, 97, 102, 103, 105, 106, 362n, 595
  new preface, 245–46
  publication, 116, 119–21, 125–28, 135
  written, 108–11, 115
Cooper, Thomas, 236–38
Copley, John Singleton. *See* Lyndhurst, Baron
Cork, Earl of, 510
Cork and Orrery, Countess of, 139, 149, 154, 192
Corn Importation Bill (1846), 253
Corn Laws, 135–36, 179, 207, 226
  debate on repeal, 249–55
  repeal, **291,** 292, 335
Correspondence Relative to the Affairs of Syria, 246
Corrupt Practices Act (1854, 1868), 463–64
Corry, Henry, 439
Corry, Montagu (Lord Rowton), 438–39, 457–58, 460, 482, 508, 510, 512, 517, 530, 544, 546, 563, **578,** 579, 581, 582, 587, 591, 595, 603, 610–11, 618, 619, 630–32, 649, 651, 654, 656–60
  letters from BD, 507, 508, 570
  made Lord Rowton, 625–26
Corsair (Byron), 82
Cottingley Allotment Gardens, 231
Coulton, David, 314–15
Count Alacros (BD), 91–92, 183, 224
Countess Kate (Yonge), 552
Courier des Dames, 198
Court Journal, 97, 140, 270
Coutts, Thomas, 69
Cowley, Lord, 205
Cowper, Lady, 453, 638
Craigie, Mrs. Pearl, 490
Cranborne, Lady, 444, 465, 467
Cranborne, Lord Robert (*formerly* Robert Cecil, *later* 3rd Marquis of Salisbury), 412, 442–44, 452, 453, 461, 465, 467
Cranbrook, Earl Frederick Stanley, 589, 626
Crichton-Stuart, Lady Dudley, 154
Crimean war, 336–39, 342–45, 360, 365, 394, 541, 597n, 601
"Crisis Examined, The" (BD political address, 1834), 159
Croker, John Wilson, 55, 61, 62, 203, 210, 212, 234, 235, 275–76, 282, 334

Cromwell, Oliver, 206n, 602n
Cromwell (Carlyle), 413
Cross, Richard Assheton, 1st Viscount, 520,
    529, 578, 626
Crotchet Castle (Peacock), 286
"Cry of the Children, The" (Browning), 228
Crystal Palace, 305–307, 394
    speech (1872), 503–506, 504, 529
Culture and Anarchy (Arnold), 487
Cumming, Dr. John, 364, 365
Curiosities of Literature (Isaac D'Israeli), 26,
    28, 39, 139
    BD memoir in preface, 19–20, 279, 286,
    308
Curzon Street house, 651–62, 652

Daily News, 554, 569, 590n
Daily Telegraph, 492, 497, 546, 608
Daisy Miller (James), 493
Dalmeny, Lord (later Earl of Rosebery),
    352–53, 506
Damiani, (expatriate Venetian), 101, 106
Dana, Richard Henry, Jr., on BD, 355–56
Daniel Deronda (Eliot), 23, 632
D'Arblay, Madame (Fanny Burney), 135
Darwin, Charles, 260, 347, 425, 428, 536n
Dasent, G. W., 439, 482, 493
Davies, Scrope, 42
Davis, Jefferson, 392, 409, 452
De Aguilar, Ephraim, 22
Dearborn Independent (Ford), 674
Defence of the Old Testament, A, 280
Delane, John T., 310, 439–40, 473, 482, 493,
    510, 580
De La Warr, 5th Earl, 333
Denison, J. E., 350, 460, 463–64
Denning, S. P., 41
Denvil, Henry, 158
De Quincey, Thomas, 42–43
Derby, 1st Earl of, 155
Derby, 14th Earl of (formerly Edward
    Stanley), 553
    on BD, 358
    and BD's succession as Prime Minister,
    459–60
    death, 479
    and Gladstone's succession to Exchequer,
    325–26
    letters from BD, 407, 411–12, 444, 459–60,
    644
    and Palmerston government, 340–42
    as Prime Minister, 313–26, 370–76,
    378–79, 417–18, 437–58
    as Tory leader, 329, 331–37, 339–42,
    344–46, 359–62, 380, 383–85, 387,
    388, 391, 393, 402–404, 406, 409,
    411–12, 416
Derby, 15th Earl of (formerly Lord Edward
    Henry Stanley), 479, 500, 511, 520,

    535, 536, 538, 539, 542–43, 546–50,
    554, 557, 559, 564, 570–74, 576, 579,
    582–89, 626, 626n, 660
Derby, Countess of (wife of 14th Earl), 81
Derby, Mary Catherine, Countess of (formerly
    2nd Marchioness of Salisbury, wife of
    15th Earl of Derby), 480, 519, 535,
    538, 573, 577, 582–85
De'Rossi, Enrichetta (great-grandmother), 21
De Vere (Ward), 53n, 77
Diaries and journals (BD), 44
    on grand tour to Flanders and Germany,
    48–50
    on Henrietta Sykes, 167
    on Samuel Rogers, 129
    on travels to Switzerland and Italy, 75–76
    on travels to Middle East and Holy Land,
    104–105
Dickens, Charles, 14, 170n, 217–18, 224,
    224n, 229, 230, 238, 241, 258, 420,
    482, 580, 632, 636
Dilke, Sir Charles, 497–98, 503, 568, 612,
    633, 654
Discourse on the Manners of the Ancients
    (Shelley), 7
Disraeli, Benjamin (Lord Beaconsfield), 54,
    122, 222, 291, 315, 407, 448, 464,
    504, 554, 567, 578, 584, 602, 662
    ambition reflected in early novels, 120–21,
    128
    ambition to become Prime Minister,
    154–55, 304–305, 411–12, 454–56
    ambition, youthful, xii–xiv, 38, 44, 56,
    66–68, 82, 97, 111–12
    Anglican baptism and conversion, xii,
    31–34, 36, 50, 148–49, 266
    birth and circumcision, 17–19, 28, 191–92
    as Chancellor of Exchequer, 302–304,
    313–26, 320–28, 370–79, 437–58
    as consultant to John Murray, 40, 55–65
    death, 431, 654–59
    and death of Sarah, 381–82
    debts, and leadership of Commons,
    258–59, 273, 304–305, 362
    debts, and marriage to Mary Anne, 188,
    189, 193–96, 401
    debts, and purchase of Hughenden, 272,
    283
    debts, and second Parliament seat, 195–97,
    200–201, 203–204, 248
    debts bought and discharged by Montagu,
    401
    debts, early, 4, 7, 12, 51, 62, 63, 76, 77, 79,
    84, 86, 88, 115, 118, 121, 129, 135,
    136, 139, 150, 165, 169–70, 179, 290
    depression, 27, 47, 70–72, 78–84, 93, 121,
    298, 316, 318, 319–20, 356–57
    dress and appearance, 5, 13, 59, 72, 84,

86–87, 91, 92, 121, 134, 139–40, 225, 230, 347, 349–50, 454, 476, 603
(created) Earl of Beaconsfield, 555, 556, 558, 558–62, 573
education, 28–44
eloquence, 154
family background and ancestry, 19–28
and father's death, 278–80, 283
father's influence on, 25, 27, 28
father's library, 280, 641
finances after death of Mary Anne, 510, 512
finances, and Sarah Brydges Willyams, 400–401
financial advice from Lionel Rothschild, 246–47
financial rewards from novels, 68, 76, 126, 135, 219, 225, 270, 482, 631–32, 654, 657
first literary efforts, 45–46
first novel, 4, 28
first publication, 51
first seat in Parliament, 3–16, 170–71, 181–82, 195
foreign policy, see Foreign policy
funeral and memorial, 657–63
and Gladstone's succession to Exchequer, 325–26
and high society, 8, 67, 68, 116–19, 121–26, 138–43
honors, Oxford D. C. L., 332; Rector of Edinburgh Univ., 354; Rector of Glasgow Univ., 499, 515–16; earldom of Beaconsfield, 558–63, 578; Garter, 599–600
(probable) illegitimate child Kate Donovan (see also Donovan, Kate), 430–36 (see also Nevill, Ralph)
illness, last, 641–43, 650–58
illnesses, 30, 169, 296, 331, 379, 457, 529, 534, 536–38, 556, 557, 559, 572–73, 577, 580–81, 595, 616–17, 622 (see also depression)
illness, venereal disease, 99, 114
inheritance from brother James, 477
inheritance from Mrs. Brydges Willyams, 307–308, 400–402
inheritance from sister Sarah, 401
Jewish background, 4–5, 17–34, 141–42, 377–78
and Jewish Oaths bill, 275–78, 337–38 (see also Jews; Judaism)
last days at Hughenden, 641–43, 649
last days in London and Parliament, 649–53
law studies and apprenticeship, 43–45, 47, 50, 52, 78
leadership threatened by Burghley cabal, 500–501, 503

leads House, 370–88
leads party under Aberdeen, 328–39
leads party under Palmerston, 339–47, 340–43, 355–69, 382–88
legislation as Prime Minister, 463, 530–32, 536–37, 549–53, 586
letters, see specific correspondents
marital life with Mary Anne, 191–92, 221, 293–95, 347–55, 419–20, 457, 642
marriage ideas, 141, 147, 149, 178–79
marriage to Mary Anne Lewis, 188–91
memoir of father, 19–21, 23, 279
mining pamphlets, 51–52, 77
mining stock speculation, 50–53, 55, 57, 61–63, 79, 86
mother's death, 272
motto, xi, xiv
name, xi–xii, 5, 18, 20, 21, 45
newspaper, starts Tory Press, 329–31
novels, xiv, 4, 7, 14n, 154, 161, 592–94, 665 (see also specific novels)
and Parliament, early attempts to win seat, 111–19, 129–36, 153, 158–62, 196–97
in Parliament, early years, 175–97
in Parliament, moves to seat of Buckinghamshire, 271–73
in Parliament, under Peel, 232–36, 235, 248–58, 251, 268
in Parliament, becomes party leader, 249–58, 269, 275–78, 280–98, 455–58
pension preserved by Charlotte Rothschild, 402
personality, 414–15, 428, 526
plagiarism charges, 319–20
political aims, in youth, 13–14, 154–55
political aims sponsored by Lord Lyndhurst, 158–68
political dinners, 190–91, 195, 225
political journalism, 163–65, 178, 329–31
political philosophy, 9, 43–44, 100, 129–30, 135–36, 143, 207–208, 212–14
political rivalry with Gladstone, 358, 360, 375–81, 394, 397, 400, 403–406, 442–47, 452, 455, 501–506, 511, 516–21, 539, 563–68
prejudice against Jews met by BD, xi–xii, 4–5, 13, 36–37, 113, 115, 116, 136, 138–39, 143, 161–62, 197, 219, 245, 248, 261–67, 276–78
prejudice against Jews experienced as Prime Minister, 458–75, 518–21, 518, 525–526, 527, 567, 573–75, 580, 585, 590–93, 597–98, 601–608
and Reform Bill of 1867, 439–55, 448, 451, 469–70
Rothschilds, friendships with, 380–81, 411, 539–40, 611–12, 635

Disraeli, Benjamin (Lord Beaconsfield)
    (cont.)
  short fiction, 138, 153, 154n, 156–57 (see
    also specific works)
  travels to Belgian Spa, then to France,
    357–59
  travels to Congress of Berlin in 1878,
    591–604, **594**
  travels to Flanders and Rhineland with
    father and Meredith, 46–50, 76
  travels to France and Flanders with Mary
    Anne, 246–48, 264
  travels to France with Mary Anne in 1842,
    204–206
  travels to Mediterranean and Middle East
    with Meredith and Clay, 82, 85–113,
    261–68, 447, 486, 541
  travels to Scotland to see Lockhart and
    Scott, 57–59, 61, 67
  travels to Switzerland, France and Italy
    with Austens, 72–76
  and Victoria, 232, 303, 386–88, 397–400,
    520–21, 546–47, 555–56, 560,
    571–72, 582, 624–26, 628, 632
  will, 431, 610–11, 660
  and women, affair with Clarissa Bolton,
    84–85, 117
  and women, relationship with Dorothy
    Nevill, 419–30
  and women, affair with Henrietta Sykes,
    143–49, 157, 163–68
  and women, after death of Mary Anne,
    512–14, 516, 528
  and women, attraction to older, 8, 37, 40,
    92, 138–39
  and women, courts Mary Anne Lewis for
    her money, 179–86
  and women, flirtation with Sara Austen,
    66–67, 71–72, 78–79, 82–84
  and women, infatuation with Lady
    Bradford, 533–34, 539
  and women, Mary Anne's jealousy, 293–95,
    319
  and women, used for political connections,
    xiv, 122–26, 138–39, 152–55, 157–58,
    638
  writes Alroy, 111–12, 121
  writes Coningsby, 211–19
  writes Contarini Fleming, 108, 110–11
  writes Count Alarcos, 183–84
  writes Endymion, 628–41
  writes Falconet, 643–48
  writes Henrietta Temple, 165–69
  writes Lothair, 479, 481–94, **483**, 495
  writes memoir of Bentinck, 308–12
  writes Revolutionary Epick, 149–52
  writes Sybil, or The Two Nations, 227–28,
    236–44, 246
  writes Tancred, 246, 248, 256, 259–72

  writes Velvet Lawn masque, 147–48
  writes Vivian Grey, 53–54, 65–70
  writes Vivian Grey sequel, 75–78
  writes Voyage of Captain Popanilla, 80
  writes Year at Hartlebury with Sarah,
    150–51, 381
  writes Young Duke, 83–84, 87
  see also Conservative party; Diaries and
    journals; Foreign policy; House of
    Commons; Jews; Jews, prejudice
    against; Speeches; and specific
    correspondents, domestic and foreign
    issues, legislation, literary works
D'Israeli, Benjamin (grandfather), 18–26, 30,
    264, 641
D'Israeli, Benjamin (of Dublin), 21
D'Israeli, Coningsby Ralph (nephew), 477,
    610, 625, 649, 661
D'Israeli, Isaac (father), **41,** 71, 84, 167, 223,
    420
  advice on ambition, 56, 64
  advice on dinner conversation, 40
  background and education, 24–28
  BD on, 28, 76
  and BD's debts, 12, 169–70, 189, 193, 259
  on BD's depression, 79–81
  and BD's education, 28–29, 33, 35, 38–44,
    52, 78
  and BD's illness and irresponsibility, 85
  and BD's law clerkship, 44, 44n
  and BD's marriage, 189–90, 201
  and BD's name, 18
  and BD's political career, 160
  on BD's speech on Jewish question, 277–78
  and BD's win of Maidstone seat, 5, 8, 11
  and BD's writing, 269–70
  birth, 22
  and Bradenham household, 134
  and children's conversions, 31–32, 31n
  death, 278–80
  on family background, 19–20
  finances, 26–28, 30
  friendship with John Murray, 40–43,
    56–60, 62, 64, 64n, 73–75
  on grand tour with BD, 47–49
  honorary degree, 134
  old age and illness, 272
  letters from BD, 72–73, 90–92, 96–98, 109,
    111–12, 113, 142
  letters to BD, 152, 176, 216
  marriage, 27–28
  moves to country, 53, 80–81
  publications and literary reputation, 26, 28,
    90, 137, 139, 141–42, 286
  resigns from synagogue, 30–31
D'Israeli, Jacobus (brother, later James), 30,
    72, 210, 279, 280, 318, 382, 417
  death, 477, 508, 642
  letters from BD, 359

D'Israeli, Kate Trevor, 477
Disraeli, Mary Anne Lewis (formerly Lewis,
    Mary Anne Wyndham), 298, 318,
    319, 331, 332, 334, 338, 345, 346,
    364, 376, 382, 395, 404, 449, 451,
    453, 496
  age and illness, 348–49, 457, 479, 495
  on BD's ambitions, 347
  and BD's debts, 194–95, 258–59
  and BD's writing, 260
  death, 506–10, 512, 661
  and Dorothy Nevill, 423, 424, 426, 428,
    430
  early life as BD's wife, 189, 192–93,
    200–201, 208, 209, 211n, 221–22,
    225, 230
  and Hughenden, 292, 293, 395–96, 401
  and Isaac's will, 279
  last letter to BD, 348
  letters from BD, 201–203, 256, 257, 284,
    286–88, 342, 441, 443, 472, 507
  letters to BD, 201, 314, 507, 512
  letters to Charlotte de Rothschild, 460
  letters to Mrs. Brydges Willyams, 385
  letters to Sarah, 232
  personality, 348–54, 381, 419–20, 454,
    629
  portrayed in Endymion, 638
  presses Peel for BD post, 199–200
  as Prime Minister's wife, 460, 463–65, 468,
    471
  and Rothschild family, 243–45, 267, 373,
    509
  (created) Viscountess Beaconsfield,
    474–75, 477, 501, 503, 626
  travels to France with BD, 204, 205,
    243–46
  See also Lewis, Mary Anne Wyndham
D'Israeli, Miriam Basevi "Maria" (mother),
    17, 18, 27, 28, 30, 39, 71, 92, 183,
    224, 279
  and BD's education, 34
  letter to John Murray, 64
D'Israeli, Naphtali (brother), 30
D'Israeli, Rachel, 21
D'Israeli, Raphael (brother, later Ralph), 30,
    72, 93, 210, 224, 279, 280, 477, 649,
    661
  letters from BD, 94, 95, 381, 382
D'Israeli, Rebecca Mendes Furtado
    (grandfather's first wife), 21
D'Israeli, Sarah (sister), 4, 18, 66, 72, 83,
    111, 147, 224, 229, 246, 248, 272,
    277, 312
  Alroy dedicated to, 142–43
  and Annie Bassett, 477
  baptized, 32
  as BD's audience and helper, 110
  and BD's marriage, 141, 190
    birth, 28
  and father's death, 279–80
  and fiance William Meredith, 45–46, 85
  death, 381–82
  fiction, 150–51
  letters from BD, 6–11, 15, 48–50, 89–90,
    93–94, 100–104, 107, 108, 109–10,
    116–119, 122–23, 126, 134–35,
    138–39, 151–52, 157–60, 163,
    166–67, 173, 177, 179, 186, 189, 190,
    193, 195, 197, 200, 204, 205, 209,
    211, 269, 278, 289, 292–96, 298, 299,
    302, 306–307, 318, 382
  letters to BD, 16, 90, 94, 111, 146, 149,
    153–55, 188, 216
  Mary Anne's letters to, 232
  portrayed in Alroy, 139; in Endymion, 634
  Sara Austen's letters to, 72–73
  Sunday school catechism published,
    148–49
D'Israeli, Sarah Shiprut de Gabay Villa Réal
    (grandmother), 18, 22–24, 26, 31
Dizzi-ben-Dizzi, the Orphan of Bagdad
    (pamphlet), 573
"Dizzy's Lament," 478–79
Doche, Madame, 126
Dodgson, Charles (Lewis Carroll), 664
Dombey and Son (Dickens), 224n, 632
Don, Gen. Sir George, 90–91, 91n
Don, Lady, 92–94
Donati, Giambattista, 373
Don Juan (Byron), 68, 429
Donovan, Agnes, 432
Donovan, Catherine Mary (possible mother
    of Kate), 431–36, 513
Donovan, Frederick, 434
Donovan, John Vincent, 431–32
Donovan, Mary, 431
D'Orsay, Count Alfred, 4, 125–26, 153, 154,
    158, 160–62, 166–68, 170–71, 183,
    192, 195, 197, 205, 255, 279, 283,
    319
  death, 290–92
  letters to BD, 184, 291–92
Douce, Francis, 26, 28
Dreikaiserbund, 549, 554
Drummond, Henry, 305, 334–35, 373–74
Ducrow, Andrew, 159
Dufferin, Lady. See Blackwood, Helen
"Duke de l'Omlette, The" (Poe), 78
Dumas, Alexandre, fils, 359
Du Pre, Caledon George, 273
Durand, Sir Henry, 475
Durham, Bishop of, 299
Durham, Earl of, 153, 158–60
Dyce, William, 444

Earle, Ralph, 360–61, 375–76, 384, 417, 439
Eastern Question, 265, 335–36, 541, 543,

Eastern Question (cont.)
    553–54, 556–57, 559–60, 563–73,
    576, 581–84, 586–97, 604, 645
East India Company, 333, 365–67
Ecclesiastical Titles Bill (1851), 305
Edinburgh, University of
    honorary degree, 354
    office of Rector, 413–15
Edinburgh Review, 270, 327, 454, 639
Education Act (1870, 1876), 480–81, 495,
    529, 531
Edward II, King, 155
Edwards, Capt. Fleetwood, 655
Egerton, Lady (Anna Elizabeth Grey-
    Egerton), 8
Egerton, Lord Francis, 8
Eglinton, 13th Earl of, 629
Eglinton Tournament (1839), 629–30, 634
Egypt, Khedive of, 611
Elections
    of 1834, 159–60
    of 1835, 160–62
    of 1837, 3–16, 170–71
    of 1847, 273
    of 1859, 378–79
    of 1865, 411
    of 1868, 469, 472–73
    of 1874, 517–20
    of 1880, 623–27
Eliot, George (Mary Ann Evans), 23, 493,
    620, 632
Ellenborough, Lord, 414
Elphinstone, Lord, 318
Ely, Jane, 576, 660
Eminent Victorians (Strachey), 309
"Endymion" (Aytoun), 630
Endymion (BD, 1880), 81, 87, 128, 222,
    300–301, 316, 378, 382, 423–24, 439,
    651
    letter to Queen on, 639–40
    written and published, 628–41, 654, 657
Enfield, Lord, 473
England and France: or a Cure for the
    Ministerial Gallomania (political
    satire), 116–19, 121, 125, 126
England and the English (Bulwer-Lytton), 137
"England's Trust" (Manners), 203
Englishman, The (newspaper), 331
Enquiry into the Plans, Progress and Policy of
    the American Mining Companies, An
    (BD's first publication, 1825), 51
Eöthen (Kinglake), 255n
Esher, 2nd Viscount. See Brett, Reginald
Ernest, Duke of Coburg, 386
Ernest, King of Hanover and Duke of
    Cumberland (Victoria's uncle), 10,
    209
Ernest Leopold Victor, Prince of Leiningen,
    538

Espinasse, Francis, 383
Essay on the Manners and Genius of the
    Literary Character, An (Isaac
    D'Israeli), 28
Eta Carinae (star), 488
Ethics of the Fathers (Akiba), 171
Eugénie, Empress of France, 192, 343, 359,
    613
Evans, John Viney, 16, 188
Evans, Thomas Mullett, 50, 79
    letters to BD, 86
Evelyn, William John, 211, 211n
Examiner, The, 151, 237
Exeter, Lord, 295, 332, 500

Factory regulatory bill (1844), 227, 228, 530
Faerie Queene (Spenser), 521
Falcieri, Giovanni Battista "Tita," 94, 95,
    107–108, 134, 278
Falconet (BD's unfinished last novel), 643–48
Fancies, Fashions and Fads (Nevill), 429
Fancourt, Charles, 10–11
Farmer, Thomas, 225
Faust (Goethe), 571
Fector, John Minet, 181
Fenians, 455–56, 465, 466, 480, 481, 485
Ferdinand VII, King of Spain, 55
Ferrand, William Busfield, 231–32
Fitz-Clarence, George Augustus Frederick
    (Earl of Munster), 8, 9
FitzGerald, Edward, 569
Fleming, Canon, 658
Floreat Etona (Nevill), 429
Flower, Constance Rothschild. See
    Rothschild, Constance de
Flower, Cyril, 509, 603
Food and Drugs Act (1876), 530
Ford, George Samuel, 194–195, 201
Foreign policy
    BD and, as leader in House of Commons,
        294–95, 395, 397, 400, 403–405
    BD and, as Prime Minister, 470–71,
        525–26, 540–46, 548–58, 563–79,
        581–602, 608–10, 613–18, 621–23
    BD and, during Derby's last illness, 455–56
    and intelligence from Rothschilds, 468,
        468n, 539–42, 572
    Palmerston's, 355, 360–61, 363–64, 366,
        367, 393
    See also Eastern Question; and specific
        events
Forester, Selina. See Bradford, Countess of
Forster, John, 224, 224n, 237
Fortescue, Chichester, 352
Fortnightly Review, 492–93
Fowler, John Kersey, 269
Fox, William Johnson, 152
Franco-Prussian War, 491
Franklin, Jacob, 270–71

Fraser, Sir William, 367–68, 499, 624, 650
Fraser's Magazine, 138, 143, 167, 243
Frederick, Crown Prince of Prussia, 366, 368, 438, 549
Frederick the Great (Carlyle), 413
Freeman, Edward
  on BD as Jew, xi, 568, 582
Free Trade, 207, 208, 234, 250, 252, 303, 306, 312, 314, **315,** 317, 321
Fremont, General, 481
Frere, Sir Bartle, 610
Friendly Societies Act (1875), 530
Frith, W. P., 350
Fun, **589**
Furniss, Harry, **558**
Furtado, Rebecca Mendes (*see also* D'Israeli, Rebecca), 21

Gabriel, Thomas, 453
Galignani's Messenger, 49, 98, 99, 108, 246
Gamaliel, 339*n*
Gans, David, 112
Garibaldi, Guiseppi, 481
Gaskell, Charles Milnes, 638
Gathorne-Hardy, Jane, 517
Gathorne-Hardy, Gathorne (*later* Lord Cranbrook), 445, 447, 447*n*, 449, 466, 479, 481, 500, 505, 508, 510, 511, 516, 520, 558, 559, 565–66, 577, 590, 609, 623–24, 653, 654
Gemara, 141
Genius of Judaism, The (D'Israeli), 141, 309
George II, King, 315*n*
George III, King, 315*n*
George IV, King, 10, 90, 634
Germany and Berlin Congress, 590, 592, 596
Gibbs, John, 273
Gibson, Mrs. (Cogan's elder daughter), 36
Gibson, Susan, 221
Gibson, Thomas Milner, 221
Gideon, Samson (Lord Eardley), 116
Gilbert and Sullivan (operettas), 443, 577
Gil Blas (Lesage), 640
Girardin, Emile de, 359
Gladstone, Catherine, 468, 508, 566
Gladstone, Herbert, 519
Gladstone, Mary, 656
Gladstone, William Ewart, 199, 224, 227, 230, 234, 236, 248, 250, 253, 275, 281, 282, 292, 296, 332, 373, 376, 384, 412, **464,** 554, **589,** 637
  Albert wants him to lead Commons, 320–21
  anti-semitism. *See* Anti-semitism, Gladstone's attempts to reunite Conservatives, 297
  on BD as Jew, xi, 276, 519–20, 601, 605–608
  BD meets young WEG, 160

BD on, 179, 564, 565, 593, 641–44
and BD's death, 657, 658
on BD's debates against Peel, 253–54
and BD's funeral, 661–63
on BD's memoir of Bentinck, 311
as Chancellor of Exchequer, 326, 328, 331, 333, 379, 392–93
debates BD on budget under Derby, 322–25
and Derby's Ministry, 317, 374–75, 391
and Exchequer robes, 328
portrayed in *Falconet,* 644, 645
as Prime Minister, after BD resigns in 1880, 604, 632, 639, 642, 649, 650, 656
leads Tory faction against BD's faction, 345
letters to BD, 508, 600–601
offered appointment by Stanley, 303–304
and Palmerston's Ministry, 340–41, 356
as party leader in Commons opposite BD, 413, 417–18
and Peel's death, 297–98
as Prime Minister, with BD as rival (1868–74), 475–83, **483,** 497, 500–506, 511, 516–21
and "rescue work" with prostitutes, 323–24, 341, 444–46, 565–66, 570
as rival, when BD is Prime Minister, 462–66, **464,** 468–71, 475, 484, 521, 526–29, **527,** 535, 538–39, 544, 546, 551, 552–53, 557, 563–69, 570–71, 574, 576, 578, 581–83, 585, 587, 588, 600–601, 605, 613, 618–26, 664
rivalry with BD, **358,** 360, 377, 394, 397, 400, 403–406, 408, 411, 416, 441, 454
rivalry with BD over Reform bill, 442–47, 452, 455
and slavery, 392–93, 408
on *Sybil,* 242
Gladstone, Robertson, 511
Glasgow, University of
  BD as Lord Rector, 515
Globe, 329
Goethe, Johann Wolfgang von, 67, 119, 488, 571, 594
Goldsmid, Sir Francis Henry, 373
  ridiculed by BD, 142, 264*n*
Goldsmid, Frederick, 373
Goldsmid, Isaac Lyon, 142, 248
Goldsmid, Julian, 373
Goldsmith, Lewis, 205
Gordon, Arthur (Lord Stanmore), 576
Gordon, Sir Robert, 100
Gore, Catherine, 140
Gorst, John Eldon, 500–501, 503, 518
Gortchakov, Prince of Russia, 592
Goschen, George, 653
Goschen, Lucy, 653

Gosse, Edmund, 633
Goulburn, Henry, 195, 323
Gower, Lord Ronald, 507–508, 641–43
Graham, Sir James, 210, 211, 226, 227, 235,
    317, 373, 374
Gramont, Duchesse de, 205
Granby, Marquis of, 282, 287, 289, 290
Granville, Lord, 310, 387, 398, 439–40, 482,
    497, 622
Grant, Ulysses S., 576
Graves, Henry, 603
Great Exhibition of 1851, 305–307, 388
Great Exhibition of 1862, 394, 397
    and Albert memorial, 399–400
Gregory, Lady Augusta, 604–605
Gregory, Barnard, 191–92
Greville, Charles Fulke, 159, 210, 236, 251,
    281, 303, 372, 284–85
Grey, Charles, 2nd Earl, 119, 126, 127, 130,
    154, 157, 458
Grey, Lt. Col. Charles (later General), 9,
    130–34, 136, 159, 455, 458, 463, 474,
    475, 520
Grey, Sir George, 235, 408
Grey, Henry George, 3rd Earl, 552
Grey de Wilton, Lord, 516
Grillon's (club), 412–13
Grote, George, 177, 332
Guardian, 55
Guérin-Meneville, F. E., 425
Guest, Josiah John, 149, 225
Guest, Lady Charlotte (formerly Lady
    Charlotte Bertie, later Lady Charlotte
    Schreiber), 149, 225, 595
Guizot, François, 247
Gull, Sir William, 556, 580, 581

Haber, Baron Moritz von, 117
Haber, Salomon, 117, 165
Hallez, Théophile, 248
Hamilton, Edward, 659, 662
Hamilton, Lord George, 473, 495, 496, 571,
    620n, 654
Hamilton, Ian, 616
Hamilton, Walter, 41
Hamley, Sir Edward Bruce, 492
Hansard, 176, 254, 288, 308, 655
Harcourt, William Vernon, 507, 568, 583
Hare, Augustus, 630
Harrison, Frederic, 492–93
Harte, Bret, 494
Hartington, Spencer Compton Cavendish,
    Marquess of, 528, 564, 574, 626, 642
Hartmann, Leo, 647
Hastings, Lady Flora, 186
Hawarden, Lord, 653–54
Hawthorne, Nathaniel
    on BD, 347
Hay, John, 415, 452

Haydon, Benjamin Robert, 224–25, 379
Haydon, Frederic, 379
Hayward, Abraham, 298, 328, 454, 493, 624
Headlong Hall (Peacock), 286
Heath's Book of Beauty. See Book of Beauty,
    The
Heenan, Jack C., 479, 479n
Helena, Princess (later Princess Helena of
    Schleswig-Holstein), 467, 604
Helps, Arthur, 515
Henrietta Temple (BD, 1836), 4, 90, 92, 139,
    143, 362n, 525
    written and published, 165–69
Henry VII, King, 155
Herbert, Edward James, 550
Herbert, Sidney, 321, 341
Heroes and Hero-Worship (Carlyle), 221
Herries, John Charles, 281, 282, 287, 289,
    290, 297
Herschel, John, 487–88
Hertford, 3rd Marquess of, 154, 203, 212,
    221, 222, 638
Heywood, John, 607
Hicks Beach, Sir Michael, 520, 577, 624
Higham Hall school, 33–38
High Wycombe, 6, 9, 23, 53, 80, 112, 158
    seat, 114, 115, 129–37, 158–60, 458
Hillel, Rabbi, 339n
Hind, John Russell, 363
History and Literature of the Israelites
    (Constance and Annie de
    Rothschild), 494
History of Men of Genius (Isaac D'Israeli), 35
History of Rothschild I, King of the Jews, 247
"History of the Baroni Family, The," 264
H. M. S. Pinafore (operetta), 577, 606
Hobhouse, Sir John Cam (Lord Broughton),
    136, 225–26, 235, 284, 286
Hogarth, William, 24
Hollams, John, 13
Hollingshead, John, 394
Hood's Magazine, 220
Hook, Theodore, 69
Hooker, Thomas, 216n
Hope, A. J. Beresford, 393, 454, 517
Hope, Henry, 204, 211, 212, 219
Hope, Lady Mildred Cecil, 517
Hornby, Adm. Sir Geoffrey, 586
Horsman, Edward, 511
Houghton, 1st Baron (formerly Richard
    Monckton Milnes), 446, 469, 482,
    510
House of Commons, xiii, 108
    and BD as PM, 531, 556
    BD becomes Opposition leader in, 269,
    280–98
    BD leads, after Exchequer loss, 334–35
    BD leads Tories in, 1858–1868, 370–88,
    391–418, 437–58, 500–21

BD leads young Tories in, 198–219
BD leaves for Lords, **558**, 558–62, 574
BD pursues seat in, 4–16, 115–19, 170–71
BD's early ambitions, 82, 111–13
BD's early attempts to win seat, 130–36, 153
BD's early years in, 176–97
BD wins first seat, 3–16, 170–71
Gladstone's memorial address on BD, 663
Jews and, 116, 267, 273–78, 292, 298, 337–38
property qualifications for, 115
House of Lords, 6, 11, 118, 258, 267, 269, 274, 278, 292, 296, 334, 338, 372, 379, 393, 404–405, 439, 452, 453, 479–82, 501, 511, 528, 588–89
BD attends during last illness, 650–53
BD moves to, 556, **558**, 558–62, 573, 574
and Reform Bill, 127, 453
Salisbury's memorial address on BD, 663–64
House tax, 321, 323
How, Jeremiah, 237
Hughenden Manor, 292, 293, 353, 379–80, **380**, 495
BD buried at, 660–62
BD's last days at, 641–50
life at, 377, 378, 395–96, 405–406, 537
Mary Anne dies at, 507–508
mortgage, 401
purchase, 259, 269, 272–73, 283–86, 312
Victoria visits, 582
Hughes, Thomas, 601–602
Hugh of Lincoln, 602, 602n
Hume, Joseph, 130, 205
Humphrey, H., 23
Hunt, George Ward, 463, 520, 577, 582
Huskisson, Mrs. William, 232
Hyndman, Henry Mayers, 654

Idylls of the King (Tennyson), 535
Ignatiev, Count, 575
Illustrated London News, The, 279
Imperium et Libertas (pamphlet), 607
Importance of Being Earnest, The (Wilde), 646
India, as jewel in crown, 504–505, 569
East India Company, 333, 365–67
Mutiny, 365–67
Victoria made Empress of, 549–53, **561**, 571–72, 620, 620n
India Bill (1853), 333–34
India Bill (1858), 368, 370–71, 376
Industrial reforms, 227
"Infernal Marriage, The" (BD, 1834), 156–57, 171
Inquiry Concerning Moral Good and Evil (Hutcheson), 321
Iolanthe (operetta), 443

Irish Arms Bill (1843), 209–10
Irish Church (Disestablishment) Bill (1869), 465–68, 470, 478–80, 482, 510
Irish Coercion Bill (1846), 252, 253, 255–57
Irish Coercion Bill (1881), 632, 649
Irish Land Bill, 480, 510
Irish University Bill (1873), 510–11
Irving, Sir Henry, 471–72
Isaac, Saul, 373
Ismail Pasha, Khedive, 541–42, 544
Israel, Abraham (1613), 21
Israel, David (of Tunis), 21
Israel, Isaac, 21
Israel, Jacob (of Tunis), 21
Israeli, Isaac (great-grandfather), 21
Israeli, Menasseh Ben, 280
Istóczy, Gyösö von, 604
Ivanhoe (Scott), 59
"Ixion in Heaven" (BD, 1832), 138, 630

Jackson (tailor), 349–50
James, Henry, xii, 493, 569, 590
Janin, Jules, 306
Jenner, Sir William, 497, 580, 655
Jerdan, William, 69, 70, 76
Jersey, 6th Earl of, 357n
Jewish Disabilities Removal Act ("Jew Bill" or Jewish question), 116, 177, 223, 267, 274, 275–78, 281, 283–84, 287, 292–93, 298, 309–11, 327
1858 compromise on, 371–73
Oaths Bill form, 243, 337–38, 361, 437
Jews
BD on, 265–66, 283–84
BD on restoring Holy Land to, 301–302, 604
and BD's career, 664–65
BD's contemporaries, xii, 142, 278, 283–84, 338
and BD's Eastern policy, 557, 567–69, **567**, 572–74, 576, 579, 582–84, 589–91, 596–97, 605–608
in BD's novels, 106, 111–12, 115, 138, 280, 280n, 568
BD's pride in accomplishments of, 229–30, 263–64, 267
BD socializes with prominent, 190, 283–84
in Coningsby, BD's self-examination as, 214–17, 216n, 229–30
in Endymion, 635, 639
in Holy Land, 105–106
legal return to England, 19
Mary Anne and, 190, 245
and state in Palestine idea, 604–605
in Tancred, 261–68, 270–71
in Trollope's writings, 363
Jews, prejudice against. See Anti-Semitism
John Bull (Colman), 68, 70, 636
Johnson, Andrew, 409

Johnson, Dr. Samuel, 25, 139, 315n
Jolliffe, Sir William, 344, 373–74
Jones, Dr. Thomas, 88, 193, 290, 334
Jones, John Paul, 56–57
Jowett, Benjamin, 270, 441, 445
Judaism
  and BD's death, 658, 660
  BD's ideas on, 364–65, 377–78
  BD's ideas on, in memoir of Bentinck,
    309–10
  BD's imagery and, 339n
  BD's knowledge of, and father's library,
    280, 280n
  in Coningsby, 214–17
  Isaac's ambivalence toward, 25–26, 35,
    141–42, 278
  in Sybil, 242
  See also Jews; Jews, prejudice against
Juifs en France, Des (Avigdor), 248
Juventus Mundi (Gladstone), 482

Kant, Immanuel, 647
Kean, Edmund, 40
Kebbel, T. E., 426–27
Kenealy, Edward Vaughan, 330–31
Kent, Duchess of (Victoria's mother), 7, 186,
  386
Kent, Duke of (Victoria's father), 90
Khelat, Khan of, 569
Kidd, Dr. Joseph, 580–81, 596, 649–52, 655,
  656, 658
Kinglake, A. W., 255, 255n
"King Pest the First" (Poe), 78
Kingsley, Charles, 242–43
Kruger, Paul, 621

Labouchere, Henry, 160–61, 473, 579
Lamb, Lady Caroline, 67n, 140
Lambert, Sir John, 450
Lamington, Baron. See Baillie-Cochrane,
  Alexander
Lancastre, Comte de, 514
Landon, Letitia E., 126
Landsdowne, Lord, 225, 341
Lara family, 377–78
Lawes, Henry, 206n
Lawrence, Alderman, 496
Lawyers and Legislators: or Notes on the
  American Mining Companies (BD,
  1825), 51–52
Layard, Austen Henry, 542, 543, 546, 575,
  577, 601, 604–605
  sees BD as a boy, 72
League, The, 223
Leaves from the Journal of Our Life in the
  Highlands (Victoria), 468–69
Lectures on the Book of Revelation (Cumming),
  364
Lee, Frederick George, 505

Leighton, Frederic, 486
Lennox, Lord Henry, 318–19, 357, 360, 498,
  596, 597, 626
Leon of Modena, 104n
Leopold, Prince, 576, 661
Leopold I, King of the Belgians, 48, 98, 243
Lesage, Alain René, 91, 640
Lesseps, Ferdinand de, 541
"Letters to the Whigs" ("Manilius"), 330
Letters of Runnymede, 176
Leveson-Gower, Lord Ronald. See Gower,
  Lord Ronald
Levy, Esther, 435
Levy-Lawson, Edward (Lord Burnham), 546,
  608
Lewes, G. H., 225
Lewis, Mary Anne Wyndham, 15, 149 (later
  Disraeli, Mary Anne)
  BD meets and becomes protégé, 123–24,
    178
  on BD's future, 16
  and BD's win of Maidstone seat, 10, 13, 16
  courted by BD, 179–86
  letters from BD, 181–86
  marriage to BD, 188–91
Lewis, Wyndham, 10, 12, 13, 15, 16, 144,
  178, 181, 348, 349
  death, 179
  estate, 259, 286, 509, 510
Liberal Party, 408–409, 413, 416, 418, 446,
  468, 487, 502–504, 510, 511, 516,
  528, 531, 550, 574, 626, 633
  and Church, 384
  election of 1868, 473–74
  election of 1874, 519
  election of 1880, 618–25
  firmly amalgamated (in 1859), 379
  Gladstone leads as Prime Minister, 469,
    471, 475, 480–99, 501–21, 626
  and Reform Bill of 1867, 443, 444
  See also Whigs
Liddell, Henry, 417
Lightfoot, John, 104n
Lincoln, Abraham, 408–409, 415, 452
  BD on, 409
Lind, Jenny, 398
Lindo, Benjamin Ephraim (B. E. L., cousin),
  11, 12
Lindo, David Abarbanel (uncle), 18
Lindo, Sarah Basevi (aunt), 12
Lister, Dr. Joseph, 497
Literary Gazette, 69
Liverpool, Bishop of, 664
Lives of the Poets (Johnson), 315n
Lockhart, John Gibson, 57–62, 85, 210, 224
Lockhart, John Hugh, 58, 60
Lockhart, Sophia Scott, 58
Lockhart, Walter, 224
Londonderry, Charles William Stewart, 3rd

Marquess of, 123, 287, 297, 334, 343, 386, 396
Londonderry, Frances Anne, Marchioness of, 8, 11, 123, 180n, 213, 269, 297, 343–44, 396
  BD on, 386
  letters from BD, 295, 312, 336–37, 341–42, 356, 367, 368, 382
London Magazine, 198
London Society for Promoting Christianity among the Jews, 265
Longman, Thomas, 482, 489, 491, 631–33, 654, 657
Longman, William, 69
Lonsdale, Lord, 334
Lopes, Sir Manasseh, 116
Lord Beaconsfield Interviewed, 607
Lord George Bentinck, a Political Biography (BD), 285
  written and published, 308–12
"Loss of Breath" (Poe), 78
Lothair (BD, 1870), 94, 154, 154n, 392, 420, 425, 503, 631, 632, 637, 646
  written, 481–91, 630
  reception of, 491–95
Lothaw (Harte), 494
Loudoun, Countess of, 507
Louise, Princess, 441, 472
Louis Napoleon, Prince (later Napoleon III), 192–93, 255
  elected President of France, 286
  declares self Emperor, 312–13, 320
Louis Napoleon, Prince Imperial (Napoleon III's son), 613–15
Louis-Philippe, King of France, 117, 192, 205–206, 246–48, 420
Low, Sampson, 362n
Lowe, Robert, 416–18, 441, 467, 469, 551–53
Lowell, James Russell, 271, 601, 623
Lowther, James, 446
Lucan, Earl of, 372
Lucas, Samuel, 329, 331
Lucy, Sir Henry, 353
Lumley, Augustus, 641
Lumley, Benjamin, 306, 308
Lyell, Sir Charles, 346
Lygon, Viscount Elmley (later 4th Earl of Beauchamp), 426–27
Lyndhurst, Baron (John Singleton Copley), 9, 11, 109, 157–160, 162–68, 177, 180, 189, 205, 210, 261, 267, 297, 637, 639
Lyndhurst, Georgiana, 180n
Lyster, Lady Charlotte, 625
Lyttleton, George, 1st Baron Lyttleton, 315, 315n
Lytton, Edith, Countess of, 550–51
Lytton, Edward Bulwer-. See Bulwer, Edward Lytton

Lytton, Lord Robert (Bulwer-Lytton's son, later Earl of Lytton), 550, 571, 574, 608–609, 615–18
  letters from BD, 627

Macaulay, Thomas Babington, 7, 118, 321, 332, 643
MacCarthy, C. J., 226
Macdermott, Gilbert Hastings, 582
McClellan, General George, 481
MacDonald, Hector, 616
Mackenzie, Forbes, 313–14, 328
Maclise, Daniel, **54, 74, 122,** 138, 167–68, 168n
Macmillan's Magazine, 493
Macready, William Charles, 40, 183, 202, 224, 282, 420
Madame Tussaud's, 327, 328
Magic Flute (opera by Mozart), 49
Maginn, William, 60, 138
Mahmoud II, Sultan of Ottoman Empire, 99–100
Maimonides, Moses, 112, 217
Major Barbara (Shaw), 14, 14n
Malibran, Maria, 149
Mallet, Sir Louis, 566
Malmesbury, Earl of, 285, 304, 316, 334, 335, 341, 345, 358, 359, 362, 376, 378, 379, 384, 510, 520
Manchester, Louise, Duchess of, 398, 461–62, 528, 639
Manfred (Byron), 128, 158
Manners, Lord John, 202–209, 212, 219, 228–29, 231, 236, 269, 276, 282, 299, 308, 319, 349, 421, 462, 495–96, 500, 501, 507–508, 520, 532, 550, 577, 626
  letters from BD, 382
Manning, R., 194
Manning, Archbishop William (later Cardinal), 27, 484, 490, 622–23, 637
Manning & Vaughan, 27
Maples, Thomas Frederick, 44–45
Marlborough, Duke of, 500, 516, 526
Marochetti, Baron Carlo, 414
Martin, Theodore, 546
Martin Chuzzlewit (Dickens), 230
Marx, Karl, 208
Maurice (Lord Byron's boatman), 72–73
Maxse, Lady Caroline
  letters from BD, 176
Mayfair and Montmartre (Nevill), 430
Mayo, Lord, 455, 481
Mazzini, Giuseppe, 491
Medea (Cherubini), 49
Medina Sidonia, Duke of, 92
Mehemet Ali Pasha, 106, 108–109, 108n
Melbourne, Viscount, 67n, 140, 168n
  BD meets, 154–55

Melbourne, Viscount *(cont.)*
  as Prime Minister, 157, 158, 161, 162, 187, 582
Mellon, Harriot, 69
Melville, Gansevoort, 5
Melville, Herman, 362n
Memoirs (Cellini), 79
Memoirs of Moses Mendelssohn, 280
Mendelssohn, Felix, 267, 346
Mendelssohn, Moses, 26, 35, 142, 278, 280
Mendes, Solomon, 25
Mendez da Costa family, 308, 378
Mendoza, Daniel, 223
Merchant Shipping Act (1876), 530, 538
Meredith, Ellen, 141, 147
Meredith, George, 290, 492, 552, 569, 623
Meredith, Georgiana, 46, 110, 141
Meredith, Mrs. (mother of William), 141
"Meredith, Owen" (Bulwer-Lytton), 550
Meredith, William, 46–49, 85–87, 89, 91–96, 98–101, 106–108, 119
  illness and death, 109–10, 147
Messer, Robert, 50–53, 56, 86, 118, 290
Metternich, Prince Klemens von, 287–88, 294–95, 590, 635, 636
Meynell, Wilfrid, 664
Middlemarch (Eliot), 632
Mill, John Stuart, 438, 439
Millais, Sir John, 603, 644, 663
Milman, Henry, 119–20
Milnes, Richard Monckton (*later* 1st Baron Houghton), 220–21, 226, 230–31, 255–56, 270, 413–14, 446
Miscellanies, or Literary Recreations (Isaac D'Israeli), 28
Mistletoe (schooner), 538
Mitford, Dr. George, 136
Mitford, Letetia, 149
Mitford's History of Greece, 44
Montagu, Andrew, 401
Montagu, Edwin, 533
Montalembert, Comtesse de (Eliza Forbes), 8, 149
Montefiore, Sir Moses, 177, 265, 597
Montefiore, Mrs., 190, 225
Montefiore, Nathaniel, 194n
Monthly Depository, 152
Monypenny, W. F., 214, 288, 290, 647
Moore, Tom, 41–43
Moran, Benjamin, 368, 408–10
Moresby, Capt. Sir Fairfax, 525
Morgan, Lady (Sydney Owenson), 124, 298
Morier, R. D., 566
Morley, John, 326, 552
Morning Chronicle, The, 177, 208, 210, 219, 221, 319
Morning Herald, 16, 289
Morning Post, 162–63, 216, 277
Morris, William, 569

Motley, John Lothrop, 139, 140, 462
Motley, Lily, 452
Moxon, Edward, 141, 152, 237, 286
Mozart, Wolfgang Amadeus, 49
Munby, Arthur, 551
Münster, Count, 591
Murillo, Bartolomé, 93
Murray, Anne, 64
Murray, John, 26, 31, 35
Murray, John, II, 45, 46, 51, 54–65, 67, 69, 77, 85–86, 88, 116, 125, 224, 315
  break with Isaac, 64, 73–75
  burns early work of BD, 46, 80
  letters from BD, 134
  as publisher and friend of Isaac, 39–43
  publishes BD's works, 119–21, 126, 135
Murray, John, III, 538
Murray, Sophia, 65

Napier, Sir Robert, 470, 471, 475, 503, 550, 613
Napoleon, 92n
Napoleon III, Emperor of France (*formerly* Louis Napoleon), 192–93, 320, 320n, 329, 335, 340, 343, 357, 359, 368, 375, 383, 395, 440–41, 498, 552, 624, 637
  on BD, 359
Nash, John, 132
Nathan, J. L., 195
Nation, 639, 659
Nevill, Lady Dorothy (Dolly) Walpole, 351, 419–30, 435, 491
  on BD, 414, 663
  on *Endymion*, 633
  and husband's death, 429
  letters from BD, 395, 425–28, 462, 495, 521
  letters to BD, 424, 424n, 425, 509, 521
  letters to Mary Anne, 424n
  relationship with BD, 420–30, 528
Nevill, Edward Augustus, 424
Nevill, Guy, 427
Nevill, Horace, 425
Nevill, Ralph (possible son of BD), 427–30, 436
Nevill, Reginald, 423–24, 427
Newcombes, The (Thackeray), 643
Newdegate, Charles, 288
Newman, Cardinal John Henry, 462, 601, 622–23, 637
  on BD, 505–506
New Monthly Magazine, 138, 156, 493
Newton, Sir Isaac, 346
Newton, Stuart, 41
"New Voyage of Sinbad the Sailor, Recently Discovered, A" (political series), 165, 169
New York Mirror, 154

New York Tribune, 465, 617
Nicholas I, Czar of Russia, 342
Niemann, E. J., **6**
Nightingale, Florence, 441, 445
Nineteenth Century, The, 601
Noel, Gerald, 500
"No Popery" Act, 302–303
Norris, John, 259
North, William, 223
North American Review, 271, 600
Northcote, Lady, 352, 653
Northcote, Sir Stafford, 325, 352, 381, 416,
    445, 467, 470–71, 478, 495, 500, 520,
    542, 558, 560, 579, 590n, 618, 626
Norton, Caroline, 140, 154, 225
Norton, Charles Eliot, 392, 601
Norton, George Chapple, 140
Novikov, Olga, 566, 568, 570, 592

Oaths Bill. *See* Jewish Disabilities Removal
    Act, Oaths Bill form
O'Brien, William Smith, 209
O'Connell, Daniel, 124, 130, 161–62, 175–77
O'Connell, Morgan, 162
O'Connor, T. P. ("Tay Pay"), 568, 597
"Old England" series ("Coeur de Lion"), 178
Oliphant, Laurence, 604–605
Oppenheim, Henry, 541
Orford, Countess of, 423
Orford, Earl of, 420, 421, 424, 426, 427
Orlov, Count Alexis, 117–18
Orton, Arthur, 331
Osborne, Bernal, 354, 370, 405, 510
    on BD, 449–50, 455
Osman Pasha, 577
Ottoman Empire, 96, 98, 100, 210, 265, 335.
    See also Eastern Question
Owenson, Sydney, Lady Morgan. *See* Morgan,
    Lady (Sydney Owenson)
Oxberry, William, 40
Oxford University, 33, 45, 134, 134n
    BD given honorary D. C. L., 332, 353

Padwick, Henry, 359
Pakington, John, 511
Palgrave, Sir Francis, 5
Pall Mall (Nevill), 429
Palmerston, Lady, 232, 284, 295, 368, 453,
    462, 469, 639
Palmerston, Viscount (Henry John Temple),
    202, 204, 210, 219, 235, 247, 284,
    288, 289, 295, 296, 313–14, 317, 320,
    329, 333, 335, 339, 552, 553, 637,
    645
    death, 413, 415–16
    as Opposition leader, 374, 375, 378–79
    as Prime Minister, 340–45, 350, 355–57,
        359, 360, 362–64, 367–69, 383–85,

387, 391–93, 395, 397, 399, 403–404,
    408, 411
"Papal Aggression" issue, 300–303, 305
Paris, Matthew, 602n
Parke, James (Lord Wensleydale), 355
Parliament, 108, 271, 371
    Jews barred from, 112–13, 116, 267,
        274–78, 337–38, 371
    See also House of Commons; House of
    Lords
Parnther, Robert, 178
Partridge, Mrs., **170**
Past and Present (Carlyle), 268
Patmore, Coventry, 453
Paxton, Joseph, 305, 394
Peace Preservation Act (1871), 350
Peacock, Thomas Love, 286
Peel, Lady Emily, 360
Peel, Gen. Jonathan, 403, 443, 444
Peel, Sir Robert, 118, 158, 162, 187, 195,
    198–202, 204, 223, 230, 267, 273,
    281, 282, 289, 290, 321, 324, 383,
    635
    BD presses, for sub-Cabinet post, 199–200,
        254–55
    BD's opposition to, 207–11, 226–27,
        232–36, **235**, 248–58, **251, 268**, 303,
        444
    in *Coningsby,* 213
    death, 296–97
    in memoir of Bentinck, 308–309, 311
    resignation of, 257–58
    resignation and return of, 247–48
    and Young England movement, 205
Peelites, 255–57, 273, 276, 296–98, 303, 304,
    311, 318, 322, 323, 328, 335, 341,
    356, 368, 379, 490
Pelham (Bulwer-Lytton), 87
Pellegrini, Carlo ("Ape"), 476
Pepys, Samuel, 19
Persigny, duc de, 378
Perugia, Maria, 650–51
Phillip, John, 350
Phillips, Samuel, 289
Phineas Finn (Trollope), 469
Phineas Redux (Trollope), 470
Phipps, Sir Charles, 388
Piccadilly (Nevill), 429
Pickwick Papers (Dickens), 170n
Pictorial Times, 221
Picture of Dorian Gray, The (Wilde), 91–92,
    490, 641
Pierre or, the Ambiguities (Melville), 362n
Piggott, Rev. John R., 293
Pitt, William, the elder, 474
Pitt, William, the younger, 326
Pius XI, Pope, 265, 299
Plat, Colonel du, 582
Plevna siege, 578, 582–83

Plimsoll, Samuel, 530
Poe, Edgar Allan, 77
Pollock, Jonathan Frederick, 314, 326
Ponsonby, Sir Henry, 520, 542, 549, 576,
    582, 585, 597, 625
Poor Law (1834), 14–15, 203, 218, 238
Pope, Alexander, 203
Portland, 4th Duke of, 251, 283, 285–86, 298
Portland, 5th Duke of (formerly Lord
    Titchfield), 312, 618
Portland, William Cavendish-Bentinck, 6th
    Duke of, 618–19, 619n
Potter, Beatrix, 36
Potter, John, 640
Potticary, Rev. John, 29–31
Powles, John Diston, 51, 52, 56, 57, 62, 77
Present State of Mexico, The (BD, 1825), 52
Press, The (BD's Conservative newspaper),
    329–31, 333, 342, 344
Primrose League, 429
Principles of Geology (Lyell), 346
Protectionism, 207, 234, 249, 250, 256–58,
    281, 282, 289, 296, 298, 299, 303,
    306, 313, 315, 316–18, 321, 322, 335,
    392
Protection of the Jews of Palestine, 280
Public Health Act (1875), 530
Public Worship Regulation (Ritualism) Act
    (1874), 531–32, 537
Punch, 219, 222–23, 234, 235, 251, 268,
    273, 291, 292, 330, 358, 360, 407,
    450, 451, 464, 475, 482–83, 483,
    504, 510, 518, 527, 554, 555, 560,
    561, 567, 584, 590, 594, 662
Purgatory of Suicides, The (Cooper), 236
Pye, Henry James, 25, 26
Pye, Mrs. Jael, 25
Pyne, William, 7, 165, 165n, 168, 178, 179,
    189, 193–95, 200

Quain, Richard, 656, 658
Quarterly Review, 39, 55, 59–61, 210, 314,
    383, 453, 454, 480, 493, 639
Quin, Dr. Frederick, 169

Radicals, 162–63, 188, 207, 231, 255, 296,
    323, 328, 339, 342, 368, 379, 408,
    445, 450, 455, 469
  BD runs as, 158–59
  and elections of 1837, 12, 14, 16
  and elections of 1847, 273
  and Liberal Party, 379
Radowitz, Count von, 593
Ralph the Heir (Trollope), 474
Ranelagh, Lord, 233
Redesdale, Lord, 600
Reform Bill (1832), 108, 111–12, 114, 115,
    118–19, 127, 129, 131, 133, 134, 159,
    187, 212

Reform Bill (1867), 354, 441–55, 448, 451,
    456, 461, 463, 469, 475, 518–19, 665
  agitation for, 437–43
  effect of, 450
Rembrandt, Ivan Rijn, 48
Renan, Joseph-Ernest, 356, 495
Reply by Rothschild the First, King of the Jews,
    247
Representative, The (newspaper), 61–65, 67,
    73–74, 329
Reschid, Mehmet Pasha, Grand Vizier, 96
Revelations of Chaos, 260
Revolutionary Epick, The (BD, 1834), 113,
    149–52, 154
Revue des deux mondes, 633
Reynold's Newspaper, 497
Ricardo, David, 116
Richard II, King of England, 155
Richmond, 5th Duke of, 318–19
Richmond, Henry Gordon-Lennox, 6th Duke
    of, 278, 454, 480, 501, 511, 520, 572,
    579
Ridley, Sir Matthew, 448
Rieti, Solomon, 27–28
"Rise of Iskander, The" (BD, 1833), 138
Rites and Ceremonies of the Jews (Leon of
    Modena), 204n
Rivers Pollution Act (1876), 530
Rivingtons (publishers), 148, 150
Robarts, Abraham Wildey, 10
Robert III, of Scotland, 334
Robert Orange (Craigie), 490
Roberts, Gen. Frederick "Little Bobs," 609,
    615
Robertson, James, 607
Roby, John, 218
Rochard, S. J., 15
Roebuck, John Arthur, 339, 340, 342–43
Rogers, Sir Frederic, 462
Rogers, Samuel, 42, 70, 129
Roman Catholicism, 6, 50, 243, 267,
    298–301, 365, 479, 481–82, 484–86,
    490, 510–11, 537
  oath in Commons, 274
Romilly, Frederick, 423
Romola (Eliot), 493
Roper, Miss, 28
Rose, Harcourt, 550–51
Rose, Sir Philip, 110, 113, 162, 259, 273,
    290, 307–308, 328, 401, 430, 431,
    439, 508, 550, 610, 611, 654–55, 658,
    660, 661
Rose, William Stewart, 59
Rosebery, 5th Earl of (formerly Lord
    Dalmeny), 506–508, 611
Rosebery, Sybil, 611
Rossetti, William Michael, 569
Rothschild, Alfred de, 243, 612, 631, 650,
    651, 652, 660

Rothschild, Almina, 652
Rothschild, Baron Alphonse de, 361
Rothschild, Annie, letters from BD, 494–95
Rothschild, Baron Anselm de, 179
Rothschild, Sir Anthony de, 179, 190, 205,
  209, 269, 283, 327, 396, 487, 494,
  509, 539, 543–44
  letters from BD, 506
Rothschild, Baron Charles de, 265
Rothschild, Baroness Charlotte de, 179, 219,
  225, 243, 267, 273–74, 278, 307, 319,
  357, 373, 381, 395–96, 401–402,
  404–406, 419, 450–51, 453, 457, 460,
  468, 496, 526, 539, 635
  BD's friendship with, 611
  letters from BD, 243, 365, 401, 515, 611
Rothschild, Constance de, 243, 396, 509, 603
  letters from BD, 494
Rothschild, Emma de, letters to BD, 633–34
Rothschild, Evelina de, 243, 245, 406, 411,
  451
Rothschild, Baron Ferdinand de, 411
Rothschild, Hannah de (later Countess of
  Rosebery), 178–79, 209, 219, 243,
  539, 611, 637–38
Rothschild, Baron Jacob James Mayer de,
  205, 269, 373, 489, 509, 539
Rothschild, Baron James de, 247, 265
Rothschild, Juliana de, letters from BD, 509
Rothschild, Leonora de, 243, 361, 395
Rothschild, Leopold de, 243, 246, 307, 395,
  401, 402, 404, 406, 419, 433, 451,
  453, 457, 496, 612, 650–51
  letters from BD, 650
Rothschild, Baron Lionel de, 179, 190, 214,
  219, 225–26, 146–47, 257, 269, 273,
  276, 327, 361, 368, 376, 380–81, 402,
  411, 440, 453, 468, 510, 572, 635
  and BD's debts, 402
  illness and death, 611–12
  letters from BD, 431
  letters to BD, 575
  and oaths debate for seat in Parliament,
    284, 297–98, 309–10, 371, 372
  and Suez Canal, 539–40, 541, 543–45,
    545n
  takes seat in Parliament, 373
Rothschild, Lady Louise (earlier Louisa) de,
  194n, 243, 283, 292, 327, 487, 494,
  509, 544
Rothschild, Baron Mayer Amschel de, 205
Rothschild, Sir (later Lord) Nathaniel Mayer
  de (Natty), 243, 373, 431, 468, 407,
  541, 633–34, 661, 664
  as executor of BD's will, 430, 611, 660
  letters from BD, 431
  letters to BD, 612
Rothschild, Nathan Mayer de, 178–79, 209,
  214

Rothschild, Baron Solomon Mayer de, 205,
  248
Rothschild and Rothschild of Wellington,
  435
Rothschild family, 61, 178, 213, 278, 283–84,
  302, 378, 516, 604
  and Kate Donovan, 433
  portrayed in Endymion, 635
  portrayed in Falconet, 647
Rous, Admiral Henry John, 513
Rowton, Baron. See Corry, Montagu
Royal Academy banquet of 1870, 482
Royal Literary Fund, 331–32
Royal Titles Bill (1876), 553, 556, 571
Rubens, Peter Paul, 48
Rumpel Stiltskin (BD), 46
"Runnymede" series (BD), 163, 165, 176
Ruskin, John, 392, 499
Russell, G. W. E., 614
Russell, Earl John, 108, 158, 177, 188, 225,
  226, 235, 247–49, 258, 269, 273–74,
  276, 284, 290, 292, 299, 335–38,
  340–42, 345, 347, 361, 372, 374, 379,
  387, 393, 398, 403, 409, 441, 446,
  597n
  as Prime Minister, 413, 417–18, 553
  resignation and caretaker government,
    302–303, 305, 312–14, 317
Russell, Lord Odo, 554, 592, 620
Russell, W. H., 310
Russell, William Howard, 414, 415
Rutland, Duke of, 213, 229, 258, 295
Ryan, Charles, 375

Saint-Cyr, Marshal Gouvion, 319
Sala, George Augustus, 125–26
Salisbury, Mary Catherine, Marchioness of
  (later Lady Derby), 333, 412, 416,
  461, 467, 479
Salisbury, 2nd Marquis of, 195, 332–33, 384,
  416, 467
Salisbury, Marchioness of (formerly Mrs.
  Robert Cecil), 531–32, 566, 581
Salisbury, 3rd Marquis of (formerly Robert
  Cecil, then Lord Cranborne), 467,
  469, 479–80, 495, 517, 519, 531–32
  on BD's death, 663–64
  after BD's retirement, 642, 650, 653, 654,
    660
  joins BD's government, 520, 538, 564, 566,
    570–75, 578, 583, 585, 586, 590,
    591n, 593, 595, 597, 599–600, 602,
    604, 613, 623, 626–27
  letters from BD, 570, 649
Salisbury, Dowager Marchioness, 11
Salisbury, Marchioness of ("Old Sally"), 333
Salomons, David, 267, 371, 373
Sand, George, 362n
Sandford, Baron, 467

Sandon, Viscount, 531
Saqui, Moses, 29
Sartor Resartus (Carlyle), 413
Sassoon, Arthur, 650
Sassoon, Louise, 650
Satirist, The, 190–92, 194
Saunders and Otley (publishers), 135, 137–38, 149–51
Saxe-Weimar, Grand Duke of, 395
Sayce, A. H., 428
Sayers, Tom, 479n
School for Scandal, The (Sheridan), 644
Scott, Sir Walter, 57–60, 65–66, 77, 81, 203
Scrope, William, 189
Seager, Robert, 607
Sebright, Olivia, Lady, 563
Second Report of the Children's Employment Commission (1843), 228
Sedgwick, Ellery, 639
Sève, D. J. A. ("Suleiman Pasha"), 255
Shaftesbury, 7th Earl of, 227, 339n, 410, 462, 557, 643
Shaw, Bernard, 14, 14n, 598
Sheil, Richard Lalor, 177
Shelley, Percy Bysshe, 7, 92, 96, 169
Sher Ali, Ameer of Afghanistan, 569, 608–609
Sheridan, Mrs. Frances, 139
Sheridan, W. B., 644
Sheridan sisters, 139, 140, 629, 643
Shiprut, Esther (great-grandmother), 26
"Shooting Niagara" (Carlyle), 453
Shuvalov, Count, 566, 570, 573, 577, 579, 582–85, 587, 590, 592
Sidney, Sir Philip, 400
Simcox, Edith, 620
Skelton, Sir John, 354, 454
"Skelton Jun[io]r" series (BD, 1836–37), 165
Smalley, George, 465–66, 617–18
Smart, Theophilus, 56
Smith, Sir Benjamin, 194
Smith, Goldwin, 490
Smith, Robert (*later* 2nd Lord Carrington), 132, 134, 136
Smith, Rev. Sydney, 161
Smith, W. H., 520, 578, 624
Smythe, George (*later* 7th Viscount Strangford), 202–205, 207–12, 219, 221, 227–29, 236, 248, 319, 516, 633, 636
    death, 367–68
    and Dolly Nevill, 421–24
Somerset, Duchess of (*formerly* Georgina Sheridan, *later* Lady Seymour), 319, 628, 629
Somerset, Duke of, 552
Song of Songs, 280
Sophia, Queen of Netherlands, 464
    letters to BD, 509

Southey, Robert, 80–81
Soyer, Alexis, 306, 306n
Speeches and debates, 665
    "ape or angel," 406, **407**
    and bad teeth, 495–96
    BD consults Metternich on, 288
    on Cobden's death, 408
    consistent themes, 163
    Crystal Palace, 503–506, **504,** 517, 529
    "drunken," on Church of Ireland, 465–66
    early, in House of Commons, 179, 201–202, 209–10
    on Eastern Question in Lords, 574
    on first budget as Chancellor of Exchequer, 321–24
    at Glasgow University, 515–16
    on government and society (Reform Bill), 410
    harvest home of 1871, 495, 596–97
    homely anecdotes in, 159
    on Jewish question, 276–78
    on journalistic irresponsibility, 329–30
    on landed interest, 331
    last to Commons, 560
    on Lincoln, 409
    maiden, in House of Commons, 175–77, 183, 198, 635
    Manchester Athenaeum, 421
    Manchester Free Trade Hall of 1872, 466n, 501–503, 517, 529
    masterful style develops, 202
    on murder of English emissaries in Kabul, 617–18
    Old Testament imagery, 339, 339n
    opposing Peel, 232, 249–50, 253–55
    "peace with honor," 597, 597n, **662**
    on Reform bill of 1867, 450–52, 456
    Stanley on BD's, 287
    on sugar duties, 226
    summing up, of 1856, 355–56
Speeches on Parliamentary Reform (1867), 442
Spencer, Lord, 519
Spencer-Stanhope, Lady Elizabeth, 230
Spencer-Stanhope, Walter, 230
Spenser, Edmund, 521
Spinoza, 214, 217, 647
"Spirit of Whiggism, The" (Runnymede letters), 163
Spofforth, Markham, 328
Spooner, Richard, 385
Stacey, Henry James John, 435
Standard, 329, 492, 633
Stanhope, Lord, 414
Stanley, Arthur Penrhyn, Dean of Westminster, 404, 660
Stanley, Lady Augusta, 463, 467
Stanley, Edward (*later* 14th Earl of Derby), 155, 226, 248, 258, 276, 281–82, 285, 296–97, 299

forms government with BD as Chancellor of Exchequer, 302–304
meets with BD after Peel's death, 297
and memoir of Bentinck, 310–11
offers BD leadership in Commons, 286–89, 292–93
as Opposition leader in Lords, 269
and Papal aggression, 301–302
reason for hostility of, 113
Stanley, Edward Henry (later 15th Earl of Derby), 292–93, 301–302, 304, 316, 320, 323, 325, 326, 329, 333–34, 344–45, 360, 362, 379, 388, 393, 397, 403, 466, 476–78, 481
and BD as Prime Minister, 460, 475
on BD, 385–86, 413
as Foreign Minister, 418, 440, 445, 468
letters from BD, 400
offered crown of Greece, 396–97
proposed leader of Conservatives, 412, 416, 417
Stanley, Frederick (later 16th Earl of Derby), 590
Stanley, Henry, 113
Stanley, Sir John (founder of family), 155
Stanley, Lady Venetia, 533
Star Chamber, 69
State in its Relations to the Church, The (Gladstone), 233–34
Stephen, Leslie, 491
Stepney, Lady, 138–39
Stevens, William, 44
Stockmar, Christian, Baron of Coburg, 326
Strachey, Lytton, xii, 309
Strangford, 6th Viscount, 202, 229, 367, 421
Stratford de Redcliffe, Viscount. See Canning, Sir Stratford
Sturt, Charlotte, 515
Sturt, Gerard (later Baron Alington), 515–16
Styles, Catherine Esther (Kate's granddaughter), 432, 434
Styles, Dorothy (Kate's daughter), 432, 435, 436
Styles, George Peter, 435
Styles, Louis (Kate's son), 435
Succinct Account of the Rules and Covenants of the Jews, 280
Suez Canal, 540–46, 554, 548, 549, 551, 590, 592, 596, 611
Sukkot, 266, 280
Sullivan, Arthur, 525
Summerhayes, Miss, 444–45
Sunday Times, The, 492
Sutherland, Duke of, 8, 516, 641
Swain, Stevens, Maples, Pearce and Hunt, 44, 47, 51, 52
Swift, Jonathan, 80, 352
Swinburne, Algernon, 569

Sybil, or The Two Nations (1845), 123, 187, 246, 531, 611
sequel, 246, 260
written, 227–29, 236–44
Sykes, Lady Henrietta, 4, 143–48, 144, 149, 151–53, 157–59, 162, 164–68
death, 255
letters to BD, 145–46, 164, 166–68, 533
Sykes, Sir Francis, 143–46, 149, 153, 164–68

Talmud, 104n, 141, 453
Tancred, or the New Crusade (BD, 1847), 103, 106, 231, 289, 307, 362, 382, 481, 549
Jewish themes, 280, 280n, 309, 568
publication and reception, 267–72
written, 246, 248, 256, 259–67
Tancredi (Rossini opera), 141
Tankerville, Lady, 154, 157
Tauchnitz, Baron, 491, 593, 594
Taylor, Col. T. E., 362, 473
Taylor, William Cooke, 223
Teck, Prince and Princess of, 353
Temple Bar, 349
Ten Hours' amendment, 227
Tenniel, John, 482
Tennyson, Alfred Lord, 535
Term of Life, The (Israel), 280
Thackeray, William M., 154, 178, 221–23, 222, 394, 494, 636, 643
Theodore, King of Abyssinia, 455, 470
Thiers, Louis Adolphe, 319, 320
Thimbleby, Rev. John, 32
Thistlethwaite, Laura, 445–46, 566, 570
Thompson, Col. Thomas Perronet, 12, 13, 15
Thomson, James, 623
Times, The, 49, 55, 61, 125, 136, 162, 163, 165, 169, 178, 202, 205, 208, 228, 233, 270, 299, 310, 311–12, 332, 371, 373, 473, 482, 493, 510, 513, 517, 579, 600, 643
Titchfield, Marquess of, 258–59, 284, 312
Tom Brown's School Days (Hughes), 601
Tomline, George, 196, 197, 200
Tooke, William, 38n
Toombs, Robert, 452
Tories. See Conservative party
"Tory Democracy," 439, 627, 665
Traditions of Lancashire, The, 218
Traditions of the Jews, The, 280
Transactions of the Parisian Sanhedrin, 280
Travelers' Club, 116
Travels of Rabbi Benjamin, 280
Tremaine (Ward), 53–54, 65, 66, 87
Trevelyan, Sir Charles, 322, 323
Treves, Joseph, 21
Treves, Pellegrin, 21
Trollope, Anthony, 362–63, 469–70, 473–74, 482, 632

True Theory of Rent (Thompson), 12
Truth, 574, 579
Turkey, Ottoman
  and Berlin Congress of 1878, 590–97, 601,
    603, 604
Turner, Sharon, 31–32, 73–75, 79–80
Turton, Dr., 27
Twiss, Horace, 202
Two Years before the Mast (Dana), 355
Tyndall, John, 428

Uncle Tom's Cabin (Stowe), 324

Van Dyck, Anthony, 48
Vane, Lord Adolphus, 343, 344
Vanguard (ship) sinking, 538
Vanity Fair (magazine), 476, **578,** 602–
  603
Vanity Fair (Thackeray), 154, 222
Vathek (Beckford), 127
Vaurien (Mendelssohn), 26, 278
Velvet Lawn (BD, 1833), 147–48
Venetia (BD, 1837), 7, 8, 30, 92, 96, 362n
  written, 169
Verulam, Lord, 630
Very Successful (Rosina Bulwer), 124
Vestiges of the Natural History of Creation
  (Chambers), 260
Victoria, ("Vicky"), Princess Royal (*later*
  Crown Princess of Prussia), 366, 368,
  461, 466, 532–33, 548, 549, 551, 560,
  588, 592, 624
Victoria, Queen of Great Britain, xii, 3, 7–9,
  11, 48, 90–91, 98n, 149, 168n, 182,
  186, 233, 265, 290, 414, 455
  and Africa, 613–15
  and Albert's death, 386–88, 394
  BD on, 376–77
  on BD, 610n
  and BD as Prime Minister, 458–61, 463,
    467–72, 474–75, 520, 529, 530, 532,
    535, 536–38, 542–43, 546–55,
    557–61, 564, 571–77, 581, 599, 608,
    613–15, 621, 622
  BD's badly chosen words about, 496–97
  BD's audiences with, 398–99, 441, 537,
    614
  and BD's death, 655, 659–63
  BD's early friendship with, 316, 345, 346,
    388
  BD's effect on, 665
  and BD's final resignation, 624–26
  BD's last dinner with, 652–53
  BD's letters and reports to, 317–18, 370,
    376, 388, 438, 447, 457, 460, 463,
    532, 536, 544, 557, 571, 575, 577,
    585, 591, 621, 624, 625, 639–40, 645,
    649, 655
  after BD's resignation, 628, 632

  and Bedchamber Crisis, 187
  and Derby, 303, 314, 320, 325–26,
    402–403, 437, 441
  early dislike for BD, 303, 306
  and Eastern Question, 585–88, 591, 596,
    597
  and Empress of India issue, 549–53, 555,
    571–72, 620, 620n
  and *Endymion,* 637, 639
  foreign policy, 397
  gifts to BD, 641, 649
  and Gladstone, 477–78, 498, 511, 554,
    565–66, 625, 626, 628
  illness, 496–99
  letters to BD, 399–400, 460, 508, 572, 576,
    585–86, 588, 624, 625, 628, 649, 655
  letters to Vicky, 466
  makes BD Earl of Beaconsfield, **555,**
    558–61
  marriage, 185n
  and Mary Anne's death, 508
  meets BD, 232
  and morals of Court, 368, 376, 423
  museum plans, 397, 399–400
  and Palmerston, 340–42, 379
  and Peel, 249, 251, 256
  seclusion after Albert's death, 415–16,
    460–61, 477–78
  visits BD's grave, 661–62
Vie de Jésus (Renan), 365, 495
Vigny, Alfred de, 359
Villa Real family, 22, 22n
Villiers, Charles Pelham, 87, 314, 317, 404,
  510
Villiers, Lord (*later* 6th Earl of Jersey) and
  Lady, 357
Vindication of the English Constitution (BD
  1835), 109, 163
Viney, Sir James, estate, 401
"Visit to the Grand Vizier, A" (BD, 1831),
  97
Vitzthum von Eckstaedt, Count, 340, 387,
  395
Vivian Grey (BD, 1826), 9, 28, 34–39, 43, 50,
  56, 62, 63, 77–78, 87, 91, 120, 128,
  138, 161, 362n
  Gladstone on, 527–28
  "keys" to, 67n, 69, 76
  written, 53–54, 65–70
Vivian Grey (sequel), 70–71, 91
  written, 75–79
Voice of Judaism, The, 271
Voltaire, 26, 43, 80, 127
Voyage of Captain Popanilla, The (BD, 1828),
  46, 53n, 80
Vyvyan, Sir Richard, 201

Waddington, Georges, 592, 595
Wakley, Thomas, 183

Waldegrave, Lady, 352
Wales, Prince Albert Edward of ("Bertie"),
    397–98, 432, 468, 472, 482, 513, 516,
    526, 544–45, 549, 550, 590, 597, 604,
    641, 650, 651, 656–57, 660–61
  India trip, 540–41
  Thanksgiving, 497–500, 597
Wales, Princess Alexandra of, 398, 468,
    528
Wales, Princess Charlotte of, 98, 98n
Walewski, Count, 340
Walker, Charles Edward, 40
Wallace (play), 40
Walpole, Frederick, 420, 426
Walpole, Horace, 420
Walpole, Lord Horatio, 353, 420, 423
Walpole, Sir Robert, 420
Walpole, Spencer, 302–303, 416, 449
Walter, Catherine, 409
Walter, John, 205, 208–209
Ward, John, 53n
Ward, Rebecca Raphael, 53n
Ward, Robert Plumer, 53–54, 53n, 65, 69, 70,
    77, 80, 87, 135
Warden, The (Trollope), 362
Warton, Thomas, 26
Waterford, Lord, 629
Watkin, E. W., 217
Watts, Charles, 605, 608
Waverley novels (Scott), 58, 65
Webster, Lt. Col. Henry, 124–25
Welch, Captain, 538
Wellesley, Dean, 472
Wellington, Duke of, 9, 52, 98, 126–27, 158,
    199, 316, 414
  BD's eulogy, 319–20
  declines dedication by BD, 152
  letters from BD, 160
Wessenberg, Baron, 288
Westall, William, 641
Westmeath, Gen. T. J. Nugent, 8th Earl of,
    440, 440n
Westminster, Dean of, 404
Westminster Review, 12
Whigs, 108, 126–27, 130, 134, 199, 225–26,
    236, 256–58, 328, 368, 371
  BD writes series of articles against, 162–63
  and elections of 1832, 136
  and elections of 1834, 159–60
  and elections of 1837, 9, 10
  and elections of 1847, 273
  and Jews, 142
  and Liberal Party, 379
  radical wing, 153
  and two nations issue, 229
  See also Liberal party; Liberals
Whigs and Whiggism ("Runnymede"),
    165n
Whistler, James A. McNeill, 20, 603

Wilberforce, Samuel, Bishop of Oxford, 332,
    374, 376, 404, 406, 456, 483–84
  on BD, xi, 420
Wilde, Oscar, 91, 246, 352, 433, 490, 492,
    641, 646
  on BD, 665
Wild Irish Girl, The (Morgan), 124
Wilhelm Meister (Goethe), 67, 119, 120,
    595
William of Norwich, 602n
William I, King of Germany, 548
William III, King of Netherlands, 464
William IV, King of England, 90, 98, 108,
    119, 127, 158, 634
  death 7–10, 168
Williams, Henry, letters from BD, 339
Willis, Nathaniel Parker, 154
Willyams, Sarah Brydges (Sarah Mendez da
    Costa), 307–308, 376, 386
  death, 401–402, 477, 508, 642
  letters from BD, 308, 336, 337, 343–47,
    356, 357, 364, 366, 367, 375–78, 380,
    381, 383–86, 391, 394–97, 400–401,
    661
Wilson, C. Rivers, 288, 455
Wilton, Marie, 409
Wiseman, Cardinal, 368
Wolcot, Dr., 27
Wolff, Georgianna, 426
Wolff, Sir Henry Drummond, 429
Wolff, Rev. Joseph, 426
Wolseley, General Sir Garnet, 525, 613,
    621
World, The, 12, 579, 657
Wortley, Stuart, 641
Wright, Richard, 219, 259
Wright, William, 58–59

Yakub Khan, Mohammed, 609
Yate, Mrs. Eleanor, 180, 201, 204
Yates, Edmund, 580, 657
Year at Hartlebury, A (BD and Sarah
    D'Israeli, 1834), 150–51, 381
Yeast (Kingsley), 243
Yonge, Charlotte, 552
Yorke, Lady Mary, 360
Young, John, 257
Young Duke (BD, 1831), 8, 63, 77–78, 85,
    93–94, 129–30, 362n
  published, 97
  written, 83–84, 87
Young England movement, 205, 206–12, 220,
    226, 228–31, 234, 236, 241, 245, 248,
    250, 253, 367, 421, 516, 531, 550
Young England or, the Social Condition of the
    Empire, 232–33

Zadig (Voltaire), 43
Zafar, Bahadur Shah, 366